Second Edition

Home, School, and Community Collaboration

For the dedicated Family Outreach Specialists at Franklin Elementary
School in Missoula, Montana. Sue Black courageously led the way
in the Franklin Family Resource Center to connect family members with
teachers through her persistence and "true" grit. Thank you for the
opportunity to learn from you.

K.B.G.

For my family, who bless me with love and laughter: Dennis,
my best friend and confidante; my mom, Wanda; my "just like sisters,"
Cathy, Debbie, and Dena; my daughters, Nicole and Natalie and their supportive
spouses, Jamie and BJ; and especially for Micah, Ava, and James, who inspire me
to help prepare teachers for supportive family engagement practice.

J.A.R.

Second Edition

Home, School, and Community Collaboration

Culturally Responsive Family Engagement

Kathy B. Grant • **Julie A. Ray**

State University of New York at Plattsburgh   *Southeast Missouri State University*

Los Angeles | London | New Delhi
Singapore | Washington DC

Los Angeles | London | New Delhi
Singapore | Washington DC

FOR INFORMATION:

SAGE Publications, Inc.
2455 Teller Road
Thousand Oaks, California 91320
E-mail: order@sagepub.com

SAGE Publications Ltd.
1 Oliver's Yard
55 City Road
London EC1Y 1SP
United Kingdom

SAGE Publications India Pvt. Ltd.
B 1/I 1 Mohan Cooperative Industrial Area
Mathura Road, New Delhi 110 044
India

SAGE Publications Asia-Pacific Pte. Ltd.
3 Church Street
#10-04 Samsung Hub
Singapore 049483

Acquisitions Editor: Diane McDaniel
Assistant Editor: Rachael Leblond
Editorial Assistant: Megan Koraly
Production Editor: Laureen Gleason
Copy Editor: Codi Bowman
Typesetter: C&M Digitals (P) Ltd.
Proofreader: Kate Macomber Stern
Indexer: Gloria Tierney
Cover Designer: Candice Harman
Marketing Manager: Terra Schultz
Permissions Editor: Adele Hutchinson

Printed in the United States of America

Library of Congress Cataloging-in-Publication Data

Grant, Kathy B.

Home, school, and community collaboration: culturally responsive family engagement/Kathy B. Grant, Julie A. Ray.—2nd ed.

p. cm.
Includes bibliographical references and index.

ISBN 978-1-4129-9074-5 (pbk.)

1. Home and school—United States. 2.Community and school—United States. 3. Parent-teacher relationships—United States. I. Ray, Julie. II. Title.

LC225.3.G73 2013
371.19'2—dc23   2011041243

This book is printed on acid-free paper.

12 13 14 15 16 10 9 8 7 6 5 4 3 2 1

BRIEF CONTENTS

Preface   xv

Acknowledgments   xxiii

SECTION I.   UNDERSTANDING FAMILY ENGAGEMENT: BUILDING A KNOWLEDGE
                BASE FOR CULTURALLY RESPONSIVE FAMILY ENGAGEMENT   1

Chapter 1.   Family Engagement and the Responsive Educator   3

Chapter 2.   Theories and Models for Family Engagement in Schools   27
                Contributing Authors Josephine Agnew-Tully and Donald Mott

Chapter 3.   Supporting Families as They Parent Today's Children   51

SECTION II.   APPRECIATING FAMILIES: TODAY'S DIVERSE FAMILIES   77

Chapter 4.   Structurally Diverse Families   79

Chapter 5.   Culturally Diverse Families   109
                Contributing Authors Luis Hernández, Lynn Zubov, Joyce Goddard,
                and Manuel Vargas

Chapter 6.   Students of Families in Transition   129

Chapter 7.   Families Overcoming Obstacles   155
                Contributing Authors John Wong, Jonathan Livingston,
                George Cliette, and Sherry Eaton

Chapter 8.   Families in Abusive Situations   175
                Contributing Author Keith Anderson

SECTION III.   FAMILY ENGAGEMENT: PUTTING KNOWLEDGE
                AND SKILLS INTO ACTION   201

Chapter 9.   Engaging Families in Their Children's Learning
                at School and Home   203

Chapter 10.   Teacher as Family Communication Facilitator   225
                Contributing Author Jeannine Studer

Chapter 11.   **Working With Families of Children
With Exceptional Needs**   251
Contributing Author Suzanne George

Chapter 12.   **Teacher as a Family Resource and Advocate**   281
*Contributing Authors Josephine Agnew-Tally,
Donald Mott, Sheila Brookes, and Kathy R. Thornburg*

Chapter 13.   **Schoolwide Family Engagement Activities: Family Events,
Family Resource Centers, and Volunteer Programs**   309
*Contributing Authors Vincent Snipes, Pamela Moses-Snipes,
Catherine Matthews, Jewell Cooper, and Carole Robinson*

Appendix A. Standards   343

Appendix B. NAEYC Code of Ethical Conduct   345

Appendix C. State Agencies for Reporting Child Abuse and Neglect   349

Appendix D. Family Engagement Program Mandates   355

**Appendix E. Developing, Implementing, and Evaluating
a School's Family Engagement Plan**   357

Glossary   361

References   369

Photo Credits   399

Index   401

About the Authors   417

About the Contributors   419

DETAILED CONTENTS

Preface   xv

Acknowledgments   xxiii

**SECTION I.   UNDERSTANDING FAMILY ENGAGEMENT: BUILDING A KNOWLEDGE
              BASE FOR CULTURALLY RESPONSIVE FAMILY ENGAGEMENT**   1

1 Family Engagement and the Responsive Educator   3

  Preparing for Family Partnerships: Actualizing the Process   4
  In the Classroom: A New School Year Begins   5
  Forming Family Partnerships: Self-Assessment Activity   6
  Benefits of Effective Family Engagement Practices   8
    Benefits for Students   8
    Benefits for Families   8
    Benefits for Educators and Schools   9
  Barriers to Authentic Family Engagement   9
    School Barriers: Educators   9
    Family Barriers: Individuals or Groups   10
    School/District/Community Barriers   10
    Barriers for Culturally and Linguistically Diverse Families   11
  The Administrator as a Responsive Leader   12
  Current Trends in Family Demographics   14
    Configuration of Today's American Families   15
      Traditional Family Configurations   15
      Nontraditional Family Configurations   16
      Single Mother/Father Families   16
      Marriage Ages and Birthrates   17
      Teen and Unmarried Birthrates   17
      Divorce   18
      Remarriage   18
      Grandparent Caregivers   19
    Economic Status of Today's American Families   19
    Race and Ethnicity of Today's American Families   21
    Summary of Demographic Information   22
  Culturally Responsive Family Engagement   22
    Culturally Responsive Teaching   23
  Ethical Practice   24
  Summary   25
  Reflection Questions   25
  Websites   25
  Student Study Site   26

2 **Theories and Models for Family Engagement in Schools**   **27**

Defining Family   28

In the Classroom: A Parent's Perspective   29

Family Systems Conceptual Framework   30

Characteristics of a System   30

The Whole Is Greater Than the Sum of Its Parts   31

A System Has Boundaries or Limits   31

A System Has a Balance of Bonding and Buffering   32

Rituals and Traditions Affect the Bonding Process   33

Systems Are Rule Governed   34

A System Is Hierarchically Organized   34

A System Is Dynamically Changing   35

A System Has Goals   36

Members of a System Have Roles   36

A System Is Self-Regulating   36

Ecological Systems Theory: Urie Bronfenbrenner   37

Family Empowerment Models: Carl Dunst   41

Social Capital: James Coleman   43

The Funds of Knowledge: Luis Moll   44

Family-School Partnerships Framework: Joyce Epstein   45

School Development Program: James Comer   48

Summary   49

Reflection Questions   49

Websites   50

Student Study Site   50

3 **Supporting Families as They Parent Today's Children**   **51**

In the Classroom: The First Meeting With a Parent   52

Stages of Parenthood   53

Infancy   53

Toddlerhood and the Preschool Years   54

The Elementary School Years   56

Attachment and Temperament   57

Parenting Styles   60

Authoritative Parenting   61

Authoritarian Parenting   61

Permissive/Indulgent Parenting   61

Permissive/Neglectful Parenting   61

Effects of Different Parenting Styles on a Child's Behavior   62

Criticisms of Parenting Styles Research   63

Children's Views of Their Parents   64

Teacher Acceptance of Differing Parenting Styles   66

Family Support for All   67

Principles of Family Support in Schools   68

Parent Education Models   73

    Parents as Teachers   73

    Even Start   74

    Systematic Training for Effective Parenting   74

    Parent Effectiveness Training   74

    Active Parenting   74

    Home Instruction for Parents of Preschool Youngsters   75

Summary   75

Reflection Questions   75

Websites   76

Student Study Site   76

SECTION II. APPRECIATING FAMILIES: TODAY'S DIVERSE FAMILIES   **77**

4 Structurally Diverse Families   **79**

Today's American Families   79

In the Classroom: Grandparents Becoming Parents   81

Nuclear Family Settings   81

    Suggestions for Working With Nuclear Families   83

Extended Family Settings   84

    Suggestions for Working With Extended Families   85

Single-Parent Families   85

    Suggestions for Working With Single-Parent Families   88

    Suggestions for Working With Families Experiencing a Divorce   90

Blended Families   91

    Suggestions for Working With Blended Families   93

Grandparents and Other Kinship Roles   95

    Suggestions for Working With Kinship Care Families   96

Same-Sex Families   98

    Suggestions for Working With Same-Sex Families   100

Adoptive Families   101

    Suggestions for Working With Adoptive Families   103

Foster Families   105

Summary   106

Reflection Questions   107

Websites   107

Student Study Site   108

5 Culturally Diverse Families   **109**

In the Classroom: The Silent Child   111

What Is Culture?   112

    Key Concepts in the Idea of Culture   113

Similarities and Differences Among Culturally Diverse Families   114

Teachers' Beliefs About Diverse Families   115

Linguistic Diversity in Families   117
    Suggestions for Working With Linguistically Diverse Families   117
Working With Newly Immigrated Families   118
    Suggestions for Working With Newly Immigrated Families   119
Diversity in Family Religious Practices   120
    Suggestions for Working With Religiously Diverse Families   123
Culturally Responsive Family Engagement   123
    Developing a Classroom Cultural Audit   125
Summary   126
Reflection Questions   127
Websites   127
Student Study Site   128

6 Students of Families in Transition   129
Family Life Cycle: Normal Transitions   130
In the Classroom: Divorce and a Five-Year-Old   131
Moving   131
Characteristics of Difficult Family Transitions   133
Students in Families Undergoing Separation, Divorce, and Remarriage   134
    Suggestions for Working With Children and Families Experiencing a Separation,
        Divorce, or Remarriage   136
Death of a Parent or Family Member   137
    Suggestions for Working With Children and Families Dealing With a Death   139
Students With Parents in the Military   140
Students With Parents in Prison   145
Students in Foster Care   148
    Suggestions for Working With Children in Foster Care   151
Summary   152
Reflection Questions   154
Websites   154
Student Study Site   154

7 Families Overcoming Obstacles   155
Families Living In Poverty   156
In the Classroom: Out of School Supplies   157
    Suggestions for Working With Children and Families in Poverty   159
Students Experiencing Homelessness   160
    Suggestions for Working With Children and Families Who Are Homeless   163
Families Affected by Violence   164
    Suggestions for Teachers Working With Children and Families in Violent Communities   165
Chronic Illness of a Family Member or Student   165
    Suggestions for Working With Families and Children Who Are Chronically Ill   167
Working With Families Who Have Experienced Natural Disasters   168
    Suggestions for Working With Children and Families Who Have Experienced Natural
        Disasters   169

Families and Children Under Stress: Risk and Resilience   170
Summary   173
Reflection Questions   173
Websites   173
Student Study Site   174

8 Families in Abusive Situations   175

Child Abuse Statistics   176
In the Classroom: Sharing Crackers   177
Types of Child Abuse and Neglect   178
    Physical Abuse   178
        Signs of Physical Abuse   179
    Sexual Abuse   180
        Signs of Sexual Abuse   180
    Emotional or Psychological Abuse   180
        Signs of Emotional or Psychological Abuse   181
    Neglect   181
        Signs of Neglect   182
Substance Abuse, Child Abuse, and Neglect   183
    Fetal Alcohol Syndrome and Drug-Affected Newborns   183
The Role of the Teacher in Reporting Child Abuse   184
Mandatory Reporting of Child Abuse: Working With CPS   185
    Facts on Teachers as Reporters   187
Working With Families in Abusive Situations   190
Domestic Violence, Families, and Schools   191
    Statistics and Definitions   193
    Children   193
    Teachers/Schools   193
    Immigrants   194
The Educator's Role After Reporting Occurs   195
The Role of the School Administrator   196
Corporal Punishment in Schools   196
Summary   198
Reflection Questions   198
Websites   198
Student Study Site   199

SECTION III.   FAMILY ENGAGEMENT: PUTTING
KNOWLEDGE AND SKILLS INTO ACTION   201

9 Engaging Families in Their Children's Learning at School and Home   203

In the Classroom: Homework and More Homework   204
Collaborating With Families on Academic Learning and Development   204
    Barriers to Collaboration   207
Communicating With Families on Standards-Based Curriculum   208

Collaborating With Families on Classroom Behavioral Challenges   211
Classroom Volunteers   213
    Variety of Roles for Volunteers   214
Homework and Home Learning Activities   215
Summary   223
Reflection Questions   223
Websites   223
Student Study Site   224

10 Teacher as Family Communication Facilitator   225
Print Communication: One Way and Reciprocal   226
In the Classroom: Spring Parent-Teacher Conferences   227
Reciprocal Communication: Informal and Formal Conferences   230
Active Listening Behaviors   232
Planning for Formal Conferences   233
Alternatives in Conferencing With Families   233
    Student Involvement   234
    Group Conferences   235
    Telephone Conferences   236
    Home Visits   237
    Community and Workplace Conferences   238
Documentation of Communication   238
Technology as a Tool for Communication   239
Communicating With Culturally and Linguistically Diverse Families   241
Barriers to Communication   243
    Teacher Attitudes and Beliefs   244
    Negative School Experiences of Families   244
    Sharing Difficult Information   245
    Hostile Families   246
Summary   246
Reflection Questions   249
Websites   249
Student Study Site   250

11 Working With Families of Children With Exceptional Needs   251
Helping Families Adjust to Having a Child With Exceptional Needs   252
In the Classroom: Another Difficult Parent-Teacher Conference   253
Cultural Considerations in Working With Families of Children With
    Differing Abilities   256
Classroom Teachers' Role in Special Education   257
Legislation Relating to the Education of Children With Exceptional Needs   258
Components of IDEA   260
Communicating With Families About Exceptional Needs   262
Families of Children With Autism   265

Referral Process and Identification   265

Screening and Testing for Exceptionality   266

Involving Families in the IEP Process   268

Collaboration With Families of Young Children: Individual Family Service Plans   269

Response to Intervention   272

Working With Families of Gifted and Talented Students   273

Summary   278

Reflection Questions   278

Websites   279

Student Study Site   280

12 Teacher as a Family Resource and Advocate   281

Asset-Based and Family-Centered Partnerships   282

In the Classroom: Setting Goals for Improvement   283

Home Visits   285

Advocacy for Children and Families: Strategies for Becoming Advocates   288

Case Advocacy   289

Class Advocacy   289

Barriers to Effective Advocacy   291

Community Resources for the Classroom and Families   292

Classroom Collaboration With Community Partners   292

Community Resources for Families   296

Parents as Decision Makers and School Leaders   298

Developing Family Leaders   298

Parent Organization Leaders   299

Advisory Council Members   300

Resource Personnel to Support Families   301

Home-School Coordinator   301

School Social Workers   303

Paraprofessionals   305

Summary   306

Reflection Questions   306

Websites   306

Student Study Site   307

**13 Schoolwide Family Engagement Activities: Family Events,
Family Resource Centers, and Volunteer Programs   309**

Preparing for Schoolwide Family Engagement Activities   309

Family Events That Support Students' Success at School   310

In the Classroom: Family Fun Online   311

Organizing, Preparing, and Hosting Family Events   312

Back-to-School Events   316

Transition Events   318

Collaboration on Cultural Events   320
Setting Up a Family Literacy Event   321
Family Math as a Cultural Event   325
Family Science Night   327
Organizing a Family Technology Night   330
Establishing a School or Classroom Family Resource Center   332
    Family Information Center (FIC)   333
    Family Resource Center (FRC)   334
School Volunteers   335
    Recruiting Volunteers   336
    Training Volunteers   338
    Retaining Volunteers   339
Summary   340
Reflection Questions   340
Websites   340
Student Study Site   341

Appendix A. Standards   343

Appendix B. NAEYC Code of Ethical Conduct   345

Appendix C. State Agencies for Reporting Child Abuse and Neglect   349

Appendix D. Family Engagement Program Mandates   355

Appendix E. Developing, Implementing, and Evaluating
a School's Family Engagement Plan   357

Glossary   361

References   369

Photo Credits   399

Index   401

About the Authors   417

About the Contributors   419

PREFACE

The second edition of this comprehensive textbook for family engagement courses uses the culturally responsive family support model to prepare early childhood and elementary teachers to work effectively with the diverse families of their students. With more than 20 contributing authors who are experts in the field representing multiple perspectives, the text features information to help teachers understand, appreciate, and support diverse families.

Home, School, and Community Collaboration: Culturally Responsive Family Engagement, second edition, can be adopted by college and university education departments in their undergraduate and graduate course work in family engagement. The text is particularly powerful in nurturing teachers' understanding of family dynamics coupled with supportive, authentic strategies to actualize classroom-family involvement.

The philosophical underpinning for the text comes from a family engagement approach, with a focus on culturally responsive family engagement. The heart of the text remains our commitment to prepare teachers to work empathetically with all families. The authors have extensive backgrounds in their work in family engagement, including experiences as a Title I home-school coordinator, elementary and early childhood teachers, family involvement teacher educators, a consultant for Goals 2000 Preservice Teacher Education in family involvement grants and parent information resource centers, NCATE accreditation program reviewer of family and school relationship standards, presenters at national conferences, and authors of articles on family engagement. These experiences have formed the basis for realistic case studies and vignettes as well as practical activities and strategies found in the text and the ancillary materials.

In addition, revisions in education law under the provisions of No Child Left Behind contain requirements for meaningful family engagement at the state, district, and local school levels. National standards from organizations, such as the Interstate New Teacher Assessment and Support Consortium (INTASC), the National Association for the Education of Young Children (NAEYC), the Association of Childhood Education International (ACEI), and the National Board of Professional Teaching Standards (NBPTS), promote principles and values intrinsic to strong family engagement programs. Teachers need to be aware of these standards to strengthen their family engagement practices.

A strong research base is embedded throughout the text chapters. Current research from peer-reviewed journals, such as *Early Childhood Education Journal, Early Childhood Development and Care, The School Community Journal, The Journal of Educational Research, The Journal of Teacher Education, Teaching Exceptional Children, The Educational Forum, Educational Leadership,* and *Phi Delta Kappan,* support a growing family engagement knowledge base for new and practicing teachers. In addition, organizations promoting healthy families, such as the Children's Defense Fund; regional educational laboratories, such as Northwest Regional Education Laboratory; and university collaboratives, such as the National Network of Partnership Schools, The Harvard Family Research Project, and Johns Hopkins University, provide best practice ideas in family engagement and support. Moreover, research from leading authors in the field of family involvement and support, such as Davies, Dryfoos, Edwards, Epstein, Hoover-Dempsey, Henderson, Mapp, Saunders, and Weiss, as well as theorists in various fields, such as Baumrind, Bronfenbrenner, Coleman, Dunst, and Kübler-Ross, add richness to the text. To support our commitment to culturally responsive family engagement, groundbreaking work by Comer, Delgado Gaitan, Espinosa, Gay, Ladson-Billings, Moll, and others have been included.

Home, School, and Community Collaboration introduces the family systems theory and family involvement models presented in a reader-friendly manner that builds the foundation for the remainder of the text. Contemporary issues are addressed throughout the text, such as working with linguistically diverse and immigrant families; families going through divorce, remarriage, or military deployment; families dealing with financial difficulties, natural disasters, or violence; as well as children who have exceptional needs, are in foster care, or are in abusive situations. Educators will read about and reflect on realistic classroom situations and the harsh realities that families face in society today, such as family homelessness, incarceration of a parent, poverty and child hunger, chronic illness, and death of a family member. Practical suggestions for partnering with families, including using the latest technology as a communication tool, hosting family event nights, having family-friendly homework practices, and using community resources are given.

Culturally responsive family support forms the framework for the second edition. Our beliefs embrace this model for reaching out to all families, and it appears as a common thread throughout the text.

- Culturally responsive teaching is defined in Chapter 1.
- The funds of knowledge model is discussed in Chapter 2.
- Differing parenting styles are delineated in Chapter 3.
- Chapter 5 is devoted to culturally diverse families.
- Communicating with culturally and linguistically diverse families as well as exploring barriers to effective communication are covered in Chapter 10.
- Cultural considerations in working with families of children with exceptional needs are discussed in Chapter 11.
- Culturally responsive advocacy for children and families is addressed in Chapter 12.
- Family math and science as cultural events are described in Chapter 13.

Useful community, school district, and classroom-family engagement suggestions abound in the later chapters. These include setting up both a school- and classroom-based family resource center; conducting home visits; establishing neighborhood support groups; organizing, preparing, and hosting family events (family science, literacy, technology, and math); a school's family involvement plan; using volunteers; and supportive family engagement efforts.

Finally, the text encourages self-reflection, self-assessment, and questioning on the part of the educator. This is a key facet in use of the text. This aspect of the book can benefit instructors by challenging the preconceptions and misconceptions held by many teachers. Unfortunately, in some districts, parents are viewed negatively and are even banned from local schools except during allotted times. By questioning "habitudes," or ingrained patterns of thinking and response toward families, teachers are afforded the opportunity to embrace and celebrate diversity in families and understand how to use the strengths that families can bring to the school setting. We believe in the powerful benefits of family engagement for schools and families as demonstrated by research and practiced by exemplary practitioners in education at all levels.

NEW IN THE SECOND EDITION

The second edition of this text features several changes to strengthen its content and ease of use in instruction. Revisions were made in regard to the intended audience, the formatting of the chapters, and updating the content. Specifically, these changes were made:

- While the first edition of the textbook focused on the knowledge, skills, and dispositions of a beginning teacher, the second edition has been expanded to address the needs of both undergraduate and graduate family involvement courses.
- The term "family involvement" was updated to "family engagement" throughout the text to reflect the current research in the field. An explanation of the terminology change is given in Chapter 1.
- Content of each chapter was updated to reflect the newest research and current trends in the field.
- Sections on working with families of children with autism and helping families understand Response to Intervention (RTI) were added to Chapter 11: Working With Families of Children With Exceptional Needs.
- The section on homework was expanded to discuss interactive home learning activities in Chapter 9: Engaging Families in Their Child's Learning at School and Home.
- A stronger discussion of domestic violence was added to Chapter 8: Families in Abusive Situations.
- To condense and streamline information, the text was shortened to 13 chapters, with the content from Chapters 3 and 15 of the first edition moved to other sections of the text. Chapters 12 and 13 from the first edition were reorganized to have a smoother, more cohesive flow of topics.
- Several new quotes and interviews, such as with a military mom, were added to make the content more real to the reader.
- Statistical information was updated throughout the text, using current U.S. Census data and other resources.
- Throughout, chapters feature more tables and figures, and long narrative sections have been broken up with bulleted lists to support readability and flow. More text boxes were added.
- Websites were updated, with new websites added for the reader to use in further study.
- The appendices were expanded, with the national standards for family engagement moved to Appendix A and the discussion of school district family engagement plans moved to Appendix E.

Even with these changes, the text remains true to its original focus of supportive family engagement practices that are culturally responsive for the diverse children and families whom teachers will be serving.

FEATURES OF THE TEXT

In the Classroom Case Studies

Each revised chapter begins with a case study designed to help readers apply chapter information to a real-world setting, and realistic vignettes featuring diverse students and families are included throughout the text. The case studies are all set in the same fictitious elementary school setting during a school year, allowing teachers to see the varying practices across different grade levels throughout a school year, as well as the importance of school faculty working together to create a climate of positive family engagement practices. The In the Classroom case studies present an opportunity for rich discussion based on creative problem solving, understanding, and best practices in family engagement; they may be used as an introduction to a chapter, as well as at the completion of each chapter as a summary or assessment tool. In surveys done with teacher candidates using the text, the case studies were consistently rated as the most favored way to learn the content of each chapter. The case studies can be given as assignments or used as a springboard for small group or class discussions. They are also useful for online course instruction.

Vignettes

Additional vignettes are interspersed through the chapters to encourage readers to pause and apply what they have learned. Again, these realistic vignettes are based on the challenges that teachers may soon face. By connecting teachers with concrete ways to engage families, they grow as practitioners who value and support not only their students but also the families of their students. The vignettes are particularly helpful for instructors who favor active teaching strategies that require critical thinking and application of course content.

Focus Questions

Each chapter starts with a series of focus questions to frame the chapter discussion. These specific questions can act as focal points for topics in chapters, expand reflective thinking, and promote authentic discourse among class participants.

Application to Practice

One of the most important goals in the revised edition is to provide readers with the opportunity to validate what they have learned about productive interactions with families. Along with enhancing critical collaborative skills with families, we also hope to nurture dispositions in teachers to work successfully with families. Developing plans for their classrooms and envisioning the possibilities inherent in cooperative family engagement are encouraged throughout this text.

Family Engagement Terminology

Key terms are defined in the chapters, as well as included in a comprehensive glossary. The authors selected key family engagement vocabulary from each chapter to add to the reader's schema.

Websites

An updated list of websites related to topics covered is found at the end of each chapter. Relevant web pages within sites are described. Exploring these sites will provide valuable additional resources for the reader to explore areas of further interest. In addition, a student study-guide website expands on current issues presented in the text and offers further opportunities for in-depth study of topics.

ORGANIZATION OF THE TEXT

The text is divided into three sections:

Section I. Understanding Family Engagement: Building a Knowledge Base for Culturally Responsive Family Engagement

Section I helps educators actualize the process of family engagement by establishing a knowledge base through the exploration of theories and models, as well as the family support approach. The notion of culturally responsive family engagement is explained along with current trends in family demographics. Finally, a chapter is devoted to help teachers understand current parenting practices in diverse families.

Section II. Appreciating Families: Today's Diverse Families

Section II focuses on helping teachers appreciate structurally and culturally diverse families, as well as understand the many challenges that today's families face. The challenges may include transitional situations, such as divorce, death, military deployment, homelessness, and incarceration, as well as long-term stresses of poverty, illness, and violence. Finally, child abuse and neglect are discussed, along with mandatory reporting requirements.

Section III. Family Engagement: Putting Knowledge and Skills Into Action

Section III helps teachers take the foundational information about families from Sections I and II and begin to apply it to their teaching practices in a supportive manner. Collaborating with families on issues such as homework, academic, and behavior challenges and helping families understand contemporary standards-based curriculum, as well as encouraging classroom volunteers are foci of the beginning of the section, followed by communicative strategies to use with families, including reciprocal communication, active listening, conferencing, and home visits. Partnering with families of exceptional children is discussed, along with asset-based practice, advocacy, and families as decision makers and school leaders. A discussion of collaborating with the community to support learning is also included in this section. Section III concludes with practical strategies for schoolwide family engagement, including how to prepare for family events; establishing a school or classroom-family resource center; and the recruitment, training, and retention of school volunteers.

Appendices

Five appendices are included to support the text chapters' content.

Appendix A describes the four major sets of national standards for both beginning and practicing teachers. This section compares the family engagement standards from the Interstate New Teacher Assessment and Support Consortium (INTASC), National Board of Professional Teaching Standards (NBPTS), National Association for the Education of Young Children (NAEYC), and Association for Childhood Education International (ACEI), and it offers guidance for teacher preparation and inservice relating to family engagement.

Appendix B features a section of the National Association for the Education of Young Children (NAEYC) Code of Ethical Conduct that relates to family engagement. This appendix will help readers better understand ethical practice with families, and it offers them a resource for making decisions when presented with ethical dilemmas.

Appendix C lists the contact information for reporting abuse or neglect in the 50 states, Puerto Rico, and the District of Columbia. It will be a helpful resource for teachers.

Appendix D provides information about federal mandates in family involvement for Title I, Head Start, and the No Child Left Behind Act. The analyses of these mandates can help teachers better recognize the importance and requirements of family engagement in their practice.

Appendix E offers guidance on how to develop, implement, and evaluate a school's family engagement plan. Examples of school districts' mission statements and one state's family involvement plan for the schools are given.

ANCILLARY MATERIALS

Instructor Teaching Site

A password-protected site, available at **www.sagepub.com/grant2e**, features author-provided resources that have been designed to help instructors plan and teach their courses. These resources include the following:

- An extensive test bank with at least 20 to 25 multiple-choice questions, 15 to 20 true/false questions, and 15 to 20 short-answer or essay questions for each chapter
- 15 to 20 chapter-specific PowerPoint slide presentations with key points and significant tables/figures appropriate for lectures

- Sample syllabi for semester, quarter, and online courses
- Discussion topics and corresponding questions based on current research topics and issues
- Access to recent, relevant full-text SAGE journal articles and accompanying article review questions
- Suggested movies and TV shows related to the discussed topics to help students connect with the subject matter discussed in the book
- A list of additional websites related to each chapter to further students' interest and spark discussion

Student Study Site

A study site is available at www.sagepub.com/grant2e. This site provides access to several author-provided study tools, including the following:

- eFlashcards to reinforce students' understanding of key terms and concepts presented in the text
- Web quizzes for student self-review
- Web resources organized by chapter for more in-depth research on topics presented in each chapter
- Learning objectives to track learning goals throughout the semester
- Access to recent, relevant full-text SAGE journal articles and accompanying article review questions

ACKNOWLEDGMENTS

We would like to acknowledge the powerful writing of our 24 contributing authors. Experts from the fields of family engagement and advocacy, parenting education, psychology, early childhood, elementary education, family support, multicultural education, literacy, counselor education, special education, social services, and math and science education left their mark on our textbook. With their knowledge and experiences relating to the wide range of topics presented, their contributions have greatly enhanced our efforts, and we are extremely grateful for their scholarly contributions.

We wish to sincerely thank our numerous reviewers for their helpful suggestions for revising and editing our early drafts, as well as those who reviewed this second edition. Our reviewers included the following:

Nancy Aguinaga, *Southeast Missouri State University*

Junie Albers-Biddle, *University of Central Florida*

Amy E. Allen, *The University of Toledo*

Rosemary Bolig, *The University of the District of Columbia*

Mary Bowne, *South Dakota State University*

Jane Tingle Broderick, *East Tennessee State University*

Claire Coleman, *University of LaVerne*

Linda Garris Christian, *Adams State College*

Anthony Faber, *Southeast Missouri State University*

Janice E. Hale, *Wayne State University*

Terry H. Higgins, *The Ohio State University–Newark*

Michelle Hughes, *James Madison University*

Ithel Jones, *The Florida State University*

Dennis J. Kirchen, *Dominican University*

Amy J. Malkus, *East Tennessee State University*

Mari Riojas-Cortez, *The University of Texas at San Antonio*

Kathleen M. Sheridan, *National-Louis University*

Sally M. Wade, *University of South Florida*

Sharryn Larsen Walker, *University of Missouri–Columbia*

Herman Walston, *Kentucky State University*

Fatemah Zarghami, *St. Cloud State University*

We appreciate the contributions of Martha Delarm, Patricia Fisk-Moody, Luanne Kicking Woman, Tami Adams, Brian Horne, Nina Smith, Jeanne Moon, Mike Maxwell, and Lisa Srokowski. Classroom teachers and social workers Dana Beussink, Emily Brune, Debbie Childers, Jeanne Dent, Renee Mayse, Lindsay Miller, Natalie Curry, and Dena Shelton shared valuable practical experiences in working with families, and the knowledge and personal insight of parents and grandparents Sharon Dees, JoAnne Dunham-Trautwein, Anne Fildes, Susan Fraser, Dave Kramer, Julia Pewitt-Kinder, DO, and Nicole Cody were also invaluable. The revisions of the second edition of this text would not have been possible without the efficiency and dedication of assistant Melanie O'Leary. Finally, we wish to thank the staff at SAGE, especially Diane McDaniel and her editorial assistants, for providing support and encouragement through the publication process.

SECTION I

Understanding Family Engagement

Building a Knowledge Base for Culturally Responsive Family Engagement

Becoming partners with families in the education of their children does not always happen automatically for teachers. It will require commitment, specialized knowledge, and skills. Section I of this text is designed to help develop an understanding of families and a positive attitude toward family engagement, as well as build on or extend the knowledge base about family engagement practices. Chapter 1 will explore the benefits of and barriers to effective family engagement and the changing demographics of today's families, as well as introduce the concept of culturally responsive and ethical family engagement practices. Chapter 2 will explore different theories and models of family engagement, with an emphasis on recognizing cultural context. Chapter 3 will present different parenting styles, cultural differences in parenting, and how educators can apply an understanding of these through the principles of family support and parent education models. Together, these chapters will help begin a journey in developing the knowledge, skills, and dispositions needed for culturally responsive family engagement in the education of students.

Chapter 1

Family Engagement and the Responsive Educator

"There is no program and no policy that can substitute for a parent who is involved in their child's education from day one."

—President Barack Obama (2010)

As an educator, the focus is on effective teaching and assessment strategies, classroom management skills, content expertise, and a myriad of other pedagogical skills and knowledge. However, a crucial aspect of development as a responsive educator is knowing how to collaborate authentically and effectively with students' families. Research has shown that the most effective teachers and schools are those with strong family engagement programs (Henderson & Mapp, 2002).

Historically, **family engagement** has been consistently mandated at both the federal and state levels, beginning with **Title I** of the Elementary and Secondary Education Act of 1965 and continuing through the No Child Left Behind legislation (1994) and currently with the reauthorization of the U.S. Department of Education (2010).

Reflects the importance of strengthening and supporting family engagement both through specific programs designed to involve families and communities and through policies that will engage and empower parents. It will ensure that families have the information they need about their children's schools and enhance the ability of teachers and leaders to include families in the education process. (U.S. Department of Education, 2010, p. 1)

This text is designed to help teachers become responsive family engagement practitioners, and, while reading this chapter, to consider these questions:

- What does it mean to become a "partner" with families?
- How do I feel about developing home-school partnerships?

- What are the benefits and barriers of family engagement?
- What are today's families like in structure and culture?
- How can I practice culturally responsive family engagement?
- What does it mean to have ethical practice in family engagement?

PREPARING FOR FAMILY PARTNERSHIPS: ACTUALIZING THE PROCESS

Working toward genuine partnerships with students' families may be one of the most rewarding experiences for a responsive educator. Establishing those partnerships may be elusive, but once established, the family's element of trust in their child's teacher may be secure. Trust is a critical component of collaborative partnerships between families and teachers, and a trusting relationship begins with teachers who are committed to and respectful of all families.

This is especially important since researchers have found that parents are more likely to be involved in their child's education if they trust their child's teacher (Adams & Christenson, 2000).

Realistically, establishing authentic partnerships with families can be challenging, undoubtedly time intensive, and many times, it depends on creative problem-solving techniques to cement the relationship. As a responsive educator, it may be apparent that some family members may not be involved in schools in the expected ways, such as volunteering in the classroom or chaperoning a field trip. However, this does not mean that they are not interested in their children's academic and social progress (Compton-Lilly, 2004). It may mean instead that you will need to develop a variety of family engagement strategies that fit today's diverse families' lifestyles, issues, and beliefs about their role in their child's education. Researchers have found that when teachers reach out to families, the families are more likely to be involved in their child's education in some way, resulting in strong, consistent gains in student performance in both reading and math (Westat & Policy Studies Associates, 2001).

Allocating extra time to nurture relationships with families throughout the school year is essential. A key research finding in effective family engagement practices is that *relationships matter*. When school staff view and treat families and community members as assets in the process of educating students as opposed to liabilities, positive relationships can develop (Henderson & Mapp, 2002). This may require several more hours during an already busy day for tasks such as meeting with a parent or updating the class website with new pictures of class activities and links for homework help. As relationships with families develop and mature, the time spent will pay big dividends, with students seeing a connection between home and school and gaining more support in teaching efforts. In reality, families generally know their children much better than the educator ever will, as the teacher, and they can be a valuable resource in helping students reach their potential.

How can the educator develop a mutually respectful relationship with families? This textbook is designed to answer that question, with a focus on adopting a **culturally responsive family engagement** approach. This approach involves practices that respect and acknowledge the cultural uniqueness, life experiences, and viewpoints of classroom families and draw on those experiences to enrich and energize the classroom curriculum and teaching activities, leading to respectful partnerships with students' families. Some ideas that will be further explored in future chapters include the following:

- How the family operates as a system and the implications this and other family involvement models have for your teaching practices
- The wide range of diversity in today's families, in structure and culture
- The difficult issues that contemporary families face that may have an impact on their ability to be involved in school
- Ways to collaborate with families on their children's education, including families of children with special needs
- Effective school-home communication practices—oral, written, and technological means of communication
- Classroom and school environments that are welcoming, with family resource centers and supportive volunteer policies and practices
- Family events that can be held throughout the year, such as literacy, math, or science family nights
- Community resources available to support families and educators

While this process of learning how to develop partnerships with the families of students may seem overwhelming, consider it as another ingredient in becoming an exemplary teacher.

IN THE CLASSROOM: A NEW SCHOOL YEAR BEGINS

Kate Harrison listened intently as her principal, Brenda Fraser, addressed the group of teachers at their first faculty meeting of the year. As a first-year teacher, Kate was excited to have a job teaching second grade at Kennedy Elementary School, but she was also nervous. She wanted to make this school year a special one for her second graders, but as Mrs. Fraser described some of the new district and state requirements for teachers and students, she wondered if she'd be able to do everything that was required of her. One of the new mandates that Mrs. Fraser was describing was something called a District Family Engagement Plan:

"Our new Family Engagement Plan requires that we do more than what we've done in the past—an open house at the beginning of school, fall parent-teacher conferences, and monthly parent newsletters are not enough. We're going to have to work at doing a better job of engaging our school's families—and that means all families. You know that our Latino population is increasing, and we need to find ways to reach out to those parents who haven't been very involved in our class activities. There are other groups that haven't been involved—for example, how many fathers volunteered in our classrooms last year, especially those divorced dads who don't have custody of their children? I want all of you to be thinking about how you're going to do that in your class-rooms, as well as how we can do a better job with family engagement as a school. I want us to move toward a more family-centered approach where we use the strengths of parents to help us educate their children. That will be the topic of our next faculty workday, and in the meantime, I'm going to ask you to work in subgroups to come up with some collaborative family engagement strategies for our different family types."

(Continued)

(Continued)

Mrs. Fraser handed out assignments, and Kate looked at hers with trepidation. She and three other teachers were given the task of improving family engagement practices with the single-parent families in the district. Kate had grown up with both parents and wasn't sure if she knew what it was like to be a single parent. She wasn't even a parent herself. While she wanted to have good relationships with the families of her students, she was also a little afraid of what they might think of her, as an inexperienced teacher. She also couldn't imagine how she was going to find time to do anything more than write a monthly parent newsletter, with trying to get lessons planned and papers graded. She sighed as she laid the paper to the side with the stack of other back-to-school tasks that the principal had given out.

You'll note that the term "parent involvement" is not used in this text. Rather, **family engagement** is the terminology chosen to reflect the changing nature of the homes in which children reside, which may or may not include a parent or parents. A mutually collaborative, working relationship with the family serves the best interests of the student, in both the school and home settings, for the primary purpose of increasing student achievement (Epstein et al., 2002). It also denotes the rich contributions of individuals beyond parents, such as grandparents, aunt, uncles, and siblings. As this text title, *Home, School, and Community Collaboration* suggests, a broader perspective than "parental connections" will be presented, demonstrating the "overlapping spheres of influence" that **school, family, and community partnerships**—a multidimensional concept that acknowledges that families, teachers, administrators, and community members jointly share the responsibility for students' academic achievement and development—have on children's education and development (Epstein & Sheldon, 2006). The term "family engagement" has also replaced the familiar "family involvement" phrase. As Ferlazzo (2011) explained:

ACTIVITY 1.1

Using the survey in Table 1.1, assess your beliefs about some of the basic premises of family engagement. Consider returning to this survey at the end of the course to determine your growth as a responsive family educator.

We need to understand the differences between family *involvement* and family *engagement*. One of the dictionary definitions of *involve* is "to enfold or envelope," whereas one of the meanings of *engage* is "to come together and interlock." Thus, involvement implies doing to; in contrast, engagement implies doing with (p. 11).

A true collaboration between school, home, and community requires active engagement of all those involved.

FORMING FAMILY PARTNERSHIPS: SELF-ASSESSMENT ACTIVITY

Perhaps the first step in becoming a responsive educator in connecting with the families of students is to reflect on beliefs about family engagement. Initially, an

TABLE 1.1   Family Engagement Attitude Survey

Directions: This survey presents an opportunity for self-reflection about some of the basic premises of family engagement. Read the following statements and indicate your level of acceptance of the statement by selecting option (a) completely, (b) somewhat, or (c) do not. Be honest in your self-assessment and be prepared to provide your reasoning in rating the statement as you did.

  a. Completely

  b. Somewhat

  c. Do not

As an educator preparing to work with families, I _____

  1. Acknowledge that the family remains the child's first teacher throughout the school years.

  2. Recognize the potential of the home as a learning environment.

  3. Believe in the strength of families and the ultimate resilience of the family unit.

  4. Tend to judge families' abilities to be involved with their child's education, based on their backgrounds, degree of education, socioeconomic status, or family structure.

  5. Empathize with the daily economic, personal, and psychological stresses in today's families.

  6. Understand how cultural differences and beliefs affect families' attitudes about their role in their child's education.

  7. Maintain an openness to communicate with families through a variety of methods.

  8. Recognize the risk factors brought on by poverty, I have knowledge of community resources and a willingness to refer families to the appropriate agencies.

  9. Respect the decisions made by families concerning the academic future of their children (my students).

  10. Welcome all my students' family members, as well as community members, to volunteer in my classroom.

  11. Complete this statement: "When I think about being a partner with my students' families in their education, I feel . . ."

educator may experience feelings of ambivalence, fear, or shyness when confronted with the idea of collaborating with families. These feelings are natural for any educator, especially if the educator is not a parent. However, an important part of the job as an educator of children will involve partnering with families in the school community, and it is important to identify any attitudes that will be a barrier to effective family collaboration practices.

Family engagement in children's education has many benefits for students, their families, and their teachers.

BENEFITS OF EFFECTIVE FAMILY ENGAGEMENT PRACTICES

As one reflects on present knowledge and skills relating to working with families, it is important to understand the benefits of a strong family engagement program, as well as barriers to its success. Research confirms that "educators need to know how to work with families and communities. . . . These competencies are required *every day of every year of every teacher's professional career* [italics added]" (Epstein, Sanders, & Clark, 1999, p. 29). The reciprocal benefits of family engagement are numerous—all constituents, including children, families, educators, and the school community, reap the positive rewards of increased family engagement.

Benefits for Students

Numerous research studies have confirmed the positive impact of family engagement on students from early childhood through high school. *A New Wave of Evidence: The Impact of School, Family, and Community Connections on Student Achievement* (Henderson & Mapp, 2002) reviewed hundreds of studies, which overwhelmingly indicated that high-quality family engagement programs improve and support student achievement. Specifically, it was found that students whose families are engaged in their education in some way

- earn higher grades and test scores,
- are less likely to be retained in a grade,
- are more apt to have an accurate diagnosis for educational placement in classes,
- attend school regularly,
- like school and adapt well to it,
- have better social skills,
- have fewer negative behavior reports, and
- graduate and go on to postsecondary education.

A key finding of this research is the importance of encouraging families to support their children's learning at home. Other researchers have found that family engagement may account for 10% to 20% of the variance in student achievement levels and that family engagement at the elementary level was a strong predictor of student achievement in urban schools (Fan & Chen, 2001; Jeynes, 2003; 2005; 2007). Family engagement appears to have a long-range effect as children progress through school, and the more families support their children's learning, the better they do in school over time (Henderson & Mapp, 2002).

Benefits for Families

Family engagement can also have benefits for parents and guardians. Studies have found that families who are engaged in their children's education tend to have more positive attitudes and be more satisfied with their child's school and teachers, with fewer mistaken assumptions between families and teachers about one another's attitudes, abilities, and motives. There is also an increase in families' skills and confidence, sometimes even leading to improving their education. As families better understand the school's structure and programs, they may move into more leadership roles in the school setting (Cotton & Wikelund, 2001). Family members may also gain a better understanding of their child's skills, abilities, and development and learn how to handle parenting issues, such as discipline, nutrition, or how to help with homework (Diffily, 2004).

Benefits for Educators and Schools

Family engagement also benefits schools and school districts. Certainly, teachers benefit from the extra support and individualized attention that families can give their child, whether it is volunteering in the classroom or helping at home. School districts can benefit in a number of ways. For example, researchers have found that schools with highly rated partnership programs make greater gains on state tests than schools with lower-rated programs (Henderson & Mapp, 2002). Family engagement can help school districts achieve the standards required under the No Child Left Behind accountability movement. Other research has shown that school safety is increased with the presence of active family and community members throughout a school's campus (Saunders, 1996). School districts may also benefit financially; families who approve of the schools that their children attend are more likely to support the school with votes for passage of school bond issues, educator raises, and may be involved in grant-writing initiatives.

A note of caution about the benefits of traditional family engagement for educators and schools—it may be a benefit to teachers and schools, but have little benefit for families. For example, attending PTA meetings or school performances, volunteering clerical assistance, fundraising, or sending in school party treats may be quite helpful to teachers or districts, but they do little to authenticate a true partnership.

BARRIERS TO AUTHENTIC FAMILY ENGAGEMENT

Although there are numerous benefits to family engagement, researchers have also identified barriers to authentic family engagement. Although the roadblocks may appear formidable, the first step in overcoming them is to recognize school barriers (teacher and administrators), family barriers (individual or group), community barriers (district or school building), and programmatic barriers (families invited to partake in workshops or training) that hinder effective family involvement.

School Barriers: Educators

Despite research to the contrary, unfortunately, some teachers think that families are not valuable resources in educating students, and hence, they do not value or promote family engagement.

Finding the time in a busy school day is also a major barrier for teachers (Lawson, 2003). Moreover, the lack of trust for parental motives, actions, or lack of respect for their life choices can create a negative attitude for teachers toward family engagement (Adams & Christenson, 2000). Middle-class teachers tend especially to view low-income families negatively, in valuing their contributions or childrearing practices (Edwards & Young, 1990). They may also fear that family members will judge their teaching performance or gossip outside the classroom about the students' abilities or behaviors. Teachers' preferences for traditional school involvement such as volunteering, chaperoning field trips, or acting as a classroom parent to organize events, may limit family engagement. This schoolcentric approach, which refers to traditional family involvement activities that are centered on meeting the teacher/school's needs without regard to a family's perspective or needs relating to their child's education, may offer few opportunities for meaningful interactions and relationship building with families (Lawson, 2003).

Family Barriers: Individuals or Group

In addition to educators' and school districts' practices, families may also have barriers that keep them from fully participating in their child's education. Similar to teachers, time is one of the biggest roadblocks to family engagement. Whether it is a work schedule or a busy lifestyle, today's families often do not have discretionary time to devote to their child's education. Teachers may inadvertently make it more difficult for busy working families by only offering school engagement opportunities between 8:00 a.m. and 4:00 p.m. on school days, with no flexibility or other options (Rich, 1998). For example, one study found that low-income working mothers or those who were attending school full-time required other means of engagement beyond the school day schedule (Weiss et al., 2003).

Adults who had negative personal school experiences may be anxious about entering a school they perceive as unwelcoming (Finders & Lewis, 1994). Direct conflicts with teachers (Lawson, 2003) or unhappiness over remarks made by teachers may cause families to avoid contact with teachers. A lack of family efficacy, or confidence in being able to help their child succeed in school (Henderson & Mapp, 2002), and the embarrassment associated with this struggle again may cause avoidance of classrooms.

All these issues will be addressed throughout this text in more detail. Although the barriers to effective family engagement seem many, creative, caring, and committed educators and families can find ways to surmount these obstacles.

School/District/Community Barriers

In today's era of school security issues, many school campuses have a forbidding appearance for nonschool personnel, with locked doors and signs demanding that visitors report to the office, creating an actual physical barrier to families wishing to visit school. Lewis and Henderson (1997) noted that an unwelcoming school atmosphere may turn families away from venturing into a school. Policies such as not allowing younger siblings to come to school with a family volunteer or not permitting family members to volunteer in their child's classroom can also be a barrier. In addition, with the new scrutiny imposed on schools to meet higher academic standards, school systems may close doors to parents, especially those who may be critical of teachers or school policies (Saunders, 2001).

A low priority of family engagement funding in high-poverty schools has been noted (Roza, 2005). Schools receiving funding under Title I must allocate a certain portion of Title I funds to developing family partnerships, but this money can be spent in other ways. School districts often bemoan a lack of positive and authentic opportunities for families to become involved (Hoover-Dempsey & Sandler, 1997). Many times, restricted thinking on the part of the district concerning what is viewed as an acceptable contribution to the school effort is constraining for families wishing to be involved in other ways.

Schools may be well intentioned in developing family engagement activities, but they may fail to recognize that not all families may be able to participate in them. For example, many elementary schools host family events, such as a Grandparents' Day luncheon, a Mother's Day tea, or a Father's Day breakfast, which by nature will eliminate some children's families from participating if they are not a two-parent family or if they do not have grandparents in the community. A family event that features a meal may eliminate some families whose culture or religion does not allow them to eat certain foods, and school holiday celebrations that honor the majority population holidays, while neglecting other cultural holidays, will exclude some cultural or religious minorities. Teachers may have children create Mother's and Father's Day gifts or complete projects, such as a family tree, which may be difficult for children who do not live with both parents or are adopted or foster children, as they may not have photos of themselves as babies or knowledge about their family heritage.

> **ACTIVITY 1.2**
>
> Table 1.2 has a list of common school activities. Which of these activities will exclude some students and their families from participating due to their family diversity, socioeconomic status, or language background? Explain how that can occur sometimes in schools. How can these activities be modified to include all families?

Barriers for Culturally and Linguistically Diverse Families

A major barrier for families who are new immigrants or English language learners (ELLs) includes the inability to understand the majority language of the school (Antunez, 2000). Furthermore, some cultural traditions (or simply some parents) believe that the role of the teacher is to educate the child (Kim, 2002) and that the family's role is to rear the child, not to be directly involved in educational practices. Olivos (2009) & Salas (2004) explore potential barriers for culturally and linguistically diverse families who have a special needs child. These include the following:

- The asymmetries of power that can take the form of explicit and implicit discouragement by educators
- Educators fluent in legal discourse of special education laws versus parents lacking that knowledge
- Parental feelings of alienation and disrespect from educators that result in disengagement, avoidance, and anger
- Parental opinions discounted in feeling their "voices were not heard"

Chapter 5, Culturally Diverse Families, explores in great detail the benefits and barriers of culturally responsive family engagement and nurturing educators who support this model of collaboration with families.

TABLE 1.2   Inclusive or Exclusive Activities

Rate These School or Classroom Activities

1. All children and their families will be able to participate fully

2. All children and their families will be able to participate, but some may be uncomfortable with the activity

3. Some children and their families will be excluded in this activity

_____ A family picnic on the last day of school

_____ Dressing in a Halloween costume for the school costume parade and inviting families to view the parade

_____ Requesting that children have their mom or dad sign a paper

_____ Creating a family tree with baby pictures as a school project

_____ Inviting grandparents to have lunch with their grandchild

_____ A classroom cooking activity with family volunteers during a religious observance, such as Ramadan, Yom Kippur, or Lent

_____ A history day show-and-tell where children and/or their parents bring an item that represents their family's heritage

_____ A nighttime parent education meeting where child care is not offered

_____ A field trip to the pumpkin patch with parent chaperones that requires an admission and snacks fee

_____ Asking a student's family members to come in and read a story to the class

How could each of these be modified so that all children and families can participate?

Although all schools face roadblocks to effective family engagement, Table 1.3 compares and contrasts the findings from recent research on the differing barriers in urban, rural, and suburban schools.

THE ADMINISTRATOR AS A RESPONSIVE LEADER

From the activities described thus far, a supportive administrator is key to the success of schoolwide family engagement practices. Research substantiates the powerful impact a principal or assistant principal committed to family engagement can have on school partnership programs in numerous ways (Davies, 2002; Sanders & Harvey, 2002; Van Voorhis & Sheldon, 2005). Without an effective administrator spearheading organized efforts toward family engagement, teachers who are at first enthusiastic about including families in all aspects of school planning and engagement often get discouraged. As one study found,

TABLE 1.3	Family Engagement Barriers: School, Family, Community, and Program-based			
	School Barriers	**Family Barriers**	**Community Barriers**	**Programmatic Barriers**
Urban	• Inappropriate teacher & school secretary attitudes • Avoidance • Fear of confrontations • Lack of understanding cultural differences • Few translators or bilingual teachers • Methods of contact unsuccessful	• Participant disinterest • Gender-specific exclusion (males) • Feelings of intimidation/ inadequacy • Prior negative school experiences • Families' past social interactions with school • Parental occupation/time limitations • Childcare and transportation issues	• Unmet physical and safety needs • Unsafe communities, school security issues: locked access • Scheduling problems: lack of facilities/ community resources • Catastrophic school closure: for example, New Orleans/Katrina	• Misconceptions about purpose of parental program • Babysitting costs: children not invited • Too many meetings offered, "less is more" • Fear of getting in trouble with spouse for attending meeting
Rural	• Itinerant teachers travel to various school	• Lack of awareness of importance of activities • Negative impression of program based on comments of other families • Persistent poverty: lack of money for anything but basic needs	• Rural communities: working poor live just above poverty line • Out-migration for employment • Geography: consolidated rural schools many miles from students' homes • Weather impediments in areas with limited services	• Transportation costs for program attendance • Learning is "threatening"; fear of attending because of limited literacy
Suburban	• School visitation notification 24 hours in advance • Parents not allowed to visit first week of school • Exclusionary and political views/ of curriculum • "Grapevine" comments judging parents' lifestyles	• Helicopter parents: overinvolvement • Divorced parents: access to records; who attends teacher meetings? • Parental privacy concerns • Children misbehaving when parent involved in school	• School reassignment can cause travel constraints • Lack of access: Internet-based school websites	• School environment too sterile • Lack of visual aids and colorful teaching material • Competing family demands • Programs focused on biological parents, not extended families

Sources: Farrell & Collier, 2010; McBride, Bae, & Blatchford, 2003; Olivos, 2009; Wanat, 2010

Principals have the power to motivate and mobilize school personnel for specific purposes and hold the purse strings for specific initiatives. Principals hold the key to initiating programs and processes. They can enlist school community support, earmark funds for specific priorities, and provide time for teams of teachers, parents, and community members to meet, plan, and evaluate their family involvement actions. When principals fail to support partnership efforts, teachers may abandon their focus on partnerships and shift their energies elsewhere. (Van Voorhis & Sheldon, 2005, p. 56)

As the ultimate host of a school, the principal must ensure that families entering the school experience a welcoming and positive atmosphere, from the friendliness of the school secretary to helpful signs in multiple languages. A principal's vision or motto for family engagement in her school should be evident to families who come there. As a family adviser, a principal's ability to effectively communicate her vision through different modes is crucial. As an instructional leader, a savvy administrator should push teachers to connect their teaching with learning at home and to work with families on issues, including family literacy, home extension activities, and learning challenges.

Moreover, a principal should function as an advocate for families, in part by establishing an information base at the school with up-to-date information about state, district, and community resources available to support families. In addition, the administrator must maintain a deep understanding of the diverse cultures within the community. He should know when to ask resource personnel for translations of important documents and when to consult cultural guides to the community. Finally, as the school's business broker, the principal should be instrumental in collaboration with a school team in seeking school-business partnerships tied to community needs. Figure 1.1 presents a model of the roles that effective family engagement administrators assume.

CURRENT TRENDS IN FAMILY DEMOGRAPHICS

Prior to effectively dealing with barriers to a family engagement program, it is important to have a better understanding of the families of the students in today's classrooms. American families are not easy to define or track because of the changing nature of families and differences in definitions of family. Although the U.S. Census Bureau (2004b) defines a family as people residing in a home who are related "by birth, marriage, or adoption," the reality in today's American families is that there is a wide range of possibilities:

- Children living in two-parent, married families
- Blended families where one parent is a stepparent
- Children living with two adults both acting as parents but who are not married (and may be opposite-sex or same-sex partners) and, therefore, defined as a single-parent household
- Children living in households with grandparents or other relatives
- Children in foster-care situations

One study of the Woodlawn community in Chicago found that first graders had 86 different combinations of adults living in households and 35 different family configurations (Demo & Cox, 2000). Therefore, the labeling of students' family types must be carefully considered.

FIGURE 1.1   Roles of Highly Effective Family Engagement Administrators

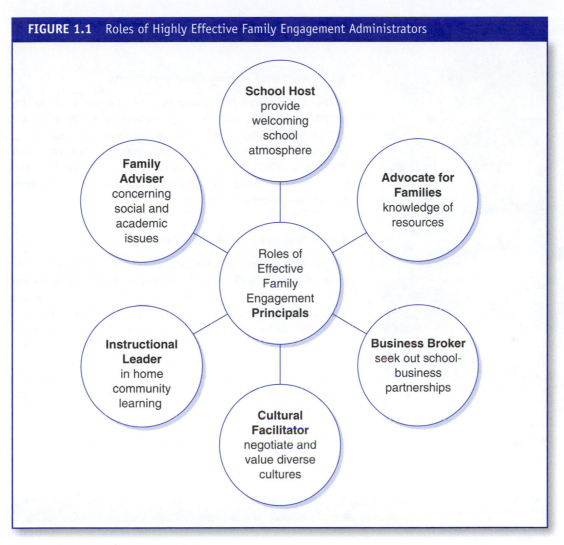

Source: Taken in part from Davies (2002).

However, the U.S. Census Bureau (2005a) provides a snapshot of today's families through data that are gathered annually in the American Community Survey, as well as the data that are collected every 10 years in the Census. Data are gathered on households and families related to number of families, type and size of families, age of children, type of housing, income, and race/ethnicity. In addition, Columbia University's National Center for Children in Poverty currently provides fact sheets on poverty in the United States.

Configuration of Today's American Families

Traditional Family Configurations

In 2008, the majority of children (67%) lived with two married parents, although this may include a number of options, such as a biological mother and father, adoptive parents, a

The proportion of single-parent households continues to increase in today's families.

biological parent and a stepparent, or grandparents who were serving as parents.

Nontraditional Family Configurations

It should be noted that these statistics do not include the nonfamily groups, such as single adults or adults who are unrelated but living together without children. Approximately 33% of all households fit this type. It should also be noted that while children may be living with a single parent, this parent may be cohabiting with another adult and, in essence, providing a two-parent household.

Single Mother/Father Families

Single-mother families have increased from 3 million in 1970 to 10 million in 2003, while single-father families have grown from half a million to 2 million. In 2008, 23% of children lived only with their mother, while 4% of children lived only with their father (Childstats.Gov, 2009). Single mothers are the heads of 44% of Black households (U.S. Census Bureau, 2002a). At the same time, the percentage of two-parent families has decreased from 87% in 1970 to 67% in 2007 (U.S. Census Bureau, 2003, 2004a).

Figure 1.2 provides more detailed information about the complexity of family types, including the presence of a cohabiting parent, which increased the percentage of two-parent homes to 70%.

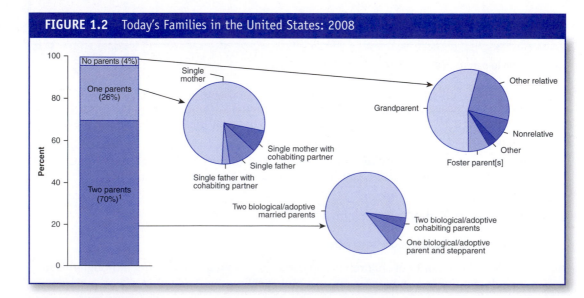

FIGURE 1.2 Today's Families in the United States: 2008

[1] Includes children living with two stepparents.

Source: ChildStats.Gov, 2009; U.S. Census Bureau, 2009

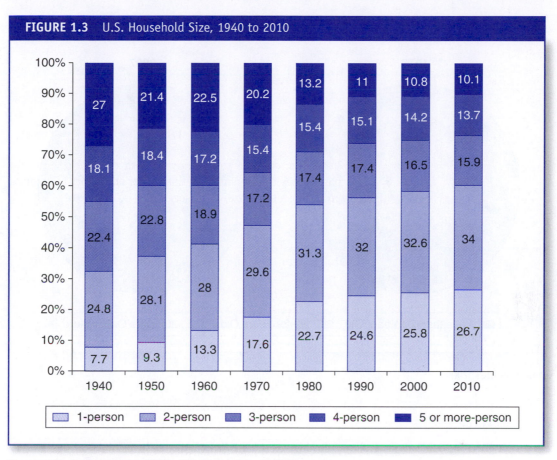

FIGURE 1.3   U.S. Household Size, 1940 to 2010

Sources: U.S. Census Bureau, 2006a; U.S. Census Bureau, 2010

Marriage Ages and Birthrates

American adults are also marrying later. In 2005, the average ages for men and women to marry were 27.1 and 25.8 years respectively. This increased from 22.8 and 20.3 years, respectively, since 1950 (U.S. Census Bureau, 2006b). American parents are choosing to have fewer children as well. There has been a downward trend in household and family size since the beginning of the century. In 2010, families had, on an average, 1.88 children, down from 2.19 children in 1955 (U.S. Census Bureau, 2010). Figure 1.3 shows the trend of smaller households from 1940 to 2010.

Teen and Unmarried Birthrates

The 2009 birthrates for teenagers ages 15 to 19 was 39.1 births per 1,000, a historic low, declining 8% from 2007 to 2009 (Centers for Disease Control and Prevention, 2011b). Preliminary 2008 data showed a decline in overall teenage childbearing. Teenage births have declined 35% since 1991 across all races and ethnicities. However, the births to unmarried women of all ages have risen steadily to 41% of all U.S. births in 2009 (Centers for Disease Control and Prevention, 2011a). Adult women over the age of 20 years have accounted for most of the increase in births to unmarried women, with historic increases in unmarried births since 2002 (Ventura, 2009). Figure 1.4 shows the trends in the ages of unmarried women having babies.

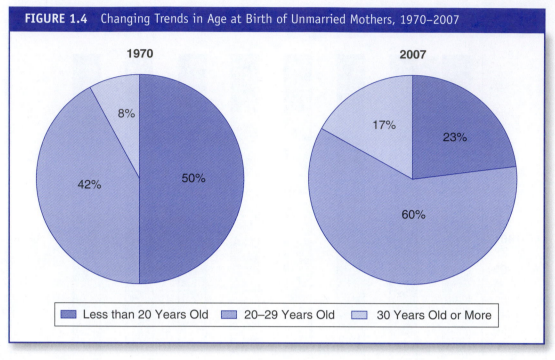

FIGURE 1.4   Changing Trends in Age at Birth of Unmarried Mothers, 1970–2007

Source: Ventura, 2009

Divorce

A growing debate exists about the divorce rate of American marriages. It has been widely reported that approximately one in two marriages will end in divorce based on the marriage and divorce statistics of each year. For example, in 2009, the National Vital Statistics System reported that there were 6.8 marriages and 3.5 divorces per 1,000 people, which is a divorce rate of approximately 51.4% (Centers for Disease Control and Prevention, 2011). However, a recent U.S. Census Bureau report (Kreider & Ellis, 2011) found that determining the divorce rate is more complicated than just comparing the number of marriages to the number of divorces in any given year. Divorce rates differ according to factors such as the length of the marriage and race. For example, divorces were more likely to occur in the first ten years of marriage, with the median length of a first marriage as eight years. Divorce rates were also lower in 2009 for Asian American and Hispanic women, with 22% of Asian American and 34% of Hispanic women's first-time marriages ending in divorce, compared to 41% of white women and 49% of Black women. Experts do agree that divorce rates, which rose sharply in the 1970s and the 1980s, leveled off and slightly declined in the 1990s, with that trend continuing in 2009 (Hurley, 2005; Kreider & Ellis, 2011; U.S. Census Bureau, 2002b).

Remarriage

Divorces and remarriages that involve children often occur when children are in early childhood or elementary school years. In 2009, the average age at which a divorce occurred was 30 for women and 32 for men. For divorced adults who went on to remarry, the average amount of time between the end of the first marriage and the second marriage was 3.8 years for men and 3.7 years for women (Kreider & Ellis, 2011).

Grandparent Caregivers

Another significant trend in today's families is the increase of grandparents raising their grandchildren, known as Grandfamilies (Children's Defense Fund, 2010). In 2009, 9% of all children (4.4 million) were living in grandparent-led households (U.S. Census Bureau, 2010). Another 1.5 million children were living with other relatives, in what is labeled Kinship Care (AARP, 2007). Clearly, there is not one typical type of family in today's American society.

Economic Status of Today's American Families

Responsive educators recognize that child poverty in America affects educational opportunities, child health, and social growth and development for children whose families experience poverty. Hardships suffered by children include food insecurity, lack of affordable housing and health insurance, and difficult daily economic struggles. Persistent or deep poverty is even more debilitating and defeating for families.

Family poverty appears to impact the following:

- A greater percentage of African American (61%) and Latino children (62%)
- Children of immigrants, who comprise 26% of children of poverty
- Young children; 20% of children younger than six live in poverty
- Southern states, as they exhibit the highest levels of extreme child poverty (20% to 56%) (National Center for Children in Poverty, 2005)

Child poverty is defined as children who live in families below the federal poverty level (FPL), which is $22,050 (2009) for a family of four. However, extreme child poverty is defined as children living in families with incomes below half the FPL. In 2005, 17% of children or more than 12 million children lived below the poverty line (National Center for Children in Poverty, 2005). While 8.5% of the children living in married-couple families were living in poverty, 43.3% of the children living with single mothers and 21.7% of single-father-headed households were below the poverty line (U.S. Census Bureau, 2006-2008). In 2009, 21% of all children were living in poverty, but poverty rates varied in different geographic regions and by race and ethnicity. Although 12% of white children lived in poor families, the number increased for children who were African American (36%), American Indian (34%), or Hispanic (33%), as shown in Figure 1.5. Children in immigrant families had higher rates of poverty, as did those living in southern states (Wright, Chau, & Aratani, 2011). In 2009, 10.5 million children were living with an unemployed parent. In addition, low-income families (defined as having income below twice the FPL) care for 41% of the nation's children—nearly 30 million in 2008 (for 2009, about $44,000 for a family of four) (Cauthen & Fass, 2010). Figures 1.5 and 1.6 display the status of children living in poverty in the United States.

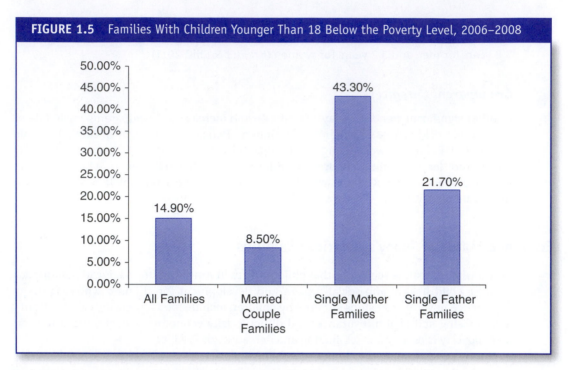

FIGURE 1.5 Families With Children Younger Than 18 Below the Poverty Level, 2006–2008

Source: U.S. Census Bureau, 2006–2008 American Community Survey

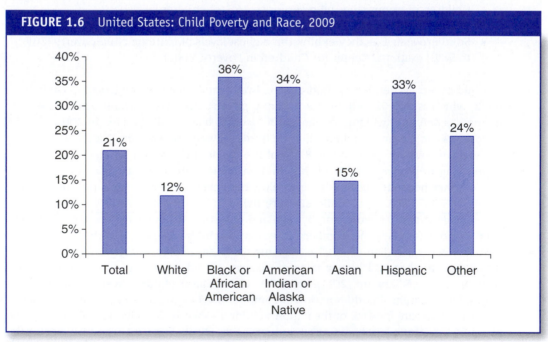

FIGURE 1.6 United States: Child Poverty and Race, 2009

Source: Wright, Chau & Artani, 2011

Race and Ethnicity of Today's American Families

As the society of the United States becomes more diverse, American families are also increasingly diverse in race and ethnicity. The Census Bureau predicts that while family size will decrease, family diversity will increase. Latino and Asian American families are projected to show the most growth, while the percentage of white families will decrease. In 2008, whites represented the majority population at 66%, blacks at 13%, Latinos at 15%, and Asians at 3%. By 2042, the Census Bureau projects that the combined minority population will be larger than the majority, white non-Hispanic population (Roberts, 2008). As Figure 1.7 demonstrates, by 2050, the Census Bureau projects that the U.S. population will include 46% whites, 30% Latinos, 13% blacks, and 9% Asians, with other minority groups increasing to 5% (Roberts, 2008). Originally, the Census Bureau had projected that the population of minority children would be larger than the white majority by 2023, but because of the rapid increase of Latino families, this is now projected to occur by 2019 (Tavernise, 2011).

FIGURE 1.7   U.S. Population by Race, 2008, and Projected, 2050

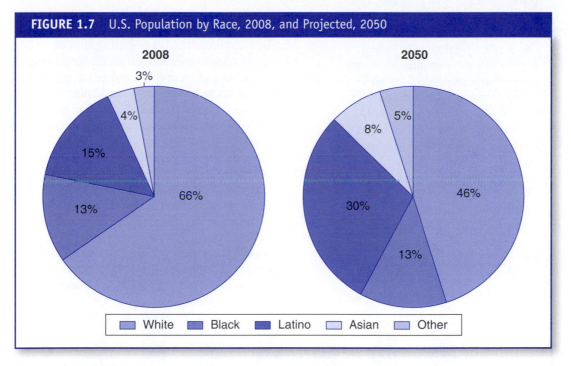

Source: Roberts, 2008

An increase in biracial and multiracial children and families is also being seen, and new guidelines were developed to "reflect the increasing diversity of our Nation's population, stemming from growth in interracial marriages and immigration" (U.S. Census Bureau, 2005b). Respondents to the Census can now indicate their race, including new categories for "two or more races" or "some other race alone." Multiracial families make up the fastest growing demographic in the United States. Approximately 9% of the U.S. population is multiracial, and it is estimated that the numbers will climb to 21 % by 2050 (Brown, 2009, p. 124). The divorce rate for interracial couples is higher than for other couples, and interracial couples are more likely to be younger than older, with 10 % of women under the age of 45 in interracial marriages, compared to 4 % of women older than 55 (Kreider & Ellis, 2011). A difference among family types has also emerged. Although white, Asian, and Latino families are more likely to be headed by married couples, the percentage decreases for black families, with 44 % of these households headed by single mothers (U.S. Census Bureau, 2002a).

Summary of Demographic Information

ACTIVITY 1.3

The chart in Table 1.4 offers you the chance to describe both your family of origin and what you perceive to be the "ideal," in family practices, beliefs, and values. Where are they similar? Where are they different? With a partner, discuss your ideas. Do you think that there is more than one way to "do family?" How will your vision of the ideal family influence your interactions with the families of students in your classroom, especially those who are different from either your family experience or your ideal family? Completing this activity may help you better understand not only the influence of your family but also how diverse family backgrounds have a major impact on the students in your classroom.

An examination of current demographic data indicates the following trends:

- There are more single-parent households because of the choice to raise children alone, divorce, or cohabitation with another adult.
- Couples are choosing to marry later in life.
- Families and households are getting smaller.
- More grandparents are raising their grandchildren.
- There has been a decline in teenage births but an increase in births to unmarried mothers.
- The divorce rate has leveled off between 40 % and 50 %, depending on how the statistics are examined.
- Both parents are likely to work; moreover, most low-income parents are employed.
- Single-parent households are more likely to be below the poverty line than married-couple households.
- Families are more diverse in both structure and race, and the population of children is rapidly growing more racially diverse. Latinos are the fastest growing minority in the United States, followed by Asians.
- There is an increase in biracial and multiracial children and families.

CULTURALLY RESPONSIVE FAMILY ENGAGEMENT

With the family demographics in mind, it is clear that today's classrooms are becoming increasingly diverse in family structure, culture, race, and socioeconomic status, as well as in other respects, such as religion or sexual orientation. Within the different cultural and racial groups, there is much diversity as well. For example, an Asian child could be Chinese, Japanese, Filipino, Vietnamese, Korean, and so on. Each of these cultures potentially represents different beliefs about education, parenting practices, religions, communication styles, and family values. The number of children who come from homes where English is

TABLE 1.4 The Ideal Family and Your Family: Are They the Same?

Briefly describe your family of origin in the different categories and then describe your vision of the "ideal family."

	My Family	The Ideal Family
Family structure		
Typical family activities		
Meal time		
Childhood chores		
Family celebrations/holidays/birthdays		
Relationships with extended family members		
Family transitions (i.e., moves, parents changing jobs, deaths, divorce, new babies)		
Types of family involvement in children's education		
Family values and goals		

not the native language is also increasing. American schools have seen a dramatic rise in ELLs, with 3.7 million ELL children in 1999 to 2000 (Bae & Clark, 2005). This growth in non-English-speaking families presents unique challenges to today's teachers in communication with children and families.

Culturally Responsive Teaching

Gay (2002) proposed that culturally responsive teaching (CRT) provides the best-quality education for diverse students. A culturally responsive teacher uses students' "cultural orientations, background experiences, ethnic identities as conduits to facilitate their learning" (p. 614). This requires that teachers first understand the influence of family experiences, race, culture, and ethnicity on learning, including becoming "critically conscious" of their cultural backgrounds and how these affect their attitudes about children and families that are different from theirs. As a responsive educator, it is important to recognize the influence of personal family experiences, which now provide the lens through which educators look at their students' families and develop CRT strategies. Researchers suggest that these strategies should include developing caring relationships with students, establishing warm, yet demanding classroom climates, and fostering collaboration and social relationships among students. Other strategies include becoming familiar with students' verbal and nonverbal communication styles, providing language support, and developing classroom activities, using a variety of teaching strategies, including appropriate assessments, that reflect students' needs (Bae & Clark, 2005; Brown, 2003; Gay, 2000; 2002).

Therefore, it will not be enough only to focus on teaching strategies that are culturally responsive. Since children cannot be isolated from their home, community, or cultural settings, an educator will also need to use family engagement strategies that are responsive to the families' cultural and community backgrounds. Students will be most successful in their education when there is continuity between home and school. When teachers are supportive of families and communicate in ways that are appropriate for each family's culture, better educational outcomes are seen in children (Keyes, 2002; Poveda & Martin, 2004). The teacher considers the family's perspective in developing family engagement practices and individualizes strategies to meet the needs of diverse family types (Ray, 2005).

This can be difficult for teachers when working with children and families from cultures different from their own. For example, if the educators have never experienced extreme poverty, how can they relate to a family who is homeless? If a teacher has been raised in a Christian background, how can one be sensitive to the beliefs and values of students' parents or guardians who may come from a Jewish, Muslim, Buddhist, or no faith background? If English is the only language that is spoken, how can an educator communicate effectively with the family of a Japanese, Bosnian, or Mexican student who speaks little or no English? Because the majority of early childhood and elementary education teachers are females from a European American, white, middle-class, monolingual background, they may know little about the beliefs, values, and behaviors of children from cultures that are different from this majority perspective (Gay, 2002). This textbook will examine all facets of family engagement from a culturally responsive approach.

ETHICAL PRACTICE

A final note about having effective family engagement practices that are culturally responsive includes understanding how to work with families in ethically and morally responsible ways. The National Association for the Education of Young Children (NAEYC) provides guidance for educators of children of all ages in working ethically with children, families, and colleagues in the *Code of Ethical Conduct* (NAEYC, 2005). In particular, Section II addresses the ethical responsibilities that teachers have to families. These include being responsible for communicating, cooperating, and collaborating with families in ways that will support children's learning and development. An ethical teacher welcomes and encourages families to be involved in their child's education and collaborates with them on making significant decisions about their child. Collaboration also means listening to families, acknowledging their strengths, and learning from them about how to best educate their child. This also involves respecting their culture, language, customs, and beliefs. In turn, teachers can help families understand the educational program and enhance their ability to support their child's learning and development. Ethical practice also means that teachers treat information about children and families with confidentiality and respect families' right to privacy relating to family matters. Families also have the right to be fully informed about anything that occurs at school relating to their child's cognitive, physical, social, or emotional development.

A complete list of the Code of Ethical Conduct Ideals and Principles relating to families is provided in Appendix B.

SUMMARY

Becoming an exemplary teacher with effective home and school collaboration practices is a lifelong task that requires a myriad skills and dispositions, such as commitment, creativity, understanding, respect, and communication. Recognizing the benefits of strong family engagement can help an educator become committed to the work involved in achieving this, and being creative in removing the barriers that present roadblocks to efforts may help you be more successful. Understanding the demographics of the families of students, having respect for their differences, using culturally responsive family involvement strategies and ethical practices will make the task easier. Developing a variety of warm, friendly communication strategies is an important part of the process. As a responsive educator, this may all seem a daunting task, but consider the following commonsense advice from a working mother who coordinates a family resource center as a family outreach specialist in a Western state:

> It is really important for teachers to know how to make a good impression, a friendly impression right off the bat. They have to lay it out, "here's how you communicate with me, here's my phone number, here's my e-mail address, this is a great time to call me because I have recess." So the parent feels welcomed, so they don't have to wait for a problem, when they are nervous about approaching the teacher. Be very approachable, that is what I am trying to say. (Grant, 2002, p. 106)

The vast majority of students' families want their children to achieve and to have a positive relationship with you. It will be up to you to help achieve that goal.

REFLECTION QUESTIONS

Reread the In the Classroom case study presented at the beginning of the chapter, and reflect on these questions:

1. What do you think it means to have a family-centered approach to family engagement?

2. Why is it important to look at different family types, in culture and structure, when developing family engagement plans? What should you consider when working with diverse families?

3. What ideas might Kate take to her first meeting about ways to work effectively with single-parent families?

WEBSITES

Building Parent-Teacher Partnerships, maintained by National Association for the Education of Young Children (NAEYC), http://www.naeyc.org/families/PT

This website provides excellent strategies to increase family involvement through links to family-based documents and resources.

Family and Community, maintained by North Central Regional Education Laboratory, **www.ncrel.org/sdrs/areas/pa0cont.htm**

This website is an excellent source for strategies, advice, and support for improving family involvement in the classroom; site also provides additional resources, through links, for subject integration, educational software, and links for parents.

Family Involvement in Children's Education: *Successful Local Approaches*, maintained by U.S. Department of Education, **www.ed.gov/pubs/FamInvolve/index.html**

This website provides excellent strategies to increase family involvement; detailed examples of successful schools that have undergone extensive transformations to form partnerships with families are highlighted. It also has contact information for both resource centers and regional assistance centers.

National Center for Children in Poverty, maintained by the Mailman School of Public Health, Columbia University, **http://www.nccp.org**

This website contains a multitude of facts, maps, and reports on child and family poverty in the United States.

STUDENT STUDY SITE

Log on to the student study site at **www.sagepub.com/grant2e** for additional study tools, including the following:

- eFlashcards
- Web quizzes
- Web resources
- Learning objectives

Chapter 2

Theories and Models for Family Engagement in Schools

Parents love their children, and if the teacher feels this same love, then parents are your friends. Be casual, be off-handed, be cold toward the child and parents can never work closely with you . . . to touch the child is to touch the parent. To praise the child is to praise the parent. To criticize the child is to hit at the parent. The two are two, but the two are one.

—James T. Hymes (1974)

Teachers often begin the school year with a commitment to having a strong family engagement program, and look for ideas, activities, or strategies to help them reach this goal. However, before beginning to collect a list of ideas, it is important to examine some of the foundational concepts underlying the idea of family involvement. Theories, along with models built on theory and research, can guide teachers in creating a cohesive family involvement approach. As you read this chapter, consider these questions:

- How is a family defined, beyond the legal definition?
- How does a family operate as a system? What are some implications of this family system theory in my family involvement practices?
- How do the home, the community, the society, the culture, and the time in which children live influence their learning and development?

Contributing Authors Josephine Agnew-Tally and Donald Mott

- What are different ways to recognize and incorporate in my teaching the strengths, knowledge, and skills that families offer children in their learning and development?
- What are some examples of how I can organize my classroom and school family engagement practices into a successful program?

DEFINING FAMILY

Before learning about different theories and models for family involvement, it is important to determine what is meant by the term "family." What exactly is a family? Is there one definition of a family? As noted in Chapter 1, the U.S. Census Bureau defines a family as a "group of two people or more (one of whom is the householder) related by birth, marriage, or adoption and residing together" (U.S. Census Bureau, 2010). Some communities have developed a legal definition of family for zoning ordinances, such as Manassas, Virginia, which adopted an ordinance that redefines family as two or more persons who are related by law or blood or three and fewer unrelated people who are living and cooking together as a single housekeeping unit (McCrummen, 2005).

Defining family in legal terms narrows the possibilities of what a family may be. However, when broadening the definition of family, difficult questions arise: Do family members have to be related by blood or by a legal contract? Can someone act as a family member in a child's life, yet not be related to the child? Can a family be a group of people who live together and are committed to one another, but are not related? Are people who are legally related, but have no bond or love for one another, a family? Do people remain a family when legal ties are severed or members move out of the home? Must a family have two adults? Must a family include children? Gestwicki (2010) offers a more global definition of family:

ACTIVITY 2.1

Think about how you would define "family" and jot your ideas down. Pair up with a classmate and compare your ideas. How similar or different are they? Is your definition more inclusive in nature or is it more specific to your particular family experience? With your partner, create a definition of family and share it with the class.

We may be related by birth or adoption or invitation.

We may belong to the same race or we may be of different races.

We may look like each other or different from each other.

The important thing is, we belong to each other.

We care for each other.

We agree, disagree, love, fight, work together.

We belong to each other. (p. 32)

Perhaps the best answer is that you must determine your definition of a family (Bigner, 2006). That definition will reflect your experiences with a family because, ultimately, family is an intensely personal construct and will have different meanings for each person.

IN THE CLASSROOM: A PARENT'S PERSPECTIVE

Driving the long commute home to Poplar Grove, Lois Chandler mentally checked off the tasks that needed to be done when she got home—dinner; laundry; dishes; and, now that school had started again, homework. She was still struggling to fit that new requirement into the few hours between the time she got home from work and bedtime for her three children. She would have liked to work closer to home, but since she and her husband had divorced the previous year, she needed the good salary that her corporate job in the city provided her. She had thought about moving the kids to the city, but she hated to add another change to their lives. The divorce had been hard enough. Besides, Kennedy Elementary was a good school, and she wanted them to have the best education possible.

Lois never dreamed that she would be a single mom. She had always imagined herself growing old with her husband and having grandchildren come and visit them someday. That dream was gone now, and it was up to her to raise the children. While Jim was faithfully making his child support payments and took the kids one weekend a month, most of the child rearing still fell on her, and she often felt like the "bad guy" when she had to enforce the rules for homework and chores. The kids frequently complained about not getting to have friends over on week nights or the "no TV until homework is done" rule, and there were times when she wondered if she was being too strict and whether she should just let them play with friends or watch TV all night.

As she pulled into the parking lot of her child-care program, she realized with guilt that she was one of the last parents to pick up her children. They met her at the door, all competing for her attention: Eight-year-old Tyler wanted to know what was for dinner, ten-year-old Shaina begged to have a friend stay overnight, and five-year-old Ella clung to her wanting to show a picture she had drawn. The noise and competition for her time and energy continued through the rest of the night, until she collapsed into a kitchen chair around midnight, with the dishes done, the latest load of laundry folded, bedtime stories read, and all three children sleeping soundly. Then she noticed the backpacks thrown by the back door and realized that she had not looked in them in several days. As she pulled out the wadded up stories, drawings, worksheets, tests, and book orders, she came across several notes from teachers and the school. Ella's teacher, Ms. Grey, requested that all children bring in $5 for their field trip to the pumpkin patch and asked for parent volunteers to accompany them. There were unfinished worksheets in Tyler's backpack and a note from his teacher, Mrs. Russell, asking to meet with his "parents" next week to discuss her "concerns" about his behavior in class. Shaina's backpack had a letter about the careers unit that they were doing, with a schedule for parents to come in and talk about their jobs. There was also a scribbled note with the words, "I am NOT your friend anymore!!!!!" All three backpacks had information about the new school fundraiser selling pizzas and a flyer about the school's upcoming PTO Fall Festival with a request for donations and volunteers to work the different booths. For a moment, Lois wished that she had never looked inside the backpacks. She felt overwhelmed and pulled in every direction, guilty at the thought of not being able to volunteer at school and worried about the note from Tyler's teacher. She had no vacation days at work left—Ella's frequent asthma attacks had taken all those and more, and Lois had gone to work sick herself a few times to save her remaining sick leave days for the children's illnesses. She also knew that she would have to limit the children's book order requests—there just wasn't enough money in the account to cover many extras—especially if she was going to have to pay for a field trip and order pizzas. Worst of all was the gnawing worry she now felt about Tyler's unfinished school work and a fear that Shaina was having problems with friends. She knew that she probably had another sleepless night ahead of her.

FAMILY SYSTEMS CONCEPTUAL FRAMEWORK

In the 1970s, a conceptual framework emerged in the field of family therapy to help explain how a family functioned. This framework has been called family process theory or family systems theory and grew out of von Bertalanffy's (1968) general systems theory and the structural functional theory developed by sociologists, which focused on the social functions of the members of a society (Broderick, 1993). Family relations specialists and therapists proposed the idea that a well-functioning family operates as a "social system," much like the other systems noted in nature, such as the solar system or biological ecological systems (Becvar & Becvar, 2008; Bigner, 2006; Broderick, 1993; von Bertalanffy, 1968). Members of a family system are interconnected, and each member influences the others. For educators, applying family systems theory to their teaching means not just focusing on individual students but rather looking at children in the context of their families to understand why children act the way they do in the class setting (Christian, 2006). To better understand what a system is and how family systems influence children's classroom behavior, it is helpful to look at the general characteristics of a system and see how these relate to families and the classroom setting.

Characteristics of a System

As you read the descriptions of the characteristics of family systems that follow, think about how each family system characteristic functioned in your family of origin. Then complete the activity for that characteristic by filling in the appropriate box in the Your Family System chart (Table 2.1).

TABLE 2.1 Your Family System	
Family Systems Characteristic	**Your Family Example**
"The whole is greater than the sum of its parts"	
Boundaries/limits	
Bonding/buffering	
Rituals/traditions	
Rules	
Hierarchical structure	
Dynamic change	
Goals	
Roles	
Self-regulation	

The Whole Is Greater Than the Sum of Its Parts

In a system, one part cannot be understood without looking at the whole (von Bertalanffy, 1968), and families operate on the "principle of wholeness" (Bigner, 2006, p. 41). This means that, as a teacher, you cannot fully understand how a child is functioning at school without considering the family. For example, a child's schoolwork may suffer when a parent develops a chronic illness, such as cancer. In such a case, if you only focused

on the child's poor school performance, you might make the mistake of thinking that the child has a learning problem or is not putting forth any effort. You must look at each student as a part of a family and not just at the student alone. This becomes more difficult when children are part of more than one family system, as in the case of binuclear families. Binuclear families occur when parents divorce and remarry and create stepfamilies, where two families share the same children. When children regularly spend time in both families and have two sets of parents raising them, teachers must learn how both families operate to better understand the child because both families have an influence on the child's learning and development.

A System Has Boundaries or Limits

A system is open enough to allow the members to get resources from the environment, yet is closed enough for them to operate as a unit. A well-functioning system will have a balance between open and closed boundaries, with the family having open enough boundaries to allow outside information and people such as teachers, friends, or neighbors to enter but closed enough to maintain some privacy and functionality. For example, children may have outside interests and friends, but there may also be a family rule that they are not allowed to take any phone calls from friends during dinner or family time, thus creating a boundary around the family unit during that family activity. Family members may have guests at the house, yet also have certain limits about when guests will be invited, such as not inviting anyone but family at holidays. Establishing boundaries helps define the family as a unit. Family boundaries may be symbolic, such as family members agreeing on the same values and rules or limits about what family members will or will not do, or actual, such as fences around a home, unlisted phone numbers, and locks on the door that keep strangers out. A family's sense of boundaries may influence how open they are to your suggestions about how to best help their child learn and develop (Christian, 2006). For example, a family with rigid boundaries may not want their child to be involved in a school-based after-school tutoring program but would prefer that their child receive extra help at home.

The **family worldview** is the lens through which the family sees the world. The family worldview causes the family to organize their lifestyle according to their attitudes about the place in which they live. For example, the family worldview influences the boundaries that are set by the family. If the family as a whole views the world as a good place and believes that people can be trusted, then boundaries may be more relaxed, with the children having outside interests and activities, than in a family that has a distrustful view of the world. Minority families who have

ACTIVITY 2.3

What boundaries or limits did your family set? Can you determine what your family's worldview was as you were growing up? Add an example to the Your Family System chart.

experienced racism or violence may have tighter boundaries than families who have not been victimized because a general distrust of society has become part of their family worldview. Similarly, a Muslim parent in the post-September 11, 2001, United States may not allow his or her child to attend a sleepover party for fear that the child would experience discrimination from the other children.

A System Has a Balance of Bonding and Buffering

Related to the boundaries set around a family unit is the concept of **bonding**. Bonding is the process of drawing close together and operating as a cohesive unit. Families who are strongly bonded have established family boundaries and emphasize togetherness, belonging, or being emotionally connected (Christian, 2006). Bonding can be measured by the amount of focused time spent together, how family members get along with one another, and how families resolve conflicts or crises. For example, when families regularly read to their children or spend time talking with them about their day at school, the family bond is strengthened.

Bonding must also be balanced with **buffering**, or allowing for space, privacy, and a healthy distance between family members. For example, children may need time alone in their bedrooms, and as children mature, they may prefer to spend time with friends, rather than do all their social activities with family. Buffering is necessary for healthy identity development and allows young adults to leave home and pursue their career interests, separate from the family identity. For a system to operate effectively, there must be a balance of both closeness and time apart, although the levels of bonding and buffering will change as the family goes through its life cycle, with families tending to be more bonded when children are small and buffering increasing as children grow older and more independent.

Systems that don't function in a healthy manner will operate at the extremes of bonding and buffering. At these extremes, families are **enmeshed** or **disengaged**. A family that is too close or overconnected becomes enmeshed, while a family that has few or no bonds may become disengaged. Some of its members may stop interacting altogether or may have **cutoff relationships**. Although cultural differences influence the definition of healthy bonding, a family can be defined as enmeshed when the connections are too close to be healthy for individual family members. One woman described her experiences in an enmeshed family:

My family is very close-knit and puts great value on family togetherness. As young children, my brother and I went with mom to our dad's softball and soccer games. We attended school picnics and events as a family and participated in church events as a family. We celebrated all the holidays with extended family gatherings. Every Friday night my mom, grandma, and I went shopping and out to eat. We enjoyed spending time together as a family, and then, I became a teenager. Everything was status quo until some of my friends and a couple of boyfriends did not make the grade. I cherished the closeness of my family, but realized that noncompliance came with a price. In fact, one year, I was 22 at the time, I was not allowed to bring my boyfriend to the family Easter breakfast and egg hunt. So I didn't go. . . . Today my parents, my uncle, and my cousin all live next door, and my sister, her husband and their three children live two houses down the street from us. And my mom sets the dinner table for 10 to 13 almost every night (R. Mayse, personal communication, June 24, 2010).

In enmeshed families, an individual's identity is strongly tied to the family's identity (Christian, 2006). Thus, it is especially important to understand the family unit when working with a child from an enmeshed family and to build strong relationships with the family members, who have such an important influence on the child.

In many cultures, the family is the center of social, financial, and child-rearing support, and what is considered enmeshed in some cultures is considered to be healthy in others. For example, many Hispanic families from rural Mexico determine success or family wealth not by material goods but by the quality of personal relationships within the family, including extended family members, who are considered part of the immediate family. Recreational or social activities are a natural extension of family functions, and independence from the family is discouraged (Welton, 2002).If a student in your classroom is newly arrived from rural Mexico or other parts of Latin America, you might find that the parents would be uninterested in attending a parent education meeting or school carnival or that extended family members, such as a grandparent or aunt, would also attend parent-teacher conferences. The concept of family bonding is a personal and cultural construct, and your judgment about whether a family is bonded or enmeshed is probably based on your personal experiences with your family. It is important to avoid letting your personal biases about what is a good family influence your interactions with families (Christian, 2006).

> **ACTIVITY 2.4**
>
> Think of examples of how your family bonded or buffered. Are there any examples of enmeshed, disengaged, or cutoff relationships in your family? Add your examples to the Your Family System chart.

At the other extreme from bonding is disengagement. In a disengaged family, members have withdrawn or become distant from one another. A disengaged family may value independence and autonomy over a sense of belonging (Christian, 2006). This may occur as family members move long distances from one another and rarely have contact, but it can also occur when families live in close proximity or even in the same house. For example, families in which the parents work long hours and rarely spend time with each other or with their children may not have a strong family bond. Another common disengaged family is one in which the noncustodial parent may only see the children during holidays or in the summer. At the extreme of disengagement is the cutoff relationship where there is no physical or emotional contact with a family member. For example, brothers and sisters who haven't spoken in years or a child who doesn't know a parent because he or she left the home have cutoff relationships. You may find that you will have to work harder to establish relationships with all family members of a student when a family is disengaged, and it is also important to understand and be sensitive to any cutoff relationships that exist in a student's life.

> **ACTIVITY 2.5**
>
> Did your family have any rituals or traditions? Did these traditions help family members bond or have a sense of closeness? Add your examples to the Your Family System chart.

Rituals and Traditions Affect the Bonding Process

One way that bonding occurs in family systems is through family rituals or traditions. These "habits" are "richly meaningful but often informal" activities in which families engage (Broderick, 1993, p. 201). Family rituals teach children what is important to the

ACTIVITY 2.6

What were the spoken and unspoken rules in your family when you were a child? Did you feel a sense of consistency between the rules at home and the rules at school? Add your examples to the Your Family System chart.

family and bring members together. Family rituals can be daily, such as saying a prayer at mealtime, singing in the car on the way to school, or reading bedtime stories together. Rituals can be related to holidays, such as birthday traditions, preparing a special recipe for a Thanksgiving meal or putting on a family fireworks display on the Fourth of July. The family's faith background may also provide religious rituals that bring family members together, such as the baptism, christening or naming ceremony of a new baby, a wedding celebration, or a funeral. Families may also have regular traditions such as a weekly dinner at a grandparent's house, a family vacation, or an annual family reunion. To better understand your students' families, you can ask them to share their favorite family traditions or rituals, which can be compiled into a booklet that is sent home for families to learn about one another's traditions (Galinsky, 2001).

Systems Are Rule Governed

Another characteristic of a system is that it operates according to rules. For families, this may mean rules about children doing daily chores, completing homework before watching television, not allowing name-calling or violence toward one another, and having an established bedtime or curfew. Rules may be explicit, as when a chores schedule chart is posted on the refrigerator, or implicit, as when everyone knows that they must take their shoes off before coming into the house or make the bed before going to school. Sometimes there may be a clash between what children are allowed to do at home and what they are allowed to do at school. For example, it may be all right for children to challenge authority at home

ACTIVITY 2.7

Who had the power in your family or made the decisions when you were a child? Can you identify the power structure among the adults and children in your family? Describe your family's hierarchical structure in the Your Family System chart.

or use profanity, and then they may not understand why such behavior is not appropriate at school. You may have to discuss the difference between "school rules" and "home rules" with them (Christian, 2006). There may also be times when students are conflicted about participating in a school activity that is not allowed in their family. For example, it would violate the rules of a family who practices the Jehovah's Witness faith to require their child to say the Pledge of Allegiance. It is important for you to understand the set of standards, laws, or traditions established in your students' families (Christian, 2006).

A System Is Hierarchically Organized

A system has a **hierarchical structure**, or a well-defined structure of power. In a family, the adults make the major decisions for the family and have more of the power. In a poorly functioning family system, the adults in a family may not assume a position of power, which forces children to make adult decisions, as when a child has to take care of an alcoholic mother and younger siblings. This is an example of a **parentified child**: a child who becomes like a parent and takes on adult responsibilities, such as grocery shopping or counseling a parent about personal problems. Parentification can be a form of child neglect, as the role reversal causes the child to "sacrifice his or her own needs for attention, comfort, and guidance in order to accommodate and care for logistical or emotional needs of the parent" (Chase, 1999, p. 5, as cited in Hooper, 2007). Well-functioning families may share power with children, depending on their age and maturity, but ultimately, the adults must be the head of the hierarchical structure. In addition to the parentified child, another unhealthy structure of power is the **perverse triangle**, which occurs when two members of a family system form a coalition and gang up against another family member. For example, if one parent sides with the children against the other parent, the power shifts away from the parents as a team to the parent/child coalition. Another unhealthy structure of power is the **detouring coalition**, which occurs when one family member becomes the scapegoat for the family's problems, and the family stress is detoured from the real cause. This may occur in a family with a child with special needs in which the child is blamed for all the family's problems. As a teacher, you can determine the hierarchical structure of a family by looking for clues, such as who signs permission forms and returns phone calls or how the student responds to male or female teachers and administrators' authority. Understanding a family's hierarchical structure and knowing "who's the boss" can help you deal more effectively with your students' families (Christian, 2006).

> ### ACTIVITY 2.8
> What changes or transitions did your family experience when you were growing up? How easily did your family adjust to the changes? Give some examples of how your family changed over time in the Your Family System chart.

A System Is Dynamically Changing

A system is continually changing over time, with loss and gain of parts in the system and new patterns of interaction that call for adaptation by the parts of the system. Families change over time, with normal family circumstances such as the birth of a baby, the children growing up and leaving home, or the death of a grandparent. Families also change because of unexpected events, such as a parent developing a terminal illness, a teenager becoming pregnant, or a spouse leaving a marriage. The family life cycle stages force family systems to go through **morphogenesis**, that is, to change and adapt; but because families cannot function well or maintain any order if they are in a constant state of morphogenesis, family systems constantly return to a state of stability or **morphostasis** (Maruyama, 1963). When families can find a balance between change (morphogenesis) and stability (morphostasis), they are in a state of **homeostasis**, or equilibrium.

Families have problems when they resist morphogenesis; for example, keeping the same rules for older children that they had when they were younger may lead to teenage rebellion. However, families also have difficulties when there is too much change at once, and they are unable to maintain any morphostasis. A family divorce may require the children and their mother to move to a smaller home and send a stay-at-home mom into the workforce. Well-functioning families adjust to the changes that life brings, although the adaptation to a new family structure may take some time, depending on the nature of the change or transition. Some common family transitions and their impact on student learning will be further discussed in Chapter 6.

ACTIVITY 2.9

What goals did your family have for you? How were those goals communicated to you? Describe your family's goals in the Your Family System chart.

Families have a variety of goals for their children, such as a college education.

ACTIVITY 2.10

Can you identify the roles in your family? What was your role? Did it carry over into the classroom? Give examples of family roles in the Your Family System chart.

ACTIVITY 2.11

How were conflicts resolved in your family? Did your family work to have a sense of equilibrium, or were there many ongoing conflicts that were not settled? Give an example of how your family regulated itself in the Your Family System chart.

A System Has Goals

The members of a system will set goals for the system. For example, families may set the goal that all their children will receive a college education. They may choose to sacrifice some of their material goods to help provide their children with a good education. You may find that not all families have the same goals for their children as you do. For example, family closeness may be the most important goal for a family, and they may not encourage their children to participate in extracurricular activities or leave home for college; instead, they may expect children to participate in family-centered activities. They may not be responsive to your suggestions about different career opportunities for their child that would take their child away from their hometown. Although you may not agree with a family's goals for their child, it is important that you respect the beliefs and values that have led to those goals.

Members of a System Have Roles

In a system, different parts play different roles. For the family, this means that mothers and fathers may have certain roles, such as caregiver or breadwinner and that children may also be expected to fill certain roles, such as being the nurturer of younger siblings, the peacemaker in conflicts, or the family clown. Family roles often carry over to the classroom, and you can better understand why a child behaves in the classroom by learning the role that the child plays in the family (Christian, 2006). For example, a student who is the family peacemaker may be especially good at resolving conflicts among his or her classmates, or the student who constantly disrupts class with joking behaviors may just be continuing in the "clown" role established at home. By learning more about the different roles in a student's family, you can work more effectively to nurture the student's strengths and deal with any negative behaviors.

A System Is Self-Regulating

A system that is always dynamically changing will regulate its conflicts and work toward homeostasis or equilibrium (Jackson & Zuk, 1981). For example, a well-functioning family does not require visits by local police officers to settle their conflicts and will work to reach a state of peace in the home.

Although it would be abnormal for a family not to have conflicts, the key to a well-functioning family is that family members are able to resolve conflicts in a mutually supportive way. It is crucial for children to have an overall sense of security and trust in the home, which may be difficult to maintain when a family goes through times of change and stress. As a teacher, it is important for you to be aware of changes and unresolved conflicts in a student's family. Although it is not your job to be a family therapist, you can provide consistency and security in your classroom routine and create a nurturing environment for a child who is experiencing an unstable home life. You can also encourage families to create or maintain stability through family rituals, such as regular bedtime stories, during times of conflict.

> **ACTIVITY 2.12**
>
> Now, share your completed Your Family System chart with your classmates, noting the diversity among families. How did the different cultures or ethnicities represented in your class impact these differences? Discuss how understanding the different characteristics of family systems may help teachers work with students and their families more effectively. Also discuss why it is important to avoid the judgmental label of "dysfunctional" when working with families.

All the characteristics of family systems exist along a continuum, and when the system is working smoothly, a family is well functioning. However, when parts of the system break down, the family may not function well, which will have an impact on the student's ability to learn and achieve. Although the term **dysfunctional** is often used to describe family systems that have broken down, this term is judgmental and stigmatizing (Walsh, 1993). A better way to describe families is to focus on how they are functioning as a family at the present time. "Dysfunctional" tends to imply that a family system is in a permanently unhealthy state. In reality, families move on a continuum from poorly functioning to well functioning because of life's circumstances. A well-functioning family may go through a period of being poorly functional when an unexpected change occurs, such as the death of a family member or the loss of a job. Well-functioning families tend to recover from these circumstances and move back into a state of homeostasis, but the nature of the transition can affect how quickly this occurs. As a teacher, it is important that you not label families in your mind as dysfunctional but, instead, seek to understand how families are operating as a system and how you can support them.

In addition to family systems theory, different theories and models for effective family involvement have been proposed by many researchers. Following are descriptions of theoretical models that have had an impact on successful family involvement practices.

ECOLOGICAL SYSTEMS THEORY: URIE BRONFENBRENNER

Bronfenbrenner (1979; 1986; 1993) proposed the ecological theory to explain how children develop and function in a family system and in the broader context of the world. Bronfenbrenner developed a model of "contexts" that children are influenced by, with the child in the center of the different settings (Figure 2.1). In the family systems theory an individual part of a system cannot be isolated but must be studied in the system's wholeness; in Bronfenbrenner's theory, all the levels of influence are reciprocal and not unidirectional, with the different contexts influencing one another (Weiss, Kreider, Lopez, & Chatman, 2005).

FIGURE 2.1   Bronfenbrenner's Ecological Model

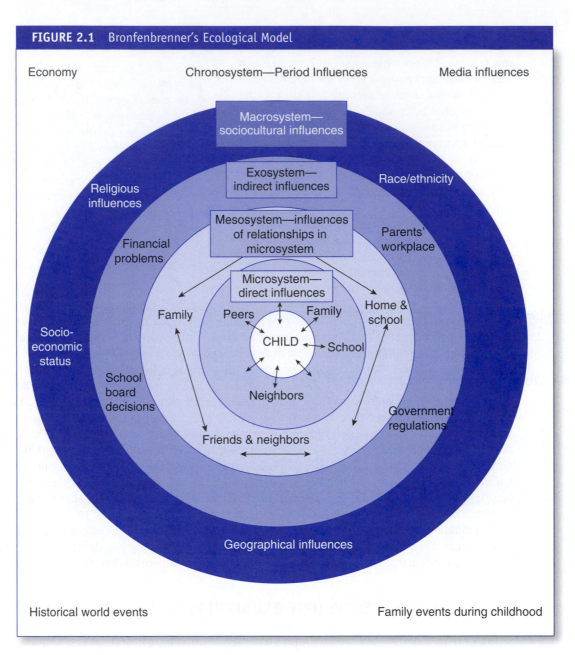

The first level of influence is known as the **microsystem**, which contains the direct contacts in a child's world, such as family members, friends, neighbors, and teachers. The face-to-face interactions that the child has with the people in his or her home, school, and community will have a strong influence on the child's growth and development, but these immediate contacts are not the only influences on a child's development. The next level, the **mesosystem**, is related to the microsystem in that it includes the influences of all the relationships or links that exist in the microsystem. For example, if a grandparent serves as a caregiver for a child, the relationship may be bonded and the influence of the grandparent may be strong in the child's life. If a parent has a substance abuse problem, the relationship with the parent may be strained and that relationship may affect how a child behaves at school both academically and socially. The child's peer relationships or lack of friendships may affect home and school life. Thus, the quality of the different relationships or the degree of connectedness that the child has with individuals in the microsystem form the mesosystem level. A child who has a thin mesosystem with few positive relationships will have little support for learning and development, while a child who has a rich mesosystem with strong, nurturing relationships will have many resources for school achievement. This may explain why research has shown that elementary-aged children with families who have high levels of communication with teachers (strong positive relationship in the mesosystem) receive higher grades and show greater initiative and independence as they get older (Bronfenbrenner, 1994).

> ## ACTIVITY 2.13
>
> As with the Family Systems theory, it is helpful to understand Bronfenbrenner's theory by applying it to your life. Using the blank diagram of Bronfenbrenner's ecological model in Figure 2.2, identify the different influences in each of the levels in your life as a child. Discuss these with a partner. What differences and similarities do you note in the influences of family, community, culture, and time? Why is it important for teachers to understand the multiple influences and relationships in students' lives to work more effectively with them and their families?

The third level of influence, or context, is the **exosystem**, which contains the influences on a child's life of people or institutions that do not have a direct contact with the child but, nonetheless, influence the child. For example, a parent's workplace may require the parent to work more hours, giving less time for the child to spend with the parent and negatively affecting the child's life. Other exosystem influences might be government regulations, such as the **Temporary Assistance for Needy Families (TANF)** work requirements or poverty level restrictions for child-care funding, which may force a family to choose a poorer-quality child-care program, negatively impacting a child's development (TANF is a federal program created by the Welfare Reform Law of 1996 and replaces what was commonly known as "welfare." It provides assistance and work opportunities to needy families, U.S. Department of Health and Human Services, 2011) or a school district's decision to change the bus routes or district boundary lines, causing a child to spend more hours on a school bus or change schools, or leaving friends and familiar teachers. Exosystem influences may also be positive, though, such as a parent's workplace that offers good health care benefits that allow a child to receive adequate medical and dental care.

The fourth level of influence is the **macrosystem**, which is the larger societal influence of cultural beliefs and values. The macrosystem can include the influences of race, ethnicity, language, religion, socioeconomic status, and geographical locations. For example, a child who lives in a homogeneous white, politically conservative, Christian, middle-class community and attends a parochial school will likely develop the attitudes and dominant beliefs of that community and religion because of the combination of the home, community, and school influences.

The fifth level of Bronfenbrenner's ecological systems model is the **chronosystem**, which is the time in which the child lives. Each historic time influences the generation growing up

FIGURE 2.2   A Personal Application of the Ecological Model

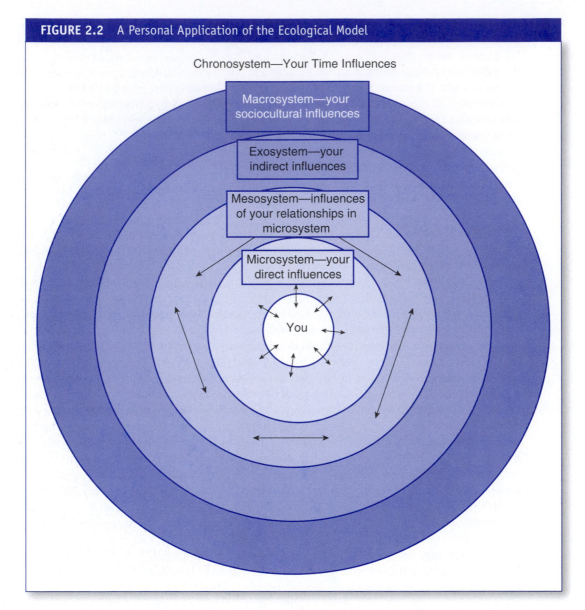

Note: Using the blank diagram of Bronfenbrenner's Ecological Model, identify the different influences in each of the levels in your life as a child.

in that time. For example, a child growing up in the Depression Era of the 1930s will have had a different outlook on life than a child growing up in the affluence of later decades. The rise in international terrorism and Middle Eastern wars continue to be an influence on today's generation of children, and, without a doubt, the rapid rise of technological advances in contemporary life, in video games, computers, cell phones, and the advancement of the Internet have a major impact on children of the 2000's decade.

Bronfenbrenner's theory provides a valuable resource for teachers to better understand how children operate within a system, as well as the influences on both children and their families.

FAMILY EMPOWERMENT MODELS: CARL DUNST

As in the family systems approach to human learning and in Bronfenbrenner's ecological theory, family empowerment models of family involvement in schools recognize that students' learning and development are strongly influenced by their family experiences. Children are more successful when they are reared in families that have adequate resources, where both parents and children are active participants in children's learning, and where parents are actively involved in goal setting and decisions regarding their children (Dunst, 2002).

Dunst's model of family empowerment is based on 30 years of research and was first widely disseminated in the now-classic book *Enabling and Empowering Families* (Dunst, Trivette, & Deal, 1988). Research conducted by Dunst and others has consistently demonstrated that interventions that support and strengthen families have a dramatic positive effect on children's development (Connors & Epstein, 1995; Dunst, 2002; Dunst, Ardley, & Bollinger, 2006; Henderson, 1987). In recent years, Dunst's family empowerment model has been described as an integrated framework for child learning and development (Dunst, 2005). A simplified version of the integrated framework is shown in Figure 2.3.

The large circle in the integrated framework represents family-centered practices, which emphasize involving parents in making decisions about their child's education and using practices that focus on the strengths of families and respect their culture and background. Family-centered practices involve family members as active participants, both in determining goals to which they devote time and energy and in taking action to achieve those goals (Wilson & Dunst, 2005).

The three inner circles of the integrated framework represent the core components of the model. Opportunities for children to learn include activities that build on their interests and assets. These opportunities occur in a variety of settings and contexts and are most effective when the students actively participate (Dunst, 2005; Raab, 2005). For example, everyday learning opportunities may include family routines, like caring for a pet or helping with a garden, attending community events, or participating in organized groups, like a sports team or scouting group (Dunst & Swanson, 2006).

Parenting supports include a wide variety of experiences that strengthen families' parenting knowledge and skills and that build on existing knowledge and skills to enhance parenting confidence and competence. Parenting supports include parenting education classes, home-based support, opportunities to participate in their children's learning activities, participation in family resource centers, and participation in informal activities, such as talking with other parents or family members (Wilson, 2005).

Family/community supports and resources include all the informal and formal resources that are helpful to families in achieving their goals. This includes resources from within the family, such as strengths and capabilities of individual family members, including parents themselves. Additionally, family/community resources include support from families' informal social networks such as friends, family members, church members, and members of community groups, as

> ## ACTIVITY 2.14
>
> What are some of the practical ways in which you can apply Dunst's family empowerment model to your teaching? With a partner, discuss strategies that you might use for the three inner core circles of the model: child-learning opportunities, parenting supports, and family/community supports and resources.

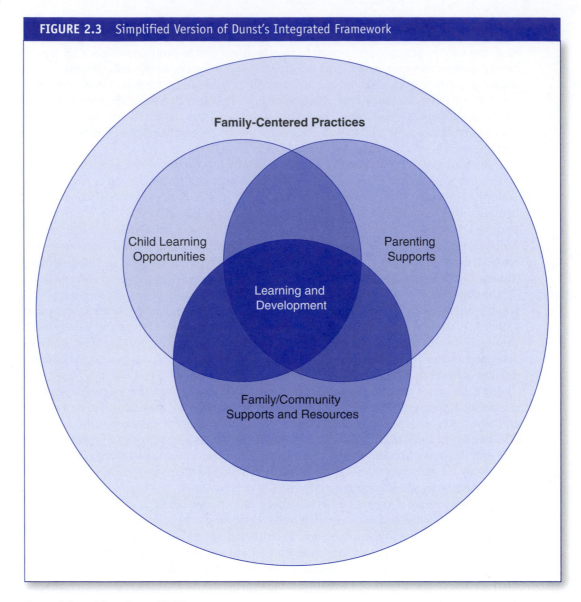

FIGURE 2.3   Simplified Version of Dunst's Integrated Framework

Source: Adapted from Dunst (2005).

well as formal support from professionals, community organizations, and agencies (Mott, 2006).

A key to understanding Dunst's integrated framework is being aware that each component of the framework is essential for children's optimal learning and development, as represented by the intersection of the three inner circles. The implications of this are especially important for classroom teachers. Although classroom teachers are typically skilled and knowledgeable in providing child-learning opportunities, the benefits of doing so are significantly enhanced when the other areas of the integrated framework are also addressed. Specifically, outcomes for children are best when children participate in learning opportunities and when (1) families receive the parenting supports that they need to support their children's learning, (2) the family has the informal and formal resources that they need to function well as a family, and (3) the family is treated with respect and is involved in the decision making and educational activities that affect their children. Only when all the previous supports exist simultaneously can it be said that teachers are effectively using the family empowerment model. Teachers who apply Dunst's family empowerment model recognize that children are more successful when their families are supported, strengthened, and, thereby, empowered.

SOCIAL CAPITAL: JAMES COLEMAN

In examination of families and how they operate, another factor to consider is the resources that are available to families through their social networks. James Coleman proposed that, in addition to financial capital, communities and families also possess social capital. **Social capital**, as defined by Coleman (Coleman & Hoffer, 1987), exists in the relations between people and provides a network of support. These could include collaborative relationships between families and teachers. In families, social capital can include the presence of adults and the richness of their interactions and relationships, while in the community, social capital can include opportunities for social networks to form through organizations or informal relationships (Powell, 1989). When families capitalize on the resources available within and from others, their well-being can be improved. For teachers, this means using all available resources within the student and family's social network, such as extended family members, neighbors, church family, and community members. In other words, when families, especially those who need to struggle to meet the demands of survival in an education-based society, turn to the resources of relatives, neighbors, supportive groups, or social connections, their lives are made better. Likewise, **human capital** (Coleman & Hoffer, 1987) or the sum of skills and capabilities that make a person productive, such as the attainment of a high school diploma or college degree, complements social capital in the area of family partnerships.

Based on research done in schools in the 1980s, Coleman argued that there has been a general erosion of the social capital needed for the proper rearing of children because of changing family demographics, an increase in individualism, and a deterioration of the sense of collective responsibility for other people's children. Coleman also warned that the social capital that exists in families is different from school resources and that schools need to provide children from socially resource-weak families with experiences that approximate those provided by homes and communities that are rich in social capital (Powell, 1989).

An anecdote recounted by Coleman (1988) is an especially powerful example of the convergence of social and human capital:

ACTIVITY 2.15

Think beyond the financial capital that your family did or did not possess as you were growing up. What social capital did your family have? Make a list of all the ways in which your family was socially rich. How was this supplemented by the human capital in your family? How can educators and schools increase social and human capital in the families in your community?

In one public school where texts for school use were purchased by children's families, school authorities were puzzled to discover that a number of Asian immigrant families purchased two copies of each textbook needed by the child rather than one. Investigation showed that the second copy was purchased for the mother to study in order to maximally help her child do well in school. Here is a case in which the human capital of the parents, at least as measured traditionally by years of schooling, is low, but the social capital in the family available for the child's education is extremely high (p. 110).

THE FUNDS OF KNOWLEDGE: LUIS MOLL

Similar to Coleman's concept of social capital is the idea of **funds of knowledge** (i.e., using the extensive experiences of minority families to add to the richness of the classroom learning environment for lesson plans or instructional units) developed by Luis Moll and colleagues (Gonzalez, Moll, & Amanti, 2005). Moll's work on this and other related topics encompasses nearly 20 years of research (Gonzalez et al., 2005). Funds of knowledge are the knowledge and skills that exist in the homes of students, or as Moll, Amanti, Neff, and González (1992) described it, the "historically accumulated and culturally developed bodies of knowledge and skills essential for household or individual functioning" (p. 133). Educators often miss the rich cultural and cognitive resources that exist in households, particularly in low-income, minority families. For example, migrant farm families have much knowledge about soil and irrigation systems and crop planting, and low-income families may have learned about repairing automobiles from having to drive unreliable, older vehicles. Rich funds of knowledge may also exist relating to child care, cooking, and moral and ethical values passed down through generations by way of stories told in the family (Moll et al., 1992). Funds of knowledge can also explain the development of social skills in young children, as found in a study by Riojas-Cortez and Flores (2009), which demonstrated that Mexican immigrant and Mexican American families were teaching the children in their home the social skills found in the Texas Prekindergarten standards, such as friendship, sharing, respect, and listening to others. The funds-of-knowledge approach allows educators to view families with a positive, strengths-based perspective that respects cultural values and practices and affirms that teachers can learn as much from families as children can learn from their schools. Rather than viewing low-income families with a deficit model or seeing them as socially and intellectually inferior, a funds-of-knowledge approach can encourage teachers to make more resources available to students in need. The approach also "reframes family-school relationship to make communication, interactions, and curriculum development a two-way process" (Weiss et al., 2005, p. xxii). When teachers better understand the occupations and daily routines of students' homes, they can develop class activities or projects that are connected to the children's lives and then ask family members to volunteer in the classroom, as experts on the topics (Weiss et al., 2005). Moll et al. (1992) suggested three avenues by which teachers may explore their students and families'

ACTIVITY 2.16

To further understand the concept of families' funds of knowledge, consider completing the class activity described in Table 2.2, where you will conduct surveys or interviews with families of students in a field placement and create a presentation on their funds of knowledge.

funds of knowledge. First, he suggests that educators research their community as a sociopolitical, historic, and economic context where the children's households reside. Learning about the history of a given community can in itself lead to immense gains in knowledge and can help transform the perspective of the educators in that community. In addition to the historic background, the community members may offer knowledge about ranching, farming, animal husbandry, construction, occupations, trade, business, and finance. It is also important to note the social networks that develop in these communities.

Second, Moll et al. (1992) recommends that teachers form afterschool study groups in which they have the opportunity to share information, reflect on their findings, and look for potential instructional applications. Finally, Moll et al. suggests that teachers reexamine classroom practices to incorporate the funds of knowledge that have been identified and make connections to students' experiences. For example, students can be encouraged to write or tell stories about individuals in their community or families (Moll et al., 1992).

FAMILY-SCHOOL PARTNERSHIPS FRAMEWORK: JOYCE EPSTEIN

One leader in the field of family involvement practices who has attempted to answer the question of how to form partnerships with families is Dr. Joyce L. Epstein, Director for the Center on School, Family, and Community Partnerships (Johns Hopkins University). Epstein has been a seminal researcher in the field of school, family, and community partnerships for more than 25 years. Like Bronfenbrenner, Dunst, and other theorists, she cites overlapping spheres of influence affecting students and acknowledges the need for

TABLE 2.2 Funds of Knowledge Activity

Connecting With Families	Goals	Activities
Teacher establishes rapport with students/families in field-based placement	To establish a trusting relationship with students and their families	Teachers spend several weeks building a rapport with students, making home visits to families, and participating in parent-teacher conferences
Teacher creates classroom-family survey/interviews	To develop a comprehensive overview of the expertise and skills held by family members and students	Teachers prepare and disseminate a survey about the jobs, hobbies, and/or specific expertise held by classroom families (a family interview may be used in place of a written survey with interpreter/translator, if needed)
Teachers create presentations on their funds of knowledge	To showcase the expertise held by family members	After watching video-taped presentations, teachers write reflective essays

Source: Gonzalez et al. (1993).

FIGURE 2.4   Keys to Successful Partnerships: Six Types of Involvement

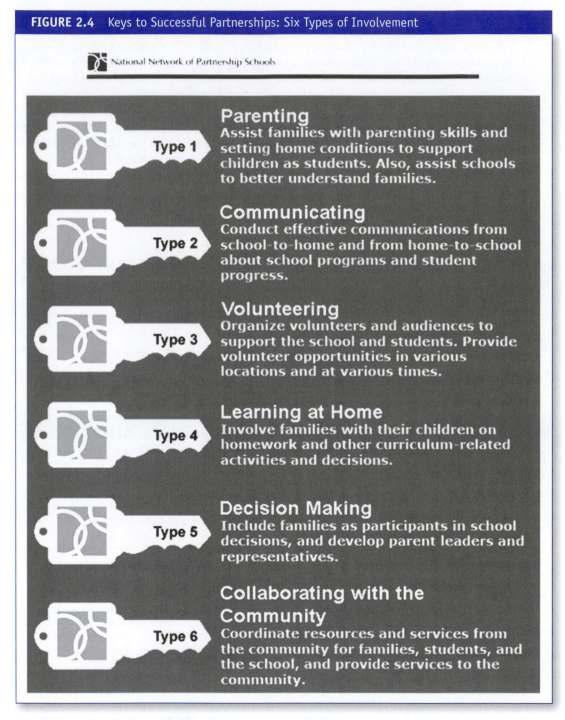

National Network of Partnership Schools

Type 1

Parenting
Assist families with parenting skills and setting home conditions to support children as students. Also, assist schools to better understand families.

Type 2

Communicating
Conduct effective communications from school-to-home and from home-to-school about school programs and student progress.

Type 3

Volunteering
Organize volunteers and audiences to support the school and students. Provide volunteer opportunities in various locations and at various times.

Type 4

Learning at Home
Involve families with their children on homework and other curriculum-related activities and decisions.

Type 5

Decision Making
Include families as participants in school decisions, and develop parent leaders and representatives.

Type 6

Collaborating with the Community
Coordinate resources and services from the community for families, students, and the school, and provide services to the community.

Source: Epstein et al. (2002). Used with permission from Corwin Press.

parents, educators, and community members to share responsibility for students' academic and social growth (Epstein, 2001).

Epstein and colleagues (2002) developed a framework of six types of family involvement necessary for successful family-school partnership programs. Figure 2.4 shows Epstein's Keys to Successful Partnerships: Six Types of Involvement.

Ideas for each type of family involvement and the challenges that are involved include the following:

Type 1: Parenting. Help families with parenting skills, their understanding of child and adolescent growth, and foster family support. Collaborate with families to make sure you understand families' backgrounds, cultures, and goals for their children.

Challenge: Make sure all information presented to parents is understandable and usable to them to support their child's academic growth.

Type 2: Communicating. Provide information about school programs and student academic progress. Ensure that two-way communication exists between home and school.

Challenge: Consider family members who do not read English well, struggle with understanding text, or need large type.

Type 3: Volunteering. Recruit, train, and schedule family volunteers. Make sure that you have time to work with volunteers and provide proper support for their work with students and the school.

Challenge: Orchestrate flexible scheduling for volunteers to match volunteer talents and their time availability to students' needs.

Type 4: Learning at home. Promote family involvement with their children in academics at home, such as homework, discussing the school day, or setting goals. Develop authentic home extension activities that are interactive for both families and students.

Challenge: Keep families aware of the content of classroom instruction and ways to help their child.

Type 5: Decision making. Offer opportunities for families to participate in school decision making, governance, and advocacy through various collaborative organizational teams.

Challenge: Train and delegate qualified parent leaders to serve as representatives for other families, which includes gathering their recommendations, voicing concerns, and relaying information back to families.

Type 6: Collaborating with the community. Coordinate community resources and services for families, students, and the school through all types of groups: businesses, cultural and civic organizations, and higher education.

Challenge: Integrate social, medical, and family services (and more) into a full-service school approach.

Learning at home is one of the keys to supporting a strong family engagement program.

ACTIVITY 2.17

As a class, divide into six groups and choose one of the keys to successful family-school partnerships to discuss. In your small group, answer two questions:

- What are ways I could implement this type of family engagement in my classroom?

- What are ways that my school district could implement this key?

Then, come back together as a class and compile the ideas into a master list, creating a class Family Engagement Plan that addresses all six areas of family engagement.

In 1996, Epstein founded the National Network of Partnership Schools to provide guidance to school districts on how this framework for family involvement could be put into practice. The organization now boasts more than 1,500 school and district participants, as well as 22 states, demonstrating the wide range of influence of Epstein's work (National Network of Partnership Schools, 2010). Research has shown that National Network of Partnership Schools (NNPS) have had positive results on student achievement, with NNPS schools having higher attendance rates, fewer discipline problems, and improved math and reading skills, especially when homework was given that required parent-child interactions to complete (Epstein, 2005).

SCHOOL DEVELOPMENT PROGRAM: JAMES COMER

Comer's School Development Program has also widely influenced school districts' family involvement practices. The School Development Program shifts the focus of effective family involvement practices to the child, with the foundational belief that all children's needs must be met before they can learn and succeed (Couchenour & Chrisman, 2000). The program's mission is the "total development of children and adolescents by helping parents, educators, and policymakers create learning environments that support children's physical, cognitive, psychological, language, social, and ethical development" (Yale School of Medicine, 2010). Comer's School Development Program began in 1968 as a collaborative effort between the Yale Child Study Center and the New Haven, Connecticut, school system. It was designed to bring improvement to two elementary schools in New Haven and has since developed into a widely respected model of family involvement (Yale School Development Program, 2004). Research on schools using the School Development Program model at high levels have shown these schools to have strong gains in student achievement and development (Yale School of Medicine, 2010). One study of five school districts implementing this model over a five-year period found that all districts had gains in reading and math achievement test scores, with significant improvement in closing the achievement gap between African American and white students (Emmons, 2010.)

The model is based on three principles: (1) making decisions based on a consensus about what is good for children; (2) collaboration between administrations and teams of teachers, staff, families, and students; and (3) focusing on problem solving rather than placing blame. Three teams guide the consensus-building process, working collaboratively without finding fault with anyone for problems that arise. The three teams are a school planning and management team that deals with curriculum, instruction, and assessment; a student and staff support team that focuses on the issues and needs of individual students; and a parent team that involves parents at all levels and integrates the school into the community (Yale School of Medicine, 2010). As a part of the school development program, three operations occur: (1) creation of a comprehensive school plan that deals with curriculum, instruction, assessment, social and academic climate goals, and communication between school and community; (2) periodic assessments of the school's programs with adjustments as necessary; and (3) staff development based on goals developed in the comprehensive school plan (Comer, Haynes, Joyner, & Ben-Avie, 1996). Comer's School Development Program Framework now functions as a comprehensive school plan in hundreds of schools in more than 20 states, as well as sites in South Africa, England, Ireland, and Trinidad and Tobago (Yale School of Medicine, 2010).

SUMMARY

With the myriad theories and models presented, is there one approach to family engagement that is better than others? What defines a public school as an exemplary family engagement site? To answer this, it will be important for you, as a teacher, to look at the community and population that your school serves. "Effective parent involvement programs match the needs of school and community in creating a positive school climate" (Barrera & Warner, 2006, p. 73). In other words, there is no one best approach, but you and your school colleagues should be familiar with different theories and models of family engagement while also acknowledging the needs and strengths of the families of your students.

Clearly, teachers who desire to collaborate successfully with families must do more than send an occasional newsletter or hold annual parent-teacher conferences. Family engagement is much more multifaceted, and one of the first steps to beginning a family engagement program is to understand the complexities of families and their influence on children's learning and development. Theories and models such as those described in this chapter can provide teachers with an understanding of how to do this.

REFLECTION QUESTIONS

Reread the In the Classroom case study presented at the beginning of the chapter, and reflect on these questions:

1. How is the Chandler family operating as a system? What family system characteristics do you see in their situation?

2. Note the family engagement strategies that the children's teachers and Kennedy Elementary School are implementing. According to Epstein's model, what types of family engagement are present or absent? What strengths do you note about the teachers' and school's family engagement efforts? How could they be improved?

For more advanced study:

1. Thinking about the family systems characteristics that you noted in the Chandler family's case, how might this change your family engagement practices as a teacher of one of the Chandler children? What are some specific strategies that you would implement as a teacher of one of the Chandler children, based on family systems theory? How can applying family systems theory to the families in your classroom help you become a better teacher?

2. Choose one of the theories presented in the chapter (Ecological, Family Empowerment, Social Capital, or Funds of Knowledge) and develop a list of strategies that you'd like to implement in your classroom that reflects the philosophy of that theory. Justify how your strategies are an application of the theory.

WEBSITES

The Comer School Development Program affiliated with the Yale Child Study Center, http://www.schooldevelopmentprogram.org/index.aspx.

This site includes the components of the School Development Program, in which family input into school decision making plays a primary role. Check out the publications page for recent articles and texts written by Comer and others.

The Connection Collection maintained by Southwest Educational Developmental Laboratory, www.sedl.org/connections/resources/bibsearch.html.

This is an excellent school-family-community publications database from the National Center for Family and Community Connections with Schools.

Harvard Family Research Project, http://www.hfrp.org/.

With a strong influence of Bronfenbrenner's ecological theory, researchers focus on approaches and evaluation of complementary learning projects (early care and education, out-of-school time, and family and community involvement in education). The site offers links to sign up for free subscriptions to their latest news and publications.

National Network of Partnership Schools (Epstein), http://www.csos.jhu.edu/p2000/.

This is a site for schools, districts, and states using Epstein's family-school partnership framework. Check out the Promising Partnership Practices page for descriptions of successful activities from partnership schools, organized by the six keys of Epstein's model.

STUDENT STUDY SITE

Log on to the student study site at www.sagepub.com/grant2e for additional study tools, including the following:

- eFlashcards
- Web quizzes
- Web resources
- Learning objectives

Chapter 3

Supporting Families as They Parent Today's Children

You don't have to give parents a college education. You just have to give them a strategy for having an interesting conversation with their third-grader about a book they're reading even if the parents haven't read the book.

—Joyce Epstein (Epstein, quoted in Russakoff, 2009, p. 17)

The primary responsibility for the development and well-being of children lies with the family, and it is within the family that children have their first educational experiences. These experiences in the home influence children's later abilities in school. Therefore, if you hope to be an effective teacher, it is important that you have an understanding of the parenting process and how it affects children's development, as well as the unique needs of families during the different stages of the family life cycle. In Chapter 2, you learned about a number of theories or approaches to being partners with families in educating their children. However, some families may have myriad needs that prevent them from embracing an active role in their child's education. With support from the school and alternative involvement strategies offered, these families may be able to help their children successfully learn and achieve in school. This chapter will examine the parenting process and ways that schools can strengthen families so they can best support their children's healthy development and, ultimately, their success in school. As you examine these ideas, think about these questions:

- What should teachers keep in mind while working with parents in different stages of parenthood?
- How do attachment between children and their families and each child's unique temperament affect the parenting process?
- What are some of the different styles of parenting? Is one style of parenting more effective than another? What are some of the cultural differences in parenting practices and beliefs?

- How do children view their parents? What do they think a good parent is?
- How do I accept parenting styles that are different from what I experienced or what I think is best for children?
- Why do all families, regardless of income, status, language, race, or ethnicity, require support to help their children learn in school?
- How can the principles of family support help me reach and work more effectively with diverse families to ensure student success?
- What steps can be taken to create a family-friendly and family-supportive school, and what are the barriers to doing this?
- What are some examples of home-based parent education models?

IN THE CLASSROOM: THE FIRST MEETING WITH A PARENT

Jan Russell glanced at the clock and noticed that Mrs. Chandler was late for their meeting to discuss Tyler's difficulties in math. She hoped that Mrs. Chandler wouldn't be much later. Jan had already stayed a half hour later than required by their principal to accommodate Mrs. Chandler's work schedule, and she had errands that she needed to run. She had samples of Tyler's work laid out and notes about her concerns, along with suggestions for what they could work on at home. She and the other second-grade teachers had worked out a weekly schedule of how many minutes per night parents should work on math facts and word problems with the second graders, and she had a copy of that schedule, in case Mrs. Chandler needed the reminder. She felt prepared for the meeting and hoped it would go quickly, so she could get to the bank before it closed.

This was Jan's first meeting with Mrs. Chandler, and she wondered what type of parent she would be. Mrs. Chandler had not come to their back-to-school picnic and didn't always send back school forms, which did not bode well in Jan's mind as a parent who was going to be very helpful. She knew from Tyler's records that his parents were divorced, and he had told her recently that his dad and "Janet" were getting married. Tyler didn't seem very happy about it, and she wondered if that might have something to do with his lack of progress in math. "Children always seem to suffer the most," she thought. "I wish these parents could get their act together." She put a smile on her face, though, when Mrs. Chandler rushed in with apologies about being stuck in traffic.

The meeting did not progress as well as Jan had hoped. Mrs. Chandler kept asking questions about the amount of homework that was required, in addition to the extra math that Jan was asking them to do. She said, "I have two other children to help at night with homework, and by the time I get home from work, get supper and the dishes done, we only have about an hour for homework total. What you're asking me to do will take more than an hour, much less than the time I need to spend listening to Ella read and helping Shaina with her homework!"

Jan felt a pang of sympathy for her and said, "I'm sure it must be hard for you, Mrs. Chandler. One thing that might be helpful to you is the parenting workshop that we're having this month on time management. A local psychologist is going to address parenting stress and busy schedules and give suggestions about how to better organize your time."

Lois Chandler looked at her and didn't reply, and there was a moment of discomfort on Jan's part. However, she firmly believed that families needed to be involved in their children's education, especially with the current pressure for good test scores, and she was determined to do whatever she could to help her students be successful, even if parents weren't always receptive to her suggestions. The meeting ended with Mrs. Chandler taking the suggestions for how to help Tyler, with the plan to talk further about his progress at the parent-teacher conferences in October. As Jan followed her out the door, she felt pleased with her efforts to engage Tyler's mother in his learning, and she made a mental note to refer Mrs. Chandler's name to the counselor's office for the new support group that the counselor was organizing for single parents

STAGES OF PARENTHOOD

Becoming a new parent can be an exhilarating experience. However, the hard work begins in raising children to be happy, successful young adults. Parenting evolves over time, as there are different stages in parenthood, each with unique joys and challenges. This section will explore those stages to help you better understand the families of your students and the different parenting issues that they face.

Infancy

When I first saw him, I don't even have words for how it felt. It felt like we'd been waiting so long to have him and now he was here. I couldn't sleep that first night because I was so in awe of him and the miracle of what he was. Once we got home, though, it was terrifying.

—Nicole, a new mom

When a couple become parents of a new baby, they are completely responsible for the child's every need, which can be exhausting for new parents as they adjust to this transition into parenthood. For a single parent, this stage of parenting can be even more exhausting, unless the single mother or father has a strong support system. New babies require round-the-clock care, and this stage of parenthood is often chaotic, with frequent interrupted sleep. If the family has older children, sibling rivalry can add stress to the home. Returning to work after the birth may bring feelings of guilt and sadness at being apart from the new baby. New mothers may also experience postpartum depression, which has symptoms such as feeling hopeless or worthless, being overwhelmed, having little energy, or withdrawing from friends and family. Postpartum depression can also cause physical symptoms, such as headaches, chest pains, heart palpitations, or hyperventilation (National Women's Health Center, 2005). As one new mother said,

I expected big demands and sleepless nights, but I never imagined I would feel the way I felt. My severe sleep problems were the most disturbing symptom. I wanted nothing more than to sleep, but I was too riddled with anxiety to relax. Even after taking pills to sleep, I'd wake up at 3 AM and would immediately feel the anxiety as if I had not slept at all. I felt incapable of mothering my baby. I felt my life was over, that I was losing my mind, and would end up dead or institutionalized.

—Amelia, 34, Teacher (Mother-to-Mother Postpartum Depression Network, 2007)

Approximately 10% to 15% of new mothers develop postpartum depression, and this number is higher for women with a history of other mental conditions, such as bipolar disorder ("Mental Disorders Among New Parents," 2007).

While infancy can present challenges for families, it can also be a period of delight, with rapid changes in the baby's physical, social, and language skills. The helpless newborn will quickly change into a responsive infant who will interact with family members through smiles, cooing, and babbling. It is during this time that secure attachments are formed between an infant and parents, as well as other family members and caregivers. Attachment theory will be further discussed in a later section.

As a teacher working with a family who has a new baby, it is important for you to understand the challenges and joys that the birth presents to a family, especially the older siblings, and be supportive as the family adjusts to the changes. If you are a teacher working with infants, it is crucial that you have close, frequent communication with families about the child's feeding and sleeping schedule, as well as any health issues. Mothers should be welcome anytime during the day for breastfeeding, with a private space provided, and the same open-door policy should be extended to all family members. Make sure that your classroom is inviting for families, with comfortable spaces for them to play with their children or read them a book. You will also want to become familiar with the families' cultural child-rearing beliefs, especially if they are at odds with your program's philosophy.

Leaving an infant in child care can be difficult for a family, and it is important that you are sensitive to their concerns and provide a safe, nurturing environment for the baby. If you are working with older siblings with a new baby, remember that family life may be chaotic, and it is important that you do not make many demands on the family. Allow the students to talk, write, or draw about their feelings about the new baby, and share children's books that show a variety of diverse family types with a new baby. You can provide important support for a family adjusting to a new infant.

Toddlerhood and the Preschool Years

My toddler is a raging storm out of control, mainly made of noise, toys, and bodily fluids. She can go from joy, to utter hopelessness, and back to bliss in nanoseconds. We communicate by her yelling her discontent and me trying desperately to find a way to make it stop. She is always looking for attention and trying to appease her is not always possible. Sounds rough, huh? I should mention that she can melt my heart with the slightest grin.

—Dave, father of a 21-month-old daughter

As children become toddlers and preschoolers, families are faced with new challenges, including the need for constant supervision to keep children safe. Toddlers go quickly from taking their first step to being mobile and constantly on the go. With this combination of new mobility skills and curiosity about their environment, toddlers must not be left unattended. This period of development has often been called the "terrible twos," and although new behaviors, such as temper tantrums and the frequent use of the word, "no" can try the patience of any caregiver, they represent a normal stage of child development, as toddlers are learning to become individuals with their own likes and dislikes. Problems with toilet training, bedtime, and finicky eating are all typical of this stage in parenting but are usually resolved with patience. Parenting skills are tested during toddlerhood, and for many families, it is during this period that parenting styles and practices evolve and are refined, as the parent or other family members determine what kind of parenting style they find comfortable (Bigner, 2006). Although toddlers can be challenging, they can also be a delight to their families, with their development of new skills and concepts daily.

If you are teaching in a toddler classroom, it will also be important for you to have regular communication with family members during drop-off and pick-up times, with phone calls or notes, and in more formal meetings. Being a partner with families of toddlers means providing information to them about their child's day and seeking their advice about caring for their child. This communication can help build a trusting relationship, which is a crucial element in working with families of toddlers. One study found that it is difficult for true partnerships to develop between families of toddlers and their teachers if teachers and families do not trust each other. Interestingly, it was more difficult for teachers to trust the mothers in the study, as they were skeptical of the mothers' ability to be partners with them, while mothers were more likely to trust the teachers in caring for their children (McGrath, 2007). If you want families to be involved in your classroom, it will be important that they sense your respect for them and your appreciation of their role as the most important people in their child's life (Poole, 2001).

> My preschooler is like a knowledge sponge. He takes in everything he sees and hears. It may not register right away, but sometime later when he repeats that bad word that you may have mistakenly said a week earlier, you know that he does listen. This age is fun for me because I can have conversations with him about how his day goes and how he feels about events in his life. I like that he and I can communicate, rather than him just yelling and me trying to find out what he needs. It's amazing to see him develop into a little man.
>
> —Dave, father of a three-year-old

During the preschool years (ages three to five), families must adjust to a developing child, who is curious about the world and rapidly acquiring language and cognitive skills and whose personality traits are emerging. Typically, the preschool years bring much pleasure to families but also challenges, as the preschooler tests limits that adults have established. Preschoolers may continue to have bedtime and sleeping problems, toilet-training difficulties, and eating problems that can create friction in the home. However, the preschool age can be a wonderful time for families, with the preschooler's eagerness to learn, improved language skills, and increased independence.

Parents often develop their parenting styles as infants become challenging toddlers.

The National Institute of Early Education Research found in 2009 that 30% of children attended a state-funded preschool program prior to kindergarten, and when Head Start (a federally funded program) was added, almost 40% of all four-year-olds were in a public program. When private preschools were also included, 74% of four-year-olds attended a public or private preschool program the year prior to kindergarten (Barnett, Epstein, Friedman, Sansanelli, & Hustedt, 2009). You may find yourself teaching in a prekindergarten classroom in a private program, public school, or Head Start center, and this may be the child and family's first experience with a school setting. Providing a smooth transition between home and school will be important, with regular communication between home and school a key factor in this transition. This communication should include information about not only the child and her development but also the preschool program's philosophy and curriculum and ways that families can be involved.

The Elementary School Years

My grandson is in kindergarten and still wants Grandma's attention. He loves it when I volunteer in his classroom. He gets along well with all the children and loves to play with them. My granddaughter is in fourth grade, and she has begun to wonder if Grandma knows anything. At this age, she seems to be more dependent on friends and less on the adults in her life. Her friends fight and don't always like each other, but she still clings to their every word. She also seems to be less likely to tell me about her day and seldom asks for my help now. The way I suggest she does her homework is never like the teacher taught her. I volunteer in her classroom too, and now she looks around at her peers to see if what Grandma said is OK. This is difficult for me, as I am no longer the main influence on her.

—Sharon, grandmother of five

During the elementary school years, families may have to worry less about attending to a child's safety or physical needs, but new challenges arise with children beginning formal schooling. Expectations for learning change, and families must now work with a school system to ensure that children are mastering academic skills. Even though children may have been in a child-care or preschool program, elementary school presents more structure in schedules and routines, with less freedom for families to schedule their activities. Children also begin to separate from their families and form bonds with peers. Parenting begins changing, as methods and strategies used with preschoolers are no longer effective or needed with children becoming more independent. While families may have exercised complete control over a child's behavior in the toddler and preschool years, the school-age years become a time of sharing regulation or negotiating rules, with the goal of children developing self-control.

Children may not need as much physical support from families for their needs, but they still need much emotional support. School-age children must develop social skills that help them form healthy relationships with friends, and they are increasingly expected to become independent problem solvers and learners, responsible for completing school tasks. For children with learning difficulties or special needs, the elementary-school-age years may be the first time that families are confronted with the news that their child has some type of disability, even if it has been suspected earlier. This news can be difficult for families, and it may take months, or even years, for families to accept and reconcile themselves to the loss of their dreams of a typically developing child (Bigner, 2006).

Although the elementary years do present new challenges, there is also great satisfaction in parenting children of this age. With children's increased independence, responsibility, and self-control, adults and children enjoy each other's company, and the family bond can be strengthened. Even though peers and others outside the family become a stronger influence, elementary-school-age

ACTIVITY 3.1

What knowledge do you have about the developmental characteristics of children of different ages and the different parenting requirements of each age? Using the questionnaire in Table 3.1, locate families with children at different age levels (infant/toddler, preschool, primary grades, and upper-elementary grades) and ask the same questions about each age level. Compare the results. How does parenting change as children grow? How will this influence your family involvement practices with children of different ages?

TABLE 3.1   Family Interview Questionnaire

1. How would you describe your child? What are some skills and abilities your child has? What does your child like to do?

2. How has your child changed as he has gotten older? How has your parenting changed with your child's different ages?

3. What are the rules in your home with your child? Who makes the rules? What happens when your child breaks a rule? What types of discipline do you use?

4. Does your child attend any kind of child-care program? What is your relationship like with your child's caregivers or teachers? What are different ways that you and your child's caregivers communicate with each other about your child?

5. Does your child attend any type of schooling? What is your relationship like with your child's teacher? Are you involved in your child's education either at home or at school? Has your child's teacher encouraged your involvement? If so, how?

6. What kinds of influences are in your child's life outside the home, such as teachers, friends, neighbors, or extended family?

children still want to please the adults in their lives and spend time with them, and this stage of parenting has sometimes been called the "golden years" of parenthood.

As a teacher working with elementary students, it is important for you to understand the strong influence that you will have on the children in your classroom and, ultimately, their homes. Bronfenbrenner's Ecological theory, described in Chapter 2, included teachers as direct influences in a child's microsystem, and your influence will help shape your student's beliefs about the world. For example, one second-grade teacher who had chosen to be a vegetarian discussed her beliefs with her class, leading several students to refuse to eat meat at home. This upset their families in the rural, cattle-farming community and created a divisive relationship between home and school. It will be important for you to understand the beliefs and values of the diverse families of your students and be respectful of those that are different from yours.

Although each of these sections has described the challenges and joys of children's different age levels as related to parenting, it is important to note that families may have children in multiple developmental stages at the same time. With the number of contemporary step- and blended families, it is conceivable that children in the same family may range in age from infants to young adults. It is also essential to remember that while the term "parenting" was used to describe child rearing, many children consider people other than their biological parents, such as grandparents, siblings, aunts or uncles, and stepparents, to be their real parents and that parenting may also be done by a single parent.

ATTACHMENT AND TEMPERAMENT

How do loving bonds form between children and the people raising them? Are there differences in the strength of these bonds, depending on the child's personality and behavior? These questions can be answered by a discussion of two concepts relating to parenting: attachment and temperament.

Ideally, bonding between a child and parent begins at birth. Researchers have studied this bonding process, hypothesizing that children who do not have a healthy bond with a parent or caregiver can have later social and emotional difficulties. These studies led to the concept of **attachment**, or a close emotional relationship between two people. Attachment often develops at birth between a child and a parent (Puckett & Black, 2005; Santrock, 1998). John Bowlby, a psychiatrist and pioneer in attachment research, believed that mothers and infants instinctively form an attachment and that newborns are biologically equipped with this survival mechanism, as they induce their mothers to care for them by the bond that has been formed between them (Gonzalez-Mena, 2006). This attachment intensifies over the first year of life, and bonds are also formed with other caregivers. Researchers have found that at about six to eight months of age, infants develop **separation anxiety**, or a state of fear and distress at being separated from a primary caregiver, and **stranger anxiety**, where they may show strong fear and avoidance of strangers and cling to their caregiver (Puckett & Black, 2005). While both of these reactions are developmentally normal, they can be disconcerting for a parent or other caregivers who find leaving the infant in child care suddenly difficult.

The quality of attachment between a child and parent can vary. Mary Ainsworth, a student of Bowlby's, researched attachment behaviors and proposed three categories of attachment: (1) secure, (2) insecure/avoidant, and (3) insecure/resistant. Securely attached infants are comfortable exploring their surroundings, but they return periodically to their mothers as their secure base for comfort and nurturing. They typically show some distress when their mother leaves and are delighted when she returns. Infants who are avoidant attached may act no differently around their mother than strangers and show little reaction when their mother leaves the room. Resistant attachment babies are less likely to explore their surroundings or leave their mother's side and are distressed when she leaves, but when she returns they may resist her efforts for physical contact and appear angry at her absence. A fourth category has been more recently proposed as the insecure/disorganized/disoriented attachment. These infants appear confused and may have contradictory behaviors of being disoriented, in a daze, or rocking in a repetitive manner when their mother returns after being separated (Gonazalez-Mena, 2006).

Although most of the research on attachment has been done with mothers and infants, studies have found that infants can form secure attachments with both mothers and fathers and that fathers play a critical role in healthy attachment behaviors that lead to positive social behaviors (Puckett & Black, 2005). Researchers have documented this connection between secure attachments with caregivers and later positive outcomes for children, including school achievement. For example, one study found that securely attached infants had better grades in third grade, while another study that followed disadvantaged children into adolescence determined that the teens who had a secure mother-infant attachment had better relationships with peers and did well in school (Egeland, 1989; Ostoja, McCrone, Lehn, Reed, & Sroufe, 1995).

Although attachment theory can be helpful in understanding the parenting process and how the relationship between children and their families can affect their later learning and development, it is important to acknowledge that much of the research done has been with the **nuclear family**, focusing on the mother, father, and children. As the demographics in Chapter 1 showed, there are many other family types than this, and in some culturally diverse families, children are raised by an extended network of family members. Children may develop attachments with multiple caregivers, including grandparents and siblings (Gonzalez-Mena, 2006; Santrock, 1998). Close bonds can also develop with a caregiver or teacher in an infant child-care setting when children experience continuity in care by the same person daily. Researchers have challenged the notion that a secure attachment to a single caregiver is critical for children's future social and emotional development and have theorized that other factors, such as a child's temperament and later social experiences, are more important than attachment theorists realize (Santrock, 1998). Regardless of which theory you think is more credible, you should recognize the importance of the strong emotional bond children have with their families that begins at birth.

How exactly does a child's temperament affect attachment and the parenting process? **Temperament**, or the distinctive personality and behavioral traits of a child, can either positively or negatively affect the attachment process, depending on the match between the child and parent's temperaments. Chess and Thomas (1977) identified three basic types of behavioral styles in a child: (1) easy, (2) difficult, and (3) slow-to-warm-up. They described the easy child as generally happy, settling into a regular routine as an infant, and adapting easily to new experiences. In contrast, the difficult child cries frequently and does not have a regular routine. The slow-to-warm-up child may seem moody and resistant to close interactions and new situations and have a low activity level. J. R. Lally and his colleagues put a somewhat more positive spin on these categories by renaming them "flexible," "feisty," and "fearful" (Gonzalez-Mena, 2006). Although heredity can certainly influence temperament, there also seem to be cultural differences among children's temperaments. For example, researchers found in two separate studies that Chinese American babies were calmer, slower to reach an excited state, easier to control when crying, and more able to stop crying themselves without being consoled by their caregivers than European American infants (Santrock, 1998).

The fit between an infant and parent in temperament can affect the attachment process. For example, if a relaxed father has an easy baby, he'll be more likely to enjoy the baby and bond quickly. However, if the baby is difficult, highly active, intense in emotions, with no regular routine for sleeping, then the father may be frustrated in caring for the infant and form a less-secure attachment. Similarly, a mother with a high energy level may provide too much stimulation for a calm baby and may wonder why the infant turns away from her (Gonzalez-Mena, 2006). Chess and Thomas (1987) state that harmony or agreement between children's and their caregivers' temperaments, or a **goodness of fit**, leads to "optimal positive development" for the child, while a poor match can lead to "maladaptive functioning" (pp. 20–21).

What do the findings of attachment and temperament research mean for families and teachers? First, it is crucial that strong emotional bonds be formed between the child, family members, and caregivers. This requires time, effort, attention, and continuity in the persons providing the care. In a child-care setting, it is best for children to have the same caregivers rather than be shuffled among numerous people. Child-care programs should also seek to minimize turnover among staff to ensure that strong bonds can develop between staff members and children over time. Second, it is also important to realize that parenting and care-giving practices may need to be different for different children depending on their temperament. Families and teachers should be sensitive to the characteristics and needs of individual children, especially if a child's temperament is different from theirs, and respect that individuality rather than trying to treat all children the same way (Gonzalez-Mena, 2006; Santrock, 1998).

Children's growth and development are optimal when there is a strong attachment with their caregivers and a goodness of fit in temperament.

PARENTING STYLES

How did your family raise you? What do you remember about your family's rules and discipline? How did your family handle conflicts? Who made the decisions in your family? Did your family talk openly about issues or were some topics off-limits? Was your family physically and emotionally affectionate? What were favorite family activities or rituals, and what did you learn from those? These questions may help you better understand the parenting style of your family and how it has influenced who you are as an adult. For example, if you had a parent who read for pleasure and shared books with you during your childhood, then you probably now enjoy reading for pleasure also, whereas if your family valued athletic activities and competition, you may find yourself having a competitive personality, regardless of whether you're involved in athletics.

Families have certain specific behaviors that they use with their children, such as helping them with their homework or reminding them to use manner words like "please" and "thank you." These behaviors are called **parenting practices**. Families also have a **parenting style**, which is the general pattern of these child-rearing practices or a set of parenting behaviors. A parenting style is characterized by the "emotional climate" of warmth and control in which families raise their children. While parenting practices, such as discipline methods, may change as children get older, parenting styles tend to stay fairly stable across time (Coplan, Hastings, Lagacé-Séguin, & Moulton, 2002; Spera, 2005). For example, families may use time-out with a preschooler, but with an older child, they can take away privileges or a weekly allowance for misbehavior. However, the general discipline style of firm control will not change.

In a series of studies, Diana Baumrind identified three different parenting styles: **authoritative parenting style**, **authoritarian parenting style**, and permissive parenting style. The permissive classification was later divided into separate categories of **permissive/indulgent parenting style** and **permissive/neglectful parenting style** (Baumrind, 1966, 1968, 1991; Maccoby & Martin, 1983). This classification of four parenting styles has dominated research in this area for almost 30 years and is based on levels of warmth and control (see Table 3.2).

TABLE 3.2 Baumrind's Parenting Styles			
Characteristics	**Styles**	**Styles**	**Characteristics**
High warmth High control	Authoritative	Permissive/indulgent	High warmth Low control
Low warmth High control	Authoritarian	Permissive/neglectful	Low warmth Low control

Authoritative Parenting

Authoritative families have a firm discipline style combined with high levels of warmth and nurturing behaviors. Authoritative families set rules and limits but have an open communication style. The adults are willing to listen to their children and adjust their parenting demands based on their children's views and opinions. In families with authoritative parenting styles, adults are concerned with helping children understand the reasons behind the rules as opposed to enforcing strict adherence to the rules (Kaufmann et al., 2000).

Authoritarian Parenting

Authoritarian families also have firm control on children's behavior but may lack the warmth or negotiation style of the authoritative family. There is little communication about the reasons for rules or limits. This parenting style may appear to be punitive, with its focus on obedience to the family demands, as opposed to understanding the reasons behind the demands. This "do as I say" and "because I said so" approach requires uncompromising obedience from children and may include punishment for breaking rules (Brenner & Fox, 1999; Gonzalez-Mena, 2006).

Permissive/Indulgent Parenting

Although this parenting style may be generally warm and loving, nonpunitive and accepting, permissive families avoid controlling children and may place few demands or limits on them. Permissive families may consult with children on family decisions and assume more of a role of guide or friend. In power struggles, permissive/indulgent families will give into children, but they may also use reason or manipulation to get desired results (Couchenour & Chrisman, 2000). For example, one parent who had grown up in a strict household declared that she would raise her children with no rules. Although she was loving and affectionate with her children, they were also allowed to do as they pleased when it came to household chores, bedtime, and activities with friends. To get them to cooperate, though, she would often resort to manipulative techniques such as questioning their love for her when they didn't obey her rules.

Permissive/Neglectful Parenting

This fourth classification was added to differentiate between two types of permissive families. Neglectful or indifferent families may place few demands or control on their

TABLE 3.3 How My Parents Raised Me

Family Practices	Recollections/Memories "Snapshots"	Influences on Teaching Practices
Family rules		
Parenting style/discipline practices		
Types of punishment or rewards		
Decision-making power in the family		
Methods to deal with conflict		
Family communication styles		
Affection/nurturing practices		
Family rituals and routines		
Family involvement in school		

children, but they will also lack warmth and nurturing and display indifference to their children. These families may be underinvolved in their children's lives and respond minimally to their needs (Brenner & Fox, 1999; Couchenour & Chrisman, 2000). For example, permissive/neglectful families may be similar to permissive/indulgent families in allowing their children to do as they please, but unlike the latter, they are uninterested in their children's activities, friends, or schoolwork.

Baumrind (1991) also described a generally flat, average parenting style that tended to fall in the middle ranges in the classifications and not fit well in any of the four categories. Baumrind used the term "good-enough parenting" to describe this parenting style characterized by low to moderate control, nurturing, and expectations (Brenner & Fox, 1999).

With classifications similar to Baumrind's, two leading psychiatrists, James Comer and Alvin Poussaint (1992), described parents as tending to consider themselves the "owners," "servants," or "developers" of their children. As in the authoritarian approach, the owners command their children, requiring complete compliance. The servants tend to be permissive, allowing children free rein over the family. Parents in the last category, the developers, allow children freedom to explore and develop necessary skills with their guidance, as seen in the authoritative parenting style.

EFFECTS OF DIFFERENT PARENTING STYLES ON A CHILD'S BEHAVIOR

Research in the years following Baumrind's classification of parenting styles has generally supported her work, including the effects of the different parenting styles on children's well-being. Baumrind and others have found that the authoritative parenting style has many positive effects on child behavior outcomes. Children of authoritative families tend to be independent, self-reliant, and responsible and to have prosocial behaviors, such as cooperation, sharing, and sympathy for others. Adolescents raised by authoritative families were less involved in drug or delinquent activities and had higher grades than other children, and their families were more likely to be involved in school and their children's academic work (Baumrind, 1995; Couchenour & Chrisman, 2000; Kaufman et al., 2000; Sorkhabi, 2005). Researchers have theorized that authoritative parenting styles lead to positive school outcomes because authoritative families provide their children with a high level of emotional security, which helps them succeed in school. Authoritative families also provide children with explanations for their actions and opportunities for two-way communication, which helps children develop strong interpersonal skills (Spera, 2005).

The authoritarian parenting style leads to less successful child outcomes. Children raised in authoritarian homes tend to be more anxious and insecure, to have low self-esteem and poor communication skills, and to be overly aggressive. They may show little independence and have acting-out behaviors and poor social problem-solving skills. Authoritarian parenting also correlates highly with poor school performance and teacher reports of children's adjustment problems to school. Children of authoritarian families tend to avoid challenging academic situations and seek easy success (Coplan et al., 2002; Couchenour & Chrisman, 2000; Kaufman et al., 2000).

The permissive/indulgent and permissive/neglectful parenting styles also are associated with negative child well-being outcomes. Children of both indulgent and neglectful families tend to have poor social skills and lack self-control. Indulgent parenting may lead to children who are disrespectful and noncompliant, and who have difficulty setting goals or handling responsibilities. Children of neglectful families tend to lack self-esteem and be at high risk for emotional and behavioral problems, including alcohol and substance abuse. Researchers have also found that both the authoritarian and permissive parenting styles are correlated with children being motivated by extrinsic rewards, as opposed to being intrinsically motivated to learn (Chan & Chan, 2005; Couchenour & Chrisman, 2000; Edwards, 1999).

Think about what this research means to you as a teacher. For example, what kind of discipline practices will you use in your classroom? Will you be an authoritative, authoritarian, or permissive teacher? How can you learn more about the parenting styles of your students' families? How can this help you adjust your discipline practices for individual students?

Criticisms of Parenting Styles Research

Baumrind's classification of parenting styles is not without criticism. Some have criticized the work because of the difficulty of assigning a parent to a single style (Coplan et al., 2002). A parent may be more authoritarian in situations where a child might be in danger but more authoritative when the situation does not appear to bring harm to a child. For example, a parent might be stern and expect unquestioning obedience with a young child when walking in a crowd near busy traffic but be more willing to negotiate with the child about changing a bedtime on a weekend. Families may also use different child-rearing styles with different children in a family based on their unique personality traits; and even when adults use the same parenting style, it may have different effects on boys and girls in the family. Researchers have also questioned whether the different parenting styles can be strictly divided into categories as Baumrind suggests (Chan & Chan, 2005; Sternberg, 1994).

Another major criticism of Baumrind's parenting styles typology is the issue of cultural differences. Baumrind's research was primarily done with white, middle-class parents, and other researchers have found that Baumrind's findings do not always translate to families from other cultures or socioeconomic status (Barbour, Barbour, & Scully, 2005). For example, some Chinese families use a parenting style that would be classified as authoritarian, yet it is not harsh and punitive but rather gentle and related to the Confucian tradition of social harmony. Chinese children raised with this approach do well in school (Gonzalez-Mena, 2006). This was demonstrated in several studies that found that Caucasian teenagers who were reared with authoritative parenting styles had higher grades than those raised with authoritarian or permissive styles, while the opposite was found for Asian teens: authoritarian parenting for these adolescents resulted in higher grades, as opposed to authoritative or permissive parenting styles (Sorkhabi, 2005). The authoritative parenting style is favored by Caucasian families, while African American, Asian American, and Latino families may use more authoritarian parenting styles. Baumrind found that authoritarian parenting led to assertiveness in African American females, and further research has shown that although this parenting style was negatively associated with a high GPA for Caucasian students, the same result was not seen with students from African American or Latino families (Spera, 2005).

Another difference was correlated with socioeconomic status, with families who experienced economic hardships tending to be more authoritarian. In one study, African American mothers from low-income neighborhoods were more likely to emphasize unquestioning obedience through an authoritarian parenting approach because of the fear they had about the crime in their neighborhood and the goals they had for their children.

Researchers have also found that there may be a difference in the effectiveness of parenting styles depending on education levels of adult family members. For example, for families in both the United States and Australia who had little education, authoritarian parenting was positively related to academic achievement (Spera, 2005). Although the research tends to support the positive effects of authoritative parenting overall, inconsistent results have been seen about the positive or negative effects of authoritarian parenting styles with families from different cultures, socioeconomic status, or education levels (Kaufman et al., 2000; Sorkhabi, 2005).

Researchers have attempted to explain why there are cultural differences in the effectiveness of parenting styles. One explanation is related to issues of independence and interdependence. In individualistic cultures, like the middle-class, white American culture, authoritative parenting seems to have positive outcomes, but in cultures that are collectivist in nature, such as the Chinese culture, authoritarian parenting is considered to be a positive type of parenting. Although there are no definite answers to which parenting style is the most effective for students from different cultures, it is clear that parenting styles do vary based on cultural beliefs and practices (Sorkhabi, 2005).

CHILDREN'S VIEWS OF THEIR PARENTS

So far, this chapter has looked at the family in terms of parenting practices, but an important part of understanding families and parenting styles is to understand children's views of their families' child-rearing practices. What do children think are effective parenting practices? In 1999, Galinsky conducted a research project, "Ask the Children," to find out how children viewed their parents. Questions about parenting styles were embedded in a larger study relating to working parents. The study revealed insights into what children viewed as positive parenting practices. When children were asked to assess parenting skills relating to their development and school success, eight critical parenting skills emerged:

1. Children want to feel important and loved.
2. Children want parents who respond to their cues and clues.
3. Children want to be accepted for who they are, but they also expect to be successful.
4. Children want parents to promote strong values.
5. Children want constructive discipline.
6. Children need predictable routines and rituals in their lives.
7. Children want their families to be involved in the child's education.
8. Children want their parents to "be there" for them. (Galinsky, 1999)

Interestingly, when children were asked to grade their parents, younger elementary-age children rated their parents more favorably than older adolescents. Of the eight parenting skills, mothers were rated high for being there when the child was sick and raising them with good values but rated low for controlling their tempers and knowing what is happening in their children's lives. Children in the study didn't necessarily want more time with their parents but wanted their parents to not be stressed or distracted by work during their time together. Galinsky found that both quality, or "focus" time, and quantity, or "hang" time, were important to children. Similarly, comedian Jeff Foxworthy (2009) wrote in an essay "What my kids taught me":

As a parent, I've found out that kids don't want "quality time" with you. They want "quantity." In fact, they want all of your time. Of course, they need interaction and communication, but just your presence there in the house means the world to them. I asked my girls, "Would you rather see me once a week and we go to Disneyland, or would you rather just have me here every night?" And they said, "Every night." (p. 18)

This research has implications for teachers:

- Encourage family engagement in your students' education. Be sure to include opportunities for fathers and other family members in your family engagement practices.
- Support **families' rituals/traditions** (regular activities families engage in that help familiarize children with the values and beliefs of the family and increase family bonding). For example, have meetings where families can share ideas for family activities, rituals, and traditions.
- Encourage adults to think about what causes stress in their lives and how that stress may be affecting their relationships with their children. Offer support in learning techniques to manage stress.
- Help families learn and improve communication skills with their children, including active listening. (Galinsky, 2001)

Certainly, an important part of parenting is listening to children. As one 12-year-old in the study said, "Listen. Listen to what your kids say, because, you know, sometimes it's very important. And sometimes a kid can have a great idea, and it could even affect you" (Galinsky, 2001, p. 28). This is also good advice for you as you seek to learn more about students and their families.

TEACHER ACCEPTANCE OF DIFFERING PARENTING STYLES

Earlier in the chapter, you were asked to think about the parenting practices that you experienced growing up in your family. Although research supports the democratic, authoritative parenting style typically found in white, middle-class families as leading to positive student outcomes, the criticisms of this research demonstrate the importance of teachers recognizing the cultural, socioeconomic, and gender differences that play a role in parenting styles. A term that is useful in considering different parenting styles is **differentiated parenting** (Edwards, 2004), which affirms that families differ from one another in their ideas, viewpoints, and abilities to work with educators. This means that just as you differentiate your instruction for the diverse learners in your classroom by modifying lesson activities so that all can be successful, you will also need to use different strategies to work with families who are different in their parenting practices and style from what you experienced or believe to be effective. You are more likely to favor the parenting style similar to your family's practices and view parenting styles different from your own in a negative light. For example, if you were raised in an authoritative family who used nonphysical discipline methods, you may not understand or accept the practice of corporal punishment found in African American and Latino families or the "shaming" discipline techniques traditionally used by some Asian groups (Harry, n.d.). You may also find yourself judging the authoritarian verbal style of a low-income African American family as harsh. However, if you consider the verbal exchange in the context of a loving parent-child relationship, you will be more likely to realize the strength of the verbal exchanges (Delpit, 1988).

An example of the importance of understanding and accepting differing parenting styles is demonstrated in the Latino culture. When you work with Latino families, it will be important to recognize the role that extended family members, such as aunts, uncles, grandparents, and cousins, play as surrogate parents in helping raise the children. The term **compadrazgo** means the relationship established between parents and godparents as a form of coparenting, with the extended family members having a strong influence on the students' learning and behavior in the classroom. Another aspect of this parenting style is what Delgado Gaitan (2004) describes as *respeto*, a term for the respect shown for teachers and education. She also describes the authoritarian parenting style as reigning supreme in many Latino homes, with the questioning of authority being considered a sign of disrespect. It will be important for you to understand and accept the beliefs and practices of different cultures as being effective for these families, even if they are different from what you experienced.

Although these examples have been from typical African American, Asian, and Latino families, you should avoid forming opinions about parenting styles based solely on cultural generalizations. Laosa (1983) recommends that teachers become familiar with the parenting practices of the different families of their students and judge their effectiveness based on their cultural relevance and individual student needs as opposed to global assumptions. For example, not all African American families may use corporal punishment and other authoritarian parenting practices, and not all Latino families may include extended family members raising the children. Ladson-Billings (2006) echoes the recommendation to teachers to become careful observers of families' culture instead of making stereotypical assumptions; one way to do this is through interacting with students and families in nonschool settings. Cultural differences among families will be further discussed in Chapter 5.

FAMILY SUPPORT FOR ALL

As noted earlier in the chapter, parenting children is a challenging task. All families need support to raise healthy children ready to learn in our schools. Economic factors alone do not designate the need for family support. The birth of a child with special needs, a change in family structure brought about by divorce or death, changes in employment, or living long distances from extended family and friends can cause families to need extra services or supports. For example, a family with a child with special needs may need information about therapies or treatments, or a family that has recently moved into a community may need basic information about local pediatricians or dentists for their children. Single-parent families may require information on extended child care or afterschool programming for their children. All families, regardless of their makeup or description, require some assistance at one or more times during their life span.

Family support is a set of beliefs and an approach to strengthening and empowering families, which will positively affect children's development and learning (Family Support America, 2001). The underlying premises to the family support model can guide you in developing family involvement strategies that are respectful and supportive of your students' families. These foundational beliefs are outlined in Table 3.4.

TABLE 3.4 Premises of Family Support

1. The primary responsibility for the development and well-being of children lies with the family.

2. Assuring the well-being of all families is the cornerstone of a healthy society.

3. Children and families exist as a part of an ecological system.

4. Child rearing is influenced by parents' unique understanding of child development; their child's unique characteristics; personal competence; and cultural traditions and customs.

5. Helping families to build on their strengths and capacities promotes the healthy development of children.

6. Developmental stages of parenthood and family life have unique needs in the life span.

7. Families are empowered when they have access to information and services to improve the well-being of their children.

Source: Family Support America (2001).

These underlying premises or values of the family support model provide guidance in developing principles that tell educators how to work with families to ensure that they are supported and strengthened. The following family support principles for educators were adapted from the original work developed by Family Support America.

PRINCIPLES OF FAMILY SUPPORT IN SCHOOLS

Principle 1: School staff work together to build positive relationships with families based on equality and respect. Teachers and other school staff recognize that families bring important information to share with teachers. They know that a family's knowledge of their children is often different from that of a teacher and acknowledge how important this input is to their understanding of each student. When teachers are practicing this principle, they are acutely aware that they are in an equal partnership with families. Each perspective is valid and valuable. They make sure to let families know that they appreciate their input and that they intend to work in partnership with the family to make sure that their child is successful in school. Teachers avoid an "expert role," in favor of a more collaborative and congenial relationship.

Principle 2: Administrators, principals, and teachers recognize the capacity of families and honor their role in supporting the overall growth and development of all family members: young children, students, and adults. Educators working with families in any school setting help them recognize their strengths. They work together with families to establish unique ways in which they can help their children learn and grow. Teachers who are practicing this principle recognize that often families are struggling to meet basic needs, and they take this into consideration when requiring families to assist with learning activities. For example, you will want to make sure that there are options for family involvement available to working families or parents who may be non-English speakers, undereducated, or illiterate. You should invite all family members to attend school functions and provide child care and transportation when needed. You should avoid making negative judgments about families who cannot or will not attend school-based activities. Instead, work on developing flexible, innovative ways to reach out to these families, with care taken to make sure that all families can find effective, respectful ways to participate in their child's education.

Principle 3: School staff understands that families are important resources to design, implement, and evaluate programs. They are resources to themselves and to other families. Each community has multiple resources, and families can be resources to themselves and to others. Schools that practice this principle find multiple ways to engage parents and other family members in the design, delivery, and evaluation of school activities. When families take ownership of activities, they are more likely to attend and participate in the life of the school. Classroom teachers, parent-teacher organizations, and the school administration need to include family input in their school-reform efforts. Successful teachers practicing this principle have creative ways to include families in their curriculum from prekindergarten through high school. One example of this is seen in Spanish-Speaking Grandmothers Help Out.

SPANISH-SPEAKING GRANDMOTHERS HELP OUT

A Los Angeles area high school planned a community meeting to discuss discipline problems in their school. The meeting was facilitated by a member of this Spanish-speaking community. The principal and the teaching staff of the school were experiencing difficulties in maintaining a peaceful learning environment. Students were disruptive and misbehaving in class. They went to the community for help. As most parents in this community worked many part-time, low-paying jobs, many could not attend the meeting. These parents did, however, send the senior members of their family to find out what was happening. The facilitator of the meeting explained the problem and suggested that they needed some volunteers to help in the classrooms. The grandmothers asked how they could help in the classroom when they did not speak English. The skillful facilitator replied, "Do you not have eyes to see?" She politely challenged the grandmothers to come to school and sit in on the classes. The grandmothers agreed to volunteer. A few weeks later, teachers reported increased attendance and a reduction in classroom disruptions. The grandmothers did their job. They reported everything that they saw in the classroom to the students' parents, godparents, and other members of the community, who addressed these behavior issues with their youth.

Principle 4: Schools and their community partners understand that successful family involvement and support programs must affirm and strengthen families' cultural, racial, and linguistic identities and enhance their ability to function in a multicultural society. A key way to improve the achievement of children from diverse backgrounds is to form partnerships with their families. Schools that embrace the family support principles work tirelessly to develop meaningful programs that are respectful and responsive to the culture of students' families. Often, this work is done in partnership with community agencies that are familiar with or are already working with specific populations. Consider the example of a cooking lesson for Russian families.

A COOKING LESSON FOR FAMILIES

A school district in suburban Seattle recognized a shift in the population with a recent influx of both Spanish- and Russian-speaking students. Using an old district office site, the district entered into a partnership with their city and a local nonprofit family support center to establish its on-site family support center. At this center, families could drop in, take a parenting class offered in their home language, or sign up for other classes of interest, such as English language or job interviewing. On-site child care and transportation vouchers were made available to the families to ensure their participation. The center staff was responsive to the needs of the families and continuously listened to the suggestions that they offered to improve their programs. For example, the Russian-speaking families indicated that they did not know much about the Thanksgiving holiday. Their children were learning about this celebration in school, but their families felt unprepared to support this holiday at home. After some discussion, it was established that a history lesson was not what they desired. The families wanted to learn how to cook a turkey! Hence, the first-ever turkey-cooking class was held at the district's family support center.

When you work to build programs that are responsive and respectful of family cultures, traditions, and needs, you will increase your understanding of diverse families. When families are treated with respect and involved in the preparation, implementation, and evaluation of these efforts, they come to understand their vital role in the school. Making the shift from thinking that school staff knows best what families need to listening to families carefully as they tell you what they need is a necessary step when practicing this principle.

Successful family engagement programs are respectful of families' cultural and racial identities.

Programs must be responsive to family needs, but they must also help families feel secure and successful in our society.

Principle 5: Schools acknowledge their role in the community that they serve and recognize that school programs that are embedded in the community contribute to the community-building process. Schools must understand their role in the community. The school is one place that families trust to care for their children and help them learn the cognitive, social, and emotional skills that they will need to be successful members of our society. Often families seek advice from a teacher, who they perceive is a trustworthy adult. Sometimes these requests do not directly pertain to their student's learning. Although teachers and other school staff cannot be expected to respond to all needs, they should know which families they can turn to for help. Most schools that follow the family support principles collaborate with community partners that have resources to help families with unique needs. Some rely on the school counselor, social worker, or nurse to make these referrals, but all staff members need to understand how to respond to a family member's questions or concerns.

Principle 6: School-based or school-sponsored initiatives for families are designed to advocate with families for services and systems that are fair, responsive, and accountable to the families and students served. As teachers work with families, they often find that some services that they require are not readily available in the community. When schools work in partnership with community agencies, they bring their concerns for families to these agencies and begin to work toward community solutions. Likewise, community agencies desire to work in schools where families often congregate. Together with family leaders, schools and their agency partners can make a significant difference in a community. They can bring information and data to community meetings and promote action by the community to address these concerns. They can advocate for services that are not available to families in need and give evidence or document how these services will stabilize or support families so that children can come to school ready to learn. Consider the example of a school and community partnership that worked.

A SCHOOL AND COMMUNITY PARTNERSHIP THAT WORKED

An Oregon Education Service District (ESD) decided to take action for poor families. According to state education law, no child may be enrolled in an Oregon school without proper immunizations. This posed a problem for many local poor migrant and immigrant families who lacked health care coverage and access in rural areas to a medical facility. After years of excluding numerous children who were unable to start the school year on time, the ESD made a bold move. They contacted Northwest Medical Teams, an international nonprofit organization that brings medical care through mobile medical units to children in developing nations. The ESD successfully worked with this agency to bring a mobile unit to many schools in this county and provide not only required immunizations but also basic health care checkups for the children and their parents. This effort not only addressed an exclusionary law but also led to early detection and treatment of children's health issues.

Principle 7: School staff members working with families mobilize both formal and informal resources to support family development and efficacy. Family-friendly and family-supportive schools help parents help themselves. **Informal supports** are developed not by schools, community programs, or agencies but by the parents themselves. Single parents, for example, often benefit from support groups developed to encourage problem solving and the sharing of needed resources. Schools have encouraged such groups by working in partnership with local agencies that have trained facilitators for community support groups or often by simply providing needed space. Parents can organize, support, and maintain these groups with a minimum of help from the school.

In some cases, schools have found unique ways to assist families in building social support networks in informal settings. Spaghetti dinners, family fun nights, and movie evenings have made it possible for families to meet each other and build friendships and support. In today's complex world, many families live in isolation and struggle with child rearing, as they have no input from extended family members or lack positive role models as parents. These informal activities give families a chance to meet and talk with other families of children the same age as their child. Powell (1991) reported that "kitchen talk," or the conversations that families engage in during breaks at school activities, can be very helpful to families, as they discuss issues such as child care, transportation, and discipline. Following is an example of an informal support network that led to a meaningful friendship for an isolated parent.

MOMS' SUPPORT SYSTEM

In the process of dropping off and picking up their children at school, two mothers of kindergarten students developed a friendship. Diane had always lived in the community and had a wide support network of extended family and friends. Jamie was new to the community and knew few people. Jamie's lack of support and isolation was magnified by the fact that her husband was a truck driver and was rarely home. With a five-year-old, a three-year-old, and a baby on the way, she eagerly welcomed the new relationship and parenting support, and the two mothers often lingered at school to converse about their children. The kindergarten teacher noticed the budding friendship and further enhanced it by asking Diane and Jamie to work together to plan the fall harvest party for the classroom. They began meeting at each other's homes, and the relationship was strengthened. When Jamie went into labor with her husband still on the road, she turned to Diane for support, who drove her to the hospital and stayed with her children until her husband could arrive. The friendship continued throughout the school year, with the two mothers providing support for each other in a number of ways, such as caring for each other's children when they were sick.

Formal supports in schools are organized efforts and may include developing parenting education opportunities. Teachers often see this as a priority need, but many times, these efforts are not successful, with meetings poorly attended. Adults routinely resist parenting classes, if they perceive that the school's motivation for offering parenting classes is judgment about the quality of their parenting. One way to avoid this issue is to support natural family or community leaders as *they* organize parenting education events in the school. These activities can be generated by the families themselves, with the motivation coming from their desire to learn more about effective ways to parent their children. Care should be taken to avoid "at-risk" labels or other negative conditions for participation.

Other formal support activities can also include information about job opportunities, English as a second language (ESL) classes for adults, and on-site health care. These resources, like parenting education, are usually accomplished by the schools in partnership with community agencies. Families are not only grateful for these services but they also tend to be more supportive of their schools. Bringing family members to the school in a nonthreatening, positive environment can help you better connect to your students' families and understand your community.

Principle 8: School-based or school-sponsored programs are designed to be flexible and continually responsive to emerging family and community issues. Family-supportive schools always keep themselves informed about community issues that affect families. Working in collaboration with community agencies, they make sure that the ease of access to these services is improved. For example, many schools offer their buildings for use by youth development programs to provide afterschool recreational and academic programs. Families of children attending these programs no longer have to worry about how their children can safely reach and attend these programs while they are at work. Some districts have begun to work to raise funds for transportation of family members to attend activities, events, and festivals at the school. Lack of safe or appropriate child care can act as a major barrier to family participation. Working with local child-care providers not only assists with these needs but also builds a bridge between the school and programs serving the neighborhood and the young children who will soon be attending their kindergartens.

Principle 9: School staff ensures that the principles of family support are modeled by all staff in their day-to-day interactions with families, in the design of all program activities, and in the district policies that govern school-based or support initiatives for families. Family support practices in schools cannot be an isolated effort of the school counselor, social worker, or an individual teacher. It is the work of the whole school to ensure that the families of their students feel welcome and have options for participation in their children's education. Family-friendly and family-supportive schools have the following characteristics:

- An open and friendly environment that welcomes families (including extended family members) to the school.
- Teachers who embrace the principles of family support in all that they do. They make an effort to try to connect with each family of their students in some way.
- Teachers who are knowledgeable about community issues and are sensitive to the needs of families and what effect these needs may have on their students.
- Teachers who have high expectations and are committed to ensuring excellence by creating curriculum that is relevant to each student's family culture and living conditions.
- Administrative staff members who understand the value of community partnerships and work in close collaboration with community agencies/programs that can bring needed resources to families.
- School administrators, teachers, and other staff who are committed to building respectful and responsive relationships with families. They avoid negative labels, patronizing, or blaming behaviors in all situations and settings.
- School boards, administrators, and other staff recognize the unique role that schools play in providing equal opportunities to learning that will support the future of the local community.

By following these principles, you, your teaching colleagues, and administrators can work together to build a family-friendly and family-supportive school that can best help all students succeed.

PARENT EDUCATION MODELS

Although teachers, with their professional preparation and experience, often view themselves as experts on teaching children, the reality is that the family is the child's first and most influential teacher (Parents as Teachers, 2005). Embedded in the web of the community, families provide what may be called the "first school for young children," and their influence is strongly felt not only in the early years but throughout life in the formation of values, attitudes, and goals (Fruchter, Galletta, & White, 1992). As noted previously, providing education relating to parenting skills is one way to implement family support principles. Nationally, several parent education models exist.

Family-friendly schools have environments that are welcoming and inviting for all families.

Parents as Teachers

One program that recognizes the importance of families as their children's first teachers is Parents as Teachers (PAT), which was developed in Missouri after concerned educators noted varying levels of learning readiness among children entering kindergarten. Based on research that showed a critical link between early learning in the home and children's development of academic skills, such as reading and writing, the Parents as Teachers program was developed as a way to help parents better understand and support their children's development from birth. Core values of the program include the belief that parents are a "child's first and foremost teacher," that all young children deserve the opportunity to succeed, and that effective service to families must include an understanding of and appreciation for the diverse histories and traditions of the families (Parents as Teachers, 2005). The program has four components:

1. Home visits by trained parent educators for families with children up to five years of age, during which age-appropriate child development information and activities are shared, using the Born to Learn curriculum

2. Regular developmental and health screenings

3. Group parent meetings on parenting and child development issues

4. The setting up of a resource network to connect families with the resources needed to fully support their children's development and learning

Since the program was fully implemented in Missouri schools in 1985, it has spread to all 50 states and several countries, including Australia, England, China, Mexico, and Germany, and has served more than three million children. PAT programs can also be found in high schools, where instead of doing a home visit, the parent educator will meet in a school classroom with teenage mothers and fathers sharing the same information. Research demonstrates that children whose families participate in a parent education model such as PAT have higher levels of school readiness at kindergarten and continue to outperform their peers in first through fourth grades (Parents as Teachers, 2005; Zigler & Pfannenstiel, 2007). This program illustrates the importance of educators partnering with families not only when they enter school but also during the crucial early years of learning and development before kindergarten.

Even Start

Even Start is a Title I program, first authorized in 1988. More recently, the program was reauthorized by the Literacy Involves Families Together (LIFT) Act of 2000 and the No Child Left Behind Act of 2001 (U.S. Department of Education, 2007). Even Start is a family literacy program that aims to join together early childhood education, adult literacy (including instruction for English language learners), parent education, and interactive parent-child activities for families with low incomes. Families with children of ages from birth to seven years who are eligible for services under the Adult Education and Family Literacy Act can receive Even Start services. Most Even Start projects operate year-round, providing support services such as child care and transportation so that families can participate in the program's educational activities. The goals of this program are to improve adult literacy or basic educational skills rates and increase school readiness for children from families with low incomes so that these children can reach their full potential (U.S. Department of Education, 2007).

Systematic Training for Effective Parenting

Systematic Training for Effective Parenting, or STEP, written by Dinkmeyer and McKay (1976), was originally designed for parents of children of ages 6 to 12 years. There are now two additional components to this video-based parenting program: Early Childhood STEP and STEP/Teen. These programs are widely used throughout the United States and are available in Spanish. STEP programs teach positive approaches to parenting. Participants in these programs are taught to appreciate the motivations of children's behaviors, to encourage children to reach their full potential, and to implement family councils to make decisions with children (Dinkmeyer & McKay, 1976). Research has shown that participation in these programs significantly improves parenting skills (Dinkmeyer, 2007).

Parent Effectiveness Training

Parent Effectiveness Training, or P.E.T., developed by Gordon (1970), teaches children to be self-reliant and emphasizes parents and children addressing problems by coming to mutually satisfactory solutions. Gordon's proposition is that when children are punished, they learn not to be caught, rather than learning not to commit the act at all. P.E.T. helps children understand why they should not misbehave. Reviews of P.E.T. programs have found that there are positive changes in parental attitudes and children's self-concepts and behaviors after completion of this program (Wood & Davidson, 1987; 2003).

Active Parenting

Active Parenting, developed by Popkin, is a video-based parent education program. This program teaches families communication and negotiation skills to encourage better child or teen behaviors. Additionally, this program teaches positive discipline techniques and responsibility.

Participants in this program report positive changes in their behavior and that of their children (Fine, 1991). There are now several versions of Active Parenting: *Active Parenting Today* (Popkin, 1993), *Active Parenting of Teens* (Popkin, 1998), *Families in Action* (Popkin & Hendrickson, 2000), and *Active Parenting Now* (Popkin, 2003). The program has been studied extensively, with research indicating that families believe that their child's behavior is better following the program (Mullis, 1999) and that this program is effective across socioeconomic levels (Brown, 1988).

Home Instruction for Parents of Preschool Youngsters

Home Instruction for Parents of Preschool Youngsters (HIPPY), a literacy-based home education program, began in Israel and was first implemented in the United States in 1984. The program now operates in more than 160 neighborhoods, nationally and internationally. Through 30 home visits per year, families are given information about how to provide educational enrichment for their preschool child. Learning materials and children's books are left in the home, and families agree to work about 15 minutes/day, five days a week on the learning activities. Evaluations of the HIPPY program have revealed positive outcomes for children, with two recent studies showing that children who participated in HIPPY performed better in reading and language arts than children with no preschool experience. There were also positive outcomes noted in the families' attitude toward their children's education and the school system. As one father said,

> I didn't have a clue as to what was required of our children going into school. But because of the HIPPY program and the weekly lessons, my children not only were ready for school, they excelled in school. I am now an involved parent. Even though I work long and difficult hours, education is a priority in my house. (Doyle, 2005, p. 28)

SUMMARY

Although it is difficult to recognize and respect different parenting styles in the context of cultural, socioeconomic, and education level differences, you are more likely to be successful in working with students when you build positive relationships with your students' families and work to support them in their child-rearing efforts, as opposed to being critical of their parenting style. Although there will not always be easy answers for how to work effectively with families, you are more likely to be successful when you seek to understand the parenting beliefs and practices of each student in your classroom and practice the principles of family support.

REFLECTION QUESTIONS

Reread the In the Classroom case study presented at the beginning of the chapter and reflect on these questions:

1. What are some needs that the Chandler family may have at this time? In what ways did Jan Russell's efforts demonstrate her understanding or lack of understanding of those needs?

2. How might the relationship between the teacher and parent have been improved if Jan had sought to understand Mrs. Chandler's parenting practices and parenting

style, as related to homework, rather than assuming her difficulties were because of poor time management?

3. What are the ways in which you would improve on this meeting with Mrs. Chandler that demonstrate a family support approach?

WEBSITES

Family Education Network, **www.familyeducation.com/home.**

Launched in 1996 as the first parenting site on the Web, Family Education Network has become the Internet's most visited site for parents who are involved, committed, and responsive to their families' needs.

Parents Action for Children, http://www.iamyourchild.org

This website was developed by Rob Reiner and his wife to help raise public awareness about the critical importance the prenatal period and the first early years play in a child's healthy brain development. Check out the *I Am Your Child* video series that addresses the mental health needs of children in diverse family settings. Reasonably priced booklets and books on many parenting topics round out the site.

Parents as Teachers, **www.parentsasteachers.org.**

This site offers research about the benefits of parent education programs and other resources, including information on home visiting programs.

Zero to Three, http://www.zerotothree.org/

This is a nonprofit site dedicated to informing, educating, and supporting adults who influence the lives of infants and toddlers. Their Parent Resources page contains science-based information and tools designed to nurture young children's development.

STUDENT STUDY SITE

Log on to the student study site at **www.sagepub.com/grant2e** for additional study tools, including the following:

- eFlashcards
- Web quizzes
- Web resources
- Learning objectives

SECTION II

Appreciating Families

Today's Diverse Families

In Section I, you developed an understanding of families through theories and models of family engagement. Section II will further help you not only understand today's families but also appreciate the strengths that diverse families possess. As you learned in Section I, today's students and families represent a wide range of diversity in family structure and culture. In the first two chapters in this section, you will learn more about how to collaborate with diverse families. In Chapter 4, you'll read about different family structures and learn practical ways to individualize your family engagement practices for different family types. Although this entire text looks at cultural diversity in family engagement practice, Chapter 5 will focus specifically on diversity in language and ethnicity, religion, and socioeconomic status, with further practical suggestions for culturally responsive practice. In addition to learning to appreciate structurally and culturally diverse families, it is also important that you recognize the many challenges that today's families face. These challenges may encompass transitional situations, such as divorce, death, military deployment, homelessness, natural disasters, and incarceration of a parent, as well as long-term stresses of poverty, illness, and violence. Chapters 6 and 7 will offer a realistic look at these challenges that families encounter, as well as suggestions for how you can remain supportive while collaborating with families in difficult situations. One of the most difficult issues that you may face in your teaching is dealing with child abuse and neglect. Chapter 8 will help you be better prepared to recognize the signs of abuse and neglect while understanding your role as a mandatory reporter. To have effective family engagement practices, it will be important for you to move beyond the basic knowledge about families to appreciate the strengths that they possess and recognize the significant partnerships formed in the education of their children. Appreciating the families of *all* your students will be key to your commitment to culturally responsive family engagement.

Chapter 4

Structurally Diverse Families

Family is where life takes root.

—Lori Borgman (2010)

What exactly is a family? Is it a group of people related by blood or marriage, or is it something larger than that? As you begin reading this chapter on diverse family types, consider these questions:

- What are the different types of families that children are living in today?
- What are the characteristics of these different family types?
- How can I work effectively with all family types? Are there different strategies and family engagement practices that I should use with different family types?

TODAY'S AMERICAN FAMILIES

One way to learn about the evolution of families in recent history is to observe how families are portrayed on American television. TV shows not only reflect current families but also help shape our definitions of family (Kennedy, 2003). For example, television of the 1950s showed the classic *Leave It to Beaver* sitcom family, the Cleavers, with their traditional family type of a breadwinner father and stay-at-home mother. Although the majority of families in the 1950s may not have looked like the Cleavers, they represented the idealized image of traditional families of the era. In the 1960s, the divorce rate began to explode, and single-parent families were depicted, as in the case of *The Andy Griffith Show, The Courtship of Eddie's Father,* or *Julia.* The single-parent status was usually because of the more socially acceptable reason of the death of a parent rather than divorce. In the 1970s, shows that depicted divorce and blended families began to emerge, such as *Maude, One Day at a Time,* and *The Brady Bunch.* Families on television, by and large, were white, though, making it difficult for children from minority families to find a family similar to theirs. *The Cosby Show* of the 1980s was a breakthrough in that it depicted not only an African American family but showed an upper-class, successful black family. In the 1990s, the comedy *Murphy Brown* created public discussion about family values when Vice President Dan Quayle criticized the fictional leading character, a single woman, for having a child out of wedlock. While other 1990s shows such as *Roseanne* and *Married . . . With Children* still had traditional, two-parent families, the families were no longer idealized. As Kennedy (2003) wrote, "Until the 1990s, television families, even the messed up ones, still exhibited a sense that the members cared for one other. But *Married . . . With Children* changed that" (para. 11). In the 2000s, the expansion of cable networks allowed more nontraditional family types to be regularly included on television, such as the HBO's series *Big Love* about a polygamist with three families; Showtime's *The L Word*, which included a lesbian couple with a child; and even the Disney Channel with its popular preteen show *The Suite Life of Zack and Cody*, which featured a single mother raising twin sons in a hotel assisted by the various hotel employees, who serve as an extended family. The show *Modern Family,* which includes a traditional family, a stepfamily, and a gay couple who adopted a Vietnamese daughter, won six Emmys in 2010, and it illustrates the acceptance of structurally diverse family types in mainstream American society.

So how do these shows help shape the definition of family? To answer these questions, spend a week observing families on television as described in Table 4.1.

Whether current television depicts the true state of today's American families is debatable, but what demographic research on current families does demonstrate is that children today live in a wide range of different family types, such as traditional, **nuclear families**; single-parent, blended, and extended families, including grandparents and other kinship care; and same-sex, adoptive, and foster families. Let's look at each of these now, noting different family engagement strategies that are effective with the different family types.

TABLE 4.1 Today's American Families in the Media

Spend a week observing television shows that depict families. Keep a journal about how the families are portrayed, noting the following:

- What are the relationships like among the different members of the TV family? What is their communication style? Is it respectful, loving, and supportive or combative and mean-spirited?

- What types of problems does this TV family have? How does the family resolve problems?

- How are the children portrayed in the TV family? Do they have more power than parents? How are decisions made in the family?

- What was the structure of the family? (i.e., two-parent, single-parent, blended, adoptive, foster care, same-sex, grandparent/kinship care, etc.)

- Do you think that this portrayal of a family is typical of real-life families? Why or why not?

- What does this TV show teach today's children about families?

Share your findings with the class and discuss your memories of television families from your childhood as compared with today's television families. How have television and other media shaped your perception of what family is?

IN THE CLASSROOM: GRANDPARENTS BECOMING PARENTS

Susan Meyer wearily walked through the door and sunk into her worn recliner. "What a day," she thought. She loved teaching second grade, but days such as this made her wonder if she had made the right career choice. Susan had been teaching for seven years at Kennedy Elementary, and she enjoyed working with the teachers in the building and respected her principal, Brenda Fraser. She appreciated the support her principal gave her, especially with difficult students or their families. Today had been one of those days that she had called on her principal for help.

Susan's class of 24 second graders was typical, with some children still struggling to recognize words, and others reading fluently in chapter books. Kennedy was a Title I School, which meant that it qualified for federal funds because of the low-income and special-needs children it served. Most of the families of Susan's students worked, and the jobs were mainly blue-collar positions, with the families living from paycheck to paycheck. Poplar Grove was a small town, with few opportunities to get ahead, and the community had taken a blow when the local factory had closed, laying off more than 200 workers and leading to several home foreclosures.

On this day, Susan's students had tried her patience, especially Zach, a lively eight-year-old boy, who was more interested in recess than reading. Zach was frequently out of his seat, noisy, bothered other students, and had difficulty getting along with his classmates when they were working in groups. Susan had tried different behavior management strategies with him, with no success. By the end of this day, she had finally lost her cool with him and sent him to talk to Mrs. Fraser.

As Brenda Fraser hung up the phone, she wished she could have called the Fosters with good news but knew they needed to know about Zach's continued behavior problems. She had asked them to come in for a conference with her and Mrs. Meyer to see if they could work out a plan for Zach. Brenda liked Zach and knew that things were tough for him and his little sister since their mom had been arrested on drug charges. She also knew that the Fosters were good, decent people who loved their grandchildren and wanted the best for them. Zach had always been active and needed a firm hand, and although Susan was a great teacher with creative teaching ideas, she didn't have the best classroom-management skills. Brenda wondered what she was going to have to do to keep the problem from escalating.

Betty Foster sighed as she hung up the phone. Brenda, the principal at the elementary school, had called to tell her about Zach's getting into trouble again at school. It seemed like the calls were getting more frequent, and she didn't know what to do. Although she had worked many years as a high school teacher, she felt at the end of her rope with Zach's behavior, both at home and school. Betty dreaded telling Ed about the principal's phone call. Ed worked long hours as an attorney and often brought work home with him. He had been talking about retirement on and off for the past five years, but she knew he wasn't really serious about it. Besides, retirement wouldn't be the way they had planned, now that they were raising an eight- and a five-year-old who had more energy than they could deal with sometimes. Betty still hoped that their daughter would eventually be able to assume her role as the children's mother when she finished the drug rehabilitation program that they had managed to get her in. Meanwhile, she and Ed were doing their best. They loved those children fiercely and would do whatever it took to raise them so that they would turn out better than their mom did.

NUCLEAR FAMILY SETTINGS

Randall and Shantel married when they graduated from high school and found jobs locally. They were excited when their first child, Jada, was born after they had been married for two years, but now after seven years of marriage and still in their 20s, their family has grown to include two more children, three-year-old Quinton and the new baby, Tia. Finances are tight for the family with day-care expenses for the two younger children and repairs to their fixer-upper house, and Shantel has used all her sick leave days for her maternity leave because of Quinton's frequent asthma attacks. Randall and Shantel both feel exhausted at night from work and caring for their small children, and the stress level often leads to arguments about their finances. Shantel has been able to volunteer a few times in Jada's kindergarten classroom and secretly wishes she could go to college to become a teacher, but doesn't know how they could afford for her to quit her job. She also worries about the future of her marriage.

The two-parent or nuclear family is often described as the ideal family with few problems, in comparison with other family types. In fact, in discussions about diverse family types, this family type is often omitted because it doesn't appear to be diverse. However, this family type is indeed an example of a diverse family, and as in the case of Randall and Shantel, the nuclear family has its share of challenges as well as strengths.

A two-parent or nuclear family may be defined as one in which the parents are first-time married; the children living with them are their biological or adopted children, and no other adults or children live in the home (Barbour, Barbour, & Scully, 2005). Since the Census Bureau no longer distinguishes whether a two-parent family has first-time married parents or is a stepfamily, it is difficult to determine precisely the number of nuclear families in America today. For example, the Census Bureau reported that in 2007, about 70% of children lived in households with married parents, but this percentage also included blended families with stepchildren (U.S. Census Bureau, 2009).

Although often thought of as being the traditional or majority family type, the nuclear family is not necessarily a dominant family culture worldwide. This family type is favored in Western industrial nations that have an **individualistic culture**, with an emphasis on independence and individuals' accomplishments, but in other countries of the world that have a **collectivist culture** (where cultural emphasis is on being a part of a group), the **extended family** is the traditional family type, with grandparents, aunts, uncles, cousins, and other family members sharing in raising children. This extended family culture favors interdependence among family members in financial and emotional support, and children are encouraged to depend on adults in the family (Georgas et al., 2001; Gonzalez-Mena, 2008).

Research on different family types has shown that growing up in an American nuclear family leads to many positive outcomes for children. For example, children in nuclear

While the nuclear family leads to positive outcomes for children, it also has its share of challenges.

families tend to have a higher educational attainment than children who grow up in single-parent or blended families (Ginther & Pollak, 2004). This may be because of more financial and emotional resources in nuclear families than in a single-parent family and the fact that stress levels may be higher in families that are attempting to blend into a new family with stepchildren and stepsiblings.

Contemporary nuclear families are not without stress, though. Only about one-fourth (24%) of married couples with children under the age of 15 had a stay-at-home parent in 2007. Mothers who chose to stay at home with their children were more likely to be Hispanic or foreign born and were also more likely to live in poverty than other mothers (U.S. Census Bureau, 2010). The Census Bureau reported that the primary reason mothers chose to stay at home with their children in 2003 was to care for their home and family, while the primary reason fathers were stay-at-home parents was because of illness or a disability (U.S. Census Bureau, 2004). In 2009, 59% of married couples with children younger than 18 were both employed, meaning that many parents are juggling long workdays with caring for children (U.S. Census Bureau, 2010). As Gilbert (2005) stated, for most dual-working parents, "There are not enough hours in the day to harmonize work and family life" (p. 12). However, in the current economy, dual working families are also struggling financially. The number of both fathers and mothers who are unemployed has doubled from 3% (father) and 2% (mothers) in 2007 to 6% and 4%, respectively, in 2009. One demographer noted, "These statistics show us that families are having a difficult time during this recession," (U.S. Census Bureau, 2010, para. 4).

In 2007, the U.S. Census Bureau changed the collection of data on cohabitation, or individuals who lived together in a committed relationship but were not married. This data showed that younger children were more likely to live with their unmarried parents than older children. For example, 10% of one-year-olds lived with their unmarried parents, while only 1% of teenagers did. This may be because of the rise in acceptance of cohabitation, as well as the fact that couples who live together have a high rate of ending their relationship, meaning that they may no longer be together when children are older (Kreider & Elliott, 2009). Although this family type does not fit the definition of a nuclear family, because of a lack of a legal marriage, it is important for teachers to recognize the presence of both parents in the home and encourage their involvement in their child's education.

It is also important to note that families are fluid in nature, changing over time. Children may live in several different family types during their childhood, For example, a preschool-aged child may live in a traditional nuclear family and then experience a family divorce, which leads to living in a single-parent home. One or both parents may choose to cohabit with a boyfriend or girlfriend, or to remarry, leading to a blended family, which can operate much like a nuclear family. Therefore, teachers should be familiar with characteristics of all family types.

Suggestions for Working With Nuclear Families

What do the characteristics of this family type mean to you as a teacher? What should you consider in being partners with the nuclear family in educating their child? Some suggestions include the following:

- Plan activities for both fathers and mothers to be engaged in their child's education. Don't just ask for "room mother" volunteers but also offer volunteer opportunities for fathers.
- Let stay-at-home parents indicate their interests, as opposed to dictating volunteer opportunities. While stay-at-home parents are often interested and willing to volunteer in their children's classrooms, it is important to not take advantage of them or assume that they will always handle family volunteer duties.
- Arrange networking opportunities for families to get to know one another, such as parent education meetings, family nights, celebrations, and other activities. For families who may not have extended families nearby for support, help them develop supportive relationships with other families.
- Arrange for parent-teacher conferences and school events after work hours for dual-working families. Schedule events at various times to accommodate different working schedules, such as a breakfast with the teachers, a Saturday morning brunch, or weeknight conference appointments.
- Be aware of children who may be latchkey children because of both parents working. Help organize an afterschool program in your district to meet the needs of working parents.
- Although you may not agree with the living arrangement of a parent(s) cohabiting, it is important to treat all families with respect, such as using the correct last name for each parent. Avoid addressing letters home to "Mr. and Mrs. _____."

EXTENDED FAMILY SETTINGS

As noted, for many cultures, the typical family structure is the extended or multigenerational family that includes additional family members, such as grandparents, aunts, uncles, and cousins. Historically, the extended family was common in Europe in the 19th century with the practice being continued by immigrants to the United States, and it was typical of farm families with more than one generation living on a farm and handling the chores. The Industrial Revolution and movement from an agrarian to an urban society caused this family type to decrease. In 1940, about 25% of family households were multigenerational, but by 1980, only 12% of families fit this type. However, analysis of recent Census Bureau data shows this family type is on the rise. In 2008, the number of extended family households had increased to 16% (Roberts, 2010). This increase in extended families may be because of difficult financial times, elderly people living longer, or immigrant families bringing extended family members to live with them. The multigenerational family is more commonly found in Latino, African American, Asian American, and Middle Eastern families (Roberts, 2010; Taylor, 2000).

Extended, multigenerational families offer a wealth of resources for nurturing and parenting of children. For example, the care of children is often shared among family members, and this can create a strong network of support for the parents and "thick" social relationships for the children (Demo & Cox, 2000). Extended family members can provide additional role models for children and share family traditions and values, as well as be another source of guidance and discipline for children. However, multiple generations living together can be a source of conflict in the home, especially when there are disagreements among the family members about how to raise children (Schwartz, 2010).

Suggestions for Working With Extended Families

For children living in extended families, the most important suggestion for teachers is to recognize the influence of all family members on the children's education and include them in school activities and communication sent home. For example, a lack of understanding of the importance of the extended family led to one teacher's being surprised when a grandmother and two aunts attended a parent-teacher conference, along with the child's mother. The teacher expressed reluctance to share information with anyone other than the mother, requiring the mother to explain to the teacher that the other family members were also vital to her child's education (Manning & Lee, 2001). Some specific suggestions for working with extended families include the following:

- Send out a survey at the beginning of the school year to find who all the members of the students' families are, their roles in the children's lives, and their expected involvement in the children's education.
- Allow children to include extended family members in any activity or assignment that involves families, such as drawing pictures of their families, writing stories about them, or making multiple gifts for family members at Christmas.
- Include extended family members in any invitations for school events and do not limit the number of family members students can bring to school activities.
- Be sure to have enough chairs and space for extended family members when meeting with them for a conference.

SINGLE-PARENT FAMILIES

Mike is the single father of six-year-old Brooke. Mike and Brooke's mother never married, but he has been an active parent in her life since she was born, and Brooke has been living with him full-time since her mom started working a night shift and decided she was unable to care for Brooke. Mike does not have any family nearby, but his parents try to visit every few months to spend time with them. Mike has dated several women, and briefly lived with one woman whom he thought might be a good mother for Brooke, but that did not work out. Mike has tried not to let his dating interfere with his parenting responsibilities, and he reads bedtime stories with Brooke every night and makes sure that the clothes she dresses herself in for school are clean. He has not volunteered for any activities at Brooke's school but did attend her parent-teacher conference. He is worried about the skills that the teacher said Brooke hasn't learned yet and isn't sure how to help her.

Single-parent families have always been a part of American life. In these families, fathers or mothers raise children on their own; a single parent does not necessarily have to be the custodial parent, and a child can have both a single father and a single mother. However, the causes of single-parent families have changed over time. In the late 1800s and through the mid-1900s, children were most likely to be in single-parent families because of the death of a parent (Berger, 2004). As health care improved and divorce rates increased, single-parent status changed because of divorce rather than death. About 25% of children in the United States are living in a single-parent household (with no cohabitating partner) (Kreider & Elliott, 2009). This rate varies geographically. As the map shows in Figure 4.1, children in the South, as well as a few states in the North and West are more likely to live in single-parent homes than children in the Midwest, North, and West. For example, 54% of households in Washington, DC, were single parent families, while only 15% in Utah fit this family type.

Recent statistics show an emerging trend leading to the single-parent family: the rise of women choosing to have children without marriage (National Center for Health Statistics, 2006). As noted in the vignette about Mike, the number of single fathers is also increasing

FIGURE 4.1   Percentage of Households With Own Children Under 18 That Are Single-Parent[1] Households by State: 2007

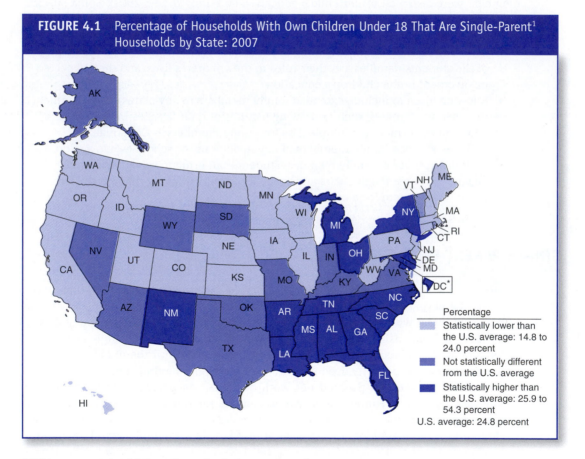

Percentage

- Statistically lower than the U.S. average: 14.8 to 24.0 percent
- Not statistically different from the U.S. average
- Statistically higher than the U.S. average: 25.9 to 54.3 percent

U.S. average: 24.8 percent

* DC is represented at 4.5 times the scale of other continental states.

[1] Excludes single parents living with unmarried partners.

Note: See www.census.gov/acs/www/Downloads/ACS/accuracy2007.pdf for further information on the accuracy of the data.

Source: U.S. Census Bureau, 2009

as courts are more willing to grant custody to fathers (although a single male parent is still a single parent, regardless of whether he has custody of his children or not). There has been a 62% increase in the number of single fathers raising their children alone since 1990 (Gilmore & Bell, 2006). Allowing single people, both male and female, to adopt children is also a relatively new process. Before 1970, there were few adoptions granted to single parents, but in the past 30 years, there has been a steady increase, both nationally and internationally, with more courts allowing both single men and women to adopt children. Census data on adopted children were collected for the first time in 2000, and that survey indicated that 22% of adopted children lived with a single parent (Kreider, 2003). Nearly one third of all adoptions in 2000 were to single parents (Gestwicki, 2007). Artificial insemination and surrogacy are also recent choices for single people choosing to become parents.

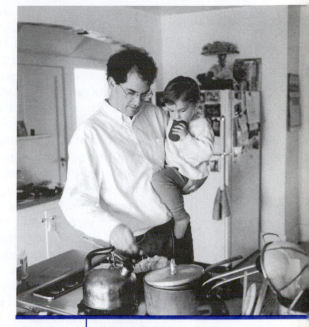

The number of single fathers with custody of their children is increasing.

Single parents face many issues in raising children by themselves, not the least of which is economic difficulties, particularly for single mothers. As noted in Chapter 1 (Figure 1.5), single-parent families are more likely to live in poverty. Although the poverty level for all children in 2005 was 17%, the number of children living with single mothers below the poverty line was 43.3%, and the percentage for children living with single fathers was 21% (U.S. Census Bureau, 2006–2008). Ethnically, black and Latino families tend to have higher percentages of single-parent households (KIDS Count Census Data, 2006).

Single parents may feel more stress because of both providing financially for the family and also taking care of the emotional and physical requirements of parenting. They may suffer from a sense of isolation (Sailor, 2004). If a divorce led to the single-parent family status, then the circumstances that surround the divorce, especially the amount and type of conflict, and the continuing relationship between the parents and with the child can have ongoing, negative effects on the child (American Academy of Pediatrics, 2003; Demo & Cox, 2000; Sun & Li, 2002). Children in single-parent homes may have to take on more adult responsibilities, such as caring for younger siblings, preparing meals, and cleaning the house. These children may also have emotional or physical difficulties because of a divorce or death of a parent, requiring more intense parenting (Wright, Stegelin, & Hartle, 2007).

Research has shown that children from single-parent families tend to be at higher risk for a variety of problems, including educational difficulties. If the single-parent status is because of a divorce, children may experience a variety of physical and behavioral symptoms, such as stomachaches, headaches, regression of behaviors such as bedwetting and tantrums, anxiety, sadness, depression, guilt, anger, denial, and disruptive classroom behavior (Richardson & Rosen, 1999; Wright et al., 2007). Generally, divorce has more of a negative impact on children than parents, and the effects are both immediate and long term (Bigner, 2006). However, it is important to note that while the average findings show divorce has serious and harmful effects on children, there are individual differences among children, with a great variation in how children respond, relating to factors such as the age when the divorce occurred, the amount of parental conflict before and after the divorce, the child's gender and resilience. These differences can even be seen among children from the same family (Dunn, 2004). Children who can distance themselves from their parents' conflicts or who have good coping strategies can adjust well after a divorce. If the new single-parent living arrangement is more stable and has a happier environment than the previous troubled two-parent home, children may actually do better. The quality of parenting may also be higher if the troubled marriage consumed much of the parents' emotional strength, and given attention and support, children can adapt to their new life situation (American Academy of Pediatrics, 2003; Demo & Cox, 2000).

Single-parent homes are often described as being "incomplete" or "broken," yet this family type has many strengths that teachers should acknowledge. Children from single-parent homes may be more independent because of increased responsibility and power in making family decisions, leading to a healthier self-image (Parron, 2008; Sailor, 2004). A close relationship can develop between children and the parent in single-parent homes, and children often report admiration for their parent in raising them alone. In fact, single-parent homes may be particularly suited for older children in foster care needing adoption because of the intense and close relationship that can develop with a single parent (Child Welfare Information Gateway, 1994).

Suggestions for Working With Single-Parent Families

What does all this information about the single-parent family mean to you as a teacher? Some suggestions include the following:

- Have conferences at times that are convenient for working single parents and offer child care.
- Encourage single parents to be involved in ways that are easy for them, such as take-home activities, rather than coming to school. Send home videos taken during the school day and class books with pictures of school events so parents know what's happening in the classroom.
- Offer extra support for children, such as afterschool tutoring, child care, or homework help.
- Give single parents support by helping them form relationships with other families in the classroom for sick child care, carpools, friendships, and advice.
- Don't assume that single parents don't care about their child's education if they don't volunteer or get involved at school. Families that live in poverty may be dealing with survival needs that are more pressing, such as keeping the heat turned on or getting a car running, and although they may want to support their child's education, basic needs have to come first.
- Be sensitive to single parents' financial needs by not sending home frequent requests for money or supplies.
- Share children's literature that includes the single-parent family type. (See Table 4.2 for suggested titles.)

| TABLE 4.2 | Children's Literature That Depicts Diverse Family Types: (a) Single-Parent Families and (b) Children of Divorced Parents ||||

Title	Author(s)	Publication Date	Suggested Grade Use
(a) Single-parent families			
Let's Talk About Living With Your Single Dad	Apel, M.	2000	2–6
Getting Through Thursday	Cooper, M.	2000	K–5
Where's Jamela?	Daly, N.	2004	Preschool–3
Totally Uncool	Levy, J.	2000	K–5
Soldier Mom	Mead, A.	1999	K–4
Junebug	Mead, A.	1999	3–6
Goodnight, Daddy	Seward, A.	2000	K–3
When Mama Comes Home Tonight	Spinelli, E.	2001	Preschool–K
Let's Talk About Living With a Single Parent	Weitzman, E.	1996	2–4
(b) Children of divorced parents			
On the Day His Daddy Left	Adams, E.	2000	Preschool–4
Speaking of Divorce	Beyer, R.	2001	2–7
What in the World Do You Do When Your Parents Divorce?	Beyer, R.	2001	2–7
Since Dad Left	Binch, C.	1998	Preschool–3
Dinosaur Divorce	Brown, M., & Brown, L. K.	1986	Preschool–3
My Parents Are Divorced Too	Ford, M., Ford, A., and Ford, S.	1998	4–7
Daddy Day, Daughter Day	King, L., & King, C.	1997	K–4
It's Not Your Fault, Koko Bear	Lansky, V.	1998	Preschool–2
Don't Fall Apart on Saturdays: The Children's Divorce-Survival Book	Moser, A.	2000	2–3
Mom and Dad Break Up	Prestine, J.	2002	K–3
I Don't Want to Talk About It	Ransom, J.	2000	K–3
Mama and Daddy Bear's Divorce	Speman, C. Q.	1998	Preschool–2
Always My Dad	Wyeth, S.	1995	2–5

Source: Gilmore and Bell (2006, pp. 284, 286).

It is important to note the special needs of the single-parent family members who have experienced a separation and divorce. Schools and communities often rally around families who lose a parent to death but tend to offer little support in the event of a divorce, which is a time in which children and their parents may be particularly vulnerable (Richardson & Rosen, 1999). A divorce is a loss and can feel like a death, in a sense, as this newly separated mother illustrated:

> I took my daughter out for dinner, and I saw these couples in the restaurant in their eighties, and that was my dream. That was who I thought we would be someday. The tears started flowing at the loss of that dream.

It is also important for teachers to understand the different custody and visitation arrangements that children may experience. Types of custody include both physical custody (the parent[s] with whom a child resides) and legal custody (the parent[s] who has legal authority to make decisions about the child). Parents may be awarded sole or joint physical and/or legal custody. Sole custody is usually awarded if one parent is determined to be unfit to be a parent, which may be because of drug or alcohol problems. However, joint legal custody may be given, along with sole physical custody, meaning that a parent may still have the right to make decisions about the child's education. This parent may also be given visitation rights (FindLaw, 2011). A review of studies of custody arrangements found that, in general, children who spent at least 25% of their time with each parent (joint custody) had better self-esteem, behavior, family relationships, and emotional adjustment than children in sole custody. The lower the conflict between the parents, the better the children did (Leon, 2009). A new trend with divorced families is coparenting, or shared parenting, where both parents work together as a team to raise their children, even though they are no longer married. Parents may develop a legal parenting plan, as a part of the divorce agreement, which includes decisions such as when a child will be with each parent, including holidays, financial support, and choices for the child's education (i.e., private or public school, summer school, tutoring, extracurricular activities) (McQueen, 2008).

Suggestions for Working With Families Experiencing a Divorce

Some suggestions for supportive family engagement practices for families experiencing a divorce include the following:

- Help organize support groups for children led by your school counselor during the school day and family support meetings at night. Meeting topics can focus on problem solving, coping, and communication skills. Make sure your programs are based on the specific needs of the children, as related to their age, gender, ethnicity, and socioeconomic status (Richardson & Rosen, 1999).
- Be aware of any court order relating to visitation and custody, as well as whether a legal parenting plan exists. Document the visitation/custody schedule of your students and become familiar with what days children are with each parent. Help parents understand your school schedule, such as the day library books are due or children need to be dressed for a PE class.

- Remain in communication with the noncustodial parent as much as possible. One way to do this is to communicate regularly with both parents by sending copies of newsletters and notes to both the custodial and noncustodial parent and, if necessary, holding separate conferences for estranged parents. Do not rely on young children to remember to show any newsletters or note to both parents.
- Although your role as the classroom teacher is not to be a counselor, you can provide parents a chance to share their emotions, including their fears about the future and the consequences of the divorce on their children.
- Maintain a classroom with security and structure and allow children to express their feelings in a variety of ways, such as artwork, puppets, and personal conversations. Table 4.2 also has suggested book titles relating to families who have experienced a divorce.

BLENDED FAMILIES

David and Kathy have each been married before. This is David's third marriage and Kathy's second, and they have been married to each other for seven years. David has three children from previous marriages (ages 16, 12, and 10), and Kathy has a daughter (age 10). Together, they are parents of Mark (age 6). David's two younger children live with their mother nearby and stay with David and Kathy every weekend and several weeks in the summer. However, David rarely sees his 16-year-old son, who lives farther away with his mother. Kathy's daughter lives with them, but visits her dad every other weekend and two weeks in the summer. Kathy dreads the weekends when all the kids are together because their house doesn't have much space and her daughter, in particular, resents having to share her bedroom with her stepsister. Although Kathy is able to get along well with her ex-husband, the relationship between David and both of his ex-wives is rocky, and his children seem to be caught in the middle of conflicts often. David and Kathy would like to be more involved with the kids' schools, but most weeks, it seems to be all they can do to just find library books that were at the other parents' homes or get homework done.

According to research, roughly 60% of divorced parents will go on to remarry within six years after the divorce, creating **blended families** or families created by the joining of adults in unions, with one or more of the adults having children brought into the new family (Desrochers, 2004). One study of children of divorce found that nearly all of their parents were dating or remarried within two years after separating (Ahrons, 2004). This means that a substantial number of children in today's classrooms are part of a blended family. Indeed, one-third of today's American children are expected to become stepchildren before they reach the age of 18 (Arnold, 1998).

Complex relationships are created with a blended family, not only with the newly married spouses but also relationships between stepparents, their natural children, stepbrothers and stepsisters, as well as the possibility of half-siblings if the newly married parents go on to have more children. Extended families also become more complicated with the addition of step-grandparents, aunts, uncles, and cousins. When divorced parents remarry, children become a part of **binuclear families,** or two different families, and must learn to negotiate living in two houses that may have different rules, expectations, parenting styles, and levels of caring.

Although remarriage may bring a higher economic level and better standard of living than the single-parent family experienced, blended families have unique problems and challenges, especially relating to children, with more opportunities for conflicts for both children and parents. There are characteristics exclusive to the blended family that distinguish them from first-marriage, nuclear families. For example, new family members are instantly created when parents remarry, as opposed to gradually adding members with the additional births of younger siblings. This instantaneous family requires immediate establishment of rules, boundaries, and roles to be well functioning, which may explain why the first few years of living in a stepfamily are especially difficult for children (Arnold, 1998; Bigner, 2006). Children in blended families also have mixed feelings of allegiance to their parents and stepparents, and the guilt they feel about a perceived lack of loyalty to their biological parent may interfere with bonding with the stepparent. Children may also have been unwilling participants in the formation of the new family. If a remarriage occurs too quickly after the parents' divorce, children may still have unresolved grief or resentment over the loss of their biological parent in the home, which can make life for the new stepfamily difficult (Bigner, 2006). In fact, Ahrons (2004) found that one-third of the stepchildren she studied thought their parents' remarriage was more stressful than their divorce. About 60% of remarriages end in divorce, and often, disagreements about raising the children is one of the issues of conflict between the new spouses (Desrochers, 2004). Developing a strong blended family requires time, as much as four to seven years (Papernow, 1993). Research has shown that blended families do not necessarily offer any benefits for children over a single-parent family. For example, one study found that the overall educational outcomes for children in stable blended families were worse than for children in nuclear families (Ginther & Pollak, 2004), leading some to question why the addition of another adult in the home to help with financial and parenting needs does not seem to offer benefits over the single-parent family. One hypothesis is that children in blended families experience higher levels of family conflict than children in nuclear families. Blended families bring the opportunity for both intrahousehold conflict and interhousehold conflict, with discord both within their home and between their biological parents' homes.

What do children say about living in a stepfamily? When asked about their thoughts of being in a stepfamily, children described being confused by the changes that occurred in their family and that these changes had not been explained well. Children felt a lack of control over decisions being made about them, such as visiting their other household. They also talked about the importance of having friends for support (Dunn, 2004).

It is important not to overlook the positive factors that blended families offer to children. Stepfamilies have often been portrayed in a negative manner, such as the wicked stepmother and stepsisters in fairy tales, but blended families can provide stability and economic security for children. Parents may find happiness with their new marriage partner and, ideally, have more time for meeting the needs of the children, as well as increased support for parenting decisions. Children now have another parent figure and gender role model and gain a new extended family (Sailor, 2004). Children may see the new stepparent as a friend, mentor, or bonus parent, in particular when the divorced parents have a cooperative relationship that doesn't cause children to feel conflicting loyalties (Ahrons, 2004). Children, as a whole, do best when living with two parents, in a stable, well-functioning family that has adequate social and financial resources and both parents are actively engaged in raising the children, and children are undeniably better off in a caring blended family as opposed to an unhappy or unloving nuclear family home (American Academy of Pediatrics, 2003; Arnold, 1998). As this parent described, creating a well-functioning blended family is a challenge, but this family type can be a nurturing environment for a child:

> After my ex-husband and I separated, my approach to "new people" in the kids' lives was that I was very protective. . . . I didn't let just anyone into their lives—I was picky because I didn't want them to get attached to someone who wasn't going to be there long term. I also took the approach that the more people who loved my children, the better. . . . The bigger the community of positive influence in their lives, the better. . . . The biggest challenge was my own baggage—letting go of feeling like a failure because of the divorce, opening myself up to a new relationship and new life with my husband and recognizing that the kids weren't just fine—they were great. . . . It's also really nice because there are truly three parents—mom, dad, and step-dad—and we all have very deep respect for the role that each of us plays in the lives of our kids. I feel so blessed that we all do things together—we carve pumpkins and trick or treat together at Halloween, we coach sports teams and go to games together, and the three of us talk all the time about things going on with the kids. In really practical terms, having three parents is fantastic for things like snow days and all the many extracurricular activities that they are involved in—there are more hands on deck! (N. Cody, personal communication, July 9, 2011)

While creating a well-functioning blended family is a challenge, this family type can be a nurturing environment for a child.

Suggestions for Working With Blended Families

These findings have implications for you, as a teacher, in working with children from blended families. Some suggestions include the following:

- Offer support for children by facilitating peer relationships and support groups. Be especially sensitive to children's needs if a parent has recently remarried, especially if the remarriage required the child to move and change schools.
- Include the noncustodial parent in communication and school activities.
- Be aware of a student's schedule for visitation with another parent, in homework assignments, library books, notes, and permission slips. When talking about visitation experiences, present it in a positive light, such as having two homes.
- Avoid using terms such as, "your mom's house" or "your dad's house," which imply that neither home is the child's, and instead, use terminology such as, "your home with your mom" and "your home with your dad."
- If making family gifts or pictures, let children draw more than one picture or make gifts appropriate for their situation, such as two Mother's Day cards.
- Be aware of family names and use the correct last name for students, parents, and stepparents.
- Recognize that the stepparent is an additional parent, not a replacement, and that this extended family member can support the child and school. One mother described her difficulty with teachers who didn't understand this:

We have to make a strong effort right up front to let them know that we do everything school-related together, which means that when we walk in the classroom for a parent/teacher conference, we do it as a unified parent team—Dad, Mom, and Step-Dad. It is a learning experience for the teachers because they usually aren't used to families like us, so we try to let the teachers get to know us very well at the beginning. It's much easier once they realize that we all have a great "working" relationship as parents and that all three of us have mutual respect for the role that we each play in the lives of our children. It takes awhile for the teachers to understand that our relationship is a positive one, which is understandable given that they are used to dealing with divorced parents who don't get along. I do wish that it wasn't such a surprise, almost a shock at times, to the teachers (sometimes it feels like they don't actually believe us), but again, we just work really hard at it, and once they take the time to get to know us, it works out OK. (N. Cody, personal communication, July 9, 2011)

- As with other family types, it is beneficial to share books that depict blended families similar to what children have experienced. See Table 4.3 for suggested titles.

One example of a successful schoolwide program for elementary children from blended families is the Positive Connections's afterschool program in Arizona. The support club includes not only typical afterschool activities, such as drama, music, dance, and art, but

TABLE 4.3   Children's Literature That Depicts Diverse Family Types; Children Living in Blended Families

Title	Author(s)	Publication Date	Suggested Grade Use
To & Fro Fast & Slow	Bernhard, D.	2001	Preschool–K
Terrible! Terrible!	Bernstein, R.	2002	K–4
The In-Between Days	Bunting, E.	1996	3–7
The Steps	Cohn, R.	2003	3–7
Jennifer Has Two Daddies	Galloway, P.	1990	Preschool–3
Falling Into Place	Greene, S.	2002	4–7
Mister and Me	Holt, K.	2000	2–5
There's Only One of Me!	Hutchins, P.	2003	Preschool–3
I Have a New Family: Understanding Blended Families	Monroe, R.	1998	K–2
I Hate Weddings	Petersen, P. J.	2000	2–5
Stepfamilies: Let's Talk About It	Rogers, F.	2001	Preschool–3

Source: Gilmore and Bell (2006, p. 283).

also guest speakers and opportunities for children to talk about their families. At the end of the first year of operation, more than 90% of the participating children said that the support club helped them understand and cope with their feelings, and 40% reported improvement in their relationship with their noncustodial parent and new family members (Killian, Bixler, Cowgill, & Cowgill, 2000).

GRANDPARENTS AND OTHER KINSHIP ROLES

Although Barbara is not considered the legal guardian of her granddaughter, Makayla, she is, by all accounts, her parent. Born to her 19-year-old daughter, Amy, Makayla has lived most of her life with Barbara. Although Amy now lives on her own, her visits with Makayla are sporadic. Amy occasionally gives Barbara money for special expenses for Makayla, like the recent prescription for medicine for an ear infection, but most of the financial burden falls on Barbara. Barbara has considered going to a lawyer to start proceedings to become Makayla's guardian, so she will qualify for Barbara's company's insurance plan, but that would require that she terminate Amy's maternal rights, and she is not sure about doing that. Besides, she is hoping that one day Amy will live up to her promises to Makayla for her to move in with her. Barbara is looking forward to the time when she can just be grandma to Makayla and not her parent.

Grandparents and other relatives are an important part of many children's lives, and they may be actually raising their grandchildren. One in twelve children is living in a household headed by grandparents (4.5 million children) or other relatives (1.5 million children) (AARP, 2007b). These living arrangements may include the parent of the child living in the home. For example, a variation of the grandparent-headed household is the **subfamily**, which is created when a family, such as a single teenage mother and baby, live with the grandparents, with the grandparents remaining as the head of the household, but the mother raising the child. In addition, grandparents may also play the important role of providing before- or afterschool care for their grandchildren who do not live in their home.

Kinship care, or grandparents or other relatives becoming surrogate parents (when parents are unable to; the arrangement may be temporary or a permanent legal guardianship), has increased dramatically in the United States, and the AARP (2007a; 2011) now offers support for grandparents in the legal, financial, educational, and health issues that they face in raising their grandchildren (Fuller-Thomson & Minkler, 2000). Grandparents and other relatives assume a parenting role for many reasons, including the death of the child's parents, parental divorce, unemployment, teenage pregnancy, and drug and alcohol abuse, which may lead to serving a jail sentence. If children are removed from the home because of abuse or neglect, a grandparent or other relative may assume custody to keep the children from going into the foster care system.

The parenting styles of grandparents vary. Some grandparents may be minimally involved while others are active participants in child rearing. Raising grandchildren can give grandparents a sense of satisfaction and a renewed sense of purpose in life as they seek to raise their grandchildren more successfully than the children's parents. Special bonds can be created between children and grandparents who live together (Edwards & Daire, 2006).

However, there are also challenges for grandparents raising their grandchildren, especially economic difficulties, with the additional expenses of the children; expenses are often not reimbursed by the parents. A total of 18% of children living with their grandparents are below the poverty line, and 23% of these children are not covered by health insurance (U.S. Census Bureau, 2003). Raising young children can take a physical and emotional toll on grandparents, especially if they have personal medical conditions. Children may have behavioral problems and emotional difficulties because of a sense of abandonment, anger, or rejection that grandparents often feel unequipped to handle (Sailor, 2004). Grandparents may struggle with how to help grandchildren with their emotions while dealing with their feelings about the situation. As one grandmother wrote:

> How do you get a 4 [year old] to understand, without trashing her mother, that her mom just doesn't want to raise her? And how do you deal with it from your own perspective, from knowing that you're doing all the work and yet all they [the child] want is someone who can't/won't provide for them and really doesn't even want them? (AARP, 2011, para. 7)

The relationship that grandparents or other relatives have with the children's parent(s) may be strained and difficult, creating tension in the family. If the grandparents have not legally adopted or do not have legal guardianship of the grandchildren, the situation has a temporary feeling, and grandparents may not have access to legal records, such as school or medical records.

Suggestions for Working With Kinship Care Families

Grandparents or other relatives raising children have special needs, and as the children's teacher, you can provide extra support for their efforts. Some recommendations for teachers include the following:

- Acknowledge grandparents or other relatives as primary caregivers by initiating contact and maintaining that contact throughout the school year. Issues of adoption and custody should be discussed and documented for future reference (Mader, 2001).
- Understand that enrollment in a school district may be problematic. Some issues that may need to be addressed include lack of proof of legal guardianship, transportation to another district, possible fees for out of district enrollment, and development of an individual education plan (IEP) for students with special needs (Mader, 2001).
- Recognize the stress (emotional, physical, and psychological) that raising young children creates for older adults. Refer grandparents to school personnel who are helpful: the guidance counselor, principal, school nurse, or school psychologist (Edwards & Daire, 2006).
- Be aware of the financial constraints that grandparents who live on fixed incomes suffer, as well as insurance coverage limits of Medicare. Make grandparents aware that financial assistance can be obtained through various agency resources, such as Department of Jobs and Family Services, Supplemental Security Income, SS

Survivors Benefits, Medicaid, Earned Income Tax Credit, or Special Supplemental Program for Women, Infants, and Children (Mader, 2001).

- Explore the possibility of forming support groups for grandparents parenting for the second time. Help grandparents find child-care sources for times when the pressure of parenting is overwhelming and they need a break (Mader, 2001).
- Although there are many children's books available that show loving relationships of children with their grandparents or grandparents living in their homes, there aren't as many available with the family type of children being raised by grandparents. See Table 4.4 for titles about children and their grandparents.

Keep in mind also that grandparents who are not primary caregivers play a very critical role in the lives of children and should be encouraged to get involved in the classroom in ways that are comfortable for them. These grandparents are often retired and have the ability to volunteer in the classroom during the school day. Invite grandparents to share

TABLE 4.4 Children's Literature That Depicts Diverse Family Types: Children and Their Grandparents

Title	Author(s)	Publication Date	Suggested Grade Use
The Wednesday Surprise	Carrick, D.	1990	K–3
Walk Two Moons	Creech, S.	1994	5–7
Picture Me With My Grandma	D'Adrea, I.	2000	K–3
Nana Upstairs & Nana Downstairs	dePaola, T.	1973	K–3
Abuela	Dorros, A.	1997	Preschool–2
Western Wind	Fox, P.	1995	4–7
Sun and Spoon	Henkes, K.	1998	4–7
Robert Lives With His Grandparents	Hickman, M. W.	1996	Preschool–2
Ghost Wings	Joosse, B.	2001	K–3
Annie and the Old One	Miles, M.	1985	K–3
Kele's Secret	Mollel, T.	1997	K–3
What Grandmas Do Best/What Grandpas Do Best	Numeroff, L.	2000	K–3
Anna's Corn	Santucci, B.	2002	1–4
Belle Prater's Boy	White, R.	1997	5–7
Visiting Day	Woodson, J.	2002	K–3

Sources: Gilmore and Bell (2006, pp. 284–285) and Relatives as Caregivers Resource Guide for Erie County (n.d.).

their hobbies or stories from their childhood with your class, and extend invitations to them for special events, such as student presentations and graduations. Extended families or blended families may have several sets of grandparents, so find out whom the parents want invited to functions. It is a good idea to check with the parents first about the degree of grandparent engagement allowed.

SAME-SEX FAMILIES

Melissa and Rachel have been together in a committed relationship for about three years. Melissa was married before she met Rachel and has two children, Alex and Adam, who are now ten and six years old. When Melissa and her husband divorced, she moved in with Rachel, although there was a bitter custody battle for the boys. Melissa's ex-husband was awarded frequent visitation rights, and the boys spend most weekends with him. The tension is often high when the boys are picked up or dropped off by their father. Separate parent-teacher conferences have to be held with each parent. In spite of the difficulties between Melissa and her ex-husband, she and Rachel have created a peaceful, nurturing home, and they both help the boys with their homework at night and attend their soccer games together.

My observation is that the harsh realities of divorce were harder on the kids than their mom's choosing an alternative lifestyle. I also see the very tight support given within the gay community to parents with children. I may be biased, but I also feel that same-sex parents start off early on to achieve balance in their child's life around their own sense of self and their own principles. Diversity, acceptance, and "not judging" are discussed around the kitchen table on a daily basis. And this is in regards to looks, race, religious convictions and a variety of current society's expectations as well as around sexual orientation. I feel that children of same sex couples are well prepared to discuss any issues that come up in the classroom regarding their parent's life choice because they have been given the tools to have that type of discussion. (Davidson, 2010, p. 1)

Another type of family that you may encounter in your classroom is the **same-sex family**, where the family is headed by two males or two females who live together in a committed relationship. It is estimated that there are two to seven million children being raised in lesbian- or gay-headed households (Gelnaw, Brickley, Marsh, & Ryan, 2004). Same-sex families face many challenges relating to discrimination. "Heterosexism and homophobia are so embedded in our society that the impact of existence of this bias is often invisible to people who are not the target" (Lesser, Burt, & Gelnaw, 2005, p. 4). **Lesbian** (a woman who is homosexual), **gay** (a man who is homosexual), **bisexual** (a person who is attracted to people of either gender), or **transgender** (a person whose identity, expressions, and behaviors in gender are not traditionally associated with his or her birth sex) parents worry about how open to be with their children's teachers and how their children may be treated by other children or parents. Harassment by peers does occur, and it is more often experienced by children of gay fathers than those who have lesbian mothers (Wright et al.,

2007). Other challenges include **LGBT** (lesbian, gay, bisexual, and transgender) parents worrying about being declared unfit parents and losing custody of their children, as courts still routinely deny custody to LGBT parents on the basis of sexual orientation (Gelnaw et al., 2004). Same-sex families face other legal issues, such as whether both parents may have access to school records, authorize emergency care for children, and have rights to insurance and death benefits.

Same-sex families face many challenges.

Although the American Federation of Teachers, American School Counselor Association, American School Health Association, and the National Education Association have all developed antidiscrimination statements about sexual orientation, some teachers and families have difficulty accepting the same-sex family, and they avoid communicating with them or involving them in the classroom. How comfortable are you working with an LGBT parent? Consider the following typical fears that teachers have about working with a same-sex family:

- I am afraid that I will have to talk about sex in the classroom if I address LGBT issues and questions from the other children.
- I am uncomfortable using the words "gay" or "lesbian" in class.
- I don't know what terms to use when addressing members of gay or lesbian families. For example, do I address both lesbian parents as their child's mom?
- I have trouble reconciling my personal or religious beliefs with my classroom responsibilities.
- I don't have any knowledge about resources for LGBT families or where to obtain information.
- I am afraid I will lose my job or make other families angry if I introduce the same-sex lifestyle in discussions or encourage LGBT parents to volunteer in the classroom (Gelnaw et al., 2004).

While these are typical fears of teachers, especially in conservative communities, if some families are explicitly ignored by educators, a message is sent to students that their family is not valued as much as others. Children who cannot talk about their families feel left out, which can negatively affect their self-esteem and academic development (Gonzalez-Mena, 2007). You should not allow any biases to prevent you from involving all family members in their child's education. For example, an LGBT parent should not be excluded from participating as a field trip chaperone. An inclusive classroom community is clearly absent when some families are excluded.

The booklet *Opening Doors: Lesbian and Gay Parents and Schools* (Gelnaw et al., 2004) includes questions for educators to ask parents while conferencing. These questions may help you understand the family constellation of the same-sex family.

1. Start with an open-ended question such as, "tell me about your family and who would you like to be included in our further discussions."

2. What are the names your children use to refer to family members? (Dad/Papa, Mom/Lisa, Mama, first names)

3. What degree of openness about your relationship do you maintain with the rest of the community? (confidentiality or, on the other hand, public disclosure might be preferred)

4. Do you know of resources that might help me learn about differing family configurations and cover this in class?

5. What explanation do you provide when you are asked how your children came to you? (Gelnaw et al., 2004)

Children can often help ease teachers' fears and also help their classmates better understand the issues that their families face. For example, in this exchange between two second graders, a lesson was taught about fairness: "Well, your parents could get married, because you have a mom and a dad, but I have two moms and they can't get married. That's not fair" (Cowhey, 2005, para. 7). Another child, Zack, an 11-year-old, simply explained his membership in a gay-headed family by stating, "I'm just a kid with parents" (Gelnaw et al., 2004, p. 4). Children, in their infinite wisdom, may be able to guide you in how to sensitively approach the topic of lesbian and gay families.

Suggestions for Working With Same-Sex Families

What can we change in schools to welcome LGBT families? School district personnel can ask themselves these questions:

- Does the school have an antidiscrimination policy that includes sexual orientation that is communicated to families (Gelnaw et al., 2004)?
- Does the school use forms that have spaces for "mother's name" and "father's name?" A space for "parents' names" or "family members" would be more appropriate.
- Do all teachers understand the appropriate terminology to use relating to LGBT families? Do they find out what a parent prefers to be called or just make an assumption?
- Does the school hold celebrations such as Mother's Day or Father's Day? It can easily be called Family Day (Gonzalez-Mena, 2007).
- Do school administrators establish a model for an inclusive environment? School leaders should set the tone for welcoming LGBT families by making sure that they do not tolerate bias toward families among the faculty and staff.
- Does the school censor materials that depict same-sex families? Will school administrators support teachers if they are criticized by other parents or the community for sharing children's books with same-sex families? (See Table 4.5 for suggested titles.)

Table 4.5   Children's Literature That Depicts Diverse Family Types: Same-Sex Families

Title	Author(s)	Publication Date	Suggested Grade Use
123: A Family Counting Book	Combs, B.	2000	Preschool–3
ABC: A Family Alphabet Book	Combs, B.	2001	Preschool–3
Heather Has Two Mommies	Newman, L.	2000	Preschool–3
And Tango Makes Three	Parnell, P.	2005	Preschool–3
In Our Mother's House	Polacco, P.	2009	K–3
Lots of Mommies	Severence, J.	1983	Preschool–3
Daddy's Roommate	Willhoite, M.	2000	Preschool–3
Daddy's Wedding	Willhoite, M.	1996	Preschool–3

Source: Gilmore and Bell (2006, pp. 291–292).

In the past 20 years, researchers have found that a parent's sexual orientation does not affect a child's gender identity, self-concept, intelligence, behavior, or personality characteristics and that children in same-sex homes have the same advantages as children whose parents are heterosexual, in health, adjustment, and development (American Academy of Pediatrics 2003; Demo & Cox, 2000; Perrin, 2005; Sailor, 2004). An American Academy of Pediatrics (2002) policy statement found that a "considerable body of professional literature provides evidence that children with parents who are homosexual can have the same advantages and the same expectations for health, adjustment, and development as can children whose parents are heterosexual" (p. 339). As a teacher, it is important that you respect the LGBT parents and work to form a partnership that will help you better understand how to educate their child.

ADOPTIVE FAMILIES

Dan and Jane tried for many years to have a child. After exploring adoption possibilities, they opted for an international adoption from China. The process was expensive, but they both agreed it was worth it when they got the picture of Su Lee, whom they now call Suzanne, from the adoption agency. She was 18 months old when they were able to bring her to America, and she is the light of their lives. As first-time parents in their forties, Dan and Jane read every book they can find on parenting, including books about adopting children from other cultures. They have tried to raise Suzanne with an awareness of her Chinese heritage, as well as enrolling her in dance, music, and gymnastics classes. They are protective of Suzanne and frequently volunteer in her kindergarten class, so they can become familiar with the other children she plays with.

International adoptions by American families can provide nurturing homes for children.

One unique family type that may also have the structure of the others listed in this chapter is the **adoptive family**, where a parent(s) is the legal parent but not the birth parent of a child or children in the family. Adoptive families can be found in nuclear, extended, single, blended, grandparent and kinship care, and same-sex households. Adoption is common in America, with between five and six million Americans being adopted; approximately 51,000 children were adopted in 2007 (U.S. Department of Health and Human Services, 2008). Adopted families are different in that they are created by legal agreements rather than by biological ties. Adoptive families may also be multiracial, multiethnic, or **transracial**, where a child of one race or ethnic group is adopted by a family from another race or ethnicity. Children may also be adopted internationally. International adoptions were at a high in 2004, with 22,990 children adopted from other countries. That number declined to 12,753 in 2009, with the highest number of children coming from China, Ethiopia, Russia, South Korea, and Guatemala (U.S. Dept. of State, 2011).

As with other family types, adoptive families also face challenges. Adoptive families may have little warning before their children arrive and may receive little information about their children, such as physical, intellectual, and emotional health history or past environmental influences, and they may not be prepared for a child's special needs. They may need extra support from teachers and caregivers in understanding their new children's learning and developmental needs. As one mother, who was herself adopted as a child and then became an adoptive mother said,

The other thing that being adopted and raising an adopted child and stepchildren has driven home for me, is that as parents, we REALLY have to work to understand our kids' strengths and differences when it comes to their learning styles and motivation with school work. I know this is true for biological children, also, but because of the stark differences in my children, it has been necessary. My brother and sister and I were all adopted, but we were not blood-related at all. However, our parents definitely had the same expectations for all of us. Of course, often their expectations were not met, and at least one of us felt like a "failure." They weren't trying to demean any of us, they just didn't get that just because we were all being raised the same way in the same environment, that didn't mean we would all learn the same way and have the same strengths and struggles. Having an adopted child and stepchildren and biological children that battle things like Fetal Alcohol Syndrome, Attention Deficit Hyperactive Disorder, and depression, has taught me to learn about each child's learning preferences and motivation for learning, etc., and then to try to accommodate them individually. I am constantly learning more about each child and often, this has meant seeking help from people who know a lot more than me about learning challenges. (S. Fraser, personal communication, April 18, 2007)

Challenges also exist relating to the nature of adoption. When children learn that they are adopted, they may have questions about who they are and why they were given up for adoption. Children who have been adopted may fantasize about their birth parents. As one mother said, "When my daughter was younger, she imagined that her birth mom was a princess somewhere, locked up in a castle and unable to come and get her." Families may also be unsure about when and how to disclose to children that they were adopted and whether to let children have any contact with birth parents. Children who are culturally or racially different from their parents may face discrimination. For example, one mother reported insensitive questions from a stranger about her daughter whom she adopted from China, such as "Is she adopted?" "Was it expensive?" "Where is she from?" which subtly implied that she was an oddity or not a true part of the family (Couchenour & Chrisman, 2000, p. 99). Children may also be adopted by a stepparent or a foster parent, and emotional difficulties may arise if the children have not resolved issues with ending the relationship with their biological parents.

Children in families created by adoption are chosen by parents who want a child to raise and love. Adoptive parents provide children with love, care, and the legal status of family. Adoptive parents typically must undergo a screening process to determine the fitness of their home to raise a child, and adoptive parents are held to a high standard. Because families may have to wait for months or years to adopt a child, children who were adopted are often cherished by their families.

As noted, adoptive parents and children are often subjected to "verbal ignorance" (Gajda, 2004, p. 163) by well-meaning individuals, including teachers, who say things like, "I can't believe he's not really yours! Do you know anything about his real parents?" (Stroud, Stroud, & Staley, 1997, p. 229). As you work with families who have children who were adopted, think carefully about your word choices and what they imply to the child or family members. Use thoughtful, positive language. For example, stating that a birth mother "made an adoption plan" is a more positive approach than "she gave away her baby," while the term "international adoption" has a less judgmental connotation than "foreign adoption." Even using the past tense when referring to an adoption, such as "he was adopted," as opposed to "he is adopted," places the emphasis on the child's place in the family and less on the adoption act (Stroud et al., 1997).

Suggestions for Working With Adoptive Families

Other suggestions for you as a teacher working with families who adopt children include the following:

- Avoid stereotyping adopted children as being more at risk of emotional, behavioral, or academic problems. Adopted children have the same capacity for academic and social success as nonadopted children (Gajda, 2004).
- Become familiar with the family situation and what children know or do not know about their biological parents. Find out what the parents want shared about the adoption in the classroom. Respect a family's wishes for privacy about the adoption.
- Avoid projects that may be difficult for adopted children, such as family histories that are based on biological family relationships and require photos or mementos. Be aware that adopted children may not have photos of themselves as babies. Be open to classroom discussion about the differences in families when discussing family histories.

- Allow children adopted from other cultures to share something about their culture of origin, but be aware that culture is learned and not biological. Children adopted from a foreign country as small children will not have an understanding of that culture unless they have been taught about it.
- For newly adopting parents, share observations and specific information about what the child is like in the school setting.
- Offer parent education materials and support groups for adoptive families to help them understand the developmental shifts that children experience about being adopted as they grow and mature.
- As with the other family types, it is important to share children's literature with your class that shows a variety of family types, including adoptive families. Suggested titles relating to adoption, including international adoption, are shown in Table 4.6.

Table 4.6 Children's Literature That Depicts Diverse Family Types: (a) Children of Adoption and (b) Children of International Adoption

Title	Author(s)	Publication Date	Suggested Grade Use
(a) Children of adoption			
I Got a Family	Cooper, M.	1993	Preschool–2
A Is for Adopted	Cosby, E.	2001	K–5
Tell Me About the Night I Was Born	Curtis, J.	1999	Preschool–1
Twenty Things Kids Wish Their Adoptive Parents Knew	Eldridge, S.	1999	3–6
Adoption Is for Always	Girard, L.	1991	K–3
Who's Who in My Family	Leedy, L.	1999	Preschool–2
Why Was I Adopted?	Livingston, C.	1997	4–6
We Belong Together: A Book about Adoption and Families	Parr, T.	2007	Preschool–2
(b) Children of international adoption			
When I Met You: A Story of Russian Adoption	Bashista, A.	2004	K–4
When You Were Born in Korea	Boyd, B.	1993	K–4
Our Baby From China	D'Antonio, N.	1997	K–4
I Wish You a Beautiful Life: Letters From the Korean Birth Mothers of Ae Ran Won to Their Children	Dorrow, S.	1999	3–6
I Love You Like Crazy Cakes	Lewis, R.	2000	PreKindergarten
The Red Blanket	Thomas, E.	2004	PreKindergarten

Source: Gilmore and Bell (2006, pp. 288–291).

FOSTER FAMILIES

Claire has always had a special place in her heart for children, which led her to become a teacher of children with special needs. After several years of trying to have children of their own, she and her husband, Nick, decided to become foster parents. In the 15 years they have been fostering children, they have seen a number of children come and go. They have cared for as many as eight children at one time, although now, they currently have four children in their home, three of whom are brothers, and a baby who was born addicted to cocaine. The three boys were taken from their mother after several episodes of neglect, and Claire's heart aches when she thinks about what they have endured in their short lives. The court is still hoping to reunite them with their mother, and she hopes it will be successful. If not, the boys have a home with them.

> ### ACTIVITY 4.1
>
> In this chapter, you have learned about several different family structures, their unique needs, strengths, and challenges. To further reflect on your work with diverse families, as a teacher, do the Quotable Minute Paper activity in Table 4.7.

TABLE 4.7   Quotable Minute Paper

The Quotable Minute Paper is a reflective quick-write activity. Select one of the quotes from the chapter about the different family types, and in one to five minutes, write your thoughts about the quote. Share your ideas with a classmate.

- Nuclear family: For most dual-working parents, there are not enough hours in the day to harmonize work and family life.

- Extended family: [In extended families], the care of children is often shared among family members, and this can create a strong network of support for the parents and "thick" social relationships for the children.

- Single-parent family: Single-parent homes are often described as being "incomplete" or "broken," yet this family type has many strengths that teachers should acknowledge.

- Blended family: Blended families bring the opportunity for both intrahousehold conflict and interhousehold conflict, with discord both within children's home and between their biological parents' homes.

- Grandparent and other kinship roles: As one grandmother wrote, "How do you get a 4 [year old] to understand, without trashing her mother, that her mom just doesn't want to raise her?"

- Same-sex family: In the past 20 years, researchers have found that a parent's sexual orientation does not affect a child's gender identity, self-concept, intelligence, behavior, or personality characteristics and that children in same-sex homes have the same advantages as children whose parents are heterosexual, in health, adjustment, and development.

- Adoptive family: Adoptive parents and children are often subjected to verbal ignorance by well-meaning individuals, including teachers.

- Foster family: The challenge for foster parents is to create a sense of family and belongingness, with the uncertainty of how long different children may be in the home.

A final family type to consider is one that is, by definition, a temporary family: the foster family. Foster families provide temporary care for children whose parents, for a number of reasons, cannot care for their children. Foster families can provide stability for children who have experienced a crisis, such as abuse or neglect. Foster parents become parents when they are granted legal guardianship of a child, but the goal of the court system is family reunification, or reuniting children in foster-care status with their birth parents, meaning that the foster family is not a permanent placement. Foster parents may care for several foster children, and the challenge for foster parents is to create a sense of family and belongingness with the uncertainty of how long different children may be in the home. The foster family is further discussed in Chapter 6, including suggestions and a book list for teachers working with children and their foster families.

In addition to reading books that focus on a specific family type, it is also important to share books with your students that show the individuality among and within families and to discuss how all families are different, but valued. Table 4.8 has suggestions of titles that will help your students understand that families come in all different sizes and types, and each is unique in its own way.

TABLE 4.8 Children's Literature That Depicts Diverse Family Types: Children in All Types of Families

Title	Author(s)	Publication Date	Suggested Grade Use
A Family Like Yours	Dotlich, R.	2002	Preschool–2
Let's Look at Families	Driscoll, L.	1999	K–4
Family Pictures	Garza, L.	1990	K–3
How My Family Lives in America	Kuklin, S.	1992	K–5
Families	Kuklin, S.	2006	K–4
Why Are All Families Different?	Maynard, C.	1997	K–2
Families	Morris, A.	2000	Preschool–2
The Family Book	Parr, T.	2003	Preschool–2
Who's in a Family?	Skutch, R.	1995	K–3

Source: Gilmore and Bell (2006, pp. 292–293).

SUMMARY

Although this chapter has examined the diversity that exists among families in their structure, it is essential that you do not develop stereotypes about families, such as viewing all single-parent families as being low-income or all blended families as having conflicts. It is also important that you realize that there is a great diversity within each family type. In fact, the results of one study suggest that it is less important to focus on the structure of the family than it is to learn about how the family functions and the relationships among its members (Georgas et al., 2001).

Rather than labeling families in your mind as "single-parent," "blended," "same-sex," and so on, you would do your students and their families the best service by getting to know each family as individuals. Family structure provides an important backdrop in understanding how a family operates, but it is only the beginning when it comes to developing relationships. True partnerships will begin when you develop deeper understandings of who each family is as an individual family.

REFLECTION QUESTIONS

Reread the In the Classroom case study presented at the beginning of the chapter and reflect on these questions:

1. What does Susan Meyer need to do to collaborate with Zach's grandparents about his behavior issues?

2. What issues should the teacher and principal consider when working with his grandparents?

3. How is this situation different when viewed from each perspective: the teacher's, the principal's, and the grandparents'?

WEBSITES

American Association of Retired Person GrandCare Support Locator. http://www.giclocalsupport.org/pages/gic_db_home.cfm.

This site offers a variety of national, state, and local resources for grandparents raising their grandchildren, including a way to connect with support groups in their area.

The Family and Work Institute, www.familiesandwork.org.

It is a nonprofit research organization studying the changing family and community. Check out their reports available for download that provide important information on the influence of work on the family.

Family Involvement Network of Educators (FINE), Harvard Family Research Project, sponsored by the Harvard Graduate School of Education, http://www.hfrp.org/.

The Family Involvement Network of Educators is a national network promoting strong partnerships between children's educators, their families, and their communities.

The Parent Institute, www.parent-institute.com/educator.

The Parent Institute encourages parent involvement in the education of their children and publishes a variety of materials, including newsletters, booklets, audio CDs, brochures, videos, and presentation kits; some are free, others are available at a low cost.

STUDENT STUDY SITE

Log on to the student study site at **www.sagepub.com/grant2e** for additional study tools, including the following:

- eFlashcards
- Web quizzes
- Web resources
- Learning objectives

Chapter 5

Culturally Diverse Families

Culturally responsive curricula include collaborative partnerships with families that are built on reciprocal trust and focus on the child and family's strengths.

—Linda Espinosa (2005)

American families are becoming increasingly diverse. What does that mean for teaching? Think about responsively engaging different family types, having experiences with people from different races, cultures, religions, and socioeconomic and language groups. How prepared do you now feel to work with culturally diverse families? Consider these questions:

- How do the changing demographics of American families influence your work with them?
- What exactly is culture?
- What are some similarities and differences between culturally diverse families?
- How can you work effectively in supporting linguistically diverse families?
- What should you consider when collaborating with families in terms of their religious beliefs or socioeconomic level?
- What is culturally responsive family engagement and how can you practice it?
- How can a *classroom cultural audit* help you welcome all families into your classroom?

Contributing Authors Luis Hernández, Lynn Zubov, Joyce Goddard, and Manuel Vargas

Part of the excitement of working in the field of education is to get a glimpse of the future of communities and the nation right in our classrooms. The children of families served today will soon be high school graduates and, one day, the adult citizens in the community. Children in the classroom reflect the next generation and demonstrate the increasing diversity of America. One illustration of this diversity is seen in the many languages spoken by children in today's American classrooms. Table 5.1 lists the top 25 languages spoken in schools currently, and Table 5.2 demonstrates that although some states do have a higher population of English language learners (ELL), diversity is found in all areas of the country.

As you encounter the changing demographics of the nation at the local level in your classroom, you will be working with children and families whose language and culture will be different from yours, as well as that of other children. Those differences pose a particular set of challenges as you seek to be respectful of all children and families. The long list of differences can range from child-rearing practices, eating and dietary habits, gender roles, attitudes about school and learning, and communication styles to complex relationships with teachers and administrators.

TABLE 5.1   Language Backgrounds of Limited English Proficient (LEP) Students in the United States and Outlying Areas, 2000 to 2001 (Sorted by Estimated Rank, Top 25 Languages)

Rank	Language	LEP Students	Percentage of LEP Students
1	Spanish	3,598,451	79.045
2	Vietnamese	88,906	1.953
3	Hmong	70,768	1.555
4	Chinese, Cantonese	46,466	1.021
5	Korean (Yue)	43,969	0.966
6	Haitian Creole	42,236	0.928
7	Arabic	41,279	0.907
8	Russian	37,157	0.816
9	Tagalog (Filipino)	34,133	0.750
10	Navajo (Dine)	27,029	0.594

Source: U.S. Department of Education (2000–2001).

Note: These numbers mask regional variations. For example, in nine states, Spanish was not the dominant language among LEPs. In Montana, Blackfoot was the top language other than spoken English, and in Maine, the top language diversity was French. In several states, Vietnamese was not the second most common language diversity. For example, Chinese ranked second in New York and Kentucky, and Serbo-Croatian was second in Missouri.

TABLE 5.2 English Language Learners Population by State

States with largest population of students with limited English proficiency (LEP) in public schools (2007 to 2008)

1. California (1,526,036)
2. Texas (701,799)
3. Florida (234,934)
4. New York (213,000)
5. Illinois (175,454)
6. Arizona (125,636)

States with highest percentage growth rates of students with LEP in public schools (1994–1995 to 2004–2005)

1. South Carolina (714.2%)
2. Kentucky (417.4%)
3. Indiana (407.8%)
4. North Carolina (371.7%)
5. Tennessee (369.9%)

Source: National Clearinghouse for English Language Acquisition (2010).

Note: Twenty states have seen more than a 100% growth in the numbers of students with limited English proficiency since 1994.

Today's classrooms reflect the increasing diversity of America.

IN THE CLASSROOM: THE SILENT CHILD

Clara Simpson didn't know what to do. She had tried everything she could think of to help Elena be successful in her third-grade classroom, but as far as Clara could tell, she had made no progress with Elena. Elena and her family had moved to Poplar Grove from Mexico in early September, and they spoke no English. Since Elena's first day in her classroom, she had not spoken one word in class. Clara had not been worried about that in the beginning, but here it was, late November of the school year, and Elena continued to be silent in the classroom. Clara knew that Elena was learning. She noticed how observant Elena was in watching the other children, and she knew that Elena comprehended some information. Just yesterday, the class had been working in groups on experimenting with simple machines. Elena had successfully done the task, needing little help from her group members. "How can she understand that a bottle opener is a lever, yet can't answer questions about a story?" Clara wondered in frustration.

Clara had tried to build a relationship with Elena's parents, but it was difficult since they spoke no English and had to rely on family members to serve as translators. At the parent-teacher conference a few weeks ago,

(Continued)

(Continued)

they had nodded at everything Clara told them about Elena's progress and seemed agreeable to helping her at home, yet Clara couldn't tell if they were helping her. As a part of the school's new family involvement plan, Clara had invited the parents in to talk about their careers, and she had hoped Elena's parents would come in and share their Mexican culture with the class. Clara knew they couldn't speak English well, but thought that might motivate Elena to speak in class, if she could translate for her parents. However, they had sent word through Elena's fifth-grade cousin that they were not available. Clara knew that they worked long hours at the family's Mexican restaurant to support themselves and guessed that they didn't have time to come to school. Elena was probably going to grow up and work in the family's restaurant business anyway, so maybe she shouldn't worry about her academic progress.

Rosario rocked three-year-old Gabriela and thought about how their lives had changed so dramatically in the last year. A year ago, the hurricane had destroyed much of their coastal fishing village of La Pesca in northeastern Mexico. Miguel's fishing boat had been demolished, and their home damaged beyond repair. It was the final straw in their decision to leave Mexico for a better life for their family in the United States. Miguel's brother, Hector, and his family had moved to the United States 10 years ago and owned a successful Mexican restaurant in town. He had been after them for a long time to come and join him in the business. "Our life in La Pesca wasn't so bad," she thought, as Miguel worked hard with his fishing business, and Rosario had been a teacher at the local school until Elena was born. Miguel and Rosario both believed that it was important for her to stay home with their children, and she had given up her teaching job to care for Elena, followed a few years later by Javier, and then Gabriela. Even without her income, they had managed to get by, until the hurricane. Now, in their new life, Miguel enjoyed the restaurant business, and she liked living close to her sisters-in-law. The Latino community in Poplar Grove was growing, and their local Catholic church offered a service in Spanish where her family could worship. Her English was slowly improving, and she hoped that one day she would speak it well enough to volunteer at the children's school. The school system was good, and she respected the teachers' opinions. Elena's teacher, Mrs. Simpson, had been concerned at their conference that Elena was not keeping up with the class, but Rosario knew from the things that Elena chattered about at home in Spanish that she was learning many new things. Elena didn't seem to be picking up English as quickly as Javier was in his kindergarten class, and some of Rosario's friends from church had told her that she shouldn't allow the children to speak Spanish at home, but it was important to Rosario that the children not lose their Mexican heritage. She wished she could help Elena more with her homework and that Elena didn't have to work two to three hours a night on it, but until Rosario's English was better, she'd have to continue to rely on her nieces and nephews for help.

WHAT IS CULTURE?

Culture is often described as the beliefs or practices of a certain group of people, but there are difficulties associated with the word "culture" in its complexity. Frequently, people are labeled as "Latino," "African American," "Asian," or "Native American," and described in characteristics attributed to their culture. Yet within each of these groups, there is much diversity. As Gonzalez-Mena (2008) stated,

> Culture is extremely complex, and people of the same culture are quite different, depending on their individuality, their family, their gender, age, race, ethnicity, abilities, religion, economic level, social status, where they live and where they came from, sexual orientation, educational level, and even appearance, size, and shape! (p. 5)

Instead of viewing culture as a description of a group of people, perhaps a more useful approach for educators is to think of culture as the lens through which people view the world based on their backgrounds and experiences. Cultural beliefs and practices, as transmitted through a student's family and community experiences, help shape their personal and family histories. This is called **belongingness**, and it is important for educators to understand all the cultural influences on a family when trying to establish a relationship with them (Villegas & Lucas, 2002).

In addition to race, ethnicity, language, age, socioeconomic status (SES), sexual orientation, disabilities, or country of origin, culture can also include religious or spiritual practices and geographical locations. For example, even though the white, Anglo-European descendant population may be similar in skin tone and language, there is a great diversity between rural and urban; male and female; upper-, middle-, and lower-socioeconomic classes; and younger and older Caucasians. Culture or diversity does not just refer to minorities but applies to the entire population.

If culture includes all these different factors, then all of us are multicultural. As Warrier et al. (2002) stated,

I might have grown up in a working class, but today I am a professional, so I may no longer identify as a working-class person. If I am multiracial, how do I identify myself? We must move from having unitary ways of understanding people to looking at the complex ways all these issues come together for different people. (p. 662)

Key Concepts in the Idea of Culture

Phillips (as cited in Couchenour & Chrisman, 2000, pp. 25–26) described six key concepts of culture:

1. *Culture is learned.* Culture is not biological, meaning that a child of a certain ethnic or racial background may not necessarily understand the practices of that ethnic or racial group if not raised in it. For example, a child adopted from China and raised in a rural, middle-class white American home may not have any understanding of Chinese culture, unless specifically taught about it.

2. *Culture is characteristic of groups and not an individual trait.* Individual personality characteristics, such as shyness or competitiveness, are not culturally determined; however, students may also have learned cultural behaviors. Children whose personality traits are in conflict with their family's cultural behaviors may feel as if they do not belong in their culture.

3. *Culture is a set of rules for behavior, but not necessarily the behavior itself.* Children are taught what is considered to be correct behavior and what is not, based on cultural beliefs. For example, if a family's worldview is one of assertiveness and speaking up for individual rights, then children will be encouraged to be equal participants in conversations and question authority, while another cultural group's belief may be to respect authority, with children taught to remain silent when adults are speaking.

4. *Cultures borrow and share rules.* Cultures change and influence one another, especially as people from different cultures interact, marry, and raise children. For

example, if two people of different faiths marry, the couple may choose to raise their children with the religious beliefs of both of their faiths, including observing holidays from both religions. Cultures may change over time unless the group protects its boundaries by discouraging members from interacting with others outside the culture. For example, the Amish culture seeks to isolate itself from the American culture and protects its cultural practices and beliefs, dating back to the late 17th century. Marriages outside the faith are not allowed (Robinson, 2006).

5. *Members of a cultural group may be proficient in cultural behavior but are unable to describe the rule.* For example, a rural southern tradition is to serve black-eyed peas and hog jowl on New Years' Eve because of the belief that if a person eats like a "poor man" on the first day of the year, the New Year will bring prosperity. Children may grow up participating in this tradition and continue it into adulthood without ever understanding why this is a traditional holiday meal.

ACTIVITY 5.1

Think about each of these six concepts of culture. Can you give an example from your family experiences of each of these concepts? For example, how embedded are you in your culture? Can you give examples of cultural rules that you were taught as a child? Share your examples with class-mates, noting how each of you has learned your cultural beliefs and practices over time, as opposed to being born with a cultural identity.

6. *Individuals are embedded to different degrees within a culture.* **Acculturation** describes the degree to which people from a certain cultural group display the beliefs and practices of that group. Families adopt cultural practices to varying degrees based on factors such as education level, socioeconomic status, the amount of time spent in the culture or removed from it, including the age of immigration from the native country, the amount of contact with people from other cultures, and urban or rural origin (Randall-David, 1989). Therefore, it is important for teachers not to expect a family to *act* a certain way because of their race, ethnicity, or language. It is important to understand individual differences, as well as cultural beliefs.

SIMILARITIES AND DIFFERENCES AMONG CULTURALLY DIVERSE FAMILIES

There are fundamental similarities among culturally diverse families that teachers can count on. Parents from all races, social classes, and ethnicities want the very best for their children. One Latino mother summed it up: "I believe every parent wants their child to be something" (Griego Jones, 2003, p. 89). To help achieve this, a significant amount of learning goes on in the home. Families may discuss the events of the school day with their children, help with homework and projects, as well as teach about the world indirectly through everyday activities in the neighborhood and community (De Gaetano, 2007). This goes counter to the notion of the **cultural deficit model** held by some educators. The deficit model is a negative view about families that presumes that some families are lacking in resources or talents to support their children in their education.

Although there are similarities among culturally diverse families, there are also differences, especially relating to the amount and type of school involvement the families will choose. Edwards (2004) described **differentiated parenting** as the recognition that families differ from one another in their ideas, viewpoints, and ability to work with educators. Some families may willingly choose an active role and partnership with the school, while other families may remain fearful and intimidated by the prospect of school involvement based on language differences, racial politics, social stigma, educational or economic level, and age. One mother related her discomfort when attending a meeting scheduled by the teacher:

> The pre-judgment before you even get there . . . your stomach starts churning, and I mean, I think that's how most parents feel. It's like, oh, I gotta go in and talk to the teacher at the teacher conference and they are going to look at me like I don't know anything. (Griego Jones, 2003, p. 91)

It is important for you to have a variety of family engagement strategies that will allow families to choose to be involved in ways that are best suited to their lifestyle and beliefs about education.

TEACHERS' BELIEFS ABOUT DIVERSE FAMILIES

While collaborating with individual parents, caregivers, and extended families, you need to reconsider your **habitudes,** or unexamined attitudes or preconceptions of cultural traits, because these preconceived notions may be inaccurate for the actual families you'll be working with (Flores, Tefft-Cousins, & Diaz, 1991). Teachers may mistakenly use the term "culture" as an explanation for student and family behaviors that appear contradictory to their expectations. Ladson-Billings (2006) described an incident where teachers had labeled certain cultures as being a problem when it came to family engagement:

Children learn from the culture in which they are raised.

> Teachers from a suburban school invite me to talk to them about a problem they are experiencing. They cannot get African American and Hmong parents to come to school. I arrive at the meeting and begin with the question: "Suppose you arrive at school tomorrow morning and every African American and Hmong parent in this school is here. What would you have them do?" The teachers sit in stunned silence. I have not given them some handy tips or a pat explanation about the culture of the students and their parents. (p. 108)

Establishing respectful relationships with families of diverse cultures first involves understanding one's personal beliefs about culture and the complex nature of family engagement.

Teachers should be wary of the following habitudes that may influence their attitudes while engaging with families:

- *Dominant cultural perspective.* The majority of American teachers come from the dominant culture: 86% of elementary and secondary teachers are white, European Americans (Gay, 2002), and they may have fixed notions of the right way to parent, leading to resistance to other worldviews. For example, teachers regularly recommend that families read books with their children and view negatively any families where books weren't read in the home. However, as one Latino mother shared, having books in the home and reading to children was not a routine in many Latino homes, but instead, they tended to tell stories. For example, many mothers would hold babies and toddlers and tell them stories, which was also a bonding time. This mother was surprised when her children entered school that families were encouraged to purchase books for the home and that reading to or listening to children read was so much stressed by the teachers (J. Goddard, personal communication, March 30, 2007).
- *Engrained notions of conventional family engagement.* It is also important to note that the dominant white, middle-class American perspective generally prevails when considering family engagement practices, and teachers often (unconsciously and consciously) feel more at ease with family engagement practices that reflect that worldview (Villegas & Lucas, 2002). This conventional approach to family engagement may feel strange to families who hold different viewpoints about their role in their child's education. For example, some families may not understand how fundraising through a bake sale or school car wash may directly contribute to the academic success of their child. They would rather help their children with homework and leave school activities to the teacher, who was trained for that (Clayton, 2003).
- *Deficit role of family in school engagement.* American teachers view favorably families who act as interventionists in their child's education, with active involvement in school activities. However, some cultures view the family's role in their child's education to be noninterventionist in nature, believing that they should not intervene in the education process or question the teacher's practices (Protheroe, 2006). "Demand parents" who hold urban and suburban schools accountable are now constituting a parent interventionist model whose voices are increasingly heard (Crews, 2007).
- *Parental disinterest.* These varied perspectives can cause teachers who value traditional family engagement activities to feel frustrated, as in the case of one teacher who lamented the lack of volunteers in her classroom, stating, "I give up my time after school for their child. They should give up a little of theirs to come to school and meet with me." This teacher never realized that her cultural perspective limited families to ways they could be involved, causing her to fail to appreciate the ways they were actually supporting their child's learning.

As this illustrates, it is important for teachers to not only understand their personal beliefs but also strive to understand other families' viewpoints and practices.

LINGUISTIC DIVERSITY IN FAMILIES

With the variety of languages spoken by American students and their families, it is important to develop skills to work successfully with those who may not speak English. This starts with an understanding of the process of second language acquisition and how families influence that process. The process of learning a second language is similar to the process of learning the first language. However, becoming fluent in a language can be highly influenced by environmental factors, including the ability to practice the language with other competent speakers and the support in the school setting. Schools may offer a variety of instructional programs for English language learners (ELLs):

1. *English immersion.* Often called ESL (English as a Second Language). This approach does not develop or have the child practice their first language. The goal is to have students learn everything in English.

2. *Bilingual education.* Sometimes called dual-language programs. Instruction in this program is divided into English and the child's first language. The goal is to maintain and support the child's first language while transitioning into English.

3. *Primary or native language programs.* Instruction is only in the child's native language, with little or no exposure to English (Espinosa, 2005).

Research indicates that helping children maintain and build their skills in their first language while building strong language skills in English should be a long-term goal for educators. When children lose the ability to speak their native language, they may suffer cultural alienation, family difficulties, and possible school failure (Espinosa, 2005; Garcia, 2003; Wong Fillmore, 2000). There is strong value in children maintaining their home language, as the home can function as a language refuge, a place where cultural bonds and linguistic ties to the extended family are nurtured. The home can also reinforce a positive attitude toward learning English, although the decision about whether to speak English at home should be a collaborative family decision and not forced because of school expectations (Clayton, 2003).

Suggestions for Working With Linguistically Diverse Families

When working with families who do not speak English as their first language, encourage them to speak with their child in the home language and support families in the following ways:

- Loan native language books, stories, and materials to families to use during interactive reading activities.
- Include families and extended relatives in the classroom as language models to read to the class in their first language or tell stories, provide translation, and teach the class new words. The United States Census Bureau (2000) noted 47 million people (over the age of five) spoke a language other than English in their homes.
- Keep families informed about their child's language development in the acquisition of English. Compared with learning only one language, bilingualism may result in a slower growth in vocabulary. Also, one language may become dominant for the

speaker, which is normal (Espinosa, 2005). This can be confusing and upsetting for families who notice the child depending on her native language less.

- Allow students to maintain their native culture and language. Research shows that students who maintain their cultural identity and native language have more academic success (Northwest Regional Educational Laboratory [NWREL], 1998).
- Recruit volunteers to serve as guides for the families' first year in a new school setting. Ideally, these mentors should speak both English and the families' native language. If that is not feasible, then offer the services of translators when possible.
- Work with your district to offer district-wide meetings for families with limited English proficiency, complete with translators to ensure information is disseminated and questions are answered (Clayton, 2003).

Although you may try to reach out to families who do not speak English and encourage them to be involved in the school setting, it is important to realize that often, families with limited English proficiency may be reluctant to become involved for several reasons. Their lack of fluency in English, plus their lack of knowledge of the cultural expectations of schools, may prevent involvement. In addition, many cultures regard attending a child's school as the delivery of bad news and possible loss of face. They are afraid they will be given suggestions by the teacher they cannot implement because of language misunderstandings. Finally, many families do not have the luxury to leave work and physically get to school during inconvenient hours for them, from 8:00 a.m. to 4:00 p.m. If public transportation does not run near the school, they may lack the means to get there.

More information about working with linguistically diverse families, relating to communicating effectively with them, will be shared in Chapter 10.

WORKING WITH NEWLY IMMIGRATED FAMILIES

Estimates provided from the Federation for American Immigration Reform (FAIR, 2007) show that, as of 2005, 13% of the U.S. population comprises foreign-born people. Although a debate has raged for several years about the positive or negative influence that immigration has had on our society, the impact of immigration has been profoundly felt in schools (Friedlander, 1991). Immigrant children are regularly found in today's classrooms, and there are a variety of reasons as to why these students' families chose to migrate to the United States. Some came for religious freedom or to unite with family members, others to escape various war-torn countries or oppressive governments and dictators, while others may have chosen to live in the United States to seek the economic possibilities the country has to offer.

Some families who reach the United States come with advanced preparation, job security, language and educational skills, family, and community support, making for an easier adjustment in adapting to their new life. Other families, who leave their country under a variety of difficult circumstances such as war, political chaos, or economic stagnation, may face greater adaptation problems because of uncertainty, separation, lack of support, low education and language skills, and general isolation. The experience of many immigrant families includes a combination of both these positive and negative experiences in their adjustment and adaptation (Igoa, 1995; Suarez-Orozco & Suarez-Orozco, 2001).

Suggestions for Working With Newly Immigrated Families

Immigrant families and their children are now part of communities in every state of the nation. As a teaching professional, your task is to focus on the well-being, adjustment, and accommodation of the family and child in the school community. By building a relationship that strengthens the adaptation journey for the family, you foster individual success in school and community life. Here are some suggestions to consider:

- Focus on helping the child become successful in school. School success is embraced and encouraged by families, most specially immigrant families.
- Provide families with resources for their lifelong learning goals by sharing resources for English classes, job training, GED classes, and job opportunities.
- As a key person in the adaptation process for an immigrant family, you may be the "ambassador" of American culture. Provide explanations and reasons for our way of life, from special celebrations and holidays to the foods served in the school cafeteria.
- Depending on the stage of adaptation, you may be using translators and interpreters with recently arrived immigrant families; as the teacher, you must always be the person responsible for a child's school progress—translators are to be the background voice during meetings and conferences. Ideally, professional translators should be used, but realistically, finding these translators is not always feasible. Teachers may need to get creative and find local resources within the community, such as military personnel who have lived abroad, or electronic translation sources, such as free or commercial Internet sites and computer programs. Remember, there may be some parents who are not literate, and you should not rely only on print communication.
- Be aware of **intercultural communication**, which includes more than just language, but also the relationships between people who are different in values, role expectations, and rules in social relationships (NWREL, 1998).
- Encourage family engagement. Many families come from cultures where teachers are not questioned and family engagement in schooling would be considered rude and disrespectful (NWREL, 1998). Thus, involvement in the educational process may be a new concept for many immigrant families. Therefore, continuously reach out to your students' families with suggestions of ways they may be involved with their child's education.
- Seek to understand the causes of immigration and particular concerns of your students' families. As stated earlier, immigrants come to the United States for various reasons, and no two immigrants' experiences are the same. Understanding why students' families immigrated will assist in developing a positive relationship with immigrant families.

As with past generations of immigrants to America, education will provide the foundation for a new life in the United States for new immigrant families. Work with these families and their children today will have a lasting, positive impact on those families as well as the community.

DIVERSITY IN FAMILY RELIGIOUS PRACTICES

Responsive teachers are often confused about diverse family religious practices: what to include in the classroom curriculum in the area of world religions and how to respect family requests concerning their religious beliefs. For example, is it all right for children to talk about their family's religious practices in class discussions, or is that a violation of the separation of church and state? Can teachers share books that show families participating in religious ceremonies and rituals without being accused of teaching about religion? The First Amendment makes it clear: "Public schools may not inculcate nor inhibit religion. They must be places where religion and religious conviction are treated with fairness and respect." This point is important enough to repeat, "Public schools uphold the First Amendment when they protect the religious liberty rights of students of all faiths or none" (Family Education, 2007, p. 1). Therefore, culturally supportive family involvement practices include respecting all families' religious beliefs and allowing children to share those freely in the classroom.

The issue of religious beliefs often surfaces around holidays. In the United States, the school calendar is built around the holidays celebrated in the Christian religion. For example, public schools are not in session on Sunday, the Christian Sabbath day, and schools rarely plan activities to be held on a Sunday or other special religious days, such as Christmas and Easter. Teachers tend to plan their curriculum around the dominant culture themes, and the classroom read-aloud often features holiday stories from an Anglo-Saxon perspective. This ethnocentric, monocultural emphasis can lead to cultural discontinuity for students from different religious backgrounds, where they feel disconnected from the overall classroom cultural environment because of a lack of connectedness with what is being taught.

Schools demonstrate equity when they ensure that the curriculum includes study about all world religions. Diverse religious holidays offer rich opportunities to teach about religion in elementary schools. Teaching about religious holidays is permissible, as opposed to celebrating religious holidays, which is not. Studying different religious holidays or festivals may not only add to students' academic knowledge about the world but also be a way to explore family and community diversity (Family Education, 2007). Table 5.3 lists a variety of ethnic and religious holidays, many of which may not be familiar to you.

TABLE 5.3 Ethnic and Religious Holidays/Celebrations		
Ethnicity/Religion	**Holiday/Celebration**	**Month**
African American	Emancipation day Black history month Rosa Park's anniversary Malcolm X's birthday Juneteenth Kwanzaa	January February February May June December to January
Buddhist	Lohri Vesak—Buddha's Birth Diwali Bodhi—Buddha's Enlightenment	January April October December
Chinese, Korean, Taiwan	Chinese Lunar New Year Lantern Festival Dragon Boat Festival Mid-Autumn Festival Double Ninth Day (Elder's Day)	January/February February/March May/June September/October October/November

Hindu	Lohri Holi Mahashivaratri (Shiva Ratri) Rama Navami Krishna Jayanti Ganesha-Chaturthi (Ganesha Utsava) Diwali	January February/March February/March April July/August August/September October
Islamic, Muslim[b]	Al Hijra—Muslim New Year Mawlid al-Nabi (Muhammad's birthday) Ramadan Eid al-Fitr (conclusion of Ramadan) Eid al-Adha (conclusion of Hajj)	January/February/March March/April/May August/September/October/ November September/October/ November/December November/December/January/February
Japanese	O-Sho-Gatsu, Japanese New Year National Foundation Day Hinamatsuri, The Doll Festival O-Bon Festival/Feast of Lanterns Autumnal Equinox	January February March August September/October
Jewish	Tu B'Shvat or Tu B'Shevat Purim Pesach/Passover Yom Hashoah/Holocaust Memorial Day Shavuot Tisha B'av Rosh Hashanah, Jewish New Year's Day Yom Kippur/Day of Atonement Sukkot Shemini Atzeret/Simchat Torah Hanukkah	January/February February/March March/April April/May May/June July/August September/October September/October September/October September/October December
Mexico	Constitution Day Flag Day Cinco de Mayo Mexican Independence Day Dia de los Muertos/Day of the Dead Las Posadas	February February May September November December
Puerto Rican	Three Kings Day Emancipation Day Commonwealth of Puerto Rico Discovery of Puerto Rico Day	January March July November

Source: Kentucky University Medical Center (2008).

Notes:

a. For specific dates for a calendar year, see, www3.kumc.edu/diversity/ethnic_relig/ethnic.html.

b. The Islamic calendar is based on lunar observation, and dates apply to North America.

One issue that sometimes turns into a battleground between teachers and families relating to religion is a family's request for their child to be excused from classroom discussions or activities for religious reasons. School officials must accommodate these requests, and if students miss school days because of religious reasons, they must be allowed to make up the work. This may be difficult for you, as a teacher, to accept, but it is important to remember that religion shapes culture, and cultural practices often reflect religious beliefs. For example, as one Muslim mother stated, "Our religion is our culture, and our culture is our religion. I cannot separate the two." For this parent, observing her faith's religious practices was more important than her child attending school that day. This illustrates the importance of teachers suspending their judgment concerning families' religious beliefs, as they will spill over into the classroom setting.

Consider the following short vignettes involving classroom situations. How would you respond to the students involved and their families?

Family Religious Beliefs

- You overhear a conversation between two students in your fifth-grade class concerning snakes and poison. One of the students describes his church, The Church of God With Signs Following, where they wave live rattlesnakes during services and drink poison (strychnine) too. If they die, their faith is probably weak. The student said that he has witnessed men fall on the floor and be carried out.
- A parent calls for a conference with you, the teacher, and the principal. She adamantly and emotionally states that she does not want her child to hear anything about the topic of religion either in the classroom or in the school environment. When information on religion comes up, she asks that her child be allowed to leave the room. She indicates that she is willing to sue the district and the teacher personally if she hears of religion being discussed.
- A new student moves into your classroom. On her first morning, her mother brings her to class and informs you that their family members are Jehovah's Witnesses and that her daughter does not celebrate holidays and/or salute the flag. That morning, during the Pledge of Allegiance, the student remains seated. Later, the other students ask why she did not participate in saying the Pledge.

Sexual Mores

- A Muslim father requests that his fifth-grade daughter never be seated next to a boy (Weinstein, Tomlinson-Clarke, & Curran, 2004). However, you often have students' desks in groups of four facing one another to promote cooperative learning. In addition, there are fewer girls than boys in your classroom this school year, so the option of placing the girl only next to other girls appears limited. You are also unsure how you will control her seating when she is in other classes, such as art or music.
- Some of the fundamentalist Christian families in your classroom believe that a gay lifestyle is against the natural order and do not want their children exposed to this lifestyle. However, your roster for the upcoming year's class includes a family with same-sex parents. You have planned a beginning of the year picnic at a local park, and all families are invited.

Religious Practices or Traditions

- It is taboo to describe the religious ceremonies of the Zuni to outsiders—secrecy is fundamental to the Zuni religion. Teaching Zuni ceremonial prayers to youths is the role of the head kachina priest (Morrell, 2007). A Zuni student in your class has missed several classes for reasons that are unclear to you. When you contact the parents, they indicate that their child has been undergoing training to be involved in a ceremony.
- You create a math classification activity for your kindergarten class where children are given small bags of colored candies and asked to sort them according to color, size, and shape. After the children sort their candies by different attributes, they are allowed to eat them. One child begins crying and says that she can't have any sweets because of her religion. Her mother sends you a note the next day that expresses her unhappiness about the incident. She writes that their Catholic family is abstaining from all sweets during the Lent season and that she does not want any more candy served in class until the end of Lent.

All these scenarios present difficult dilemmas that teachers find themselves facing, relating to religious diversity. What can teachers do to be better prepared for family religious diversity in their classrooms?

Suggestions for Working With Religiously Diverse Families

- Research the major religions or belief systems practiced within your school community. Take notes on any restrictions within the religion that may influence your classroom instruction and your students. Investigate festivals or celebrations that could add richness to your curriculum.
- Be aware of school district policies relating to how religious information is shared, and also make sure families are aware of the district policies and legal rights concerning religion. Have a chat with your principal about his approach to working with families who bring up faith-based concerns. You may be reluctant to approach the issue of religion with families; however, to be respectful of all families, you must be aware of any religious limitations for particular students.
- Remember, students also have the right to express their religious views during a class discussion or as a part of a written assignment or activity. Young students' opinions are often based on their families' values and may be controversial, but warrant a discussion. Be prepared that certain units of study, such as evolution or religious holidays, may lead to questions and discussions relating to faith or religious beliefs.
- Recruit another teacher as a mentor to help you with community religious issues. If you are concerned that a conversation with a family member about religious concerns may become confrontational or accusatory, ask your administrator, mentor teacher, or family involvement coordinator to be a part of the meeting.

Your faith background (or lack thereof) helps define who you are as a member of your culture, yet as a public school teacher, it is important that you suspend judgment concerning families' religious beliefs and be respectful of those beliefs different from yours.

CULTURALLY RESPONSIVE FAMILY ENGAGEMENT

Recent researchers have described the importance of a culturally responsive curriculum that meets the needs of all learners, including those who are diverse in race, ethnicity, language, ability, gender, language, religion, and SES (Gay, 2002; Ladson-Billings, 1995; Villegas & Lucas, 2002). In Chapter 1, you were introduced to the similar concept of **culturally responsive family engagement**, where teachers go beyond the traditional activities associated with schools and families and seek to have a strong awareness of cultural differences, while also affirming the views of all families (Villegas & Lucas, 2002, p. 27). This culturally responsive family engagement requires multiple communication opportunities with families, such as the beginning of school year survey in Table 5.4 or by conducting home visits (which will be further discussed in Chapters 10 and 12).

Culturally responsive family engagement must go beyond your classroom practices, though, and also include your school's policies and practices. The state of Alaska has developed Standards for Culturally Responsive Schools to provide "a way for schools and communities to examine the extent to which they are attending to the educational and cultural well-being of the students in their care" (Alaska Native Knowledge Network, 1998, p. 2). The Standards are listed in Table 5.5.

TABLE 5.4 Beginning of the Year Survey for Families

1. What does your child like to do at home? What do you like to do together?

2. Does your child like to read or be read to? What does your child like to read?

3. What kind of activities does your child do at home that requires work with numbers or math?

4. How do you help your child learn different things that are important to your family, such as your family's values and beliefs?

5. How does your child contribute to your daily family routines? What special jobs within the family does your child do?

6. What hobbies or sports does your child enjoy? Do other family members participate in these hobbies or sports? If so, who?

7. What goals do you have for your child this year?

8. What else would you like me to know about your child or your family?

TABLE 5.5 Alaska Standards for Culturally Responsive Schools (1998)

Cultural Standards for Educators

Culturally responsive educators work closely with parents to achieve a high level of complementary educational expectations between home and school. Educators who meet this cultural standard

1. Promote extensive community and parental interaction and involvement in their children's education

2. Involve elders, parents, and local leaders in all aspects of instructional planning and implementation

3. Seek to continually learn about and build on the cultural knowledge that students bring with them from their homes and community

4. Seek to learn the local heritage language and promote its use in their teaching

5. Exercise professional responsibilities in the context of local cultural traditions and expectations

6. Maintain a close working relationship with and make appropriate use of the cultural and professional expertise of their coworkers from the local community

Source: Reprinted with permission from Alaska Native Knowledge Network (1998).

Note that the recommendation that culturally responsive educators actively participate in the community and connect with community members in meaningful ways. This can be a powerful tool to strengthen partnerships with families (Villegas & Lucas, 2002). If the community that students come from is having a celebration, by all means attend. It is painfully clear when parents realize that some teachers avoid involvement in their cultural events, whether at school or in their community setting. For example, Latino parents noticed with surprise and sadness that both new and veteran teachers sometimes appeared afraid to venture into their communities and wanted to leave quickly (Griego Jones, 2003).

Developing a Classroom Cultural Audit

Another important aspect of culturally responsive family engagement involves the classroom environment. It's easy to send a subtle message of acceptance or rejection each time a student or family member walks into the classroom. During the first year of teaching, seek to create a classroom community that values the cultural contributions of all families and is a risk-free environment where students respect different cultures. Watch attitude, tone of voice, and behavior while interacting with students and families; this will serve as a model for students and is the essence of **culturally sensitive caring,** where teachers are placed in an ethical, emotional, and academic partnership with ethnically diverse students who are anchored in honor, integrity, resource sharing, and deep belief in the possibility of growth (Gay, 2002). When children feel accepted (or rejected) at school, they will communicate this to their families.

In addition to behavior in the classroom, the environment should also clearly represent the children's lives through home, school, and community connections (McIntyre, Rosebery, & Gonzalez, 2001). Gay (2002) described the hidden or **symbolic curriculum** that is communicated through classroom materials and displays. By portraying a wide variety of age, gender, ability, race, ethnic, religious, and social class diversity through the classroom environment, the message is given that all people are valued. Rotating classroom displays, portfolio collections, photo albums or scrapbooks, bulletin board exhibits, student projects, tape recordings, or videos that represent family diversity can draw attention to the accomplishments of all families and help them feel that they are partners with the teacher in educating their children. It also gives the children a sense of belonging and continuity between school and home.

One way to ensure this is to conduct a family-friendly classroom cultural audit. By looking at classroom displays and exhibitions of family cultural artifacts, classroom projects, and the ways in which you have authentic contact with families, you can determine your level of cultural responsiveness. Table 5.6 presents a checklist of ideas for ways in which you can further develop culturally responsive family engagement through your classroom environment.

TABLE 5.6   Family-Friendly Classroom Cultural Audit

How does your classroom rate? Check if your classroom has the following elements:

Classroom Displays

Recruit families as collaborators in designing a family-friendly classroom:

- Display a world map on the wall indicating where everyone is from, linking children's pictures with yarn. Encourage families to add their pictures next to their child's in the collection.
- Record children's songs based on community themes (McIntyre et al., 2001). Have a tape recorder available to families to listen to their children's songs.
- Record children's dance demonstrations, whether they are ethnic, regional, or community based. Have a television available for families to view when they stop by.

(Continued)

TABLE 5.6   (Continued)

- Label items throughout the classroom in multiple languages and use these to build vocabulary. Consider rotating terms rather than leaving them all year. When possible, integrate into the curriculum.
- Set up a family-based classroom museum with families contributing artifacts on a rotating basis.
- A family member might be willing to take on the role of curator (on a rotating basis).
- Create a bulletin board exhibit of photos of ceremonial dress or clothing worn in the native country.
- A volunteer might be willing to be in charge of changing the exhibit periodically.
- As a project for the year end, put together a portfolio (using a pictorial overview) of the cultural artifacts families have contributed.

Projects Tied to Family/Community Interests

Enlist families as partners with their children in project development:

- Embed home language into projects through the year (McIntyre et al., 2001). Make sure to alert families about contributing to projects in which they may have particular expertise.
- Integrate cultural knowledge by storytelling in the classroom (Delgado Gaitan, 2004). Record the event for other families to view later.
- Compare current projects in your classroom with those completed by families (e.g., raising chicks) (McIntyre et al., 2001). Encourage families to tell their children about their school projects similar to the ones in which they are currently engaged.
- Ask students about special food dishes, breads, or candies from their communities of origin (Cortina, 2006). Provide ingredients for families to make recipes if they are willing.

Cultural and Community Demonstrations

Cultural and community-learning opportunities engage students:

- Have families act as guides in local area mapping activities during a classroom geography lesson.
- Integrate funds of knowledge held by family members relating to a specific classroom lesson.

Opportunities for Authentic Contact With Families

Deepen your understanding of family dynamics:

- Exchange journals between families and teacher (Finnegan, 1997).
- Look for opportunities for interactions with family members during pick-up or drop-off times.
- Try to allow for discussions about hobbies, sports interests, and academics.
- Display multicultural books and use them for interactive reading and make them available for children and families to read at home through a classroom lending library.

SUMMARY

Respecting and honoring the different families represented in your classroom through your teaching practices and classroom environment is not an easy task. In fact, it will be a lot of work! However, as a professional in the field of education, you will be supporting the basic principle of family engagement as a part of healthy child development and learning for children from diverse families. Your work will also benefit your entire class, as all your students learn to accept and appreciate each other's similarities and differences.

REFLECTION QUESTIONS

Reread the In the Classroom case study presented at the beginning of the chapter, and reflect on these questions:

1. What attitudes or preconceived notions does Clara Simpson have about Elena and her family? How does that affect her teaching effectiveness with Elena?

2. What family engagement strategies has the teacher tried? Have they been effective? Why or why not?

3. Using a model of culturally responsive family support, what other family engagement strategies should the teacher try to help Elena be successful in class?

WEBSITES

Children's Defense Fund, **www.childrensdefense.org.**

This site includes information on family income research and policies affecting families, including food insecurity, poverty statistics for states and cities, and minimum wage increases.

The Education Alliance, maintained by Brown University, **www.alliance.brown.edu.**

This website offers suggestions to foster family relationships, family involvement, and cultural awareness.

National Clearinghouse for English Language Acquisition (NCELA), funded by the U.S. Department of Education, maintained by George Washington University Graduate School, **www.ncela.gwu.edu.**

Promotes educator's cultural competence to better serve culturally diverse students.

Parent Teacher Home Visit Project at **www.pthvp.org.**

This partnership between a faith-based community group, a local teachers union, and a school district began in 1998 as an effort to address the cycle of blame that existed between parents and teachers at several Sacramento schools.

The Urban Institute, **www.urban.org.**

Urban Institute experts study public policies affecting families and parents. Look under their section on families and parenting.

STUDENT STUDY SITE

Log on to the student study site at **www.sagepub.com/grant2e** for additional study tools, including the following:

- eFlashcards
- Web quizzes

- Web resources
- Learning objectives

Chapter 6

Students of Families in Transition

Change is inevitable, except from vending machines.

—Anonymous

As described in Chapter 3, families go through normal changes that include marriage, the birth of children, and the children growing up and leaving home. Although cultural or socioeconomic influences may cause the timing of these events to vary, these transitions are a normal part of family life. What happens, though, when a family experiences an unexpected change such as a divorce or a death in the family? Do these family transitions require any special knowledge or skills on your part as a teacher? Consider the following questions that relate to changes that families and children may experience:

- How can I help a new student who has moved from another school to be successful?
- What kind of support does a student need when her parents separate and divorce? Does the transition into a blended family create any special issues for students?
- What should my response be to a student who has lost a sibling, parent, grandparent, or other significant family member?
- How can I work effectively with military families, who are often in transition owing to deployments or moves?
- How does having a parent in prison affect students' ability to learn and be successful at school?
- How can I help children in foster care feel secure in my classroom, even though their family may be temporary?

All these questions address difficult transitions that families and children may experience and that may affect the children's learning. This chapter will explore both normal family transitions and those changes that are unexpected and difficult for families; the chapter then offers suggestions as to how teachers and schools can respond to the changes.

FAMILY LIFE CYCLE: NORMAL TRANSITIONS

When I was really young I wanted a sister, but I think that was a mistake. Now I want a brother, an older brother, who can drive a car.

—Noah (quoted in Kurklin, 2006, p. 10)

Think about your life from birth to the present. What significant transitions have occurred in your life, such as the birth of a younger sibling, a family move, the death of a grandparent, or a family divorce or remarriage? Using a timeline format, create a chronicle of your life, with labels for these significant transitions. How many transitions have you experienced? Reflect on these transitions: Were some more difficult than others? Your experiences can better help you understand the students you'll have in your classroom and the changes they experience in their family life.

Today's students undergo a significant number of transitions. A stay-at-home parent entering the workforce or changing jobs, the family moving to a new area, children changing schools, older siblings leaving home, or the death of a grandparent are just a few of the normal **life events** that may occur in a family. (A life event is a significant experience that has an impact on a person's psychological condition.) Although change is inevitable, even changes that are positive and desired, such as the birth of a new baby, can cause stress for children and have an impact on student learning (Pryor & Rodgers, 2001).

One of the primary reasons that transitions are difficult for children appears to be the way a change affects the quality of parenting and the relationship between children and their parents or caregivers. If a transition causes the family to be under stress, then parenting abilities may suffer, leading to negative outcomes for the children. However, if families are able to maintain strong relationships and the adults have good parenting skills during the transition, then children appear protected from the risks associated with the change (De Vaus & Gray, 2003). For example, if parents prepare siblings for the arrival of a new baby and continue to meet the older sibling's emotional and physical needs, children tend to adjust more easily to the change in their family. Conversely, if a parent's new job requires a family move, the move may have a negative impact on a child if the new job is demanding, with long hours affecting the quality of parenting. Transitions do not affect all children the same way because children are different in resilience and adaptation to change, but one common factor in whether a transition has a major impact on children appears to be how the adult family members handle the transition and the quality of parenting during the transition (De Vaus & Gray, 2003).

IN THE CLASSROOM: DIVORCE AND A FIVE-YEAR-OLD

It was a busy morning in Ms. Tamika Grey's kindergarten classroom. The children were working in their literacy stations on a variety of tasks while she worked with small groups on beginning reading skills. At the reading table, she helped Javier, Ella, and James write a sentence about the pictures they had drawn. Javier and James were both concentrating as they "stretched out" the words and tried to write the sounds they heard. Ella, however, seemed to be a million miles away. "Ella," Tamika said gently, "what would you like to write about your picture?" Ella shrugged her shoulders and then scooted her chair closer to Tamika's and continued to look at her paper without writing anything. Tamika noticed that Ella had gotten clingier in the last month, and she wondered if it had anything to do with the changes that had happened at home.

At the fall parent-teacher conferences, Ella's mother, father, and new stepmother had all come for her appointment. Tamika hadn't realized that Ella's father had remarried, and she wished that she had scheduled separate conferences for the parents because Lois Chandler, Ella's mother, looked uncomfortable and tense during the conference. She remained briefly afterward and quickly told Tamika that Ella's father had recently remarried and the children were not adjusting to the change well. Lois's eyes had filled with tears as she asked Tamika to let her know if Ella was having any problems with her schoolwork and then quickly left.

Tamika wasn't sure how to handle the situation now. Ella was having more problems at school, both socially and academically. Tamika did not believe that she had learning problems, but she just seemed unable to concentrate or focus on anything, and her work was often unfinished. She also did not want to play with her classmates at recess but, instead, wanted to stand close to Tamika or whatever teacher or aide was on recess duty. Tamika knew that she should share this information with Ella's parents, but she hated to add to the stress that Mrs. Chandler seemed to be feeling. Mr. Chandler obviously cared about his children, and his new wife had seemed interested in Ella's schoolwork at the conference, but Tamika didn't know whether she should notify both parents and ask them to come in again or just contact Ella's mom. She made a mental note to talk to their school counselor about the situation and get her advice. At the beginning of the year, the counselor had started a support group for children whose families had experienced a divorce, and she had recently expanded it to include monthly parent meetings at night. Maybe it would help Ella to be a part of that group. Meanwhile, Tamika put her arm around Ella's shoulders and said brightly, "Let's see if we can think of something to say about that great picture you've drawn!"

MOVING

"You ruined my life!" I screamed at my parents. "I'm not moving, and if you try to make me, I'm running away from home!"

Mom told me that running away from home was the same thing as moving, except you have to cook all your own meals. I don't know how to cook.

That's when I knew I was stuck moving.

—Mallory (quoted in Friedman, 2004, p. 7)

Moving can have a negative effect on student learning and requires special family support.

One normal family transition that deserves special attention from teachers is a family move. The Department of Education reported that, in the early 1990s, one in six third-grade children had attended at least three different schools since the beginning of first grade (U.S. General Accounting Office, 1994). This number may be higher for children from low-income families. In urban schools, as many as 20% of students may change schools during the year (Weissbourd, 2009). Many students move during the early childhood and elementary school years, and research has generally shown that a move can have a negative effect on student learning. Studies have found that students who experience a move have lower test scores and grades and a higher chance of being held back, and they are more likely to receive special education services. Possible explanations for these negative outcomes are the loss of social relationships, both with community and peers, as well as a lack of continuity from one school curriculum to another. Other reasons are that a move may be accompanied by a negative life event, such as a divorce or a parent losing a job, or that families that move tend to be lower in socioeconomic status than nonmoving families. However, one study found that even children who lived with both biological parents and were from a high-income family tended to have a decline in test scores if they moved. Moving appears to be difficult for all children (Alexander, Entwisle, & Dauber, 1990; Hartman, 2006; Pribesh & Downey, 1999).

Schools and teachers can ease the transition to a new school by being sensitive to new students' needs and creating a welcoming atmosphere. Moffett Elementary School in Los Angeles, California, which serves a large Latino population and receives 4 to 10 new students each month, provides extra help and attention to these transfer students, connects them with counselors, assigns them a student ambassador or friend to help them find their way, and works to involve new families in school. Other suggestions for schools include keeping good records on students and offering transportation assistance to homeless students or those who move only a short distance to keep them from having to change schools, at least until the end of the school year (Hartman, 2006).

For classroom teachers, it is important to provide extra support and attention until the student has adjusted to the classroom routine and demands and to help the student develop new friendships in the classroom to replace those that were lost in the move. School records may not arrive quickly, so you should conduct informal assessments as soon as possible to determine the student's abilities, such as reading level, and curriculum concepts that the student may have been exposed to at the last school attended. Sharing books with the class about children who move to a new school can open discussions about the difficulties a move creates in a student's life. A list of children's literature for family transitions, including moving, is included at the end of this chapter in Table 6.3. You should also reach out to the families through a phone call or note and try to form a relationship quickly, although it is important to realize that family life after a move may be chaotic. Informing families about community resources, such as pediatricians or dentists, park and recreation activities, library services, and other family-friendly resources in the community, can be a big help. If you are teaching in a community that is growing in population with new students regularly moving to the area, you can create a "welcome" packet of helpful information for families about your school, classroom, and community.

CHARACTERISTICS OF DIFFICULT FAMILY TRANSITIONS

It was what Mom would have said. What Mom would have done. Jane's voice was soft, as Mom's would have been. But this wasn't Mom. Mom had died three years ago. This was Jane.

—Laura (quoted in Bunting, 2000, p. 21)

Although a birth of a new baby or a move may be a planned, expected transition, some transitions are unexpected, or nonnormative, such as a young parent dying of cancer or a mother of grown children finding out that she's pregnant. Obviously, **nonnormative transitions**, or changes in a person's life that do not occur at the physically, socially, or culturally expected time in the normal life cycle, are more difficult for families to handle, and teachers need to be sensitive to the family stress created by both normal and nonnormative transitions. Certain characteristics can make transitions more difficult for families. These include the following:

- *Timing.* The transition lasts too long or the timing is off. Examples include a teenage pregnancy, a parent remarrying too quickly after a divorce, or a parent suffering a long battle with cancer. There is more social support for transitions that occur at the normal time, as in a baby shower that precedes the planned birth of a baby. This may explain why, in one study, children rated the birth of a new sibling as a low stressor, compared to a parent's divorce (Bagdi & Pfister, 2006).
- *Control.* Transitions are more difficult if the family members have no control over them, as when a spouse walks out on a family or the family has to move owing to the relocation of the family breadwinner's workplace. A less stressful transition would occur if the breadwinner chose to leave a job and take a better one and if the move was based on a family decision.
- *Rite of passage.* Transitions are easier on families if there is a ritual or ceremony to mark the transition, such as a graduation ceremony that signals the move from childhood to adulthood, a wedding that celebrates the beginning of a new family, or even a funeral that marks the ending of a person's life. Transitions that have no ritual, such as a separation or divorce, may be more stressful for a family.
- *Warning.* Transitions that occur without warning are often difficult for families to cope with, such as a family member being killed in an accident. Having time to prepare for the transition, such as the months leading up to the birth of a baby, knowing the

ACTIVITY 6.1

Think back to the timeline you created at the beginning of the chapter. Choose the three most significant transitions you've experienced thus far in your life. Using the list of characteristics of difficult transitions just presented, reflect on your three transitions in timing, control, rite of passage, warning, and status loss. Did you find these characteristics to be true of your transitions? What made your transitions easier or more difficult? Finally, reflect on actions that your teachers took or didn't take during these transitions. What was helpful? What do you wish your teachers might have done to better support you or your family during the transitions? What does this mean to you, as a teacher?

baby's gender, and even having a planned date for a delivery, can ease the stress of the transition.

- *Status loss.* Transitions that involve a loss of status, role, identity, or self-respect can be difficult for family members. For example, the loss of a job, a divorce that requires the family to move into a smaller home, or children leaving home causing a stay-at-home mother to feel a loss of identity as a mom can all be more difficult than a transition that involves a gain in status, such as a job promotion or a move into a larger home in a good neighborhood.

All these characteristics of transitions can add stress to a family, and the more of these that are seen in a family, the more likely it is that the family would be struggling to be well functioning. Offering parent education programs or newsletter tips on how to minimize the impact of these characteristics can be helpful to families. For example, one mother described how she tried to give her children more control during the transition of a remarriage and move to help them adjust:

When we moved from our apartment into my husband's home after we got married, we did have to talk about it a lot because they really loved [the apartment]. One thing we did was give them pieces of paper, and they wrote down different things like "my bed" or "my chair" and then they put those papers where they wanted their stuff to go. It was really cute to see them "set up" their rooms before moving day, and then when they came back over, everything was where they had asked for it to go. (N. Cody, personal communication, Feb. 5, 2011)

STUDENTS IN FAMILIES UNDERGOING SEPARATION, DIVORCE, AND REMARRIAGE

"Ms. Beartrice," says KoKo, "my daddy doesn't live with us anymore."

"That must be hard for you, KoKo. Is that why you did not finish your picture of your family?" she asks.

"I don't know where to put any of us," says KoKo.

—KoKo (quoted in Lansky, 1998)

One difficult transition that many children experience is the separation and divorce of their parents. As noted in Chapters 1 and 4, a significant number of children will experience a separation and/or divorce of their parents. One estimate is that 40% of American children's parents will divorce (Barbour, Barbour, & Scully, 2005).

Although research suggests that children and adolescents who go through the family transition of separation and divorce have more academic, social, and emotional difficulties than students who live with two biological parents, there is marked individual variability in how students adjust to the change. While some adapt well, others experience short- and long-term negative effects. The difference seems to be related to the number and nature of the negative life events, such as a family divorce that they undergo, as well as the resources and supports that they have to help them adapt to the changes. Students who have greater accumulations of negative family transitions have more academic, behavioral, and emotional problems than those who experience few negative life events. If a parent also has emotional problems, such as depression, and becomes self-absorbed or withdrawn, then students may exhibit acting out behaviors as well as develop emotional problems. However, effective parenting practices and strong emotional support can reduce these negative effects (Doyle, Wolchik, Dawson-McClure, & Sandler, 2003; Martinez & Forgatch, 2002; Wood, Repetti, & Roesch, 2004). As one mother said,

> It has taken every ounce of God-given courage I have to acknowledge the kids' feelings and comfort them and to delicately answer their questions about why. I absolutely believe that they do not need to hear my adult feelings. I don't think they would know how to process them, so it wouldn't be fair to share them. So, in some ways, I get strength to get through the day just by being their mom, and vowing that I will not subject them to that. I am honest in terms of telling them that "yes, I am sad, also," but I always follow-up with a strong, "but we will be okay. Daddy will always be your daddy and I will always be your mommy. I will not leave. We will always be a family and will help and support and love each other." Sometimes, I have to literally bite my tongue, and I usually have to pause and choose my words with loving discernment because there are days when my adult feelings of anger, resentment, and sadness are my prevailing thoughts; but by keeping theirs and my routines the same, and by being open to talking about things without bitterness, they are seeing every day that my reassurances aren't just empty words. I am noticing their comfort in that. (S. Fraser, personal communication, April 18, 2007)

When parents are able to maintain a sense of security and provide emotional support for children, the negative effects of this difficult transition can be reduced.

When parents remarry and create blended families, children experience another difficult transition, as demonstrated by this 11-year-old:

> As for my blended family, we're going on our second year, and it's been really rough. I haven't made it any easier, I must admit, but there is so much going on inside my head that it is really hard for me to reverse roles and put myself in my step-parent's shoes. . . . We'd been pretty much running wild and having a good old time for close to a year, and now we were suddenly told we had to conform to rules set forth by our parents along with their new significant others. Did this go over well? NO—I don't THINK so. We were all convinced that the changing of the rules were due to the new wicked step-parents. We didn't like it one bit. We decided to stick together and rebel. (Goebel, 2001, p. 14)

As noted in Chapter 4, students who transition from a single-parent family to a blended family have to adapt to new rules, roles, and boundaries, as well as the possible instant addition of new family members, such as stepsiblings, stepgrandparents, and other members of the extended family of the new parent. The transition may be more challenging for children if it has the characteristics of difficult transitions listed earlier, such as occurring too quickly after parents' separation and divorce, the child having no choice or input into the parents' decision to remarry, and the child feeling a loss of status, such as having to share his bedroom with a new stepsibling. However, with time to adjust to the changes and the opportunity to be involved in decisions, as well as attention from parents throughout the process, children may also be able to readily adjust to the new blended family. One mother describes her family's experience of becoming a blended family:

> So when we decided to get married, [the children's] response seemed very natural—like "Ok, neat, so what's for lunch?" We had a very casual wedding, and our only attendants were the children. We tried very hard to involve them as much as possible and to make them feel that it was "our wedding," rather than their mom's wedding. The other thing that really helped a lot was how supportive their dad, my ex-husband, was of it. He recognized that the wedding was very important for them to be involved in (agreed to change our parenting plan so that the kids could be with us longer to attend everything), and he always had positive responses for the kids whenever they talked about it, which I think helped them feel safe and comfortable no matter where they were. (N. Cody, personal communication, February 5, 2011)

Suggestions for Working With Children and Families Experiencing a Separation, Divorce, or Remarriage

Teachers and schools can also provide support for students from families experiencing a separation, divorce, or remarriage by helping children deal with their feelings and encouraging all parents to stay involved with their child's schooling (Frieman, 1997).

The following specific suggestions for teachers may be helpful:

- Allow students to talk about their feelings, but do not quiz them about their family situation. Help them express their feelings in acceptable ways.
- Respond to students in a way that shows you are willing to listen and care about them and their family.
- Be alert to changes in behavior or schoolwork and stay in contact with parents about these changes.
- Be sensitive to problems with getting work completed, concentrating in class, or acting out behaviors, as students are sorting through the many psychological, emotional, and physical changes occurring in their lives.
- Encourage noncustodial parents to remain active in their child's schooling and extracurricular activities.
- Send all communications, such as newsletters or notes, to both parents' homes, rather than asking the child to communicate information to the noncustodial parent.

- Be as neutral as possible when parents separate and remember that it is not your role to judge either parent.
- Include both parents and stepparents in conferences or meetings; offer separate conference times if parents do not want to meet together.
- Keep both parents informed about the child's schoolwork, such as projects or long-range assignments that may need to be completed on weekends when a child is visiting the noncustodial parent.
- Make a special effort to involve noncustodial parents in classroom activities by inviting them to volunteer in the classroom or on field trips, have lunch with their child, or attend school functions.
- Use age-appropriate children's books with the whole group, small groups, or individuals to give children an opportunity to discuss divorce and remarriage and share their responses to the books through art, writing, or other creative expressions. (A list of children's literature for transitions is given at the end of the chapter in Table 6.3).
- If a student seems to be seriously affected, seek professional help from the school counselor or social worker. Consider organizing a support group, facilitated by the school counselor, with children in the school experiencing a divorce and consult with the counselor about specific classroom problems.
- For schools with limited in-house counseling resources, consider seeking community mental health professionals to volunteer for sessions with both children and parents.
- Propose to your school administrator that your school offer parenting seminars on the effects of divorce and remarriage on children and the emotional support and positive parenting strategies that are effective.
- Propose to your school administrator that your school offer inservice training for teachers to help them better understand some issues of divorce and remarriage relating to school achievement and some ways in which they can better provide support for students and families (Frieman, 1997; 1998; Hodak, 2003; Kramer & Smith, 1998).

DEATH OF A PARENT OR FAMILY MEMBER

> One spring, Grandmother became thin as smoke. She didn't make tortillas; she was too tired. She said, "It's almost time for the butterflies to leave. Come with me to the Magic Circle, and we'll say goodbye."
>
> —Ghost Wings (Joosse, 2001)

The death of a parent or both parents in the life of a child is an exceptionally traumatic event. A total of 3.5 % of children in the United States lose a parent to death before the age of 18 (Haine, Wolchik, Sandler, Millsap, & Ayers, 2006). Children who have lost a parent may suffer from anxiety, depression, anger, sleep disorders such as nightmares, and may exhibit behavior problems such as aggression or acting out. Children may also have physical symptoms. For example, after her father died unexpectedly, one 12-year-old student developed eczema, a skin disorder, and a nervous habit of repeatedly scratching her scalp, which led to partial hair loss. Younger children may not be able to express their emotions about a parent's death or be able to explain why they are angry or sad. In addition, they may feel that their behavior in some way contributed to the death of their parent. Students may withdraw into themselves, have difficulty concentrating on schoolwork, and avoid it out of frustration (Schlozman, 2003; Willis, 2002; Worden, Davies, & McCowen, 1999).

The death of a sibling is also traumatic for children and occurs more frequently than many teachers realize. As noted in the characteristics of difficult transitions, a death that is unexpected or occurs without warning is especially hard, and accidents are the leading cause of death in the United States of children younger than 14, with motor vehicle crashes, drowning, and fires being the leading types of accidents. In 2007, 41.8% of deaths due to injuries were caused by motor vehicle crashes (Centers for Disease Control and Prevention, 2011). The Children's Defense Fund reports that every day in America, 32 children or teens die from accidents, and 78 babies die before their first birthday (Children's Defense Fund, 2009). Second to accidents, the most common cause of death of children is cancer, such as leukemia or brain cancer. However, the good news is that because of advances in medical treatment, childhood cancer survival rates have improved, and the number of childhood deaths from cancer has decreased since 1990 (Centers for Disease Control and Prevention, 2009).

When a child loses a sibling, the survivor's guilt may compound the horrendous feelings of sadness and depression (Doran & Hansen, 2006). Besides guilt and sadness, children may also feel anger, fear, hopelessness, rejection, self-doubt, anxiety, worry, and impaired cognitive functioning or poor school performance. They may have a preoccupation with thoughts about death and be unable to concentrate. Children who lose a sibling may also have physiological symptoms such as headaches, stomachaches, skin rashes, allergies, and bed-wetting. While dealing with their grief, parents may also be incompetent to provide the support that surviving siblings need (Birenbaum, 2000). Children's emotional well-being during this stressful time can benefit from grief counseling or intervention from a doctor (KidsHealth, 2007).

Families may respond differently to the death of a child in the family, depending on cultural and religious beliefs, as well as different coping mechanisms. One study of Mexican American families after the death of a child found that parents sought support from their extended family network and their church and that families participated in rituals such as celebrating the **Day of the Dead** (a Mexican holiday typically celebrated on November 2) and attending church masses as a way to connect with the deceased and honor their memory. Many parents used storytelling, keepsakes, and pictures to maintain a sense of the child's presence (Doran & Hansen, 2006). Family responses to grief may vary widely. Some families may not want to talk about their deceased child, while others may find it therapeutic. For example, one parent said, "Our closest friends are fine, they'll bring up [child's name], but a lot of people . . . won't sort of bring up the topic . . . and that's what I think we need. Other people might not need that but we need to include him" (Hynson, Aroni, Bauld, & Sawyer, 2006, p. 807).

The death of a relative, especially a grandparent who may have been actively involved in raising a child, can leave a huge void in the life of a student. As noted in Chapter 4, a significant number of children (4.5 million) are being raised by their grandparents (American Association of Retired Persons, 2007), and the death of the grandparent can have the same impact as the death of a parent. However, even when a grandparent is not actually raising a child, the death represents a significant loss in the child's life. In the normal life cycle process, especially with parents delaying having children until later in life, elementary-age children may face the loss of one or more grandparents.

Suggestions for Working With Children and Families Dealing With a Death

It is important that you remember that grief is a process that takes time. Kübler-Ross (1969) identified stages of grief that people may experience after a death: denial, anger, bargaining, depression, and acceptance. However, she later wrote that these stages "were never meant to tuck messy emotions into neat packages. . . . There is not a typical response to loss, as there is no typical loss. Our grief is as individual as our lives" (Kübler-Ross & Kesler, 2005, p. 7). Children do not respond to grief in the same way as adults, and they may have difficulty in understanding that death is permanent, irreversible, and final. They may not be able to express their emotions or ask for what they need, and they may exhibit unacceptable classroom behaviors (Willis, 2002). However, there are several steps you can take to help the child cope with the loss:

- Keep routines as regular as possible.
- Offer extra nurturing, as adults in the child's life may be emotionally unavailable.
- Be patient with the child if she regresses in behaviors, such as bed-wetting, or displays aggressive, acting-out behaviors or irrational fears.
- Answer the child's questions honestly, but also be sensitive to the family's cultural or religious beliefs about death.
- Assure the child that he did not cause the death and help family members recognize that it is not disrespectful for children to play and have fun, even while the family is grieving.
- Encourage the child to express feelings or remember the loved one through artwork, creative drama, and writing letters to or stories about the person.
- Expect that holidays or the anniversary of the death may be a difficult time for the child; be ready to provide extra support at these times.
- Provide the child with an opportunity to do something in memory of the person who died, such as making a memory book about a grandparent or creating a treasure box for special keepsakes from a deceased sibling.

You may be unsure of how to respond to a family after a death, whether to reach out to the family or respect their privacy by limiting your contacts. It is important to recognize that individuals respond differently to grief and to accept that personal responses will vary widely within and between families. The following general suggestions about how to support a family dealing with a death may be helpful:

- If the family is receptive, schedule a home visit through a personal note or a phone call to the family. Deliver class cards or notes to the family through this family visit. Later visitors might include the school principal, your district/school social worker or parent coordinator, community members, or other teachers who had contact with the family member. However, be sensitive about overwhelming the family with visitors. Always call ahead before the visit to make sure that the family is ready for visitors.
- Recognize that cultural influences have an impact on the grief process. Some cultures historically tend to deny death and suppress their grief, while other cultures may be open and demonstrative in their grief.
- At school functions, arrange for the deceased parent whose presence had been expected to be represented by school staff or a friend.
- At holiday times, avoid assigning projects that require children to create gifts for a deceased family member, such as making Mother's Day or Father's Day presents.
- Seek a grief support program for the family or the individual child. Notify parents of the existence of the support program and explain the benefits, but let the parents or a relative follow through.
- Honor the deceased in the school community. Often trees are planted in memory of a loved one, but mental health professionals warn that if the tree dies, this can create further traumatic feelings for children and their families. (Armstrong, 1997; Doran & Hansen, 2006; Haggard, 2005; McEntire, 2003; Willis, 2002)

STUDENTS WITH PARENTS IN THE MILITARY

All summer long, I knew Dad would have to leave again when school started in the fall. When the time came, he reminded me, "The ship pulls out in three days to go on a cruise."

I felt sad and mad and scared all at once, like a big ball of yarn had gotten tangled inside my stomach. I knew he would be gone for a very long time.

—Emily (quoted in Pelton, 2004)

Being part of a military family involves frequent transitions, and it can, ultimately, include losing a parent in war. Many teachers are unaware of the challenges faced by military families affected by deployment—career military, guard members, or even reservists (Allen & Staley, 2007). Mobility is an accepted way of life for military families; they spend an average of three years at a military installation before reassignment, and children may transition from school to school from six to nine times from kindergarten through high school (Titus, 2007). One study found that 15% of students in military families had moved at least 11 times during their schooling. These students reported moving as their most stressful experience, along with being separated from a parent or parents (Bell, Booth, Segal, Martin, Ender & Rohall, 2007). Children of military personnel are often called resilient by principals and counselors, as they have to endure frequent school changes, long parental separations, missing friends, and forming new friendships (Hardy, 2006). However, this does not mean that these students and families don't need support, even if they are only in your classroom for a short time. As one teacher said, "Even when the parent comes in and says we'll only be here for four months, we always say, 'We are glad to have you for whatever time you are here.' That's what our school is about" (Farrell & Collier, 2010, p. 14). Another teacher said,

> They've already been to four schools and they are in fourth grade. They already have a certain opinion of what school is, whether they've had a good experience or a bad one. Then, how do you get them involved? They may be moving again in six months or a year. . . . Even though it's only one year of the child's life, *you* make it important. (Blum, 2005, p. 14)

Waiting for a parent to return from a military deployment can be difficult for children.

Research has shown that second to families, schools are the most important stabilizing force in students' lives, and that is especially true for military families.

Districts bordering military bases tend to be sensitized to the needs of military children, while the staff in other schools may not even be aware that a child has a family member currently in the military (Hardy, 2006). By opening lines of communication with military families, you can better understand their situational needs and attempt to keep them in the academic loop. If you are a teacher of military children, it is important that you become an emotional anchor for the children to help build coping skills and that you strive to create a caring, stress-free classroom, where regular school routines reinforce a feeling of security for children and their military families (Allen & Staley, 2007). It is also important to become more educated about military life and its effects on children. Table 6.1 illustrates some issues that children from military families may experience.

Some suggestions for classroom teachers of military children include the following:

- Include instructional practices that incorporate the military life, such as teaching military time or doing math activities that include counting the number of soldiers in a troop, brigade, or battalion.
- Encourage classroom conversation that helps build relationships and support among military and non-military students. For example, in a geography lesson, have students show on a map where their fathers/mothers are or include information about family deployments in classroom newsletters.
- Initiate more frequent contacts with military parents than the typical parent-teacher conference; for military families who may move or be deployed before the traditional fall or spring conferences, schedule a special conference before they leave (Farrell & Collier, 2010).

It is important for schools and teachers to be proactive about working with military families through family-friendly policies and practices, such as having an orientation

TABLE 6.1 Effects of War on the Children of Soldiers	
Statistics	• More than two million American children have had a parent deployed to Iraq or Afghanistan • At least 19,000 children have had a parent wounded in action • More than 2,000 children's parents have died from one of the conflicts • High rates of mental health, trauma, and related problems • Military life is a source of psychological stress for children
Behavior	• Changes in school performance • Anger issues • Worrying, hiding emotions, and disrespecting parents and authority figures • Feeling a sense of loss • Symptoms consistent with depression
Media Influences	• Media coverage of war a significant source of stress • Negative effect on children of deployed parents
Home Issues	• Increased rates of child maltreatment (physical, emotional, or sexual abuse) during deployments • Rates 42% higher when the soldiers are on combat-related deployments than nondeployment

Source: National Center for Children in Poverty. *Exploring the Effects of America's Ongoing Wars on the Children of Soldiers* (2010)

process set in place for new military students, as well as making sure that all school personnel understand the fundamentals of military life and incorporate that understanding in their teaching (Farrell & Collier, 2010). If you are informed of a child in your classroom with a parent on active duty, you should connect with resource personnel such as the school psychologist or counselor, who may be able to provide advice, counseling, and support. One example of a support group for children of deployed parents is the Kit Kat Club (Keeping in Touch, Kids and Troops) at Ringgold Elementary School in Clarksville, Tennessee. This group was organized by the school psychologist, and the children sent e-mails, photos of school activities (even report cards), and letters to the parents overseas (Hardy, 2006, p. 12). In Killeen, Texas, the school counselor taught a "worrying" unit for military children, helping them cope with constant anxiety about their parent. The unit helped children identify what was out of their control or "worries you have to let go." Children constructed a "worry doll" to comfort them when they found themselves getting anxious (Hardy, 2006).

The parent or family member left at home also needs special consideration and patience. Living with uncertainty and anxiety about their loved one is part of the commitment to the military way of life. You should strive to remain in contact with the child's caregivers through phone calls, personal notes, and visits, and you should invite them to the classroom for school events and volunteer activities or to simply spend time with their children (Allen & Staley, 2007). You should also inform the parent about a child's behavioral changes that may have been brought on by the transition. Be aware that the

TABLE 6.2 Websites for Military Families	
Blue Star Families	http://www.bluestarfam.org/
Camaraderie Foundation	http://www.camaraderiefoundation.com/about/
Military Interstate Children's Compact Commission	http://www.mic3.net/
Military Child Education Coalition	http://www.militarychild.org/
Military HOMEFRONT, supporting our troops and their families	http://www.militaryhomefront.dod.mil/
National Military Family Association	http://www.militaryfamily.org/
National Guard Family Program	http://www.guardfamily.org/FP/
National Military Spouse Network	http://www.nationalmilitaryspousenetwork.org/
Operation Shower	http://operationshower.org
Our Military Kids	www.ourmilitarykids.org
REACH MCNC: Reach Every Military Child in North Carolina	http://www.fortbraggmwr.com/sls/remcnc.php
Student Online Achievement Resources, a program for military families and the school districts that serve them	http://www.soarathome.org/
Substance Abuse and Mental Health Services Administration	http://www.samhsa.gov/militaryfamilies/
Tutor.com for U.S. Military Families	http://www.tutor.com/military/

remaining parent may be called away if the military parent is injured and that grandparents or other relatives may have to assume the parental role temporarily (Hardy, 2006). Establishing a military support group for parents and other family members at school, in conjunction with the children's group, might be beneficial (Allen & Staley, 2007). You can also share helpful information, such as websites for military families. Table 6.2 lists some examples.

Parents who are deployed may choose to remain active partners in the education of their children, and with today's technology, that is possible. Students can communicate with the absent parent through letters, phone calls, e-mail, and blogs; they may use a webcam; and they may supplement their personal communications with class newsletters, videotapes of school events, class-generated Web pages, class or individual photographs, art work samples, or other classroom artifacts. Be sure to get permission from the child's primary caregiver before sending items to the deployed parent (Allen & Staley, 2007).

When the deployed parent returns from active duty, it is a reason to celebrate, but return dates can be subject to change, which creates a great disappointment for children and their families. When parents do arrive home, the family will have another transition to adjust to: the addition of a new family member. In the parent's absence, new routines and roles were established, and it may take a while for families to function effectively again. Deployed parents may also feel disconnected from their child's school, and you can establish a feeling of school connectedness by inviting returning parents to have lunch at school with their child, share their experiences with the class, or attend family night events. However, it is important to give returning parents time to adjust to being home again before bombarding them with requests for school engagement.

For some students, their military parent or family member may not return home. Since 2003, more than 4,400 U.S. soldiers have died in Operation Iraqi Freedom, and there have been more than 1,800 deaths in Afghanistan's Operation Enduring Freedom (U.S. Department of Defense, 2011), leaving military children to grieve the loss of a parent, sibling, or other significant family member. Although many of the suggestions in the preceding section may be implemented with military families, the death of a family member in war is somewhat different and may need special attention. For example, when people die in service to their country, children are often told that they should be proud of their family member. Although the sentiment is admirable, it is important to recognize that children may have a variety of feelings, such as anger or intense pain, and that telling them how they "should" feel may not help them in their grief process (Children's Grief Education Association, 2006). One resource for families who have lost a loved one in a war is the Tragedy Assistance Program for Survivors (TAPS), which provides comprehensive services free of charge to grieving military families (TAPS, 2007).

On a wider scope, school district personnel should develop intervention plans to assist military families at several levels. School crisis teams, consisting of an administrator, counselor, and school psychologist can work to meet the needs of individual families (Allen & Staley, 2007). The crisis team can also provide training for teachers on strategies to use when working with children from military families.

Lisa, the wife of a career Air Force officer noted, "Strengths of military families include resilience, respect for authority, global experiences and perspectives, and a high value placed on education." She stated, "Issues facing military families include the following:

- Children moved every two to four years: They may be going to or coming from overseas schools; discrepancy in kindergarten age requirement among school districts.
- Change of schools includes record transfers, graduation requirements, lack of connection with extracurricular activities.
- Quality of schools and teachers directly impacts the quality of life for military families. Families need regular communication, personal contact, and feedback.
- During time of deployment and separation, school is the most important element of stability for military families. Most important thing is strong home-school connections."

She mentioned some things teachers should consider:

- "New families need transition support and communication; in the military, they are used to communication and order.
- Teachers need to know their students well and tune into their emotions. Become aware of deployment and family separation changes.
- Children need support, stability, caring and kindness, similar to children of parents who are separating, divorcing or suffering the death of a parent.
- Use technology through Skype, Google Earth, and e-mail or blog like a working journal. Use deployments to teach geography lessons."

We have written Bono's Antarctic Adventures. Dad took the school mascot, Bono, a stuffed monkey, all over with him on his travels. We wrote a narrative from the perspective of his travels. We know of another dad who writes on a blog from the perspectives of the emperor penguins viewing the military personnel. (Lisa S., 2011, personal communication).

STUDENTS WITH PARENTS IN PRISON

> When my mother was sentenced, I felt that I was sentenced. She was sentenced to prison—to be away from her kids and family. I was sentenced as a child, to be without my mother.
>
> —Antoinette (Quoted in Bernstein, 2005, p. 122)

Another difficult transition for children occurs when a parent is sentenced to jail and taken from the home. It is estimated that nearly two million children in the United States have at least one parent incarcerated (imprisoned or jailed) in a state or federal prison (Family & Corrections Network, 2009b); nearly half of these children are younger than 10. In 2007, one in 43 children had a parent in prison nationwide. This percentage is even higher for African American and Latino children (Family & Corrections Network, 2009a). The number of children affected by parental incarceration can be inferred from statistics of the year 2000 at the Ronald McPherson Correctional Facility for Women in Arkansas, where the 685 women inmates had nearly 1,500 children of minor status (Bilchik, Seymour, & Kreisher, 2001).

"Children carry a lot of the burden around with them" (Bilchik et al., 2001, p. 108) when they feel guilt over a parent's imprisonment, according to Dr. Justin Skiba, coordinator of the Treatment for Residents With Incarcerated Parents Program (TRIP) in Dobbs Ferry, New York. Children mourn the absence of their parent and may develop emotional and behavioral difficulties, including withdrawal, aggression, and anxiety. Furthermore, risks of poor academic performance, low self-esteem, and drug/alcohol abuse exist for these children. In addition, children of incarcerated parents are six times more likely to enter the criminal justice system themselves (Bilchik et al., 2001). Young children may be clingier and regress in behaviors, such as returning to thumb sucking or having bathroom accidents, and they may develop sleeping or eating problems. They may startle easily, and teachers may see violent themes in their drawings, storytelling, and play (Roznowski, 2010). If children witnessed the arrest of their parent, their feelings of loss, helplessness, and trauma may be intensified, leading many to exhibit symptoms of post-traumatic stress disorder (Family & Corrections Network, 2009a). The extent to which children are affected by their parent's imprisonment will depend on factors such as their age, the strength of their relationship with their parent, their presence at the arrest, and the length of the parent's sentence (Roznowski, 2010).

Prison visits are one way that children can remain connected with their parents, but these visits are often a humiliating process because of the procedures children must endure to visit an inmate. For example, children visiting parents in prison may only be allowed to visit once or twice a month, often traveling a distance of 100 miles or more from their home for a visit. Public transportation typically does not exist for prisons, prohibiting some children from being able to visit. In some cases, the parent may be transferred to a distant facility, making visitation even more difficult. Forty-three percent of parents in federal prisons live more than 500 miles from their children (Family & Corrections Network, 2009a). Prison visits may be as long as four hours, but the children may not be allowed to have any type of physical contact with the parent, and the visit may be inexplicably cut short (often for head counts). Children may also have to endure body searches and close checks of their personal belongings. These prison visits can be filled with emotions, including guilt on the part of the parent (Mansour, 2003). Some correctional facilities are beginning to use technology for prison visits. For example, in Florida, two prisons allow children and their mothers to have visits through videoconferencing in the "Reading Family Ties: Face to Face" program (Hoffman, Byrd, & Kightlinger, 2010). If you have a child in your classroom who has an incarcerated parent, it's important to be in contact with the child's caregiver to know about prison visits, and you should be sensitive to the child's emotional state—depression, anger, or withdrawal—when she returns from a visitation.

Children who have a parent in prison may live with the remaining parent, a grandparent, other family member, or in foster care. These caregivers often have numerous challenges, such as the stigma and shame from an incarcerated family member, financial difficulties, and a lack of resources and support in raising the children. These caregivers may need guidance about what is best for the children, information about services available to them, and respite care or some relief from caring for the children (Family & Corrections Network, 2003b). For example, offering an afterschool program with homework help can be a support for these caregivers.

How do children of incarcerated parents feel about their family situation? What needs do they have? Children often have many questions and need a safe place to express their emotions and get reassurance for their fears. One study of 12- to 18-year-olds with a parent or family member in prison found that students' greatest needs were to know what was happening to their parent or family member and to be kept informed about everything that was happening. Being kept up-to-date helped them make decisions about what to tell others about their family. Their next most pressing concern was confidentiality. Students did not want their classmates to know that they had a family member in prison because of their fear of being labeled (Newnham, 2002). For younger children, their most pressing questions for their parent are, "Where are you?" "Why are you there?" "When are you coming home?" and "Are you okay?" If they are not able to talk with their parent, the caregiver may have to be the one to answer those questions (Family & Corrections Network,

2003a). Caregivers may need help in knowing how to answer these questions honestly, but in a developmentally appropriate way. In 2003, the San Francisco Children of Incarcerated Parents Partnership created the Bill of Rights for Children of the Incarcerated, based on interviews and experiences of children. The eight rights include the following:

1. I have the right to be kept safe and informed at the time of my parent's arrest.
2. I have the right to be heard when decisions are made about me.
3. I have the right to be considered when decisions are made about my parent.
4. I have the right to be well cared for in my parent's absence.
5. I have the right to speak with, see, and touch my parent.
6. I have the right to support as I face my parent's incarceration.
7. I have the right not to be judged, blamed, or labeled because of my parent's incarceration.
8. I have the right to a lifelong relationship with my parent (San Francisco Children of Incarcerated Parents, 2005).

Based on these ideas, some helpful suggestions for teachers include the following:

- See children as individuals, rather than the label of "child of a parent in prison."
- Avoid treating the child as a victim or being overprotective.
- Acknowledge the child's preferences for sharing information about his parent. Find out what the child has been told from the caregiver.
- Avoid asking about the crime (Newnham, 2002).
- Provide a safe, secure classroom environment, and do not allow any negative peer comments about the child's parent.
- Provide opportunities for children to tell their stories through artwork or writing.
- Be a good listener, but remember to be nonjudgmental; the child has not committed a crime (Roznowski, 2010).
- Be supportive of the child's caregiver, but understand that she may not be willing to share information about their family. Work to build a trusting, respectful relationship.

One example of supports provided to children and families of an incarcerated parent by the Cambridge Community Partnerships for Children, working with the Cambridge, Massachusetts, school system, are literacy bags that teachers make and send home for parents or caregivers to use with children. The bags contain children's books, such as *Mama Loves Me From Away* or *Visiting Day,* or homemade books that are specific to the child's situation, age level, and emotional maturity. The bags also contain a list of resources for families and children, such as the Bill of Rights or pamphlets with helpful suggestions on how to talk to children about their parent, and materials for the child to write letters to the parent or create artwork. Some parents may not want to use the bag with their children, if the children have not been told their parent is in prison, so it is best to meet with the parent or caregiver about the bag before sending it home.

Once the incarcerated parent is released, there are new challenges for the family in the transition from life with the parent being away to life with the parent returning to the home. For the newly released parent, opportunities for employment are extremely limited, finding housing is challenging (public housing is off limits), and public assistance will be denied (42 % of incarcerated mothers relied on public assistance before being incarcerated) (Children's Defense Fund, 2005). Children who have been living with relatives or in foster care for an extended time may have difficulty adjusting to a parent who is more like a stranger. The newly released parent may also avoid being involved in any school activities because of the embarrassing stigma of prison time.

Parent education programs have been developed to help ease the transition and strengthen parenting skills for the returning family member (Bushfield, 2004). One example is the "Books Without Barriers" parent education program for incarcerated parents, developed through a collaboration of the Multnomah County Library in Portland, Oregon, with the local sheriff's department. This program teaches inmates about the importance of shared reading with their child. Parents learn about brain development, the benefits of early reading, and ways to choose appropriate books for children. The culminating activity is a videotaping session where parents read aloud a favorite story on a videotape, which is then sent to the child (Arnold & Colburn, 2006). Another program designed to strengthen family ties is the "Girl Scouts Beyond Bars" program where incarcerated mothers meet together and plan activities for visits with their daughters, and the girls have meetings together in the community with supportive peers. Research has found that the participating girls had a decrease in behavior problems at school and improved grades, and were less angry, sad, or worried they would lose their mothers. Their relationships with their mothers were strengthened (Hoffman et al., 2010). Another example of a successful parent education program is the North Idaho Correctional Institution's "boot camp" parenting education program, which includes four modules:

1. Normal child development—birth through adolescence

2. Fathering issues and concepts (criticality of fathers in the lives of children, unique roles of fathers)

3. Communication and effective discipline

4. Home literacy (reading, creating a home learning environment)

Interviews with the 32 participants serving convictions for drug or burglary crimes showed the success of the program. As one father reflected, "My outlook on life is different. For once in my life, I really want to change, not because I have to, but because I want to. I want to be a part of my children's lives" (Bushfield, 2004, p. 113). Research on prison parenting programs suggests that parents who participate are less likely to return to prison and more likely to have a successful reentry into the family (Family & Corrections Network, 2009a).

STUDENTS IN FOSTER CARE

"This is your family tree," the substitute teacher said. She smiled as she passed out the papers. She acted like this assignment was special. . . . I'm a foster kid. Ben Watson, child of the system. I could write, "Division of Family and Child Services" on one of my twigs. I guess I belong to them. But the system is not exactly what you would call "family." It's an office in Greenfield County, Virginia. It pays real families to take in kids who don't have one.

I think of all the foster families I've been with. I don't belong on their trees; I don't want them on mine.

—Ben (quoted in Quattlebaum, 2001, pp. 1–2)

As noted in Chapter 4, when a parent is incarcerated or dies, and no one is available to care for the family's children, foster care may be the only option. Children may also be placed in foster care because of parental neglect or abuse. Foster care is a temporary placement of children with families outside their home, and is not intended to be a permanent state. The goal of foster care is the reunification of families, or if that alternative is not available or in the best interest of children, to find a new permanent home that is stable, safe, and nurturing. Although the goal is to find a permanent home as quickly as possible, reuniting children with their birth parents or permanent placement with a relative or adoptive family may take years (National Foster Parent Association, 2007a).

The United States has a long history of families taking in children who need a home, but this hasn't always been done with the best intentions. In early American foster care, children were often indentured servants or became slave laborers for the family. It wasn't until the early 1900s that foster parents were supervised and records kept. Social agencies began working with natural families to reunite them with their children, and foster parents became part of the professional teams formed to find safe, healthy, permanent homes for foster children (National Foster Parent Association, 2007b).

The Adoption and Foster Care Analysis and Reporting System (AFCARS) of the U.S. Department of Health and Human Services (2010) reported that 423,773 children in the United States were in foster care in 2009. The average age of a child in foster care was 9.6 years, and the average length of stay was 26.7 months. As noted in Chapter 4, the goal of the foster care system is to reunite children with their families, and this does occur for the majority of children who leave foster care. However, not all children will return to their families once they are placed in the foster care system. Some children are adopted, the majority by their foster parents. While 66% of adoptive families were headed by married couples in 2009, 28% of adoptive parents of foster children were single women. Figure 6.1 shows the outcomes for children who exited the foster care system in 2009.

To be in foster care is to be a life in transition, which for many children does not lead to a positive outcome. Children who stay in foster care for years may be moved from one community to another with little notice (Children's Defense Fund, 2007a). They may also be separated from siblings. The average child in foster care moves to three different families while in foster care (Krinsky, 2006). Many of the characteristics of difficult transitions listed earlier in the chapter can be found in the foster child's life. For example, foster children have little control over their placements or moves from one home to another. Being placed in foster care may occur without warning, such as when a parent's arrest in the middle of the night in a drug raid causes the children to be put in protective custody. No rite of passage marks the transition from one family to another, and although foster care may provide a safe, healthy home for the child, being a "foster child" entails a sense of loss of status from being a child living with his biological family.

Children in foster care, or "looked after children," often do more poorly in school than those in permanent homes, and many do not succeed educationally (Coulling, 2000; Martin & Jackson, 2002). Because they may have attended school only sporadically before being placed in foster care or have been in families where education was not a priority, foster children tend to be behind academically. Even after being placed in foster care, children may

FIGURE 6.1   Outcomes for Children Exiting Foster Care: 2009

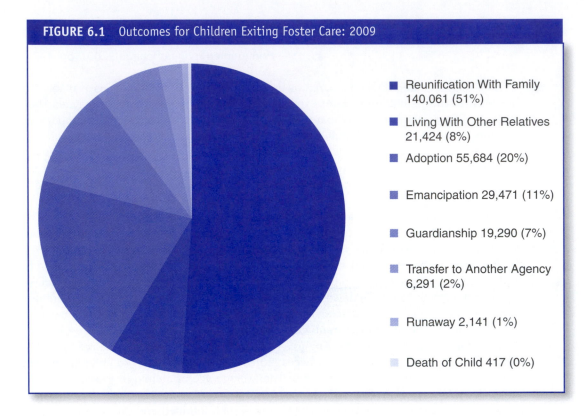

- Reunification With Family 140,061 (51%)
- Living With Other Relatives 21,424 (8%)
- Adoption 55,684 (20%)
- Emancipation 29,471 (11%)
- Guardianship 19,290 (7%)
- Transfer to Another Agency 6,291 (2%)
- Runaway 2,141 (1%)
- Death of Child 417 (0%)

Source: U.S. Department of Health and Human Services (2010): Adoption and Foster Care Analysis and Reporting System (AFCARS) Data Submitted for FY 2005 (10/1/08 through 9/30/09).

frequently be late to school because of appointments or be absent because of moves between schools in the middle of a term (Martin & Jackson, 2002). These children may also have had to focus on taking care of themselves and younger siblings and have little energy left for schoolwork. Children placed in foster care may also have emotional and behavioral issues and may blame themselves for being removed from the home. They may lack in social skills and use aggression as a way to solve problems (Noble, 1997). All these issues present special challenges to teachers and call for extra effort to help children in foster care succeed.

Although children in foster care are often viewed negatively because of the difficulties they may present to a teacher, it is important to look at the potential of the foster child and have high expectations. One way to do that is to listen to the "voices" of former foster care children who have succeeded. Although little research exists about successful ex-foster children, one such study (Martin & Jackson, 2002) examined the opinions of high achievers who had lived for at least a year in residential or foster care. When asked what could be done to improve the opportunities for children in foster care, nearly all stressed the importance of being treated like other people or not wanting to stand out, of having a sense of a normal life with typical childhood activities like sports or scouting. The need for encouragement, support, and an active interest in the child's education from everyone, including caregivers, social workers, and teachers, was also vital. These high-achieving former foster children also reported feeling discrimination or stereotyping, a sense of shame or stigma as a result of their foster care status, and described feeling "set up to fail." More than half of those surveyed said that their foster homes lacked basic necessities for a child's success in school, like books or a quiet place to study. A few stated that their teachers did not expect them to be intelligent or succeed and that teachers should help children realize their full potential, expect success, and encourage them to attend college someday.

In another study of successful "looked after children," the researcher found that being successful in school had little to do with the children's academic abilities and was more related to the support they received from their foster caregivers and teachers (Coulling, 2000). In an era of educational agendas such as No Child Left Behind and Race to the Top, it is important for teachers to expend the extra effort needed to help children in foster care reach their full potential.

Suggestions for Working With Children in Foster Care

As a teacher of a child in foster care, you may play a vital role in his or her life. As Coulling (2000) noted,

> It is clear that for a child in foster care to stand any chance of succeeding in the mainstream environment, the nurture and support of caring teaching staff are essential—staff who are able to understand the individual needs of the child and look behind the presenting, sometimes difficult, behavior; who are able to work in conjunction with car[egiv]ers, birth families, and social workers to provide the best possible chance of a long-term, stable school experience. (p. 34)

Some suggestions for how to work effectively with children and families of foster care include the following:

- Teachers and other school staff should establish a good relationship with the child's foster care family and social worker and stay in frequent communication.
- Be an advocate for children, making sure they get the necessary emotional and academic support to be successful.
- Because a child in foster care may have had little security or stability in the past, make the classroom a haven of safety, with regular and predictable routines.
- Provide extra support for the child to fit in socially in the classroom, including teaching her how to answer classmates' personal questions about the child's life in foster care.
- Be aware of the danger of foster children being ridiculed or bullied by classmates and provide extra attention, if needed, without singling the child out as being different.
- Involve the foster family in the classroom and in school activities, although it is important to realize that if they have several foster children, they may not be able to participate beyond helping the child at home.
- Be sensitive about assignments that relate to families, such as requiring children to bring in baby pictures or create a family tree.
- Share books that include family types other than biological families; include books that show multiracial families. (See the list of children's literature for transitions at the end of this chapter in Table 6.3.)
- Be a positive role model or mentor for the child or provide opportunities for mentoring from community volunteers such as Big Brothers, Big Sisters, or an adopted grandparents program.
- Have high expectations and encourage the child to set goals, including the goal of going to college (Martin & Jackson, 2002; Noble, 1997).

SUMMARY

This chapter has examined some of the many transitions that children may encounter during their school years. Some transitions may be normal and expected, such as the birth of a new baby or the move into a new home, while other, more difficult transitions, such as those occurring when a military parent is deployed or with the death of a parent, can have a major impact on students' academic success. Teachers who are sensitive to these changes and supportive of students and families during transitions can make the difference as to whether students succeed in their education. To further support your teaching, a list of children's books that feature the kind of transitions described in this chapter is provided in Table 6.3.

TABLE 6.3 Children's Literature for Family Transitions

Title	Author	Date	Grade Use
Moving			
Alexander, Who's Not (Do You Hear Me? I Mean It!) Going to Move	Judith Viorst & Ray Cruz	1998	PreK–Grade 2
Coming to America: A Muslim Family's Story	Bernard Wolf	2003	Grade 2–5
Eagle Song	Joseph Bruchac	1997	Grade 3-4
I Like Where I Am	Jessica Harper	2004	PreK–Grade 2
Ira Says Goodbye	Bernard Waber	1998	Pre K–Grade 4
Jorah's Journal	Judith Caseley	1997	K–Grade 3
Mallory on the Move	Laurie B. Friedman	2004	Grade 2–4
Moving Day	Ralph Fletcher	2006	Grade 3–6
What You Know First	Patricia MacLachlan	1995	K–Grade 3
Where's Jamela?	Niki Daly	2004	Grade 4–7
Separation, Divorce, and Remarriage			
Dear Mr. Henshaw	Beverly Cleary	1983	Grade 2–5
Dinosaurs Divorce	L. K. And M. Brown	1986	K–Grade 3
It's Not Your Fault, KoKo Bear	Vicki Lansky	1998	PreK–Grade 2
Jigsaw Puzzle Family: The Stepkids' Guide to Fitting It Together	Cynthia MacGregor	2005	Grade 4–8
Mom and Dad Break Up	J. S. Prestine	1998	K–Grade 3
There's Only One of Me!	Pat Hutchins	2003	Pre K – Grade 2
To & Fro, Fast & Slow	Durga Bernhard	2001	PreK–K
Two Homes	Claire Masurel	2001	PreK–Grade 1

Title	Author	Date	Grade Use
Death of a Parent or Family Member			
Can You Hear Me Smiling? A Child Grieves a Sister	Aariane Jackson	2004	Grade 2–4
Ghost Wings	Barbara M. Joosse	2001	K–Grade 3
Gran-Gran's Best Trick	L. Dwight Holden	1989	Grade 4–7
Janna and the Kings	Patricia Smith	2004	Grade 2–4
The Memory String	Eve Bunting	2000	K–Grade 3
Nana Upstairs and Nana Downstairs	Tomie DePaola	1997	PreK–Grade 2
Papa's Latkes	Michelle Edwards	2004	K–Grade 2
Upside-Down Cake	Carol Carrick	1999	Grade 2–4
Military Parents			
Love, Lizzie: Letters to a Military Mom	Lisa Tucker	2005	K–Grade 3
Mercedes and the Chocolate Pilot	Margot Theis Raven	2002	Grade 3–5
Peacebound Trains	Haemi Balgassi	1996	Grade 3–5
Pilot Mom	Kathleen Benner Duble	2003	Grade 2–4
When Dad's at Sea	Mindy Pelton	2004	K–Grade 2
While You Were Away	Eileen Spinelli	2004	K–Grade 3
Parent in Prison			
Harry Sue	Sue Stauffacher	2005	Grade 4–8
An Inmate's Daughter	Jan Walker	2006	Grade 5–8
Mama Loves Me From Away	Pat Brisson	2004	Grade 1–3
My Daddy's in Jail	Janet M. Bender	2003	K–Grade 3
Visiting Day	Jacqueline Woodson	2002	K–Grade 3
Foster Care			
The Great Gilly Hopkins	Katherine Paterson	1978	Grade 4–7
Grover G. Graham and Me	Mary Quattlebaum	2001	Grade 4–6
Mama One, Mama Two	Patricia MacLachlan	1982	K–Grade 3
Maybe Days: A Book for Children in Foster Care	Jennifer Wilgocki	2002	K–Grade 3
The Moccasins	Earl Einarson	2004	Grade 4–7
The Pinballs	Betsy Byars	1977	Grade 4–7
Welcome Comfort	Patricia Polacco	1999	K–Grade 3

REFLECTION QUESTIONS

Reread the In the Classroom case study presented at the beginning of the chapter and reflect on these questions:

1. What characteristics of transitions have affected Ella and her family in a positive or negative way?

2. What should Tamika do that will be supportive of Ella, her parents, and her new stepmother? To whom should she communicate her concerns, and what would be the best communication method?

3. What strategies could Tamika use in her classroom to help Ella adjust to the transitions of divorce and remarriage?

WEBSITES

Hospice, http://www.hospicenet.org/html/child.html.

This site for patients and families facing life-threatening illnesses has links relating to children and death, including articles on how to talk to children about death and available bereavement camps for kids.

The Military Child Initiative, http://www.jhsph.edu/mci.

This website, hosted by The Johns Hopkins Bloomberg School of Public Health and the Johns Hopkins Center on School, Family, and Community Partnerships, offers resources for educators working with military children.

National Foster Parent Association, http://www.nfpainc.org/.

This website offers support for foster families, including a Forum for discussions with other foster parents and social workers, the Foster Child and Foster Parent Bill of Rights, and an extensive list of websites relating to foster parenting.

National Resource Center on Children and Families of the Incarcerated at Family & Corrections Network, http://fcnetwork.org/.

This website provides support for families of the incarcerated and has resources, research, and advocacy information, including the Bill of Rights for Children of the Incarcerated Project. Of particular use to teachers and caregivers is the Children of Prisoners Library, which includes helpful articles for parents and caregivers.

STUDENT STUDY SITE

Log on to the student study site at www.sagepub.com/grant2e for additional study tools, including the following:

- eFlashcards
- Web quizzes
- Web resources
- Learning objectives

Chapter 7

Families Overcoming Obstacles

A fair number of [my] students are struggling with a host of issues that should never have to worry the average seven year old.

—Second Grade Teacher in Georgia
(Phillips, 2009, p.101)

As a classroom teacher, you will meet students from all walks of life, including those from families beset by personal, psychological, social, and economic problems. You will be presented with the challenge—indeed, the privilege—of helping these students overcome obstacles and become successful young adults. To prepare for this task, consider the following questions:

- How are families and students affected by obstacles such as poverty, homelessness, violence in the home and community, chronic illness, and natural disasters?
- How do these obstacles affect children's behavioral development, and the ability to succeed educationally? What are the ways in which I can be supportive of children and families experiencing these problems?
- How can I help students develop resilience to these stresses? What factors at home, at school, and in the community can lead to resilience?

In Chapter 6, you learned about difficult transitions that affect student learning, such as students having to move; go through a family separation, divorce, or remarriage; the

Contributing Authors John Wong, Jonathan Livingston, George Cliette, and Sherry Eaton death of a family member; living a military life; a parent being incarcerated; or a student being placed in foster care. However, there are also family stresses that are ongoing and may not be related to a change. For some children, daily living is confusing, difficult, and distressing. Their families may be poor and have to struggle constantly to obtain food, health care, a home, and other necessities needed to subsist. They may live in a home or community where violence is prevalent. They may live with a family member, who has a chronic illness, or they may endure the physical and emotional toils of chronic illness themselves. They may experience a natural disaster. Although many of these problems will be out of your control, you can help students develop resilience that will help them cope and overcome obstacles in their lives. This chapter will explore some major stresses that families face, and discuss the concepts of risk and resilience as related to student learning.

FAMILIES LIVING IN POVERTY

A fundamental measure of the character of a nation is how it treats those who are poor.

—Children's Defense Fund (2005)

In this chapter, we will explore the unique challenges of working with families in poverty. America may be the "Land of Plenty," but the poverty level has climbed drastically based on recessional unemployment. The U.S. government annually determines the poverty line, the minimum amount of income a family needs to subsist. For 2009, the federal government set the poverty line at $22,050 for a family of four and $18,310 for a family of three (National Center for Children in Poverty, 2010, p.1). In 2009, 43.6 million people struggled in livelihoods below the poverty line (Catholic Charities USA, 2011). As noted in Chapter 1, children living in a single-parent household, or certain minorities, such as African American, American Indian, or Hispanic, are also more likely to live in poverty (KIDS Count Census Data, 2006). In addition to those living in poverty, the standard of living for many more Americans teeters on the poverty line. More than one-third (34.2%) of Americans live in poverty at least two months during the year (U.S. Census Bureau, 2003). Almost half will live in poverty for more than a year before they turn age 60 (Catholic Charities USA, 2006).

The majority of families below the poverty line include one or two workers in the family, shattering the myth that families are poor because of unemployment or dependence on government assistance. In 2004, 71.5% of poor children lived in families where someone worked, and 34.4% of these poor children lived with a full-time, year-round worker (Catholic Charities USA, 2006; Children's Defense Fund, 2005). However, for families in poverty, the jobs are often low wage and lack benefits, such as health insurance, leading families to struggle to make ends meet and provide for basic necessities. Children who are poor are more likely to have health problems and inadequate food and housing, which can greatly affect school achievement, with the children in poverty more likely to receive lower scores in math and reading (Children's Defense Fund, 2005).

IN THE CLASSROOM: OUT OF SCHOOL SUPPLIES

Clara Simpson tried not to let her frustration show as Keisha again asked to borrow crayons and glue for the solar system project the class was doing. "Keisha, did you tell your mom and dad that you need new crayons and glue?" she asked. "Yes, ma'am," Keisha said, "but mama said it would have to wait." Clara directed her to get what she needed from the closet and decided she would send a note home to Keisha's parents, stressing the importance of her having the necessary school supplies for her class work. Brenda, the principal, had been urging the teachers to have better communication with families this year, and while Clara hadn't done the weekly phone calls that Brenda had suggested, she had been sending home more notes when there were problems. She couldn't tell that the increased communication had helped that much, though, as her students still struggled in many areas.

Later that day, after the children had left, Brenda stopped by her classroom for a chat. Brenda and Clara had worked together for many years at Kennedy Elementary. In fact, Brenda had at one time been a third-grade teacher with Clara before she had gone back for her masters and specialists degrees in administration and had become the school's principal. They were more like friends than administrator and teacher.

"Brenda, are we going to get a bigger budget for classroom supplies next year?" Clara asked. "It's only January, and I've about gone through all my school supplies. I think I gave out my last bottle of glue to Keisha Wallace today. It sure seems like parents today just don't care anymore about their kid's education. Keisha said she told her mom she needed more school supplies, but her mom didn't buy them."

Brenda considered this for a minute, and then slowly said, "Clara, do you really think Keisha's parents don't care about her? I can think of a dozen ways the Wallaces show that they care about their children. Keisha and her little brothers, Da Shon and Deon, are at school every day, clean, dressed, and as far as I can tell, they have their homework done. That's pretty amazing, considering that Mr. Wallace has to work the night shift at the convenience store and does odd jobs during the day. Mrs. Wallace just lost her job at the factory, and now she's having to care for her mother who had a stroke, and that's a big financial burden on their family. Did you know about that?"

Clara paused thoughtfully and said, "I knew that Keisha's grandma was living with them, but I didn't know about her stroke or about her mom losing her job. I wonder if that's why they didn't come to our literacy night last week."

Brenda continued, "Well, you know the cost of gas these days. I think we forget sometimes about the financial burden that school can be for families. It's what I've been trying to say all year. We need to get to know our students' families, really get to know them before we pass judgment on them."

"OK, OK, you don't have to lecture me," Clara said with a rueful smile as they walked out the door together, "I wonder what else I don't know about my students' families."

"Low levels of parental education are a primary risk factor for being low income" (National Center for Children in Poverty, 2010, p. 4). Poverty is a difficult barrier to overcome in becoming successful. Those living in the lowest income level are only 10% as likely to achieve a college education as those in the highest income level. One study found that when parents in **generational poverty** had a low education level, there was a lack of conversation in the home about the importance of education and an "almost total absence of educational goals" (Beegle, 2003b, p. 14). As one participant said, "I could not imagine finishing high school. . . . If I did, it would be an incredible accomplishment because no one I knew went beyond the eighth grade." This study also found that 89% of those who grew up in generational poverty felt that their teachers did not believe in them or have high expectations for their success. They felt shame and humiliation as children, with physical, emotional, sociological, and economic barriers to literacy and education at all stages in their lives (Beegle, 2003b).

Americans generally show compassion for the plight of the poor. In 2010, an average of 1,858,192 families received temporary financial assistance (U.S. Dept. of Health and Human Services, 2011).

However, there is also a critical view toward the poor, with the belief that those who live in poverty are an **underclass** (poorest of the poor who often have difficulty finding a place in mainstream society), who are more likely to be illiterate, use drugs, be involved in crime, have unstable relationships, and not care about their children or their education (Auletta, 1982). Those who subscribe to this **cultural deficit model**—the belief that cultural values, as transmitted through the family are dysfunctional and the cause of poverty and lack of education—say that the poor live in a "culture of poverty" that is their fault (Solorzano & Yosso, 2001; Yeich, 1994) and that they do not have capacity to pull themselves out of their plight.

Although this view came to the forefront in the 1970s, the cultural deficit model once again gained attention in the 2000s and is used to frame poverty in schooling for poor students. In her popular book, *A Framework for Understanding Poverty,* and other writing, Payne (2003) described how generational poverty hinders educational success. She wrote, "Often in generational poverty, parents will fear their children getting educated because then they leave their home and neighborhood" (Payne, 2006, p. 2). She further attributed a set of hidden rules as the explanation for the behavior of parents and children trapped in generational poverty and also described the rules under which middle- and upper-class society operate. These rules are hidden because most educators operate with middle-class values and do not see the manifestations of the cultural norms of people living in generational poverty. Examples of such rules for those living in poverty are (1) physical fighting is how conflicts are resolved; (2) destiny and fate, not choice, are in control; and (3) entertainment and relationships are more important than achievement. According to Payne, educators should understand student behavior in light of these hidden rules and help students adapt to the rules that will bring them success in school and in work (Payne, 1996; Tough, 2007).

Although many schools have used Payne's work in helping their teachers understand the low-income students in their district, it has been criticized widely as being oversimplified, a form of "thinly veiled bigotry" and lacking in factual research (Bohn, 2006; Tough, 2007). Others have stated that this approach is not supportive for children and families in poverty, and it ignores the overwhelming evidence that poorly funded and low-quality schools are the reasons for poor education (Gorski, 2005).

When thinking about working with families in poverty, it's important to note these misconceptions:

- Most low-income parents (74%) are employed, most likely in service industries.
- Nearly a third of children in poverty live in homes without public benefits.
- Official poverty statistics are deeply flawed; consideration should address state-to-state differences as well as urban versus rural settings.
- Taking into account family expenditures to accurately reflect food, clothing, housing, medical care, and transportation, millions more children would fall under the poverty level (National Center for Children in Poverty, 2010).

Suggestions for Working With Children and Families in Poverty

As a responsive teacher, you will probably encounter other educators who identify with Payne's theory that poverty is caused by cultural traits and values that hinder and oppose educational success. You may also find that some teachers and administrators believe poverty-stricken students tend not to succeed because they do not receive the same opportunity to learn and thrive as children from more affluent backgrounds. You may be unsure of your beliefs. However, to be successful in working with families, you must suspend whatever beliefs you may hold about the roots of poverty.

- Learn about each family individually. Studies have found that teachers who are able to successfully involve all parents in their child's education do not prejudge those who are poor and single parents, while those teachers who have stereotypical view of poor families tend to have low levels of family involvement (Epstein & Dauber, 1991).
- Show understanding—not judgment based on generalizations and misconceptions. Express appreciation for their efforts as parents, and do not assume that a lack of involvement in education means that they do not care about their children. As one author said, "My mother, for example, never went to a school conference. She'd say, 'I ain't going in there and make a fool of myself,' yet I have the most caring mother you could ever want" (Beegle, 2003b, p. 19).
- Focus on the common ground that you share with the family—you both care about their child. If your focus is only on education, you may have difficulty connecting with the family. Ask them to tell you about their child, and share with them what you have learned about their child (Beegle, 2003a).
- Empathize with the parenting challenges of families trying to overcome poverty, and help build a network of support. Recognize family risk factors and refer the family to appropriate community services for assistance. Develop a resource file of those in your community who are working to address poverty issues. Always report problems to authorities when necessary.
- Families in poverty may have had negative experiences with schools when they were children. Work to offer positive school experiences for these families and their children. Show them that you value their child, and give children the message that they are special, valued, and have great potential (Beegle, 2003b).
- Homework may not be a high priority for families living in poverty, where survival needs are more crucial. As one author said, "Asking a single mother with a sixth-grade education and three children to spend an hour reading or helping with homework is unrealistic" (Beegle, 2003b, p. 19). Consider that most of the

academic learning for students in poverty will occur during the school day, and find other ways to provide support for homework, such as with in-school or afterschool tutorial programs.

- Cultivate a respectful relationship with families based on open communication and collaboration on the goals and activities concerning the academic future of their children.

One area where you may see an impact of poverty on the students in your classroom is hunger. The persistent threat of food insecurity, or children who are hungry on any given day, affects more than 500,000 households in the United States. In 2009, 17.4 million households, or 15% of all U.S. households, suffered from food insecurity (Food Bank for New York City, 2010).

Providing a free breakfast and lunch is crucial for children living in poverty.

Hunger can have a negative impact on students, leaving them apathetic, passive, withdrawn, and unmotivated. Furthermore, children who are chronically undernourished suffer from health problems and a lack of emotional well-being. Schools receiving the School Breakfast Program and the National School Lunch Program offer the best opportunity for children leaving home hungry (Ashiabi, 2005).

You may notice that some families receiving free or reduced lunches for their children are embarrassed by the designation and may initially refuse to process the paperwork involved. The very poor rely on community food pantries to supplement their monthly food stamps, which may be spent 5 to 10 days before the end of the month (Daponte, 2000). Educators in high-poverty schools have found families very appreciative of a family-fun-night meal near the end of the month, by which time they had depleted their monthly food stamps. As a teacher, do not assume that all families can adequately feed their children; many families live on the edge of hunger daily.

STUDENTS EXPERIENCING HOMELESSNESS

People who are homeless are not social inadequates. They are people without homes.

—Sheila McKechnie (Scotsman.com, 2004)

Children living in poverty may, at some time in their lives, become homeless. Homelessness for children can be a traumatic and confusing time, as they are caught in a complex set of circumstances beyond their control. Children often worry about situations that may be difficult for you to imagine: a spot to sleep that is warm and safe, where they will get their next meal, what will happen if they are sick or hurt, and even the possibility of being separated from other family members and having to end friendships. They may also feel shame, and perhaps even guilt, for their situation.

Parents who are homeless often feel extreme **stress** (experiences, situations, and events that lead to severe strains). They may be anxious, responding to many requirements, such as working, attending school/training, looking for permanent housing, and keeping themselves and their families safe and in some form of shelter. Some may be escaping from domestic violence or may struggle with alcohol or drug addictions and mental illness. A homeless life is characterized by risk and uncertainty for both parents and children. A social worker with the homeless described it in this way:

> Working with families experiencing homelessness can highlight the desperation that extreme poverty can cause. While families may be able to access shelters, some are unable to stay because there may not be a shelter available that appropriately meets their needs, or there may not be a shelter in their community at all. Families who are homeless can experience crises with finding ways to feed and clothe their children, in addition to meeting their basic hygiene needs (such as where they can safely use the bathroom and shower), as well as somehow finding a way to keep their children in school. For many families, these stressors are never ending—they may need to find a way to purchase birth certificates for their children, apply for public assistance for medical insurance, or arrange transportation to school. Even so, families in such crises can survive and even thrive, as the family system can be quite resilient. Many families can receive the education and support they need to overcome the crisis and never return to homelessness. (N. A. Curry, July 24, 2011, personal communication)

The face of homelessness has changed significantly over the past few decades. Your image of the homeless may be men on city sidewalks asking for spare change or "bag ladies" living on streets. However, the homeless may be of all ages, including teenagers and young adults with no home, or underemployed fathers and mothers and their children. Estimates of the number of homeless vary, as their transient nature makes it difficult to count them (Drever, 1999). People experiencing homelessness are also reluctant to identify themselves and be counted as such because of the stigma of being homeless. On a single night in January 2009, there were an estimated 643,067 sheltered and unsheltered homeless people nationwide. Nearly two-thirds of the people homeless on a single night were homeless as individuals (63%), while more than a third (37%) were homeless as a part of a family (U.S. Department of Housing and Urban Development, 2009).

This count, however, ignored the doubled-up population. Families who lose their homes because of economic hardships are likely to move into the homes of relatives and friends before seeking help at public shelters. Families living in a doubled-up situation are considered under law as homeless (Indiana Department of Education, 2007). Although this study was done at a single point, other broader studies have identified higher estimates than this study. One report stated that between 2.3 million and 3.5 million people experience homelessness over the course of a year in the United States (Satcher, 2004). Families with children comprise 42% of the total homeless population according to another analysis (Kasindorf, 2005). A total of 200,000 children in the United States are estimated to be homeless each day (Satcher, 2004).

How does being homeless affect children? One in 50 children experience homelessness in America each year. That's more than 1.5 million children (National Center on Family Homelessness, 2010).

One study found that the average school-age child who was homeless moved 3.6 times in a year (Rosenheck, Bassuk, & Salomon, n.d.). The majority of these students did not attend school regularly and may attend more than one school during a school year. According to one study, 41% of the students who were homeless attended two different schools over a given year, and 28% attended three or more different schools (National Center on Family Homelessness, 1999).

The experience of being homeless has a devastating impact on children and youth and can result in the following:

- Higher rates of acute and chronic illnesses, including ear infection, stomach problems, and asthma (National Center on Family Homelessness, 2010)
- Higher rates of developmental delays, including speech problems (Molnar, Rath, & Klein, 1990) and learning disabilities (National Center on Family Homelessness, 2010)
- Higher incidence of emotional problems: 47% of children and youth experiencing homelessness suffered from anxiety, depression, or withdrawal compared with 18% of housed children (National Center on Family Homelessness, 2010).

How do schools or teachers respond to the homeless? Unfortunately, it is not always positive. Some school personnel do not welcome these families into their school district. They feel resentment toward families who do not pay taxes in the town but add to the burden of education and other social services, particularly in cases where resources are already stretched thin. Moreover, some school officials may fear that the inclusion of homeless children will lower their academic achievement test scores in an era of high-stakes testing and school accountability. By law, schools may also require up-to-date immunization records and other documentation that a homeless family may not have for their children. However, a teacher's sensitivity and support should be the cornerstones of any relationship with these children and their families. In the midst of chaos, a teacher can be a source of hope, encouragement, and positive reinforcement in relationships with the family. A teacher can make the school a place where a student who is homeless can find security, acceptance, and a safe haven (Wong, Peace, Wang, Feeley, & Carlson, 2005).

What resources are there for schools and teachers in working with children who are homeless? One possible resource comes from the McKinney-Vento Homeless Education Act, which was reauthorized in 2001 (National Law Center on Poverty and Homelessness, n.d.). This law states that schools must provide the same level and quality of services to students who are homeless as are provided to other students—including transportation, educational services, and nutritional and health services (Wong, Salomon, Elliott, Tallarita, & Reed, 2004). This act establishes clear mandates that a teacher or school can use to get needed services and programs for students who are homeless.

The McKinney-Vento act requires that school districts appoint a **homeless liaison**. Liaisons serve a pivotal role in coordinating and providing services to students experiencing homelessness. A liaison knows the requirements of the McKinney-Vento act, understands the legal rights of families who are homeless, is aware of school services that are available to assist students, and is familiar with public and private programs in the community available to both children and parents. A liaison tries to build a formal referral and collaborative network in the school district and the community. As the central contact for services and programs for families who are homeless, a district's homeless liaison is a key support for family involvement.

Suggestions for Working With Children and Families Who Are Homeless

You may feel apprehensive about having a student in your classroom who is homeless or about working as a partner with this student's family. However, not only is it mandated by law that students who are homeless be provided with a quality education but it is also your ethical and moral responsibility to do so. Some suggestions for collaborating with the families of your students who are homeless include the following:

- Work with your homeless liaison to provide an afterschool program for these students. Family life in shelters, publicly funded motels, and other temporary living space is life lived in public or shared space, often cramped, with little privacy or areas for doing homework. Cars, temporary campsites, and other substandard living spaces do not come equipped with study rooms, bookshelves, computers with Internet access, educational toys, and other materials that constitute a learning environment many people take for granted. Therefore, it is important that schools and teachers make up for these lost learning opportunities. For example, in one school, teachers rotated tutoring duty after school for homework help, while in another, teachers were hired by the shelter to come at night to the shelter and provide extra assistance.
- Consider going outside the classroom or school to find what the child needs. For example, community resources such as library reading programs, scouting or athletic programs, and community counseling resources are often beyond the realm of possibility for children who are homeless. Work with community leaders to help your students have access to community resources.
- Besides community resources for students, work with your homeless liaison or school social worker to obtain resources for parents. Children's welfare is directly related to the well-being of their parents, and resources such as housing subsidies and vouchers, domestic violence protection, legal aid, job training and career development courses, GED preparation, life skills training, English as a second language (ESL) classes and language training, counseling, substance abuse prevention, and mental health services may provide the needed help to leave a homeless situation.
- Try to suspend any judgment about families who are homeless. These families have the same goals for their children as other parents, but they also must overcome difficult barriers. As you find out about the unique situation and challenges of your student's family, you must be sensitive to their dignity and self-esteem.
- Understand that by yourself, you cannot address the complex, interrelated problems that your students may be facing. As one educator who has assisted many homeless families in her school district said, "Collaboration and cooperation are the only ways to produce an effective program and to meet the educational needs of students experiencing homelessness" (Wong et al., 2005, p. 9).

FAMILIES AFFECTED BY VIOLENCE

Children cannot learn and live up to their full potential when violence and drugs threaten their safety in schools.

—President Bill Clinton, referring to the 1997
school shooting in West Paducah, Kentucky

For some of the estimated 7 million children ages 5 to 13 who return to empty homes after school, the notion of "safe communities" may not be in their experience (Dryfoos & Maguire, 2002). Living in a high-crime neighborhood may negatively affect a child's academic performance (Aisenberg & Ell, 2005). In a Canadian survey, teachers in inner-city schools indicated that high-crime neighborhoods and the presence of street gangs were their biggest concerns of risk factors for their students. They expressed an intense frustration and a sense of being powerless to make a change. "Crime and violence on neighborhood streets set an example of behavior for young children who come to adopt the norms of the community" (Johnson, 1997, p. 19).

Gangs, with their related violence, have been an integral part of the American culture and can be traced back to as early as the Industrial Revolution. Gang membership has continued to increase, and by 2000, membership had reached more than 1 million (Savelli, 2001). However, there has been considerable change in the nature and focus of gang activity over the years. Shifts in the economy and urban renewal have moved much of the gang activity to rural areas. Thus, gang activity has increased in many small southeastern and midwestern cities. Consistent with that of earlier urban gangs, many of the members recruit at local junior, middle, and high schools. Given the pressure to belong and the need for acceptance, rural youth may be just as susceptible to gang involvement.

The widespread assumption is that gang involvement is more prevalent among low-income inner-city youth. However, recent trends indicate that gang involvement has increased among the middle class and children in rural communities. Why do young people join gangs? Table 7.1 lists some possible reasons.

TABLE 7.1 Why Do Youth Join Gangs?

1. *A sense of belonging*. Youth, no matter what background or social station, want to belong to something. Often young people reach out to gangs as a way of attempting to fulfill the sense of family, acceptance, and encouragement they may be missing from their familial context (Scheidlinger, 1994).

2. *Safety*. The belief that there is power in numbers provides a sense of safety for many youth. Youth of low economic status may join gangs for protection.

3. *Respect and power*. Youth may perceive that joining a gang will offer them respect and a sense of power among their peers.

4. *Financial gain*. Youth may believe that being in a gang will be a way to make money in a lucrative drug trade. If they are pressured to help provide for their family, there may be limited opportunities to make money, causing them to turn to gang criminal activity.

5. *Absent fathers or mothers*. Children in inner cities are most vulnerable economically and socially when fathers are absent or both parents are frequently in and out of the prison system.

Suggestions for Teachers Working With Children and Families in Violent Communities

Although you may feel powerless to make a difference in community violence or gang involvement, you can play a key role, as a teacher, in keeping your students safe and reducing violence among the youth of your community through your classroom activities and school district programs. Some suggestions for teachers in preventing community violence and gang activity through school and classroom activities include the following:

- Be a part of a team of teachers, students, families, law enforcement, juvenile justice officials, and community leaders to help develop a safe school plan where students feel secure and safe during the school day.
- Help establish before- and afterschool programs where children can be supervised while families are at work. Offer activities that include tutoring, homework help, counseling, community service, and recreation.
- In your classroom, help students learn conflict resolution skills through direct teaching and everyday classroom activities. Help students learn to manage their anger, solve problems, negotiate with their peers, listen actively, and communicate effectively.
- Have regular class meetings where conflicts in the classroom are discussed and resolved as a group. Allow students to have some power in making class decisions, such as rules for behavior that will keep everyone safe and foster a productive learning environment.
- One of the most critical factors in preventing violence among youth is having a positive, supportive relationship with an adult. Encourage adults in the community to become involved with the school and to develop mentoring relationships with students.
- Learn to recognize warning signs of students affected by community violence. Communicate your concerns to the student's family, and use school and community resources for appropriate help.
- Do not tolerate bullying, harassment, name-calling, or teasing among students in your classroom or as a school. Develop school and classroom policies to create a positive school climate.
- Encourage students to share their fears and concerns and to report threats or criminal activity without fear of reprisal. Have a system in place in your school for handling suspicions. (National Youth Violence Prevention Resource Center, 2003)

CHRONIC ILLNESS OF A FAMILY MEMBER OR STUDENT

I think illness is a family journey, no matter what the outcome. Everybody has to be allowed to process it and mourn and deal with it in their own way.

—Marcia Wallace (Great-Quotes.com, n.d.)

Another obstacle that children and families face is **chronic illness**, which is defined as an illness that lasts more than three months, affects a child's normal activities, and

Chronic Conditions (not limited to)

Asthma (most common)	Diabetes
Cerebral palsy	Sickle cell anemia
Cystic fibrosis	Cancer
AIDS	Epilepsy
Spina bifida	Congenital heart problems

Source: University of Michigan Health System, 2007

may require ongoing medical attention. Approximately 15% to 18% of American children are affected by chronic illnesses (University of Michigan Health System, 2008). Examples of chronic illnesses are asthma (the most common), diabetes, cancer, severe allergies, epilepsy, cystic fibrosis, sickle-cell anemia, or congenital heart problems (University of Michigan Health System, 2007). These conditions can affect a child's ability to succeed in school and require close collaboration with the family.

You may feel unprepared to meet the classroom health concerns of chronically ill children with potentially fatal or debilitating conditions. However, as with the other obstacles described in this chapter, you should not try to handle the situation alone. A comprehensive team approach is needed to support the child, and this team should include the student, family members, other teachers, the school counselor, the school nurse, and the child's health care professionals. The team should develop a coordinated systematic approach to meet the needs of a student with severe health issues (National Asthma Education and Prevention Program et al., 2003). Examples of questions that the team might consider include the following:

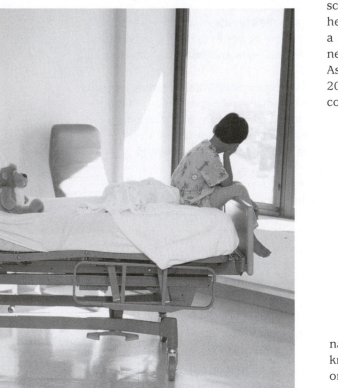

Close collaboration with families is important for children with chronic illnesses.

- Should a home visit with the school health professional and/or teacher be conducted?
- Who will initiate and maintain contact, the school or the family, if the child requires hospital or home care?
- How should you approach the family about remaining active in school and classroom events if the child has left the class due to illness? Will they want to remain involved with the child homebound or in the hospital?

Teachers must remain sensitive to the complex nature of chronic illnesses. Never assume that you know how a child or family feels, either physically or emotionally. Sometimes young children feel they are to blame for the condition, while older children may rebel against the disease. Students may be embarrassed by their appearance or procedures required by the illness, such as children who have lost all their hair because of cancer treatments, or children with cystic fibrosis, who need frequent postural drainage procedures. A family's ability to cope with either a fatal illness or chronic debilitating illness cannot be predicted by the teacher. The importance of establishing routines for both the child and family members in support of the child can lessen the anxiety about the illness (Schlozman, 2002).

Besides working with the child and family, it is also helpful to give guidance to the other students in the classroom about how to be supportive of their classmate who is ill. You may discuss whether the class should send a get-well card to the family residence if the child is housebound or attending school intermittently (Schlozman, 2002). As noted, children who are ill or have been out of school for a long time may be anxious about returning and fear what other children will think or say about them. You can help prepare your class for the child's return with discussions about the condition and how to talk with their classmate in a way that is not insensitive or embarrassing. For example, you might conduct a role-play of what to say and do if a classmate starts wheezing at recess or returns to school wearing a wig or, as a class, visit websites such as Kidshealth.org or Bandaides and Blackboards for Kids to find ways to best help ill classmates. It is important to create a caring classroom climate, where a child with a chronic illness that requires special equipment or procedures or that causes a change in the child's appearance is not ridiculed or made to feel like an outsider. You can also find mentors or friends for the child in other students who have had long-term illnesses. A friend can go a long way in easing the isolation caused by the illness (American Academy of Pediatrics, 1999).

Chronic school absenteeism is a consequence of a chronic illness and can create difficulties for both teachers and students. By law, all children are entitled to an education in the "least restrictive setting." This means that a child with a chronic illness is entitled to any additional services that will help the child be successful in school, and you may not exclude a child from school activities such as a field trip or deny help in making up assignments after an absence (American Academy of Pediatrics, 1999). Although families and health care professionals will ultimately make the decision about whether their child is well enough to attend school, communicating clearly with families about school activities and the importance of attendance may reduce unnecessary absenteeism (Sheldon & Epstein, 2004).

Suggestions for Working With Families and Children Who Are Chronically Ill

Families of children with a chronic illness are often anxious about their child's care and worry that school personnel may not provide needed supervision or meet their health needs. It is important to reassure them that not only will their child's education needs be met but also their health care. Following is a list of suggestions for working with children who are chronically ill:

- Keep updated medical records in both your files and the school nurse's office, noting any special dietary needs or activity limitations. Make sure that this information is shared with those who work with the student, such as the art, music, or physical education teachers, as well as substitute teachers, cafeteria staff, bus drivers, and adults on recess duty.

- Stay in close communication with the student's family about daily classroom activities; ask them to tell you activities that should be avoided or modified. Check with the family before any field trips, special events, or activities that are out of the ordinary. Emphasize to parents the importance of keeping you informed of any changes, such as a change in the child's daily routine, condition or treatment, events in the home that may affect the child's behavior, emergency contacts, and so on. Special emergency plans should be renewed and sent to school.
- Communication with the family may be difficult if they are overwhelmed by the severity of the illness, reluctant to supply private information in a timely manner, or even forget to provide an adequate supply of the student's medicine in pharmacy-labeled containers. Have a staff person, such as the nurse or yourself (as the child's teacher), delegated as the contact person to get needed health information from the family. If necessary, send thoughtful reminders to the family or be persistent in communication efforts to get needed information. Post telephone numbers where you can reach parents (and alternate emergency contacts) at all times. Make sure the emergency contacts and phone numbers are current.
- If the student needs supplies for health care, be sure to notify families if supplies are running low. Make sure that anyone who works with the student knows where the supplies are stored. Also, remember that prescribed medication cannot be administered without authorization from parents and a physician. Update cell phone numbers and those of relatives.
- Confidentiality of student health issues is the law. Do not share student health information with anyone other than those who work directly with the child.
- Become educated about the child's illness and how this illness may affect the child's development and learning. Learn what may trigger an emergency situation; how often a crisis might occur; and how the child might behave before, during, and after the crisis. Have a plan in place for handling emergency situations, such as an epileptic seizure, asthma attack, or diabetic emergency. This plan should be developed by the health team and communicated to all those who work with the student. The plan should include information about whether to call for additional help (American Academy of Pediatrics, 1999; Greenstein, 1998; National Asthma Education and Prevention Program et al., 2003; Weller, Doren, Burbach, Molgaard, & Ngong, 2004).

WORKING WITH FAMILIES WHO HAVE EXPERIENCED NATURAL DISASTERS

The loss of loved ones, community resources, and security [in a natural disaster] can be devastating upon one's sense of psychological wellness. Putting the pieces of one's life back together can be a cumbersome task and is usually precipitated by a myriad of emotions.

—Jonathan Livingston and Sherry Eaton (2007)

Over the past 30 years, with changes in climate and shifts in populations, there have been a number of natural disasters that have affected the lives of U.S. families and children. Whether it has been the hurricanes that have hit U.S. coasts, including the devastating Hurricane Katrina that affected New Orleans and Mississippi, the severe tornadoes and flooding experienced throughout much of the Midwest, or earthquakes and wildfires in California, no geographical area is immune to a natural disaster. Communities are often unprepared for the damaging effects of a natural disaster, and lives of families and children may be changed forever. Recovery is often agonizingly slow. For example, even five years after Hurricane Andrew, families were still living in makeshift communities in southern Florida.

Although the disasters themselves may only last for a short time, the subsequent destruction (e.g., flooding, fires, landslides, tremors) can compound the emotional and psychological trauma. Survivors of a natural disaster can experience emotional stress and trauma years after a natural disaster has occurred. A natural disaster may include the loss of family members or the family's home, as well as the loss of neighbors or familiar community dwellings such as churches, schools, or neighborhood stores. For example, the devastating 2011 tornado in Joplin, Missouri, a city of approximately 50,000, killed 159 people, destroyed 7,000 homes, and severely damaged 10 public school buildings (Zagier, 2011, p. 3A). Damages to businesses may cause a loss of employment or vital services for families, creating additional stress. As one flood survivor, on the edge of hysterics when she arrived at a flood assistance center described, "I was a disaster when I came in. I was bawling. . . . It's been like one disaster after another." This victim lost her home, nearly all her possessions, including all the food in her refrigerator, and then her job and paycheck when her place of employment flooded (DiCosmo, 2008, pp. 1A, 5A).

For many families, trying to put the pieces back together after a natural disaster can be a challenging and time-consuming task, yet doing so takes their mind off the surrounding stressors. However, children may not have this emotional outlet, and the impact of a natural disaster on a child can be quite devastating. Children may experience the closing of their school, parks, or playgrounds; the loss of playtime with friends; and a breakdown in the consistency and structure of their daily world. The effect of a natural disaster on a child will depend on key factors, such as exposure to the actual event, personal injuries or loss of loved ones, and levels of parental support and physical destruction (Lazarus, Jimerson, & Brock, 2002). Because families are preoccupied with rebuilding their lives, they may not recognize serious changes in their children's emotional or mental development.

Suggestions for Working With Children and Families Who Have Experienced Natural Disasters

One of the first steps taken by human service professionals and educators should be identifying families who are at high risk. In particular, children should be recognized first. Although children are resilient, they take their cues from adults. What can you do in your classroom to help children who have experienced a natural disaster? Some suggestions from Lazarus et al. (2002) are as follows:

- Remain calm and reassuring. Children need to be reassured that family and friends will take care of them and that things will return to normal.
- Acknowledge children's emotions. Allow them to talk about their feelings, about what happened to them during the event, and ask any questions about the natural disaster.

- Foster strong peer support. Build on children's friendships by giving them plenty of opportunities to share, play, and discuss the impact of the storm on their community.
- Use mental health professionals as a resource. Although you can be a support in the healing process, trained mental health professionals can be invaluable when working with the children and families at this vulnerable time.

FAMILIES AND CHILDREN UNDER STRESS: RISK AND RESILIENCE

One of the most important and consistent findings in resilience research is the power of schools, especially of teachers, to turn a child's life from risk to resilience.

—Bonnie Benard (2004)

As noted in previous chapters, today's families and children face many obstacles and stresses that put students at risk of failing academically. Changes in family structure because of parents separating, divorcing, and remarrying have meant that parents may not have the emotional reserves to provide needed support and that the home may not be a base of strength and protection for children. Other factors such as drug and alcohol abuse, domestic and community violence, poverty, and physical or mental illness may lead students to being **at risk** (conditions or factors that put a child in jeopardy of failure; negative outcome that an individual or an organization could likely experience) for failure. For many years, educators tended to focus on identifying children considered to be at risk and on the deficiencies of these students and their families, rather than looking at their strengths that can lead to success. This focus on what is wrong, rather than what is right, created a self-fulfilling prophecy, where expectations for students to fail led to failure (Frey, 1998). In the 1980s, researchers began to look at factors that led to students overcoming obstacles and develop a strengths-based approach based on the idea of resilience. Resilience is the ability to cope with, adapt to, and prevail over adversity. Resilience research

challenges educators to focus more on strengths instead of deficits, to look through a lens of strength in analyzing individual behaviors, and it confirms the power of those strengths as a lifeline to resilience. It shows what is "right" in the lives of people, overlooked until recently, which can build a path of triumph over all that was "wrong." Most importantly, it indicates what must be in place in institutions, especially schools, for resiliency to flourish in the lives of students and adults who learn and work there. (Henderson & Milstein, 1996, p. 3)

Researchers examined students who tended to achieve against all odds and looked at the characteristics or **protective factors**—conditions that negate or oppose negative outcomes—that seemed to help students cope with difficult circumstances and become successful adults. For example, what helped children who experienced abuse, neglect, and difficult foster care situations go on to become successful young adults? How did students with many risk factors, such as poverty, a parent with mental illness or substance abuse problem, or homelessness, still achieve in their education and develop into socially and emotionally healthy adults?

What can teachers and schools do to support these students? Resilience research seeks to answer these questions and can offer you insights to help your students succeed.

Researchers have identified both personal characteristics of students, as well as environmental factors that help children overcome adversity and achieve success. Personal characteristics include the following:

- Social competence, such as having good social and communication skills, positive relationships, a sense of humor
- Problem-solving skills, such as the ability to think abstractly, flexibly, and come up with alternate solutions
- Autonomy, such as a sense of independence, power, self-esteem, ability to separate oneself from a poorly functioning family
- Sense of purpose and future, such as having goals, expectations, a sense of hopefulness (Benard, 2004)

These characteristics can be found in all ethnicities, cultures, genders, and geographic areas. Resilience is not a characteristic of a few but can be found in all youth. However, it is the responsibility of caring adults, including teachers, to nurture these protective factors in students (Ryan & Hoover, 2005). After analyzing decades of resilience research and intervention programs, Benard (2004) concluded that schools and teachers, youth development organizations, family support programs, and other community institutions have played critical roles in helping children overcome risk factors and become resilient. In particular, research seems to indicate the importance of the "single relationship" or "turnaround relationships," where an adult in a student's life, through a caring, mentoring relationship, can bring about a positive change (p. 109). For many resilient youth, it is a teacher who provides that special relationship. Indeed, a favorite teacher is the most frequently encountered positive role model in resilient children's lives (Edwards, 2000).

Besides personal characteristics, Benard (2004) has identified three common variables that can be found in families, schools, and communities that are environmental protective factors for resilience. These include the following:

- Caring and supportive relationships
- High expectations
- Opportunities for participation

In the school setting, caring and supportive relationships between teachers and students are crucial. As Nel Noddings (2007) wrote,

In an age when violence among schoolchildren is at an unprecedented level, when children are bearing children with little knowledge of how to care for them, when the society and even the schools often concentrate on materialistic messages, it may be unnecessary to argue that we should care more genuinely for our children and teach them to care. However, many otherwise reasonable people seem to believe that our educational problems consist largely of low scores on achievement tests. My contention is, first, that we should want more from our educational efforts than adequate academic achievement and, second, that we will not achieve even that meager success unless our children believe that they themselves are cared for and learn to care for others. (p. 1)

TABLE 7.2   Fostering Resilience in Your Students

With a classmate, discuss the following questions, giving specific examples of how you will apply the concepts about resilience in your classroom:

- How can you encourage the development of the personal characteristics in your students that lead to resilience, such as strong social skills and a sense of humor?
- How will you develop caring and supportive relationships with your students and their families?
- Do you expect that all your students can succeed, even those who have difficult home lives?
- What are ways you can communicate that expectation to your students?
- What are specific, meaningful opportunities you will give your students for participation in your classroom? What are the suggestions for your students' meaningful participation at home?
- How can you make sure your students are not alienated and that strong bonds are developed among the children?
- What boundaries will you set for student discipline and behavior that will foster positive behaviors in your classroom?
- What are ways you can teach conflict resolution, communication, and problem-solving skills? How can you partner with your students' families to work on these skills together?

Caring is "not just a warm, fuzzy feeling," but instead it involves developing relationships with students and their families that give them the message that we want the very best for them and that our goal is for the students to become competent, caring people who will make positive contributions to the world (Noddings, 1995).

Although most teachers would not say they expect some students to fail, they may unconsciously have low expectations for students. Besides caring and supportive relationships, it is important that teachers have high expectations for students by challenging them academically and repeatedly giving the message to students that they can be successful. When students are told by their teachers, "you are bright and capable," they have a sense of purpose and belief in a bright future. For example, every year, the kindergarten teachers in an elementary school that serves primarily low-income families in Cape Girardeau, Missouri, take their students and family chaperones on a field trip to the local university to expose them to the possibility of a college education and regularly encourage them to "dream big" for their future.

When students have opportunities for participation in the classroom and home, it communicates to children that they are not only capable but indispensable in the operation of the classroom and home. For example, assigning students class jobs or home chores, such as caring for pets in the classroom or at home, creating a class or school newspaper, or helping prepare dinner, can give children a sense of empowerment and the belief that they have something valuable to contribute.

Besides these three areas, Henderson and Milstein (2002) suggest additional strategies for educators in promoting resiliency. These include the following:

- Increase social bonding and reduce alienation among students.
- Set clear and consistent boundaries for student discipline and behavior.
- Teach life skills, such as conflict resolution, communication, and problem solving, to help students cope with and overcome stresses.

When these protective factors are in place, students feel connected to learning and to the school community, build confidence about challenges ahead, and possess the self-esteem and skills to overcome obstacles in their personal and home lives. Boundaries are set, not to exclude and alienate troubled students but to prevent disruptions to learning. Students feel that their voices are heard and issues addressed, and learning is meaningful.

What does this mean to you as a teacher? With a classmate, discuss the questions in Table 7.2.

SUMMARY

Today's families and children have many obstacles, and as a teacher, it is important that you consider these stresses in your family involvement practices. Families living in poverty or families dealing with a chronic illness, domestic violence, or the aftereffects of a natural disaster may have little time, energy, or desire to participate in the education of their children in traditional ways, such as volunteering at school. The federal No Child Left Behind act requires that schools involve not only parents who readily participate in school activities but also those who find it difficult to do so (Epstein, 2005). To accomplish this, it is important that you believe in the strength of families and the ultimate resilience of the family unit, treat them with dignity and respect, and collaborate with families to help their children overcome risks and build resilience.

REFLECTION QUESTIONS

Reread the In the Classroom case study presented at the beginning of the chapter and reflect on these questions:

1. How could looking at the Wallace family from a strengths perspective help Clara collaborate more effectively with Keisha's parents? What are the other strengths of the family besides what the principal listed?

2. How can Clara be more supportive of Keisha and her family in her education?

3. What are the ways in which a district or school, such as Kennedy Elementary, can support and ensure a high-quality education for all children in the district, including those who live in poverty?

WEBSITES

American Academy of Pediatrics (AAP), **www.aap.org**.

The mission of AAP is to attain optimal physical, mental, and social health and well-being for all infants, children, adolescents, and young adults. The AAP has compiled resources to assist in these efforts, including a resource guide to help children cope with natural and other disasters at www.aap.org/new/disasterresources.htm.

Bandaides and Blackboards for Kids **http://www.lehman.cuny.edu/faculty/jfleitas/ bandaides/contkids.html.**

> This is a child-friendly informational websites to help children and students understand illness and medical problems.

Kidshealth.org **http://kidshealth.org/.**

> This websites covers all matters of health. A great resource for children through to adults. It is also an excellent classroom resource.

Healthfinder.gov and Healthfinder.gov kids, **www.healthfinder.gov/kids.**

> An award-winning federal website that can guide families to the best government and nonprofit health and human services on the Internet. Teachers can download free reproducible health brochures in multiple languages.

Mental Health America (MHA), **http://www.mentalhealthamerica.net/go/information/ get-info/coping-with-disaster.**

> MHA has several resources available to help survivors cope with tragic events, loss, and other related issues. Tip sheets are available for download on numerous youth and adult mental health topics, including coping with natural disasters, war and terrorism, and divorce.

National Coalition for the Homeless (NCH), **www.nationalhomeless.org.**

> NCH is a national organization of individuals committed to ending homelessness and changing the attitudes that prevail about homeless families. Check out research-based fact sheets on issues such as "Homeless families with children," "Who is homeless?" and "Education of homeless children and youth."

STUDENT STUDY SITE

Log on to the student study site at **www.sagepub.com/grant2e** for additional study tools, including the following:

- eFlashcards
- Web quizzes
- Web resources
- Learning objectives

Chapter 8

Families in Abusive Situations

If we are ever to turn toward a kindlier society and a safer world, a revulsion against the physical punishment of children would be a good place to start.

—Dr. Benjamin Spock

One of the most difficult situations that you will face in your career as a teacher is working with children who are victims of abuse or neglect. You may have many questions such as these about how to work with children and families in abusive situations:

- How prevalent is child abuse and neglect in the United States?
- What exactly is considered child abuse or neglect? What are the signs of abuse or neglect?
- How does family members' drug or alcohol abuse affect children physically or emotionally?
- What is my role as a teacher in reporting abuse or neglect? How can I work effectively with **Child Protective Services (CPS)**?
- What is my role as a teacher in working with abusive families? How can I work effectively with these families after abuse or neglect has been reported?
- What is the role of my school administrator in abusive situations?
- Is corporal punishment considered physical abuse? Is it legal for teachers or administrators to spank children?

Identifying signs of child abuse or neglect and reporting the case to a child protection agency can be confusing and uncomfortable for teachers who worry about the ramifications

Contributing Author Keith Anderson

of such action for a child, the family, and even their teaching career. Teachers are often uncertain about whether abuse or neglect has occurred and how to handle their suspicions. This chapter aims to resolve some of the uncertainties that are influential in this critical decision-making process.

CHILD ABUSE STATISTICS

Child Protective Services (social service organization charged by the state with the collection and investigation of child abuse reports) agencies respond to the needs of children who are alleged to have been maltreated and ensure that they remain safe. (CPS may be referred to differently, depending on the location.) Approximately, 3,503,000 American children received an investigation by CPS agencies in 2004, and of those, an estimated 872,000 were found to be victims. As Figure 8.1 illustrates, this represents a 32.4% increase from 1990, when 36.1 per 1,000 children received an investigation, to 47.8 per 1,000 children in 2004. However, the rate of substantiated victimization decreased from 13.4 per 1,000 children in 1990 to 11.9 per 1,000 children in 2004 (DePanfilis, 2006).

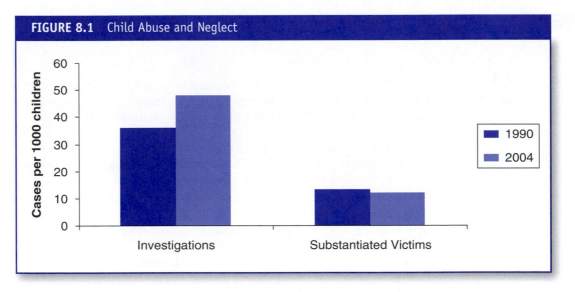

FIGURE 8.1   Child Abuse and Neglect

Source: DePanfilis, 2006.

According to Besharov (1992), an estimated 40% to 70% of suspected abuse and neglect cases still go unreported. These figures reflect a general increase in the awareness of child abuse, resulting in an increase in investigations and overall reduction in actual child abuse, as indicated in Figure 8.1. Regardless of this decrease, child abuse continues to be a serious problem, as shown in Table 8.1.

TABLE 8.1   Scope of the Problem
• Nearly 3 million reports concerning 5 million children were filed in 2000, and about 1 million children were confirmed victims of abuse or neglect.
• Boys and girls are equally likely to experience neglect and physical abuse. Girls are four times more likely to experience sexual abuse.
• Children of all races and ethnicities experience child abuse.
• Children of all ages experience abuse, but the youngest children are most vulnerable.
• Most abuse happens within families (DHHS, 2003).

Source: National Association for the Education of Young Children (2004). © Copyright of the National Association for the Education of Young Children.

Child abuse and neglect occur among all socioeconomic family environments and cultures. No one factor can predict that child abuse will occur; abuse is a systemic problem, with family violence often a symptom of problems that exist within the family system. No one solution will prevent child abuse, either, but preventive measures include ensuring that children are wanted, making the families know that there are resources available, increasing public awareness of child abuse, increasing the number of CPS staff, providing supports for good mental health, and finally, offering more education for children about child abuse. Although these actions won't prevent all abuse or neglect from occurring, they do offer hope for improving the problem.

IN THE CLASSROOM: SHARING CRACKERS

As the second graders excitedly ran outside for their morning recess, Travis lingered at the door and said, "Miss Harrison, do you know what we're having for lunch today?" Kate realized this was the third time that Travis had mentioned lunch this morning and felt a warning signal go off in her head. She said, "Travis, would you like some crackers from my desk drawer? I keep a supply handy for when I need a morning snack. How about we share some together?" Travis quickly came to Kate's desk and ate the crackers she put on a napkin. As they ate and talked, Kate gently tried to question Travis about his breakfast that morning and learned that he hadn't had any. "Mom was sleeping, and there wasn't no cereal left. Joe said he'd get some money from mom's purse tonight and go to the store and get some food." Kate realized that Travis was talking about his brother, Joe, in fifth grade.

"Oh, is your mom sick?" she asked.

"Nah, she just came home late and that's why she was in bed."

"Is she working at night now?" Kate asked, as she quickly tried to remember where Travis's mom worked. She had met Travis's mom at the fall parent-teacher conferences, but she hadn't come to any other school events. Kate remembered her as being a young parent, who had said little at the conference and seemed glad when it was over.

"No, she was just doin' stuff," he said matter-of-factly.

After Travis went out to play, Kate pondered the situation and decided to start keeping notes about anything relating to Travis's care and family situation. Over the next few weeks, she noticed there were several instances where Travis came to school hungry or in the same clothes as the day before. He also did not have gloves or hat for the cold winter days, and she was glad to be able to get some from the closet that had been stocked by the Poplar Grove Rotary Club. As their morning recess shared snack became a routine event, she learned more, including the disturbing information that Travis, his 10-year-old brother, Joe, and six-year-old sister, Tiffany, were often left alone at night, sometimes overnight. Although Travis never said anything about his mother's activities, it was obvious that he and his siblings were fending for themselves on a regular basis.

TYPES OF CHILD ABUSE AND NEGLECT

The first step in helping abused and neglected children is understanding the different types and warning signs of abuse and neglect. The federal Child Abuse Prevention and Treatment Act (CAPTA), as amended by the Keeping Children and Families Safe Act of 2003, defines child abuse and neglect as follows:

> Any recent act or failure to act on the part of a parent or caretaker which results in death, serious physical or emotional harm, sexual abuse or exploitation or an act or failure to act which presents an imminent risk of serious harm. (U.S. Department of Health and Human Services, 2005, p. 1)

In other words, when adults take action that causes serious physical or emotional harm to a child, or when their inaction leads to the child being hurt in some way, abuse or neglect has occurred. The major categories of child abuse and neglect include physical abuse, sexual abuse, emotional/psychological abuse, and physical/emotional neglect.

Physical Abuse

Physical abuse is an injury to a child, such as beating, kicking, punching, shaking, and burning. Often, physical abuse is the easiest form of abuse to identify because it may leave visible injuries, such as bruises, burns, or broken bones. However, the lack of noticeable injuries does not rule out the presence of abuse.

By definition, physical abuse is not accidental, but neither is it necessarily the adult's intent to injure the child. Physical abuse may result from overdiscipline or an adult's use of punishment for disciplinary purposes. One study found that in the majority of physical abuse cases (69%), the abuse occurred because of an adult's intent to give punishment as a disciplinary action (Durant, 2005). Therefore, it is important to make a distinction between the terms **discipline** (action taken by an adult designed to correct, shape, or help a child develop acceptable behavior), **punishment** (a form of physical or nonphysical discipline that is designed to stop undesired behavior), and **abuse** (action or inaction of an adult that causes serious physical or emotional harm to a child). Table 8.2 provides further discussion about these terms.

Although these definitions in Table 8.2 are easy to understand, they are harder to interpret. For example, when does punishment become abuse, and who should decide? There are cultural and religious differences relating to parental beliefs in what is appropriate discipline or punishment for children. State statutes demonstrate this difficulty in determining the difference between punishment and abuse. In 14 states' statutes, the physical punishment of a child is an exception to the definition

ACTIVITY 8.1

During a morning reading activity, you notice one of your students holding her wrist during writing. Later, at recess, the child yelps out in pain after a brush with another student. When you question her, she tells you that she hurt her wrist when her mom's boyfriend pushed her down the stairs in anger. You are unsure whether to send her to the nurse, talk to the counselor or principal, or call her mother yourself. What should you do?

TABLE 8.2   Is It Discipline or Abuse?

Discipline: Action taken by an adult designed to correct, shape, or help a child develop acceptable behavior. The term discipline comes from the Latin word "disciplinare," which means "to teach" (Encyclopedia of Children's Health, 2006). The focus of discipline is on guiding the child to develop self-control and may include modeling appropriate behavior, positive actions, such as praise and rewards, or negative actions, such as time-out (isolating a child for a short period). Discipline may be physical.

Punishment: A type of discipline that is designed to stop undesired behavior. Punishment may be nonphysical, such as a child losing privileges or a verbal scolding, or physical, as in a spanking. Although spanking is accepted by many parents, its use is controversial, with the potential of severe spankings becoming physical abuse (Encyclopedia of Children's Health, 2006).

Abuse: Action or inaction of an adult that causes serious physical or emotional harm to a child (U.S. Department of Health and Human Services, 2005). Abuse may be distinguished from discipline or punishment by the severity of injury to a child.

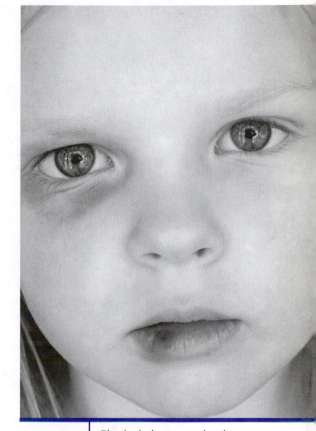

Physical abuse may be the easiest type of abuse to identify because injuries are often visible.

of abuse, if it is "reasonable" and does not cause bodily injury (U.S. Department of Health and Human Services, 2005).

Signs of Physical Abuse

Prevent Child Abuse America (2007) offers these warning signs of physical abuse:

- A child has unexplained injuries.
- A child has fading bruises or other marks after an absence from school.
- A child appears frightened of or protests going home at the end of the school day.
- A child shrinks at the approach of adults.
- The parent or caregiver's explanation for the child's injury conflicts with the child's explanation, or there is no explanation given.
- The parent or caregiver uses severe physical discipline with the child. (p. 2)

ACTIVITY 8.2

A second grader in your class has had increasing bathroom accidents because she does not want to go to the restroom. When you question her, she says it hurts to defecate. You are becoming concerned about the obvious health issue and notice that the child appears to cower when her uncle routinely picks her up after school. Should you share your suspicions with anyone?

Sexual Abuse

While physical abuse may be readily visible, victims of sexual abuse may suffer in silence. The CAPTA defines sexual abuse as follows:

> Employment, use, persuasion, inducement, enticement, or coercion of any child to engage in, or assist any other person to engage in, any sexually explicit conduct or any simulation of such conduct for the purpose of producing any visual depiction of such conduct. Rape, and in cases of caretaker or inter-familial relationships, statutory rape, molestation, prostitution, or other form of sexual exploitation of children, or incest with children. (U.S. Department of Health and Human Services, 2005, p. 2).

It should be noted that children, by legal definition, are not considered capable of giving consent for a sexual act (Berger, 2008). Of the children who were classified by CPS as being abused in 2000, 10% had been sexually abused. During the seven-year period from 1986 to 1993, the Third National Child Abuse Incidence study reported an 83% to 125% increase in sexual abuse cases (Thomas, 2003). However, recent statistics indicate that sexual abuse may be declining because of more public awareness, prevention programs, and incarceration of sexual offenders. Sexual abuse cases continue to be difficult to detect, though, as the majority of sexual offenders (80%) are family members or acquaintances (Berger, 2008).

Signs of Sexual Abuse

Some possible warning signs of sexual abuse of a child, as noted by Prevent Child Abuse America (2007) include the following:

- The child appears to have difficulty sitting or walking.
- The child does not want to change clothes for gym or participate in physical activities.
- The child displays inappropriate or mature sexual knowledge or behavior.
- The parent or caregiver does not allow the child to have contact with other children.
- The parent or caregiver appears to be secretive and isolates the family. (p. 3)

Emotional or Psychological Abuse

Where physical and sexual abuse involves harming a child's body, emotional or psychological abuse harms the child's spirit. Rather than striking a child with fists, it is akin to hitting a child with "words or actions." Emotional or psychological abuse is defined as "injury to the psychological capacity or emotional stability of the child as evidenced by an observable or substantial change in behavior, emotional response, or cognition, or as evidenced by anxiety, depression, withdrawal, or aggressive behavior" (U.S. Department of Health and Human Services, 2005, p. 4). Emotional or psychological abuse can include behaviors such as belittling, humiliating, shaming, terrorizing, or rejecting children. Examples might be a parent who calls a child "fat" or "stupid" or threatens to leave a child stranded on the road or harm his pet. Emotional or psychological abuse can potentially be even more harmful than physical abuse because of its long-lasting effects. According to Lewis (2000),

Emotional abuse is one type of abuse that can truly scar your mind and soul forever if you allow it to. It is the one abuse that leaves all of its scars on the inside where they are not visible to people around you. (para. 2)

Differentiating between children who have been emotionally abused and children with emotional disturbances is a difficult task. In observing parents with an emotionally disturbed child, they may acknowledge that their child has a problem, and as such, they are often anxious about their child. However, the parents of an emotionally abused child may be less attentive to their child or perhaps even blame the child for her difficulties. There are a number of reasons why emotional abuse is the most difficult form of child abuse to identify. One reason is that the manifestations of emotional abuse, such as learning problems, speech disorders, and delays in physical development, are also present in children who have not suffered from psychological abuse. In addition, these effects might not become apparent until later in the child's maturation. Emotional abuse may also function as a secondary type of abuse after sexual or physical abuse has occurred (M. Delarm, personal communication, June 4, 2007).

> ### ACTIVITY 8.3
>
> After the school counselor's presentation to your fourth-grade class on bullying, one of your students reveals privately that his mom does many of the things that the counselor had described as bullying tactics. He shares that his mother regularly calls him names, such as "ungrateful moron" and has also told him that her life would be better if he had never been born. Although you have not observed any warmth from the student's mother toward him, you are shocked and unsure how to respond. Should his mother be reported for child abuse?

Signs of Emotional or Psychological Abuse

Prevent Child Abuse America (2007) describes these potential signs of emotional or psychological abuse:

- The child has extremes in behavior from being overly compliant and passive to overly demanding and aggressive.
- The child's behavior is at the extremes of adult-like, such as wanting to take care of other children, or immature, such as frequent rocking or thumb sucking.
- The child's emotional development seems delayed or the child exhibits suicidal thoughts.
- The child does not appear to have a secure attachment to her parent or caregiver.
- The parent or caregiver makes insulting, belittling comments about the child or blames the child for all the family's problems.
- The parent or caregiver does not appear concerned about the child and does not seek assistance for any problems the child may be exhibiting. (p. 3)

Neglect

Neglect occurs when adults do not provide for the physical, emotional, or developmental needs of their growing children. Neglect is the most frequently reported form of child abuse.

ACTIVITY 8.4

You notice that one of your third graders doesn't seem to be eating his lunch. His face also appears swollen and puffy. You ask the nurse to check out the problem, and she finds that several of his teeth are decayed and need to be extracted. When his parent is called, she says, "Yeah, I know, he has a toothache, but I don't have the money for a dentist." The school nurse offers to arrange free dental care for the child through a community program, but even after free dental care is set up, his mom still doesn't make an appointment. What can you or the nurse do about this?

In 2000, 63% of children classified by CPS agencies as abused had experienced some form of neglect (Thomas, 2003). Neglect can include adults not providing for children's basic needs, such as food, shelter, clothing, health care, supervision, and protection. Neglect can also include not making sure a child attends school. The symptoms of neglect can be harder to define than some of the other categories of child abuse. Manifestations of neglect often get worse as the child gets older. Neglected schoolchildren are often described as inattentive, uninvolved, and lacking in creative initiative. In addition, they tend to be more teacher dependent, more helpless, passive, withdrawn, and more easily frustrated. Living in a home environment with less stimulation may result in language difficulties, acute learning problems, and lower standardized-test scores in reading and math (Dubowitz, 1996). As children get older, neglect may become more apparent, demonstrating the "cumulative malignant effects" of neglect (Egeland, 1988, p. 18). Although a poor diet can lead to medical problems, deformities, and lifelong poor health, severe neglect can result in death (Munkel, 1996).

Signs of Neglect

Two reports provide comprehensive data on the characteristics of neglected children and their families: The National Incidence Study-3 (NIS-3) (Sedlack & Broadhurst, 1996) and a report from the U.S. Department of Health and Human Services (1999), which is based on the National Child Abuse and Neglect Data System (NCANDS). Based on the findings from these reports, boys and girls are neglected at approximately the same rates. Findings regarding the children's age, however, differed between the two studies. The NIS-3 reported that children age six and older suffer from neglect at higher rates than children five and under. However, U.S. Department of Health and Human Services reported that the rates of neglect are highest for children ages from birth to three and decrease as children get older. The studies also found strong associations between neglect and

- single parenthood,
- poverty,
- parental substance abuse,
- parental impulsivity,
- parental low self-esteem, and
- a lack of social support for the family.

Certain factors seem to put children more at risk for neglect, and this risk increases as the number of risk factors increases (Brown, Cohen, Johnson, & Salzinger, 1998). Although they are no guarantees that neglect is occurring, these risk factors from the Prevent Child Abuse America (2007) can raise red flags for a teacher:

- A child frequently misses school.
- A child steals classmates' money or food.
- A child does not get appropriate medical, dental, or vision care.
- A child does not have appropriate clothing for the weather or is unclean.
- A child appears to have to take care of himself at home.
- The parent or caregiver appears to be indifferent to the child's needs.
- The parent or caregiver appears depressed or behaves in an irrational manner.
- The parent or caregiver has a substance abuse problem. (p. 2)

SUBSTANCE ABUSE, CHILD ABUSE, AND NEGLECT

> ### ACTIVITY 8.5
>
> After a lesson with the DARE officer, one of your fifth-grade students confides in you that his parents smoke pot in their bedroom after he has gone to bed and that he is sometimes afraid when "weird" people come over late at night. You have worked hard to establish a relationship with his family in the past, through repeated phone calls and notes, and you do not want to jeopardize the progress you've made with accusations of illegal behavior that may or may not be true. However, you are also concerned about your student's safety. You are unsure whether to tell the DARE police officer about this, your administrator, school counselor, or talk to the students' parents first. What should you do?

It is estimated that 9% of children in this country (6 million) live with at least one parent who abuses alcohol or other drugs. Research has demonstrated that children of substance-abusing parents are more likely to experience abuse (physical, sexual, or emotional) or neglect than children in nonsubstance-abusing households (Chaffin, Kelleher, & Hollenberg, 1996; DeBellis et al., 2001; Dube et al., 2001). Children of drug addicts or alcoholics are more likely to have poorer physical, intellectual, social, and emotional outcomes and are at greater risk of developing substance abuse problems themselves (U.S. Department of Health and Human Services, 1999). Some CPS agencies estimate that substance abuse is a factor in as many as 70% of all the child neglect cases they serve (Gaudin, 1993). Substance-abusing adults may divert money that is needed for basic necessities to buy drugs and alcohol (Munkel, 1996). In addition, family substance abuse may interfere with aspects of daily living, including the ability to maintain employment, further limiting the family's resources (Magura & Laudet, 1996) and possibly influencing decisions related to appropriate child rearing. The substance-abusing behaviors may expose the children to dangerous people and/or situations. Substance-abusing families may be emotionally or physically unavailable and unable to adequately supervise their children. Children living with substance-abusing families are more likely to model inappropriate substance use behaviors and experiment on their own. Heavy drug use can interfere with a family's ability to provide the consistent nurturing that promotes children's development and self-esteem.

Fetal Alcohol Syndrome and Drug-Affected Newborns

One serious issue relating to mothers' substance abuse is fetal alcohol syndrome (FAS) and drug-affected newborns. Recent studies suggest that 5.5% of pregnant women used some illicit drug

TABLE 8.3 Signs of Fetal Alcohol Syndrome

Fetal alcohol syndrome is one of a group of disorders that occurs after prenatal exposure to alcohol via the maternal bloodstream. The most apparent symptoms include distinct facial features, including a groove between nose and upper lip, a thin upper lip, and smaller eye openings. Other features may include the following:

- Small head
- Heart defects or other organ dysfunction
- Deformities of joints, limbs, and fingers
- Slow physical growth before or after birth
- Vision or hearing problems
- Mental retardation or delayed development
- Behavior problems

It is important to remember that teachers may identify a problem, but only trained health professionals may make a full diagnosis.

during pregnancy, resulting in 221,000 babies that had the potential to be born drug exposed (National Institute of Drug Abuse, 1999). Although the outcome of this drug exposure is difficult to predict, some forms of prenatal exposure may result in physical and neurological deficits, slower growth, heart problems, and long-term developmental abnormalities, including learning and behavior problems and language difficulties. Table 8.3 lists other typical signs of FAS.

Fetal alcohol exposure is the leading preventable cause of mental retardation, with a cost to society of an estimated $4 billion per year. Currently, five states now include some type of prenatal substance exposure in their statutory definitions of reportable child abuse and neglect (U.S. Department of Health and Human Services, 2000), while others consider prenatal exposure to be child abuse per se, mandating health care workers to file a report to and receive a response from CPS. This requirement is intended to identify those children at risk of child abuse and neglect (primary prevention) so that appropriate intervention services can be delivered to the infant and mother.

THE ROLE OF THE TEACHER IN REPORTING CHILD ABUSE

You will probably have many questions about whether to report your suspicions of abuse or neglect. Recent research has suggested that the decision-making process for reporting child abuse, for teachers as well as other professionals, is influenced by several factors. These include a teacher's uncertainty of symptoms that might define abuse, indecision about the reporting process, concerns about liability, and potential consequences to the child once a report is filed, as well as reluctance to report abuse because of the tremendous consequences that reporting can have on families involved (Alvarez, Donohue, Kenny, Cavanagh, & Romero, 2004; Hinson & Fossey, 2000; Thomas, 2003).

When making decisions about reporting child abuse, you should be guided by your school's internal administrative policies for reporting abuse. Sometimes, however, these policies can be confusing. Some schools encourage educators to report suspected abuse internally before contacting CPS. Nevertheless, state and federal laws mandate educators to report suspected child maltreatment directly to the appropriate agency. As such, allowing school administrators to determine if a teacher's suspicions should be reported is unlawful. Many teachers have, unwittingly, violated the law by only reporting suspected child abuse to a principal instead of the appropriate agency.

Because you, as the teacher, are not a trained investigator, it is especially important for you to document and report any suspicions of abuse or neglect that you have and not assume the responsibility of determining whether a child has been abused. Appendix C provides a comprehensive review of the child abuse phone numbers for each state, as well as the appropriate website that discusses each state's laws regarding the mandatory reporting of child abuse in that state.

MANDATORY REPORTING OF CHILD ABUSE: WORKING WITH CPS

All 50 states have passed some form of a mandatory child abuse and neglect reporting law to qualify for funding under the CAPTA (January 1996 version as cited in DePanfilis, 2006). CPS, a division usually found within state and local social service agencies, is the organization charged with the collection and investigation of child abuse reports. In most areas, CPS employs a wide variety of social service personnel who are expected to conduct an initial assessment or investigation of reports of child abuse or neglect. Table 8.4 offers more information about the reporting process and advice for teachers from the perspective of a CPS caseworker.

Note that CPS does not work alone. Many community professionals are mandatory reporters. They can include law-enforcement officers, health care providers, mental health professionals, legal and court system personnel, teachers, and substitute care providers. Some states have statutes that require all persons to report cases of suspected abuse, regardless of their occupation or profession.

Reporting child abuse can be a simple process with complex consequences. To make an accurate and useful report, it is important to maintain objectivity and collect as many facts as possible. Before calling CPS, you should have important documentation, including the child's name, date of birth, address, and telephone number; details of the suspected abuse; and if possible, information about the perpetrator. You should begin this documentation process at the first suspicion of abuse or neglect. Without proper documentation at the time an incident occurred, it is difficult to recollect a prior incident accurately. Descriptive information about bruises, marks, or other physical signs of abuse may help determine the degree of physical risk that is currently present. Information about family members may help determine if the child is at risk if she returns home. Clarity in the report is critical. As statements become more vague or ambiguous, the CPS screener will have more difficulty making an appropriate determination for the case.

If you feel, as a mandatory reporter, that the person taking the report over the telephone doesn't understand the extent of your concern, by all means, ask for a supervisor. A supervisor generally has years of experience dealing with abuse/neglect, and if there is some dispute about whether to report, the supervisor may help make the final decision.

It is the responsibility of CPS to assess all reports with enough information for possible investigation. Without adequate identifying information, CPS may not be able to initiate an inquiry or acquire further information. Although social workers attempt to clarify the

TABLE 8.4   Interview With a Child Protective Services Caseworker (2007)

Martha Delarm has worked in the upstate New York Adirondack area for 20 years as both a Child Protective Services (CPS) caseworker and a school-based probation officer for Warren County. She offers some advice for teachers starting their work with students (age: birth to 18 years) and families needing support from social service agencies. (Note that this information applies to a particular county of New York State and the protocols may vary for other counties throughout the United States).

How is your office notified of suspected child abuse or neglect as reported by school staff members who are mandated reporters?

The New York State Child Abuse Registry accepts hotline reports (on a 24-hour basis) that are investigated by my local CPS office. New York State supplies a form for the mandated reporters, which includes what happened, what the child said, what marks or bruises were noticed, and other pertinent information. It is important to know if your school has a specific set of protocols that are followed for reporting abuse and neglect, as often the principal or school nurse are designated reporters.

What is the advantage of using designated reporters?

Designated reporters know what words to say, their training provides them with the terminology. Sometimes teachers are reluctant about reporting, just knowing their name is on the form, or they may be fearful of retaliation.

What else is important for teachers to know?

Teachers do not have to investigate what they report; it is not part of their job. CPS personnel are trained to interview students in a child-friendly manner and spot inconsistencies if they exist. Also, CPS will work closely with the school to ascertain the needs of the child. For a young teacher starting in the classroom, they can be shocked to witness the effects of abuse or neglect; they may be devastated by the situation. Others may be in denial that the situation even exists. However, many teachers will send the child to the school nurse, who is a critical liaison, especially for special-needs students. My best advice is to trust your instincts. On the average, teachers will make one to two reports a year. Many times teachers never hear the results from their reports, which can be frustrating.

What other school personnel are critical to help teachers in reporting abuse or neglect?

If your school has a social worker, get to know that person well. Often, a team approach is very success-ful for at-risk students with inclusion of the guidance counselor. One area school has a team meeting every Friday to discuss students whose social, academic, and emotional risk factors are present. This team approach can also work effectively with parents resistant to intervention.

What kinds of reactions can teachers expect to see from parents who have been reported?

All kinds of reactions. Some parents may make vague threats, some may indicate they are going to home-school their child, many will be angry, and yet some will readily admit the abuse/neglect. In my work, I find 90% of the reports involve neglect: a lack of food in the home, educational neglect, students not attending school on a regular basis, lack of parenting skills, or families involved in drug and alcohol use.

What advice can you give to teachers working with families who have been "hotlined"?

Again, work within your school team to interact with parents. School team intervention can be highly successful. Have patience and persistence in working with families whose child has been referred to CPS.

Source: Used with permission of Martha Delarm, Probation Officer, Warren County, Queensbury, New York.

concerns of a reporter, in some cases, calls may be referred to other agencies. It is the responsibility of CPS staff to make an initial determination of which agency is most suited to identifying a case and pursuing the complaint or initiating a more thorough and detailed investigation. Figure 8.2 shows the CPS process in dealing with abuse.

Part of your role in the reporting process will be to ask a child open-ended questions that will provide enough information to CPS to determine if an investigation is necessary. When talking to children about suspected abuse, several issues are very important. Finding the appropriate setting is an important aspect of gathering information, as children are more likely to talk freely when other students are not present. However, it may be appropriate to have another trusted person present, such as your administrator, school nurse, or counselor. Also, it is critical that you avoid asking leading questions or insert information that has not been revealed by the child. Asking leading or inappropriate questions can result in much otherwise useful information being discarded or discredited. As much as possible, the incident should be conveyed in the child's words. It is important to keep in mind that these records will eventually become accessible by all those who are involved in investigating the case, including attorneys, investigators, social workers, psychologists, police detectives, and judges.

Facts on Teachers as Reporters

Reporting child abuse or neglect is a difficult decision and one that many teachers do not feel adequately prepared to handle (Tite, 1994; Wurtele & Schmitt, 1992). As one teacher said,

> Even though this is my first year of teaching, I have had to hotline [report] five out of my 26 students this year—one for sexual abuse, two for physical abuse and neglect, one for drug use in the home, and another for a child being hit in the middle of a domestic abuse, which is considered neglect. Emotionally this has been a very hard year. The hardest part for me through this whole year was struggling with the ethical decision of, "Is it better not to tell because the child could get punished by the parents for telling someone at school?" or "Is it worse not to hotline because next time the child could die or be so emotionally scarred they would like to die?" Of course, I hotlined the families anyway, and yes, some of the parents will not speak to me because they suspect it was me, but at least, they are aware of the consequences they could face for endangering their child. (Anonymous, personal communication, May 3, 2007)

Researchers have found that when teachers do report abuse or neglect, they are better at reporting physical abuse over emotional abuse, which may be because of the difficulty in recognizing red flags of emotional abuse that might be similar to other childhood developmental difficulties (Walsh, Farrell, Bridgstock, & Schweitzer, 2006). Teachers may delay reporting until they feel they have sufficient evidence or may not report if they feel the abuse or neglect is not severe enough. Teachers also may have concerns and fears for families and children about the negative legal consequences of reporting (Wurtele & Schmitt, 1992). If teachers had prior negative experiences with reporting, are afraid for their personal safety after reporting, are afraid that the child will be punished or that parents will deny the report, then they may choose not to report their suspicions of abuse or neglect (Smyth, 1996; Zellman, 1990). Characteristics of the family may also sway teachers' decision about whether to report their suspicions. For example, if the parents are law-abiding citizens, have a positive attitude toward the teacher, or view their child as

FIGURE 8.2 Overview of Child Protective Services Process

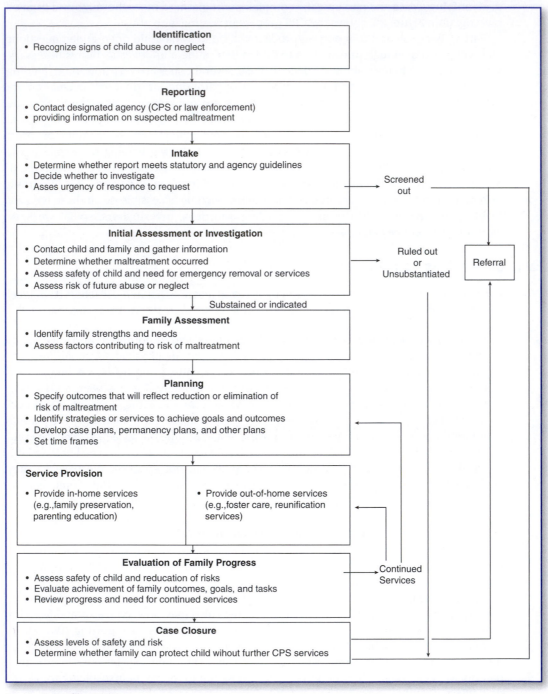

Source: DePanfilis (2006)

inherently good, then the teacher may be less likely to make a report (Alter, 1985). Other researchers have found that teachers strongly consider the consequences of reporting or not reporting in reference to the quality of relationships with the child, the family, and themselves (Zellman & Bell, 1990). Dalgleish (1988) calls this the **judgment threshold** (relationships with the child, family, or teacher that affect a teacher's judgment about reporting suspected abuse or neglect). Teachers will factor in the strength of their suspicions, or the **action threshold** (strong suspicions that lead a teacher to take action and report suspected abuse or neglect). "If the potential negative outcomes for the child and the quality of their suspicions are below teachers' thresholds, they will decide to take action by reporting, otherwise they will not report" (Dalgleish, 1988, p. 72).

You will be required to make complex judgments concerning your suspicions. "Like social workers, teachers must make child protection decisions—that is, they must detect it, they must gather and organize information to assess the presence of abuse or neglect to develop a suspicion" (Walsh et al., 2006, p. 72). Although you may be hesitant to report abuse or neglect, it is clear that you have a legal responsibility to children and families to protect them from further harm by reporting any suspicions. As the Missouri Department of Social Services (2004) advises,

> Err on the side of *over*-reporting [italics added]. If you have the thought "Maybe I should call . . . "—DO! Not all calls to the hotline are determined to be abuse/ neglect. However, Children's Division can often provide services and assistance that can help families *prevent* [italics added] abuse. (Section 2)

Besides your legal responsibility, you also have an ethical responsibility relating to child abuse and neglect. The National Association for the Education of Young Children's *Code of Ethical Conduct and Statement of Commitment* (2005) provides guidelines for educators for ethical practice in regards to child abuse and neglect, as shown in Table 8.5.

TABLE 8.5 National Association for the Education of Young Children Code of Ethical Conduct

Ethical Guidelines: Principles for Educators Relating to Child Abuse and Neglect

P-1.8: We shall be familiar with the risk factors for and symptoms of child abuse and neglect, including physical, sexual, verbal, and emotional abuse and physical, emotional, educational, and medical neglect. We shall know and follow state laws and community procedures that protect children against abuse and neglect.

P-1.9: When we have reasonable cause to suspect child abuse or neglect, we shall report it to the appropriate community agency and follow up to ensure that appropriate action has been taken. When appropriate, parents or guardians will be informed that the referral will be or has been made.

P-1.10: When another person tells us of his or her suspicion that a child is being abused or neglected, we shall assist that person in taking appropriate action in order to protect the child.

P-1.11: When we become aware of a practice or situation that endangers the health, safety, or well-being of children, we have an ethical responsibility to protect children or inform parents and/or others who can.

Source: National Association for the Education of Young Children (2005). © Copyright of the National Association for the Education of Young Children

WORKING WITH FAMILIES IN ABUSIVE SITUATIONS

To be most effective, your family engagement practices must be based on principles of empowering families, always respectful of cultural differences, and when possible, building on strengths already possessed by the family. These principles may provide some useful suggestions for you when working with abused or neglected students. Suggestions for teachers working with families in abusive situations include the following:

Be aware and respectful of cultural differences. It is important that you are aware of long-standing cultural beliefs and differences among individual families. Without this awareness, you will be forced to make assumptions about families that may be incorrect. It is important that you build relationships with families to understand their cultural beliefs and practices, which may lead to actions that appear to be abusive or neglectful. You can learn more about families' cultural beliefs and practices relating to guidance and discipline, not only by talking with families but also by researching the culture, talking with colleagues and others in the community, reading professional literature, and even attending workshops or courses relating to different cultural beliefs (McIntrye & Silva, 1992).

Religious beliefs or practices may appear to be child abuse or neglect. For example, a Christian scientist parent may choose not to seek medical treatment for a child because of religious beliefs, while families in other religions may use the act of prayer as a sole means of healing. The tradition among some mothers of not addressing children's misbehavior in public may appear to be neglect, when, in reality, it is a sign of respect for the spirits of the children (Warrier et al., 2002). Other religious practices that may seem like abuse or neglect include excessive punishment or folk cures, such as home remedies, healing practices, or treatments. However, keep in mind that these families may consider the frequent middle-class cultural practice of isolating a misbehaving child in time-out as being neglectful because it involves an emotional separation (McIntrye & Silva, 1992).

As noted in Chapter 3, parenting practices vary among cultures and punitive, physical punishment may be more acceptable among some religious, socioeconomic, or ethnic groups. However, when punishment goes beyond "reasonable" or causes "serious harm," it is not legal or acceptable, regardless of the cultural beliefs and practices.

Understand the importance of outreach and community. Families experiencing abuse or neglect tend to have fewer resources and may be more removed from social contact with others. Therefore, effective interventions might include efforts to make contact with the family and, when possible, to make use of available community resources. Collaboration is a key element in working with the family and engaging the community. Many schools have "crisis" or "care" teams that consist of faculty members identified to provide resources and support for children in difficult situations. A care team may include the school counselor, a psychologist, a social worker, a school nurse, an administrator, and teachers. These teams can connect families with available community resources.

Establish a helping alliance and partnership with the family. Besides connecting families with outside resources, it will also be critical for you to work to establish a collaborative relationship with the family. That will present one of the biggest challenges of your teaching career. For example, a parent who is abusing his child may have difficulty communicating with those who could provide help. While realizing that your role as a teacher is often very limited, consider engaging the family in an active partnership when possible. This partnership must be carefully crafted to forge an alliance with families, yet avoid the potential pitfalls often associated with going beyond the role of the teacher. The partnership can also include key school personnel, such as counselors, nurses, and administrators.

Always emphasize family strengths. One way you can work toward forming an alliance with families is to focus on their strengths and existing competencies. All families have strengths or the potential for strengths, even those that aren't functioning well. For example, if parents are abusive or neglectful, there may be allies for the child in the extended family. Focusing on a family's potential may provide some impetus to begin the process of making changes. Although it is easy to view abusive families in a negative, critical manner, this negative approach will not be helpful in building relationships and working to improve the situation for the child.

Become an advocate for children in preventing abuse and neglect in your community. Even if you are not faced with the challenge of working with abusive families and children in your classroom, it is your ethical and professional responsibility to speak out against the problem and work to reduce abuse and neglect incidents in your community. As a way to develop your advocacy skills, complete the activity in Table 8.6, using the suggested websites as a resource.

Chapter 12 will present further strategies on becoming an advocate for students and families.

> ### ACTIVITY 8.6
>
> A new student in your sixth-grade classroom often appears depressed, withdrawn, and avoids the close physical proximity of other students. You know that this child was recently removed from her home and placed in foster care after her previous school reported severe emotional abuse from his drug-addicted parent, who is now incarcerated. What are the ways in which you can support this student?

DOMESTIC VIOLENCE, FAMILIES, AND SCHOOLS

Domestic violence not only affects those who are abused, but also has a substantial effect on family members, friends, co-workers, other witnesses, and the community at large. Children who grow up witnessing domestic violence are among those seriously affected by this crime. Frequent exposure to violence in the home not only predisposes children to numerous social and physical problems, but also teaches them that violence is a normal way of life—therefore, increasing their risk of becoming society's next generation of victims and abusers.

—The United States Department of Justice, 2011, para. 8

Many children live in homes where they witness domestic violence among the adults in their family. A total of 8.8 million children are living in family settings where they have been exposed to domestic violence (Kilpatrick & Saunders, 1997). All races, ethnicities, and socioeconomic classes experience domestic violence. Domestic violence is about power and control using physical violence, emotional or economic abuse, intimidation or isolation, coercion, or threats (American Bar Association, 2001).

Table 8.6 Advocacy Plan: Develop a Plan to Prevent Child Abuse in Your Community

It is important for educators to speak up about issues that affect children and families, such as child abuse. Develop an advocacy plan to prevent child abuse in your community. The advocacy plan should include the following components.

Research the problem of child abuse in your community. Find the statistics and types of abuse seen, the significant issues your community faces, barriers to solving this problem, and the key decision makers or those who have the power to make changes. The following websites can be a resource for information, but also explore your state and local website resources, such as state advocacy groups and community health and counseling agencies.

Develop a realistic plan of action. In your plan, identify other groups of people in your community with similar concerns with whom you could collaborate and the steps you would take in your plan.

Tell how you would educate others about this problem, such as letters to the editor, parent newsletters or programs, radio announcements, or personal conversations. If your plan involves legislative issues, indicate how you would contact your legislative representatives.

Tell how you would monitor and evaluate the success of your advocacy plan and what further steps you would take.

Website Resources for Advocacy Plan

American Academy of Pediatrics: www.aap.org

Annie E. Casey Foundation: www.aecf.org

Center on Budget and Policy Priorities: www.cbpp.org

Center for Law and Social Policy: www.clasp.org

Child Care Law Center: www.childcarelaw.org

Child Trends: www.childtrends.org

Child Welfare League of America: www.cwla.org

Children Now: www.childrennow.org

Children's Advocacy Institute: www.caichildlaw.org

Children's Defense Fund: www.childrensdefense.org

Children, Youth and Family Consortium Electronic Clearinghouse: www.cyfc.umn.edu

I Am Your Child: www.iamyourchild.org

Kids Campaign: www.sparkaction.org

National Association of Child Care Resource and Referral Agencies: www.naccrra.org

National Association for the Education of Young Children: www.naeyc.org

National Association for the Education of Young Children's Champions Action Center www.capwiz.com/naeyc/home

National Association for Family Child Care: www.nafcc.org

National Black Child Development Institute: www.nbcdi.org

National Center for Children in Poverty: www.nccp.org

National Child Care Association: www.nccanet.org

National Conference of State Legislators: www.ncsl.org

Project Vote Smart: www.votesmart.org

Public Agenda: www.publicagenda.org

Stand for Children: www.stand.org

U.S. Census Bureau: www.census.gov

U.S. Department of Education: www.ed.gov

U.S. Department of Health and Human Services ACF Head Start Bureau: www.acf.hhs.gov/programs/ohs

Zero to Three: www.zerotothree.org

Statistics and Definitions

- Domestic violence is also called intimate partner violence. Nearly one-third of American women will experience intimate partner-related physical assaults and rapes (End Abuse, 2010).
- Intimate partner or spousal abuse. Not only occurring in heterosexual relationships, domestic violence happens in same-sex partnerships.
- Child witnesses of family violence. "The witnessing of domestic violence can be auditory, visual, or inferred, including cases in which the child perceives the aftermath of violence, such as physical injuries to family members or damage to property. Children who witness domestic violence can suffer severe emotional and developmental difficulties that are similar to those of children who are victims of abuse" (Schecter & Edelson, 1999, p.10).
- Restraining orders and schools. A restraining order, also called an abuse prevention order, is a court order issued to protect a parent or child from being abused by certain other people. "A restraining order, whether issued in the District Court or Probate and Family Court, may contain additional protections to ensure that children are safe in school or day care. These protections may include an order prohibiting the abusive parent from going to the school, from gaining access to the child's school records, prohibiting the abusive parent from meeting with school personnel, or generally preventing the abusive parent from involving himself or herself in the child's school or education" (Mass Legal Help, 2011).

Children

Teachers and parents need to be aware of how domestic violence at home can affect a child in the school setting. A student may demonstrate the following:

- Always watch for danger or perceived danger
- Be unmotivated both in and out of class; appear depressed, powerless, or lethargic
- Become a "people-pleaser" or overachiever
- Be tense and fearful at drop-off or afraid to go to school
- Have attention or behavioral problems
- Challenge teacher's authority ("Domestic violence can affect your child at school" pamphlet)

Teachers/Schools

Children who have been exposed to domestic violence sometimes experience serious problems at school as a result. Abusive parents sometimes try to interfere with their children's safety at school, their education, and with the ability of custodial parents to support their children's education (Mass Legal Help, 2011).

Mandatory reporting of child abuse or neglect is a legal requirement of all teachers and professionals working with children (and others depending on the state statute) under the Child Abuse Prevention and Treatment Act of 1974 (Smith, 2006). As with students who live in violent communities, it is important that your classroom be a safe haven for children who have experienced domestic violence, with a secure, predictable routine and a sense of cooperation among peers. Schools need to collaborate with parents who have restraining orders and help them meet the safety needs of themselves and their children.

- Meet with the parent who has a restraining order and review each of the terms of the order with the parent so that the meaning of each term is mutually understood.
- Place a copy of the order in the student's school record.
- Provide copies of the key school personnel who may have contact with the abusive parent.
- Note the expiration date of the order.
- Have a conversation with the parent about whether he has any particular safety-related requirements for methods of communication between school personnel and him.
- Have a conversation with the parent about her plans concerning extending the order when it is set to expire.
- Have a conversation with the parent about how, within the terms of the order, the school can best support the order being obeyed.
- Discuss with the parent whether and how school personnel should communicate with him about violations of the order.
- Discuss and implement a secure means for communicating the information developed in these conversations to key school personnel.
- Make school personnel who have regular or frequent contact with the parent or child available to the parent, at the parent's request, to discuss the terms of the restraining order and the child's safety needs.
- Develop and implement a policy whereby key school personnel inform the principal
  - if a student or the student's parent has a restraining order,
  - if they are contacted by the abusive parent, or
  - if they observe the abusive parent in or near the school.
- Develop and implement a policy whereby, at the parent's request, a dated note is placed in the student's record indicating that the parent wishes to be informed if the abusive parent contacts the school or comes into or near the school.
- Review the school directory information with the parent, and inform the parent that the directory information can be released without her prior consent; offer her the opportunity to request that the information not be released without her prior consent, and honor requests not to release directory information.
- Honor a parent's request not to release directory information (Mass Legal Help, 2011).

Immigrants

Recent immigrants to the United States may be fearful of reporting incidents of domestic violence. They may wonder if they will be deported if they call the police or get a protection order or if their husband or intimate partner might be deported or arrested.

Immigrants can be more vulnerable to abuse and violence for the sole fact of being immigrants. This vulnerability increases even more when the person is undocumented. The fear of deportation is a constant factor that limits them in reporting that abuse or violence to the authorities. (WomensLaw.org, 2008, para. 4)

Your role as the teacher is not to end family violence, investigate claims, or recommend a student's removal from the family. School social workers or other advocates are trained to assist families in nonjudgmental ways (Kearney, 1999). Your role is to provide the underlying support for the student's cognitive, social, and emotional development and academic success in the midst of the stressful living situation. Your role is to also be an advocate for your students and families by helping establish supportive school practices, such as support groups for children affected by community or domestic violence (Kearney, 1999), as well as community supports, such as shelters for adults and children fleeing domestic violence.

THE EDUCATOR'S ROLE AFTER REPORTING OCCURS

Teachers are often nervous about what actions to take with children and families once an abuse or neglect report has been filed. One important area to consider is the classroom environment. Although you will have little control over your students' home environments, you can work to provide a safe, secure, warm, and inviting classroom and school environment for children. Another factor within your control will be your school curriculum. For example, when your classroom activities and teaching practices stress communication and conflict management, you can encourage children to break the cycle of abuse (Bancroft, 1997). You can also help students learn how to set boundaries and gain respect, as victimized children may not have learned how to say no or understand the concept of personal space (Blume, 1990). It is also important for you to "believe the child is not to blame for the abuse, and [understand] there is nothing the child can do to prevent or stop the abuse" (Blume, 1990, p. 86). In addition, schools can provide for the physical needs of a child, including clothing through the school nurse or establishment of a clothing closet, availability of snacks, and showers through the physical education department (Bancroft, 1997).

Finally, it is vital that you respect the confidentiality necessary to deal with situations of abuse and neglect and that children understand their privacy will be respected. Although you are ethically and legally bound to report abuse and neglect to CPS, the information should not be shared with anyone other than those directly involved with the child's education (Gullatt & Stockton, 2000).

Children in abusive or neglectful situations need safe, secure, and nurturing classroom and school environments.

ACTIVITY 8.7

A new school principal assumes the helm of a school known for its high teacher turnover. Realizing many of his teachers are unsure about mandatory reporting laws and have never been exposed to child abuse or neglect to the extent apparent in his school, he sees the necessity of providing training in this area. He also decides to establish a multidisciplinary crisis team consisting of teachers, the school nurse, the school psychologist, community members, and social workers. However, by midschool year, no workshops have been scheduled, and the crisis team has not been able to meet consistently. How do you think the confusion among the faculty about the process for reporting abuse/neglect may negatively affect the school? How can it be remedied?

THE ROLE OF THE SCHOOL ADMINISTRATOR

Working with abused children must be a collaborative process, between the family and the school, in which people plan and carry out goals together with the clearly stated intent of improving the life of a child. The school administrator should initiate the development of procedures and training programs and work with the community to provide information about the crime of child abuse. Your school should have written procedures, developed by a multidisciplinary team, that provide support to you in your role as a mandatory reporter of abuse and neglect. Information to include in the school policy follows:

- Definition of child abuse and neglect
- Explanation of mandatory reporting laws
- Steps to be followed in reporting
- Signs of abuse and neglect—red flags
- A list of child welfare contacts

In addition, administrators should suggest a school staff member be present during an interview by the social service agency. Finally, it is important that administrators are involved with community child-abuse committees and review school-community practices, such as fundraising activities, that might place children at risk (McClare, 1990).

CORPORAL PUNISHMENT IN SCHOOLS

A final comment relating to child abuse is about the use of corporal punishment in schools. As noted earlier, corporal punishment, or spanking, is a discipline practice common to many cultural groups and, as such, may be a socially acceptable form of discipline for use by educators in certain communities. Families may even request that teachers or administrators spank their children when they misbehave, creating a dilemma for educators who do not believe in the use of corporal punishment. Typically, corporal punishment is more often found in rural, southern areas. For example, a U.S. Department of Education report on the use of corporal punishment in U.S. schools in the 2005–2006 school year found that the highest incidence of corporal punishment occurred in Mississippi and Arkansas, where 7.5% and 4.7% of the total number of students enrolled were hit as a form of discipline. Alabama, Oklahoma, and Louisiana rounded out the top five states in the use of corporal punishment. Almost 40% of all corporal punishment cases in U.S. public schools occurred in Mississippi and Texas. Currently, 19 states permit corporal punishment (Center for Effective Discipline, 2010). Although there has been a steady downward trend in the use of corporal punishment, it continues to be accepted and even requested by parents or administrators. As one Fort Worth, Texas, middle school administrator stated, "I'm a big fan. I know it can be abused. But if used properly, along with other punishments, a few pops can help turn a school around. It's had a huge effect here" (Hyman, 2006, para. 2).

A disturbing fact about corporal punishment is the increased incidence of physical punishment for African American children. During the 2005–2006 school year, African American children represented 17% of the population in public schools, yet they received 36% of the paddlings administered to children in the United States (Center for Effective Discipline, 2010). According to the U.S. Department of Education Office of Civil Rights, African American schoolchildren are disproportionately affected by corporal punishment. They are hit at twice the rate of other students, and in some large city school districts, they are hit at five times the rate of other children. In many of the largest cities where corporal punishment is allowed, African American students make up a majority of the school population. A proclamation opposing school corporal punishment spearheaded by Dr. Alvin Poussaint, Professor of Psychiatry at Harvard Medical School, and EPOCH-USA (End Physical Punishment of Children) was signed by numerous African American leaders, including Marion Wright Edelman and Julian Bond, urging "all school boards to ban corporal punishment and . . . state legislators in all states allowing its use to pass legislation ending school corporal punishment (Center for Effective Discipline, 2004). Organizations such as the American Academy of Pediatrics, National Association of School Psychologists, American Medical and Bar Associations, and National Education Association have come out in public opposition to corporal punishment.

As a teacher, you will need to seriously consider the detrimental effects of corporal punishment on students and whether to support a district's policy or parental request to administer corporal punishment. Viable alternatives to corporal punishment include emphasizing positive behaviors of students, setting realistic rules that are consistently enforced, crafting instruction that reaches all students, conferencing with students for planning acceptable behavior, calling parent-teacher conferences about student behavior, using school staff such as psychologists and counselors, or holding detention, in-school suspension, or Saturday school. The most effective way to deal with student misbehavior is through prevention strategies (Center for Effective Discipline, n.d.).

How should you respond when faced with the decision about whether to use corporal punishment? Questions you may ask include the following:

- Even if it is legal to use corporal punishment, is it ethical for me to strike someone else's child?
- How can I collaborate with families as partners in educating their child when they ask me to use spanking as a form of discipline?
- Am I being culturally disrespectful by refusing to use a practice common to the community and families?
- Will my administrator consider me weak disciplinarian if I don't use corporal punishment?

Perhaps the clearest guidance for teachers is offered in the National Association for the Education of Young Children's Code of Ethical Conduct and Statement of Commitment (2011, p. 3). This guideline to ethical practice states, "Above all, we shall not harm children. We shall not participate in practices that are emotionally damaging, physically harmful, disrespectful, degrading, dangerous, exploitative, or intimidating to children. This principle has precedence over all others in this Code."

SUMMARY

This chapter has examined a facet of teaching that educators hope never to face. However, when armed with information about the types and signs of child abuse or neglect and the role of the teacher in documenting, reporting, and working with abusive families, you will be better prepared to deal with the problem and make a difference in the lives of students in your classroom.

REFLECTION QUESTIONS

Reread the In the Classroom case study presented at the beginning of the chapter, and reflect on these questions:

1. Should Kate report this situation to anyone? If so, to whom?

2. What other school personnel and community members should be involved in this situation? What school and community resources are available for Kate in working with Travis? What resources are available for Travis and his family?

3. Should Kate communicate her concerns directly to Travis's mother? If so, what communication strategies would be best? How can she be supportive of Travis's mother while also protecting Travis's interests?

WEBSITES

American Bar Association's Commission on Domestic and Sexual Violence, **http://www.americanbar.org/groups/domestic_violence.html.**

This website contains state-specific domestic violence information, downloadable publications in six languages (e.g., English, Spanish, Chinese, Japanese, Korean, and Vietnamese), domestic violence safety tips for you and your family, 10 myths about custody and domestic violence and how to counter them, and a listing of attorneys specializing in domestic law.

Futures Without Violence, **www.futureswithoutviolence.org.**

Instrumental in developing the landmark Violence Against Women Act passed by Congress in 1994, Futures Without Violence has continued to break new ground by reaching out to address violence prevention.

National Child Traumatic Stress Network: **http://www.nctsnet.org/resources/audiences/school-pesonnel/trauma-toolkit.**

Numerous resources are available to use when working with traumatized children, including a toolkit of fact sheets for educators and parents and a DVD on students and trauma.

National Council on Child Abuse and Family Violence (NCCAFV), **www.nccafv.org.**

Founded in 1984, NCCAFV provides intergenerational violence prevention services by bringing together community and national stakeholders, professionals, and volunteers to prevent domestic violence (spouse/partner abuse) and child abuse.

YWCA, **www.ywca.org.**

The YWCA is an organization that provides safe places for women and children and conducts programs that empower women, advocate for women's rights and civil rights in Congress, and promote racial justice.

STUDENT STUDY SITE

Log on to the student study site at **www.sagepub.com/grant2e** for additional study tools, including the following:

- eFlashcards
- Web quizzes
- Web resources
- Learning objectives

SECTION III

Family Engagement

Putting Knowledge and Skills Into Action

Now that you are armed with the knowledge, skills, the commitment to culturally responsive family engagement, and have a better understanding of your many roles in supporting families, the final section of this text will help you put your ideas into practice. Practical suggestions for how to plan for culturally responsive family engagement in your classroom, and beyond that in the larger school setting, will be given in Section III. Chapter 9 discusses a classroom volunteer program, collaboration with families on issues such as homework, academic and behavior challenges, as well as helping families understand contemporary standards-based curriculum. Chapter 10 continues the discussion by focusing on one of the most important aspects of family involvement: communication. Chapter 11 will help you understand the special skills and knowledge needed when supporting and partnering with families of children with exceptional needs. Chapter 12 discusses your role as a resource for families, in particular through asset-based practice, advocacy, helping family members become decision makers and leaders in their child's education, and the use of community resources. Chapter 13 concludes the text with a discussion of schoolwide family-engagement practices, such as family events, a family resource center, and school volunteers. This final section completes the journey that you've taken in understanding, appreciating, and supporting families to putting your commitment, knowledge, and skills about family engagement into action.

Chapter 9

Engaging Families in Their Children's Learning at School and Home

One of the best-kept secrets in Washington is that families are educators' most powerful allies.

—Theodora Ooms (Ooms & Hara, 1991)

As the preceding chapters have noted, a sound understanding and appreciation of families is vital for effective family engagement practices. Now, it is time to examine how you can apply your knowledge about families to your classroom practices. In this chapter, you will learn how to engage your students' families in their children's learning and development. Some questions to consider as you learn about this task include the following:

- What should you consider when collaborating with families on academic learning and development? What are barriers to having a full partnership with families?
- How can you help families understand highly technical educational terminology in this standards-based era?
- How can you effectively collaborate with all families on classroom behavioral concerns?
- How can classroom volunteers support students' learning and development?
- What are appropriate homework or interactive home learning activities for children of different ages?

IN THE CLASSROOM: HOMEWORK AND MORE HOMEWORK

Reggie Turner was one of the few male teachers at Kennedy Elementary in Poplar Grove. He was known both for having firm control over his fourth-grade students and for making learning fun. His class regularly conducted scientific experiments, such as testing the properties of the local river water or experimenting with different types of soil for growing plants in the garden behind the school. The class took field trips to the local courthouse, where on one occasion they participated in a mock trial; and recently, they went to the bowling alley, where they not only learned how to bowl but also sharpened their math skills while keeping their score. Mr. Turner had been an athlete in college, and his students clamored for him to play basketball with them at recess, which he only consented to do if they all made A's on a test. He was one of the most popular teachers at Kennedy Elementary, and families often requested that he be their child's teacher.

Mr. Turner was also known for giving homework—lots of homework. His homework assignments were designed to give his students more practice in the skills and concepts they were learning, such as the math worksheet on long division he had given the previous day. He also assigned projects for students to complete over time because he believed that it helped them develop critical-thinking skills as well as a sense of responsibility, which they would need when they went to middle school next year. He knew that the projects were a lot of work, and at his back-to-school meeting with families, he had stressed the importance of their helping their children with homework. He remembered his mom sitting at the table with him, making sure his homework and projects got done, and he knew he owed much of his academic success to her. He didn't have much patience with families who didn't take time to make sure their child's homework got done.

Currently, his class was working on a social studies project relating to their community's history and heritage. His students were researching their family history and relating it to what they had learned about Poplar Grove's history. It was one of his favorite projects because it required his students to interview family and community members, and it helped him learn more about his students and their families. The students had three weeks to complete the project, and he was looking forward to their presentations on Friday.

Shaina stared at the pile of books and the blank poster board in frustration. She had math problems to do, review questions from her science chapter to answer, and her family history poster to make. She didn't know how she was going to get it all done. Her mom's rule about "no TV until homework is done" meant that she rarely watched TV on weeknights. "It just isn't fair," she thought. She considered asking her mom to help, but knew she was busy helping Tyler. Ever since that meeting with Tyler's teacher, her mom spent all her time at night helping him, leaving Shaina to clean up the dishes and try to get Ella to bed. Sometimes she wished that she could live with her dad and Janet. It was a lot more fun at their house, and they let her talk on the phone with her friends as much as she wanted. She wondered if she should put Janet on her family poster, but she knew it would probably make her mom mad if she did. Mr. Turner had told them to put the important people in their family on it and to tell about the history of their family. They were supposed to interview their grandparents, but her mom's parents were both dead, and her dad's mom and dad were divorced and lived out of state. She hadn't seen them since she was six. "Maybe I'll just make something up," she thought, as she got out her math worksheet and started on the problems.

COLLABORATING WITH FAMILIES ON ACADEMIC LEARNING AND DEVELOPMENT

Parent involvement appears to account for between 10 and 20% of the variance in a student's achievement, and parent expectations of their child's success in school consistently have the strongest relationship with achievement.

—Thorkildsen and Scott Stein (1998)

The recognition that families and communities shape students' learning and development is the cornerstone of family engagement practices. In establishing productive relationships with parents or caregivers, successful teachers first consider the needs and beliefs of the family when planning family engagement activities. That is, they take a family-centered approach, as opposed to a school-centered approach (one based on the school or teachers' needs), in their planning (Foster & Loven, 1992). Think about which approach the teacher took in the following case:

Second grader Cicely Reid was excited to start school again in the fall. Although she had struggled with reading comprehension during first grade and was placed in the remedial one-on-one Reading Recovery program for 30 minutes, three times a week, she did not receive these intensive services until after Christmas. When her first-grade teacher called her parents to set up a meeting to discuss placing Cicely in Reading Recovery, they were surprised and dismayed to hear this. During the meeting, they said they didn't understand Cicely's reading problems, as they had bought books for her to have at home. They stated they wanted her to do well in school and someday to go to college because that was some-thing they had not had the opportunity to do. The teacher complimented them on realizing the importance of having books in the home, and asked more about their reading habits, such as whether they read and re-read the books with her. The parents described, some-what defensively, how Cicely often looked at books at night while they watched television after dinner. The teacher went on to explain the importance of actually reading the books with Cicely, identifying the reading skills she needed help with, and gave the parents a sheet of home activities to increase reading interest and motivation. Cicely's parents admit-ted they didn't realize that reading and re-reading books aloud was that important. They described their busy work schedules and hectic nights with taking care of Cicely and her younger siblings and how their television viewing was a chance for them to relax together for a few minutes. The teacher listened attentively and empathized with them about the difficulties of two working parents with small children. Together, the teacher and parents came up with a plan for one of them to try to listen to Cicely read books sent home by her reading teacher for 20 minutes a night after her younger siblings were put to bed. The teacher promised to send regular updates on Cicely's reading progress and offer further suggestions or guidance. They also agreed to meet again at the end of the school year to share their observations about her reading abilities and discuss some fun summer reading activities. By the end of summer, Cicely's reading skills had greatly improved, and more important, her bonds with her parents were strengthened by the special times she spent reading with one of them each night.

At first, the teacher may have been quick to judge these parents as uninvolved and uncaring, but further dialogue helped her better understand the parents and Cicely's home life. Think about these questions:

- What family strengths did Cicely's parents demonstrate? Did the teacher exhibit respect for the parents' ideas and roles as Cicely's first and most influential teachers?
- What incongruities appeared to exist between the teacher's idea of reading and book usage and the parents' idea of the act of reading? What did the teacher do to help overcome these differences?

- Is there anything that this teacher or Cicely's kindergarten teacher could have done differently to help prevent her reading difficulties before this meeting with her parents?
- How was the teacher able to support the parents in their willingness to work with their child at home? Was the **home-school connection** enhanced or hurt by this meeting?

Although not all interactions with families will have a positive result, as in this situation, there are lessons to be learned from it. First, it is important not to assume that all parents understand what occurs at each grade level or the academic requirements of a particular classroom. Second, it is also important to suspend judgment while you learn more about families. Third, although you should be prepared with suggestions for help, it is also important to listen to families' ideas and work together with them on a plan for their child's learning. Finally, you should also take notes, or **annotate with purpose** (the act of taking notes during parental meetings and using those notes to reflect on enhanced student learning), during conversations with parents to later reflect on ways to enhance your student's learning. These notes will provide you with a window through which the student's home learning can be viewed.

Some of the problems with Cicely's reading might have been avoided if her kindergarten and first-grade teachers had made more efforts to share information with her parents about **family literacy practices**, or the practical things families can do at home that embed reading, writing, and viewing (as well as other domains) into daily life as critical components in the quest for higher literacy. Part of collaborating with families is to share information with them about topics such as these:

- The school's educational mission and philosophy
- Your personal teaching philosophy
- Classroom expectations for academic success
- The everyday academic schedule of the classroom and the supplies students will need to have
- In-school resources that can help students who struggle academically
- Developmental stages common to children at the specific grade level
- Academic concepts, skills, and subjects children will be learning at the specific grade level
- How family members can help their children at home—for example, doing interactive home learning activities together
- How to assess children's progress in both strengths and challenges (Gregg, 1996)

Cicely's teachers also failed to focus with her family on **transfer of learning** activities, or the application of the reading skills she learned at school to at-home learning activities. For example, her teachers could have made suggestions for home reading activities beyond sharing books, such as reading recipes together while preparing dinner. Woolfolk (2001) suggests inviting parents for an evening of "strategy learning" in which students teach family members a reading strategy they have learned in class. She also suggests that teachers ask family members to include children in at-home projects that require math skills, such as estimation, measurement, and reading word problems. When you create small, family-friendly settings during class meetings, potluck dinners, parent-teacher conferences, or family breakfasts, families may feel more open to discuss the ways in which they interact with their children at home. They may listen more willingly to suggestions about ways in which they can support their child's learning and development (Henderson & Mapp, 2002).

Barriers to Collaboration

Although it is unclear from the short scenario why Cicely's parents had not spent time reading with her, one reason some families may not help their children is a lack of confidence in their ability to make a positive difference in their child's education. A **sense of efficacy,** or feeling of competence in helping one's child succeed in school, is an important factor in successful home-school collaborations (Hoover-Dempsey & Sandler, 1997). This sense of efficacy is also important for teachers; teachers may be hesitant to encourage family engagement in the classroom for fear of being judged or criticized. Family members' lack of engagement may also be influenced by their experiences as children and by whether their families were extensively involved in school and in home-based learning activities (Mapp, 2003).

As noted in Chapter 1, there are many other barriers to family partnerships from the perspective of teachers and families. Figure 9.1 summarizes some of these common barriers.

FIGURE 9.1a   Family Barriers Affecting Engagement in Children's Classroom Learning

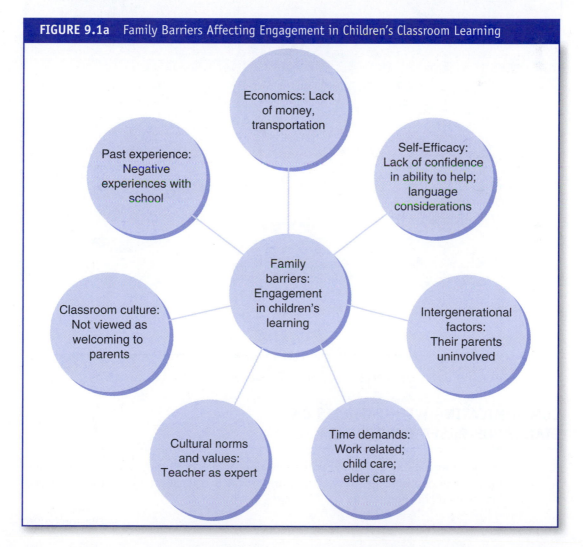

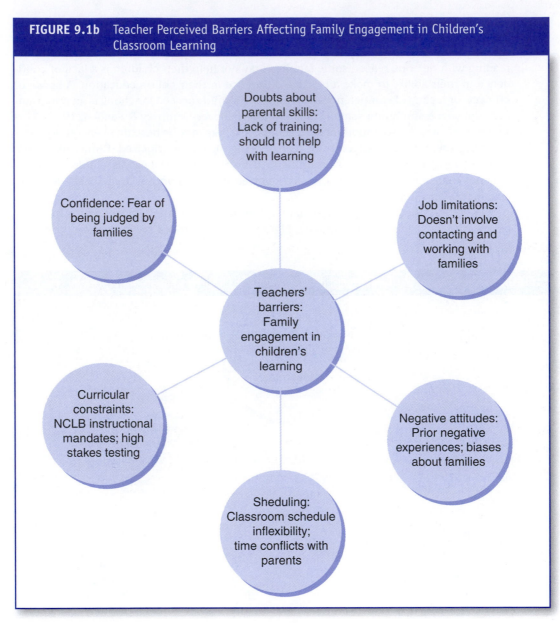

FIGURE 9.1b Teacher Perceived Barriers Affecting Family Engagement in Children's Classroom Learning

Sources: Gonzalez-Dehass & Willems, 2003; Mapp, 2003; Trumbull, Rithstein-Fisch, & Hernandez, 2003.

COMMUNICATING WITH FAMILIES ON STANDARDS-BASED CURRICULUM

Many times parents do not know the questions to ask or, if they know the questions, may not understand the answers that are provided. Education has its own language, just as medicine and law do.

—Tileston (2006)

In the current atmosphere of high-stakes testing and standards-based curriculum, anxious parents have every right to be confused by the complex issues involved in setting educational standards and assessing student performance. The terminology itself may appear highly technical and disconnected from any educational experiences that parents have ever had. To compound this problem, newspaper and magazine articles regularly employ terms such as "state report cards," "differentiated instruction," "mastery," "subgroups," and "adequate yearly progress" (AYP) without defining them succinctly and clearly for readers. Table 9.1 provides a handout that may be given to families to explain unfamiliar terminology in everyday language.

Family and community members can also be asked to participate in developing standards and curriculum for the local school district. Schools that are committed to family input as they wrestle with standards-based changes often form a parent advisory group to help craft a curriculum. Although family or community members may not be curriculum experts, they can provide valuable input on how their children best learn and on the interests of their children. They can also help to tie curriculum content to community-based resources and culture. For example, educators worked with Native American parents and tribal elders to develop a **native-focused curriculum (**a curriculum developed in collaboration with tribal members that infuses in its daily lessons/units values important in Native American culture) in the Honor, Respect, and Responsibility (HR2) Grant Project in Box Elder, Montana. Teachers linked particular topics in the curriculum, such as character traits, with aspects of the local culture, such as beliefs about how a certain color may represent a particular quality, into their daily teaching. The HR2 project helped to break down long-standing barriers between the families in the community and the school district (Northwest Regional Educational Laboratory, 2007).

Families may also be confused by report cards, progress reports, or achievement test results that describe student's levels of academic performance based on the attainment of standards with terms such as "proficient," "meets standard," "moderately effective," or "partial evidence." For example, one parent complained in a local newspaper about a school's new report card:

> I am not interested in how my child compares to district or state standards. How does that relate to how my child is doing? . . . I am not interested in comparisons or vague terms like beginning to demonstrate, approaching, meeting, or exceeding district and state levels. Are we afraid to give an F if that's what the student has earned? (Southeast Missourian, 2010).

Guskey (2004) offers valuable advice for teachers working with parents to explain different levels of student performance based on learning goals or standards.

ACTIVITY 9.1

With a classmate, brainstorm how you might eliminate some barriers to family partnerships. For example, on the families' side, how could you overcome the barrier of your low-income families not having transportation to attend parent-teacher conferences? How could you work effectively with families who believe that their role is to raise their child and your role is to educate the child, and that you are not doing your job when you ask them to help their child with school work at home? On the teachers' side, how could you or your school strive to change negative attitudes toward families in the community? How could you eliminate the belief that some families are not capable or do not care about helping their child be successful in school?

TABLE 9.1   Key Terms in Standards-Based Curriculum and No Child Left Behind (NCLB) Legislation

Accountability: As a teacher, I am accountable for your child's learning and academic growth. Furthermore, this state sets academic standards for what your child should know and learn. Your child's academic achievement is measured in different ways throughout the year.

Achievement: This refers to the level of success on an academic task or assessment. As your child's teacher, I look for your child to show academic achievement in many ways during the school year.

Adequate yearly progress (AYP): Adequate yearly progress is the minimum level of academic improvement that our school strives to achieve each year. As a part of that effort, I have goals for each student's academic progress. In a larger way, school districts and states measure and determine AYP and work with schools based on those results.

Alignment: When I prepare to instruct students on new information, my lessons must cover specific concepts I plan to assess students on. I cannot test students on information I have not presented. What teachers teach is in accord with, or aligned with, what the curriculum says will be taught and what is assessed on official tests.

Assessment: As a teacher, I am responsible for measuring what students know based on specific learning goals by assessing how they are able to demonstrate new knowledge. As a parent, you are probably used to tests as the main type of assessment, but there are other types, including observing or watching children, using a checklist, or having them give a demonstration.

Benchmark: This is a standard for judging your child's performance. Some schools name benchmarks to tell what students should know by a particular stage of their schooling. For example, "By the end of sixth grade, students should be able to locate major cities and other important geographical features on each of the continents."

Criterion-referenced tests: In this type of test, children are tested against themselves to show the level at which they know what has been taught.

Differentiating instruction: As a teacher, I strive to provide for the range of student differences in the same classroom by using different learning materials, assigning different tasks, and using other activities, such as children learning in pairs or small groups.

Disaggregated data: In the school, test scores or other data are divided into various categories so that they can be compared. For example, schools may break down the information for the entire student population to determine how different groups of students compare with others.

High-stakes testing: This term refers to state and national testing that occurs in schools and that can determine school standing, according to whether schools have met yearly progress goals.

Highly effective teachers: The goal is for every classroom to have a highly effective teacher as demonstrated through teacher licensing, involvement in district professional development, and other methods.

Mastery: Our school strives to have all students master, or acquire a deep knowledge of each area of a subject before moving to the next level.

Public school choice: A provision of NCLB may allow parents to transfer their children to another public school if their state deems their school needs improvement.

Response to intervention: Our school is using this three-tiered approach to give immediate help to students who are struggling, rather than waiting and letting them fail. All children are in Tier 1, and some children may need small group or one-on-one help with a teacher for specific skills in Tiers 2 or 3.

School district report cards: Each school within a district receives a report card that provides families with specific information concerning the educational success of students in the school.

Standard: These are specific criteria (knowledge or skills) that our students are expected to learn and be able to do.

Standardized tests: These are tests developed by a commercial company to measure how well children perform as compared with others at the same age or grade level or relating to specific criteria.

Supplemental services: Outside tutoring or academic assistance for students that is provided if a school falls within a certain category of need. You can choose the appropriate services for your child from a list of approved providers.

Sources: Tileston, 2006; Association for Supervision and Curriculum Development, 2007; U.S. Department of Education; 2007.

1. *Be consistent in your grading practices and knowledgeable about the grading system:* Parents are used to letter grades as a basis for interpreting their child's progress. They may query you about the grade equivalent and ask questions such as "Does receiving a *proficient* translate to an A or a B, grade-wise?"

2. *Avoid language that compares students:* Parents should revise their perspective from "How is my child doing compared with others in the class?" to "How is my child performing in relation to the learning expectations at this level?" Help them understand how these expectations relate to grades.

3. *Be prepared to present student work samples at various performance levels:* Examples of student work at various levels, illustrating terms such as *beginning, novice, proficient, apprentice, distinguished, or exemplary,* should be displayed and explained to parents.

4. *Be prepared to illustrate other assessment concepts:* Indicators of what students are able to do (quality of work) can be confused with how often they do it (frequency of display). Parents might ask what frequency of display means; be prepared to provide examples to illustrate terms such as *rarely, occasionally, frequently,* and *consistently.* (p. 328)

A back-to-school night early in the school year can offer families an opportunity to explore standards-based curriculum and assessment issues with educators. Regular communication via newsletters, the class website, or personal conversations can help clarify any confusion families have about the standards-based approach.

COLLABORATING WITH FAMILIES ON CLASSROOM BEHAVIORAL CHALLENGES

> Parents who know their children's teachers and help with their homework and teach their kids right from wrong—these parents can make all the difference.
>
> —President Bill Clinton, State of the Union Address, 1994

Research has shown that when families get involved in their children's learning, children not only achieve more academically but are also more likely to be better behaved and have a positive attitude about school (Family Involvement Partnership for Learning, 1998). There are numerous ways to collaborate with families to improve children's classroom behavior. Ladson-Billings (1994) speaks of the importance of creating a **community of learners** (a family-like atmosphere in the classroom that values contributions that each student makes to the overall positive atmosphere of the classroom) (p. 69). Some teachers make discussions and activities about families a regular part of the curriculum. Inviting family members to be a part of the classroom community can help promote family pride as well as classroom cohesiveness and can lessen any alienation that some students may feel. Teachers can also hold class meetings in which students discuss issues relating to learning and behavior and work cooperatively to solve problems. Class meetings have been found to have a positive impact on children's interactions both at school and at home, especially when a family component, such as a parent survey, a student's journal entry, or a discussion of family, has been included in the meetings' agendas (Potter & Davis, 2003).

TABLE 9.2 Student Behavioral Survey

Global Questions: What are your goals for your child's education? How would you like to see your child interacting with other students in the classroom this year?

1. What strengths have you observed in your child at home in the area of behavior and getting along with others?

2. What concerns, if any, do you have about your child's behavior at home?

3. How does your child communicate with you or other adults in the home about frustrations she may be experiencing that may lead to misbehavior?

4. How does your child interact with other children in cooperative settings? Can you give me some examples of incidents that illustrate this?

5. What does the term *respect* mean to your child in the family setting? How does your child interact with siblings or extended family members?

6. How do you praise your child for exemplary behavior as a form of positive reinforcement?

7. What advice could you give me, as your child's teacher, concerning ways in which I could help reinforce positive behavior, communication skills, and goal-setting habits?

One example of a parent survey is the Student Behavioral Survey (Table 9.2), which can be modified to meet the particular needs of the families of students in your classroom. After this questionnaire has been filled in, teachers can have a discussion with families about behavioral concerns or specific behavioral incidents. The questionnaire could be given orally as a part of a parent-teacher conference, or it could be sent home to be returned after a specified period. When families and teachers team up to nurture children's competent classroom behavior, positive results are more likely to occur. An example of a Student Behavioral Survey can be found in Table 9.2.

Collaborating with families about their children's behavior may place teachers in the uncomfortable situation of discussing problem behaviors, which are naturally upsetting to parents. What steps should you consider when confronted with family members who are upset about their child's behavior in the classroom?

1. *Stay objective.* When families are upset, they may struggle to stay composed. You, too, may have trouble staying calm if accusations are leveled. Don't return the anger.

2. *Listen actively.* Allow the child's family to have their say. Try to see their point of view and reiterate it. For example, "I can see why that playground incident last Tuesday would have upset you." Pinpoint the event if possible to keep the conversation specific.

3. *Look for common ground.* If you aim to resolve the problem, you need to be willing to compromise. Taking the high ground and "winning" will stymie your efforts to forge effective partnerships with families. Mutually acceptable solutions can be agreed on. (Truby & Dollarhide, 2006)

As you collaborate with families about behavior, it is also important to implement culturally competent classroom management strategies, or strategies that take into account cultural diversity, in your classroom. Respecting students' cultural diversity is a critical component of effective classroom management (Weinstein, Tomlinson-Clarke, & Curran, 2004). Definitions of and expectations about correct behavior are culturally bound, and teachers of children from different cultural backgrounds may wrongly interpret students' actions. European American teachers generally expect students to listen quietly and then respond individually to a teacher's questions on his prompting. Students from cultures that value interpersonal harmony may be reluctant to compete against others during question and answer sessions. Such students may be seen as not fully participating in class activities (Weinstein et al., 2004). Other cultural groups may respond in ways that teachers with a lack of multicultural knowledge may deem inappropriate or disruptive. For example, students from cultures with more participatory and active styles of learning may be seen as being interruptive. Williams (2007) quotes one parent as saying,

> After a while, black kids want to let the teacher know that they know the answers, so they start shouting out the responses. When they do, the teachers say they're disruptive and need to be in self-contained classes. (p. 254)

Culturally responsive family engagement in the area of behavioral challenges means shared problem solving between teachers and families. Often teachers dictate solutions to families without ever asking for advice; but true collaboration means mutual decision making and a "posture of cultural reciprocity" (Harry, Kalyanpur, & Day, 1999, p. 251), with explicit dialogue with families about differing cultural values and practices in school and in the home. Teachers must never forget that children come to school influenced by their cultural socialization, which shapes their classroom demeanor and attitudes (Williams, 2007).

CLASSROOM VOLUNTEERS

One of the more traditional forms of engaging family members in their child's education has been as a classroom volunteer. By definition, a volunteer is someone who performs a task without pay. In the school setting, volunteers are typically thought of as individuals who come in during the school day and help in the classroom, library, or office, or as field trip chaperones. However, a **classroom volunteer** can have a much broader definition. The term can include not only those who assist during the school day but also those who support children's learning in any way, at any time (National Network of Partnership Schools, 2006). It can include not only parents but also extended family members, such as grandparents, and community members. Epstein et al. (2002) include volunteering among their "Keys to Successful Partnerships," noting benefits for students, families, and teachers. Student learning can increase with the extra assistance that a volunteer can provide, and students enjoy interacting with volunteers. Families gain confidence in their skills and have a better understanding of the educational process, and teachers are better able to give individual assistance to students with the volunteers' help (DeCusati & Johnson, 2004; National Network of Partnership Schools, 2006). Another important benefit is improved school-community relationships. One study found that volunteers had greater respect for teachers and administrators than they had before volunteering, were more interested in educational issues, and had a better understanding of how schools operate (Brent, 2000). As it is difficult for many family members to volunteer during the school day because of employment, transportation issues, language barriers, lack of confidence, or past negative experiences in the school setting, you should plan for opportunities to involve families not only during the school day but also outside the school day.

Variety of Roles for Volunteers

There are a variety of roles for volunteers to perform both inside and outside the school setting. One study found that the most common role of volunteers in the classroom setting is as tutor for individual or small groups of students. Being a field trip chaperone is another common volunteer task (Brent, 2000). The variety of roles for volunteers is as broad as a teacher's or a volunteer's creativity. For example, one kindergarten classroom volunteer, a stay-at-home mother with a preschool child, assisted weekly for two hours in her son's classroom, helping with clerical tasks, such as restocking the take-home learning kits, making classroom materials, and copying papers. While she was volunteering, her preschool daughter participated in the classroom activities along with her older kindergarten brother. As the year progressed and the mother became more comfortable in the room and with the children, she began helping them at their learning centers, such as assisting with a "green eggs and ham" cooking activity during Dr. Seuss week. By the end of the year, she was suggesting activities that she could do with the children, and she once brought in materials to help the children make kites for a spring unit. The volunteer role changed with time from teacher directed to a more equal partnership. Turner (2000) suggested these different tasks for volunteers who come to school:

- Read stories to children; listen to them read.
- Assist children one-on-one with tasks such as writing, art projects, or computer work.
- Do clerical tasks, such as copying or laminating materials, preparing bulletin boards, typing a class newsletter, or contacting families about upcoming school or classroom activities.
- Gather and/or prepare learning materials, such as learning center games, books on tape for a listening center, or bring library books to class.
- Work one-on-one with students with special needs, such as English language learners, students with learning problems, or gifted students.
- Share information about occupations or teach a skill or hobby to the children.

For those who cannot help during the school day, volunteers might be asked to make materials at home that can be used at school, such as a learning game.

Once family or community members are in the classroom, it is important to be welcoming and enthusiastic about their contributions of time and energy. One way to show your enthusiasm is to have a work area with an adult-sized chair set aside for classroom volunteers. You can be prepared for volunteers at any time by having a volunteer file with folders that are labeled with various tasks for volunteers to do (Inspiring Teachers, 2006). It is also important that you provide clear directions about tasks to be done and information about where materials are located. Monitor the volunteer to make sure there aren't any questions; if volunteers have to ask you repeatedly what to do and where materials are, they may not return (Craven, 2006). For example, if a volunteer is helping a group of children at a learning center, make sure that the volunteer has all needed materials and is comfortable with the activities and noise level of the children. It is also important that you make sure your students treat all volunteers with respect and courtesy and that you do not allow any misbehavior to continue when students are working with a volunteer. Giving the volunteer feedback afterward and checking to see if her experience was positive can ensure that volunteers return to the classroom. A way to make sure that volunteers will have a positive experience is to ask them what their interests, skills, and

Students enjoy interacting with volunteers, and family members can gain a better understanding of the curriculum through volunteering.

talents are in helping in the classroom. You should also use your insights into people as you plan volunteer activities. Giving a variety of tasks so that the job doesn't become boring may be helpful to one volunteer, while another may prefer the security and routine of doing the same tasks each visit. It is important to get to know your volunteers' likes and dislikes for classroom tasks. Finally, it is courteous to recognize volunteers for their time and efforts in some way, such as with a personal thank you note or recognition in your class newsletter. This recognition should include volunteers who help in any way, not just in the classroom.

HOMEWORK AND HOME LEARNING ACTIVITIES

> I didn't know how interested my son is in reading and learning new things until we played those games you sent home with him.
>
> —Parent's note to her son's kindergarten teacher (Barbour, 2010, p. 3)

The subject of homework, the amount assigned, and parental help with homework can easily become a hot-button issue in a classroom. Homework is generally defined as a "teacher-assigned task that students are expected to complete outside of school hours" (Barbour, 2010, p. 19). Research in the area of educational reform has debated whether assigning homework actually enhances student academic achievement; in fact, some schools have limited homework assignments or have banned them altogether. With the push for rigorous state academic standards in the 1990s, homework came back in vogue (Cooper, 2007). One study found that homework has increased in the lower elementary grades, with six- to eight-year-olds now spending more time on homework than in the past (Gill & Schlossman, 2004). Of first graders'

Age-appropriate home learning activities can reinforce the school curriculum.

parents, 38% reported their children did homework five or more times a week, increasing to 51% for fifth graders. Teachers in schools that served high-minority populations expected more homework than teachers in lower-minority schools (U.S. Department of Education, 2008). For many families of kindergarten or elementary students, homework sessions are severely exasperating and cause family strife and anxiety (Shumow, 2001). Yet nightly homework episodes do not have to be horrific!

Research has shown that homework has different benefits, depending on the age of the student. Homework is most effective for high school students and moderately effective for middle school students. Several studies found few or no benefits from some homework, such as preparation for tests for elementary-age children (Cooper, 2001). Although this does not mean that homework is not beneficial for younger children, it does mean that the goals of homework may be different for younger students than older ones. For example, homework may help students make the connection between what they are learning at school and their home, help them become more independent learners, develop responsibility, and give families an opportunity to see what their children are learning and to encourage their learning. It also means that the activities and time required for younger students may be different from those for older students.

Traditional homework assignments typically serve a variety of purposes and come in four basic types:

1. *Practice* homework that reinforces skills already introduced to help students move toward mastery

2. *Preparation* homework that introduces material presented in future lessons

3. *Extension* homework that applies skills already learned to new situations

4. *Integration* homework that applies many skills learned to a single task, such as a report or science project (U.S. Department of Education, 2003, p. 4)

However, a new approach to homework is emerging: **interactive home learning activities**, or homework assignments that are based upon real-life or authentic experiences and designed so families and children will have interactions relating to what they are learning. Much like parent-education, lecture-based meetings are being replaced by more participatory family events; traditional worksheet homework completed in isolation by students is being replaced by interactive home learning activities that families complete together, encouraging conversations about the assigned curriculum concepts. Barbour (2010) described the characteristics of interactive home learning activities:

- Assignments individualized to students' needs, such as reading books at the child's reading level
- Culturally relevant activities that link schoolwork to the home and real-life situations (e.g., discussing fractions in a recipe while cooking a meal)

- Family members, including siblings, participate in the activity, such as playing a game together
- All materials for activities supplied, with clear directions
- Student confidence built while completing activities, such as interviewing parents or sharing their ideas with family members
- Flexibility in choice of activities and time frame for completing activities

Table 9.3 gives examples of different types of interactive family home learning activities for different subject areas.

Table 9.3	Interactive Home Learning Activities Examples		
	Take-Home Kits	**Family Activities and Games**	**Family Projects**
Language and Literacy	Writing suitcase—variety of writing supplies and paper with suggestions for meaningful writing, such as grocery lists, letters, stories, notes, cards Book backpacks—books, puppets or stuffed animals, laminated pictures from story for sequencing or retelling story, discussion questions, journal	Scavenger hunt—look for items around the house that start or end with certain sounds, or items whose names rhyme Labels—child uses Post-it notes (provided by teacher) to make labels for items around house or adult makes label and child has to find the object; for English language learners, label items in both languages Hangman—play hangman and other word games together, using words on child's reading level	Class cookbook—each family chooses a favorite recipe and completes a recipe form, with child drawing of family meal time; recipes compiled into a book and copies made for each family to try out each other's recipes
Math	Telling time kit—clock with movable hands, stopwatch, hourglass, calendar, books relating to time, suggestions of time-telling activities	Cooking together—read and follow directions from a recipe or box mix, discuss fractions, measurements, (i.e. "how much is needed if we double the recipe?") Estimation jar—fill a clear container with items like macaroni, beans, cotton balls, have everyone guess amount and then count together to see who winner is	Family calendar—provide 12 monthly calendar pages for each family to mark family events, religious or cultural celebrations, and school activities; encourage children to draw pictures on the calendar How many—send home weekly items to count and tally how many are in home, such as, "How many wheels?"

(Continued)

TABLE 9.3   (Continued)

	Take-Home Kits	Family Activities and Games	Family Projects
Science	Magnets backpack—assorted magnets of varying strengths and items to test; chart to record results and draw conclusions	Weather watchers—record weather on form each day and discuss how it changes in seasons; draw and label pictures of different types of clouds Nature walk—scavenger hunt to find specific kinds of birds, trees, flowers	Mystery bag—parents help children choose a mystery object to place in bag, relating to science topics being studied; children write three clues about object for classmates to guess
Social Studies	Family history kit–timeline with major historic events marked, writing and drawing supplies, directions for completing by adding family special events	Neighborhood map—take a walk and then draw map of neighborhood; try different routes and add these to map Needs and wants—using newspaper sale ads (teacher provided) and a pretend amount of money to spend, child and family choose items to buy and discuss budgets, needs, and wants	Come visit my town—brainstorm all the good things about the community and create a travel brochure, billboard, or tourism commercial convincing someone to come and visit; include a map with tourism sites marked
Creative Arts	Music backpack—rhythm instruments, books like *My Family Plays Music* (Cox, 2003), activity sheet with ideas to experiment with different sounds, rhythms, patterns Self-portrait kit—multicultural crayons, markers, colored pencils, yarn, glue, drawing paper, mirror; family members look in mirror and draw self-portraits, then compare how everyone is similar and different Home Olympics gym bag—masking tape, bean bags, sidewalk chalk, plastic cups and tennis ball, laminated medals, list of home Olympic outdoor activities, such as 50-yard dash, long jump, bean bag toss or balance, hop scotch, cup bowling	Homemade play dough—using teacher-supplied recipe, create homemade play dough and use to create sculptures Water painting—use a paintbrush (teacher provided) and a bucket of water to paint house, building, sidewalk, fence, etc. Pictionary—create a family list of items to draw; divide into teams and see which team can guess the most objects being drawn Concerts—provide families with list of local free or inexpensive concerts in area to attend together Parks—provide families with list of parks in the area, with suggestions of activities to do together	All about my family—create a family book using templates provided for each page, such as "The People in My Family," "One Special Thing About My Family," and "This is What My Family Likes to Do." Family You've Got Talent show—everyone performs his or her best talent; children sing songs they learned at school; children dance to music family enjoys Copy cats—one person does a certain movement or skill, such as jumping on one foot, bouncing ball with left hand, shooting basketball, or dribbling soccer ball, and rest of family has to try and copy it; see who can come up with skill no one can copy

Source: Learning at Home PreK-3: Homework Activities That Engage Children and Families, Barbour (2010)

When planning your homework program, there are four keys to a successful home learning program:

- Age appropriate homework
- Individualized homework that meets each student's needs
- Communication with families about homework expectations
- Consideration of diverse family views about homework

Although all types of homework can be used with children of different ages, it is important that you choose age-appropriate activities for your students. Young children learn best through hands-on activities, so paper-and-pencil assignments that focus on drill or isolated skills may not be the most effective homework assignment for a kindergarten or first- or second-grade classroom. Younger students also benefit from being able to talk about what they're learning and get support from adults or older siblings. Interactive homework, such as the take home activities or "mobile learning centers" shown in Table 9.3 are effective with preschool and primary-grade children (Trahan & Lawler-Prince, 1999, p. 66). For older students, paper-and-pencil assignments may be more appropriate, although students of all ages will be more engaged in homework that is meaningful and interesting. Older students are also capable of planning and completing long-range homework assignments, such as a science fair project, a report on the community's history that includes interviews with older members of the community, or creating a book of favorite poetry.

The time required for homework should also be set based on the age of the children. According to what is often called the "10-minute rule," 10 minutes per grade level is adequate. This means that for kindergarten and first- and second-grade classrooms, homework should not last any longer than 10 to 20 minutes per day, while homework for third- through sixth-grade classrooms should not require students and families to work more than 30 to 60 minutes per day (Cooper, 2001). Homework requirements should also be flexible for busy families. For example, you may give a weekly homework packet that students complete during the week as the family's schedule permits. If homework assignments are a comprehensive project, consider breaking the project into manageable sections with benchmark due dates.

The second key to effective home learning activities is individualizing the requirements based on the students' needs. Today's classrooms differentiate instruction, based on individual needs, and homework should reflect this individualization. Families are frustrated when children have busywork or have to spend hours completing assignments that are too difficult for their children. If all students are to spend approximately the same time on homework, homework assignments may need to be modified for some children. For example, when sending practice math or spelling homework sheets home, it is appropriate to create a variety of levels and numbers of math problems or spelling words that reflect the student's needs. Homework does not have to be the same for each child.

Two-way communication between home and school concerning homework is also crucial. Although parents may be anxious to help with their child's learning, they may also be unsure about how to go about it and have concerns about the time required for homework assignments (Walker et al., 2004). Remember that homework affects family leisure time, work commitments, and family scheduling of afterschool activities. Make sure that you have an academically valid reason for giving homework. Be prepared for questions that families may pose about homework, particularly on these topics:

1. *Time concerns.* Should it be taking my child this long to complete the assigned homework? My child rushes through the nightly homework in 10 minutes; is this enough time? When my child says something is due in one week, shouldn't he be starting the work well before it comes due?

2. *Homework assistance.* Should I help my child with challenging assignments? Are we supposed to do this activity together? What should I do if I am asked for help and I don't understand how to solve the problem or answer the question? If I provide help with homework in some way, is that considered cheating on my child's part?

3. *Record keeping.* Should my child be keeping a daily assignment notebook to keep track of homework? What if she leaves it at school and can't remember what was due? Is there another way to retrieve the assignment, such as a homework telephone hotline or website list? Should I check my child's assignment notebook daily to ensure homework is completed?

4. *Grading homework.* How do you grade homework? What percentage of the total subject grade is part of the homework? If my child is absent and unable to complete the homework, what is the grading policy then? Are make-up homework assignments given if my child completely misses the point of the homework? Do you formally grade every assignment; if not, how do you manage feedback?

One way to assure that families see their children's homework is to require a signature on it. However, a parent signature gives you little meaningful information from the families. Instead, consider using a standard form that allows families to give you feedback on how their child did on the homework, such as the example from the Teachers Involve Parents in Schoolwork (TIPS) program math homework template in Figure 9.2. The form invites conversation with families about the homework and offers them an opportunity to give you regular feedback on their child's success with home learning activities.

FIGURE 9.2   Homework Signature Form

Dear Family,

Please give me your reactions to your child's work on this activity by checking one of the following:

_____ 1. OK. My child seems to understand this skill.

_____ 2. PLEASE CHECK. My child needed some help on this, but seems to understand this skill.

_____ 3. PLEASE HELP. My child still needs instruction on this skill.

_____ 4. PLEASE NOTE (other comments).

_____

_____

_____

Signature_____Date_____

Source: National Network of Partnership Schools, TIPS Math—Elementary (2006)

The part you expect families to play in your students' homework activity should be reviewed at the beginning of the year. You should elicit collaborative ideas from them. An open house or group parent meeting can give you a chance to discuss home learning activities, answer questions, and get feedback from families about your suggestions for activities that would meet the needs of individual students (Trahan & Lawler-Prince, 1999). You can model or role-play some homework situations that may prove sticky, and you can share homework tips, as well as ask other parents to share suggestions for completing homework successfully.

Don't assume that families know about homework hotlines, spelling lists, writing portfolios, or the participatory nature of interactive home learning activities. Explain and demonstrate everything! Discuss reasonable time expectations for homework completion. Explain when parents should sound the alarm if they think their child is spending too much time on certain tasks. You will also want to send the information home in written form for those families who didn't attend the open house or parent meeting. It is helpful to send ongoing information about home learning activities as a part of your class or school newsletter or other written communication.

Finally, it is important that you recognize and honor that diverse families may respond to home learning activities differently. Past studies have found that Chinese American parents considered the amount of U.S. school homework to be insufficient to boost the academic performance of their children. However, a recent survey of Chinese American parents' attitudes about the amount of homework their children were given indicated that they felt it was appropriate (Li, 2006). Delgado Gaitan (2004) stated, "Homework is not an equal opportunity activity" for all students (p. 47). Although Latino parents routinely express high expectations for their children in the area of homework completion, those who have less experience with school or speak limited English may find themselves isolated from school in helping with homework yet hesitant to contact the teacher; or they may try to assist their children but supply the wrong answers. Some suggestions for improving homework practices with Latino or other non-English-speaking families include the following:

- Organize a public announcement with Spanish radio stations that suggests ways for families to help children with homework.
- Set up a bilingual hotline number that families can call to get advice on helping their children at home.
- Develop individual contracts with families and students, with all three of you agreeing on homework responsibilities. Consider recommending study groups as a form of homework support.
- Open a bilingual homework center along with offering workshops for families and students. (Delgado Gaitan, 2004)

Although non-English-speaking families may be hesitant to contact teachers about homework issues, one study found that low-income African American mothers often used homework as an impetus for contacting the teacher or stopping by school. These parents also monitored their children's progress closely, and they provided routines and structures for homework completion. The researchers found that parents worked hard. As one mother said,

Just getting over the hurdle with this new math about how to make sure that I'm learning it so I can teach it to her and make sure I'm doing it with her right. So that was like the biggest hurdle with this new math. (Jackson & Remillard, 2005, p. 63)

How can teachers help families of students who have special needs with homework? Richards (2004) recommends that parents help their child assemble a homework survival kit at the beginning of the school year. This kit can contain materials necessary for effective studying, starting out with a large calendar for assignments. Richards suggests that parents model strategies, including preplanning, teaching their children to use **mnemonic devices** (tricks to help memorize something), and creating visual organizers to "pull in processing strengths while compensating for processing weaknesses" (p. 3). Motivational devices such as a reward spinner, a customized game spinner with each section listing a reward (e.g., earning five extra points toward the 20 points needed to go to the amusement park), can expedite the completion of homework. A timer can help parents to monitor children's time on task as well as to meet the expectations outlined on a homework contract. Using some of the previous suggestions of interactive family home learning activities that are highly motivating and individualized for students' needs can be especially beneficial for a student with special learning needs.

As a teacher, you can help your school establish an infrastructure to promote homework success. The organization of a homework club after school with tutors can support students who may not get homework help at night. Offering parent workshops on study skills and homework hints, along with a meal and child care, can encourage families to connect with homework activities. Organizing a schoolwide interactive home-learning program using similar forms, such as recommended by TIPS, can provide consistency across grade levels and be especially helpful for new teachers in developing interactive homework based on specific learning goals (The Center for School, Family, and Community Partnerships, 2001). District policies on homework can vary greatly, with some districts requiring a set amount of homework each week and others leaving it up to the individual teacher. If your district has a homework policy, it is important that families receive copies of the policy, with translation if necessary.

Here are some questions or comments from parents concerning homework. Based on what you've learned about effective home learning activities, how would you respond to these situations?

- You told us at the open house at the start of school that homework would average 20 minutes for each subject. There is no way! What is going on?
- Will there be homework on weekends? Tanya lives with her father on weekends, and it is difficult to check on her finishing it with him in control. I want to make sure she gets things done, but we don't communicate at all.
- Kasey spends so much time completing five addition problems. She has no time for the rest of her reading, science, or social studies homework. It is already past her bedtime. Is this normal?
- You never seem to send home stories that have children who are like Mia or our family. I don't think this is fair, and she doesn't seem to connect with the stories.
- Mario's father and I do not read English so well at this time. When he brings home reading homework and asks us to help him with a word, we have to check in the Spanish language dictionary for the English meaning and then try to draw a picture or somehow get the meaning across. It doesn't work well; how can we help him with homework? (Translated from Spanish)

- I am sick of teachers not knowing how to teach. All they give the kids to do is research papers. I have other things to do than take my child to the library.
- I try to help Sam with worksheets he brings home, but when I do, he gets angry and tells me I am showing him the wrong way to do it.
- Thanks for sending home the writing suitcase. Abby loved writing her grandmother a letter, but was very sad when she had to return it to school. When will she get it again?

Each of these questions represents a facet of homework that you'll want to consider when developing your home learning policies.

SUMMARY

In this chapter, you have learned about engaging families in the classroom. By recognizing families and communities as children's first and most influential teachers, you can collaborate effectively with them to support your students' learning and development through home learning activities. Your role as a teacher also involves helping families better understand the terminology and concepts of the current standards-based curriculum and collaborating with families to address students' behavioral challenges. Partnering with families also means actively seeking and providing a variety of opportunities for volunteers. Successful family engagement includes both understanding and appreciating families *and* implementing supportive classroom-family engagement practices.

REFLECTION QUESTIONS

Reread the In the Classroom case study presented at the beginning of the chapter and reflect on these questions:

1. Are Mr. Turner's homework practices family friendly? Why or why not?

2. Evaluate the appropriateness of the family history project. What are the advantages and disadvantages of a homework assignment like this? Who might have difficulty or be unable to complete this homework assignment?

3. What are appropriate examples of homework for different age students, such as kindergarten and first, second, third, and fourth grades?

WEBSITES

¡Colorín Colorado! http://www.colorincolorado.org/families/.

A bilingual site for teacher and families; the family section offers suggestions for families to help their child learn to read and succeed at school, as well as how to build strong parent-teacher relationships.

Parental Involvement: Title I, Part A, **www.ed.gov/programs/titleiparta/parentinvguid.doc.**

The purpose of this guidebook is to assist state education agencies, districts, and schools in administering the parental involvement provisions of Title I, Part A of the Elementary and Secondary Education Act (ESEA).

Parents Toolkit, **www.ed.gov/parents/landing.jhtml.**

This site, sponsored by the U.S. Department of Education, offers help in explaining the No Child Left Behind legislation to families, along with tips on monitoring homework and helping children learn to read, with a special toolkit for Hispanic families.

Teachers Involve Parents in Schoolwork (TIPS) Interactive Homework: **http://www.csos.jhu .edu/P2000/tips/index.htm.**

This site offers guidelines for interactive homework, with examples for language arts, math, science, and social studies, as well as blank templates to use for creating activity sheets.

STUDENT STUDY SITE

Log on to the student study site at **www.sagepub.com/grant2e** for additional study tools, including the following:

- eFlashcards
- Web quizzes
- Web resources
- Learning objectives

Chapter 10

Teacher as Family Communication Facilitator

Nevertheless, no school can work well for children if parents and teachers do not act in partnership on behalf of the children's best interests. Parents have every right to understand what is happening to their children at school, and teachers have the responsibility to share that information without prejudicial judgment. . . . Such communication, which can only be in a child's interest, is not possible without mutual trust between parent and teacher.

—Dorothy H. Cohen (1972)

As noted in previous chapters, it is important that school personnel have the necessary skills and knowledge to build collaborative, trusting relationships with families. A key factor in building such relationships is strong communication with families that is "frequent, personal, and consistent" (Powell, 1998, p. 65). As you think about your current communication skills, consider these questions:

- What are effective one-way and reciprocal methods of print communication with families?
- How can I have successful informal and formal conferences with families?
- What are active listening skills that I need to successfully communicate with families?
- What are some alternative ways I can reach all families, beyond traditional conferences?
- What documentation is important to keep when communicating with families?

Contributing Author Jeannine Studer

- How can I use technology as a communication tool?
- How can I communicate effectively with culturally diverse families and those who may not speak English well?
- What are barriers to effective communication between home and school?

PRINT COMMUNICATION: ONE WAY AND RECIPROCAL

Dear Families,

Thanks for all your help with our schoolwide food drive before Thanksgiving. Our class alone brought in 297 food items that were donated to the local food pantry! As a school, we collected 2,474 food items for families in our community who are in need this holiday season.

Thank you for your support!

Mr. Thompson

The first technique that responsive teachers often use in their communication efforts with families is one-way communication, such as weekly or monthly newsletters, other school informational handouts, or personal notes that require no return response from the family. These types of communication can convey much information in an efficient manner and keep families up-to-date on what is occurring in the classroom or school.

A newsletter may be the first document in your regular communication efforts. Creating a template for newsletters can save you time and make it easier to send out newsletters on a regular basis. Newsletters are more likely to be read if they are attractive with larger font, graphics, and interesting, short articles. Of course, it is crucial that newsletters and other print communication be free of grammatical and spelling errors. Remember, these newsletters may be displayed on someone's refrigerator!

Families enjoy seeing their child's name in print, so including positive information about children in your room regarding accomplishments, kind deeds, hard work on projects, or even samples of work, such as poetry or short stories, can increase interest in a newsletter. It is also important to acknowledge families who have supported the classroom in any way, and asking families to contribute to your newsletters with short articles on parenting or suggestions of fun family activities can also make your newsletter more interesting to all families. Examples of ideas for a class newsletter are in Table 10.1.

Another way to have ongoing communication with families is regular notes. Teachers often make the mistake of only sending notes home when there are problems, causing both students and families to dread notes from the teacher. Make an effort to send regular notes home, reporting positive things your students have done, in addition to notes that inform parents about their children's school day, such as if their child did not seem to be feeling well, got hurt, or was upset about something. Other forms of one-way communication include building or district newsletters, school handbooks, and school telephone information systems. Some schools use a 24-hour telephone information line that has deadlines and upcoming school events and activities; teachers may also have classroom homework hotlines that families can call for homework information. Obviously, it is crucial that these lines are updated regularly and out-of-date information deleted (Riggins, 2003).

TABLE 10.1 Suggestions for Class Newsletters Information

The teacher, students, and families can all contribute to a class newsletter.

Information written by the teacher could include the following:

- Current skills and concepts students are working on
- Suggestions of home activities to support classroom skills and concepts
- Calendar of events for classroom and school; upcoming activities, such as field trips
- Class news, such as getting a new student, class pet having babies, earning a class award for good lunchroom behavior
- Recognition of students for positive behavior and learning, such as kind deeds performed or hard work on projects
- Acknowledgment of any help provided by families, such as donating class supplies, helping with a school clean-up project, or volunteering for a field trip

Information written by students could include the following:

- Sample writing, such as poetry or short stories
- Sample art work, cartoons
- Student interviews of other students, school personnel
- Student quotes or conversations overheard in the classroom

Information written by family members could include the following:

- Parenting tips, such as how to motivate children to do homework or how to handle sibling rivalry
- Suggestions for family activities, such as fun, inexpensive day trips in the area

IN THE CLASSROOM: SPRING PARENT-TEACHER CONFERENCES

Kate placed the last folder on the stack with a sigh of satisfaction. Her student portfolios were all complete and ready for the spring parent-teacher conferences that would start on Monday. "I'm so much more ready this time than I was last fall," she thought. Kate remembered the uneasiness she had felt at the beginning of the school year about working with families and the sleepless night she had before her first parent-teacher conference. She had been prepared with what she wanted to tell her students' families and had even written out an outlined script of what to say at each conference. "I didn't let them get a word in edgewise," she thought ruefully, "I was so worried that they wouldn't think I was a competent teacher for their child." However, the conferences had gone well for the most part. Most families had attended, although three had not come for their conference, and one student's parents had come but had not been pleased at their son's reading grades and test scores. They had even hinted that Kate was not teaching him the necessary skills he needed to be a good reader. Since the conferences, she had worked to improve her communication with his parents, as well as all her other students' families. It had helped when all the second-grade teachers met, at the principal's request, and brainstormed

(Continued)

(Continued)

ways to have better communication. They sent a survey to the families of all the students asking them to indicate the best way to communicate with them, and since then, Kate had tried a few new methods. She had started sending out regular e-mails to the families that had e-mail addresses. With the help of the district's technology coordinator, she had also added an interactive link to her class website where families could e-mail her, and she was pleased that several parents, including a couple of noncustodial dads, were using that option to contact her. She had even made her first home visit, along with the school's social worker, to visit Travis's grandmother, who was now caring for him and his brother and sister after Child Protective Services had taken them out of their home because of their mother's neglect. Since last fall, Kate had learned much about building relationships and communicating with her students' families and felt more confident in her abilities.

Kate's first conference on Monday after school was with Travis's grandmother. His grandmother came straight from her job as a home health aide and was obviously tired when she walked in. Before Kate had time to thank her for coming in, she pulled out a letter that Kate had sent home with suggestions for home math activities and said, "Can you just tell me what this means? I don't know what skip counting or math arrays are. I don't see how giving Travis egg cartons to play with is going to help him learn math. I never had anything like that when I was in school, and I think he should be learning his math facts. I don't have time for this kind of foolish stuff, with three kids to take care of now."

She glared at Kate, obviously waiting for an answer.

The media and community businesses can also provide a means for communication with families. Radio or public access television shows can inform families and the community about the school events, and a regular newspaper column about a school can feature student writing, awards, and other positive news. Posting notices in frequently shopped stores, such as grocery or discount stores, can be another way to inform families about school and classroom news (Stevens & Tollafield, 2003).

Although all these examples of one-way communication, including newsletters, can inform families about your school and classroom, they will not help you build strong relationships with families. You must also include two-way communication or reciprocal communication in your teaching repertoire for teaching to be truly effective. In this kind of communication, teacher and families equally share information, ask questions, and express opinions. One of the standards of the National PTA for promoting family involvement in schools states that schools should have "regular, two-way, meaningful communication between home and school" (PTA Issues Standards for Parent Involvement in Education, 1997, p. 16). Newsletters do not allow for this responsive communication. However, newsletters and notes can become forms of two-way communication by adding questions, short surveys, or a space for comments, with encouragement for families to return these to you. Teachers often use a folder system, such as "Friday folders," which are sent home at the end of the week with information about what happened in class that week, student work samples, suggested home activities, and a place for parents to write comments to return. Families know to look for the folder and that a reply is expected. One teacher described her version of reciprocal print communication:

I use a "Good News Notebook" as one way to communicate with parents. This notebook goes back and forth each day to home/school. I write a weekly letter telling the parents what the classroom theme is and activities their child will be involved in that particular week, and usually give a family activity suggestion and put it in the notebook. I also include other information such as monthly calendars. The other component of the notebook is a place the parents write a comment or two regarding their child's evening at home. They say something POSITIVE about their child. During circle time each day, I take turns calling each child up to me and together we read what their parent has written. It gives me an opportunity to know the family better, and also to use the notebook as a language activity with the child. After we read the notebook, all the children clap for that child. Reading the notebooks are a favorite part of the day. (D. Childers, personal communication, June 28, 2007)

When creating print communication, it is important to consider the unique needs of the families of your students.

- For example, how will you communicate in print with a parent who does not read or is blind?
- What about families who do not speak English?

Communicating with *all* families may require extra effort and creative solutions, such as the school that bought a Braille machine and sent all communication in Braille home to a blind parent, or the teacher who made arrangements with the neighbor of an illiterate parent to read all school communication to her. If any of your families have limited English-reading or English-speaking abilities, then it is important that they receive communication in their native language. Many websites, such as Babel Fish (www.world.altavista.com), now provide translation of print sources in many other languages, although you should always be cautious about the literal translations of your print and not rely on that as your sole source of communication. Communication in print on school and classroom websites should also provide translation for families who do not speak English. For example, at Bayless Intermediate School in St. Louis, Missouri, 46% of the students are immigrants with 11 different languages spoken. On the school district's website, a link to literal translation of the website in Spanish, French, Korean, Chinese, German, Italian, Portuguese, and Japanese is offered (Bayless School District, 2008).

One way for you to learn more about successful print communication strategies is to query another educator. Interview questions might include:

- How do you communicate with your students' families?
- How do you ensure that written information gets home to families?
- What are examples of one-way and reciprocal communication that you use with families?

Also ask for samples of notes, newsletters, and other forms of personal communication with families. If the teacher has a class Web page, ask how it is used as a communication tool. Beyond this interview, continue to collect samples of different newsletters, surveys, forms, and other print communication used by other teachers. These samples can serve as an excellent resource for your classroom.

RECIPROCAL COMMUNICATION: INFORMAL AND FORMAL CONFERENCES

> After a long day at work, she rushed across town, wove her way through corridors, located the room, signed in, and waited nervously for 30 minutes. On entering the room alone and approaching the waiting group at the conference table, she felt apprehensive, overwhelmed, and outnumbered. A newcomer in an unfamiliar situation, feeling small and on trial, she sat down at the table for the conference and held her breath.
>
> —Stevens and Tollafield (2003, p. 521)

One of the most common methods of connecting the family with the school are the routine, regularly scheduled parent/guardian and teacher conferences that are conducted during the academic year (Minke & Anderson, 2003). Yet this approach is based on a model that dates from a time when the traditional family structure consisted of a father who worked to support the family and a mother who stayed at home. Despite vast changes in family structures, school conference models have unfortunately not transformed. A study by Hirsch and Altman (1986) revealed that approximately 42% of the families surveyed were dissatisfied with educational conferences and approached them with trepidation. Surprisingly, even though teachers did acknowledge the positive outcomes when families and teachers communicate, they also reported that these conferences created some of the greatest occupation-related stress, with conferences disliked as much by teachers as parents (Huber, 2003; Stevens & Tollafield, 2003). Not only did first-year teachers express anxiety but experienced teachers also experienced stress, particularly when their decisions were questioned (Simmons, 2002).

The good news is that conferencing with families does not have to be stressful or painful for either teachers or families when teachers employ techniques designed to build a relationship. The first step is to not wait until formal conference time, often late in the fall of the school year, to get to know families. Informal conversations can occur through back-to-school nights, open house, before or after school, or through invitations to visit the classroom to view students' projects, volunteer in the classroom, read a story to the class, or have lunch with the children. For families who are unable to come to school, regular phone calls to update them on their child's progress or answer any questions, or an exchange of personal notes and e-mails can help create a trusting relationship long before the structured parent-teacher conference.

Whether it is an informal discussion with a father before school when he drops his child off at the door, or a formal scheduled conference with all family members, there are communication strategies that a teacher can use to help create a positive exchange of information. The first factor to consider is your classroom environment and whether it is conducive to good communication. The teacher's classroom is where most conferences are held. When teachers are aware of and attend to issues such as seating, privacy, and atmosphere, a more comfortable environment may be created. Table 10.2 offers considerations for conferencing with family members.

TABLE 10.2   Conferencing Considerations

Seating

- Always offer adults an adult-size chair, even if it means hunting them down from another classroom or workroom.
- Have multiple chairs available for extended family members attending the conference.
- Consider seating arrangement. Desks may function as physical barriers but the teacher may also be perceived as taking an authoritarian stance.
- Cultural differences are also considerations. You can determine appropriate space and distance by observing whether family members move chairs closer together or further apart as a means to create a comfortable distance for communication.

Privacy

- According to the Federal Educational Rights and privacy Act (FERPA), all academic and health information about a student should be kept confidential and only shared with the students' parents/guardians, the student, and those involved in educating the student (U.S. Department of Education, 2007).
- Find a private area to talk or set up another meeting time to talk when no other students or parents are present.
- If conferences run late, ensure conversations may not be overheard by families waiting outside the room.
- It is also important to shield families from observation by others if they become upset when given unexpected or disappointing news.

School Atmosphere

- Provide a welcoming atmosphere in school and classroom.
- Provide necessary parking, visitor pass, and map information.
- Post signage in families' native language. One mother described how a school's welcoming atmosphere led her to eventually becoming a school volunteer: "And well, there I didn't know hardly anyone, right? And I began to get to know them and, well, I began to like the environment. I liked the feeling. And because of that I stayed there" [translated from Spanish] (Quintanar & Warren, 2008, p. 121).
- Be organized; have all important documents and papers available.
- Put any confidential information about other students, such as a grade book, papers, or testing information out of sight.

Nonverbal Communication

- Body language (communication through body mannerisms and facial expressions) communicates to families an interest and willingness to form a collaborative partnership.
- Verbal messages say one thing and the body says another. Posture, hands, and feet are more difficult to control (Gorden, 1992). In fact, some experts suggest that 80% of all communication is nonverbal (Welch & Gonzalez, 1999; Young, 2005).

(Continued)

TABLE 10.2 (Continued)
• A teacher's body language sends messages to parents that may be misread by families from cultures different from theirs (Clayton, 2003). For instance, in Finland, folded arms are considered a sign of arrogance, while this gesture may be seen as a sign of anger or discomfort to a middle-class American. In Iran, an "up and down" head movement indicates "no," whereas a downward tilt of the head with a slight turn signals "yes." In contrast, in Lebanon a head nod indicates "yes," while "no" is indicated with the head pointed sharply upward with raised eyebrows (LeBaron, 2003). • Studies show that when eye contact is held, speakers are seen as more credible than those who do not maintain this gaze (Young, 2005). In some cultures, direct eye contact is considered rude (Welch & Gonzalez, 1999), while in other cultures direct eye contact is the norm. Lack of eye contact could suggest disinterest; however, if eye contact lasts more than two or three seconds, it may also be perceived as being too intimate (Gorden, 1992). • Nonverbal communication will also include your body position or posture. An effective communication stance for you when meeting with parents is one that is relaxed, slightly leaning forward, with open arms and uncrossed legs (Poindexter, Valentine, & Conway, 1999; Welch & Gonzalez, 1999). • People communicate feelings through their facial expressions, and emotions such as happiness, sadness, pain, and anger, are easily observed. If your facial expression is perceived as suggesting disagreement or judgment, communication may immediately halt. • Silence is one of the most useful communication skills and can be used to either contemplate issues or give family members an opportunity to discuss an issue of their choice.

ACTIVE LISTENING BEHAVIORS

I tried telling the teacher about how hard it was for me to listen to D'Marcus read at night on the days I get home late from my night classes. She didn't even seem to hear me, but just lectured me about the importance of reading books with him. I don't know why I even tried to explain things to her.

Listening is key to reciprocal communication and will help you understand new perspectives you may not have considered when working with students. Some of the active listening skills that you can learn and demonstrate include paraphrasing and questioning. Table 10.3 describes each of these.

TABLE 10.3	Reciprocal Communication
Paraphrasing	Restating the content of the message and the feelings portrayed.
	Encouragers are nonverbal and verbal invitations to talk, to expand on information, and to show that listening is taking place (Skovholt & Rivers, 2004). Head nods, gestures, and prompts such as "uh-huh" are all examples of encouragers.
	Reflection involves restating the content of the message and the feelings portrayed (Poindexter et al., 1999) with the purpose of the listener recognizing and identifying the speaker's emotions by paying attention to what is being stated. This gives the parent a chance to clarify what he is expressing, and the teacher can make corrections if needed, so they have a mutual understanding.
	Cultural factors should be considered when using paraphrases. For example, in some cultures, such as certain Asian populations, emotional control is valued, and when extensive attention is placed on feelings, a family member may feel discomfort or embarrassment (Skovholt & Rivers, 2004).

Questioning	Use of questions is one of the most misused communication skills used by individuals. Excessive questioning may be perceived as an interrogation when questions are stated in a manner that can be generally answered with a one- or two-word response.
	Closed questions (questions that have one right answer and limit conversation) require a "yes" or "no" response and do not give the family member an opportunity to disclose more insightful information.
	Open questions (questions that have many possible answers) allow for greater disclosure and verbalization. Typically, open questions begin with the words "what" or "how" (Ivey, 1994) and can help bring out useful information. Open-ended questions can help families reflect and/or examine issues, give them a sense that their ideas are being heard, and help create an atmosphere where the teacher and family members can jointly identify a plan of action to support student learning and development.

PLANNING FOR FORMAL CONFERENCES

In addition to considering the classroom environment and active listening strategies, you should also plan for successful formal parent-teacher conferences. Typically, these formal conferences are held in the fall and spring, scheduled during and after school. Often, schools will allot a short period, such as 15 minutes, for conferences, which is not enough time for meaningful communication between teachers and families. Although it takes more of your time to have longer conferences, the benefits of improved communication and relationships with families is worth the effort.

Successful conferences do not happen without careful planning. Table 10.4 lists ideas to consider before, during, and after your conferences.

Although a parent-teacher conference should not be your only type of communication with families, it can be one of the building blocks in constructing strong relationships.

ALTERNATIVES IN CONFERENCING WITH FAMILIES

In evaluating my own communication strategies, home visits are probably my favorite and get the best response. I sometimes do home visits just to let a family know that I am there if they need anything; sometimes they find it surprising. I do this especially if I feel like I will have to come back for worse reasons later on in the year. It starts a good relationship with the parents. One of the most difficult forms of communication for me is by telephone (J. Dent, school social worker, personal communication, June 28, 2007).

When traditional methods for home-school collaboration are not reaching the desired outcome, new approaches are needed. Identifying new methods may require brainstorming sessions between community, families, teachers, administrators, and other educators with solutions that better meet the needs of families and the school. What works in one community and school district may not work in another, and educators must identify the particular issues they are facing in achieving effective communication. For example, e-mail may be a very effective communication tool in a district that serves middle- and upper-class professional families, while home visits may be more effective in a low-income

TABLE 10.4 Suggestions for a Successful Formal Conference

Before the Conference

- Gather samples of students' work that demonstrate progress in skills and knowledge.
- Regularly document all areas of students' development and learning (i.e., social, emotional, physical, and cognitive skills and abilities).
- Survey families about questions and issues they would like to address in the conference.
- Schedule conferences with families; offer a variety of times and days that fit busy families' schedules, and consider offering conferences off-site, if necessary.
- Set up a conference area in the classroom that is comfortable and private.
- Prepare the classroom to be inviting for families.
- Have all materials organized and ready to show families.
- Have an outline or plan for the conference.

During the Conference

- Explain the purpose of the conference and your plan; allow families to make suggestions about topics they would also like to discuss.
- Begin with a positive attitude, sharing a positive story about the child.
- Show samples of the child's work or other documentation to illustrate points.
- Use active listening strategies, and encourage families' questions and comments.
- Be aware of the time schedule; if more time is needed, discuss with families the best way to continue the conversation at another time.
- End conference by summarizing main topics and developing a plan for improvement for both home and school.

After the Conference

- Jot down notes about the conference: family comments, questions, plan of action.
- Follow-up with a note of appreciation to families for attending conference.
- Go back and review notes periodically to make sure plans for improvement are being addressed.

community that has a high population of families who do not speak English as a first language. Following are some optional ideas of communication methods, including increasing student involvement in conferences, holding group conferences, having telephone conferences, making home visits, and using technology to connect school and home.

Student Involvement

Because students are the focus when families and educators meet, it makes sense to include students in the process. Three-way conferences that include students can be one way to increase family engagement and interest. For example, West Carrollton Middle School (Ohio) had an increase in family attendance at conferences from 30% to 78% when students were included in the conferences, and Talent Middle School (Oregon) saw an even more dramatic increase from 45% to 92–95% attendance when they implemented parent-teacher-student conferences (Ingram, 2006; Kinney, 2005). Being involved in making decisions about their academic and personal growth can affect students and can give everyone an opportunity to be engaged (Stevens & Tollafield, 2003). As one third grader said, "I got to know what you're talking about and how I can improve" (Ricci, 2000, p. 54).

The teacher's role in three-way conferences is to help students prepare ahead of time by selecting work samples together, teach students to self-evaluate and reflect on their work, and develop goals for future progress. Some teachers also help students write a script that can be used during the conference (Kinney, 2005). The teacher's guidance in the process will depend on the age and developmental levels of the students, but children as young as kindergarten can be involved in sharing their learning with their families, discussing what they are proud of and what they want to work on in the future.

Including students in parent-teacher conferences can increase family participation and student responsibility.

During the conference, the teacher can facilitate the conversation, helping refocus if the conversation gets off topic. For younger children, it is important to consider the time when conferences are scheduled, as children may be tired, inattentive, or easily distracted in later evening hours or immediately after school (Howe & Simmons, 2005). Teachers may choose not to include students in the entire conference and allow time for private conversation with parents. If the relationship with the family is strained or they are opposed to the child being a part of the conference, then it is best not to include the student (Howe & Simmons, 2005). One teacher also found that student-led conferences was not a good fit for her Latino families because putting the child in a leadership role in the conference violated the family culture of children looking up to and respecting their parents as authority figures (Quiroz, Greenfield, & Latchet, 1999).

Group Conferences

As a part of the Bridging Cultures professional development program in California, teachers experimented with alternatives to the traditional parent-teacher conference. One teacher found that holding group conferences for her Latino families was particularly effective. She divided her class into three groups, with a translator provided for her two Spanish-speaking groups, and she held three separate group conferences. The families and their children sat in a circle and were given a folder with information about their child, including their report card. The teacher explained the folders' contents and discussed what her plans were to help the students progress further in their skills as well as ideas for family activities that would help support student learning. After the group session, the children escorted their families, including siblings, to their desks to share their portfolios and give a tour of the room and work that was displayed. Parents could then sign up for a private conference, if they desired. She described the outcome:

A comfortable and warm feeling came across during the conferencing. Many parents had questions that benefited the others. . . . The group conferencing was relaxing for the parents. It was a less threatening environment than the individual conferencing style; parents supplied support and were company for one another. This format provided a group voice from the parents rather than an individual voice. . . . My new format was successful. I saw all 28 parents in three days. (Quiroz et al., 1999, p. 69)

The social format of this conference reflected the collectivist cultural view of the Latino families of the students, which emphasizes harmonious group interactions over individualistic one-on-one interactions with the teacher. The Latino families also viewed the teacher's ability to coordinate the group conference favorably as evidence of her skills as a leader of the classroom (Quiroz et al., 1999).

Telephone Conferences

With the majority of families having home or cell phones, the telephone offers a practical way to communicate with families, especially those who are unable or reluctant to attend a conference at school. As one first-year teacher reported,

The most successful type of communication for me has been the phone calls home. My student's parents really opened up over the phone. I believe this is because there was not a time constraint on how long we could talk and it is not as confrontational as the fall conferences. (L. Miller, kindergarten teacher, personal communication, June 28, 2007)

Telephone conferences should not be saved just for bad news or reports of problems, but should be done regularly to share positive information about students and see what questions families may have. It is helpful to make notes ahead of time of the main points and questions you'd like to cover in the phone call. It is important to make the first phone call early in the year as a way to begin that personal communication with families. However, it is important to find out when is the best time to call. Some parents may prefer a phone call at work to one at night when they are busy with dinner, homework, and bath, while other parents may have employers who frown on personal phone calls during the workday. A survey sent to families at the beginning of the school year asking for phone numbers and preferred time for calls can help assure that a family member will be responsive to your phone calls (Howe & Simmons, 2005). Although many teachers start the school year with good intentions of regularly phoning, they often find that months have passed without any phone calls home. Therefore, it is also helpful to create a system or schedule for phone calls, such as calling four families a week, every week, meaning that every family gets a phone call about every six weeks.

Some teachers feel overwhelmed at the prospect of making regular phone calls to families every week. One solution is to also use the assistance of other school personnel, such as the parent coordinator, social worker, counselor, Title I reading teacher, or even the administrator. For example, at Theodore Roosevelt Elementary in Rochester, New York, the parent coordinator called parents to invite them to school activities such as a DARE celebration or choir performance. Attendance at these events exceeded expectations of school staff, requiring them to set up more chairs at the events. The personal phone calls communicated to families that they were important, and the school found that "once they've promised to be there, they are likely to keep their promise" (Kirschenbaum, 1999, p. 20). In another elementary school, the principal carried a cell phone in her pocket, and whenever she spotted a child exhibiting a positive behavior, such as picking up trash in the lunchroom or comforting a classmate who got hurt on the playground, she immediately called the parent to share the positive behavior and then put the child on the phone for praise from the parent. Families in this school loved getting a phone call from the principal.

As noted earlier, it is important to know the community you serve, as phone conferences may not work with all family groups. For example, low-income families may not have phones or may have frequent termination of their service, making it difficult to contact them. If you are teaching in a highly mobile area, you may find that your families' phone numbers change frequently, requiring you to regularly update the contact information. A final caution about phone conferences is related to using a cell phone during the school day. Although your phone call may have legitimate school-related reasons, it may appear to be for personal reasons or it could be perceived as unprofessional behavior. Be prepared to justify your use of the telephone during the school day.

Home Visits

Home visits will be discussed in detail in Chapter 12, but the concept deserves a mention here as an alternative to the traditional school-based parent-teacher conference. For those families who feel uncomfortable or are unable to come to school, a visit in the home can offer another option for communication and relationship building. As one teacher said,

> When I first started making home visits, I looked for opportunities that felt natural and nonthreatening to the families and myself. I have stopped by to deliver forgotten homework, or shown up with a Popsicle for a sick or injured student. . . . Some of my visits have been for a specific purpose, perhaps an effort to gain more support from parents regarding homework or discipline issues. Like phone calls or any type of communication, a visit aimed at achieving a desired outcome is often more effective if a relationship has been established through our prior visits. . . . The primary reason I make home visits is to show my students that I care about them. Upon being hired, our superintendent spoke to a group of us newly hired teachers and challenged us to adopt as our motto: "What happens to you, matters to me." I have this motto hanging on the wall in my classroom, but I feel like I walk my talk when I make a home visit. (Worthy & Hoffman, 2001, p. 517)

Although the content of the conference may not differ in the home setting from in the school setting, there are some special considerations, such as the following:

- Make an appointment and state the purpose for the visit.
- Try to schedule home visits early in the year to provide a foundation for future communication.
- Respect the family situation and do not make judgments about the living conditions of the family. Take time to find something of interest, such as a family photograph, to talk about.
- Include the child in the visit.

- Discuss how future communication can be done, such as phone calls or notes, if the parent is not able to come to school.
- Use caution in visiting a neighborhood or remote rural area that may be unsafe, and team up with other school personnel if necessary. (Howe & Simmons, 2005)

It is critical to have training sessions for teachers prior to home visits that focus on how to build relationships, establish a true listening stance, and engage in "courageous conversations" (Henke, 2011, p. 40). Other sensitive issues include the following:

- Choosing alternate meeting places, such as parks or coffee shops, so parents don't feel school district personnel are inspecting their homes.
- Understanding that parents may have a fear of judgment and defensiveness concerning issues of race, socioeconomic status, or language fluency (Henke, 2011)

Community and Workplace Conferences

Similar to the idea of holding a conference in the home, there may be convenient locations for families and teachers to meet, such as a community center that is within walking distance of students' homes for those families who do not have transportation. Another option is workplace conferences. In one school system, school personnel were able to establish regular communication with parents by scheduling meetings at their workplace during lunch hours. School personnel contacted the managers of the community industries who employed the largest number of family members, and permission was given to schedule lunchtime meetings with them to provide information to interested employee/parents. This goodwill gesture allowed more families to receive information regarding significant events and deadlines and to have questions answered without missing work (Evans & Hines, 1997).

DOCUMENTATION OF COMMUNICATION

Sept. 8: Phone conference, 10 min. Get-acquainted phone call with family. Spoke with father. Step-mom works night shift, and dad cares for children at night. Tia sees her mom on the weekends. Paternal grandmother also provides afterschool care (needs to be included in any future communication efforts). Dad expressed concern about Tia's behavior at school after she returns from mom's house because of differences in rules and discipline. Promised to observe behavior and call back in one month.

After an informal or formal conference with families either in person or by telephone, it is important to document what was said for future reference. Summarize what the purpose of the conversation was, the primary points of the discussion, and any plan of action that was made. For example, it is easy in a casual phone conversation to promise parents that you will update them on their concerns about their child's problems with friends in the classroom and then forget to do so. Filing documentation of conversations in children's folders or on files on the computer and regularly reviewing them can help prevent misunderstanding and improve regular open communication with families (Howe & Simmons, 2005). An example of a documentation form is in Table 10.5.

TABLE 10.5   Family Communication Form

Date and time of communication _____

Child's name _____

Family member and relationship to child _____

Type of communication

_____ Telephone call   _____ E-mail   _____ Informal conference   _____ Formal conference

_____ Note   _____ Text   _____ Online chat   _____ Website/Blog comments

_____ Other: _____

Purpose of communication: _____

_____

_____

Family comments: _____

_____

_____

Teacher comments: _____

_____

_____

Action to be taken: _____

_____

_____

TECHNOLOGY AS A TOOL FOR COMMUNICATION

Technology has been useful with two of my parents. I have one mother who cannot receive phone calls at work unless it is an emergency. She does not have a home phone, so I communicate with her via e-mail. She can access a computer in the employee lounge to check her messages during her breaks at work, so this has been helpful. Another parent works from home on her computer, and getting a response with her is easier through

A classroom website can be an effective communication tool and a means for children to share their school activities with their families.

ACTIVITY 10.1

One way to gather ideas for your classroom website is to regularly examine school and classroom websites, evaluating them for effectiveness in communicating information to families. You can do a search of school and classroom websites of schools in your area or surf the teacher websites available at School Days Top Ten Classroom Websites: http://schooldays.top-site-list.com. Critically view the websites from a family's perspective: What information can you learn about the school and teacher? What information would you still like to know? Was the website user and family friendly, easy to navigate? Was it up-to-date? Did it offer opportunities for communication between home and school? What information or links were on the website that you would like to put on your classroom website?

e-mail than over the phone. If my concern needs further attention, she will call me immediately. (D. Beussink, special education teacher, personal communication, June 28, 2007)

Today's technology is rapidly developing and offers many new ways to communicate with families. School and class websites, blogs, e-mail, online chats, text messaging, and pagers are just a few of the examples of technology-based school communication methods. Many schools have district- or building-level websites with individual teacher Web pages. These websites can be a rich source of information for families and offer a quick and easy form of reciprocal communication for families with computers. Typical information found on a classroom website includes information about current projects, homework assignments, upcoming class activities, parent resources, and photographs of the class at work or special activities, such as a field trip. For working families who are unable to volunteer in the classroom or attend a field trip, these photographs and descriptions of activities can help them better understand their child's school day and give them a tool for conversation with their child about school. Suggested links for families on parenting topics and ideas for home activities can also be placed there. A link to e-mail the teacher can change a website from a one-way form of communication to another opportunity for responsive communication.

The information on a website is usually general in nature and not specifically geared to a specific child, but some teachers have begun creating personalized access sites for each family, where they can find specific information about a child and make comments or ask questions (Howe & Simmons, 2005). Obviously, this requires time and attention to keep it current, and families may not visit the site regularly if the information is not updated or their comments/questions are not addressed. Another disadvantage to the class website is that families will only receive the information if they choose to visit the website. However, one teacher used her website both as a learning tool for the students and as a way to communicate with families. Together, she and her first-grade students designed the website and chose the pictures of their daily activities to place on it, with captions that they wrote themselves. For example, after making "Rabbit Pizza" as a part of a unit on nutrition, pictures of the children making the snack and the recipe for it were put on the class website, which led to families visiting the website to get the recipe for themselves. The teacher and students updated the website weekly with new pictures and information, and the teacher sent home cards with, "Look! We've updated our website!" as reminders to encourage families to regularly check the website. She found the website to be an effective communication tool, with families regularly checking it (D. Shelton, personal communication, June 29, 2007).

E-mail is a quick and efficient way to communicate with families if they have easy access to a computer, such as at work during the day. E-mails are usually better for informal communication, similar to a personal note, and may not be the best way to communicate formal information, such as a test report or discipline notice. Because e-mails do not relay body language or emotions, they can be easily misinterpreted. However, e-mails offer much promise in a teacher's efforts to have regular, ongoing reciprocal communication, as more and more families use e-mail at home or work.

E-mail can also serve as a classroom learning tool in addition to a family communication strategy. In one first-grade classroom, a teacher developed an electronic pen pal program with children's families, including grandparents, noncustodial parents, older siblings away at college, and other extended family members. The children wrote their e-mails together as a class, telling class news and ending the e-mails with a question for their families to respond to. This allowed long-distance grandparents to be involved in their grandchildren's classroom via technology. For one student whose extended family lived in Mexico, the students used an online translation source to translate e-mails that were sent and received from her grandmother (Ray & Shelton, 2004). Although it is important to get the parent's or guardian's permission before including extended family in e-mail communication, e-mails can provide an easy way to communicate with all family members. In addition to e-mail sent from the class computer, smartphones or other digital devices can be useful e-mail tools. Teachers can jot down notes or anecdotal records about a child and send them directly from the device, via e-mail.

For a new generation of parents, e-mail is quickly being replaced as a communication tool by social media, such as Twitter and Facebook. Many schools are experimenting with these and other electronic communication tools. For example, the Nixa, Missouri, school district not only has district and school websites but also encourages parents to follow the school news on Twitter, Facebook, and YouTube. Parents can get daily tweets from a principal through a Twitter account, view a video orientation to the high school on YouTube, or get news and photos from the school and interact with other parents on Facebook (Nixa Public Schools, 2011).

Many school districts also use a private Parent Portal where grades, attendance, lunch account balances, homework assignments, or other school and classroom information can be accessed from a home computer. The Kentucky Department of Education collaborated with a telecommunications company to develop a free mobile phone app for Parent Portals in school districts across the state. This phone app can be used on Apple iOS devices (e.g., iPod Touch, iPhone, iPad). "'Instead of being tied to a computer, you can check [the portal] on your phone,' said Laura James, [Hopkins County] district technology integration specialist" (Hopkins County School District, 2011, para. 2).

COMMUNICATING WITH CULTURALLY AND LINGUISTICALLY DIVERSE FAMILIES

A Latina immigrant mother remembers a parent-teacher conference with her daughter's first-grade teacher:

> I couldn't understand what the teacher was trying to communicate when she commented on my daughter's performance. I particularly recall two confusing comments that this teacher made: "Your daughter is very sociable" and "Your daughter

is outstanding in. . . ." My tendency as a Mexican mother was to feel very happy she was sociable; after all, that was what I was fostering. However, I did not know what to do about her being "outstanding;" I had tried to show my daughter not to "show off," but it seemed that it was not working. (Quiroz et al., 1999, p. 68)

The previous example illustrates one of the difficulties in communicating with families from diverse cultural or language backgrounds, as the mother interpreted "outstanding" as "standing out," something that was to be avoided in her culture (Quiroz et al., 1999). Misunderstandings about terms or phrases, limited command of English, and differing communication styles makes communication with families from other cultures or language backgrounds challenging for a teacher.

Research has shown that expressive language is **culturally encoded**, or highly influenced by cultural socialization (Cazden, John, & Hymes, 1985). The dominant American culture predominantly exhibits a **passive-receptive communication style**, whereas other ethnic groups practice a more **active participatory communication style**. In a passive-receptive communication style, the teacher will take an active role in explaining information to parents (one way), with the parents passively listening and posing questions at the end of the session. This style features the teacher in an authoritarian role, with the parent as a dormant receptor of information. Conversely, an active participatory communication style involves both the teacher (speaker) and parents (listeners) actively engaged in a conversation, with fluidity between roles of support and affirmation for each other's ideas (Gay, 2002). When teachers use a passive-receptive communication style, families whose cultural background includes a more active participatory role may make comments such as, "She (the teacher) just threw information at me about my child. I couldn't get a word in," or "When the teacher said things about my child, I wanted to interrupt and give her information, but I didn't feel she wanted to hear my side." Families who prefer an active participatory communication style may feel a higher level of satisfaction with conferences when teachers allow them to contribute to the interactions.

Furthermore, it is important to pay attention to how conferences are conducted. Many teachers try to establish a comfortable atmosphere by using an informal approach when meeting with parents/guardians. Yet people from cultures in which there is a strict **hierarchical** (a structure or order of authority), formal approach between families and teachers may be offended by this casual manner (Copeland, 2007). For example, one Chinese American mother expressed discomfort with a young teacher who used the parents' first names in their conference, instead of addressing them formally.

It is also important to note cross-cultural ground rules for conferences. Different cultures have varied notions of time and what it means to be late. The dominant culture of American schools embraces the **monochronic** (sequence of events occurring one at a time) emphasis on time as demonstrated by the stress on orderliness, timeliness, and one-on-one interactions. The opposite notion of time is labeled **polychronic** (several things at a time), where several interactions can occur at the same moment in time (Clayton, 2003). The idea of lateness— one minute, five minutes, twenty minutes, or several hours is culturally relative. In the dominant culture, it is viewed as a sign of courtesy to attend at the clock appointed time, while in other cultures, the bounds of courtesy extend within a time range acceptable in their culture (Gonzalez-Mena, 2008).

For families who do not speak English as their first language, conferencing with the teacher can be challenging for both parties, yet it also offers opportunities for educators to authentically involve these parents in their child's education. Because of the language barriers, many times these conferences end up as one-way communication sessions with the teacher disseminating all the information, allowing the family members little possibility for input, with the teacher talking "over their heads." One second-language parent described the fear and intimidation felt about conferences with teachers: "IEP meetings are bad enough if you speak English, what if you don't understand English?" (Alexandria City Public Schools, 2004). Espinosa (2005) suggested beginning conversations with families by sensitively gathering background information concerning language usage with questions such as the following:

1. What language did your child learn when she first began to talk?
2. What language does your child hear most frequently at home?
3. What language does your child speak most frequently at home?
4. What is your child's strongest language?

For parents with a limited knowledge of English or recent immigrants to the country, a translator is mandatory at the meeting. Individuals hired by the district as translators, the home school coordinator, bilingual teachers, or administrators may provide language conversion support, or extended family members who have a stronger grasp of English may be available. It is usually not the best practice to use the child as a translator, as students may choose what to tell their families. For example, one teacher described a Latino student in her class whose parents spoke limited English. The student served as an interpreter for her parents during a school conference. When the teacher tried to explain the difficulties the student was having with her schoolwork, the student translated the messages to her advantage. Instead of telling her parents about her problems, her translation was that she was doing very well in school. The teacher later discovered that her parents never did learn the truth behind the grades (J. Studer, personal communication, February 25, 2007).

The most important considerations when using a translator are that the family feels a level of comfort and confidence in the ongoing translating and that the translation is accurate. The translator should have a familiarity with educational references and, if possible, should be briefed prior to the meeting on items to be discussed. The translator acts as a conduit for communication between the family and educators to field questions, provide information, and make decisions.

One last point: Families who are not native English speakers appreciate monolingual teachers who are willing to attempt to learn key phrases in their language. One study of Latino families who did not speak English found that when teachers, administrators, or other staff members attempted to speak some Spanish with the families, the parents were encouraged to attempt to speak English in return (Quintanar & Warren, 2008). To be able to speak even simple phrases in the families' native language communicates a message of caring and cultural inclusiveness.

BARRIERS TO COMMUNICATION

Barriers can interfere with effective communication, and working to overcome these can lead to a more collaborative home-school relationship. These barriers can include teachers' negative attitudes and beliefs, families' negative school experiences, difficult information, and hostile family members.

Teacher Attitudes and Beliefs

Why is it that the only parents who show up for parent-teacher conferences are the parents of students who are getting straight A's in my class—the ones I don't really need to talk to? I would really like to talk with the parents of my students who are having problems, but those are the parents who don't come for a conference. When I call them or send home notes, all I get are excuses as to why they can't come in.

Attitudes such as the one expressed here can create barriers to home-school collaboration. When educators view families negatively without getting to know them first, it is difficult to salvage a positive working relationship. As Chapter 7 noted, some teachers mistakenly believe that lower-income families are less interested in their child's education than families from higher socioeconomic groups. However, studies have shown that lower-income families were not less interested in their child's education, but it was their uncertainty over how they could be involved in the educational system, particularly when work hours make it difficult to attend school events during the day or help with homework at night (Evans & Hines, 1997). Additionally, some families may not have a reliable mode of transportation or means of communication. Approximately 6% of all households in the United States do not have a phone, and another 21% of parents/guardians are unable to read; in some cases, families may even be homeless (Stevens & Tollafield, 2003). When families do not respond to communication efforts, teachers may leap to false conclusions that they are not interested in their child's education, when in actuality, there may be other issues preventing them from meeting educators halfway. It is important to suspend any judgment about families and work to get to know more about the issues they face that may prevent school involvement.

It is also a common misconception that conferences with families are only needed to address learning or behavioral problems and that conferences are not needed with families of successful students. Although that may be the basis for having a conference, there are many other reasons to conduct them. Teachers should also view conferences with families as a chance to share successes and accomplishments of children and plan together for future learning. All families enjoy hearing good news and being praised for their efforts in raising children, and conferences are one way to do that. Perhaps the most important reason to have a conference with families, though, is to help families and teachers develop stronger relationships to support their children's learning (Georgiady & Romano, 2002).

Negative School Experiences of Families

I don't understand Cody's parents' attitude. Even though he hands in his homework and participates in class, he does poorly on tests. When I told his parents that I thought he needed to improve on his study habits, they seemed defensive and left my classroom with resentment. I don't get it—I just wanted them to know that their son wasn't doing well in my class.

As revealed in this statement, teachers may not be aware of personal attitudes held by families because of unresolved feelings when they attended school as students.

These feelings may be exacerbated when their child attends the same school district in which they were students or is taught by some of the same teachers or administrators with whom they had difficulties. Old feelings and resentment can resurface when invited to the school. For example, a parent may have thoughts such as, "my son will never be treated fairly because the teachers will think that he is trouble, just like they used to think of me." Without considering the cause of these feelings, a resentful attitude may put the teacher in a defensive mode and create a perpetual cycle of hostility. Again, the key to working effectively with families is to get to know them personally, including learning more about their experiences with school as a child.

Sharing Difficult Information

Dear Mrs. Williams,

   Could we meet next week to talk about Taylor's progress in reading? The reading teacher has completed her evaluations, and we'd like to share with you the results and talk about ways to help Taylor be more successful in reading. Please let me know what day and time are convenient for you.

Sincerely,
Lakeesha Walker

Communicating unpleasant news about a student's learning or behavior problems to families is difficult and often creates stressful responses for both the giver and the receiver of the news. For example, in one study, a majority of the parents reported displeasure in the way they were told that their child was diagnosed with a disability (Auger, 2006). Teachers may be torn, when giving unpleasant news, between wanting to give realistic information and presenting it in a sensitive, caring manner. Teachers may also avoid a difficult conference by delaying telling the families negative information or hiding it from them until it is too late. This can only add to the problems, as one teacher noted:

Don't hide anything or keep any issues from families. It is better for them to find something out the first time it happens, and not let it escalate into something more. They will be more upset if they know they could have done something to help at an earlier time. Just let it be known that the lines of communication are always open! Make it known that you are there as a partner, not the enemy. (E. Brune, second-grade teacher, personal communication, June 28, 2007)

Negative information is more likely to be received well when teachers communicate that they are genuinely interested in working together with families in helping the child succeed. If families perceive a caring, accepting attitude by the teacher, they are more likely to be open to addressing the problems. One way to do this is to approach the situation with the attitude of "What can we do together to solve this problem?" Using active listening strategies and brainstorming with families about different tactics to try both at home and at school can help build a sense of collaboration (Howe & Simmons, 2005). Table 10.6 has suggestions for conferences with families on difficult issues.

TABLE 10.6 Suggestions for Talking With Families About Tough Issues
• *Differentiate the behavior from the person*. Although teachers may disapprove of a particular behavior, they need to show that they still value and care for the student. • *Protect against infectious negativism*. At times, challenges may discourage parents and teachers, who may be inclined to see the student's situation as hopeless. It is important to remain realistic but optimistic. No child is beyond help or hope. • *Make a plan*. It is vital to have a clear, specific plan that will focus on and resolve identified concerns. The plan should clearly describe each participant's role in solving the problem. • *End positively and stay in touch*. Always attempt to end the meeting on a positive note. When teachers and parents work together, even very difficult problems get solved.

Source: Based on Howe and Simmons (2005).

Hostile Families

Responsive teachers are probably most fearful of encounters with hostile parents. For teachers who work hard to have positive, trusting, collaborative relationships with families, these encounters are rare. However, families deal with many other stressful personal issues that can spill over into the home-school relationship. If a meeting with a family member becomes confrontational, it is important to remain calm, use a level voice, and try to better understand the cause of the anger. For example, one experienced teacher addressed an upset parent in this way: "I can appreciate your feelings of frustration, but remember that I really do want to support you. . . . Please help me to understand how I can help you" (Howe & Simmons, 2005, p. 33). Arguing with a parent or pointing out the inappropriateness of his behavior is not productive and can cause the hostility to escalate. Often anger can be defused by allowing the family member to vent about the situation, with the teacher calmly listening, using the active listening strategies described earlier. You can also write down the family's complaints or suggestions, indicating that they are being taken seriously. Once the parent has had an opportunity to be heard, then emphasize the importance of working together to solve the issue and make plans to follow up on the issue (Georgiady & Romano, 2002).

In some instances, it is best to end the conference or call for additional assistance. If a family member is intoxicated, using profanity, or exhibiting potentially violent behavior, a meeting will not be productive, and you should call for an administrator, arrange for another conference time, and if necessary, politely but firmly end the conference. Any confrontational conferences should be documented carefully and reported to the administrator (Georgiady & Romano, 2002; Howe & Simmons, 2005). Your safety should always be a priority in working with families who have a history of bullying or aggressive behavior.

SUMMARY

This chapter has presented skills and concepts needed for successful communication with diverse families. A checklist is provided in Table 10.7 for you to use as a guide to evaluate your communication skills and to serve as a reminder of essential factors when communicating with families in print, informal, or formal meetings.

TABLE 10.7   Checklist of Communication Skills

_____ I strive to have regular and frequent written and oral communication with families.

_____ The majority of my communication efforts are reciprocal, rather than one-way.

_____ I am aware of attitudes or beliefs that may negatively affect my communication efforts and relationships with families.

_____ My seating arrangement is one that invites conversation.

_____ I make an effort to make the conference setting free from distractions and one that invites privacy.

_____ I make certain that the school environment is inviting and comfortable.

_____ I am aware of my nonverbal communication patterns, the messages sent through eye contact, my body position and posture, and how my facial expressions facilitate or hinder communication.

_____ I am aware of how silence provides parents and guardians an opportunity to speak.

_____ I use active listening strategies, such as paraphrasing, to show an understanding of feelings and content and open-ended questions to generate more information from families.

_____ I strive to find innovative ways to communicate with my families and do not rely solely on traditional newsletters or conferences in my communication efforts.

_____ I use technology as a way to communicate with families, when appropriate.

_____ I document all communications with families and review these communications to better understand families.

_____ I am willing to learn more about the knowledge, attitudes, and communication skills of diverse cultures.

_____ I make an effort to be sensitive to the communication challenges that may be present with families who speak English as a second language.

_____ I am aware of the anxiety or wariness some families feel when entering schools.

_____ I am aware of how families may react to negative news, and I try to be sensitive when I am delivering news that may be unpleasant.

_____ I individualize my communication efforts, using a variety of methods, to meet the needs of individual families.

Table 10.8 also offers an evaluation form for schools to use in assessing school communication practices.

TABLE 10.8 Assessing School-Family Communication				
Indicators	**Consistently Evident**	**Frequently Evident**	**Seldom Evident**	**Not Evident**
Educators use a variety of communication tools to facilitate regular, two-way interaction				
Families and educators discuss student interests and strengths				
School provides clear information regarding expectations, activities, and services				
School provides clear information on policies, discipline procedures, assessment tools, and goals				
Educators hold conferences with families that accommodate varied schedules, language barriers, and child-care needs				
When concerns arise, the school promotes immediate contact between educators and families				
Educators distribute student work for family review on a regular basis				
The school translates communications to assist non-English-speaking families				
Educators communicate with families regarding positive student behavior and achievement, not just misbehavior or failure				
Families have opportunities to communicate with principals and other administrative staff				
The school holds informal activities and formal events at which families, staff, and community members can interact				
The school provides staff development regarding effective communication techniques and the importance of regular two-way communication between schools and families				

Source: U.S. Department of Education (2006).

Note: Communication between the school and students' homes should be regular, two-way, and meaningful.

When families and educators keep lines of communication open and are comfortable in sharing thoughts and feelings, the ultimate winner is the student, who will benefit from the strong relationship between home and school.

REFLECTION QUESTIONS

Reread the In the Classroom case study presented at the beginning of the chapter and reflect on these questions:

1. What strengths is his grandmother exhibiting? What concerns does she have?

2. What can Kate do to turn this conference into a positive communication experience for both herself and Travis's grandmother?

3. Noting the types of communication that Kate has used at this point, what types of follow-up communication could be done with Travis's grandmother to improve the home-school relationship and provide her support for educating Travis?

WEBSITES

Family Communications, **www.fci.org/**.

A nonprofit organization founded in 1971 by Fred Rogers, this site encourages families with "important talk"—talk about thoughts, feelings, and concerns. Parent resource articles support communication with the children in their lives. Neighborhood newsletters offer resources for parents and educators on dealing with communication issues.

Head Start Information and Publication Center, **www.headstartinfo.org/**.

Communicating With Parents: Training Guides for the Head Start Learning Community provides an online module for communications with parents, with the goal of building partnerships with families.

Scholastic Parents, **http://www.scholastic.com/parents/school-help/parent-teacher -relationships/**.

It includes a free parent newsletter, message boards and blogs, as well as articles on teacher-family communications: "Policies & Practices: Family Communications—Ideas That Really Work" (Moore, 2002).

The Whole Child, sponsored by PBS, **www.pbs.org/wholechild/providers/f-s.html**.

Links to series on PBS, available through video cassettes, and telecourses. Look for the article on "Establishing Strong Family-School Communications," as well as many others on family communication.

STUDENT STUDY SITE

Log on to the student study site at **www.sagepub.com/grant2e** for additional study tools, including the following:

- eFlashcards
- Web quizzes

- Web resources
- Learning objectives

Chapter 11

Working With Families of Children With Exceptional Needs

Our kids are normal. They just aren't typical.

—Jim Delisle (n.d.)

When parents are expecting a child, most have already envisioned their child's future. They think about their child starting school, high school, and college; they think about graduation, marriage, and children. When a child is diagnosed as having exceptional needs, these thoughts often have to be changed. This can be a difficult time for parents and other family members. As a teacher, you will work with them as they go through a realignment of thoughts and dreams. You will strive to meet their needs, as well as their children's needs. This may include families of students who are gifted or talented, as their exceptional needs are often not addressed in the regular classroom, and close collaboration between home and school is necessary to help these children reach their potential. As you think about your work with families of children with exceptional needs, consider these questions:

- How can I help families adjust to the news that their child has an exceptional need?
- What cultural considerations are there in working with diverse families of children with exceptional needs?
- What is my role as a classroom teacher in working with students with exceptional needs?
- What are the key pieces of legislation that guide the education of students with exceptional education needs, such as the Individuals with Disabilities Education Act (IDEA)?

Contributing Author Suzanne George

- What are the things to keep in mind as I communicate with families of students with exceptional needs?
- What role will I have in the special education process if I refer a student for an evaluation?
- What is my role in the development and implementation of the **individualized education program (IEP),** a plan that guides the delivery of special education supports and services for students, ages 3 to 21?
- What is my role in working with families of young children to develop and implement an **individualized family service plan (IFSP),** a plan that guides families and schools in the development and education of children with exceptional needs who are birth to three years old?
- How can I help families understand and be involved in **response to intervention (RTI),** a process schools use to help children having academic or behavioral difficulties by providing early interventions through "tiers" within the general classroom setting, as well as identifying those who need special services (National Dissemination Center for Children with Disabilities, 2010a)?
- How can I work effectively with the families of students who are gifted and talented?

HELPING FAMILIES ADJUST TO HAVING A CHILD WITH EXCEPTIONAL NEEDS

The determination of a physical or cognitive exceptional need may occur at birth or in the very early years of a child's life. IDEA has defined disabilities that qualify for early intervention or special education services. For children under the age of three, a disability is defined as a developmental delay in cognitive, physical, communication, social, emotional, or adaptive development or a physical or mental condition that may result in a developmental delay (National Dissemination Center for Children With Disabilities, 2010b). For children ages 3 through 21, IDEA has defined a list of 13 categories of disabilities, and these are provided in Table 11.1.

TABLE 11.1   Disability Categories

IDEA defines 13 different disability categories under which three- through 21-year-olds are eligible for services. A disability must affect the child's educational performance for the child to qualify for special education services. These are the disability categories:

1. Autism
2. Deaf–Blindness
3. Deafness
4. Emotional disturbance
5. Hearing impairment

6. Intellectual disability (changing from "mental retardation" in the last authorization of IDEA, based on Rosa's Law)

7. Multiple disabilities

8. Orthopedic impairment

9. Other health impairment (e.g., limited strength, vitality, or alertness that affects a child's educational performance)

10. Specific learning disability

11. Speech or language impairment

12. Traumatic brain injury

13. Visual impairment (including blindness)

Source: National Dissemination Center for Children With Disabilities (2010b).

Notes: Children may not be identified as having a disability because they do not speak or understand English well.

IN THE CLASSROOM: ANOTHER DIFFICULT PARENT-TEACHER CONFERENCE

After the difficult parent-teacher conference with Travis's grandmother, Kate's confidence was shaken, but it helped when Jane Gregory, the school counselor, stopped by and talked to her briefly. Jane's counseling abilities extended to her relationships with the teachers in the building, and she had a way of listening and saying the right things to make them feel better after a rough day.

Jane asked, "Have you talked with Kyle Barker's parents yet about your decision to refer him for testing for special reading services?"

Kate said, "No, their conference is later tonight. It shouldn't be a surprise to them, though. I started telling them about his problems last fall at our first conference, and I've sent several notes home since then asking them to help. I'm afraid they may not take the news well, though."

Jane said, as she patted Kate's shoulder and walked out the door, "It's normal to not want to share bad news with parents, but I'm sure you'll be able to handle it. Just remember that you both have the same goal—you both care about Kyle, and you want to help him become a better reader. Let me know if I can help any with them."

The Barkers seemed tense when they came in, and Kate found herself immediately becoming defensive when Mr. Barker's first words were, "Well, what have you been doing to teach Kyle to read?"

Kate took a deep breath and proceeded to show the Barkers the documentation she had gathered on Kyle's reading abilities as well as on the other subjects, on his work habits, and on his social skills. After she showed writing samples and reading test scores, she said, "As you can see, I've tried several different strategies with Kyle, including extra one-on-one help as a part of our response to intervention program. I know you've been working with him at home, too. He's just not making the progress that he should, and I think the next step is to refer him for testing to determine if he needs special help in reading."

Mrs. Barker said, "You don't mean special education, do you? Kyle doesn't need that. What if we don't want him tested?"

Mr. Barker jumped up and said, "I think what Kyle needs is a new teacher. He doesn't need any testing. C'mon, Donna, let's go see the principal about this."

When the diagnosis of an exceptional need occurs, the family may be overwhelmed by the needs of their child, by the professionals who suddenly appear in their lives, and by the decisions they need to make. Parents and family members may enter the school system with knowledge and perhaps with memories of both good and bad experiences with professionals and services provided by other institutions. The determination of an exceptional need may also occur after a child has started school. Again, families may be overwhelmed with terminology, meetings, and decisions that have to be made about educational placement. They may experience confusion, fear, anger, and grief. As families grieve following the diagnosis of a disability, they may display their grief through physical changes, such as stomach and chest pains, sweating, higher heart rate, aches and pains, and so on, or through behaviors such as increased aggression, changes in sleeping and eating patterns, changes in activity patterns, and avoidance of certain people or places (Novita Children's Services, 2007).

Not all families will react in the same way when receiving the diagnosis of an exceptional need, however. One parent stated, "I cried for two days. I was grieving for the baby we had expected, the only one we thought we were prepared for" (Dwight, 2001, p. 33). Another mother said, "Finding out our child had Down syndrome was like being told that the baby we dreamed of had died, and now we had this other child that we knew absolutely nothing about" (J. Pewitt-Kinder, D.O., personal communication, March 19, 2008). Ebenstein (2001) stated, "I wish I had known that the intense sadness a parent experiences on learning of a child's disability is called mourning. For whom do we mourn when the child is alive? We mourn for lost hopes and possibilities" (p. 156). Another emotion that families may feel is frustration over the lack of control of their emotions and that the "grief may hit you when you least expect it—during a Christmas shopping trip . . . when you buy baby toys for a nine-year-old" (Naseef, 2001, p. 207).

It is common that families of children with exceptional needs go through the same stages as someone who is facing a serious or terminal illness when they first learn of their child's diagnosis (Novita Children's Services, 2007). In Elisabeth Kübler-Ross's classic book, *On Death and Dying* (1969), she described the stages of grief. These include denial, anger, bargaining, depression, and acceptance. You may see some of the same feelings and behaviors in families with children with exceptional needs as in families facing terminal illnesses. Teachers may not understand these normal reactions and may be frustrated by them: "That mother is still in denial," "The family is the real problem; they are demanding and unpredictable," or "If the dad would get over his anger, we would be able to work together better" (Ulrich & Bauer, 2003, p. 20). The family's reaction will depend on the age of the child, the severity of the exceptional need, and the family's cultural view of disabilities, but in most cases, common stages are (a) shock and denial, (b) emotional disorganization, and (c) emotional adjustment (Muscott, 2002). Some families may never reach a stage of acceptance, and even those who do may go through the cycle of grieving again whenever new reminders of the child's exceptional needs occur in the child's development.

Some parents have criticized this "grief paradigm" as being condescending and patronizing. They feel that it is not indicative of all families' experiences. Ulrich and Bauer (2003) proposed another approach by using the concept of "levels of awareness." They specify the following levels:

Level 1. The ostrich phase—a lack of awareness. Parents are not denying their child's exceptional needs, but they do not realize that there is a disability. For example, a parent may say, "He's all boy. He just doesn't like to sit still and read a book."

Level 2. Special designation—a transformational experience. Parents realize that their child has a "special" need and want services to be provided. They may become confrontational in seeking help in addressing their child's disability, and they may make demands for professional resources for their child.

Level 3. Normalization—minimizing the differences. At this level, parents want their child to be like other children and may actually argue for a decrease in services in favor of more general education classroom time with peers. This may seem contradictory, but normalization reflects the family's adjustment to the exceptional need and their faith in the child's ability to fit in and learn with other children.

Level 4. Self-actualization—including the child in educational decisions. As parents adjust to the disability diagnosis, they accept it and recognize that their child needs extra support, including support in learning about her exceptional need and how to cope with it.

When working with families, it is important to learn more about how they view their child's exceptional needs. When conflicts or miscommunications occur, it may be because the teacher and family are operating on different levels or stages of understanding. Active listening strategies (described in Chapter 10) can be helpful for understanding a family's perspective. As a teacher, you will need to be aware of families' feelings and allow them the opportunity to express themselves. Additionally, you will need to be careful with the language you use as you work with families with children with exceptional needs. For example, the term "disability" focuses attention on what a person cannot do, rather than the abilities that a person has. Families of children with exceptional needs want to know what their child *can* do and want you, as their child's teacher, to see their child's full potential. Terminology in the field of special education, such as "handicap," has become outdated with the recognition of the abilities and potential of children with special needs. For example, Rosa's Law in Maryland replaced the term "mental retardation" with "intellectual disability" in state services and residential center names (Abilities Network, 2010). You will probably also feel compassion for families and may think that you are helping by saying things such as, "I know how you feel." However, unless you have a child with an exceptional need, you do *not* know how it feels to have one. Your best tool is listening. Families know their children better than anyone, and you will learn a great deal from them about what works well with their children.

Finally, one of the hardest things for families to do in their adjustment to a child's exceptional need is to abandon or change their dreams. One parent described the loss of carefree innocence and a new sense of the unpredictability of life (Salomans, 2001). Another mother realized that although her dreams for her daughter would not come to fruition, there would be other goals: "Jesse will have dreams of her own. They may not be like those of other children, but they will be her dreams, just the same" (Waldrop, 2001, p. 113). Yet another parent described how finding out about her child's exceptional need meant the death of the dreams she had had about games, party invitations, vacations, college, and so on (Kaster,

2001). Listening to families as they express their varied feelings, grieve their loss, and adjust their dreams for their child is one of the most important things you can do as a teacher.

CULTURAL CONSIDERATIONS IN WORKING WITH FAMILIES OF CHILDREN WITH DIFFERING ABILITIES

Just as there are cultural differences in parenting and beliefs about education, there may be different reactions from families to the diagnosis of an exceptional need and to your efforts at collaboration. Lamorey (2002) described some examples of differences among cultural groups in beliefs and attitudes about exceptional needs:

- A survey found that 63% of Korean American parents of children with exceptional needs attributed the cause of their child's disability to a divine plan or "God's will," as well as to their mistakes or to "poor 'Tae Gyo,' which translates to 'education during pregnancy'" (p. 68).
- In a survey of Chinese American parents of young children with exceptional needs, one-third of them believed that supernatural or metaphysical elements caused the disability.
- A study of Mexican American parents of children with exceptional needs found that they thought that the disability was because of a medical problem (genetic diseases or birth trauma); a supernatural cause, such as divine retribution for past sins; or a sociocultural cause, such as negative parental attitudes.
- American Indian families may view having a child with an exceptional need as happening to them for a reason and feel that there is a purpose for this child to be born into the family; or instead, they may be at a loss to know how to adjust family life for a child with an exceptional need (Nichols & Keltner, 2005).

Of course, as a professional, you must remember that these are generalizations about different cultures and that all families, regardless of background, should be treated as individual entities that may respond in unique and unexpected ways to the diagnosis of a disability.

Religion may also play a role in a family's attitudes toward and perceptions of their child. For example, in the study of Korean American parents noted previously, the majority of families were members of Korean ethnic churches, and their faith and involvement in their church gave them a sense of hope and support in parenting their child. Other studies found that a family's religious beliefs seemed to give them a sense of hope, support, and resilience (Lamorey, 2002).

Cultural beliefs may also influence the type of relationship that a family would like to have with educators working with their child. For example, one study (conducted in Japan) of Japanese mothers of children with exceptional needs found that the fundamental quality they desired in their child's teacher was one of respect for the child as a human being with dignity. They communicated to the professionals working with their children that they wanted their child to be treated as a human being with "irreplaceable value" and not as a "case, an object, or a number to study, process, or categorize" (Kasahara & Turnbull, 2005, p. 255).

As noted throughout this text, it is essential to learn about and respect a family's cultural beliefs and practices. However, because of the wide diversity among ethnic groups, it is also important to make efforts to get to know each individual family. For example, in one study of Japanese mothers of children with exceptional needs, a mother who was also a Japanese school counselor noted her perception of Japanese culture as tending to see individuals with exceptional needs as "abnormal" and the disabilities as "deviant and unacceptable, and therefore, as something that needed to be fixed" (Kasahara & Turnbull, 2005, p. 256). However, the mothers who participated in this study strongly rejected this cultural belief and considered their child's disability a normal part of human life. These parents also did not share the traditional Japanese acceptance of a hierarchical structure of authority, but instead wanted to be equal partners with educators in making decisions about their children's education (Kasahara & Turnbull, 2005). Diversity exists among families of the same culture, and it is important not to make assumptions about a family's beliefs based solely on their ethnicity or race.

CLASSROOM TEACHERS' ROLE IN SPECIAL EDUCATION

For more than 35 years, students with exceptional needs have been receiving a variety of special services in their public school systems. An increasing number of students with exceptional needs are obtaining a considerable amount of instruction in general education classrooms. Although the amount of time in the general education classroom is dictated by each student's IEP (or IFSP for infants and toddlers), more general educators are providing instruction to students with a variety of disabilities (U.S. Department of Education, 2007). It is therefore imperative that *all* teachers understand their role in the special education process, as well as the roles and responsibilities of family members.

As a classroom teacher, one of the more challenging parts of your job will be working with families who have children with exceptional needs. You must gain knowledge of the special education and referral process and specific regulations in your state and school district. You, the teacher, hold the unique position of knowing the students better than any other school personnel, and typically, you are the first person to talk to family members about concerns you may have. Advocating for and providing information to families is part of your job. You will be an employee of a school district; hence, you will walk a fine line as an advocate for the student and family who must adhere to district policies.

As a source of information on disabilities and the special education process, you may often find yourself in a collaborative role with students and families. This collaboration and cooperation consists of ensuring that students and families understand timelines, process, paperwork, meetings, and IEP/IFSP development and implementation. Of course, having a collaborative and cooperative relationship with families will assist in the education of all children, particularly those having difficulty at school.

To get a full picture of your roles and responsibilities in relation to families of children with exceptional needs, this chapter focuses on key pieces of legislation regarding the special education process, with particular attention to the IEP and to the benefits of the involvement of families in the special education process.

LEGISLATION RELATING TO THE EDUCATION OF CHILDREN WITH EXCEPTIONAL NEEDS

Legislation providing for the education of students with exceptional needs began with the establishment of the U.S. Department of Education in 1980. Initially, the Department assisted states in the development of school systems. Within the next 20 years, the Department added oversight of higher and vocational education to its duties (U.S. Department of Education, 2006b).

Special education legislation was not developed until later. It was aided in development by antipoverty and civil rights legislation. The landmark *Brown v. Board of Education* (1954) led the way for the implementation of legislation for providing education for those with disabilities (Pardini, 2002). The Civil Rights Act of 1964, Title IX of the Education Amendments, and Section 504 of the Rehabilitation Act of 1973 provided additional rights for those with disabilities. With these pieces of legislation and the formation of strong parent advocacy groups, the special education movement began. There has since been additional federal legislation concerning the education of children with disabilities (U.S. Department of Education, 2006b).

Some major pieces of legislation are presented in Table 11.2.

TABLE 11.2 Major Pieces of Legislation Affecting Children With Exceptional Needs	
Legislation	**Original Provisions and Later Modifications**
Elementary and Secondary Education Act (1965)	• Protected and provided for education for students from disadvantaged backgrounds • Established the free and reduced-cost lunch program • Encouraged states to create and improve programs for students with disabilities • Revised in 1970 as the Education of Handicapped Act (PL 91–30); continued to support state-run programs for students with disabilities but with no specific guidelines provided • Continues to be revised every five to seven years; latest revision was the No Child Left Behind Act of 2001
PL 94-142 (1975) Education for All Handicapped Children's Act	• Required states to provide FAPE for every child from ages six to 21 years with a disability • Required school districts to include families in the decision-making efforts regarding these children; required the development of an IEP for each child • Stated that students must be placed in the least restrictive environment and that evaluations must include nondiscriminatory tests completed by multidisciplinary teams • Added due-process procedures
PL 98-199 (1983) Education of the Handicapped Act Amendments	• Formed parent training and information centers that provided information to parents about how to protect the rights of their children

Legislation	Original Provisions and Later Modifications
PL 99-372 (1986) The Handicapped Children's Protection Act	• Allowed parents or guardians to be reimbursed for reasonable legal costs if they win a court action or hearing
PL 99-457 (1986) Amendment to the Education of the Handicapped Act (also known as the Early Intervention Amendment)	• Extended special education services to all children ages three to five years; created a new program for infants and toddlers
PL 100-407 (1988) Technology-Related Assistance for Individuals Act	• Focused on students with disabilities' need for special equipment to perform better and more independently during educational activities • Provided funding for states to create statewide systems of technological assistance for these students
PL 101-392 (1990) The Carl D. Perkins Vocational and Applied Technology Act	• Required that vocational education be provided for students with disabilities in the least restrictive environment and that a vocational option be part of an IEP • Provided equal access to vocational programs for individuals with disabilities
PL 101-476 (1990) Individuals With Disabilities Education Act (IDEA)	• Renamed the Education of Handicapped Children's Act as IDEA • Changed "handicapped" to "disabled" • Reaffirmed FAPE; extended the ages of eligibility for services from three to 21 years • Added assistive technology as a related service • Allowed for services for infants and toddlers • Required that a transition plan be in place to assist students (at age 16) in continued education and/or employment
PL 105-17 (1997) Individuals With Disabilities Education Act Amendments	• Reauthorized IDEA, clarified FAPE, strengthened the role of parents, ensured accessibility to the general education curriculum, and allowed states to expand the definition of developmental delay to include six- to nine-year-olds
PL 108-446 (2004) Individuals With Disabilities Education Improvement Act	• Reauthorized the original legislation (effective July 2005) with additional components • Key changes included (a) attention to disproportionality of those identified for special education (including over- and underrepresentation), (b) emphasis on early intervention, (c) new methods for identification of specific learning disabilities, (d) a provision for highly qualified special education teachers, (e) new information on IEP meetings and changes to the IEP

Sources: Hardman, Drew, & Egan, 2008; Law and Exceptional Students, 1998; National Education Association, 2008); U.S. Department of Education, 2006b.

Note: FAPE, free and appropriate public education; IDEA, The Individuals With Disabilities Education Act; IEP, individualized education program.

COMPONENTS OF IDEA

In 1975, the Education for All Handicapped Children's Act (PL 94–142) was established. In 1990, this legislation was renamed IDEA (**Individuals With Disabilities Education Act**), which is the legislation that guides the education of students with exceptional needs, and it was reauthorized in 2004. There are many provisions in the legislation dealing with use of funds, responsibility of local education agencies, and so on. There are five major provisions in IDEA that are still in effect today:

1. *A free and appropriate public education (FAPE).* At no cost to the families, an appropriate education and related services (e.g., speech and language services, occupational therapy, and physical therapy) must be provided to students with disabilities. An ideal education does not need to be provided, but an appropriate and beneficial one is required.

2. *Nondiscriminatory, multidisciplinary assessment.* Students must be assessed in their native language by a team of professionals. The assessment procedures must be free of cultural or racial discrimination, and the assessment instruments must be used for their intended purposes.

3. *Parental safeguards and involvement.* The purpose of the safeguards for the family is to help ensure that they are involved in the education of their children. Parents or guardians must give consent for their child to be evaluated and receive special services. They can request an independent evaluation at public expense, and they can view their child's records. Parents or guardians have the right to participate in the development of the IEP, and they can request a due process hearing if needed.

4. *Individualized education program (IEP) or individualized family service plan for children under three years old (IFSP).* More specific information regarding the IEP will be provided later in this chapter. Briefly, families and professionals work together to develop a plan for an appropriate education for an individual child. The IEP helps determine the type of special services required for this student.

5. *Education in the **least restrictive environment** (LRE).* IDEA required school districts to develop a continuum of services and placements for students with disabilities. This continuum provides options ranging from a general education class to a homebound or hospital type program. The goal of the LRE provision is to ensure that each child is provided with an education and related services in a program as much like a general education classroom as is appropriate for the student (Hardman, Drew, & Egan, 2008).

Additionally, IDEA has a strong linkage to the No Child Left Behind (NCLB) Act of 2001. This act has been a major influence on IDEA in two primary areas. One area of influence is on standards and school accountability. NCLB supports a standards-based approach that has a focus on student achievement, an emphasis on maintaining challenging academic standards for all students, and a strong reliance on achievement testing. This approach is different in the way special education students were treated in the past. Historically, many students with exceptional needs were left out of standards-based education and standardized achievement tests.

The second area in which NCLB has been influential is that of "highly qualified teachers." Federal legislation now describes what is meant by highly qualified; this is a change, as teaching certification had earlier been left up to the states and local school districts. "Highly qualified" means that the individual has full state certification or has passed a state licensing exam. Elementary special education teachers must have subject knowledge in reading, mathematics, writing, and other areas in which they will be teaching. Secondary special education teachers must be highly qualified in one subject area and will have two years from the date of employment to demonstrate competence in the additional core academic subjects (Hardman et al., 2008).

As you think about your role as a general education classroom teacher who works with families of children with exceptional needs and who is responsible for communicating to them their legal rights, consider this situation:

IDEA states that all children are entitled to a free and appropriate education in the least restrictive environment.

> Ninjin is a student in your third-grade class. She and her family have not been in the United States for very long. Ninjin attended part of first grade and all of second grade in your school, and according to school records, she has done fairly well in learning English. However, her parents have limited English language usage. Her father speaks some English, but her mother speaks only their native Mongolian language. You have some concerns that Ninjin may have some learning difficulties that go beyond the language issue. Even with a fairly good command of the English language, she is having difficulty in most academic areas. You would like to refer her to the special education team but are concerned that Ninjin's parents will not understand either the process or their and Ninjin's rights according to the law.

What can you do? What obligations does the school district have if the special education referral process goes forward regarding the families and students when English is not their first language? What about the evaluation process—if Ninjin gets tested, what guarantees must be in place?

COMMUNICATING WITH FAMILIES ABOUT EXCEPTIONAL NEEDS

If you have felt overwhelmed and confused as you read through the last section on legislation relating to children with exceptional needs, imagine how families feel when laws, regulations, procedures, and terminology are sent home in paperwork or discussed in an IEP conference. Initial, ongoing, and meaningful communication that helps families understand all the issues relating to educating their child is critical. As noted earlier in this text, communication with all families is vital, but it is especially so for families of children with either a suspected or a confirmed disability.

There are many different ways to communicate, and the best ways will vary depending on family needs. Some suggestions for successful communication with families include the following:

- Keep them informed at the beginning and throughout the school year, and continue communication efforts through a variety of methods, including formal and informal conferences and meetings.
- Include positive dialogue so that the first thing families hear from you is not a problem or a concern. Communication should be honest and open—there should be no "sugarcoating" of bad news—yet be tactful and sensitive. Do not imply blame (Blue-Banning, Frankland, & Summers, 2004; U.S. Department of Education, 2006a).
- View the child from a strengths perspective, rather than a deficit model, and reflect this in your communication with families. For example, talk about what the child *can* do and not just the disability. Parents typically see their whole child and not just the disability and will appreciate a teacher who recognizes that their child learns differently and has abilities, interests, and skills beyond the special need.
- Avoid using educational jargon and acronyms when discussing tests and diagnoses. For example, terms such as LD, BD, ADHD, OT, PT, and so on can be confusing to someone not working in education. The same holds true for test names, such as WISC-R (Blue-Banning et al., 2004; Salend, 2006).
- Use respectful and people-first terminology, which will instill trust with families. Saying "a child with special needs" instead of "a special needs child" shows that you understand that the child is a child first and the disability is secondary. For example, "Ella has blond hair, blue eyes, and Down syndrome" better reflects who she is than "Ella is a Down syndrome kid" (J. Pewitt-Kinder, DO, personal communication, March 19, 2008). **People-first language** demonstrates that you are viewing the child as someone who has abilities and is deserving of your respect (Logsdon, 2011). Another term to avoid is "normal," which implies that children with exceptional needs are "abnormal."
- Also demonstrate respect in your interactions for their contributions and efforts in parenting their child. Ask them to share with you their experiences and acknowledge that they are the experts about their child and may have gone to great lengths to help their child grow and develop. For example, think about the importance of acknowledging the efforts of this parent:

My pregnancy was high-risk full placenta previa and high blood pressure. I had an emergency C-section at 31 weeks. Anna had a chest-tube and was in the NICU [neonatal intensive care unit] 40 days. When she was released from the hospital, she came home on oxygen, and it was imperative while under the care of her lung doctor that she not be in any day care, malls, church, or around other small children till after the age of two. In the event she would catch RSV, it could have been life threatening. I took my job seriously and literally sheltered her from the outside world. Anna knew everything, her ABCs, colors, states. I taught her everything. . . . A typical mother of a child on the [autism] spectrum spends countless hours on the Internet looking for a cure. That is exactly what I did. I read books, websites, etc. Here are just a few things I have done—read books, started her on the gluten-free diet, vitamin therapy, detoxifying/ridding her of all metals, the list goes on (A. Fildes, personal communication, April 26, 2011).

- Have two-way discussions with families encouraging them to express the dreams or goals they have for their child. Listen nonjudgmentally to their viewpoints (U.S. Department of Education, 2006a). As the previous mother stated, "I have no doubt that my daughter will lead a productive life. She takes piano lessons and had her first recital. She is going to cheerleading camp this summer and is such a delight to be around" (A Fildes, personal communication, April 26, 2011).
- Document each student's progress; it is essential that you keep good records on students' academic progress and on behavioral issues. This documentation can be used in sharing information with family members, in planning instruction and interventions for the student, and in planning meetings with intervention teams for possible special education referral (U.S. Department of Education, 2006a). In addition, keep track of family communications, including dates and contents of communications.
- Obtain translation services for families who do not speak English as a first language. Translators should have the family's confidence and understand legal and ethical guidelines relating to confidentiality. Make school reports simple and use graphics or icons to convey information. Provide written materials translated into the native language (Al-Hassan & Gardner, 2002; U.S. Department of Education, 2006a).
- Although families typically communicate most readily with classroom teachers, they should be given the opportunity to communicate with school and district administrators, therapists, and other school professionals as well. Make sure that families know they have the right to be part of the decision-making process (U.S. Department of Education, 2006a).
- Hold meetings that offer families the opportunity to meet and learn more about the different services their children receive. For example, with **inclusion**, or the principle that children with disabilities benefit by learning side-by-side general education students in the least restrictive environment (LRE) possible, many children with exceptional needs are in the general education classroom for much of the day, and families may be confused about who is their child's real teacher. Explaining how team teaching, with the general education classroom teacher, special education teacher, speech and language pathologist, physical therapist, or occupational

therapist working with all students, can help them better understand the educational process. Guest speakers, including family members of children with exceptional needs, can share their experiences and provide encouragement (Salend, 2006).

- Coordinate with others involved in providing services for children so that all important information is shared with families. For example, when parents stumble onto information about their child, they worry about what other information they haven't been told (Blue-Banning et al., 2004).

Many family members will be fearful of the special education system and process, but this is particularly true of families who differ in their culture, language, and practices from the majority culture. Despite more than 35 years of legislation mandating family involvement, there is often a lack of involvement of parents from diverse cultural and linguistic backgrounds (Al-Hassan & Gardner, 2002). Among the reasons why this may occur are a lack of English proficiency, a large amount of intimidating paperwork, a number of complicated legal procedures, the belief that their opinions are not valued, a lack of overall trust in professionals, and the cultural insensitivity of educators. Family cultural beliefs may also play a role in avoidance of the special education system. For example, because of the extended family structure of some Latino and African American families, there may be some hesitancy to allow help from outside of the family (Hardman et al., 2008). This may also hold true in some Asian American families, where, depending on the family background, there may be pressure on children to achieve academic excellence (Kim & Yeh, 2002) or, by contrast, a need to protect the student with disabilities from the outside world or even from the extended family (Tsao, 2000). Additionally, what is noted as a disability in the majority culture may be considered typical in the student's culture (Hardman et al., 2008).

Families from diverse backgrounds are more likely to collaborate with teachers when they believe that teachers are genuinely interested in their children and are making an effort to understand their culture. For example, attending community festivals, neighborhood parties, or church events can communicate a sense of caring and can help build trust between home and school (Matuszny, Banda, & Coleman, 2007). Newly immigrated families may be unfamiliar with educational practices in American schools, and may not be informed about their legal rights, as many developing countries do not have laws about educating children with disabilities. New immigrants may not ask for services for their children (Al-Hassan & Gardner, 2002). As the classroom teacher, it will be important that you advocate for the child's needs and fully explain the referral and testing process to families in a way that they can understand.

As you think about communicating with families of children with exceptional needs, consider this situation:

As a second-grade teacher, you have not had a good relationship with a particular parent. Carl's parent is a single mom raising three children. She does not come in to school often or contact you, but when she does, she is usually unhappy about something. You have tried to be very pleasant but are getting frustrated with her complaining. Carl misses quite a bit of school and is falling behind in his academic work. He also has some difficulty getting along with his classmates. You have decided to send Carl's mom a letter through the mail requesting a meeting to discuss Carl. You want to talk with her about his academic and behavior problems. You schedule the meeting during your 30-minute lunch period. She is 10 minutes late so you only have 20 minutes in which to express your concerns. You jump right in and talk with her about his problems. After about 10 minutes, Carl's mom looks at her watch and says she has to go. You weren't able to get your points across and weren't able to discuss next steps.

What could you have done differently? What communication tips could you have used to make this a more productive meeting?

FAMILIES OF CHILDREN WITH AUTISM

According to the Centers for Disease Control, autism is diagnosed in 1 out of 110 children today, making autism more prevalent than childhood cancers, multiple sclerosis, and cystic fibrosis combined (Autism Education Network, 2011, para 1).

A special note should be made about working with families of children with autism. Research has demonstrated that parents of children on the autism spectrum disorder (ASD) do not always feel valued as equal partners with educational professionals. However, teachers with positive dispositions toward students with autism increase the trust parents feel in schools and their resources. An ongoing program (PACE) involving parent-professional training that articulated its theme as "knowledge is power" noted awareness of the following dynamics with families of students with autism:

1. Families differ in experiential background based on the severity of the child's autism. Parents of children with severe ASD frequently experienced difficulty relating to parents of children with milder forms of ASD.

2. Family stories function as powerful learning tools for educators unaware of the characteristics of ASD. In addition, parents of children with special needs can be positively affected by these stories (Murray, Ackerman-Spain, Williams, & Ryley, 2011).

As noted in the earlier quote from a mom of a child with autism, "cybermothers" of children with ASD often surf the Internet in search of supportive solutions to the unique challenges of raising their children. They establish social networks through blogs and interactive websites and seek current research articles as well as practical ideas to help their children. School districts can take advantage of this driving interest to connect with parents of students with autism by using their school website to post articles or set up blogs. Family resource centers can serve as the locus for online peer-support networks (Zeman, Swake, & Doktor, 2011).

REFERRAL PROCESS AND IDENTIFICATION

General education teachers are crucial to the entire special education process. As mentioned previously, you are typically the professionals who notice that a student is having learning and/or behavioral problems, and you are the one who communicates with the family first. You are the one to try different interventions to assist the student. It is imperative that you understand the processes, timelines, and procedures for students to receive special services so that you can explain them to the family. The family often will not know other school personnel (psychologists, speech and language pathologists, therapists, etc.) and will look to you to explain what is happening with their child.

Screening and Testing for Exceptionality

Students do not automatically enter special education programs. For their protection, and to make sure placement is done carefully and accurately, there are various steps in accomplishing this. Family members should be involved and informed about every step of the process. These steps include the following:

1. *Referral.* Parents or guardians, school personnel, students, or others may make a request for an evaluation. The referral typically is directed to a school team made of special services personnel, administrators, and general education teachers. Often, the team will make recommendations to the classroom teacher about initiating and/or continuing interventions he may conduct in the general education classroom. The classroom teacher does this and reports to the team. The team may then recommend proceeding with an evaluation. Throughout this first step, the family is kept in the communication loop, often providing additional information to the team.

2. *Assessing eligibility for special services.* This must be a full and individual evaluation using a multidisciplinary team and nondiscriminatory instruments and procedures. Parents or guardians must give written permission for an evaluation. The purpose of the assessment is to determine eligibility for special education services and to assist in the development of the IEP. If the district refuses to conduct an evaluation, it must notify families and let them know their rights. If a child is not eligible for services, families have the right to disagree with the decision. Families also have the right to an independent educational evaluation.

3. *Development of an IEP.* If a child is eligible for special education and parents or guardians agree, both parties will plan the child's IEP at an IEP meeting. (An IFSP for children younger than three years will be discussed separately.) The IEP states what special services a child will need, including measurable annual goals and objectives as well as benchmarks to record progress. Additionally, the IEP specifies (a) who will deliver services, (b) what criteria will be used to assess progress, (c) the extent to which the student will have access to the general education curriculum, (d) the extent to which she will participate in statewide or school assessments, (e) a behavior plan (if needed), and (f) a process for reporting progress to families.

4. *Determining placement.* Placement decisions are made after the IEP is written. These decisions may occur at different meetings. Placement must be made into the LRE appropriate for the child, and it must be based on annual goals and on the special education services needed. An IEP meeting must be held at least once a year. Parents or guardians are part of these meetings and must consent in writing to the contents of the IEP. If families disagree with the IEP and/or the proposed placement, a compromise agreement is attempted.

Cultural and linguistic diversity can play a major role in the identification and education of students with exceptional needs. In some instances, students from diverse cultures that differ from the mainstream culture are overrepresented in the special education population, and the rate at which minority students are placed in special education is increasing (The Civil Rights Project, 2002). Data from the 2002 Annual Report to Congress on Implementation of IDEA, submitted by the U.S. Department of Education's Office of Special Education Programs (OSEP), showed that from ages 6 to 21 years,

> [the percentage of] American Indian/Alaska Native and Hispanic children receiving services for specific learning disabilities, the percentage of Asian/Pacific Islander children receiving services for speech or language impairments, and the percentage of Black children receiving services for mental retardation were somewhat higher than the percentages for all students served under IDEA. (U.S. Department of Education, 2002, p. II-24)

A recent analysis of minorities in the different disability categories found that African American students were more likely to be labeled as intellectually disabled, learning disabled, or emotionally disturbed than white students, and they were also more likely to be excluded from general education classrooms (Jordan, 2005). Some believe that the overrepresentation of African American males in special education is because of biased testing and lack of cultural competence on the part of those making the referrals for evaluation. Teachers should be aware of cultural differences that sometimes manifest themselves in the classroom and should be given staff development opportunities to learn to understand culturally sensitive testing practices (T. Moody, personal communication, March 5, 2008).

Families in low-socioeconomic conditions, especially minority families, are often the most vulnerable, and it is vital that accurate documentation of the students' abilities be obtained before beginning the special education referral process. Williams (2007) recommends that school leaders focus on the following three areas to ensure that ethical, thoughtful, and culturally competent practices are standard throughout the referral process.

1. *Facilitate a school atmosphere of transparency, trust, and collaboration with families.* Many families receive overt and covert messages that their experiences and opinions about how their child learns best are of little importance to the school.

2. *Attract, recruit, and retain teachers who practice culturally responsive family involvement.* These teachers should continually ask themselves, "What do I expect from parents, why do I expect this, and how does it support the child's education?" (Williams, 2007, p. 260). These teachers are aware of both the narrowly defined ideas of parental roles and obligations held by some educators and the expanded community-based roles families actually assume.

3. *Recognize the sociocultural, political, and historical realities that shape the experience of students and affect educational outcomes.* Remember that families are shaped by their worldviews and community interactions.

As you think about your role in the referral, screening, and evaluation process, consider this situation:

A parent of a student in your fourth-grade class sets up a conference with you. He believes his son has a learning disability and wants him placed in special education. When you explain that there is a process and timelines to be followed, he doesn't understand and thinks the district is trying to deny help to his son. You have some concerns about this student's academic progress, but there are others in your class you believe have more serious problems. At this conference you intend to explain the process to this father and hope that you can come to a shared understanding of the situation.

What will you tell this parent about the special education process? How will you explain to this parent that the timelines are for his son's protection? What other things could you do with this student and parent while you are going through the special education process?

INVOLVING FAMILIES IN THE IEP PROCESS

By reviewing the special education process, you can see that the IEP is one of the most critical parts of ensuring appropriate education for children with disabilities. A school district must ensure that families are notified and that they have a chance to participate in the development of the IEP. Besides providing the date, time, and location of the IEP meeting, notification of this meeting must include the names of those who will be attending and the purpose of the meeting. All efforts should be made to make sure that families can attend this meeting. The IEP team must include the parents or guardians of the student, at least one general education teacher, a special education teacher, and a representative of the district who knows the general education curriculum and knows the available resources for students with disabilities. Others may attend at the discretion of the family or the school district (Hardman et al., 2008).

How do you prepare yourself for the IEP meeting? Again, remember that other than the family, you know more about the student than anyone else. Armed with information from the evaluation that has been completed, you can compare that evaluation with classroom work the student has done for you; you will then be able to bring to the meeting some general goals and benchmarks and to suggest criteria for determining whether these benchmarks have been reached. In addition to preparing yourself for the meeting, you can assist the family members in their preparations. Prior to the meeting, make sure that the family has been notified and that the date and time are convenient for them. Students with exceptional needs are more likely than others to be raised by single mothers or other female caregivers. Because of this, the balance between work and family is often an issue, and the scheduling of an IEP meeting should take this into account (Cohen, 2006). When preparing families for the meeting, tell them who will be there and what these people's roles are in the process. It can be overwhelming to walk into a room with five or six school professionals present. Families should also know that they can bring guests to the meeting, but they should inform the IEP team that they will be doing so. Advise the parents or guardians as to what will go on during the meeting, emphasizing their role and importance to the meeting. Encourage them to think about the goals they have for their child and bring those up at the meeting. They should also be encouraged to question anything that is said at the meeting that they don't understand. They should make sure that they agree with the IEP before they sign (Hardman et al., 2008; PACER Center, n.d.).

It is important to remember that the IEP meeting is to develop, with family input, a plan for the student's education. According to IDEA, the IEP is supposed to be written by parents or guardians, teachers, and administrators who know the child. In some cases involving low-income or minority families, educators may be hesitant to include them in the initial drafting of the student's IEP. Instead, they will write the IEP without family input and only ask for the parents' or guardians' signature when they arrive at the IEP meeting. Williams (2007) writes that this practice is not only illegal, but also "immoral and grossly unethical" (p. 255). As the teacher, it is important that you be an advocate for students and families in ensuring that their legal rights are observed and that they do participate in the planning process.

After the entire process is completed, the child often continues to spend part of each school day in your classroom. You should familiarize yourself with the IEPs of the students in your classes and be clear on your responsibilities with regard to their education. A carefully developed IEP will provide the appropriate framework for the student's education.

As you think about your role in the IEP process, consider this situation:

As a new first-grade teacher, this is the first time you have had a student in your class who was found eligible for special education. You worked through part of the process by providing alternative strategies for the student to use in the general education classroom, and you have kept good documentation of the student's progress. You have been in communication with the family of the student throughout the process. It is now time for the IEP conference, and it has been scheduled at a time when you are in class.

What should you do about this time conflict and how should you prepare for the IEP meeting? What is your role in the IEP conference?

COLLABORATION WITH FAMILIES OF YOUNG CHILDREN: INDIVIDUAL FAMILY SERVICE PLANS

Part of IDEA (Part C) deals with children under the age of three years with exceptional needs. Instead of the IEP, the guiding plan for the child as well as the family is called the individual family service plan (IFSP). There are differences between the IEP and the IFSP, with the primary difference being the greater focus on the family in the IFSP. See Table 11.3 for a summary of differences between the IEP and the IFSP.

Besides containing information about the services the child will need, the IFSP includes information on what is necessary to facilitate the family's capacity to enhance the child's development.

The IFSP contains the child's present level of development; the family's resources, priorities, and concerns; the major outcomes to be achieved by the child and the family; and the services necessary to achieve the outcomes. The services are to be implemented in the natural environments

An IFSP is developed for children under the age of three years with exceptional needs.

TABLE 11.3 Key Differences Between the Individualized Education Program (IEP) and the Individualized Family Service Plan (IFSP)

Individualized Education Program	Individualized Family Service Plan
Ages 3 to 21 years	Birth to 3 years
Focus is on the child.	Focus is on the family and their role in supporting the child's learning and development.
Outcome objectives are focused on the child.	Outcome objectives are focused not only on the child but also on the family.
School and classroom environment are the focus of the plan. Services are provided in the school setting.	The concept of natural environments is introduced. Natural environments include places where learning may occur outside of school. Services may be provided in the home.
Local school district manages the child's services.	Because of the age of the child, many agencies may be involved in providing services for the child. The IFSP should integrate these services.
The IEP process is coordinated by the school district.	A service coordinator is named. The service coordinator assists the family in the implementation of the IFSP.
The goal of the IEP meeting is to develop long-term and short-term goals for the student and to plan accommodations and modifications, services, and placement.	The goal of the IFSP meeting is to offer information and resources to family, define various agencies' roles, and clarify financial responsibility.
The IEP meeting is typically held once a year.	The IFSP meeting is typically held every six months.

Sources: Bruder, 2000; Concord Special Education Parent Advisory Committee, 2001; PACER Center, 2000

of the child. Like the IEP, the IFSP also contains dates and duration of services, service providers' names, and the steps that will be taken to support transition to preschool or to other types of services (Bruder, 2000).

It is obvious that families are critical in the development and implementation of IFSPs. For many families, this will be the first interaction with any type of "system" as it relates to their child; it is critical that professionals offer services in a family-centered way. Some key principles of family-centered care include (a) the family is the constant in the child's life, (b) collaboration is important, (c) sharing of information between families and professionals is necessary, (d) family diversity and strengths should be honored, and (e) services should be flexible (Shelton & Stepanek cited in Batshaw, 2002).

How might you help a family prepare for the development of an IFSP? Recognizing that it is based on a child and family's strengths, their concerns, and their priorities is the first step. More than ever, families should take the lead in this system. As a professional, you may need to help guide families to recognize their strengths and priorities, and you should be sensitive to a family's culture, routines, and values. Table 11.4 provides guidelines for helping families prepare for the IFSP meeting.

Table 11.4	Helping Families Prepare for an Individualized Family Service Plan (IFSP) Meeting

Teachers and other professionals can help families prepare for an IFSP meeting in the following ways:

- Suggest that families talk with others who have been through the process to gain some insight.
- Make sure families know as much as possible about their child's developmental delay or physical or mental condition that may lead to a delay.
- Have families list their questions and concerns in writing prior to the meeting.
- Suggest that families invite those they believe are critical to the successful implementation of the IFSP to the meeting.
- Make sure that families understand that they have the right to provide input as to the day, time, and location of the meeting.
- Have families think ahead of time about where they want services for their child to be delivered.
- If needed, help families identify their concerns, strengths, and priorities, as they will be asked to share on these topics in the meeting.

Source: Adapted from North Bay Regional Center (n.d.).

When children with exceptional needs reach the age of three years, they will move into the public school realm, and this transition can be difficult for some families. Consider that, prior to this, the child may have had the same therapists for three years, with therapy done in the familiar home or child-care setting. Now, the services are shifted to a public school setting. This typically involves new testing, lengthy meetings, and much paperwork. Families may have to learn education laws, and they must learn the IEP process and get adjusted to new therapists and teachers. One mother said her experience made her feel all these feelings:

- *Sad:* "Overnight, our child went from being a baby to being a school girl!"
- *Overwhelmed:* There were lots of new things to learn.
- *Tired:* It was hard to juggle meetings, therapy, and paperwork.
- *Angry:* Strangers were telling us what they think is best for our child based on a test score.
- *Surprised:* We didn't know we would have to "fight" for our daughter's rights.
- *Comforted:* Most parents describe the IEP process in the same way. We weren't alone. (J. Pewitt-Kinder, D.O., personal communication, March 19, 2008)

Because of fears of a special education label, some parents may be hesitant to have their child evaluated for special services by the public school. One parent described her fears:

I noticed at around 2 ½ Anna wasn't saying more than one or two words. She did a lot of holophrasing, and we all knew what she wanted, so we gave it to her. At her third-year check up, I voiced my concerns to my pediatrician. She suggested speech therapy. I contacted [a local] university and had her evaluated and started in their program working with graduate students. She did two semesters with a student and participated in a play-group setting. The coordinator suggested I have Anna evaluated for a diagnosis—suggesting

> Asperger's syndrome, sensory [disorder], etc. I took her to a neurologist and he gave her the diagnosis of PDD-NOS [Pervasive Developmental Disorder—Not Otherwise Specified]. Up to that point, I had never heard of PDD-NOS. Further, he didn't tell me it fell on the [autism] spectrum. He advised me to have her evaluated by the public school and enroll her in a preschool. She already was in a private preschool two days a week. The last thing I wanted to do was have her evaluated by the public school. Personally, I felt like they were going to label her and it would turn into this vicious never-ending cycle. (A. Fildes, personal communication, April 26, 2011)

If you are working with a family who is transitioning from an early intervention program to the school setting or entering a public school setting for the first time, it is important that you be understanding and patient and realize the importance for the family of a positive first experience with school.

As you think about collaborating with families of young children with exceptional needs, consider this situation:

> Your first job is working for an agency providing services to families of children with exceptional needs who are under the age of three years. You have been hired to travel to the homes of children to deliver early intervention services with a speech and language therapist. Because of the unique nature of the settings, you encounter families of different cultures, living conditions, beliefs, and practices. Becky, the speech therapist, is experienced, and you are relying on her to help you through the first IFSP meeting in which you will be participating. She tells you that the parents have somewhat limited abilities, and she is unsure of their reading ability. When you get to the house, you notice that Becky already has the IFSP forms filled out, and at the meeting, she goes through the forms quickly. You can tell that the parents are confused, but they do sign the forms. You also notice that the parents obviously love their child and are doing a good job raising her.

Is there anything you could have done differently during this IFSP meeting? How will you prepare for the next IFSP meeting in which you will participate? What might this experience teach you about differences in families?

As you can see, your role as a child's primary teacher is of critical importance in getting the appropriate assistance and services for students in your class who have disabilities. You are a key person in this rather complicated process. Obtain the knowledge needed to work with other professionals and families and to do what is right for your students.

RESPONSE TO INTERVENTION

A new approach that is becoming increasingly prevalent in schools to address the learning difficulties of all children is response to intervention, or RTI (Dunn, 2010). This model uses a three (or more) tiered approach where each level offers increasingly intensive interventions for struggling learners (Byrd, 2011). Figure 11.1 illustrates how the process works in primary grades reading instruction. All children are given instruction in Tier 1, with regular testing or universal screening to determine if children are making progress or having difficulties. Children who need help with specific skills will receive interventions in Tier 2, through small group instruction with other children who are having similar difficulties. This instruction is designed to help them catch up with peers and not fall behind. It is expected that 90% to 95% of students will be successful in school through instruction in Tiers 1 and 2 (Hoover & Love, 2011). For the small number of children whose needs are not met in the general classroom or small group instruction, Tier 3 offers intensive one-on-one instruction and support. RTI is often depicted in a pyramid model, illustrating that all children receive high-quality instruction in Tier 1, with fewer students needing help in Tier 2, and a small percentage needing the intensive intervention of Tier 3. Although the model is most commonly used with reading in the primary grades, schools are also implementing this approach in other subjects, such as mathematics, as well as for behavior issues. Research has shown that RTI is having a positive impact on student learning, with a decline in special education placements from 4.5% to 2.5% in schools using RTI (Dunn, 2010).

The RTI approach differs from the "wait to fail" model of the past with its preventive approach (Dunn, 2010; Hoover & Love, 2011), and it may be difficult for parents or caregivers to understand the new terminology and methods. Terms like "progress monitoring," "intervention," or "universal screening" represent educational jargon to families, and in many schools, there has been little attention to the families' role in RTI or how to educate them about this new process (Byrd, 2011). Helping families understand that RTI is a general education initiative for all families and how it differs from traditional special education practices requires the efforts of everyone: administrators, classroom teachers, the parent liaison, and the school's RTI team. Communicating throughout the interventions process regularly can also help the transition for children to special education, as families better understand all the efforts that have been made to help their children. Following are some suggestions for communicating about and involving families in RTI:

- Have parent education meetings to explain RTI; create DVDs of the presentations for families who were unable to attend.
- Provide all families with print and online information (translated for families who do not speak English) about RTI. The National Center on Response to Intervention offers helpful handouts that can be given to parents.
- Ask parent leaders, such as PTA officers, to serve on the school's RTI team.
- Have family members share the RTI process from their perspective in newsletter or newspaper articles, as well as at parent education meetings (Byrd, 2011).

WORKING WITH FAMILIES OF GIFTED AND TALENTED STUDENTS

Until every gifted child can attend a school where the brightest are appropriately challenged in an environment with their intellectual peers, America can't claim that it's leaving no child behind.

—Jan and Bob Davidson (2005)

FIGURE 11.1 RTI Diagram

Response to Intervention Framework in Primary Grade Reading

Response to Intervention (RtI) is a framework for supporting students who are potentially at risk and assisting them before they fall behind. RtI is grounded in high quality core classroom instruction for all students which is then supplemented as necessary by progressively more intensive interventions for students who may struggle with reading or mathematics. Key components of RtI are periodic universal screening to determine which students may need additional instruction and ongoing progress monitoring to ascertain the effectiveness of additional instruction. The RtI framework represents a continuum and is often depicted as a triangle with three tiers of progressive intensity.

Tier 3: Intensive Support
Most intense, often one-to-one

Tier 1: Core Instruction
All students

Tier 2: Interventions
Small group, more intense instruction
focused on specific skills

TIER 3: INTENSIVE SUPPORT

TIER 2: INTERVENTION

TIER 1: CORE

UNIVERSAL SCREENING

TIER 3
TIER 2
TIER 1

All Students
Universal Screening
–Create RtI team to implement screening
–Select measures based on:
   reliability, efficiency, validity
–Screen all students
–Use benchmarks to set cut-points

All Tiers
Progress Monitoring and Differentiation
–Use screening data to differentiate in Tier 1 and
   progress monitoring data to differentiate in
   Tiers 2 and 3
–Differentiate by varying time, content, and support
–Provide training on data collection and
   interpretation
–Establish decision rules for using data

Tiers 2 & 3
Systematic Skill Instruction
–Provide small group instruction at Tier 2
–Focus on a few skills in daily sessions at Tier 3
–Use an intervention curriculum based on foundational
   reading skills
–Intense instruction features:
   modeling, scaffolding, thinkalouds, practice, and
   corrective feedback

DOING WHAT WORKS, http://dww.ed.gov
U.S. Department of Education

Source: U.S. Department of Education, *DOING WHAT WORKS,* http://dww.ed.gov

Students who are gifted and talented are often not considered when people discuss the topic of exceptional needs. As you may have noted, gifted and talented is not one of the categories defined by IDEA as requiring special educational services. Because gifted and talented students just seem to know information and learn faster than other students, some people question whether any intervention is needed. However, as one parent of a student who is gifted stated, "We are often portrayed as antidemocratic because we want special classes for our children. The simple fact is that students with special needs require special services" (Martin, 2002, p. 3). As with any student who has an exceptional need, gifted students have a right to a "free and appropriate education." However, as opposed to the other exceptional needs with federal legislation requirements, there are no national mandates for gifted education programs, and your school may provide services for students who are gifted and talented. Gifted education programs are under the supervision of state laws, which vary greatly, and family involvement in planning a gifted student's educational program has not received the same attention by states or school districts as for students in special education (Hertzog & Bennett, 2004). Because of this lack of national requirements for gifted education, a student who is gifted may not have access to a teacher who specializes in gifted education, and the general education classroom teacher may be the student's primary educator (Milligan & Nichols, 2005).

The Department of Education defines students who are "gifted and talented" as

> children or youth who give evidence of high achievement capability in areas such as intellectual, creative, artistic, or leadership capacity, or in specific academic fields, and who need services or activities not ordinarily provided by the school in order to fully develop those capabilities. (U.S. Department of Education, 2004)

Typically, most programs in schools focus on students who are intellectually advanced (gifted) rather than students who have artistic, creative, or leadership talents. Families must often find enrichment for their talented children through extracurricular or private activities. Therefore, this discussion will focus on working with families of students who are gifted.

As with students with exceptional needs, identifying children who are gifted is one of the first steps in meeting their needs. About 80% of parents of gifted children can identify their child's giftedness by age four or five years (often more accurately than teachers), and they can provide the most realistic information about their children's abilities and needs. Therefore, consulting with them is a good place to start when beginning the testing process (Smutny, 2000). However, this does not mean that all families understand the characteristics and needs of gifted children. Families need accurate information about giftedness and the testing involved in the identification process. As the classroom teacher, you need to communicate this information in a way that is free of educational and psychological jargon.

Once a child has been identified as gifted, the next issue that families and educators face is how to best meet their child's needs, apart from those that can be met by the general education classroom curriculum. Families may have to make decisions such as whether their child should attend a magnet school for gifted students or stay in the same school but leave the classroom to spend a portion of the school day in a gifted pullout program. Gifted children may also be accelerated, or advanced, to a higher grade for some or all sub-jects or stay in the general education classroom but receive differentiated instruction, such as **cluster grouping** (students who are gifted are placed together in a classroom with other students of mixed abilities with a teacher who has training in how to teach stu-dents with exceptional abilities) or **curriculum compacting** (strategy for differentiating instruction for gifted students, where they move at a quicker pace through classroom material and then have time to study other topics of interest in more depth). They may even be home schooled if the school cannot meet their needs. Students who are gifted are quite different from one another, and their abilities may be uneven. For example, a verbally highly gifted child may lack math skills, and a cognitively gifted child may be uninterested in physical activities. Students may also be **twice-exceptional**, or both gifted and learning disabled. This can make placement decisions difficult for both families and teachers. Other factors for families to consider are the social and emotional issues that may arise if children are accelerated to a higher grade and spend the school day with older students. These issues add to the difficulty of choosing an appropriate education for an individual child, as there are no clear-cut recommendations, and every child is different. As one parent said, "Every year the decision-making process is painful, and the fear of doing the wrong thing is always on my mind" (Reinisch & Reinisch, 1997, p. 242).

One of the problems in making placement decisions for their gifted children is that families do not always feel like equal partners with educators while these decisions are made, and educators may have misconceptions about what "giftedness" is. For example, a teacher may not want to send a student to a gifted program because the student does not complete his work in class, when, from the family's perspective, the student is not being challenged and is refusing to do busywork. One study found that parents reported that they felt they had little control over the education their children received at school, and they supplemented what they thought was lacking in their children's education with extracur-ricular activities. As one parent stated, "I don't have any control. I feel I can only make suggestions and hope the teacher uses them" (Hertzog & Bennett, 2004, p. 102). Because the general education classroom curriculum may not be the best match for children who are gifted, communication and collaboration with their families are crucial in meeting these children's needs.

As with all families, it is important to listen to the fears, worries, and suggestions of parents of gifted children about their children's education. Sadly, parents of students who are gifted often report that their most difficult relationships are with educational profes-sionals (Stephens, 1999). Often perceived by teachers as being a "pushy parent who expects special favors" (Reinisch & Reinisch, 1997, p. 246), the mother of a child who is gifted typically has had to be an advocate for her child. One parent described how, in meetings with school personnel to discuss her child's needs, she felt she was in an "us versus them" situation (Reinisch, & Reinisch, 1997, p. 248). Adversarial situations such as this benefit no one, especially not the child. It is important to recognize that families and teachers have the same goal: to help children reach their highest potential. Although teachers may not agree with parents about how best to reach that goal, collaboration is the key to the process (Strip & Hirsch, 2001).

Families of children who are gifted can provide incredible insights into their children's abilities and needs, and they can be a great support to you in your teaching efforts. Some tips for working with families of gifted students include the following:

- Learn as much as possible about the characteristics and the needs of gifted students. If possible, form a study group on gifted education with other teachers at your school and seek to be a resource for families.
- Seek families' input in learning about how to meet the needs of gifted students. Recognize that parents know their child's abilities better than anyone; listen to their ideas about how to meet their child's needs.
- Help families be informed and help them understand the mandated process for identifying and referring gifted students. Explain which tests are used and when they are given.
- Work together with parents to find creative ways to help the child reach her full potential. Gifted children may require a combination of different approaches, such as **acceleration**, or advancement to a higher grade; enrichment in the classroom; home schooling for some subjects; or a part-time pullout program; and the requirements may change over time. Look beyond traditional approaches and work with families, not against them.
- Consider the family's perspective when conflicts arise; look at the situation through their eyes (Strip & Hirsch, 2001).
- Help families find needed resources such as information or organizations on parenting gifted children; create a resource center in your building with literature on gifted children.
- Families of students who are gifted report feeling isolated. Help them connect by starting a support group for families of gifted children, if none exists in your community (Reinisch & Reinisch, 1997; Stephens, 1999).
- Offer parent education programs on topics that families have shown an interest in, such as the social and emotional needs of gifted children or community resources for enrichment.
- Ask parents and extended family members to volunteer in the classroom in a variety of ways, including helping with special projects or trips, to help you to provide enrichment for their child; develop an instructional partnership with parents and extended family members in which they make regular contributions to their child's education beyond the class curriculum. Share the role of instructor with them (Radaszewski-Byrne, 2001).
- Keep ongoing documentation about the child's cognitive development and share this information regularly with families. This information will be helpful to them in making decisions about their child's educational placement. Also, observe whether a gifted student may be struggling socially or emotionally and communicate this information to families.

As you think about working with families of students who are gifted, consider this situation:

A week before school begins, a mother of one of your prospective kindergarten students brings her daughter to meet you and visit your classroom. The mother tells you that her daughter is quite advanced, and she is concerned that she won't be challenged enough by the kindergarten curriculum. You assure the parent that you will provide the challenge the student needs. As the child explores the room, she sees a poster featuring characters from Milne's *Winnie the Pooh* and begins quoting complex passages from the book, using different voices for the characters. In your housekeeping area, she asks if the red plastic apple in the cupboard is a Red Delicious, a Jonathan, or a McIntosh, and then proceeds to tell you that if the apple were green or yellow it could be . . . and names off many apple varieties, some of which you have never heard of. As the child looks at the other wall decorations, she reads the names of the children on the posted class list and says, "Lauren Ann Jones—that must not be the Lauren Jones in my preschool class last year because she is Lauren Sue Jones." Her mother smiles fondly at her and tells you, "She is really reading well now. She loves *The Boxcar Children* series and just recently devoured *Mary Poppins*." As the parent and child continue to walk around the room, you think about your reading lesson plans for the first week of school on beginning consonant sounds and wonder what you're going to do with this child. (J. Trautwein, personal communication, July 12, 2007)

What do you already know about this child from the encounter with her and her mother? What do you still need to learn about her? What resources can you use to meet this child's needs? How can you develop a plan for this child, similar to an IEP, to help her reach her potential?

SUMMARY

This chapter has explored the crucial role that you will play in working with the families of students who have exceptional needs. Many suggestions from past chapters for building strong relationships with families apply here; in fact, it is even more important that you have special skills and knowledge to be successful with these families. Understanding how families view having a child with an exceptional need, and knowing the legislation relating to disabilities and your role in the referral and evaluation process are all crucial. Respecting families' beliefs and their ideas on how to help their child be successful is also essential. With all families, communication is the key to success.

REFLECTION QUESTIONS

Reread the In the Classroom case study presented at the beginning of the chapter, and reflect on these questions:

1. Why do you think Kyle's parents reacted as they did? Is their reaction typical of parents who are told that their child might have a disability? If so, how?

2. What are Kyle's parents' legal rights in this situation? If Kate believes that Kyle needs specialized services, can testing and subsequent placement be done without their permission?

3. How should Kate proceed with the Barkers after this conference? Should she involve anyone else in the situation? If so, who? What steps should be taken to repair the home-school relationship? If testing determines that special placement is needed, how can Kate work effectively with the Barkers through the IEP process?

WEBSITES

Council for Exceptional Children, **www.cec.sped.org/AM/Template.cfm?Section = About_ CEC.**

> This is an organization focused on meeting the needs of exceptional children and their families. Check out their publications and products page for downloadable information on advocacy, as well as books to purchase on issues of diversity in special education.

The Family Center on Technology and Disability, funded by the Office of Special Education Programs, **www.fctd.info/about/purpose.php.**

> This resource is designed to support organizations and programs that work with families of children and youth with disabilities. The site includes free Family Information Guides to Assistive Technology as well as a series of fact sheets and a parent glossary for terms associated with assistive technology (in Spanish and English).

National Association for Gifted Children, **www.nagc.org.**

> This site offers information for families and teachers on how to support the needs of high-potential learners. The site includes numerous resources for teachers on hot topics and offers sample lesson plans and ideas on how to challenge gifted learners.

Through the Looking Glass, funded by the National Institute on Disability and Rehabilitation Research, U.S. Department of Education, **http://lookingglass.org/index.php**.

> This site includes online articles focusing on parents and/or children with disabilities, publications on the legal program for parents with disabilities, and many other resources supporting families with disabilities.

Wrightslaw, **http://www.wrightslaw.com/.**

> This site offers a wealth of information relating to special education laws and advocacy for children with disabilities. It has a long list of topics relating to special education, updates on IDEA 2004, with links to free flyers, publications, and free subscription to The Special Ed Advocate newsletter.

STUDENT STUDY SITE

Log on to the student study site at **www.sagepub.com/grant2e** for additional study tools, including the following:

- eFlashcards
- Web quizzes

- Web resources
- Learning objectives

Chapter 12

Teacher as a Family Resource and Advocate

Experience in many schools and districts points to some common characteristics of successful school-family partnerships. Schools that succeed in involving large numbers of parents and other family members in the education of their children invest energy in finding solutions for problems, not excuses.

—U.S. Department of Education (1997)

As a teacher, you will have much knowledge about children's development and learning. Hopefully, you also will have learned the skills and understanding needed to have strong home-school partnerships. You will use this knowledge and these skills to be a resource and advocate for families and children in many ways. You can also use your understanding of the importance of collaborating with families to help them become resources and leaders for the school and other families. This chapter will focus on your role as an advocate for families. As you think about this role, consider these questions:

- How can I recognize the strengths that families have as I'm considering my role as an advocate for them?
- What are some ways in which a school can provide resources for families in the home?
- How can home visits be an effective resource for families?
- What resources are available for families in the community?
- How can I help families develop leadership skills, including the ability to advocate for their children and other children in the community?

Contributing Authors Josephine Agnew-Tally, Donald Mott, Sheila Brookes, and Kathy R. Thornburg

ASSET-BASED AND FAMILY-CENTERED PARTNERSHIPS

Family-centered partnerships based on strong relationships between families and professionals promote outcomes that are meaningful to the child and family.

—Tennessee Early Intervention Services Coordination (2007, p. 2.1)

Before considering how to be an informational resource and support for families, it is important to consider the underlying beliefs you have about your role in being a source of knowledge and support for families. Consider the following discussion between two kindergarten teachers, Jan and Deandra:

Jan: I think we need to offer a parent education workshop on discipline. It seems like the kids coming to kindergarten are getting worse and worse in their behavior. I don't think today's parents know how to discipline their children.

Deandra: Yes, that would be a good topic for a meeting. We could ask the school counselor to share some discipline strategies, and then we could talk about ways that parents can set and enforce rules in the home. Let's see if we can get it approved with the principal.

What beliefs do you think these teachers have about families and their knowledge about parenting their children? Do they view themselves as experts on child development and learning, as well as parenting? Do they view their role as one of solving families' problems or focusing on the deficits of the families? Did they consider the families' perspectives when thinking about how to best support them? Do they see the home-school partnership as one of involvement or engagement? Questions such as these relate to whether schools have **asset-based** and **family-centered partnerships**.

Many educators do not fully understand the specific characteristics and consequences of family-centered and asset-based practices (Dunst, Trivette, & Cutspec, 2002). Being asset based means focusing on existing and potential abilities (Curran, 1983; Dunst, Trivette, & Mott, 1994; Kretzmann & McKnight, 1993). For example, you will find in your teaching that regardless of what a child cannot do, there are many things the child can do or can learn to do. Even when a child has significant disabilities or challenges, being asset based means that the focus of time and energy is on promoting the child's abilities. This does not mean that disabilities or challenges are ignored; it simply means that the teacher understands (and helps families understand) that solutions are more likely when interventions build on the child's abilities. An asset-based approach can also be applied to your work with families. Just as all families have challenges and concerns, all families have strengths. It is far too easy to focus on families' problems and forget that they have strengths. Yet evidence clearly shows that outcomes are better for children when teachers and other practitioners focus on supporting families and building on their strengths (Bruder, 2004; Dunst, 2000).

Besides having an asset-based focus, it is also important to consider how, as a resource for families, you can be family centered. Being family centered means providing help that is respectful, flexible, and culturally sensitive and that involves the family both as decision makers and as active participants in planning and implementing support programs

(Dunst, 1997; Dunst & Trivette, 1996). There are two key ways in which you can be a resource in a family-centered manner: *relational support* and *participatory support* (Dempsey & Dunst, 2004). Relational support refers to the way that you will form relationships and interact with families. Many of the ideas shared in previous chapters are examples of how to provide relational support, such as using an open and honest communication style, developing trust and rapport, being responsive to families' values and priorities, being flexible with scheduling and place of contact, and treating the family with respect, including respecting their cultural or ethnic background. Participatory support refers to parent education strategies that promote family members' confidence and competence in learning new skills and knowledge, including parenting their children. Research shows that participatory support is essential for families of young children and that the best outcomes occur when both relational and participatory support strategies are used (Dempsey & Dunst, 2004; Dunst, Boyd, Trivette, & Hamby, 2002; Dunst, Trivette, & Hamby, 1996).

IN THE CLASSROOM: SETTING GOALS FOR IMPROVEMENT

Brenda rapped lightly on the table to get everyone's attention at the monthly faculty meeting.

Let's get started, so we can be done quickly. First on our agenda is a report from our newly formed Action Team for Partnership. If you remember from the memo the superintendent sent out, this is a group of interested family and community representatives, teachers, and school support staff who are going to work to set goals for the schools in our district to improve what we do, including our family-engagement practices. Tamika and Susan are our school's faculty representatives, and the group had their first meeting last week. They came up with some big goals for our school. I'll let them share the group's ideas with you.

"Well, it was a good meeting," said Susan, "although it took us a while to get started. It was hard to sit back and let the parents on the committee speak up, and in the beginning, the teachers were the only ones who were talking. However, once we got going, it really turned into a brainstorming session about what we can do to improve the school."

"Yes," said Tamika, "there were several ideas tossed out, but the group came to the consensus that the biggest need we have is a good afterschool program where kids will have child care and not have to go home to an empty house, and they can also get tutoring or homework help. Maybe we could even offer some fun classes like a foreign language, dance, or sports."

Susan added, "We know there are many obstacles in the way of making that happen, with the biggest being funding, but the group was excited about the possibility, and several of the business leaders on the committee pledged financial support. Some of the family members said that they would also volunteer their services to help, and we are looking into what kind of state or federal funding or grants might be out there. We'd like to have this up and running at the beginning of our next school year."

Reggie spoke up, "Well, I don't want to be a wet blanket, but that sounds like a big project, and I don't think you should count on much family support. Most of our families work, and the ones who don't have a job probably don't have transportation to get to school on a regular basis. I just don't think parents are reliable or responsible enough to handle a project like that, and it's probably going to all fall on us teachers to do all the work."

"Reggie's right," Clara agreed. "I know our superintendent thinks this is a good idea, but I'm not sure I agree that our students' families should be setting goals for our school. That's really up to us, I think. They can focus on making sure their children do their homework and have their necessary school supplies and let us focus on running the school. Don't get me wrong, I like parent volunteers, but I don't want them in charge of our school."

(Continued)

(Continued)

Kate listened to the discussion and felt torn. She thought an afterschool program was a great idea and agreed with the committee's assessment that it was the biggest need their school had. She could think of several children in her room who would benefit from a good afterschool program. She wanted to speak up in support of it, but as a first-year teacher, she still hesitated to give her opinion in their faculty meetings. Besides, she didn't want any more responsibilities than she already had. If Reggie was right, they'd not only have to teach all day but also run the afterschool program. She kept silent as the debate raged on around her.

Both families and teachers benefit when partnerships reflect asset-based and family-centered practices. When teachers and families establish positive partnerships based on these practices, both are empowered. When teachers use family-centered practices in their support of families, there are numerous benefits, including "parent/family empowerment; parent/family well-being; parents' judgments regarding their parenting competence and confidence; and parents' judgments about their children's behavior" (Dunst & Trivette, 2005, p. 3). When you consider family strengths as a starting place for providing support, you are more likely to be successful in your efforts to be a resource for families.

With a partner, discuss the activity in Table 12.1 to apply your understanding of asset-based, family-centered practice.

TABLE 12.1   Applying Your Understanding of Asset-Based, Family-Centered Practice

Read the following two scenarios about Jose, a child whose family has recently immigrated to the United States. Which one demonstrates that the teacher has looked at the strengths of the child's family, as opposed to viewing the family and child from a deficit, problems-based perspective? How could the teacher build on the strengths demonstrated to support Jose's learning and development? How could she use the resources available in the family's informal support network, such as friends, church, and family? What are the examples of family-centered practices that the teacher should use?

Scenario 1

Four-year-old Jose and his family are from South America. His mother, father, and older sister speak limited English, and his grandmother, who is his babysitter, hardly speaks English. They attend a church where the services are delivered in Spanish. The family does not have transportation to attend school functions and has to rely on family or friends for it. At our last meeting, his parents said that they were feeling homesick for Colombia (their former home), where many of their relatives live.

Scenario 2

Four-year-old Jose and his family are from South America. His parents are avid soccer fans. They spend a good deal of time each week participating, watching, or talking about soccer, and they often spend time teaching their son to kick a soccer ball. He is also interested in books, and his parents read books to him in both Spanish and English. His parents spend a lot of time with him all day. They also talk to him frequently, in both English and Spanish, although their English-speaking skills are still somewhat limited. They encourage his sister, Sonia, to talk with him in both languages and to read books to him. The family also is active in their church, where they typically attend Spanish-language Masses and activities. However, they have assimilated the American culture in many ways, particularly through their employment, their older child's public school education, and their interest in American entertainment, such as movies and hip-hop music. Although they are nostalgic about Colombia and have many relatives who live there, they also say that they have migrated to America "for good" and plan to become U.S. citizens. They seem very connected to their informal network, and they've used their network to accomplish outcomes, particularly by sharing transportation to attend church and soccer games and by exchanging babysitting with other families. Jose's maternal grandparents live nearby and are a major resource for the family. His grandmother speaks only Spanish and helps by babysitting.

You can be a resource of information and support for families in a variety of ways, including helping families become resources for one another and the school. Besides asset-based, family-centered support, another conceptual framework developed by the Harvard Family Research Project is known as **complementary learning.** For children and youth to be successful from birth to adolescence, it is described as

an array of linked learning supports [that] includes families, early childhood programs, schools, out-of-school time programs and activities, higher education, health and social service agencies, businesses, libraries, museums, and other community-based organizations. Complementary learning is characterized by discrete linkages that work together to encourage consistent learning and developmental outcomes for children. These linkages should be continuously in place from birth to adolescence, but the composition and functions of the network will change over time as children mature. (Harvard Family Research Project, 2006/2007, p. 3)

HOME VISITS

The two educators sat on the couch. . . . Antonio's dad smiled at his visitors. "Ain't nobody ever come to the house before," he said. "This is real amazing to me. When I told my aunt, she said it might be a prank call. [The assistant principal] laughed heartily. "No," he said. "We're no prank. We're just here to see how things are going and if there are ways we can make sure that Antonio gets the most out of his school experience."

—Henke, 2011, p. 28

There are multiple reasons for school districts to implement an organized home visitation program (see Table 12.2). A study by Meyer and Mann (2006) found that home visitation programs with early elementary students increase the likelihood of a strong home-school partnership. "Customer friendly educators," teachers who are committed to connecting with their families, begin their home visits early in the school year (Jeynes, 2011, p. 160). Home visitation becomes a vital and natural component of their annual outreach to families. Many teachers schedule these visits or invite families to meet outside the home before the school year commences (Jeynes, 2011).

TABLE 12.2   Reasons for Home Visits

Home Visitors	Purpose/Reason	Goals
Teacher, principal, cultural liaison, district translator, board members, home-school coordinator, family liaison	Relationship building	Welcome wagon; translation of materials; introduction to school services; establishing credibility
Teacher, assistant principal, cultural liaison, home-school coordinator, family liaison	Personalizing service	Improving attitudes about school on the part of parents and students
Teacher, special education teacher, tutor	Academic concerns	Courageous conversations about academics; share testing results
Advisory group members, PTA members, principal	Expanding parental engagement	Gathering information about strengths of home environment; asking about what information parents need about school; joining PTA or advisory group
Nurse, social worker, assistant principal, school-based physician	Health care	Updating inoculations, home nurse visit, health or psychological concerns, concerns about abuse/neglect
Assistant principal, teacher, middle school assistant principal	Discipline concerns	Tackling at-risk student behavior in intermediate students; discipline concerns; at-home suspension
HIPPY liaisons, Parents as Teachers Home-Visit Program Head Start Early Head Start	Home-based education programs	In-home education; early childhood parenting skills; promote school readiness

Source: Henke, 2011; Jeynes, 2011; Reglin, 2002; U.S. Department of Education and Human Services, 2007

Some benefits of an organized home visitation outreach programs have been startling for school districts:

- Discipline referrals significantly down
- Student attendance daily in school increased
- Parent attendance at open houses up
- Parent involvement in advisory groups

Furthermore, one study of fifth- and sixth-grade students classified at risk found that 91 % of the parents stated that visits to their home by school personnel would help them better support their children's education, especially if the home visitor was their child's teacher (Reglin, 2002). Teachers found it easier to make sensitive phone calls when they had already established positive communication with parents (Henke, 2011).

A home-visiting program can also be effective in building home-school relationships with new immigrants. When using a family strengths perspective and operating with the belief that immigrant families have worthwhile knowledge and competencies, teachers can approach home visits with the expectation of not only sharing information with families about their new school but also learning about families. "As teachers listen to stories about living in refugee camps in Kenya, negotiating the health care system in Seattle, and becoming self-sufficient by working three jobs, they are reminded of the strength and determination of the families they serve" (Ginsberg, 2007, p. 60). This example illustrates that home visits can have a broader purpose than just educating families; they can also be learning experiences for teachers (Worthy & Hoffman, 2001).

There are some caveats to keep in mind when examining home-visiting programs. Not all programs have been successful, and not all models have been rigorously tested on various populations. Brookes, Thornburg, Summers, Ispa, and Lane (2006) found, in a study of Early Head Start home-visiting programs, that the relationship between the home visitor and the family had a strong influence on the family's outcomes in relation to the home visitation program. In interviews with parents in another study of the effectiveness of a Parents as Teachers home-visit program, factors such as,

Students are often excited to have their teachers visit their homes.

The home visitors' background characteristics (e.g., being parents themselves, age, ethnic background); personal characteristics (e.g., genuine caring for the parent and child, a nonjudgmental attitude, sociability, achieving a balanced perspective); and skills (e.g., professional, ability to balance roles, attunement, belief in the benefits of the PAT program) may all contribute to home visits' effectiveness. (Wagner, Spiker, & Linn, 2003, p. 184)

Before beginning home visits, safety issues must be a priority; do not venture alone into neighborhoods unknown to you, and always take a partner, such as the principal, school nurse, or family advocate, with you. It is also a good idea to have a cell phone for emergencies and to conduct visits during daylight hours. Make sure that you have notified your school office of where you are going. If you are wary of making a visit to a certain home or neighborhood, consider meeting in a neutral location, such as a nearby restaurant, coffee shop, or park. However, there are some considerations for a successful home-visit program:

- Before making a home visit, become familiar with general information about the family, including its structure, members, and cultural beliefs and practices.
- Schedule appointments with the family.
- Have a plan for the home visit and have all materials organized. Include time in the plan to become better acquainted with the family; get their input about their child's abilities and their aspirations and goals for their child. Take all materials needed to do any suggested activities. Leave a written handout with family education ideas or suggestions.
- Do not be judgmental of the family's home or neighborhood, but use the information to better understand the student. Respect family privacy and keep the shared information confidential.
- Consider doing follow-up home visits that can further strengthen relationships with families. "Home visits are the ultimate way to show a family respect" (Kugler, 2011, p. 35).

According to a veteran elementary teacher who had instituted home visitations as part of the "way she does business," "one of my favorite things is watching the parents' faces as they realize this is a real conversation. They relax and speak naturally" (Henke, 2011, p. 40).

ADVOCACY FOR CHILDREN AND FAMILIES: STRATEGIES FOR BECOMING ADVOCATES

Never adjust to an unjust world or be satisfied with the status quo.

—Children's Defense Fund (2004)

- Almost 7 million children are home alone after school; this is partially because of a scarcity of afterschool programs in inner-city and rural areas (Children's Defense Fund, 2002).
- In neighborhoods where the poverty rate is highest, teachers are the least qualified (Children's Defense Fund, 2004).
- Nationwide, 26% of the care paid for by the Child Care Development Fund (CCDF) is nonregulated (Administration for Children and Families, 2002).
- Only 17% of children living in poverty are reported to have a good diet (Forum on Child and Family Statistics, 2007).
- Prevent Child Abuse America has estimated that the total annual cost of child abuse and neglect in the United States is more than $94 billion (Fromm, 2001).
- The average age of children in foster care waiting for adoption is eight years, and 53% of the waiting children are African American (Children's Defense Fund, 2002).
- Of eighth graders, 68% performed at or below the basic level in mathematics, and 29% performed at or above the proficient level (National Center for Education Statistics, 2006).

These facts are just a few of the reasons why child advocates are needed. Advocacy is another area of family leadership. Teachers, too, must join with families in being a strong voice for children and family needs. No one better than teachers and families understands how these serious societal problems affect children's lives.

Advocacy, the process of supporting a person, group, or cause, benefits individual children (case advocacy) and groups of children and families (class advocacy). More specifically, child advocacy involves sensitizing society, and even more specifically decision makers, such as political leaders, to the needs of children and to society's responsibility to meet those needs. However, new teachers do not have to be fearful of the advocacy process. All of us advocate regularly when we express our opinions about issues relating to teaching, children, and families. Formal or legislative advocacy is just a specialized form of advocacy that is directed at policy makers at the local, state, and national levels (National Association for Gifted Children, 2005).

Teachers and families can join to be a strong voice of advocacy for children and families.

Examples of how you as a teacher can advocate, both for children and families in their classrooms (case advocacy) and at the policy level (class advocacy), are listed here.

Case Advocacy

- Help a family find a community-based program where the child can get free screening for hearing.
- Offer to take a new family who is struggling to the local food bank.
- Assist a family with obtaining a tutor for a child who is reading below grade level.
- Provide information about local before- and afterschool child-care programs for families.

Class Advocacy

- Collaborate on writing a grant to fund the federal program 21st-Century Community Learning Centers, which is intended to complement school performance through high-quality arts, enrichment, and recreation (David, 2011).
- Make school meals a public health initiative. Work on eliminating highly processed and nonnutritional foods. Most schools spend less than one dollar per child per day; raise the federal reimbursement rate for lunch by one dollar (Cooper, 2011).
- Sign up for e-mail alerts regarding state and federal legislation that may affect the teaching profession or children and families. One example is the National Association for the Education of Young Children's (NAEYC's) Action Center, which sends out regular updates and action alerts on important child and family issues being considered by Congress and the administration (www.naeyc.org/policy). When those alerts call for action, act!

Families can be encouraged to become advocates for both their children and those in the community. Some current and ongoing advocacy projects efforts, similar to the work of traditional community organizers, include the following:

- Latino and black parent activists in Southgate, California, organized a boycott to protest a year-round school calendar and a strike to demand adequate textbooks guaranteed by law and won (Oakes, Rogers, & Lipton, 2005).
- At a high-poverty, predominantly Latino school in Los Angeles, parents give back to the school with fathers helping on school beautification day, mothers cooking hundreds of tacos and tamales for fundraisers, as well as working with community groups to protest expansion of a nearby landfill (Auerbach, 2011).
- At Luther Burbank High School, a home visit to a family of Hmong immigrants uncovered the need for computers and Internet connections in their homes so they could complete an online literacy course. Through this beginning effort, parents and the school sought computer access for immigrant families to increase their English skills (Ferlazzo, 2011)

One effective advocacy method to support change includes sending e-mails or writing letters to those relating to the issue. For example, as noted earlier in Chapter 8, corporal punishment is legal in 19 states. Teachers and families might work to change this policy and abolish corporal punishment in their state with a letter-writing campaign to their state legislators and local school board members. A sample letter to a state legislator is shown in Table 12.3.

TABLE 12.3   Sample Letter to a State Legislator
Your name Your address Date The Honorable Senator _____ Your State Capitol Building Your Capital City, Your State Dear Senator _____: I am writing to express my concern regarding Senate Bill 60. This bill would increase the foster care reimbursement and the adoption subsidy rates over a four-year period. Every citizen realizes the importance of providing all children with a good home. By voting yes on this bill, you will encourage more people to participate in this process of finding children good homes. The cost of raising children raises increases every day. It is only fair that we help provide these generous families with the means to help take care of the children that they have taken in. As citizens, we owe it to the children in the state's custody. Please help Missouri's foster children by voting yes on Senate Bill 60. Thank you for your efforts on behalf of Missouri's children. Sincerely yours,

Source: Association for the Education of Young Children–Missouri (2005).

Taking the time to write a letter to your local newspaper or your state and national legislators is one of the simplest, yet effective ways to be an advocate. In a recent independent poll of congressional offices, the two top influences on how legislators voted was the communication that they received from their constituents (both face-to-face and letters) and opinions expressed in the local media, such as letters to the editor (International Reading Association, 2007).

Another simple advocacy strategy is to make telephone calls to key decision makers relating to an issue. When phoning legislators or other key decision makers, it is important to give your name and position, focus on one issue or bill, and identify the bill by number and name. Make sure to ask for your legislator's position on the bill (International Reading Association, 2007).

Getting involved in advocacy can be an uncomfortable process for teachers who have never been active in the political process, yet it is one of the most valuable ways in which you can be a resource for families. The Association for the Education of Young Children–Missouri (2005) offers these tips on becoming an advocate:

- *Define your cause or issue.* Identify the issue that you are most passionate about. Why is this important to you? What do you want to see changed regarding this issue? What are the possible outcomes of change?
- *Know your subject—get the facts.* Do your homework! Find out what is happening now that is related to this issue. Locate research available to support your cause. Look at what other related organizations are doing that might be related to your issue. Sign up to receive legislative action alert e-mails to stay informed.
- *Network—join with others.* Develop contacts in your community who are also interested in the issue. Join a professional organization, such as the National Association for the Education of Young Children (NAEYC), Association for Childhood Education International (ACEI), or International Reading Association (IRA). Membership in a professional organization is a form of advocacy and one of the best ways to stay involved and up-to-date with issues that affect education, children, and families.
- *Develop an action plan.* Identify the steps you can take to affect change. How can you make your voice be heard? Try to anticipate the possible roadblocks to change. What can you do to overcome those roadblocks?

Barriers to Effective Advocacy

By far, the greatest barrier to advocacy is apathy. Too often, Americans do not even vote, believing that their one vote will not make a difference. Voting is the most basic form of advocacy, and it is important that you become informed about issues that affect children and families and support them with your vote. Another barrier is a lack of knowledge about where to begin or how the political process works. One way to become informed is to explore the public policy sections of professional organizations websites, such as ACEI (www.acei.org/advocacy.htm), NAEYC (www.naeyc.org/policy), IRA (www.reading.org/association/advocacy), or Children's Defense Fund (www.childrensdefense.org/site/Page Server?pagename = policyareas). All these websites offer support for the beginning advocate, including information about the legislative process.

A final source of support for you in your beginning advocacy efforts are mentors in your school or local professional organizations who are already involved in advocacy and can guide you in your beginning efforts. Believing that one person cannot make a difference can lead you to feeling powerless to bring about important changes, so do not hesitate to reach out to more experienced advocates.

COMMUNITY RESOURCES FOR THE CLASSROOM AND FAMILIES

If schools are going to realize a profitable collaboration, then the administration must look beyond the parents of the students and into the larger community. These are the community partners; the businesses where parents are employed, and other local entities can provide valuable linkages for involvement. These partners can lend expertise to problems and be visible partners for education.

—Indiana Department of Education (2001, p. 17)

Classroom Collaboration With Community Partners

Besides the school providing support and resources for families, the community can be an additional source of support for both you as a teacher and for families in parenting their children. As a teacher, look for opportunities to connect with key **community stakeholders** in your students' lives. These do not necessarily have to be prominent businesses or community leaders, but may also include extended family members, neighbors, clergy and congregation members, storeowners, and others who have relationships with your students and who contribute to positive ongoing school relationships. Community collaboration is not limited to the physical classroom but can take the form of community walks, field trips, home Internet connections, or school-site-based activities. Classroom collaboration with the community tends to be teacher driven; however, a parent advisory group can act as a sounding board for possible community connections. Student input can also help define the classroom's goals for its collaborations with community institutions. Students can also express service-learning (i.e., community-based volunteering) preferences.

Hiatt-Michael (2006) warns of the consequences of ignoring community ties, "Lack of educators' and policymakers' attention to the community results in difficulties for both schools and communities. The self-contained classroom, the content-based department, and the graded school structure foster isolation and independence, not interdependence, of persons, activities, and agencies" (p. 18). Think about the following questions to determine the resources in your community. Start by exploring a small number of possible partnerships with individuals and groups representative of the classroom population.

1. *Support community.* Who are the people or organizations with whom you could connect? Who represents the support community for the families in your classroom? Whom do your students' families consult for advice and financial support?

2. *Physical neighborhood.* Look at the area adjacent to the school—the neighborhood. Where does learning take place outside the school? Consider where students tend to congregate, such as the YMCA or Boys and Girls Club, the mall, a church, or neighborhood stores. How could community learning settings contribute to academic learning in the classroom?

3. *Communicative networks.* What communicative forms do your students use to connect with family or the larger community? Examples might be e-mail, instant messages, telephone and text messages, or visits with extended families and other community members. How could you harness these communicative resources to nurture partnerships with key individuals and organizations?

4. *Academic connections.* How can the formation of a community partnership enhance your students' academic learning and motivation? How would you measure the impact of these connections? How can you ensure that your community collaborations support involvement of all families from diverse backgrounds (Senge et al., 2000)?

Potential partners for community connections are numerous. *Building School-Community Partnerships: Collaboration for Student Success,* an excellent resource by Mavis Sanders (2006), inventories partnership categories that can be filled by specific groups, as shown in Table 12.4.

As you tap into community resources, consider doing so with an attitude of reciprocity or giving-back to the community. Just as your classroom benefits from the involvement of

TABLE 12.4   Potential Classroom—Community Partners and Activities

Community Partners	Activities
Community individuals/groups: parents, caregivers, mentors, relatives, friends, neighbors, educators, senior citizens, professionals, community activists, community historians, neighborhood groups, fraternities and sororities, and service organizations	Mentoring activities, lesson presentations on funds of knowledge, demonstrations, volunteering, helping with science experiments, participating in panel discussions and field trips, offering apprenticeships, being e-mail pals and pen pals, and being a big brother or big sister Example: The Galena Quilting Project ties together math skills, social skills, art, and service (quilts donated to ill children).
Local businesses (small and large): bakeries, groceries, barbershops and salons, banks, utilities, florists, insurance companies, local small businesses, and health-food stores	Support for learning: math—interpreting bills, interest rates science—flowers, electricity, health—healthy nutritional choices Example: A representative from a utility company helps students read a power bill and brainstorm ideas for conserving energy at home
Educational and government organizations: universities, high schools, fire departments, police, airports, food banks, chambers of commerce	Service learning, cross-age tutoring, educational and mentoring programs, school-to-career preparation Example: Southwest Airlines's Adopt-A-Pilot Program has students shadow an active pilot to learn about airline occupations, plane maintenance, and flight regulations

(Continued)

TABLE 12.4 (Continued)	
Community Partners	**Activities**
Cultural and recreational institutions: museums, children's museums, local parks, planetariums, galleries, zoos, YMCA/YWCA, and health clubs	Workshops, integrated curricula (arts-based, environment-based, or health-based), problem-solving activities Example: Infusion of art into the curriculum through viewing art works at galleries and museums
Media organizations and sports associations: local newspapers, Internet services, television and radio stations, and local teams	Funding for classroom projects, donating school equipment, or gift certificates Example: Minor league baseball team reading incentive program—Ozzie's Reading Club Game Night

Source: Based on Sanders, 2006

the community, see that the community benefits from its involvement with you and your students. For example, one senior citizen center regularly hosted a local kindergarten classroom for holiday parties, and in return, the children created holiday decorations and prepared holiday songs to perform for their "adopted" grandparents. On a larger scale, consider the community organizer model where schools have worked with local religious congregations, businesses, neighborhood groups, and labor unions to tackle community problems. One school built a partnership to help stop toxic incinerators from being built, assisted in getting approvals for affordable housing, and worked with officials to increase neighborhood safety (Ferlazzo, 2011).

Every community is unique and offers specific opportunities for collaboration. The following are ideas for short- and long-term collaborations along content-specific area lines for elementary school classrooms. These actual classroom-based projects encouraged family participation in meaningful ways.

- **Math.** In a classroom partnership with a neighborhood bank, students deposited money into savings accounts, and bank personnel explained interest accrual and account types. Interactive homework included a family discussion on money management.
- **Language arts.** A parent-child mailbox activity had a many-slotted mailbox with students' names on labels for each space. Students wrote their parents a letter, depositing it in the slot, and the parents picked up their mail and wrote a letter in return. For this activity, parents of English language learners can write in their native language and receive help with the translation of their children's letters.
- **Reading.** Members of a university basketball team read aloud to students and talked about the importance of literacy. They next paired off with students during lunch to listen to oral reading and share experiences. Books chosen by team members reflected the accomplishments of minority athletes. The books were sent home for rereading (an important comprehension skill).

- **Drama.** A community repertory theater partnered with a classroom to perform creative expression exercises. Students were then invited to audition for roles in upcoming productions. Parents with an acting interest were also encouraged to try out.
- **Science.** A local nursery supplied advice and materials to develop a butterfly garden outside a classroom, which could be used by the whole school. Students and families provided the labor and researched the types of plants and bushes that attract butterflies.
- **Health.** A service learning project had students visiting selected nursing home residents to chronicle the important events in their lives. They compiled these life remembrances into a book that they bound and presented to the nursing home library.
- **Physical education.** A student's uncle was a member of the U.S. Olympic tae kwon do team for several years. He talked to the class about the Korean martial art form, explained some of the commands, and stressed rules for fair conduct.
- **Art.** Students took a virtual tour of building murals created by local artists in their downtown. The murals depict community themes that define the area, such as religious affiliations (Moravian), commercial endeavors (brick making and tobacco growing), and the diversity of inhabitants, including African American and Latino populations. A community mural artist visited the classroom to help students understand this artwork form.
- **Music.** A community-based reggae musician provided handmade instruments for students to play to generate their classroom song with interpretive dance.
- **Foreign language.** Students established e-mail pals with children at a school where many speak Spanish. Language exchanges helped bridge the gap between cultures, and students learned from one another.
- **Technology.** A major computer manufacturer invited students to job shadow, or observe employees as they went about their daily tasks at work in their local facility. During the field trip, the employees demonstrated the latest innovative software and talked to students about careers in technology.

This kindergarten field trip to a local university is an example of community collaboration that enriches the classroom curriculum.

- **Social studies.** The local neighborhood historian, or "keeper of local information," took students on a brief walking tour of the neighborhood and noted transformations that have occurred with the passage of time. Students found areas that particularly interested them and discussed how changes had affected the neighborhood.

These are just a few examples of creative ways in which a classroom teacher can expand the curriculum to make connections with families using community resources.

In the tradition of best educational practices, you, too, should seek out resources using the local community and environment to teach subjects across the curriculum. This kind of place-based education emphasizes hands-on learning, solving real-life issues affecting the community, and getting students into the community and out of the classroom to learn (National Retired Teachers Association, 2007).

Community Resources for Families

Although the community can provide numerous resources to support the school's efforts to educate students, it can also be a source of support for families in parenting their children. By becoming familiar with the resources within your community, you may be able to help connect families with them. This is especially important for families who are new to the area.

One way to do this is to help your school develop and maintain a print or electronic directory of the resources available in your community, county, or state that can help meet some of the needs of the families served. These resources can be organized by the specific needs served, and it is particularly important to identify organizations that have personnel who can communicate with families in their native language, either orally or in print. Yellowstone County (Montana) Head Start's (2001–2002) *Community Resource Booklet* contained information on emergency services, including violence and shelter information, medical services, addictions, disability services, education, employment, emotional/psychiatric treatment, financial, food/nutrition information, home and family needs, housing, legal services, pregnancy/newborn services, and preschool/child care. Keep in mind cultural and religious organizations that may be welcoming to families who have newly arrived at the school; for example, in Catawba County, North Carolina, Centro Latino at St. John's United Methodist Church, and Catawba County Hispanic Ministries connected with families in Spanish. When compiling your list of resources for families, consider the following:

- Always include a first-responder organization for dire family emergencies or families seeking specific information on particular services. It is best if families are able to contact this organization 24 hours a day.
- Families can profit from joining a support group. Many exist to help deal with various issues, such as child behavior, teen challenges, divorce, stepfamilies, substance abuse, spousal abuse, and grandparents raising children. Nonprofits such as Big Brothers/Big Sisters, private grant-funded organizations such as Families First, and local hospitals offer various types of support. Be aware that some may charge fees, or may have a sliding scale fee, which make joining them prohibitive for families.
- Food banks can provide emergency supplies of food for families experiencing temporary financial setbacks, while the local federal public assistance office can be a source for food stamps. In addition, food pantries and clothes closets provide nutritious food and warm winter clothing.
- Local colleges and universities often have volunteer action services with student volunteers participating in adult education, mentoring young children and teens, providing technology expertise, or transporting families to community services.

Table 12.5 shows examples of how to organize a community resource file for families.

TABLE 12.5 Community Resource File for Families

Physical/Medical Needs

- Public health department information
- Contact information for government assistance programs, such as **Women, Infants, and Children** (WIC) nutrition program
- List of pediatricians and dentists in the area
- Free clinics
- Service organizations that provide financial support or supplies for medical treatment (such as Lions Club eyeglasses program or Shriners' Hospital burn and orthopedic care)
- Local food banks
- Shelters and programs for homeless people
- Organizations and programs, such as Goodwill or Salvation Army, that provide clothing, housing, and other assistance
- Developmental screening resources
- Religious organizations in the area that provide financial support for needy families

Mental Health/Counseling

- Community counseling centers
- Agencies, such as United Way, that may provide family counseling
- Private counselors
- Agencies that provide counseling for victims of physical and sexual abuse
- Contact information for safe homes for abused women and children
- Organizations with a specific focus, such as Alcoholics Anonymous, Parents Without Partners, or a support group for grieving parents, such as Compassionate Friends

Parenting Support

- Afterschool child-care programs
- Service programs, such as Big Brothers and Sisters
- Child-care resource and referral agencies
- Parenting education programs, such as those offered by hospitals for new parents

Recreational Opportunities

- Local parks, playgrounds, swimming pools
- Child-friendly restaurants
- List of educational and sporting activities for children, such as classes offered at a community center or university or sporting leagues
- Seasonal events and activities, such as fall hayrides or county fair

Educational Opportunities

- GED (general educational development) or English classes
- Continuing education classes at a local community college or university
- Cultural attractions, such as museums

TABLE 12.6 An Example of a Community Resource File
Spanish Language Adult Education
Centro Latino/St. John's United Methodist Church (sponsors)
(828) 404-2490 contact person Maria Sanchez (best days Monday to Wednesday, no e-mail)
Great presenter willing to come to schools! (needs two-week notice)
2000 Cool Park Road, Hickory, NC (located in old middle school near mall)
Purpose: Helps Spanish-speaking parents learn English, also adult basic skills
Child care and transportation available, no fees, language texts provided
Classes held Tuesdays 12–3 p.m. and Thursdays 4–7 p.m.

ACTIVITY 12.1

Think about your community. What resources are available for families and children? Using Table 12.5, brainstorm a list of community resources that you are currently aware of in each category. Note the areas that you are unsure about. Where can you find more information about community resources in these areas?

It will also be helpful for you to make notes in the file about community agencies and other organizations that might serve as referrals for families. Table 12.6 is an example of information that could go in a file for a community resource.

This cheat sheet can be referred to when providing vital information to families as concerns arise during conferences, over the phone, or person-to-person. When you are fully informed about community services for families, you can become a valuable ally in supporting the basic needs of families.

In helping families find needed resources, it is also important not to forget the need for social networks or support provided by other family members, friends, neighbors, and community members. Many families live in isolation, which can have a negative effect on families by limiting role models for children and increasing stress, even abuse, that can occur as families raise children (Gonzalez-Mena, 2005). Helping families find a broad base of support, where they have social contacts to call on when under stress, is important. Although some of your students' families will have strong social networks within their extended family, neighborhood, or religious institution, it is also important to help those parents who are isolated, in particular single parents, connect with other formal or informal groups for social support. Introducing parents to one another and doing get-acquainted activities at school events is one way to do this.

PARENTS AS DECISION MAKERS AND SCHOOL LEADERS

Developing Family Leaders

Parents on our site-based decision-making council become truly educated on how a school works from the inside.

—Principal, Cane Run Elementary School, Louisville, Kentucky

Part of your role as a resource for families can also include helping them become leaders in the education of their child and, perhaps, the community's children. The educational setting offers a number of opportunities for family leadership, such as leading parent organizations or serving on district advisory councils.

Parent Organization Leaders

There are many parent-teacher organizations for schools today. The National Parent Teacher Association (PTA) may be the most familiar, as it has the longest history. The PTA influences millions of parents, past and present, to get involved in their children's education. They are a national, nonprofit organization; neither the organization nor its leaders receive any financial benefit from PTA activities. They are composed of more than 5 million volunteers in 25,000 local units; they are run by volunteers and led by volunteers, and are accountable to parents and schools (National PTO, 2011). However, schools may choose to have independent organizations that are not affiliated with a national organization: These may be called Home School Associations (HSA), Parent Communication Councils (PCC), or Parent Teacher Organizations (PTOs) (PTO Today, 2007). Don't forget that parent organizations welcome and value the inclusion of teachers; make it a point during the school year to join your local parent organization and attend meetings when you can. Families may begin their engagement in school by attending a parent-teacher organization meeting and eventually move into leadership roles within the organization. For example, Chuck Saylors, installed as the first male president-elect of the National PTA in 2007, began his school involvement in his local PTA by selling hot dogs at his son's school (Miller, 2007). Tim Sullivan, father of four and founder and president of PTO Today encourages parents to get involved in their school parent groups by doing the following:

- Modeling for your child that involvement with school is critical to his academic success
- Take an active role in new endeavors; don't just give advice on what to do
- Pace yourself when assuming a leadership or volunteer role; make it fit you and make it last
- Look for a mentor; parent groups can function as social outlets for families (Williams, 2011, pp. 1–2)

Joyce Shoemake, a PTO president at Sugarland Elementary School in Sterling, Virginia, first began her involvement doing simple tasks, such as collecting tickets or passing out pizza at the school's bingo and movie nights. She described her development of leadership skills through her activities with the local organization: "As I got more involved, I found I could do these things" (Beck, 2007, para. 2). Eventually, she became the organization's vice president and then president. As a parent leader, she, along with other concerned parents, spoke to the local school board about needed renovations to the school and was able to convince them to begin the renovation work four years ahead of the originally planned date (Beck, 2007). Hispanic parents may feel uncomfortable attending parent-teacher association meetings (PTA), so one school organized outreach initiatives including monthly meetings translated into Spanish (Zimmerman-Oroco, 2011). School should also ask "current family leaders to serve as mentors for newly involved families" (Kugler, 2011, p. 36).

Another option for families to assist in taking on leadership roles is parent university. Through this program, parents became interested in learning more about how schools operate. Then teachers, school staff, and local university faculty came together with parents to develop a curriculum that met their needs. This program often attracts as many as 100 parents, and sessions are translated simultaneously in Hmong and English (Ferlazzo, 2011).

Advisory Council Members

In addition to parent-teacher organizations, families may also become leaders in a school system by serving on advisory councils or committees, guiding school administrators and teachers in making decisions that lead to positive changes for children's education. The Head Start model is a good example of this. With its emphasis on family engagement and leadership development of its low-income families through policy councils, policy committees, and parent committees, families are encouraged to have an active role in making decisions about their child's educational experiences in the Head Start program (Administration for Children and Families, 2006). Benefits can be seen as success stories abound from former Head Start parents who have become community leaders because of involvement in the policy council at their child's Head Start program (DeRose, 2005; Schumacher, 2003).

School closings are occurring with more frequency based on budget cuts or sanctions from No Child Left Behind legislation. Averill Park Central School District recently closed an elementary school based on district declining enrollment. However, administrators were proactive in forming a transition team of parents, staff, and students when school consolidation was considered. Moreover, the principal established a blog to defend controversial issues. An environmental study was conducted to explain why the school closing was necessary financially (DeWitt & Moccia, 2011).

At Highland Park Elementary School in Manchester, Connecticut, a principal's advisory committee, composed of parents, community members, teachers, and the principal, makes key decisions for the school, with families being equal members in the decision-making process and providing immediate feedback to the principal and teachers about what is working and what is not working at the school. Through relationships formed on the committee, families provided training for the teachers. For example, parents helped faculty design a school website (Deojay & Novak, 2001).Leadership teams can become involved in conducting home visits, riding the buses to trailer parks to listen to grievances, and intervening in home situations when children's health/safety are at risk (Zimmerman-Oroco, 2011).

School advisory councils can exist alongside parent-teacher organizations and provide guidance in making decisions about issues such as the school's code for behavior or dress, curriculum and program goals and priorities, and community use of school property (Damaren, 2000). For example, one parent advisory council spent a year studying issues relating to homework. They looked at research about homework, examined homework policies of other schools, and surveyed students, teachers, and families about their feelings about homework. At the end of the year, the advisory council created a homework policy that led to greater family involvement and better communication between school and home about homework (McKenna & Willms, 1998).

For the development of family leaders, it is important that power is shared and that family members are not seen as "token" members of the committee but that their views are taken seriously (Damaren, 2000). This is especially true of low-income, minority families, where the typical type of family involvement that schools have encouraged is "monitoring the school cafeteria, helping with bulletin boards, or doing school fund raising" (Civil, Bratton, & Quintos, 2005, p. 64). The Math and Parent Partnerships in the Southwest (MAPPS) project included a parent leadership component, where Latino families were encouraged to become advocates for not only their child but all children in the district and to help facilitate parent education workshops. One parent described the difficulties in working as an equal partner with teachers:

> They are "the best." They don't give you the opportunity that you may know more or bring other ideas. . . . Now we are more equal. Now they rely on me, they check with me, they make you feel that you are important to them. One teacher once told me "you just hand out papers" and I was upset. (Civil et al., 2005, p. 64)

Teachers can be hesitant to share leadership with families in meaningful ways. One survey found that teachers welcomed family engagement in classroom volunteers but did not want families to be involved in developing school goals, budget planning, or staff hiring (McKenna & Willms, 1998). However, evidence shows that families can provide leadership for a school, which can ultimately benefit children.

RESOURCE PERSONNEL TO SUPPORT FAMILIES

When discussing the topic of teachers as a resource and advocate for families, it should be noted that there are many other individuals in the school setting who can provide resources for strong family engagement in a school district. These include the home-school coordinator, the school social worker, and paraprofessionals with various duties.

Home-School Coordinator

The role of the home-school coordinator or parent coordinator in today's schools is undergoing a dramatic shift in emphasis. The traditional role of coordinator was to report to the principal on family issues and work with teachers to support the academic growth of students. However, a coordinator may now find herself working in a district with changing demographics in which multiple languages are spoken. Her role has evolved into that of a **family liaison** (this position may replace the traditional home-school coordinator in outreaching to culturally diverse families and connecting them to community services) and advocate; she is more of a **cultural broker** (paraeducators, family advocates, or school liaisons who are able to cross boundaries into differing cultural milieus and promote open communication between groups of teachers and parents) or mediator with active responsibilities toward the families of the children studying in her school. Table 12.7 contrasts the school-based roles of the home-school coordinator with the family-centered roles of the family liaison.

	TABLE 12.7 The Evolving Role of the Family Engagement Coordinator	
Characteristics	**Role of School Liaison (Family Centered)**	**Traditional Home-School Coordinator (School Centered)**
Job description	• Act as cultural broker or mediator • Manage conflict resolution • Facilitate family participation (e.g., hiring translators) • Direct family support groups • Refer families for special education services • Assist teachers with ongoing parent communications • Oversee programs for English language learners	• Make home visits based on academic deficits (as requested by teachers or principal) • Do outreach to new families • Coordinate family events • Recruit school volunteers • Refer parents for adult education
School designations	• Support adult education • Family advocate, family liaison, cultural liaison	• Home-school coordinator, parent involvement coordinator, family involvement specialist
Funding sources and administrative responsibilities	• Funding from special education and student services budgets and from nonprofit community organizations • Reports to school social worker/ coordinator, special education, or ESL coordinator	• School district funds, Title 1, other discretionary funds • Reports to principal, Title 1 director
Training/preparation	• Urban community activist/ organizer • Family social worker • Juvenile probation officer • Special education degree • Parent	• Adult education background • Undergraduate education degree • Parent

Source: Taken in part from Howland, Anderson, Smiley, & Abbott, 2006.

As mediators or facilitators who are representatives of community cultures, home-school coordinators or family liaisons have successfully navigated the educational system. They can help families understand school requirements (Chrispeels & Rivero, 2000). Strong interpersonal communication skills, a sense of empathy, and a willingness to provide emotional encouragement to families often characterize effective home-school coordinators (Howland, Anderson, Smiley, & Abbott, 2006). As they assist families, family liaisons often perform the following tasks:

- *Explaining family rights, especially pertaining to special services, in language comfortable for families.* As one parent said,

I'm thinking maybe we need more people for Spanish-speaking. I'm Mexican—I come from another country. I don't understand the schools. I want to know what the school can do for my child. She [the family liaison] takes me by the hand and she say, "this is your school, this is what they should do for you. These are your rights." I want to know everything and she tells me much, and you know, all in Spanish. She tell me everything she knew with my son, what is good for my son. (Howland et al., 2006, p. 61)

- *Explaining educational terms to families, particularly during special education placements.* A parent comments,

Our oldest son, he had a learning disability. . . . And so he took some tests . . . and they explained it to us, but we still didn't really know how to deal with it. Well I need a dictionary to understand what they were telling me, cause I mean, because when they go through those tests, I didn't know what they were talking about. I mean it took her [the family liaison] to really break it down to explain it . . . you know, explained it in laymen's terms, and she helped us get on the right track on how to deal with his problems. If it weren't for her, we would be totally lost. (Howland et al., 2006, p. 61)

- *Offering direct support to families, such as help with meeting their basic physical needs or with gaining access to programs that supply food, clothing, transportation, or medical care.* One parent had this story to tell about a helpful family liaison:

They sent her an email . . . where they asked her to help me with my son. . . . he needed glasses. . . . And she helped participate in buying, helped him with getting some nice glasses. And she took us to the appointment. She called me and made sure I had somebody to keep my kids while I take him to the appointment. She came and took us and sat there with me, talked to the people with me and with him to make sure his glasses fit. And then we couldn't even get his glasses the same day, so she came back to take me the next day to go get the glasses for him. (Howland et al., 2006, p. 60)

Clearly, the role of the traditional home-school coordinator is rapidly assuming new dimensions for many school districts. You should make contact with your district or school family liaison or coordinator; she will be a valuable resource and source of support for your classroom families.

School Social Workers

School social workers assist and advocate for children's welfare and educational needs; inform teachers of differences in cultural values; engage in program development; act as liaisons between families, teachers, and school administrators; engage in training teachers; advocate for resource procurement for children; promote diversity; contribute to the social work professional knowledge base; provide information to school systems; examine school-related social and environmental factors identified as important; and develop relationships with neighborhood and community agencies.

—Teasley (2004, p. 22)

TABLE 12.8 The Traditional Role of School Social Workers
School social workers are the link between home, school, and community. As members of the educational team, school social workers promote and support students' academic and social success by providing specialized services that may include the following: • Assessment of student needs through observation, interviews, and testing • Treatment of mental and emotional disorders • Individual and group therapeutic services • Crisis prevention and intervention • Working with students in both general education and special education settings • Advocacy for students, parents, and the school district • Education and training for parents and guardians • Information and referral • Professional case management • Collaboration and consultation with community agencies, organizations, and other professionals • Staff and policy development

Source: Minnesota School Social Workers Association (n.d.).

As this description illustrates, today's school social workers perform myriad duties for a school district. Traditionally, school district social workers have been the first contact for mandatory reporting of child abuse and neglect, dealing with family and child mental health issues, and addressing attendance issues. It is common for one social worker to serve all schools in a district. The social worker would traditionally be responsible for investigating reported abuse or truancy, advocating for children, and generating reports. Maintaining a rigorous schedule of home visitations would often leave little time for other family-centered activities. The Minnesota School Social Workers Association (n.d.) outlines the traditional role of school social workers, describing them as the link between home, school, and community, in Table 12.8.

As school and community demographics rapidly change, culturally competent school social workers are assuming a new persona (Teasley, 2004). Today's school social workers must have special skills and knowledge to work effectively with all families in a school district. They may also assume the role of **family advocates** (social workers embracing the family support model in their ongoing engagement with families) employed by a school district or partner agencies, such as nonprofit organizations devoted to bettering the lives of families. Luanne Kicking Woman and Tami Adams, from Women's Opportunity and Resource Development, Inc. (WORD), in Missoula, Montana, describe the unique role they play as family advocates in bringing families and schools together:

> The school districts work from an agenda. Districts don't always understand the stress that many of the families we work with are under and therefore do not often lead with empathy. A lack of communication between families and schools during times of crisis often exists; both groups are unaware of who to contact or why it might make a difference. Also, mandatory testing for resource referrals within the district is a big issue. Testing seems to be the method schools use if they don't understand family dynamics rather than asking the family questions about their child's needs and strengths. (T. Adams & L. Kicking Woman, personal communication, February 6, 2008)

If your school district does not employ a school social worker or family advocate, inquire about community organizations or nonprofit groups in your community that may provide the services of family advocates through agency agreements with school districts.

Paraprofessionals

Instructional aides' relationships with parents have a lot to do with the school climate, the teachers' relationship with parents, the aides' relationship with students, aides' perceptions of the parents, and aides' perception of their status in the school.

—Lewis (2004, pp. 101–102)

Instructional aides may have the title of teacher aide, teaching assistant, auxiliary personnel, education support personnel, paraeducator, or **paraprofessional** (instructional aides or teacher's aides who have traditionally worked with students in academic support roles, but now they may be interacting with families as school-based liaisons or coordinators of Family Resource Centers). "Instructional aides were among the most rapidly increasing staff categories, rising by 110 percent between 1980 and 2003" (U.S. Department of Education, 2005). The traditional role of the instructional aide was to "prepare materials for teachers or monitor lunchroom activities," but these have been replaced with new tasks (Lewis, 2004, p. 92). Most paraeducators now work alongside teachers in the area of instructional support, and many now interact significantly with families. Optimally, instructional aides and teachers should be collaborating as a team (Lewis, 2004).

Although instructional aides can be a resource in family collaboration, district administrators should be cautioned against relying solely on aides to serve as cultural brokers between school and home. The assumption that instructional aides who live in the community automatically know how to best communicate with families in the surrounding school neighborhoods may not be true. Aides may not be prepared to assume a family-involvement role, or they may be temperamentally unsuited for it. They often have little training or professional preparation in how to work with families. It is important for school districts to provide paraprofessionals with regular in-service workshops relating to family involvement (Lewis, 2004).

One example of a specialized paraprofessional is the **family outreach specialist (FOS)**. This paraprofessional has been trained specifically for intensive outreach efforts to school families. He often works in the school's **family resource center (FRC)** and can function as a valuable conduit to families. Some tasks that an FOS might do include the following:

- Make telephone calls to all families throughout the year to invite them to the school's FRC.
- Coordinate a school's FRC activities under the direction of the school principal or Title 1 coordinator. The center may house adult education resources, computers for family use, a clothing closet, and a parenting library of books and materials, and some FRCs offer food and coffee.
- Take part in home visits to welcome new families; provide information about the school and about community resources available to them.
- Work with the principal and teachers to recruit classroom volunteers; assist with family events.

- Serve as a cultural negotiator to bridge the gap between the school and hard-to-contact families whose first language is not English; coordinate translations for school notices sent homes to non-English-speaking families.
- Connect families with family advocates or social workers when the families are not able to meet basic needs, such as food, housing, medical care, and clothing.

As the list indicates, FOSs (or other paraeducators under different titles) can be instrumental in providing assistance and even leadership in a school's family engagement program.

SUMMARY

This chapter has examined your role as a resource and an advocate for families in myriad ways. Through your relationships with families, you can be a source of information and support for them in the parenting and education of their children, as well as helping them become leaders and advocates. This chapter has also highlighted the importance of community resources for families. When families have needed resources and are able to do a better job advocating for their children, schools can do a better job in educating them.

REFLECTION QUESTIONS

Reread the In the Classroom case study presented at the beginning of the chapter and reflect on these questions:

1. Do you think teachers should share leadership of a school, including setting goals for school improvement, with family and community members? Why or why not?

2. How could the teachers ensure strong participation and support of families and community members for a project, such as an afterschool program?

3. What advocacy strategies could the group use to get necessary funding for the afterschool program?

WEBSITES

Parent Teacher Home Visit Project, **www.pthvp.org.**

Works with school districts to set up home visit projects within their districts and evaluates the results.

National Even Start Association, **http://www2.ed.gov/programs/evenstartformula/index.html.**

The National Even Start Association's mission is to provide a national voice and vision for Even Start Family Literacy Programs. Visit their legislation and advocacy page.

Parental Information and Resource Center, **www2.ed.gov/programs/pirc/index.html.**

> PIRCs are U.S. Department of Education grant-funded centers that help implement and support effective family involvement efforts in schools and communities. The site contains articles on engaging parents in education and other topics.

Children, Youth and Families Consortium, sponsored by the University of Minnesota, **www.cyfc.umn.edu/welcome.html.**

> This website is a bridge to a wide range of information and resources about children and families by connecting research, teaching, policy, and community practice. Their current theme addresses educational disparity, which includes their ecological model "The Circles of Influence" Framework.

Stand for Children, **www.stand.org.**

> Stand for Children is a citizens' advocacy organization whose mission is "to teach everyday people how to join together in an effective grassroots voice to win concrete, long-lasting improvements for children at both state and local levels." The website offers information about how to be an advocate and provides examples of successful state and local advocacy campaigns.

STUDENT STUDY SITE

Log on to the student study site at **www.sagepub.com/grant2e** for additional study tools, including the following:

- eFlashcards
- Web quizzes

- Web resources
- Learning objectives

Chapter 13

Schoolwide Family Engagement Activities

Family Events, Family Resource Centers, and Volunteer Programs

PREPARING FOR SCHOOLWIDE FAMILY ENGAGEMENT ACTIVITIES

Visit 10 schools randomly in the United States, and you will discover in nine of them that most teachers and administrators still hold parents at arm's length. You will see many of the tried-and-true forms of parent involvement—an open house in the fall, two or three short parent conferences a year, parents attending student performances and sports events, some teachers calling parents when a child is misbehaving, an annual multicultural fair, a parent association that raises money, and a business association that donates equipment. But you'll observe few if any parents or community representatives actively involved in the school's efforts to make changes in curriculum, teaching, student rules, homework policies, or scheduling.

—Davies (2002)

Contributing Authors Vincent Snipes, Pamela Moses-Snipes, Catherine Matthews, Jewell Cooper, and Carole Robinson

One of the themes throughout this textbook has been the importance of establishing respectful relationships with the families of your students. Trusting relationships do not happen without effort and require that teachers and families actually spend time together, getting to know one another, and learning about one another's perspectives (Kyle, McIntyre, Miller, & Moore, 2006). One way in which this can occur is through schoolwide family engagement activities. In this chapter, you will learn some practical ways in which you can organize successful family events throughout the school year. This chapter will also discuss how to establish effective volunteer programs and family resource centers. As you think about the variety of family engagement activities that schools can offer, consider these questions:

- How can family events, volunteer programs, and family resource centers support students' success in school?
- What do I need to consider when preparing for, organizing, and hosting a school or classroom event involving families?
- How can back-to-school or transition events pave the way for teachers, students, and families to have a successful school year?
- How can I ensure that all families are comfortable attending a school cultural event? How do the roles of community collaborators facilitate inclusion of school cultures?
- How can I organize successful family events that focus on a specific content area, such as family literacy, math, science, and technology events?
- How can teachers set up classroom family information centers (FICs) and assist in establishing schoolwide family resource centers (FRCs)?
- How can volunteers be recruited and trained for a variety of roles in the school and community setting? What policies should school districts adopt concerning volunteers? What strategies are effective in retaining school volunteers?

FAMILY EVENTS THAT SUPPORT STUDENTS' SUCCESS AT SCHOOL

At times, conducting a family night is a lot of work. So why do it? All of us agree that the pay-off is well worth the extra effort. Much is made easier for the teacher for the rest of the year because of the positive relationships that are formed between parents and teachers at these events. Mutual trust is invaluable.

—Kyle et al. (2006, p. 152)

All families have the potential to contribute as mentors for their children in a productive home learning environment, but frequently, families need ongoing support and continuing communication with the teacher to help their children be academically successful. School-based family events can provide the impetus for families to gain confidence in their ability to work with their children at home.

The extensive research supporting the inclusion of families as prime contributors in the education of their children is conclusive and overwhelming (Padak & Rasinski, 2006). For linguistically diverse families, **family-centered initiatives** (which focus on the authentic needs and goals of families when planning and enacting family events) that have specific academic outcomes have yielded higher gains for children when their families participate in these experiences than when they do not (Garcia & Hasson, 2004). Interactive family events are replacing the traditional "audience member" parent meetings with much success. For example, St. Bernard-Elmwood Place School in Cincinnati, Ohio, had only a handful of involved families in their PTO, but at their first back-to-school event, 75% of the school's families attended (Wheat, 2006). Some examples of family-centered initiatives include celebratory events, such as back-to-school events, transition events, or cultural events as well as events that focus on the content subjects, such as family literacy, math, science, and technology events.

IN THE CLASSROOM: FAMILY FUN ONLINE

Susan Meyer, Kate Harrison, and Jan Russell, the second-grade teachers at Kennedy Elementary, surveyed the school's computer lab one last time. Tonight was their first family event night, a technology night. As part of their district's family engagement plan, each grade level hosted a family activity throughout the year, and April was the second grade's scheduled month. The teachers were excited about their plans, yet somewhat apprehensive about whether they would have good attendance. They had learned from the mistakes that some of the other teachers in different grades had made. For example, the third-grade teachers hadn't thought about providing child care for their literacy night, and there had been chaos during the story time with younger siblings crying, while other parents had chosen not to come because they couldn't afford a babysitter for their younger children. The fourth-grade science night also didn't have very good attendance, but it was because it was scheduled on the same night as the high school's basketball district championship game. None of the family events had strong involvement from the Latino families in the community, but the second-grade teachers were hopeful that this would not be the case with their technology event, Family Fun Online! They had made a special effort to invite the second-grade Latino families by using their parent facilitator who spoke Spanish and had made individual phone calls to all the families. Jan had also been able to get donations of appetizers from the Rodriguez's Mexican restaurant, since the family had a daughter in her classroom, in exchange for publicity for their restaurant. The Rodriguez's had also promoted the event in both English and Spanish on their store's sign on the town's main street.

The teachers went over their plans one last time.

Susan said, "First, we're going to meet in the school's library, where we'll do a presentation using the Smart Board on Internet safety. We'll have the children go to the gym with the high school child development students to do some games while we talk to the parents about the dangers for their children online."

"Do you think there will be enough supervision with the high school students? What if the games get out of hand? One of us better stay in there with them," said Jan.

"Good idea," said Susan, "Then we'll have the kids come back and join their parents. We'll divide them into groups to go to our classrooms, the computer lab, and the library to use the different software programs and try the different family-friendly websites."

"I've got the website addresses copied to give as handouts," said Kate, "and I also copied that evaluation survey we wanted to give at the end of the session."

"I think we're all ready," said Susan. "Let's go get some supper and get back before the parents get here."

As the teachers walked out the door, Kate hoped that they hadn't forgotten anything. The teachers had spent two months planning this event, and she couldn't believe that it was finally here. She wanted this first family event to be successful, and one that was worth her students' families' time and effort.

ORGANIZING, PREPARING, AND HOSTING FAMILY EVENTS

As a first-year teacher, Ms. Kelly was looking forward to connecting with the families of her students early in the school year. She decided to host a family barbecue at a local park mid-August, well before school, on a Sunday. In talking to colleagues, they encouraged her to organize the event pretty much on her own (since families are not reliable to hold up their end, according to a veteran teacher). Being new to the growing town of Charlotte, North Carolina, Ms. Kelly was unfamiliar with local parks and regulations governing use of park facilities, so she drove around looking for a park that appeared to have enough picnic tables to seat 25 families. To save time, Ms. Kelly decided to purchase southern foods, including fried chicken and pork barbecue, potato salad, rolls, and sweet tea at the grocery store. In the written invitation, she failed to mention the menu, assuming families would all like the choices and appreciate the meal. To her credit, she called each family during the week and left reminder messages about the event, but she failed to leave a contact number at which she could be reached should any families have questions.

On the Sunday of the event, scheduled for noon, Ms. Kelly arrived early at the designated park. Because the park that she chose was outside the school district parameters, she hoped families knew where it was located, having forgotten to supply directions on the invitation. As some families trickled in, she introduced herself and talked briefly to them about her hopes and goals for the upcoming school year. Only five families had arrived by noon, the time indicated for the picnic gathering. Sensing Ms. Kelly's frustration, one grandparent noted that this side of town was not familiar to many school families and that church had not yet let out by noon. As families started to eat, one mother pointed out that she was a vegetarian and would pass on the meal while another Muslim family said they did not eat pork. As the sky started to darken with impending rain, Ms. Kelly, very flustered and apologetic, wished she had sought a park with a picnic shelter in case of rain. Staying until the rain came, Ms. Kelly left the park discouraged and wondering what she could have done differently, knowing she spent many hours planning for the gathering with limited attendance.

What went wrong in this scenario? How might better systematic planning and a deeper understanding of community cultural considerations have resulted in a more successful opening family event for Ms. Kelly? Although a situation such as this might lead a teacher to assume that the families of her new students were not interested in being involved in their child's education, and that her efforts were in vain, a closer look shows several errors on the teacher's part in planning and organizing this family event. With careful planning and organization, family events can yield positive results.

The first step in planning a successful family event can be to conduct a specific needs assessment of families concerning their demographic background, personal goals, and individual knowledge and experiences. Families might be surveyed concerning the following:

Cultural events can offer students and their families a chance to spend time together doing activities that honor diverse cultures.

- Needs for transportation and/or child care
- Convenient times and location for events
- Language or bilingual formats
- Knowledge or experiences with the technology being used
- Questions or concerns that they may have about the topic of the event

In addition, teachers should have specific objectives in mind for the events, followed by revisions for future events, based on family responses, with the goal of increasing family-centered learning (Garcia &Hasson, 2004). Family events can have various designations, depending on their purposes or the goals that you decide to pursue. One-shot events whose purpose is to provide an evening of informal family fun, such as a family fun night, are much different from a more structured, monthly bilingual **family literacy night,** where academic support through family literacy and language interactions is the goal and where literacy activities, such as games, book reading, or dramatic activities, are enacted to encourage further home literacy interactions. Table 13.1 lists a sampling of some different event categories with different levels of structure.

TABLE 13.1 Examples of Family Events			
Teacher/School Planning	**Less Family Engagement**[a]	**Medium Family Engagement**[b]	**High Family Engagement**[c]
High: A group of teachers/families or whole school involved for several weeks/ month of planning	Family fun nights, Dr. Seuss celebrations	Literacy rally, community showcase, academic portfolio night, understanding standards night	Back-to-school night, family literacy nights/ programs, bilingual family literacy nights, cultural nights, diversity celebration, or funds of knowledge events
Medium: Individual teachers or small group, several weeks of planning	Family socials or teas, meet and greet events	Family reading nights, literacy lunches, family math or science event, homework preparation night	Night at the museum, science family fun night, family technology night
Low: Social food event	Donuts for dads or muffins for moms, grandparents' day	Gym night, field days	

Sources: Based on Ferguson (2005) and Quezada (2003).

Notes:

a. Generally fun, low-key family-child interactions, may be leisure-reading activities, family physical activities, or social events/food events.

b. Based on understanding academic requirements, disseminating social service information, promoting family reading, or low-key academic activity with child.

c. Family members acting as students, translated information vital (all types), academic standards and expectation demonstrated and explained, technical math, science, or reading information is hands-on and taken home for follow-up activities.

Preparing for a family event also means carefully selecting activities that have a clear cultural connection to the community and the participants; this may determine the ultimate success or failure of your event. Moreover, the inclusion of **school facilitators** who are familiar with the culture of the school and community is critical. School facilitators can act as guides to the various cultures found within a school setting. Make every attempt to include key stakeholders in the community, such as local religious representatives, elected officials, or community specialists, on your planning committee and as a part of the event. Activities that are reflective of community values will increase families' level of comfort and result in cultural cohesiveness between school and home.

It is vital that the schools provide facilitators who have been trained to promote adult learning of particular activities. Family events have turned chaotic when volunteers or unprepared facilitators simply monitored **learning stations** (typically used in family math, literacy, or science activities, learning stations function as stopping-off points to engage in learning activities with specific directions for completion) or activities with little knowledge of their purpose. Always supply a set of directions for the activities in family responsive languages; also consider videotaping a simulation of the steps necessary to complete the center or activity.

Make sure to prepare a brief anonymous exit survey slip to solicit family responses after the gathering. This will provide important feedback that can guide planning for future family events. Two or three brief questions with an open space for suggestions, as shown in Table 13.2, works well.

TABLE 13.2 Family Event Exit Questionnaire

Please complete this evaluation. Your honest input will help us plan future family events. Thank you in advance!

1. Share at least one important thing you learned tonight that will benefit your child at home:

   _____

   _____

   _____

   _____

2. What was your most and least favorite family event activity?

   a. Most favorite: _____

   b. Least favorite: _____

3. What suggestions do you have for upcoming family events?

   _____

   _____

   _____

   _____

In addition, **community liaisons** (individuals who act as agents for outreach in particular community settings) can provide follow-up after the event by conducting home visits and maintaining contact with families to assess the success of the event through follow-up learning activities. The community liaison can be a family volunteer who lives in the community and speaks the language of the community.

A checklist to assist in your planning and organization of a family event that is culturally responsive to your students and their families is provided in Table 13.3.

TABLE 13.3   Checklist for Culturally Responsive Family Events

Directions: Consider the following checklist as you prepare for your family event responsive to the needs of families in your school community. Keep referring back to this checklist as your planning group prepares for the event. Remember, thoughtful planning and collaborative decision making can mean the difference between a successful event and the one in which families are disengaged.

- Yes, I have considered this and included it in planning the event.
- No, I have yet to include this in planning the event.

1. _____ *Funds of knowledge of families*. Skills, hobbies, and occupations of family members and relatives surveyed to formulate ideas for responsive family events.

2. _____ *Community focus*. Conversations with families focusing on "What is important to the community at this time?" and "What kinds of activities or significant events create a sense of pride for community members?"

3. _____ *Parent guides*. Family participants from the community help increase teacher understanding of community goals, challenges, and their commitment to school engagement.

4. _____ *Planning group*. Establish a planning group early in the process. This should include family members, community liaisons, resource personnel (counselors, school social worker, nurse, and librarian), teachers (foreign language, media, and social studies), staff (custodians, secretary, and teacher's aides), administrators (curriculum coordinator, principal, and ESL coordinator), and students.

5. _____ *Budget and funding sources*. Solicit school and parent organization funding, grants, and community donations to cover the expenses of materials, supplies, and food/drinks.

6. _____ *Outreach efforts*. Effective means for outreach to families investigated through ongoing parent-teacher dialogues and planning group input.

7. _____ *Language considerations*. The primary spoken languages of families are identified and factored into presentations. Are translators available on event dates?

8. _____ *Detailed invitations*. Invitations give explicit and clearly written information about the event in families' primary language (purpose of event, time, location, rain date (if outside), child care provided, who is invited, sponsoring organizations).

9. _____ *Contact information*. Translated notices include contact information (through phone, e-mail, or personal contact) for the event.

10. _____ *Healthy food choices*. Consider meals or snacks, including healthy choices that families would like for their children instead of high-calorie choices.

(Continued)

TABLE 13.3   (Continued)

11. _____ *Ethnic food choices*. Make sure whether serving ethnic food is authentic to the particular culture; also, method of serving and portions should be considered.

12. _____ *Anticipated agenda*. Brainstorm activities, learning stations, experiments, presentations, or lessons to be included. Check with parent guides to address adults' comfort levels with activities. Also, make sure activities are age appropriate for student involvement.

13. _____ *Event format*. Think about the format you want to use to engage families—more or less structured, collaborative learning, presentations, workshops, large group activities, or learning stations or modules.

14. _____ *Event sessions*. Decide early on if your event will be a one-shot offering or held multiple times throughout the year. Strongly consider the times families can allocate for attendance.

15. _____ *Backup activities*. Consider backup activities if agenda fails to engage families or confusion ensues.

16. _____ *Exit survey*. Develop a short survey based on what you hope families have learned after attending the event. Also query families as to whether the event was scheduled at a good time or ask them to propose other times that might be more convenient.

17. _____ *Reflection sessions*. Debriefing sessions with planning group. What went right? What changes should be instituted the next time the event was hosted?

BACK-TO-SCHOOL EVENTS

Contrast this back-to-school event with the earlier scenario.

> Mr. Jamison, a first-year teacher, was anxious to meet his third-grade students and their families and decided to host a classroom party in mid-August before school started. He had gone through the files of his students and noted that there were a high number of single parents and that most family members were employed full-time; therefore, a weekday event might be more difficult for the families to attend. Being new to the community, he wasn't sure what type of event might lead to a high attendance, so he sought the advice of his school's parent liaison, and together, they decided that a Sunday afternoon ice cream party in the classroom would create the highest interest among families. She also recommended two parents, who had been actively involved at school the previous year, to help him in the planning. When he contacted them, they were pleased to be asked and made several suggestions he hadn't considered, including the importance of having enough ice cream for little brothers and sisters. They also told him that several of the students would be involved in the youth softball league tournament that night, and it would be important that the event last no longer than an hour and a half. Even though Mr. Jamison had sent out welcoming postcards to his students with an invitation to the event, they offered to help contact all the families with a reminder phone call the week prior to the party.
>
> On the day of the event, curious families and students showed up to meet the new teacher. Mr. Jamison introduced himself by telling about an incident that happened to

him in elementary school, which had led him to decide to be a teacher. He then had the families and students do a family scavenger hunt where they had to find others with different characteristics, such as, "Find someone who has a pet," or "Find someone who is new to this school." At first, the group seemed reluctant to leave their seats, but the parent volunteers and the school's parent liaison provided the model, and soon, everyone was chattering with one another. With the help of his parent volunteers, ice cream was passed out, and he informally talked to the group, asking them to tell him about the school and community. He made mental notes of which family members were more talkative and which seemed reserved, with the goal of making an extra effort to reach those who did not participate in the discussion in future communication. As the party ended, he asked the families to write suggestions for future events. Several of the families and their children invited him to attend the softball tournament that night and seemed pleased when he took them up on the offer. As he collected their responses, he realized that he had met the majority of his students and their families before the school year had even started.

Celebratory back-to-school events, such as the one described in the scenario, send the message that families are vital ingredients in the recipe for a healthy classroom community. It is common for whole school events to be offered; however, a classroom-based event can also be a teacher-family bonding experience. These informal events recognize the beginning of school as a benchmark event for building a learning community as well as connecting with families. Outreach attempts through phone calls, postcards, e-mails, and letters should be initiated far in advance of the planned gathering to allow families the opportunity to adjust their schedules; be sure to follow-up with contact to encourage attendance. This may be the opportune time to recruit family members to contact others via a **telephone tree**, which "branches" out family contacts by asking them to contact a specific number of other families, thereby spreading out the outreach tasks.

A back-to-school celebratory event can also provide an opportunity to connect families with one another, their children, and school staff. Therefore, the importance of introducing family members should be emphasized. For example, families can do a fun icebreaker activity that requires them to learn one another's names, such as finding people who have the same number of letters in their first name as their name. You can also develop a brief video to welcome families, including an introduction, tour of the school, a lesson demonstration, and an invitation to become involved (Aronson, 1995). Back-to-school events can be based in the community, the school, or an individual classroom. Ideas for a variety of back-to-school nights are given in Table 13.4.

Besides helping families connect with one another, back-to-school events can also give teachers the opportunity to learn about their new students and families. This can be a good time to get to know families and demonstrate your desire to collaborate with them on educating their child. This may be an unfamiliar concept to families, as one teacher described:

On Open School Night, I asked mothers and fathers to write down anything they knew about their children that might help me: how they learned, their talents, skills, interests. Much to my surprise, I got very little information back. Now I understand those parents couldn't believe that their everyday knowledge, their own experience, would be valuable to me, the expert. (Markova, 2002, p. 153)

TABLE 13.4   Back-to-School Programs

Community-Based Back-to-School Events	School-Based Back-to-School Events	Classroom-Based Back-to-School Events
Picnic in the park—dinner (barbecue) or dessert (ice cream sundaes)	Family meal event—takes place in cafeteria for welcoming meal/dessert	Family welcoming event—classroom pot-luck supper or dessert; families provide picture for classroom bulletin board
Service organizations, YMCA, Boys and Girls Club; athletic activities involving parents, teachers, and children	Take-a-family-member-to-school day; camp out on the playground with community speakers	Saturday event with families constructing birdhouses in the classroom with ice cream sundaes provided
Community read-in—families and students are provided with books, oversized pillows, and refreshments to enjoy an evening of book sharing	What do you remember? Collect stories from family members about their experiences in school. Stories placed on school website (Ferguson, 2005)	A summer orientation for ELL students and their families, guided tour of the school and classroom, introduction to routines/materials. Glossary/Pictionary of important words and phrases (Davis & Yang, 2005)
Getting to know your community and school night; chamber of commerce; community organizations	Musical performances by teachers and principal to welcome families to school	Morning meeting format—a greeting, a sharing, a group activity, and news and announcements (Davis & Yang, 2005)

A well-planned back-to-school event can be the beginning of a partnership relationship with your students' families.

TRANSITION EVENTS

The cafeteria tables were covered with food, and the white paper tablecloths were decorated with crayon drawings, letters, and numbers that children drew when they arrived. As children, families, and teachers ate and visited, high school volunteers circulated pouring drinks and clearing the tables. With the meal winding down, the principal addressed the group, welcoming them. She invited a group of six-year-olds, who completed kindergarten a few months earlier, to the front, and they performed, with gusto, songs from their spring music concert. The preschool children in the audience were then invited to go into the kindergarten classrooms where they were paired with the former kindergartners to do learning center activities together, under the supervision of the local community college's child development students. The principal showed a short video to parents of a typical day in kindergarten, and then a panel of six adults—two mothers, a father, and a grandmother of former kindergarten students, along with two kindergarten teachers—answered questions raised by the families of the preschool children about kindergarten, such as if children liked the school lunches and how long they had to ride the school buses. The principal then gave the audience a handout about the developmental characteristics of typical kindergarten students, the curriculum standards for kindergarten, a school supplies list, and information about the first parent-teacher organization meeting in September. The children were invited to return to the cafeteria, where the preschool children, along with their new kindergarten friends, performed a finger play they learned, to the delight of their families. As a souvenir of the meeting, the incoming kindergarteners were given a school folder and a small box of crayons, which were donated by the local bank. As the crowd left the meeting, one five-year-old was overheard saying, "This was fun! Can we come back here tomorrow?"

When planning a transition event, it is important to include teachers and family representatives from both sides of the transition on a planning committee. For example, the Altoona Middle School Partnership Committee at Altoona, Wisconsin, included family and teacher representatives from different grade levels. When planning for how to help students transition from elementary to middle school, fourth-grade families shared the concerns they had about the difficulties their children might face when they went to fifth grade in the middle school. Fourth- and fifth-grade teachers reviewed this input and brainstormed activities to address the families' concerns (Kaiser, 2000). The planning committee can also include community representatives, who may provide funding support for events in trade for publicity for their businesses. This is particularly effective for a transition event at the beginning of a school year for new students and families who have moved into the district over the summer and are unfamiliar with the community and its businesses.

One of the biggest needs of families going through a transition is information—information about what to expect with the new school and resources available for support, which may include school personnel, other families, or community resources, and area agencies. One way to find out what information families need is to send a survey to families of students registered to attend the new school in the upcoming year, asking what questions or concerns they have about the new school. Surveys are more likely to be returned if a postage-paid return envelope is included. This survey can be included in a mailing with an invitation to the transition event. Survey information can then be used by the planning committee to address those questions and concerns.

Often, families of children who are new to a school district or a building are wary of the unfamiliar and may be hesitant to participate in a formal family education event. This is especially true of families who are non-English speaking. One way to ease their discomfort is to serve food prior to a meeting. At the Montgomery County, Maryland, Public School Family Night Out, designed to help families of children transition from Head Start to kindergarten, parents, grandparents, and other relatives, along with teachers and the principal, enjoyed a meal together before children left for activities and families gathered for discussions. The mealtime was an important part of the event. As one principal stated,

Of course, people are of differing backgrounds, but at Family Night Out, everyone is equal. The very act of eating together unites people." Another said, "Parents have to feel comfortable in the school. So many of our parents are recent immigrants, totally unfamiliar with the culture of our schools. Family Night Out helps them feel a measure of comfort and security in the school." (Seefeldt, 1998, p. 60)

Transition family events can have benefits that go beyond helping ease students and families' first-day jitters at a new school. A family event that helps students transition to a new school can help families learn to trust teachers, and teachers learn to respect and understand families. This foundation can be a good beginning of a partnership relationship between home and school (Seefeldt, 1998).

COLLABORATION ON CULTURAL EVENTS

The Bulldog Beat class, a percussion ensemble of students from C. M. E Middle School in Greenville, North Carolina, celebrated an evening of drumming for significant adults in their lives. The Bulldog Beat class used a curriculum based on World Drumming Music (www.worldmusic drumming.com). During class, students had learned the songs, as well as their deeper cultural significance and origins before they performed them in concert. Students had learned the techniques of echo drumming to mimic drumming patterns, as well as basic drumming forms, such as question and answer, call-and-response, and rhythm complements. During the evening event, Bulldog Beat students served as mentors and assistant teachers to family members, helping them learn drumming techniques. By building a sense of pride and accomplishment for these students, "music class was no longer a place to memorize facts about dead composers" (Feller & Gibbs-Griffith, 2007, p. 49). The event presented an opportunity for students and their families to be engaged in a multigenerational activity with everyone performing together.

Planning cultural events to honor the diversity of student cultures is a powerful undertaking requiring collaboration between staff and school families. Recruiting parent guides to explain and demonstrate customs and traditions that are pivotal in the daily life of community members can lead to an openness, awareness, and acceptance on the part of educators and school participants. However, while planning and scheduling a school or a classroom cultural event, beware of what Derman-Sparks (1989) terms the tourist curriculum—a focus on superficial contact with cultural artifacts, such as food, clothing, folktales, or celebrations. For example, an "around the world" celebration that features Mexican, Chinese, Mediterranean, Russian, and Native American food, with music and dances from the different cultures, may be entertaining to families but will do little to lead to a deeper understanding of families from these cultures. Event attendees may simply view the cultural showcase as foreign, yet interesting, without recognizing the cultural dynamics that affect the lives of its people. To avoid planning a one-dimensional family event, consider these suggestions from Longwell-Grice and McIntyre (2006):

1. *Recruit a planning team.* Hold consecutive planning meetings with parent guides early in the school year. Seek to have different cultural groups represented on the planning committee and provide translators if needed. Collaboratively decide on meeting dates and offer child care for families who attend the planning meetings.

2. *Consider the constituency of your planning committee.* Don't have staff, administrators, or educators outnumber family representatives. Plan meetings in a nonthreatening location that is convenient for families; consider off-school sites that reflect different cultures represented in the community (restaurants, community centers, or parks).

3. *Practice* **facilitative communication**. This type of communication with parents is not one-way but reciprocal. Teachers encourage parent input by supportive comments, focused questions, and reiterating key points of the conversation. The purpose of facilitative communication is a shared dialogue between parent and teacher. Seek advice and genuinely listen to families; allow them to voice their ideas and bounce them around as you would with educators. Make sure to take notes on all ideas after the initial brainstorming session; review these for all attendees. You will need to return to those suggestions in future meetings.

4. *Be sensitive to cultural misconnections.* For schools represented by students from multiple cultures, consider hosting a cultural fair in a larger setting. Be especially attuned to cultural nuances that can be taken for granted by those outside their cultural environment. For example, a family event that featured competition was not successful when done with Hmong students and families, a cultural group that does not emphasize competition or drawing attention to themselves. The teacher found that the students and families hung back and did not participate in the competitive activities. However, she found that group activities, such as a readers' theater done in a small group setting, was more successful and students enjoyed getting into the different characters' roles (J. Goddard, personal communication, July 31, 2007).

SETTING UP A FAMILY LITERACY EVENT

Juan, a first grader, was looking forward to his parents attending a Saturday afternoon reading achievement award event, celebrating his completion of a successful year in reading recovery, an intensive one-on-one program for first-grade students experiencing reading difficulties. As Juan and his parents entered the media center, he could see it was different from the way it usually looked, with tables covered in white tablecloths, a delicious looking cake, and little candies in cups. When Juan's name was called, he went up to the podium to receive his reading achievement certificate for completing the reading recovery program. As he left the stage, he received activity books and writing materials (in a beach pail with a shovel) to continue his summer reading. He beamed as his principal and teacher applauded for both him and his parents and thanked his parents for their help with his reading.

This wasn't the first time Juan's parents had come to school for a literacy event. They had come earlier in the school year after Juan's teacher had invited them to observe a reading recovery lesson. She had given them a handout explaining the different parts of the lesson and why each was beneficial to Juan. During the lesson, she made sure to use prompts or questions when he didn't know a word, so he would use problem-solving strategies. Juan's parents shared that this helped them more than anything else in knowing how to assist him at home. Before that, they didn't know what else to do except either "tell him the word," or say, "sound it out," neither of which seemed to help him much. Because of the support from Juan's teacher, they felt comfortable attending their first family literacy night, where children and their parents enjoyed a pizza dinner while volunteers set up more than 12 stations around the school. At each station, Juan and his parents played a literacy-related game, such as a word search puzzle, Concentration (a memory game), word bingo, and at one station, his parents read a book to him that was provided. Juan was given a card that listed each station so he could keep track of how many stations he visited. At the end of the night, Juan turned in his card and got to pick out a free book that was written in both English and Spanish. Juan's parents got a take-home bag of materials and instructions so they could recreate the games at home. Because of the family events provided by his school, Juan was well on his way to being a successful reader, and his parents were no longer fearful of coming to school to meet with his teachers.

The developmental literacy needs of students in the early childhood or elementary grades offer a starting point to develop plans for a family literacy event in the classroom. A literacy event can focus on one or two foundational reading skills that families can easily practice at home with materials at hand or provided by the school. Darling (2005) noted the strategies in the area of literacy instruction that teachers can share with parents in the five key areas of reading: (1) phonemic awareness, (2) phonics, (3) fluency, (4) vocabulary, and (5) text comprehension. These strategies can form the basis for family literacy activities of an ongoing nature; however, without reciprocal knowledge of what happens in the home and in the classroom, families and teachers are hampered in working together to promote literacy skills. There are distinct differences between school and community literacy activities, and both should be valued. School literacy focuses on traditional reading practices (assignments, oral reading, homework, skills set, etc.), while community literacy serves as an information-gathering function for the family (grocery list writing, newspaper reading, checking bus schedules, etc.). Literacy events that emphasize everyday uses of literacy can encourage family replication of developmental reading skills (Longwell-Grice & McIntyre, 2006). Table 13.5 has suggestions of home literacy activities that can be modeled and practiced at a literacy event.

Family literacy events can be held in a variety of settings, including a school or public library.

TABLE 13.5 Strategies for Engaging Families in Home Support of Reading Acquisition				
Phonemic Awareness/Print Concepts	**Phonics**	**Fluency**	**Vocabulary**	**Text Comprehension**
Read stories that their child chooses. Make a book with their child, using large print and illustrations	Talk with the teacher about their child's phonic progress	Read aloud often, encouraging their child to read aloud	Talk with their child about daily events and about books they read together	Ask their child to predict what might happen next in the story
Point out letters, especially letters in their child's name	Encourage children to point to words and say them aloud when writing	Model reading for fun and pleasure	Use word lists provided by their child's teacher in natural conversation	Ask who, what, where, when, and why questions about a book
Talk about where reading begins on the page and show how the words flow left to right	Help children sort words by long- and short-vowel sounds	Act out a book or a story	Search for new words in texts with their child and look them up in the dictionary	Ask their child questions about the topic of a book before reading it
Play games to match lowercase and uppercase letters	Play "I spy something that starts with . . ." using letter sounds instead of colors	Read aloud a sentence and then invite their child to read the same sentence (i.e., echo reading)	Help their child learn new vocabulary based on hobbies or interests	Ask their child about books being read at school and be familiar with them to extend conversation

Source: Darling (2005)

A well-attended **literacy lunch** event (informal lunchtime activity where parents and their children are engaged in some type of reading or writing activity as supervised by a teacher, family outreach personnel, or an aide), held at the Emma Dickinson Elementary School Family Resource Center in Missoula, Montana, coupled parents and relatives (many aunts and grandmothers attended) with primary children for a brief 30-minute lunch time literacy activity. Employing *Ed Emberley's Drawing Book of Faces* (Emberley, 1992) to thumb-print and draw family or holiday scenes, children either wrote a caption to explain the picture or dictated their story to families. Teachers and family outreach specialists (teachers' aides) had the opportunity to talk one-on-one with attendees and read books aloud at the end of the session to model fluent reading to children.

Some other examples of family literacy events include the following:

- Southwest Elementary School, in Hickory, North Carolina, a school with significant populations of Latino and Hmong students, held a family literacy night in the cafeteria, hosting three rotating, translated presentations (in Hmong and Spanish) on reading nonfiction texts, employing literacy games, and promoting family spelling activities. Cultural booths highlighted Mexican and Hmong cultural artifacts and dress (with cultural presentations), and families left the event with a children's book. A pizza supper was provided.

- Bryn Mawr Elementary School, in Loma Linda, California, a school with 27 different languages spoken, hosted a family literacy rally (promoting family reading, writing, and communication activities, the rally sparks family interest while providing necessary materials such as books, pamphlets, or games, as well as family service information). Held in an apartment complex with many low-income families, the rally provided free books, promoted adult literacy, and distributed Healthy Family insurance forms (Quezada, 2003).

- Jefferson Elementary School, in Cape Girardeau, Missouri, a school with 92% free/reduced lunch population, held literacy nights based on popular children's literature, such as *The Very Hungry Caterpillar* and *Curious George*. Kindergarten children and their families rotated among stations in the gym doing hands-on activities together. Local college students facilitated the stations while the teachers and principal chatted informally with families. All children received free books, and a pizza dinner was provided with funds donated by the school's partner, a local bank.

Keep in mind that teacher demonstrations and reading role-play activities (teachers model reading skills for parents to undertake) are essential to help families absorb the literacy activities you wish them to replicate at home with their children. Do not assume that all families feel at ease with the extent of their literacy knowledge; what you might consider the simple act of reading stories together may prove anxiety provoking for families with emerging English language skills. An open forum providing opportunities for discussion and questions is also recommended. Take the time to develop a PowerPoint presentation with questions families might pose to initiate the discussion if they appear reticent or embarrassed to ask questions.

Another important resource to provide families at a literacy event is information about books appropriate for their child's developmental reading levels. Giving families a concise list of children's books with reading levels and information about where they can be found can be helpful. However, locating children's books through libraries or book sales can prove prohibitive for some families. Allington (2001) noted, "Paperback book sales are largely a middle-class phenomenon" (p. 63). Therefore, lower-income schools may consider a free book distribution program. A lending library of classroom books available for family check-out encourages continued home literacy activities. Follow-up phone calls or home visits can offer debriefing opportunities with families as a way of encouraging continued home literacy activities and checking on access to reading materials.

A lack of funding for family events can be perceived as a barrier and cited as a justification for not hosting family literacy events. However, with foresight and making good use of business connections, schools can obtain seed money, food, or actual book donations. It is important to begin planning well in advance of the event (six months at least) and seek donations early; many larger businesses (such as Wal-Mart or Target) allocate donations on a monthly first-come-first-serve basis. Private organizations, such as the Barbara Bush Foundation for Family Literacy or Reading is Fundamental (RIF) (see websites at end of chapter), offer monetary awards and book donations for ongoing family literacy programs.

FAMILY MATH AS A CULTURAL EVENT

James and Terry were fifth-grade students and athletes who loved math and hands-on activities. Their school sent out flyers to their families and spoke at their church to invite the congregation to the family math night that would be held on the local university's campus. They found out that the mathematics education program at the university was partnering with a local middle school and an African Methodist Episcopal Zion church located in the school district to host a family math night.

University professors and college students, congregation members from the church, and middle school teachers and families decided on a theme that would grab the interest of the community. The theme used for the family math night was "March Madness: On the Championship Road." The culture of the school's North Carolina community strongly supported sporting events. In addition, this piqued the interest of James and Terry because basketball reigns supreme in North Carolina, and one of the local high schools was on the road to win the state basketball championship.

All the activities were related to basketball. The activities covered the mathematics topic of data analysis and used game statistics of the high school basketball team. From the game data, groups calculated things such as field goal and free-throw percentages of certain players, the three-point percentage of the team, average number of rebounds per game for the team, and the average number of points scored per game by the team. One mathematics activity had everyone in the group shoot five free throws, and the participants had to find the mode for the number of free throws made, the average number of free throws made by each player, and the team free-throw percentage.

All the participants were actively involved in a topic that was important to their community's sense of pride and accomplishment. At the end of the night, James and Terry asked the college students when they would be back to hold another family math night!

In 1981, the Family Math Program was created by the Lawrence Hall of Science, a public science center and research and development unit in science and math at the University of California, Berkeley (Carlson, 1991). The program's objectives included having families participate in mathematics activities together with their children, developing problem-solving techniques and self-confidence in the use of mathematics, and sharing information about equity issues concerning mathematics (Carlson, 1991). Since the creation of the Family Math Program, the Lawrence Hall of Science at the University of California, Berkeley, has published several activity books for families with children ages five to 13 years (Coates & Stenmark, 1997; Coates & Thompson, 2003; Stenmark, Thompson, & Cossey, 1986; Thompson & Mayfield-Ingram, 1998). Family math events can provide a comfortable, welcoming atmosphere for families where understanding mathematics can be made simpler (Kelly et al., 1998; Schussheim, 2004). They can also provide an opportunity for interesting challenges to be presented for mathematics to be learned, shared, and made fun (Schussheim, 2004).

Family math nights are beneficial to schools, teachers, families, and especially students. Family math activities are a wonderful tool for schools in building school-home-community partnerships. Teachers benefit by gaining another resource in families to help them in their efforts to teach mathematical skills and concepts, and families can learn mathematics strategies so that they can help their children with mathematics homework and gain a feeling of support from the school. Students also benefit from improved feelings of self-confidence, an increase in positive academic experiences, and family involvement in their education. Therefore, all parties involved in family math nights can benefit from this event.

Although family math events can be beneficial to participants, there are also possible obstacles that can hinder the success of the event. Teachers may be uncomfortable interacting with families from diverse backgrounds, or depending on the age of the students, they may question the families' abilities to be successful with the mathematics activities. They may also feel that they do not have the time required for planning and organizing such an event. Some parents may be hesitant to participate in a family math activity because of mathematics anxiety. Additionally, some may feel intimidated coming to a school because of their lack of school success in mathematics. For these reasons, a family math event may have a better turnout at a church or community center.

As with family literacy events, a family math event can help students and their families see that mathematics is a part of their everyday life. It can decrease the possible fear that families may have about helping their children with their math homework, as well as help children enjoy math. For example, on the exit survey of a math night at Orchard Elementary School in Jackson, Missouri, five-year-old Allie wrote, "I like win my ant Hailey helpd me make numburs with plabo" [Play-doh] (Personal communication, W. Bandermann, November 1, 2009). When students and families have an enjoyable experience at a family math event, they are more likely to return for future events and approach working with their students on mathematics activities in a positive way. Some ideas for family math events are located in Table 13.6.

TABLE 13.6 Examples of Family Math Events

1. *Sports team theme nights.* Use professional baseball, basketball, or football teams that the community supports as a theme, such as St. Louis Cardinals night, and have a variety of activities that require mathematical calculations of the team's statistics.

2. *Family game nights.* Have a variety of board games appropriate for the age level of the students that require mathematics computations. Games can be commercially bought, such as Trouble, which requires problem-solving skills, Monopoly, which focuses on counting money and making change, or homemade such as a blank board game with problems provided to determine the number of spaces moved. Families can also check out games to play at home ("Promote Literacy—And Many Other Skills—Through Board Games," 2004).

3. *Adults-only "math academies."* While students are doing separate math enrichment activities in another room, teachers conduct short seminars, full of hands-on activities, to refresh their families on key math concepts and problem-solving exercises ("Boost Student Achievement by Enrolling Parents in Math Academies," 2005).

4. *Math literacy events.* Events that use children's literature as a basis for math activities can integrate the learning of literacy and mathematics. For example, *The Doorbell Rang* by Pat Hutchins (1986), *Eating Fractions* by Bruce McMillan (1992), and *Apple Fractions* by Jerry Pallotta (2003) all deal with dividing food into fractions, and they can be used as the basis for a family math night on fractions that combines stories, food, and math activities for students and families.

FAMILY SCIENCE NIGHT

Damion, Latisha, and Katie were excited. They were going back to school tonight with their parents, grandparents, and siblings. Tonight was family science night at Park View Elementary School. When they arrived at the school at 6:30 p.m., they were warmly welcomed by the school counselor, who registered them and assigned them a group number. All family members received the same group number. Damion, his sister, and their grandmother went to Room 3; Latisha, her mother, and aunt went to Room 4; and Katie, her brother, and father headed to Room 5. Each room had about six students, the family members, and a science facilitator. The science facilitators included three teachers and one teacher's assistant at Park View, the two student teachers from second-grade classrooms, a local chemist whose daughter attended Park View, and two high school science teachers—one of whom had a spouse who taught at the school and the other who coached some of the Park View students on a basketball team. Before the first activity period began, each of the nine facilitators welcomed the students and their families to the family science night at Park View. After brief introductions, everyone got to work. All the nine classrooms had a 20-minute science activity for students and families to try. In Room 3, Damion and his family first guessed how many drops of water fit on a dime and then tried to get as many drops as they could on the dime. In Room 4, Latisha and her family predicted how water would flow out of a gallon jug that had three vertical holes that were covered with masking tape. Then, they removed the tape and watched the water flow. Katie and her family attempted to pour water down a string. After spending most of the time doing the activity, repeating the activity, and discussing results of repeated trials, the facilitator led the group in a discussion about a science concept that they had just experienced; the concept of water pressure in Room 4 and the concepts of adhesion and cohesion in Rooms 3 and 5. Tonight, facilitators in all the rooms were doing science activities that focused on various properties of water.

Participants moved to the next room and the facilitator in the new room began the activity again. Volunteers made sure that facilitators had everything they needed, that families could find the rooms where they needed to be, and that everyone stayed on schedule. Everyone did the three different activities in three different rooms, and they then reported to the cafeteria, where a chemist talked briefly about her work and did a series of demonstrations with water. As families left the school, they were each given a handout with four simple science investigations to try at home. All needed materials were included in a gallon Ziploc bag. Damion, Latisha, and Katie hurried home to try one of the activities before bedtime.

Family science night is a way for families and children to talk and work together in a nonthreatening environment while developing their scientific thinking. It provides a time and place where communication can take place between the classroom teacher and the family. Often, additional science activity ideas are sent home with families to encourage further science study at home to support their child.

The goals and objectives of hosting a science family night might include opportunities to do the following:

- Help families and children develop a deeper understanding of science concepts and processes by engaging in simple science activities, investigations, and experiments, especially those science experiences that most easily occur after school, such as astronomy nights or night hikes.
- Meet scientists, science educators, or teachers with a special interest in science.
- Help family members work together to practice skills such as problem solving and critical thinking.
- Create interest and enthusiasm in families and students for science and encourage them to see science as a part of everyday life.
- Strengthen relationships between teachers and families.

As with the other family events, organizing a family science event requires a team effort among teachers, school, and community. A planning committee might include family representatives from the parent-teachers organization, teachers from the grade levels served, science coordinators, and individuals in the community who have a high interest in or knowledge of science, such as the local meteorologist, pharmacist, or university science educators. Table 13.7 is a checklist to help you organize a family science night for your school. Note that this checklist could easily be adapted for literacy and math nights or for other family events.

TABLE 13.7 Family Science Night Planning Checklist

Planning is essential for a successful family science night. Use the checklist to help you plan and organize your first event.

Six Months Ahead

- Establish goals (Is there a particular topic or learning strategy that will be taught?)
- Determine location (Where will the event be held? Cafeteria, classrooms, gymnasium?)
- Predict attendance (How many people will be invited? Certain grades? Entire school?)
- Choose a date and time (Does an evening or Saturday work better for parents? Make sure to check community and school calendar for conflicts.)
- Recruit staff members (Individuals could fill roles such as event coordinator, publicity.)
- Assign coordinator duties: event coordinator, activities coordinator, food/prize coordinator, community coordinator, and volunteer coordinator
- Determine time allotment during event (How will time during the event be broken up? Will you have activity centers followed by a time to reconvene and discuss experiences with the activities, the learning that occurred, and how this might be used in the home setting?)
- Decide how to promote and publicize the event (Consider letters/announcements/flyers to families, teachers, and the press. Multiple times in multiple ways increase attendance.)
- Recruit presenters

Three Weeks Ahead

- Send flyers home
- Recruit assistants
- Decide whether you will prepare/serve food or refreshments

Two Weeks Ahead

- Prepare activity schedule
- Make room assignments for each activity
- Order activity supplies
- E-mail reminder to presenters
- Send press release to newspapers, television, and radio stations
- Confirm teachers/staff to help with greeting families
- Create an evaluation form for the event
- Purchase activity supplies

Two or Three Days Ahead

- Purchase food for presenters' dinner
- Prepare program, sign-in sheets, door signs, name tags, evaluations copies
- Call newspaper and TV stations to remind

Family Science Day

- Confirm photographers (buy disposable cameras for each session and ask participants to take pictures) and film
- Make any copies needed of handouts

At Family Science Night

- Distribute to presenters: program, name tag
- Put signs on classrooms
- Set up registration table (sign-in sheets and signs, programs, name tags, markers/pencils)
- Set out box for completed evaluations (either a box lid or clear plastic container)
- All parents and students sign in and make name tags

Day After

- Summarize numbers attending by grade/parent
- Summarize parent evaluations
- Send summary to school principal
- E-mail thank-you message to all presenters; send evaluation summary
- Turn in receipts and reimburse presenters

Source: Based on the Family Science Night Check List. Used by permission from Joan Chadde and the Western U.P. Center for Science, Mathematics and Environmental Education and Michigan Technological University, www.wupcenter.mtu.edu.

Since most family science nights will last only a couple of hours, with families moving through several learning activity centers or stations, you will need resources for simple science activities. Some excellent collections of materials will help you get started. Examples include the Exploratorium (the first hands-on science museum in the United States, located in Berkeley, California), which has a valuable website, www.exploratorium.edu, with downloadable activities that can be used for family science night, and Steve Spangler Science (www.stevespanglerscience.com/experiments), which has simple eye-catching experiments that explore the "whys" of science concepts. Once the different activities have been chosen, it is advisable to have a meeting of the planning committee where the different science experiments are modeled with feedback from the group. Materials will need to be gathered, making sure that you have enough to repeat the activities several times with different groups of families and students.

Although family science events can take time and effort to plan, organize, and gather materials, they can be an extremely positive experience for families, students, and teachers. Teachers get to interact with students and their families in a less formal environment. Scientists get to interact with an interested public, including young children who may be encouraged to pursue science or whose interest in science is sparked by an activity, a question, or exposure to a field of science that they've never heard of before the family science event. Families get interested in science and their children's science education, and they learn more about science themselves and how to help their children with science homework. Family engagement is crucial to a child's success in school, and this is especially important in mathematics and science, which are subjects that are perceived to be more difficult for student and families.

ORGANIZING A FAMILY TECHNOLOGY NIGHT

Sara eagerly ran ahead of her mom and her older brother, Adam, into the school door for Terrific Tuesday, a night when her school was open for families and children to use the school's computer lab together. Most of the time, there were no scheduled activities, but this Tuesday was special because Mrs. Gallagher, the school's technology specialist, had planned a program about Sara's favorite author, Dr. Seuss. During Sara's library class that day, she had used the Smart Board to show them some of the activities they would be doing that night, and Sara couldn't wait to show her mom. She always checked out Dr. Seuss books from the school library, and her mom read them to her at night. She could read "Hop on Pop" by herself now! Sara's mom had first been hesitant to come to school to use the computer lab because she didn't know very much about computers, but Sara and Adam had begged, and after a while, she enjoyed coming and watching them play games. Adam had even showed her how he could make a PowerPoint presentation for his science report. Tonight, Mrs. Gallagher first shared a Dr. Seuss story with the group, encouraging the children to read along. She then gave the group directions on how to log onto a "webquest" she had created about Dr. Seuss. Sara, Adam, and her mom searched Dr. Seuss's website and other websites that Mrs. Gallagher provided to find out answers about the author's life and his books. When they were finished, the reward was playing one of the games on Dr. Seuss's website (www.seussville.com). Sara's mom was proud of how quickly Sara and Adam were able to find the answers to the questions, and Adam had even taught her something new when he had explained what a "search engine" was, a term Mrs. Gallagher used that was confusing. She wished that she was able to afford a computer for the kids to have at home, but was glad that their school opened the computer lab weekly for family use.

A final family event that has proven to be successful in involving families with their children's learning is a family technology night, an event that can provide an opportunity to showcase technology-based hands-on learning experiences for families and students. An evening for families and students dedicated to technology can do the following:

- Engage families in the latest technology, so they understand what and how their children are learning
- Provide information on how to help their children at home, using technology
- Further build social connections among families and with teachers

Many different activities can be done at a family technology event. For example, students can do a presentation about a topic they researched, using PowerPoint, or they can demonstrate to their families how to use a form of technology such as a Smart Board (an interactive whiteboard). Families can then be encouraged to do an activity together, such as completing a simple assignment, using classroom software, such as drawing a tree using the Kid Pix graphic software, or completing a webquest, an inquiry based activity where students must use Internet resources to discover answers to questions posed on a topic. A family technology event can also include separate sessions for children and adults, with teachers presenting information on topics, such as Internet safety, to adults, while children participate in technology-related activities in classrooms. Other examples of family-technology-night experiences are listed in Table 13.8.

There are special considerations in planning a family technology event because of the equipment needs. The location will be based on the availability of equipment and electric and Internet connections. Therefore, it is important to plan in advance when choosing a date and time and securing the necessary permission for the location. A planning committee that includes the district's technology staff can facilitate the planning and organization of the event. It is important to have technology support throughout the planning and implementation of the event. For example, equipment needs to be tested prior to the event, with contingency plans for technology problems such as a power failure, computer crash, or the network going down. Replacement equipment, such as projector bulbs, computer mice, or batteries for remote controls, should be stored in a central location to which all event coordinators have access. If computer stations are being used, it is important to consider the comfort of all body types, sizes, and disabilities. A final dress rehearsal test of each computer station and electronic equipment before families arrive can prevent unnecessary surprises. Safe use of equipment should also be considered, such as extension cords, wires, plugs, or any electric devices that may be harmful to children. Trash receptacles at each door can be used to encourage families to throw away all food and drinks before interacting with the technology. The size of the group must also be considered to make sure that all have the hands-on experiences with technology. Although a presentation by a teacher on Internet safety can be helpful for families, events that also include actual use of technology by families and students are of high interest. Families may be hesitant in using technology with which they are unfamiliar, but students can be trained to serve as guides for their families, demonstrating how to use equipment and software. Completed technology-assisted class projects and student work around the room and near computer stations can also generate interest among families as students explain how they created the work.

TABLE 13.8 Ideas for Family Technology Night Experiences

- Offer mini question-and-answer sessions about how teachers integrate technology into the curriculum.
- Address how your teachers use e-mail and/or websites for home-school communication.
- Provide families a chance to play with their child's school software programs and equipment. This can prepare them to help when their children have questions.
- Distribute class rules about computer-generated homework and provisions for computer access for students who do not have computers.
- Showcase your computer station setup and other school technology. Include platforms (PC or Macintosh), models, equipment age, district/school plans to upgrade, and networking capabilities, and give demonstrations of how the latest technological equipment (i.e., Smart Boards, Smart Tables, iPads) are being used in classrooms.
- List and demonstrate frequently used software titles (including versions) for learning and remedial assignments. This helps families understand how different titles tie into their child's schoolwork.
- Supply a list of teacher-recommended instructional programs and software for home use (word processing, spreadsheets, AppleWorks, etc.).
- Provide a recommended list of school-authorized online resources for student learning and discovery.
- Introduce tips for securing a safe online environment.
- Provide adult-child Internet awareness information including a contract to read with their child, and have her sign it.
- Explain the school's Acceptable Use Policy (AUP)—a required written agreement between the school and the student (younger than 18 years of age) with parental/guardian consent about proper use of e-mail, the Internet, and the consequences for not doing so.
- Present how the Internet is used in instruction and how the students are monitored for safety when online in the classrooms and labs.
- Offer tips encouraging a balance between computer and noncomputer activities at home. Include reading, outdoor activities, hobbies, and family games into the balance.
- Demonstrate ergonomics for setting up a computer study area in the home for promoting and maintaining healthy posture and good study habits.
- Introduce an informational website demonstrating your school's technology use. Content may include class projects, student work, and online family activities.
- Take digital photographs to give to participating families. These photos may also be used to enhance your school's website and advertise upcoming family nights.
- Make tee shirts. Demonstrate student creativity using a simple software program. Print the design on transfer paper. Press the designs on tee shirts with a hot iron.

ESTABLISHING A SCHOOL OR CLASSROOM FAMILY RESOURCE CENTER

A Family Resource Center is a place in a school that is set aside for the purpose of making the school accessible to families and encouraging adult involvement in children's education. A center may be located in a spare classroom, a section of the library, or a quiet hallway. Many schools are so crowded that a small nook at the school becomes a Center.

—Women's Opportunity and Resource Development, Inc. (n.d.)

In addition to family events, schools committed to family engagement may set aside physical space in the school building for families. This may be a FRC that serves a school building or a FIC that is located in an individual classroom. Both the FRC and FIC can provide essential information to families, and a FRC may also provide a space for family members to meet and socialize.

Family Information Center (FIC)

An FIC, located in a classroom, is designed to enhance and build on the particular strengths and to help meet the needs of classroom members and their families. The FIC can serve as a center for sharing vital classroom information, such as homework information or a schedule of upcoming classroom events. According to the space available, the information center should be housed in a location easily accessed by visiting family members. The information center can be something as simple as a bulletin board and table. If room space is severely limited, the center can even be placed on a rolling cart, located within a closet area, or in the hallway outside the class. Families can be encouraged to check out the information center before and after school or at other times if the school maintains a "drop in" policy, with families welcome at any time.

If your school is in a rural area, with children primarily riding a bus to school and families seldom in the building, families can still receive packets of information through the mail. Another option is a virtual FIC on the classroom website with all information from the FIC, making it accessible for families with home Internet access. This information can be a starting point for conversations and telephone conferences. A classroom website thus can offer the same opportunity for dialogue as the real presence of those families who are able to visit the classroom.

Some suggestions for a classroom FIC follow. The list is far from exhaustive. If you have non-English-speaking families, be sure to offer translated materials. Permanent announcements should be laminated for durability. Also, consider involving families in developing and maintaining your FIC.

- Class calendar of events with sign-up sheets for volunteers
- Photographs of class activities with student quotes or thoughts (Make sure you have a parent's or guardian's permission to use any students' pictures in this display or on your classroom website.)
- Classroom policies
- Surveys or questionnaires
- School and teacher contact information with best times for contact
- Biographical information on the teacher

Parents will recognize and appreciate the extra effort you take to establish an FIC. Not all families will be able to visit or take the time to browse at an information center, yet creating an FIC gives you an opportunity to reach at least some families and build relationships with them.

Family Resource Center (FRC)

Besides creating an FIC in your classroom, you can also be an advocate for creating an FRC in your school. The FRC is an area in the school building that is designated specifically for family members. FRCs vary from school to school according to the space available and the funding allotted for materials and personnel, but most FRCs follow this general description:

> [Family Resource] Centers provide a variety of resources including community and school information, lending libraries, workshops, friendly and knowledgeable staff, and a good cup of coffee. Generally they include comfortable furniture, a work area with computer and telephone, an area for young children with toys and books, a bulletin board announcing school and community events, brochures and information on school and community resources, and perhaps a clothing closet where families can swap clothing of fast growing children. Working with parents and teachers, Literacy Support Corps members, often known as Family Resource Center Coordinators [staff members responsible for oversight and running of the school's family resource center, including outreach efforts to families, working with teachers on family involvement projects, and connecting families with social services] in schools, facilitate a wide variety of activities for parents and families designed to strengthen learning in classrooms, homes and the community. They create an environment where strong partnerships between families and schools flourish. (Women's Opportunity and Resource Development, Inc., p. 1)

An FRC may provide useful information to families as follows:

- List of community resources
- Brochures, booklets, and magazines on different topics of interest to families
- Parenting tips

Besides providing information, FRCs can also be venues for activities (J. Moon, personal communication, September 6, 2007). One example is the FRC post office. Students could write letters and deliver them to the FRC. Then the letters would be mailed or the family members would be called to pick up their letters at the school. While picking up their children's letters, family members could sit in the FRC and write letters in reply, which would then be delivered to the children's classrooms. Chris Yankoviak, of Mt. Jumbo Elementary School, in Missoula, Montana, described her school's FRC post office:

> I recently started a "Post Office" in our Family Resource Center to encourage family members to write to each other. The activity has been a success—the kids love it and it has had a profound effect on the school. The first day, the kids were so excited they were jumping up and down as they walked to the Post Office in the Family Resource Center. Some were so excited they wrote two letters! The Post Office has also shown the generosity and hope that the kids bring to our community. Two examples of the positive effect of this program stand out. First, one of the kids wrote to the school superintendent and he graciously wrote back. That was one excited and enthused little girl. But more importantly, that letter from an excited student must have been exactly

the positive interaction that a superintendent of a large and complicated school district needs to keep going when faced with the myriad of problems that he must face. Second, and more powerful, is that one of our adopted grandparents through the RSVP [seniors who volunteer in the school] program recently passed away. Post Office was the next day and several of the kids wrote letters to the grieving spouse, who also happens to be an adopted grandparent from RSVP. These letters were delivered to the funeral, and the hope and joy that this kindness offered is beyond words. (Women's Opportunity and Resource Development, n.d., p. 3)

The FRC can also be a place for volunteers to work. Volunteers in one study cited the presence of a volunteer space as being a critical factor in their commitment to volunteering on a regular basis. Although the space provided for them varied from a former classroom to a converted supply room, the volunteers described it as a "place of joy" and a "second home." They also stated that having a space for them to connect with other family members gave them a support network (Quintanar & Warren, 2008, p. 121).

To establish an FRC, you will first need to get the support of your administration in the form of adequate space and funding. A leadership group of teachers, administrators, family volunteers, and community members can help develop the FRC. Coordination of the center can initially be handled by volunteers; eventually, a paid coordinator could be hired with district or grant funds. One way to start a center economically is to enlist **AmeriCorps volunteers** to develop one. These volunteers would receive training on how to do outreach to families, hold family activities, and operate an FRC (J. Moon, personal communication, September 6, 2007). AmeriCorps members serve with more than 2,000 nonprofits, public agencies, and faith-based and community organizations. AmeriCorps opens the door for citizens to serve in a variety of ways. Through their service and the volunteers they mobilize, AmeriCorps members address critical needs in communities throughout America, including the following:

- Tutoring and mentoring disadvantaged youth
- Fighting illiteracy
- Improving health services
- Teaching computer skills
- Managing or operating afterschool programs (www.americorps.gov)

SCHOOL VOLUNTEERS

A volunteer program was introduced in Chapter 10 as an important source of support for a classroom teacher. A volunteer program can also be a help in the larger schoolwide setting. Schoolwide volunteers can do tasks that help improve the functioning of a school such as the following:

- Organizing and participating in a school work day in which volunteers paint or repair school equipment and buildings or plant flowers
- Assisting in an afterschool program or club, such as a cake decorating course or afterschool tutoring sessions

- Organizing a fundraising project
- Working in non-classroom settings, such as assisting in the school office with newsletter mailings, or helping the school media specialist process new library materials

An important volunteer position in schools with diversity in languages is that of bilingual volunteer. This volunteer can be a parent or community member who speaks the first language(s) of your school's English language learners. For example, one school that had a significant number of children who spoke Japanese, because of the presence of a Japanese manufacturing plant in the community, recruited a retired military officer who had been stationed for most of his career in Japan to help transition new students and families to the school. Bilingual volunteers can perform several tasks. Haynes (2004) suggests these ways in which bilingual volunteers can assist in schools:

- Become a liaison between the school and non-English-speaking families by contacting them as necessary and translating school correspondence.
- Explain practices and procedures of schools in the United States. Families who do not speak English may not understand current teaching strategies, such as invented spelling, cooperative learning, or math manipulatives, and they may not understand teachers' expectations that they play a partnership role in their children's classroom education. Bilingual volunteers can create handbooks about school programs, procedures, and practices to give to new families who do not speak English.
- Establish a telephone chain among families to pass on information about emergency school closings or other important messages from school to home.
- Help with new student registration and tours of the school. The presence of a volunteer during these procedures can assist the school in getting necessary information from the family. It also offers the family a chance to ask questions of someone who speaks their language.
- Support the classroom teacher in the instruction of English language learners.
- Provide information about other languages and cultures to teachers in the building. For example, bilingual volunteers can teach faculty phrases to use with students who do not speak English.
- An effective volunteer program, whether it is for classroom volunteers or those who assist in schoolwide activities, includes three key components: (1) recruitment, (2) training, and (3) retention. A volunteer program is more likely to be successful if it is well organized, with thought going into all three of these areas.

Recruiting Volunteers

Tina Walker listened with interest at the open house presentation where the kindergarten teacher showed photos on the projector screen of scenes from the previous year's class working with volunteers on different tasks, such as putting puzzles together, matching word cards on charts, and making words with magnetic letters on metal cookie sheets. The teacher encouraged family members to consider volunteering in the classroom this year. "Maybe that wouldn't be so hard," she thought, and she told the teacher after the meeting that she might be interested in being a volunteer, although her work schedule and lack of reliable transportation might prevent her from volunteering regularly. She secretly questioned whether she could really help the children. She had gotten a GED degree after having negative experiences with school. However, she knew that her son would be excited to have his mother in class, and she was determined that he would be more successful in school than she had been. (Adapted from DeCusati & Johnson, 2004)

Since families are more likely to volunteer to help their child's education outside the classroom than during the school day (National Center for Education Statistics, 1998), recruiting families for involvement at school can be a challenge. However, a strong schoolwide recruitment program can increase the number of volunteers and is more likely to be successful if families are offered flexible opportunities to share their time and talents (National Network of Partnership Schools, 2006). It is especially important to reach out to families who may be hesitant to volunteer. Studies have found that families who have a low socioeconomic status, belong to an ethnic minority, speak a language other than English as a first language, or have a child in special education are less likely to volunteer. There are several reasons for this, such as a lack of transportation or child care for younger siblings, inflexible work schedules, lack of paid leave, a feeling that the adults in the family have nothing to offer the school, or a negative view of school (Brent, 2000; DeCusati & Johnson, 2004). Building relationships with these families and extending personal invitations to them to volunteer can also help to recruit reluctant family members.

You may be hesitant to ask family members who are limited English speakers to volunteer, but they can be valuable assets who can provide an extra pair of hands with jobs such as making bulletin boards or photocopies (Haynes, 2004). Volunteering may help them improve their English as well. Delgado Gaitan (2004) suggests these strategies to recruit Latino parents as school volunteers:

- Have each teacher suggest one or two family leaders who have shown interest by their questions or their presence at school to reach out to others with recruitment efforts.
- Hold regular meetings with these Latino parents to help make decisions on issues pertaining to Latino students and their families, such as communication strategies.
- Make meetings short, informative, and pertinent to the business of children's learning.
- Use the Latino family group to identify other families who can get involved in school events (p. 73).

Quintanar and Warren (2008) found that encouraging Latino parent volunteers to recruit other parents was a productive strategy. As one mother said,

I also invited the mothers that I would see staying around a little bit there, and I would say, "Would you like to become a volunteer?" And many times they would tell me, "Well, yes, I would like to be a volunteer." (p. 121, translated from Spanish)

Note that these strategies can be effective for all families and not just Latino families.

Recruitment efforts are more likely to be successful if volunteers are offered flexible opportunities. Having a rigid requirement of a certain day and time for volunteering is likely to limit the number of adults who sign up to volunteer (DeCusati & Johnson, 2004; National Network of Partnership Schools, 2006). Recruitment should also be done for volunteer activities outside the school day. For example, the Spooner Elementary School in Spooner, Wisconsin, began the "High Five After-School Program" to raise the achievement levels of students from low-income families. After surveying families about possible course offering, clubs were created and volunteers from the community were recruited to teach fun skills such as drama, cooking, and crafts. One group of community volunteers formed the Master Gardeners and teamed up with the 4-H Club to teach students a gardening unit. Because of the positive feedback from teachers, families, and students, more community members showed interest in volunteering (Collins, 2006).

As seen in the previous example, recruitment should not be limited to parents. Extended families, including grandparents, can be a good source of school volunteers. Grandparents who are retired may not have a daily work commitment and may be more available during the school day than other family members. For example, one kindergarten student's grandfather and grandmother came two days a week and helped children write stories in the school's computer lab. The children in the class received individual attention and came to see their classmate's grandparents as their "grandma and grandpa," which pleased the grandparents, who enjoyed having the special time with their granddaughter and her classmates. The teacher had more time to help other students who were struggling with beginning literacy skills. In addition to extended family members, community members can also be recruited to volunteer. Local business leaders, medical professionals, and community service workers can share their knowledge and skills with students as guest speakers or teachers of short lessons on topics such as money, dental health, or fire safety.

Training Volunteers

Although training of volunteers is not done in all school districts, it can help ensure that volunteers are following school policies and can also help volunteers know what is expected of them. A nationwide survey done by the National Center for Education Statistics (1998) found that approximately 39% of all K–8 schools provided some training for classroom volunteers. Schools that were located in cities, were part of large districts, or had more minority students than other schools were more likely to provide training for classroom volunteers. Volunteer training can be given to groups during an orientation session at the beginning of the year, or individually as family and community members sign up during the year. Having one staff person in charge of volunteer orientation, such as the home-school coordinator, school administrator, counselor, or social worker, can ensure that volunteers get consistent training and information. Volunteers should also be given a handbook or manual that clearly outlines school policies and general expectations of volunteers.

Policies for volunteers can be established by an advisory committee that includes an administrator, teachers, and families. Legal issues should be considered, as well as the need for policies that are family friendly. Many schools now require a background criminal check for any nonschool employee who works with students in any capacity. Health screenings such as TB (tuberculosis) tests may also be required. Schools can seek outside funding to cover the costs of these criminal checks and health screenings to make sure that they do not prohibit families or community members from volunteering.

An important policy to discuss with all volunteers is that of confidentiality. Volunteers should understand the privacy rights of students and the importance of keeping any information about students' abilities and skills private. Having volunteers who gossip about students' classroom performance or behavior is unacceptable and can damage school-home relations and the volunteer program itself. Volunteers should also not have access to any assessment information about students. It is best that volunteers not grade papers or record grades in a grade book or online grading system; and no testing information, such as a student's individual education plan information, should be in view when a volunteer is in the classroom.

Because volunteers are not school employees, for liability reasons, they should not be left solely in charge of students. For example, volunteers can assist with lunchroom or playground supervision but should not be left alone to supervise students. This also includes field trips, when volunteers must not take students off alone but must stay with the group and the teacher. A policy should clearly explain the role of volunteers in supervising students.

Another issue that a committee will need to consider in setting policies for volunteers is whether a student's younger siblings will be allowed to come to school with the volunteer. The advantages of allowing this is that family members do not have the burden of childcare expenses while volunteering and a school may attract more volunteers. However, the disadvantage is that a younger sibling may create distractions in the classroom and keep a volunteer from doing the assigned tasks.

Policies for school-day volunteers also apply to volunteers in afterschool programs that are school sponsored. Having well-thought-out policies that are clearly understood by all volunteers can prevent problems from occurring and make the volunteer program a positive experience for all involved.

Several topics can be covered at a training or volunteer orientation session. School and classroom rules should be explained so that volunteers understand what behavior is expected of students. Any rules that affect adults should also be covered, such as smoking bans or dress codes. The training session can also include information about how to use any equipment, such as copy or laminating machines. There may also be certain instructional techniques that are important for volunteers to understand if they are helping with classroom instruction. For example, explaining the questioning techniques to be used when sharing a story with students can help make the storytelling session more productive. It may be beneficial to ask the volunteers to observe several literacy or math lessons to become familiar with the curriculum and teaching techniques before working with students by themselves (Craven, 2006).

Retaining Volunteers

It is important to not only recruit and train volunteers, but also give attention to retaining them once they begin volunteering. Giving attention to how volunteers are treated is one way to build and keep a strong group of committed volunteers. It is important that volunteers have clear directions about their tasks, with all materials provided, and that they are shown respect and courtesy by school staff and students. Surveying volunteers about their experience and what could be done to improve it can ensure that they return. Mentor volunteers can also work alongside new volunteers, creating bonds and making it a pleasant experience. Finally, it is crucial that volunteers are recognized and their efforts appreciated. A personal thank-you note from an administrator is important, as well as public recognition, such as names and photos on a school sign or bulletin board, or listed in a school newsletter. School staff might consider hosting a volunteer recognition event, where volunteers are treated to a meal and a celebration of their efforts. Volunteers can also be publicly recognized at a school board meeting or in newspaper articles.

SUMMARY

This chapter has described a variety of ways to engage families in their child's education through school-based activities. The examples of family events in this chapter move beyond the traditional "audience member" level of participation for families that is typically found in school events such as a science fair or an open house to an active level of participation where families and children are learning together. Creating an FRC within a school sends the message that families are partners with school staff in educating their child, and developing a strong volunteer program will offer families another way to support the school's efforts to educate the children of their community. Although planning, organizing, and implementing these schoolwide family engagement activities can be time-consuming, the benefits that teachers, families, and students can reap outweigh the disadvantages, and these activities can go a long way toward building a partnership with families.

REFLECTION QUESTIONS

Reread the In the Classroom case study presented at the beginning of the chapter and reflect on these questions:

1. Using Table 13.3, Checklist for Culturally Responsive Family Events, evaluate the teachers' plans. Did they consider everything necessary to have a successful event?

2. Family events, such as this one, require much time and effort on a teacher's part. What are the benefits of organizing and hosting an event like this? Do you think it is worth it?

3. How can these second-grade teachers use this experience to plan other successful family events?

WEBSITES

Barbara Bush Foundation for Family Literacy, **www.barbarabushfoundation.com.**

This website offers information about grants available for family literacy activities, which must include intergenerational activities where the parents/primary caregivers and children come together to learn and to read.

Education World, **www.educationworld.com.**

> This website has a wealth of resources for teachers, including professional development articles on hosting family events. Check out the family fitness nights, where kids and families engage in physical activities together: www.educationworld.com/a_curr/ profdev/profdev095.shtml.

LearnNC: Science Family Fun Night, **www.learnnc.org/lp/pages/810.**

> One night a month a North Carolina teacher opens her classroom to families where they work together to solve logic problems and conduct experiments. Through this monthly fun night, she increases family involvement in her students' education and finds ideas for science experiments and other classroom science projects.

Parent Information and Resource Centers Grantees (PIRCS), **www.ed.gov/programs/pirc/ grantees.html.**

> A statewide list of organizations receiving grants to develop, expand, or maintain FRCs. The site can provide start-up ideas for educators interested in beginning the process.

PTO Today, **http://ptotoday.com/boards/school-family-events.**

> This page highlights family events message boards where successful ideas for family events can be spotlighted and discussed through online interactions. Some ideas included "Inside Winter Games," a "Read-A-Thon," and a "Family Arts and Crafts" night.

Reading Is Fundamental (RIF), **www.rif.org.**

> This site offers numerous resources to support literacy, including information on Family Literacy Events. RIF is also a source of free books and literacy resources for needy children and families.

STUDENT STUDY SITE

Log on to the student study site at **www.sagepub.com/grant2e** for additional study tools, including the following:

- eFlashcards
- Web quizzes
- Web resources
- Learning objectives

APPENDIX A

Standards

Four sets of national standards guide family engagement practices in early childhood and elementary education. The Interstate New Teacher Assessment and Support Consortium (INTASC) developed core teacher licensing standards for the beginning teacher in 1992, which may then be used by states in developing teacher licensure systems. These 10 standards were revised in 2011 to be performance standards for the different developmental stages of a teacher's career. Standard 10 relates to family engagement. The National Board of Professional Teaching Standards (NBPTS) was created in 1987. Whereas the INTASC standards address the knowledge and skills required of beginning teachers, the NBPTS standards include five core propositions that characterize an accomplished practicing teacher, the National Board Certified Teacher (NBCT). Throughout these propositions, the importance of being able to collaborate with students' families is highlighted. There are also specific family engagement standards for different age levels. The National Association for the Education of Young Children (NAEYC) provides guidance on collaborating with families for future and practicing teachers who work with children from birth through the age of eight years in the NAEYC Professional Preparation Standards, which were revised in 2010. Standard 2, Building Family and Community Relationships, relates to family engagement. Although the NAEYC standards relate to practice in early childhood, the Association for Childhood Education International (ACEI) has, for many years, outlined the pathway for elementary education teachers to be successful in working with children, as well as their families. ACEI developed the Program Standards for Elementary Teacher Preparation programs, and Standard 5 (professionalism) addresses the importance of elementary teachers being able to collaborate with families and communities in ways that support children's learning and development. The following summarizes and compares the four major national standards for teachers, relating to family engagement.

Standard	INTASC	NBPTS	NAEYC	ACEI
Target audience of standards	Beginning and experienced teachers	Experienced teachers	Beginning and experienced teachers	Beginning teachers
Age level	All content and grade levels	Generalist standards for ages 3 to 15 years	Birth to 8 years	Kindergarten to 6th grade

(Continued)

(Continued)

Standard	INTASC	NBPTS	NAEYC	ACEI
Standard relating to family involvement	Standard 10	Early childhood to Standard 7 Middle childhood to Standard 9 Early adolescence to Standard 11	Standard 2	Standard 5
Focus of standard	Collaborating with learners, families, colleagues, other school professionals, and community members to ensure learner growth, and to advance the profession	Initiating positive interactive relationships and using a variety of strategies to engage families in their child's education	Understanding, supporting, and engaging families and community in children's learning and development	Establishing and maintaining positive and collaborative relationships with families and community to promote child well-being

NATIONAL FAMILY INVOLVEMENT STANDARDS' WEBSITES

The Interstate Teacher Assessment and Support Consortium (InTASC)

http://www.ccsso.org/Resources/Publications/InTASC_Model_Core_Teaching_Standards_A_Resource_for_State_Dialogue_(April_2011).html

National Board of Professional Teaching Standards (NBPTS)

http://www.nbpts.org/the_standards

National Association for the Education of Young Children (NAEYC) Standards for Professional Preparation

http://www.naeyc.org/ncate/standards/initialAdvancedPrograms

Association of Childhood Education International (ACEI) Elementary Education Standards

http://acei.org/affiliations/ncate.html

ACTIVITY

Using the links to the standards, examine the full description of each family engagement standard. Reflect about your strengths and where you still feel uncomfortable in your work with your students' families, and choose one or two of these goals to work on this semester. Think about possible actions that you can take that will help you improve in these areas. Write a short reflective paper describing your goals, why you chose them, and how you intend to reach those goals. At the end of the semester, revisit your goals and evaluate your progress. How have you grown in your skills and knowledge relating to family engagement? What goals do you need to set next? Setting goals based on these national standards can be a tool to professional growth as a supportive family engagement practitioner.

NAEYC Code of Ethical Conduct

SECTION II: ETHICAL RESPONSIBILITIES TO FAMILIES

Families[1] are of primary importance in children's development. Because the family and the early childhood practitioner have a common interest in the child's well-being, we acknowledge a primary responsibility to bring about communication, cooperation, and collaboration between the home and early childhood program in ways that enhance the child's development.

Ideals

I-2.1: To be familiar with the knowledge base related to working effectively with families and to stay informed through continuing education and training.

I-2.2: To develop relationship of mutual trust and create partnerships with the families we serve.

I-2.3: To welcome all family members and encourage them to participate in the program.

I-2.4: To listen to families, acknowledge and build on their strengths and competencies, and learn from families as we support them in their task of nurturing children.

I-2.5: To respect the dignity and preferences of each family and to make an effort to learn about its structure, culture, language, customs, and beliefs.

I-2.6: To acknowledge families' child-rearing values and their right to make decisions for their children.

I-2.7: To share information about each child's education and development with families and to help them understand and appreciate the current knowledge base of the early childhood profession.

I-2.8:   To help family members enhance their understanding of their children and support the continuing development of their skills as parents.

I-2.9:   To participate in building support networks for families by providing them with opportunities to interact with program staff, other families, community resources, and professional services.

Principles

P-2.1:   We shall not deny family members access to their child's classroom or program setting unless access is denied by court order or other legal restriction.

P-2.2:   We shall inform families of program philosophy, policies, curriculum, assessment system, and personnel qualifications, and explain why we teach as we do—which should be in accordance with our ethical responsibilities to children (see Section I).

P-2.3:   We shall inform families of and, when appropriate, involve them in policy decisions.

P-2.4:   We shall involve the family in significant decisions affecting their child.

P-2.5:   We shall make every effort to communicate effectively with all families in a language that they understand. We shall use community resources for translation and interpretation when we do not have sufficient resources in our own programs.

P-2.6:   As families share information with us about their children and families, we shall consider this information to plan and implement the program.

P-2.7:   We shall inform families about the nature and purpose of the program's child assessments and how data about their child will be used.

P-2.8:   We shall treat child assessment information confidentially and share this information only when there is a legitimate need for it.

P-2.9:   We shall inform the family of injuries and incidents involving their child, of risks such as exposures to communicable diseases that might result in infection and of occurrences that might result in emotional stress.

P-2.10: Families shall be fully informed of any proposed research projects involving their children and shall have the opportunity to give or withhold consent without penalty. We shall not permit or participate in research that could in any way hinder the education, development, or well-being of children.

P-2.11: We shall not engage in or support exploitation of families. We shall not use our relationship with a family for private advantage or personal gain, or enter into relationships with family members that might impair our effectiveness in working with their children.

P-2.12: We shall develop written policies for the protection of confidentiality and the disclosure of children's records. These policy documents shall be made available to all program personnel and families. Disclosure of children's records beyond family members, program personnel, and consultants having an obligation of confidentiality shall require familial consent (except in cases of abuse or neglect).

P-2.13: We shall maintain confidentiality and shall respect the family's right to privacy, refraining from disclosure of confidential information and intrusion into family life. However, when we have reason to believe that a child's welfare is at risk, it is permissible to share confidential information with agencies, as well as with individuals who have legal responsibility for intervening in the child's interest.

P-2.14: In cases where family members are in conflict with one another, we shall work openly, sharing our observations of the child, to help all parties involved make informed decisions. We shall refrain from becoming an advocate for one party.

P-2.15: We shall be familiar with and appropriately refer families to community resources and professional support services. After a referral has been made, we shall follow up to ensure that services have been appropriately provided.

Source: www.naeyc.org/positionstatements/ethical_conduct.

NOTE

1. The term *family* may include those adults, besides parents, with the responsibility of being involved in educating, nurturing, and advocating for the child.

APPENDIX C

State Agencies for Reporting Child Abuse and Neglect

Each state designates specific agencies to receive and investigate reports of suspected child abuse and neglect. Typically, this responsibility is carried out by Child Protective Services (CPS) within a Department of Social Services, Department of Human Resources, or Division of Family and Children Services. In some states, police departments may also receive reports of child abuse or neglect. For more information or assistance with reporting, please call Childhelp, 800-4-A-CHILD (800-422-4453) or your local CPS agency. In most cases, the phone numbers listed here are only accessible from within the state listed. If calling from out-of-state, use the local (toll) number listed, or call Childhelp for assistance. Also listed are links to state websites, which can provide additional information.

Alabama
Local (toll): (334) 242-9500
Website: www.dhr.alabama.gov/services/Child_Protective_Services/Abuse_Neglect_Reporting.aspx

Alaska
Phone: (800) 478-4444
Website: www.hss.state.ak.us/ocs/default.htm

Arizona
Phone: (888) SOS-CHILD (888-767-2445)
Website: www.azdes.gov/child_protective_services/

Arkansas
Phone: (800) 482-5964
Website: www.state.ar.us/dhs/chilnfam/child_protective_services.htm

California
Website: www.dss.cahwnet.gov/cdssweb/PG20.htm
Go on the website above for information on reporting or call Childhelp (800-422-4453) for assistance.

Colorado
Local (toll): (303) 866-5932
Website: http://www.colorado.gov/cs/Satellite/CDHS-ChildYouthFam/CBON/1251579373548

Connecticut
TTY: (800) 624-5518
Phone: (800) 842-2288
Website: www.state.ct.us/dcf/HOTLINE.htm

Delaware
Phone: (800) 292-9582
Website: http://kids.delaware.gov

District of Columbia
Local (toll): (202) 671-SAFE (202-671-7233)
Website: www.cfsa.dc.gov/DC/CFSA/Support + the + Safety + Net/Report + Child + Abuse + and + Neglect|

Florida
Phone: (800) 96-ABUSE (800-962-2873)
Website: www.dcf.state.fl.us/abuse

Georgia
Phone: 404-651-9361
Website: www.dfcs.dhr.georgia.gov/portal/site

Hawaii
Local (toll): (808) 832-5300
Website: http://hawaii.gov/dhs/protection/

Idaho
Phone: (800) 926-2588
Website: www.healthandwelfare.idaho.gov/Children/AbuseNeglect/tabid/74/Default.aspx

Illinois
Phone: (800) 252-2873
Local (toll): (217) 524-2606
Website: www.state.il.us/dcfs/child/index.shtml

Indiana
Phone: (800) 800-5556
Website: www.in.gov/dcs/protection/dfcchi.html

Iowa
Phone: (800) 362-2178
Website: www.dhs.state.ia.us/consumers/safety_and_protection/abuse_reporting/child abuse.html

Kansas
Phone: (800) 922-5330
Website: www.srs.ks.gov/Pages/HotlineNumbers.aspx

Kentucky
Phone: (877) 597-2331
Website: www.chfs.ky.gov/dcbs/dpp/childsafety.htm

Louisiana
Phone: 855-4LA-KIDS (855-452-5437)
Website: **www.dss.louisiana.gov/index.cfm?md = pagebuilder&tmp = home&pid = 109**

Maine
TTY: (800) 963-9490
Phone: (800) 452-1999
Website: **www.maine.gov/dhhs/ocfs**

Maryland
Website: **www.dhr.state.md.us/cps/report.htm**
Go to the website for information on reporting or call Childhelp (800-422-4453) for assistance.

Massachusetts
Phone: (800) 792-5200
Website: **http://www.mass.gov/eohhs/gov/departments/dcf/**

Michigan
Phone: (800) 942-4357
Website: **www.michigan.gov/dhs/0,1607,7-124-5452---,00.html**

Minnesota
Phone: Contact the individual county offices listed on state website
Website: **http://www.dhs.state.mn.us/main/idcplg?IdcService = GET_DYNAMIC_CONVER SION&RevisionSelectionMethod = LatestReleased&dDocName = id_000152**

Mississippi
Phone: (800) 222-8000
Local (toll): (601) 359-4991
Website: **http://www.mdhs.state.ms.us/fcs_prot.html**

Missouri
Phone: (800) 392-3738
Outside Missouri (toll): (573) 751-3448
Website: **www.dss.mo.gov/cd/rptcan.htm**

Montana
Phone: (866) 820-5437
Website: **www.dphhs.mt.gov/index.shtml**

Nebraska
Phone: (800) 652-1999
Website: **http://dhhs.ne.gov/children_family_services/Pages/cha_chaindex.aspx**

Nevada
Phone: (800) 992-5757
Local (toll): (775) 684-4400
Website: **www.dcfs.state.nv.us/DCFS_ReportSuspectedChildAbuse.htm**

New Hampshire
Phone: (800) 894-5533
Local (toll): (603) 271-6556
Website: **http://www.dhhs.nh.gov/dcyf/cps/index.htm**

New Jersey
TTY: (800) 835-5510
Phone: (877) 652-2873
Website: www.state.nj.us/dcf/abuse/how

New Mexico
Phone: **(855) 333-SAFE (7233)**
Local (toll): (505) 841-6100
Website: www.cyfd.org/node/26

New York
TTY: 1-800-638-5163
Phone: (800) 342-3720
Local (toll): (518) 474-8740
Website: www.ocfs.state.ny.us/main/cps

North Carolina
Phone: Contact the individual county offices listed on state website
Website: www.dhhs.state.nc.us/dss/cps/index.htm

North Dakota
Phone: Contact the individual county offices listed on state website
Website: www.nd.gov/dhs/services/childfamily/cps/#reporting

Ohio
Phone: (800) 4-A-Child (1-800-422-4453)
TTY: 1-800-2-A-Child (1-800-222-4453)
Website: www.jfs.ohio.gov/ocf/reportchildabuseandneglect.stm

Oklahoma
Phone: (800) 522-3511
Website: www.okdhs.org/programsandservices/cps/default.htm

Oregon
Website: www.oregon.gov/DHS/children/abuse/cps/report.shtml
Go to the website for information on reporting or call Childhelp (800-422-4453) for assistance

Pennsylvania
Phone: (800) 932-0313
Website: www.dpw.state.pa.us/forchildren/childwelfareservices/index.htm

Puerto Rico
Phone: (800) 981-8333
Local (toll): (787) 749-1333
Spanish information on Website: www.gobierno.pr/GPRPortal/StandAlone/Agency Information.aspx?Filter = 177

Rhode Island
Phone: (800) RI-CHILD (800-742-4453)
Website: www.dcyf.ri.gov/

South Carolina
Phone: Contact the individual county offices listed on state website
Website: https://dss.sc.gov/content/customers/protection/cps/index.aspx

South Dakota
Local (toll): (605) 773-3227; (866) 847-7335; each area maintains an additional local number, and many areas have individual toll-free numbers
Website: www.dss.sd.gov/cps/protective/reporting.asp

Tennessee
Phone: (877) 237-0004
Website: www.state.tn.us/youth/childsafety.htm

Texas
Phone: (800) 252-5400
Website: www.dfps.state.tx.us/Contact_Us/report_abuse.asp

Utah
Phone: (855) 323-3237
Website: www.hsdcfs.utah.gov

Vermont
Phone: (800) 649-5285
Website: www.dcf.vermont.gov/

Virginia
Phone: (800) 552-7096
Local (toll): (804) 786-8536
Website: www.dss.virginia.gov/family/cps/index.html

Washington
TTY: (800) 624-6186
Phone: (866) END-HARM (866-363-4276)
After hours: (800) 562-5624
Website: www.dshs.wa.gov/ca/safety/abuseReport.asp?2

West Virginia
Phone: (800) 352-6513
Website: www.wvdhhr.org/bcf/children_adult/cps/report.asp

Wisconsin
Phone: Contact the individual county offices listed on state website
Website: www.dcf.wi.gov/children/CPS/index.htm

Wyoming
Phone: Contact the individual county offices listed on state website
Website: http://dfsweb.state.wy.us/protective-services/cps/index.html

Family Engagement Program Mandates

Program	Provisions	Collaborative Decisions
Title I Title I (Part A of the Elementary and Secondary Act [ESEA] of 1965—reauthorized in 2001) parental involvement provisions through No Child Left Behind stress the involvement of families in the education of their children	A written parental involvement policy jointly developed by parents/periodically updated An annual meeting at convenient time/place for all parents notifying of requirements of Title I and their involvement rights School-parent compact (compact for learning, parent-student-teacher compact, family involvement compact) Critical importance of communication between parents and the school	Translated parental involvement policy Parent notification School funds for transportation, child care, or home visits to disseminate information School-parent compact jointly developed by parents, teachers, and administrators Open access by school community to document Outlines shared responsibility for academic growth, statewide content standards, high-quality curriculum and assessments tied to student proficiency levels Timely information about student progress Access to all staff Annual parent-teacher conferences Ways to support children's learning discussed Annotating and acting on parental suggestions

(Continued)

(Continued)

Program	Provisions	Collaborative Decisions
No Child Left Behind The No Child Left Behind (NCLB) Act of 2001 (through reauthorization of ESEA) provides parents with information on their children's strengths and weaknesses; describes how well schools are performing and allocates other resources for helping children if schools are chronically in need of improvement.	Key components of the requirements under the NCLB legislation include the following: Annual report cards Schools identified for school improvement, corrective action, or restructuring Limited English proficient students, students having IEPs	Title I parental advisory councils (or board) Volunteer opportunities for parents, caregivers, and relatives through family resource centers or individual classrooms Annual report cards: local education authorities (LEAs) distribute to parents, schools, and the public Adequate yearly progress: information on aggregate achievement, graduation rates, performance of LEAs Highly qualified teacher requirements Explanation of what school identification means, reasons for school's response, how parents can become involved, parents' choices for their children, and supplemental services Notification of language instruction education programs Inform parents of a child with disability, how language instruction meets objectives of IEP
Head Start Head Start is a comprehensive federal program focused on child development that has traditionally served low-income children and families since 1965. Parental involvement is mandated by the Head Start Program Performance Standards and involves both classroom volunteerism and program administration.	Head Start programs are required to help families do the following: Build relationships/ involvement opportunities through Head Start attendance Work toward goals and link to or provide necessary services Access programs involved in curriculum development Gain volunteer opportunities Enhance parenting skills, access child health care by making community services more responsive, transition children into school, and become involved in program decision making and governance.	Home-based program options Head Start Family Literacy Initiative Intergenerational Literacy Fatherhood Initiatives Parent involvement transition activities Meetings respectful of each family's diversity and cultural/ethnic background Recruiting for diversity; honoring needs of community Spanish version—Early Childhood Center Provide medical, dental, nutrition, and mental health education programs Family assistance with nutrition Head Start Parent-Mentor Training program Parenting education Family and community partnerships Advocacy for families Head Start leadership policy council Shared decision making

Sources: California Department of Education (2006), National Head Start Association (2006), No Child Left Behind (2004), Schumacher (2003), U.S. Department of Education (2005), and U.S. Department of Health and Human Services, Administration for Children and Families (2008).

Developing, Implementing, and Evaluating a School's Family Engagement Plan

Formal schoolwide programs and policies such as the family engagement plan cannot be created in a vacuum. Schools can set up a site-based family engagement team to design, implement, and monitor the school's family engagement plan (Patrikakou, Weissberg, Redding, & Walberg, 2005, p. 186). Epstein et al. (2002) recommend creating Action Teams for Partnership (ATP) that are responsible for reviewing family engagement practices, organizing new partnership efforts, coordinating activities, evaluating progress, and planning next steps (p. 18). The various titles used by districts and individual schools to designate family engagement planning groups include school effectiveness team (SET), school council, school redesign committee, school improvement team, and family involvement coordinating committee (Epstein et al., 2002). Whatever committee designation is chosen, the group's collaborative nature should be made evident through inclusion of stakeholder groups: family members, community representatives (advocates, business owners, religious leaders, and social service personnel), educators, administrators, and staff.

The importance of a school's family engagement policy should be reflected in a well-crafted mission statement that articulates the beliefs held within the school concerning collaboration with families. Taking the time to seek suggestions from school community members when writing a mission statement is vital. Two examples of school mission statements concerning family engagement policies are presented next.

SAMPLE SCHOOL MISSION STATEMENTS CONCERNING FAMILY ENGAGEMENT POLICIES

Mission Statement: Seattle Public Schools

Our purpose is to help schools learn how to integrate and institutionalize best practices of family involvement into their academic and building goals. We seek to create equal and active partnerships between schools and families in order to eliminate disproportionality and ensure that all students succeed.

Mission Statement: Cambridge Public Schools[1]

The Cambridge school system is committed to providing your children with high quality education. This system recognizes that families are their children's first teachers. As each of us desires and deserves respect for our family and cultural differences, we encourage each student, family member, and educator to be sensitive to and respectful of human differences in the entire school community.

Once the mission statement has been jointly written, the team may brainstorm achievable goals for implementation during the first year. It is best to start on a small scale with realistic goals. The goals, written in family-friendly language, should be accompanied by a timeline for implementation, extension, and debriefing, as well as a statement of how the school's progress toward the goals will be assessed. Materials and provisions to carry out the activities to be implemented as well as the cost of the undertaking (in monetary terms as well as in teacher and family hours) should be outlined in the plan. Modifying goals based on input from participants and also teachers and administrators will cycle the committee through their next round of planning.

A family engagement plan can be organized around goals that the group has set. Missouri's family involvement policy is based on Epstein et al.'s (2002) Keys to Successful Partnerships: Six Types of Involvement, described in Chapter 2. School districts in Missouri are required to develop schoolwide family involvement plans that include activities in six areas of family engagement.

Missouri Parent/Family Involvement Policy[2]

Parents/families of all economic, racial/ethnic, cultural, and educational backgrounds can, and do, have positive effects on their children's learning. The State Board of Education recognizes the importance of assisting school districts in eliminating barriers that impede parent/family involvement, thereby facilitating an environment that encourages collaboration with parents/families and the community.

The State Board of Education supports the development, implementation, and regular evaluation of a parent/family engagement plan and expects all school districts to include in this plan the following six elements and goals:

1. Promote regular, two-way, meaningful communication between home and school

   Examples: personal visits beyond parent-teacher conferences, electronic/telephone contact, use of translators

2. Promote and support responsible parenting

   Examples: parenting workshops, parent resource centers, parent support groups

---

1. Seattle Public Schools, 2007; Cambridge Public Schools, 2007.

2. Missouri Department of Elementary and Secondary Education (2005).

3. Recognize the fact that parents/families play an integral role in helping their children learn

   Examples: parent curriculum night, family literacy programs, postsecondary planning activities

4. Promote a safe and open atmosphere for parents/families to visit the school that their children attend and actively solicit parent/family support and assistance for school programs

   Examples: training of volunteers and staff, family activities at school, identifying parent volunteer opportunities in and out of school

5. Include parents as full partners in decisions affecting their children and families

   Examples: shared parent-teacher expertise on individual students, student academic planning, advisory councils (e.g., technology, nutrition/wellness), parent leadership development

6. Use available community resources to strengthen and promote school programs, family practices, and the achievement of students

   Examples: use the knowledge and skills of senior citizens, retired teachers, and veterans; encourage education-friendly practices in local businesses and parent information centers; identify links to current, quality resources

The State Board of Education expects school districts to include parents/ families in the annual evaluation of the content and impact of this policy. The evaluation will be used to improve and/or create practices to enhance parent/family involvement.

Because communities and families vary greatly, family engagement plans vary tremendously in their design, implementation, and evaluation (Patrikakou et al., 2005). However, all schools' family partnership programs must be able to demonstrate how they contributed to students' development and learning (Davies, 2002). In this era of standardized testing and accountability, schools often measure the effectiveness of their family engagement plan through achievement test scores and improved school attendance (Dryfoos & Maguire, 2002). Epstein et al. (2002) suggest that effectiveness in family engagement can be measured by finding out whether more families have been included in partnership activities that benefit students each year. This can be done by developing a three-year outline that identifies areas for growth and that includes a one-year action plan specifying activities, a timeline for implementation, and indicators of how each activity will be assessed (Epstein et al., 2002).

Your school might assess ongoing programs by means of the following methods:

- Interviews, focus groups, or discussions with parents/families/students
- Evaluation forms completed at specific events
- Pre- and postactivity surveys
- Checklists or rating scales that rate engagement efforts
- Telephone or Internet-based surveys
- Collecting anecdotal evidence in the form of stories or quotes

Evaluations can measure whether family engagement activities accomplished the following:

- Deepened alliances with families, especially those considerend hard to reach
- Demonstrated participants' understanding of the inner dynamics of families and their preferences for working with their children
- Were useful in promoting family collaboration and partnership in dealing with academic and behavioral issues, as well as in fostering students' social and emotional development.

Evaluation results can lead to suggestions for program improvement; thus, it is important that schools track longitudinal assessment data. Note that it may take three or more years of sustained programmatic effort before improvement is seen. Teachers may get discouraged when they do not see immediate improvement. However, annual evaluations with adjustments in programming can lead to long-term success (Patrikakou et al., 2005).

GLOSSARY

Abuse: Action or inaction of an adult that causes serious physical or emotional harm to a child.

Acceleration: Advancement to a higher grade.

Acculturation: The degree to which people from a certain cultural group display the beliefs and practices of that group.

Action threshold: Strong suspicions that lead a teacher to take action and report suspected abuse or neglect.

Active participatory communication style: Speaker and listener equally engaged in an interaction with both taking active roles in the conversation.

Adoptive family: Family type where a parent(s) is the legal parent but not the birth parent of a child or children in the family.

Advocacy: The act of arguing in favor of something, such as a cause, idea, or policy (National Association for Gifted Children, 2005).

AmeriCorp volunteers: Volunteers who serve more than 2,000 nonprofits, public agencies, and faith-based and community organizations.

Annotate with purpose: The act of taking notes during parental meetings and using those notes to reflect on enhanced student learning.

Asset-based: Focusing on existing and potential abilities.

At risk: Conditions or factors that put a child in jeopardy of failure; negative outcome that an individual or an organization could likely experience.

Attachment: Strong emotional relationship between two people; often develops at birth between a child and parent.

Authoritarian parenting style: A firm discipline style; may lack warmth and involve little communication.

Authoritative parenting style: A firm discipline style, combined with high levels of warmth and nurturing behaviors; open communication style.

Belongingness: How group membership has shaped personal and family histories.

Binuclear families: Families created when two households share in raising children, such as two divorced parents who have remarried.

Bisexual: A person who is attracted to people of either gender.

Blended families: Families created by the joining of adults in unions with one or more of the adults having children brought into the new family.

Bonding: Drawing close together; being a cohesive unit as a family.

Buffering: Pushing apart; having distance, space, and privacy as an individual within the family unit.

Child Protective Services (CPS): Social service organization charged by the state with the collection and investigation of child abuse reports.

Chronic illness: An ongoing illness that requires regular medical attention and can affect a child's normal activities.

Chronosystem: The influence of the time or era in which a child lives.

Classroom volunteer: Someone who offers support for children's learning in some way.

Closed questions: Questions that have one right answer and limit conversation.

Cluster grouping: Students who are gifted are placed together in a classroom with other students of mixed abilities with a teacher who has training in how to teach students with exceptional abilities.

Collectivist culture: Cultural emphasis is on being a part of a group; interdependence.

Community liaisons: Individuals who act as agents for outreach in particular community settings. The role of community liaison can be a formal job position or more informal through a school as a volunteer. Oftentimes, community liaisons speak the language of the community and may live there.

Community of learners: A family-like atmosphere in the classroom that values contributions that each student makes to the overall positive atmosphere of the classroom (taken in part from Ladson-Billings, 1994).

Community stakeholders: Key persons or groups within a community who contribute to positive ongoing school relationships—for example, parents, relatives, extended families, clergy, business owners, storeowners, teachers, mayors, and town council members.

Compadrazgo: The relationship established between parents and godparents as a form of coparenting.

Complementary learning: Links between families, early childhood programs, schools, out-of-school time programs and activities, higher education, health and social service agencies, businesses, libraries, museums, and other community-based organizations that work together to encourage consistent learning and developmental outcomes for children from birth to adolescence.

Coparenting: Where both parents work together as a team to raise their children, even though they are no longer married.

Cultural broker: Paraeducators, family advocates, or school liaisons who are able to cross boundaries into differing cultural milieus and promote open communication between groups of teachers and parents.

Cultural deficit model: The belief that cultural values, as transmitted through the family, are dysfunctional and the cause of poverty and lack of education.

Cultural discontinuity: When students feel disconnected with the overall cultural environment of the classroom because it does not reflect their culture.

Culturally encoded: Language that is influenced by culture and socialization experiences.

Culturally responsive family engagement: Practices that respect and acknowledge the cultural uniqueness, life experiences, and viewpoints of classroom families and draw on those experiences to enrich and energize the classroom curriculum and teaching activities, leading to respectful partnerships with students' families.

Culturally sensitive caring: Teachers placed in an ethical, emotional, and academic partnership with ethnically diverse students who are anchored in honor, integrity, resource sharing, and deep belief in the possibility of growth.

Culture: The beliefs or practices of a certain group of people.

Curriculum compacting: Strategy for differentiating instruction for gifted students, where they move at a quicker pace through classroom material and then have time to study other topics of interest in more depth.

Cutoff relationship: No contact with a family member; emotionally cut off.

Day of the Dead: Mexican holiday where families remember their dead, typically celebrated on November 2.

Detouring coalition: Child or other family member is the scapegoat for the family's problems, parental conflict is taken out on child, and stress is detoured from the real cause.

Differentiated parenting: Different ideas, viewpoints, and abilities to work with educators that exist among families (Edwards, 2004).

Discipline: Action taken by an adult designed to correct, shape, or help a child develop acceptable behavior.

Disengaged: Family members withdraw from one another, become distant.

Dysfunctional family: Stereotypical description of a family that is poorly functioning as a system.

Enmeshed: Too close; overconnected.

Exosystem: The indirect influences on a child's life.

Extended family: Family type with additional family members, such as grandparents, aunts, uncles, and cousins living in the home, caring for the children.

Facilitative communication: This type of communication with parents is not one way but reciprocal. Teachers encourage parent input by supportive comments, focused questions, and reiterating key points of the conversation. The purpose of facilitative communication is a shared dialogue between parent and teacher.

Family: People residing in a home who are related by birth, marriage, or adoption (as defined by the U.S. Census Bureau, 2005a).

Family advocates: Social workers embracing the family support model in their ongoing engagement with families.

Family-centered initiatives: Instead of school-centered initiatives, these focus on the authentic needs and goals of families when planning and enacting family events.

Family-centered partnerships: Relationships with families that are respectful, flexible, culturally sensitive, and involve the family both as decision makers and active participants in planning and implementing support programs.

Family engagement: A mutually collaborative, working relationship with the family that serves the best interests of the student, either in the school or home setting, for the primary purpose of increasing student achievement; active engagement by the home, school, and community to come together and help students learn and develop to their full potential (Epstein et al., 2002; Ferlazzo, 2011).

Family liaison: This position may replace the traditional home-school coordinator in conducting outreach to culturally diverse families and connecting them to community services.

Family literacy night: An event where literacy activities, such as games, book reading, or dramatic activities, take place to encourage further home literacy interactions.

Family literacy practices: A family's commitment to literacy endeavors through at-home practical activities, which embed reading, writing, and viewing (as well as other domains) as critical components in the quest for increased literacy competence.

Family literacy rally: Promoting family reading, writing, and communicative activities, the rally sparks family interest while providing necessary materials (books, pamphlets, or games) as well as family service information.

Family outreach specialist (FOS): An instructional aide trained specifically for intensive outreach efforts to school families; an FOS may also coordinate a family resource center.

Family resource center (FRC): A room or area within a school or community setting set up as a place for families to use for various educational and social purposes. An FRC may house a parenting library, provide food and beverages, and be staffed by outreach personnel or a social worker.

Family reunification: Reuniting children in foster care status with their birth parents.

Family rituals/traditions: Regular activities families engage in that help familiarize children with the values and beliefs of the family and increase family bonding.

Family support: A set of beliefs and an approach to strengthening and empowering families that will positively affect children's development and learning.

Family worldview: How the family views the world; whether they see the world as a place to be trusted or mistrusted determines how the family organizes their lifestyle and attitudes about the world.

Formal support: Support efforts for families, organized by schools or community agencies, such as parent education opportunities.

Foster family: Family type where children are given temporary care because of a crisis, such as abuse or neglect, or a parent being unable to care for them.

Free and Appropriate Public Education (FAPE): At no cost to the families, an appropriate education and related services (e.g., speech and language services, occupational therapy, physical therapy) must be provided to students with disabilities.

Funds of knowledge: Using the extensive experiences of minority families to add to the richness of the classroom learning environment (i.e., for lesson plans or instructional units).

Gay: A generic term used to describe the lesbian/gay community or specifically a person who is homosexual.

Generational poverty: Being in poverty for at least two generations.

Goodness of fit: Harmony or agreement between a child and his or her caregiver, in personality and behavioral characteristics, or temperament.

Habitudes: Unexamined attitudes and prejifices that influence habitual practices.

Hierarchical: A structure or order of authority.

Hierarchical structure: The organization of power and authority in a family.

Homeless liaison: Coordinator between a school district and families who are homeless.

Homeostasis: A state of equilibrium, balance, or lack of conflict.

Home-school connection: This particular connection between the home and school serves as a means of ongoing communication with families about the educational needs of their children. When parents and educators collaborate effectively and understand each other, children reap the benefits of a positive partnership.

Human capital: The sum of skills and capabilities that make a person productive, such as the attainment of a high school diploma or college degree; complements social capital in the area of family partnerships.

Incarcerated: Imprisoned or jailed.

Inclusion: Children with disabilities are educated in a general education classroom setting, as much as the disability will allow.

Individualistic culture: Cultural emphasis on the individual; independence.

Individualized education program (IEP): A plan that guides the delivery of special education supports and services for students with a disability (U.S. Department of Education, 2007).

Individualized family service plan (IFSP): Plan that guides families and schools in the development and education of children, birth to three years old, with disabilities.

Individuals with Disabilities Education Act (IDEA): Legislation that guides the education of students with special education needs.

Informal support: Support efforts for families that are not organized or developed by schools, community programs, or agencies, but emerge from the families themselves.

Interactive home learning activities: Homework assignments that are based upon real-life or authentic experiences and designed so families and children will have interactions relating to what they are learning.

Intercultural communication: "Communication between two or more people who are somewhat to very different from each other on important attributes such as their value orientations, preferred styles of communicating, role expectations, and perceived rules of social relationships" (NWREL, 1998, p. 53).

Judgment threshold: Relationships with the child, family, or teacher that affect a teacher's judgment about reporting suspected abuse or neglect.

Kinship care: Grandparents or other relatives raising children when parents are unable to; the arrangement may be temporary or a permanent legal guardianship.

Learning stations: Typically used in family math, literacy, or science activities, learning stations function as stopping-off points to engage in learning activities with specific directions for completion.

Least Restrictive Environment (LRE): To ensure that each child is provided with an education and related services in a program as much like a general education classroom as is appropriate for the student.

Lesbian: A woman who is homosexual.

LGBT: Lesbian, gay, bisexual, and transgender people.

Life event: A significant experience that has an impact on a person's psychological condition.

Literacy lunch: Informal lunchtime activity where parents and their children are engaged in some type of reading or writing activity, as supervised by a teacher, family outreach personnel, or an aide.

Macrosystem: The cultural and societal influences on a child.

Mesosystem: The quality of relationships among the people in a child's microsystem.

Microsystem: Immediate contacts in a child's life who have a direct influence, such as family, teachers, neighbors, and friends.

Mnemonic devices: Aid or trick to help a person memorize something.

Monochronic: Sequence of events occurring one at a time.

Morphogenesis: Change in a system.

Morphostasis: Stability in a system.

Native-focused curriculum: A curriculum developed in collaboration with tribal members, which infuses in its daily lessons/units values important in Native American culture.

Nonnormative transitions: A change in a person's life that does not occur at the physically, socially, or culturally acceptable time in the normal life cycle.

Nuclear family: Family type in which the parents are first time married; the children living with them are their biological or adopted children; and no other adults or children live in the home.

Open questions: Questions that have many possible answers and lead to continued conversation.

Paraprofessional: Instructional aides or teacher's aides who have traditionally worked with students in academic support roles but now may be interacting with families as school-based liaisons or coordinators of family resource centers.

Parentified child: A child becomes like a parent, taking on adult responsibilities in the family.

Parenting practices: Specific child-rearing behaviors used by the family members who raise children.

Parenting style: General pattern or set of child-rearing practices, which may be classified according to the level of warmth and control.

Passive-receptive communication style: Speaker has the active role in an interaction, with the listener passively listening and posing questions at the end of the interaction.

People-first language: Referring to people first before their disability.

Permissive/indulgent parenting style: Low level of control, combined with high levels of warmth; nonpunitive style.

Permissive/neglectful parenting style: Low level of control and warmth; indifferent style.

Perverse triangle: Coalition of two members ganging up against another, such as a parent siding with children against the other parent; unhealthy coalition.

Polychronic: Several events occurring at the same time.

Protective factors: Conditions that negate or oppose negative outcomes.

Punishment: A form of physical or nonphysical discipline that is designed to stop undesired behavior.

Reciprocal communication: Two-way communication where teacher and families equally share information, ask questions, and express opinions.

Respeto: Term for the respect shown for teachers and education by Latino families (Delgado Gaitan, 2004).

Response to intervention (RTI): A process schools use to help children having academic or behavioral difficulties by providing early interventions through "tiers" within the general classroom setting, as well as identifying those who need special services

Restraining order: Additional legal protections to ensure that children are safe, such as prohibiting an abusive parent from having contact with the child at home or at school

Same-sex family: Family type headed by two males or two females who live together in a committed relationship.

Schoolcentric approach: Traditional family involvement activities that are centered on meeting the teacher/school's needs, without regard to a family's perspective or needs relating to involvement in their child's education (Lawson, 2003).

School facilitators: School facilitators can act as guides to the various cultures found within a school setting.

School or classroom volunteer: Someone who supports children's learning without compensation.

Sense of efficacy: A sense of feeling competent in carrying out the task at hand.

Separation anxiety: Fear and distress at being separated from a primary caregiver.

Single-parent family: Family type where a father or mother is raising children on his or her own; a single parent does not necessarily have to be the custodial parent, and a child can have both a single father and a single mother.

Situational poverty: A lack of resources due to a particular set of events, such as a death, chronic illness, or divorce.

Social capital: Relationships among individuals that provide a network of support.

Stranger anxiety: Fear and avoidance of strangers.

Stress: Experiences, situations, and events that lead to severe tension or strain.

Subfamily: Family type where a parent and child(ren) live with the child(ren)'s grandparents, with the grandparents remaining the head of the household but the parent raising the child(ren).

Symbolic curriculum: The classroom environment includes bulletin boards, school walls, trade books, and so on, ensuring that images portrayed represent student cultures found within.

Telephone tree: "Branches" out family contacts by asking parents to contact a specific number of other families, thereby spreading out the outreach tasks.

Temperament: The distinctive personality and behavioral traits of a child.

Temporary Assistance for Needy Families (TANF): Federal program created by the Welfare Reform Law of 1996; replaces what was commonly known as "welfare." TANF provides assistance and work opportunities to needy families.

Tourist curriculum: Derman-Sparks's (1989) term for a focus on superficial contact with cultural artifacts, such as food, clothing, folktales, or celebrations.

Transfer of learning: The application of knowledge and skills learned in one subject or during a lesson being applied to at-home learning activities.

Transgender: A person whose identity, expressions, and behaviors in gender are not traditionally associated with his or her birth sex (Gelnaw et al., 2004).

Transracial: A child of one race or ethnic group is adopted by a family from another race or ethnicity.

Twice-exceptional: Both gifted and learning disabled.

Underclass: The poorest of the poor, who often have difficulty finding a place in mainstream society (Paulette, 1982).

WIC (Women, Infants, and Children): Federal program that provides nutritious foods to supplement diets, information about healthy eating, and referrals to health care for low-income women, infants, and children up to the age of five years.

REFERENCES

CHAPTER 1

AARP. (2007). State fact sheets for grandparents and other relatives raising grandchildren. Retrieved June 25, 2011, from http://www.grandfactsheets.org/state_fact_sheets.cfm.

Adams, K. S., & Christenson, S. L. (2000). Trust and family-school relationships: Examination of parent-teacher differences in elementary and secondary grades. *Journal of School Psychology, 38,* 477–497.

Antunez, B. (2000). *When everyone is included: Parents and communities in school reform.* Retrieved January 26, 2007, from http://www.ncela.gwu.edu/pubs.

Bae, S. J., & Clark, G. M. (2005). Incorporate diversity awareness in the classroom: What teachers can do. *Intervention in School and Clinic, 41*(1), 49–51.

Brown, D. F. (2003). Urban teachers' use of culturally responsive management strategies. *Theory Into Practice, 42*(4), 277–282.

Brown, M. R. (2009). A new multicultural population: Creating effective partnerships with multiracial families. *Intervention in School and Clinic 45,* 124–131.

Cauthen, N. K., & Fass, S. (2009). *Ten important questions about child poverty and family economic hardship.* Retrieved June 25, 2011, from http://www.nccp.org/publications/pub_829.html#question5.

Centers for Disease Control and Prevention. (2011a). Birth data. Retrieved October 30, 2011, from http://www.cdc.gov/nchs/births.htm.

Centers for Disease Control and Prevention. (2011b). U.S. teenage birth rates resume decline. Retrieved October 30, 2011, from http://www.cdc.gov/nchs/data/databriefs/db58.htm.

Centers for Disease Control and Prevention/National Center for Health Statistics National Vital Statistics System. (2011). *National marriage and divorce rate trends.* Retrieved June 25, 2011, from http://www.cdc.gov/nchs/nvss/marriage_divorce_tables.htm.

Children's Defense Fund. (2010). Retrieved December 27, 2010, from http://www.childrens-defense.org.

ChildStats.Gov. (2009). *America's children: Key national indicators of well-being, 2009.* Retrieved June 25, 2011, from http://www.childstats.gov/americaschildren09/famsoc1.asp.

Compton-Lilly, C. (2004). *Confronting racism, poverty, and power: Classroom strategies to change the world.* Portsmouth, NH: Heinemann.

Cotton, K., & Wikelund, K. R. (2001). *Parent involvement in education.* Northwest Regional Education Lab (NWRLB). Retrieved December 29, 2007, from http://www.nwrel.org/scpd/sirs/3/cu6.html.

Davies, D. (2002). The 10th school revisited: Are school/ family/community partnerships on the reform agenda now? *Phi Delta Kappan, 83*(5), 388–392.

Demo, D. H., & Cox, M. J. (2000). Families with young children: A review of research in the 1990s. *Journal of Marriage and the Family, 62*(4), 876–895.

Diffily, D. (2004). *Teachers and families working together.* Boston, MA: Pearson.

Edwards, P. A., & Young, L. S. J. (1990). Beyond parents: Family, community, and school involvement. *Phi Delta Kappan, 74*(1), 72–80.

Epstein, J. L., Sanders, M. G., & Clark, L. A. (1999). *Preparing educators for school-family-community partnerships: Results of a national survey of colleges and universities* (CRESPAR Report No. 34). Baltimore: John Hopkins, Center for Research on the Education of Students Placed at Risk. Retrieved July 17, 2008, from http://www.csos.jhu.edu/crespar/techReports/Report34.pdf.

Epstein, J. L., Sanders, M. G., Simon, B. S., Salinas, K. C., Jansorn, N. R., & Van Voorhis, F. L. (2002). *School, family, and community partnerships: Your handbook for action* (2nd ed.). Thousand Oaks, CA: Corwin.

Epstein, J. L., & Sheldon, S. B. (2006). Moving forward: Ideas for research on school, family, and community partnerships. In C. F. Conrad & R. Serlin (Eds.), *SAGE Handbook for research in education: Engaging ideas and enriching inquiry* (pp. 117–138). Thousand Oaks, CA: Sage.

Fan, X., & Chen, M. (2001). Parent involvement and student's academic achievement: A meta-analysis. *Educational Psychology Review, 13*(1), 1–22.

Farrell, A. F., & Collier, M. A. (2010). *Improving Schools, 13*(1), 4–20.

Ferlazzo, L. (2011). Involvement or engagement, *Educational Leadership, 68*(8), 10–14.

Finders, M., & Lewis, C. (1994). Why some parents don't come to schools. *Educational Leadership, May,* 50–54.

Gay, G. (2000). *Culturally responsive teaching: Theory, research, and practice.* New York, NY: Teachers College Press.

Gay, G. (2002). Culturally responsive teaching in special education for ethnically diverse students: Setting the stage. *International Journal of Qualitative Studies in Education, 15*(6), 613–629.

Grant, K. B. (2002). *Preservice teacher preparation in family involvement: An emerging model.* Unpublished doctoral dissertation, University of Montana, Missoula.

Henderson, A., & Mapp, K. (2002). *A new wave of evidence: The impact of school, family, and community connections on student achievement.* Austin, TX: National Center for Family and Community Connections with Schools.

Hoover-Dempsey, K., & Sandler, H. (1997). Why do parents become involved in their children's education? *Review of Educational research, 67*(1), 3–42.

Hopkins County School District. (2011). *New mobile app provides access to Parent Portal.* Retrieved January 13, 2012, from http://www.hopkins.ky schools.us/news.cfm?story = 82823&school = 0.

Hurley, D. (2005, April 19). Divorce rate: It's not as high as you think. *The New York Times.* Retrieved July 18, 2008, from http://www.nytimes.com/2005/04/19/ health/19divo.html?pagewanted = print& position.

Jeynes, W. H. (2003). A meta-analysis: The effects of parental involvement on minority children's academic achievement. *Education and Urban Society, 35*(2), 202–218.

Jeynes, W. H. (2005). A meta-analysis of the relation of parental involvement to urban elementary school student academic achievement. *Urban Education, 40*(3), 237–269.

Jeynes, W. H. (2007). The relationship between parental involvement and urban secondary school achievement: A meta-analysis. *Urban Education, 42*(1), 82–110.

Keyes, C. R. (2002). A way of thinking about parent/teacher partnerships for teachers. *International Journal of Early Years Education, 10*(3), 177–192.

Kim, E. (2002). The relationship between parental involvement and children's educational achievement in the Korean immigrant family. *Journal of Comparative Family Studies, 33*(4), 529–540.

Kreider, R. M., & Ellis, R. (2011). Number, timing, and duration of marriages and divorces: 2009. *U.S. Census Bureau Current Population Reports.* Retrieved June 25, 2011, from http://www.census.gov/prod/2011pubs/p70-125.pdf.

Lawson, M. A. (2003). School family relations in context: Parent and teacher perceptions of parent involvement. *Urban Education, 38*(1), 77–133.

Lewis, A., & Henderson, A. (1997). *Urgent message: Families crucial to school reform.* Washington, DC: Center for Law and Education.

McBride, B., Bae, J. & Blatchford, K. (2003). Family-school-community partnerships in rural preK at-risk programs. *Journal of Early Childhood Research, 1*(1), 49–72.

National Association for the Education of Young Children. (2005). *Code of ethical conduct and statement of commitment.* Retrieved January 29, 2007, from http://www.naeyc.org/about/positions/ethical_conduct.asp.

National Center for Children in Poverty. (2005). Retrieved December 27, 2010, from http://www.nccp.org/.

National Retired Teachers Association. (2007, Spring). Trends: Your town is your classroom. *NRTA Live and Learn, 6*(1), 2.

Nixa Public Schools. (2011). *Quick news.* Retrieved October 23, 2011, from http://myemail.constant-contact.com/QuickNews-From-Nixa-Public-Schools.html?soid = 1101610527853&aid = IljK Mn0kAe0.

Obama, B. (2010). *Supporting Families and Communities.* Retrieved December 27, 2010, from http://nccp.org/.

Olivos, E. M. (2009). Collaboration with Latino families: A critical perspective of home-school interactions. *Intervention in School and Clinic (45),* 2, 109–115.

Poveda, D., & Martin, B. (2004). Looking for cultural congruence in the education of Gitano children. *Language & Education, 18*(5), 413–435.

Ray, J. (2005). Family-friendly teaching: Tips for working with diverse families. *Kappa Delta Pi Record, 41*(2), 72–76.

Rich, D. (1998). What parents want from teachers. *Educational Leadership, 55*(8), 37–39.

Roberts, S. (2008, August 13). *In a generation, minorities may be the U.S. majority. The New York Times.* Retrieved June 26, 2011, from http://www.nytimes.com/2008/08/14/washington/14census.html?pagewanted = 1.

Roza, M. (2005). *President Bush's No Child Left Behind Act appears to be leaving children behind.* Retrieved January 27, 2007, from http://www.news.medical.net/?id = 12551.

Salas, L. (2004). Individualized educational plan (IEP) meetings and Mexican American parents: Let's talk about it. *Journal of Latinos and Education, 3,* 181–192.

Sanders, M., & Harvey, A. (2002). Beyond the school walls: A case study of principal leadership for school-community collaboration. *Teachers College Record, 104*(7), 1345–1368.

Saunders, M. G. (1996). School-family-community partnerships focused on school safety: The Baltimore example. *Journal of Negro Education, 63*(3), 369–374.

Saunders, M. G. (2001). A study of the role of "community" in comprehensive school, family and community partnership programs. *Elementary School Journal, 102*(1), 19–34.

Tavernise, S. (2011, April 6). *Number of children of whites falling fast. The New York Times.* Retrieved June 26, 2011, from http://www.nytimes.com/2011/04/06/us/06census.html.

U.S. Census Bureau. (2002a). *Demographic trends in the twentieth century: Census 2000 special reports.* Retrieved January 30, 2007, from http://www.census.gov/prod/2002pubs/censr-4.pdf.

U.S. Census Bureau. (2002b). *Number, timing, and duration of marriages and divorces: 1996: Household economic studies.* Retrieved January 30, 2007, from http://www.census.gov/prod/2002pubs/p70–80.pdf.

U.S. Census Bureau. (2003). *Children's living arrangements and characteristics: March 2002.* Retrieved January 30, 2007, from http://www.census.gov/population/www/socdemo/hh-fam/cps2002.html.

U.S. Census Bureau. (2004a). *America's families and living arrangements: 2003: Population characteristics.* Retrieved January 30, 2007, from http://www.census.gov/population/www/socdemo/hh-fam/cps2003.html.

U.S. Census Bureau. (2004b). *Current population survey (CPS): Definitions and explanations.* Retrieved January 6, 2006, from http://www.census.gov/population/www/cps/cpsdef.html.

U.S. Census Bureau. (2005a). *American community survey; Puerto Rico community survey: 2005 subject definitions.* Retrieved January 30, 2007, from http://www.census.gov/acs/www/Downloads/2005/usedata/Subject_Definitions.pdf.

U.S. Census Bureau. (2005b). *American factfinder: Fact sheet.* Retrieved January 30, 2007, from http://factfinder.census.gov/servlet/ACSSAFFFacts?_sse = on&_submenuId0 = factsheet_1&_ci_nbr = &gr_name = &ds_name = &reg = &_industry.

U.S. Census Bureau. (2005c). *Number, timing, and duration of marriages and divorces, 2001: Household economic studies.* Retrieved January 30, 2007, from http://www.census.gov/population/www/socdemo/marr-div.html.

U.S. Census Bureau. (2006a). *Families and living arrangements: Historical time series. FM-3 average number of own children under 18 per family, by type of family: 1955 to present.* Retrieved October 3, 2011, from http://www.census.gov/population/socdemo/hh-fam/fm3.pdf.

U.S. Census Bureau. (2006). *Families and living arrangements: Historical time series. MS-2 estimated median age at first marriage, by sex: 1890 to the present.* Retrieved January 30, 2007, from http://www.census.gov/population/www/socdemo/hh-fam.html#ht.

U.S. Census Bureau. (2006–2008). *American community survey.* Retrieved October 10, 2010, from http://factfinder.census.gov/servlet/STTable?_bm = y&-geo_id = 01000US&-qr_name = ACS_2008_3YR

_G00_S2501&-ds_name = ACS_2008_3YR_G00_& -redoLog = false.

U.S. Census Bureau. (2010). *America's families and living arrangements: 2010.* Retrieved June 26, 2011, from http://www.census.gov/population/www/socdemo/hh-fam/cps2010.html.

U.S. Department of Education. (2010). *Supporting families and communities.* Retrieved June 25, 2011, from http://www2.ed.gov/policy/elsec/leg/blueprint/faq/supporting-family.pdf.

Van Voorhis, F., & Sheldon, S. (2005). Principals' roles in the development of U.S. programs of school, family, and community partnerships. *International Journal of Educational Research, 41*(1), 55–70.

Ventura, S. J. (2009). *Changing patterns of nonmarital childbearing in the United States: NCHS data brief, no 18.* Hyattsville, MD: National Center for Health Statistics. Retrieved June 26, 2011, from http://www.cdc.gov/nchs/data/databriefs/db18.pdf.

Wanat, C. L. (2110). Challenges balancing collaboration and independence in home-school relationships: Analysis of parents' perceptions in one district. *The School Community Journal, 20*(1), 159–187.

Weiss, H. B., Mayer, E., Kreider, H., Vaughan, M., Dearing, E., Hencke, R., et al. (2003). Making it work: Low-income working mothers' involvement in their children's education. *American Educational Research Journal, 40*(4), 879–901.

Westat & Policy Studies Associates. (2001). *The longitudinal evaluation of school change and performance in Title I schools.* Washington, DC: U.S. Department of Education, Office of the Deputy Secretary, Planning and Evaluation Service.

Wright, V.R., Chau, M., and Aratani, Y. (2011). *Who are America's poor children? The official story.* National Center for Children in Poverty. Retrieved June 26, 2011, from http://www.nccp.org/publications/pub_1001.html.

CHAPTER 2

Barrera, J. M., & Warner, L. (2006). Involving families in school events. *Kappa Delta Pi Record, 42*(2), 72–75.

Becvar, D. S., & Becvar, R. J. (2008). *Family therapy: A systemic integration* (7th ed.). Upper Saddle River, NJ: Allyn & Bacon.

Bigner, J. J. (2006). *Parent-child relations: An introduction to parenting* (7th ed.). Upper Saddle River, NJ: Pearson.

Broderick, C. B. (1993). *Understanding family process: Basics of family systems theory.* Newbury Park, CA: Sage.

Bronfenbrenner, U. (1979). *The ecology of human development: Experiments by nature and design.* Cambridge, MA: Harvard University Press.

Bronfenbrenner, U. (1986). Ecology of the family as a context for human development: Research perspectives. *Developmental Psychology, 22,* 723–742.

Bronfenbrenner, U. (1993). The ecology of cognitive development: Research models and fugitive findings. In R. H. Wozniak & K. W. Fischer (Eds.), *Development in context: Activity and thinking in specific environments* (pp. 3–44). Hillsdale, NJ: Lawrence Erlbaum.

Bronfenbrenner, U. (1994). Ecological models of human development. In *International Encyclopedia of Education,* (Vol. 3, 2nd ed.). Oxford, United Kingdom: Elsevier.

Christian, L. G. (2006). Understanding families: Applying family systems theory to early childhood practice. *Young Children, 61*(1), 12–19.

Coleman, J. (1988). Social capital in the creation of human capital. *The American Journal of Sociology, 94,* 95–120.

Coleman, J. S., & Hoffer, T. (1987). *Public and private high schools: The impact of communities.* New York, NY: Basic Books.

Comer, J. P., Haynes, N. M., Joyner, E. T., & Ben-Avie, M. (Eds.). (1996). *Rallying the whole village: The Comer process for reforming education.* New York, NY: Teachers College Press.

Connors, L., & Epstein, J. (1995). Parent and school partnerships. In M. Bornstein (Ed.), *Handbook of parenting: Vol. 4. Applied and practical parenting* (pp. 437–458). Mahwah, NJ: Lawrence Erlbaum.

Couchenour, D., & Chrisman, K. (2000). *Families, schools, and communities: Together for young children.* Albany, NY: Delmar Thomson Learning.

Dunst, C. J. (2002). Family-centered practices: Birth through high school. *Journal of Special Education, 36,* 139–147.

Dunst, C. J. (2005). Framework for practicing evidence-based early childhood intervention and family support. *CASEinPoint, 1*(1), 1–11.

Dunst, C. J., Ardley, J., & Bollinger, D. (2006). Influences of family resource program participation on elementary school achievement. *CASEinPoint, 2*(8), 1–3.

Dunst, C. J. & Swanson, J. (2006). Parent-mediated everyday child learning opportunities: II. Methods and procedures. *CASEinPoint, 2*(11), 1–19.

Dunst, C. J., Trivette, C., & Deal, A. (1988). *Enabling & empowering families: Principles & guidelines for practice.* Cambridge, MA: Brookline Books.

Emmons, C. (2010). Yale Child Study Center School Development Program impact of systemic reform. Retrieved July 27, 2010, from http://medicine.yale.edu/childstudy/comer/images/SDP%20Systemic%20achieve%20impact_tcm147-22562.pdf.

Epstein, J. L. (2001). *School, family, and community partnerships: Preparing educators and improving schools.* Boulder, CO: Westview Press.

Epstein, J. L. (2005). Developing and sustaining research-based programs of school, family, and community partnerships: Summary of five years of NNPS research. Retrieved July 27, 2010, from http://www.csos.jhu.edu/p2000/pdf/Research%20Summary.pdf.

Epstein, J. L., Sanders, M. G., Simon, B. S., Salinas, K. C., Jansorn, N. R., & Van Voorhis, F. L. (2002). *School, family, and community partnerships: Your handbook for action* (2nd ed.). Thousand Oaks, CA: Corwin.

Galinsky, E. (2001). What children want from parents—and how teachers can help. *Educational Leadership, 58*(7), 24–28.

Gestwicki, C. (2010). *Home, school, and community relations* (7th ed.). Belmont, CA: Wadsworth.

González, N., Moll, L., & Amanti, C. (Eds.). (2005). *Funds of knowledge: Theorizing practices in households and classrooms.* Mahwah, NJ: Lawrence Erlbaum.

González, N., Moll, L., Floyd-Tenery, M., Rivera, A., Rendon, P., Gonzales, R., et al. (1993). *Teacher research on funds of knowledge: Learning from households.* Santa Cruz, CA: National Center for Research on Cultural Diversity and Second Language Learning.

Henderson, A. T. (1987). *The evidence continues to grow: Parent involvement improves student achievement.* Columbia, MD: National Committee for Citizens in Education.

Hooper, L. M. (2007). The application of attachment theory and family systems theory to the phenomena of parentification. *The Family Journal: Counseling and Therapy for Couples and Families, 15*(3), 217–223.

Hymes, J. (1974). *Effective school-home relationships.* Sierra-Madre, CA: California Association for the Education of Young Children.

Jackson, D. D., & Zuk, G. H. (1981). The question of family homeostasis, with homage to Don D. Jackson. *International Journal of Family Therapy, 3*(1), 3–15.

Maruyama, M. (1963). The second cybernetics: Deviation-amplifying mutual causal processes. *American Scientist, 5*(2), 164–179.

McCrummen, S. (2005, December 28). Manassas changes definition of family: Activists criticize new housing limits as anti-immigrant. *The Washington Post,* p. A01. Retrieved from http://www.washingtonpost.com/wp-dyn/content/article/2005/12/27/AR2005122701216.html.

Moll, L., Amanti, C., Neff, D., & González, N. (1992). Funds of knowledge for teaching: A qualitative approach to developing strategic connections between homes and classrooms. *Theory Into Practice, 31,* 132–141.

Mott, D. W. (2006). Checklists for measuring adherence to resource-based intervention practices. *CASEinPoint, 2*(3), 1–8.

National Network of Partnership Schools. (2010). *Our growing network: Member tally.* Retrieved July 27, 2010, from http://www.csos.jhu.edu/p2000/map.htm.

Powell, D. R. (1989). *Families and early childhood programs.* Washington, DC: National Association for the Education of Young Children.

Raab, M. (2005). Interest-based child participation in everyday learning activities. *CASEinPoint, 1*(2), 1–5.

Riojas-Cortez, M., & Flores, B. B. (2009). Supporting preschoolers' social development in school through funds of knowledge. *Journal of Early Childhood Research, 7*(2), 185–199.

U.S. Census Bureau. (2010). *Current population survey (CPS): Definitions and explanations.* Retrieved July 23, 2010, from http://www.census.gov/population/www/cps/cpsdef.html.

U.S. Department of Health & Human Services. (2011). Temporary assistance for needy families (TANF) overview. Retrieved June 25, 2011, from http://www.hhs.gov/recovery/programs/tanf/tanf-overview.html.

Von Bertalanffy, L. (1968). *Organismic psychology and systems theory.* Worcester, MA: Clark University Press.

Walsh, F. (Ed.). (1993). *Normal family processes* (2nd ed.). New York, NY: Guilford Press.

Weiss, H. B., Kreider, H., Lopez, M. E., & Chatman, C. M. (Eds.). (2005). *Preparing educators to involve families: From theory to practice.* Thousand Oaks, CA: Sage.

Welton, D. A. (2002). *Children and their world: Strategies for teaching social studies* (7th ed.). Boston, MA: Houghton Mifflin.

Wilson, L. W. (2005). Characteristics and consequences of capacity-building parenting supports. *CASEinPoint, 1*(4), 1–3.

Wilson, L. W., & Dunst, C. J. (2005). Checklist for assessing adherence to family-centered practices. *CASEtools, 1*(1), 1–6.

Yale School Development Program. (2004). *Transforming school leadership and management to support student learning and development.* Thousand Oaks, CA: Corwin Press.

Yale School of Medicine. (2010). *Comer school development program.* Retrieved July 27, 2010, from http://medicine.yale.edu/childstudy/comer/index.aspx.

CHAPTER 3

Barbour, C., Barbour, N. H., & Scully, P. A. (2005). *Families, schools, and communities: Building partnerships for educating children* (3rd ed.). Upper Saddle River, NJ: Pearson.

Barnett, W. S., Epstein, D. J., Friedman, A. H., Sansanelli, R. A., Hustedt, J. T. (2009). *The state of preschool: 2009 state preschool yearbook.* National Institute of Early Education Research, Rutgers Graduate School of Research. Retrieved September 7, 2010, from http://nieer.org/yearbook/pdf/yearbook.pdf.

Baumrind, D. (1966). Effects of authoritative parental control on child behavior. *Child Development, 37,* 887–906.

Baumrind, D. (1968). Authoritarian vs. authoritative parental control. *Adolescence, 3,* 255–272.

Baumrind, D. (1991). Parenting styles and adolescent development. In J. Brooks-Gunn, R. Lerner, & A. C. Petersen (Eds.), *The encyclopedia of adolescence* (pp. 746–758). New York, NY: Garland Press.

Baumrind, D. (1995). *Child maltreatment and optimal caregiving in social contexts.* New York, NY: Garland Press.

Bigner, J. J. (2006). *Parent-child relations: An introduction to parenting.* Upper Saddle River, NJ: Pearson.

Brenner, V., & Fox, R. A. (1999). An empirically derived classification of parenting practices. *Journal of Genetic Psychology, 160*(3), 343–356.

Brown, D. L. (1988). *Implementing the Active Parenting program in the Baltimore County Public Schools: A final report.* Abstract retrieved August 26, 2008, from http://www.activeparenting.com/Research AbstractsAPDP4.htm.

Chan, K., & Chan, S. (2005). Perceived parenting styles and goal orientation. *Research in Education, 74,* 9–21.

Chess, S., & Thomas, A. (1977). Temperamental individuality from childhood to adolescence. *Journal of Child Psychiatry, 16,* 218–226.

Chess, S., & Thomas, A. (1987). *Origins and evolution of behavior disorders from infancy to early adult life.* Cambridge, MA: Harvard University Press.

Comer, J. P., & Poussaint, A. F. (1992). *Raising black children: Questions and answers for parents and teachers.* New York, NY: Plume.

Coplan, R. J., Hastings, P. D., Lagacé-Séguin, D. G., & Moulton, C. E. (2002). Authoritative and authoritarian mothers' parenting goals, attributions, and emotions across different childrearing contexts. *Parenting: Science and Practice, 2*(1), 1–26.

Couchenour, D., & Chrisman, K. (2000). *Families, schools, and communities: Together for young children.* Albany, NY: Delmar Thomson Learning.

Delgado Gaitan, C. (2004). *Involving Latino families in schools: Raising student achievement through home-school partnerships.* Thousand Oaks, CA: Corwin.

Delpit, L. (1988). The silenced dialogue: Power and pedagogy in educating other people's children. *Harvard Educational Review, 58*(3), 280–298.

Dinkmeyer, D. (2007). *Step into parenting.* Bowling Green, KY: Step.

Dinkmeyer, D., & McKay, G. D. (1976). *Systematic training for effective parenting.* Circle Pines, MN: American Guidance Service.

Doyle, M. E. (2005). HIPPY: Home Instruction for Parents of Preschool Youngsters program. *New England Reading Association Journal, 41*(2), 28–29.

Edwards, C. D. (1999). *How to handle a hard-to-handle kid.* Minneapolis, MN: Free Spirit.

Edwards, P. A. (2004). *Children's literacy development: Making it happen through school, family, and community involvement.* Boston, MA: Pearson.

Egeland, B. (1989, January). *Secure attachment in infancy and competence in the third grade.* Paper presented at the meeting of the American Association for the Advancement of Science, San Francisco, CA.

Family Support America. (2001). *Guidelines for family support practice* (2nd ed.). Chicago, IL: Author.

Fine, M. (1991). *The second handbook of parent education.* San Diego, CA: Academic Press.

Foxworthy, J. (2009, September 20). What my kids taught me. *Parade, p. 18.*

Fruchter, N., Galletta, A., & White, J. (1992). *New directions in parent involvement.* Washington, DC: Academy for Educational Development.

Galinsky, E. (1999, August 30). Do working parents make the grade? *Newsweek, 134*(9), 52–56.

Galinsky, E. (2001). What children want from parents—and how teachers can help. *Educational Leadership, 58*(7), 24–28.

Gonzalez-Mena, J. (2006). *The young child in the family and the community* (4th ed.). Upper Saddle River, NJ: Pearson.

Gordon, T. (1970). *Parent effectiveness training.* New York, NY: Three Rivers Press.

Harry, B. (n.d.). *Developing cultural self-awareness.* CASAnet Resources. Retrieved February 12, 2007, from http://www.casanet.org/library/culture/culture-aware.htm.

Kaufmann, B. A., Gesten, E., Santa Lucia, M. S., Salcedo, O., Rendina-Gobioff, B. A., & Gadd, R. (2000). The relationship between parenting style and children's adjustment: The parents' perspective. *Journal of Child and Family Studies, 9*(2), 231–245.

Ladson-Billings, G. (2006). It's not the culture of poverty, it's the poverty of culture: The problem with teacher education. *Anthropology and Education Quarterly, 37*(2), 104–109.

Laosa, L. M. (1983). Parent education, cultural pluralism, and public policy: The uncertain connection. In R. Haskins & D. Adams (Eds.), *Parent education and public policy* (pp. 331–345). Norwood, NJ: Ablex.

Maccoby, E. E., & Martin, J. A. (1983). Socialization in the context of the family: Parent-child interaction. In P. H. Mussen (Ed.) & E. M. Hetherington

(Vol. Ed.), *Handbook of child psychology: Vol. 4. Socialization, personality, and social development* (4th ed., pp. 1–101). New York, NY: Wiley.

McGrath, W. H. (2007). Ambivalent partners: Power, trust, and partnership in relationships between mothers and teachers in a full-time child care center. *Teachers College Record, 109*(6), 1401–1422.

Mental disorders among new parents. (2007). *Child Health Alert, 25,* 4–5.

Mother-to-Mother Postpartum Depression Network. (2007). *Straight talk from mothers who recovered.* Retrieved April 5, 2007, from http://www.postpartumdepression.net/excerpts.html.

Mullis, F. (1999). *Active parenting:* An evaluation of two Adlerian parent education programs. *Journal of Individual Psychology, 55*(2), 225–232.

National Women's Health Center. (2005). *Depression during and after pregnancy.* Retrieved July 28, 2008, from http://www.womenshealth.gov/faq/postpartum.htm.

Ostoja, E., McCrone, L., Lehn, L., Reed, T., & Sroufe, L. A. (1995, March). *Representations of close relationships in adolescence: Longitudinal antecedents from infancy through childhood.* Paper presented at the meeting of the Society for Research in Child Development, Indianapolis, IN.

Parents as Teachers. (2005). *What is Parents as Teachers?* Retrieved June 10, 2007, from http://www.parentsasteachers.org/site/pp.asp?c = ekIRLcMZJxE&b = 272092.

Phillips, T. (2009). Teaching Is Like a Box of Chocolates: A Special Story. *Kappa Delta Pi Record,* Spring 2009, 101–103

Poole, C. (2001). How to involve families in the classroom. *Scholastic Early Childhood Today, 15*(4), 26–27.

Popkin, M. (1993). *Active parenting today.* Kennesaw, GA: Active Parenting.

Popkin, M. (1998). *Active parenting of teens.* Kennesaw, GA: Active Parenting.

Popkin, M. (2003). *Active parenting now.* Kennesaw, GA: Active Parenting.

Popkin, M., & Hendrickson, P. (2000). *Families in action.* Kennesaw, GA: Active Parenting.

Powell, D. (1991). *Strengthening parental contributions to school readiness.* Washington, DC: U.S. Department of Education, Office of Education Research and Improvement.

Puckett, M. B., & Black, J. K. (2005). *The young child: Development from prebirth through age eight* (4th ed.). Upper Saddle River, NJ: Pearson.

Russakoff, D. (2009). How do families matter? Understanding how families strengthen their children's educational achievement. *Foundation for Child Development*. Retrieved Oct. 6, 2011, from http://fcd-us.org/sites/default/files/FINAL%20How%20Do%20Parents%20Matter.pdf.

Santrock, J. (1998). *Child development* (8th ed.). Boston, MA: McGraw-Hill.

Sorkhabi, N. (2005). Application of Baumrind's parent typology to collective cultures: Analysis of cultural explanations of parent socialization effects. *International Journal of Behavioral Development, 29*(6), 552–563.

Spera, C. (2005). A review of the relationship among parenting practices, parenting styles, and adolescent school achievement. *Educational Psychology Review, 17*(2), 125–146.

Sternberg, R. (1994). *In search of the human mind*. Fort Worth, TX: Harcourt Brace.

U.S. Department of Education. (2007). *Even Start*. Retrieved on March 5, 2007, from http://www.ed.gov/programs/evenstartformula/index.html.

Wood, C. D., & Davidson, J. A. (1987). PET: An outcome study. *Australian Journal of Sex, Marriage, and the Family, 8,* 131–141.

Wood, C. D., & Davidson, J. A. (2003). Helping families cope: A fresh look at parent effectiveness training. *Family Matters, 65,* 28–33.

Zigler, E., & Pfannenstiel, J. (2007). *The Parents as Teacher Program: Its impact on school readiness and later school achievement.* Parents as Teachers National Center. Retrieved June 18, 2007, from http://www.parentsasteachers.org/atf/cf/{00812ECA-A71B-4C2C-8FF3-8F16A5742EEA}/Executive%20Summary%20of%20Kind.%20Rea_singlepgs.pdf.

CHAPTER 4

Ahrons, C. (2004). *We're still family.* New York, NY: HarperCollins.

American Academy of Pediatrics. (2002). Policy statement: Coparent or second-parent adoption by same-sex parents. *Pediatrics, 109*(2), 339–340.

American Academy of Pediatrics. (2003). Family pediatrics report of the task force on the family. *Pediatrics, 111*(6), 1541–1571.

AARP. (2007a). *Help for raising grandchildren.* Retrieved April 6, 2007, from http://www.aarp.org/families/grandparents/raising_grandchild.

AARP. (2007b). *State fact sheets for grandparents and other relatives raising children.* Retrieved January 20, 2011, from http://www.grandfactsheets.org/state_fact_sheets.cfm.

AARP. (2011). *Raising grandchildren.* Retrieved January 20, 2011, from http://www.aarp.org/online-community/groups/index.action?slGroupKey=Group1882.

Arnold, C. (1998). Children and stepfamilies: A snapshot. *Center for Law and Social Policy.* Retrieved March 22, 2007, from http://s195559714.0nlinehome.us/publications/children_stepfamilies.pdf.

Barbour, C., Barbour, N. H., & Scully, P. A. (2005). *Families, schools, and communities: Building partnerships for educating children* (3rd ed.). Upper Saddle River, NJ: Pearson.

Berger, E. (2004). *Parents as partners in education: Families and schools working together* (6th ed.). Upper Saddle River, NJ: Pearson.

Bigner, J. J. (2006). *Parent-child relations: An introduction to parenting* (7th ed.). Upper Saddle River, NJ: Pearson.

Borgman, L. (2010). *Family is where life takes root.* Retrieved July 9, 2011, from http://www.loriborgman.com/Archives/2010/10-October/Family%20is%20where%20life%20takes%20root.html.

Child Welfare Information Gateway. (1994). *Single parent adoption: What you need to know.* Retrieved March 20, 2007, from http://www.childwelfare.gov/pubs/f_single/f_single.cfm.

Couchenour, D., & Chrisman, K. (2000). *Families, schools, and communities: Together for young children.* Albany, NY: Delmar Thomson Learning.

Cowhey, M. (2005). Heather's moms got married: Second graders talk about gay marriage. *Rethinking Schools Online, 19*(3), 1–5.

Demo, D. H., & Cox, M. J. (2000). Families with young children: A review of research in the 1990s. *Journal of Marriage and the Family, 62,* 876–895.

Desrochers, J. E. (2004). Divorce: A parents' guide for supporting children. *NASP Resources* (National

Association of School Psychologists). Retrieved March 22, 2007, from http://www.nasponline.org/ resources/parenting/divorce_ho.aspx.

Dunn, J. (2004). Understanding children's family worlds: Family transitions and children's outcome. *Merrill-Palmer Quarterly, 50*(3), 224–235.

Edwards, O. W., & Daire, A. P. (2006). School-age children raised by their grandparents: Problems and solutions. *Journal of Instructional Psychology, 33*(2), 113–119.

FindLaw. (2011). *Types of child custody.* Retrieved January 10, 2011, from http://family.findlaw.com/child-custody/custody-types/.

Fuller-Thomson, E., & Minkler, M. (2000). America's grandparent caregivers: Who are they? In B. Hayslip Jr. & R. Goldberg-Glen (Eds.), *Grandparents raising children: Theoretical, empirical, and clinical perspectives* (pp. 3–21). New York, NY: Springer.

Gajda, R. (2004). Responding to the needs of the adopted child. *Kappa Delta Pi Record, 40*(4), 160–164.

Gelnaw, A., Brickley, M., Marsh, H., & Ryan, D. (2004). *Opening doors: Lesbian and gay parents and schools.* Washington, DC: Family Pride Coalition.

Georgas, J., Mylonas, K., Bafiti, T., Poortinga, Y., Christakopoulous, S., Kagitcibasi, C., et al. (2001). Functional relationships in the nuclear and extended family: A 16-culture study. *International Journal of Psychology, 36*(5), 289–300.

Gestwicki, C. (2007). *Home, school, and community relations: A guide to working with parents* (6th ed.). Albany, NY: Delmar.

Gilbert, N. (2005). Family life: Sold on work. *Society, 42*(3), 12–17.

Gilmore, D. P., & Bell, K. (2006). We are family: Using diverse family structure literature with children. *Reading Horizons, 46*(4), 279–299.

Ginther, D. K., & Pollak, R. A. (2004). Family structure and children's educational outcomes: Blended families, stylized facts, and descriptive regressions. *Demography, 41*(4), 671–696.

Gonzalez-Mena, J. (2007). *50 Early childhood strategies for working and communicating with diverse families.* Upper Saddle River, NJ: Pearson.

Gonzalez-Mena, J. (2008). *Diversity in early care and education: Honoring differences* (5th ed.). New York, NY: McGraw-Hill.

Kennedy, J. W. (2003). The ideal TV families? *OldSpeak* [Online publication of The Rutherford Institute]. Retrieved March 19, 2007, from http://www.rutherford.org/Oldspeak/Articles/Art/oldspeak-families2.asp.

KIDS Count Census Data. (2006). *2000 Census data: Income and poverty profile for United States.* Retrieved January 30, 2007, from http://www.aecf.org/cgi-bin/aeccensus.cgi?action = profile results&area = 00N&areaparent = 00N& printer friendly = 0&section = 5.

Killian, E., Bixler, M., Cowgill, D., & Cowgill, T. (2000). Helping children adjust as members of a "blended family," *CYFERNET: Children, youth and families education and research network.* Retrieved March 22, 2007, from http://ag.arizona.edu/fcs/ cyfernet/cyfar/nowg_bul_child_2.pdf.

Kreider, R. (2003). *Adopted children and stepchildren: 2000.* Census 2000 Special Report. Washington, DC: U.S. Census Bureau.

Kreider, R. M., & Elliott, D.B. (2009). America's families and living arrangements: 2007. *Washington, DC: U.S. Census Bureau.* Retrieved Oct. 19, 2010, from http://www.census.gov/population/www/socdemo/hh-fam/p20–561.pdf.

Leon, K. (2009). *The effects of dual residence custody arrangements on children.* MissouriFamilies. Retrieved January 10, 2011, from: http://missourifamilies.org/features/divorcearticles/divorcefeature31.htm.

Lesser, L. K., Burt, T., & Gelnaw, A. (2005). *Making room in the circle: Lesbian, gay, bisexual and transgender families in early childhood settings.* San Rafael, CA: Parent Services Project.

Mader, S. L. (2001). Grandparents raising grandchildren. *Delta Kappa Gamma Bulletin, 68*(1), 33–35.

Manning, M. L., & Lee, G. (2001). Working with parents: Cultural and linguistic considerations. *Kappa Delta Pi Record, 37*(4), 160–163.

McQueen, C. (2008). *For our children learning to work together: Co-parenting guide.* Office of the Attorney General of Texas: Division of Families and Children. Retrieved January 10, 2011, from https://www.oag.state.tx.us/AG_Publications/pdfs/coparenting.pdf.

National Center for Health Statistics. (2006). *New report shows teen births drop to lowest level ever.* Retrieved July 28, 2008, from http://www.cdc.gov/nchs/pressroom/06facts/births05.htm.

Papernow, P. L. (1993). *Becoming a stepfamily.* San Francisco, CA: Jossey-Bass.

Parron, A. (2008). *Advantages of single-parent families.* Retrieved January 10, 2011, from http://www.articlesbase.com/parenting-articles/advantages-of-single-parent-families-301620.html.

Perrin, E. (2005). *Kids of same-sex parent do fine.* American Academy of Pediatrics Conference and Exhibition, Washington, D.C., Retrieved January 20, 2011, from http://www.cbsnews.com/stories/2005/10/12/health/webmd/main938234.shtml.

Relatives as Caregivers Resource Guide for Erie County. (n.d.). Suggested reading for grandparents and grandchildren. Retrieved February 21, 2008, from http://www.erie.gov/depts/seniorservices/rac/suggested_reading.phtml.

Richardson, C. D., & Rosen, L. A. (1999). School-based interventions for children of divorce. *Professional School Counseling, 3*(1), 21–26.

Roberts, S. (2010, March 18). Report finds shift toward extended families. *The New York Times.* Retrieved January 10, 2011, from: http://www.nytimes.com/2010/03/19/us/19family.html.

Sailor, D. (2004). *Supporting children in their home, school, and community.* Boston, MA: Pearson.

Schwartz, A. (2010). *The new extended family.* Retrieved January 10, 2011, from http://www.mentalhelp.net/poc/view_doc.php?type = doc&id = 36511.

Stroud, J. E., Stroud, J. C., & Staley, L. M. (1997). Understanding and supporting adoptive families. *Early Childhood Education Journal, 24*(4), 229–234.

Sun, Y., & Li, Y. (2002). Children's well-being during parents' marital disruption process: A pooled time-series analysis. *Journal of Marriage and Family, 64,* 472–488.

Taylor, R. L. (2000). Diversity within African American families. In D. Demo, K. Allen, & M. Fine (Eds.), *Handbook of family diversity* (pp. 232–257). New York, NY: Oxford University Press.

U.S. Census Bureau. (2003). *Children's living arrangements and characteristics: March 2002.* Retrieved January 30, 2007, from http://www.census.gov/prod/2003pubs/p20–547.pdf.

U.S. Census Bureau. (2004). *America's families and living arrangements: 2004.* Retrieved July 9, 2011, from http://www.census.gov/prod/2004pubs/p20–553.pdf.

U.S. Census Bureau. (2006–2008). *American Community Survey.* Retrieved October 10, 2010, from http://factfinder.census.gov/servlet/STTable?_bm = y&-geo_id = 01000US&-qr_name = ACS_2008_3YR_G00_S2501&-ds_name = ACS_2008_3YR_G00_&-redoLog = false.

U.S. Census Bureau. (2009). *America's families and living arrangements: 2007.* Retrieved July 9, 2011, from http://www.census.gov/population/www/socdemo/hh-fam/p20–561.pdf.

U.S. Census Bureau. (2010). *Census Bureau reports families with children increasingly face unemployment.* Retrieved Oct. 19, 2010, from http://www.census.gov/newsroom/releases/archives/families_households/cb10–08.html.

U.S. Department of Health and Human Services. (2008). *Trends in foster care and adoption.* Retrieved January 20, 2011, from http://www.acf.hhs.gov/programs/cb/stats_research/afcars/trends.htm.

U.S. Department of State. (2011). *Total adoptions to the United States.* Intercountry Adoption: Office of Children's Issues. Retrieved January 20, 2011, from http://adoption.state.gov/news/total_chart.html.

Wright, K., Stegelin, D. A., & Hartle, L. (2007). *Building family, school, and community partnerships.* Upper Saddle River, NJ: Pearson.

CHAPTER 5

Alaska Native Knowledge Network. (1998). *Alaska standards for culturally responsive schools.* Retrieved April 13, 2007, from http://www.ankn.uaf.edu/publications/standards.html.

Clayton, J. B. (2003). *One classroom, many worlds: Teaching and learning in the cross-cultural classroom.* Portsmouth, NH: Heinemann.

Copeland, A. P. (2007). Welcoming international parents to your classroom. *Kappa Delta Pi Record, 43,* 66–70.

Cortina, R. (2006). *From rural Mexico to North Carolina.* Retrieved March 25, 2007, from http://www.learnnc.org/lp/ pages/988.

Couchenour, D., & Chrisman, K. (2000). *Families, schools, and communities: Together for young children.* Albany, NY: Delmar.

Crews, R. (2007). *Only connect: The way to save our schools.* New York, NY: Farrar, Straus, and Giroux.

De Gaetano, Y. (2007). The role of culture in engaging Latino parents' involvement in school. *Urban Education, 42*(2), 145–162.

Delgado Gaitan, C. (2004). *Involving Latino families in schools: Raising student achievement through home-school partnerships.* Thousand Oaks, CA: Corwin.

Edwards, P. A. (2004). *Children's literacy development: Making it happen through school, family, and community involvement.* Boston, MA: Pearson.

Espinosa, L. M. (2005). Curriculum and assessment considerations for young children from culturally, linguistically, and economically diverse backgrounds. *Psychology in Schools, 42*(8), 837–853.

Family Education. (2007). *A parent's guide to religion in the public schools.* Retrieved April 1, 2007, from http://school.familyeducation.com/religions/school/38774.html.

Federation for American Immigration Reform. (2007). *Immigration's impact on the U.S.* Retrieved July 29, 2007, from http://www.FAIRUS.org.

Finnegan, E. M. (1997). Even though we have never met, I feel I know you: Using a parent journal to enhance home-school communication. *The Reading Teacher, 51*(3), 268–269.

Flores, B., Tefft-Cousins, P., & Diaz, E. (1991). Transforming deficit myths about learning, language, and culture. *Language Arts, 68,* 369–379.

Friedlander, M. (1991). *The newcomer program: Helping immigrant students succeed in U.S. schools* (Program Information Guide No. 8.). Washington, DC: National Clearinghouse for Bilingual Education.

Garcia, E. E. (2003). *Student cultural diversity: Understanding and meeting the challenge.* Boston, MA: Houghton Mifflin.

Gay, G. (2002). Preparing for culturally responsive teaching. *Journal of Teacher Education, 53*(2), 106–116.

Gonzalez-Mena, J. (2008). *Diversity in early care and education: Honoring differences* (5th ed.). New York, NY: McGraw-Hill.

Griego Jones, T. (2003). Contribution of Hispanic parents' perspectives to teacher preparation. *School Community Journal, 13*(2), 73–97.

Igoa, C. (1995). *The inner world of the immigrant child.* Mahwah, NJ: Lawrence Erlbaum.

Kentucky University Medical Center. (2008). *CY 2008 ethnic and religious dates.* Retrieved March 10, 2008, from http://www3.kumc.edu/diversity/ethnic_ relig/ethnic.html

Ladson-Billings, G. (1995). Toward a theory of culturally relevant pedagogy. *American Educational Research Journal, 32*(3), 465–491.

Ladson-Billings, G. (2006). It's not the culture of poverty, it's the poverty of culture: The problem with teacher education. *Anthropology and Education Quarterly, 37*(2), 104–109.

McIntyre, E., Rosebery, A., & González, N. (2001). *Classroom diversity: Connecting curriculum to students' lives.* Portsmouth, NH: Heinemann.

Morrell, V. (2007). The Zuni way. *Smithsonian, 38*(1), 76–83.

National Clearinghouse for English Language Acquisition. (2010). *Frequently asked questions.* Retrieved Dec. 30, 2010, from http://www.ncela.gwu.edu/faqs/.

Northwest Regional Educational Laboratory. (1998). *Improving education for immigrant students: A resource guide for K-12 educators in the Northwest and Alaska.* Retrieved October, 2006, from http://www.nwrel.org/cnorse/booklets/immigration/ index.html.

Protheroe, N. (2006). Cultural diversity and the school-family connection. *Principal, 85*(4), 52–55.

Randall-David, E. (1989). *Strategies for working with culturally diverse communities and clients.* Bethesda, MD: Association for the Care of Children's Health.

Robinson, B. A. (2006). The Amish: Practices of various groups. *Ontario consultants on religious tolerance.* Retrieved March 26, 2007, from http://www.religioustolerance.org/amish4.htm.

Suarez-Orozco, M., & Suarez-Orozco, C. (2001). *Children of immigration.* Cambridge, MA: Harvard University Press.

Villegas, A. M., & Lucas, T. (2002). Preparing culturally responsive teachers: Rethinking the curriculum. *Journal of Teacher Education, 53*(1), 20–32.

Warrier, S., Williams-Wilkins, B., Pitt, E., Reece, R. M., McAlister Groves, B., Lieberman, A. F., et al. (2002). Culturally competent responses and Children: Hidden victims (Excerpts from Day 2 Plenary Sessions). *Violence Against Women, 8*(6), 661–686.

Weinstein, C. S., Tomlinson-Clarke, S., & Curran, M. (2004). Towards a conception of culturally responsive classroom management. *Journal of Teacher Education, 55*(1), 25–38.

Wong Fillmore, L. (2000). Loss of family languages: Should education be concerned? *Theory Into Practice, Autumn,* 203–210.

CHAPTER 6

Alexander, K. L., Entwisle, D. R., & Dauber, S. L. (1990). Children in motion: School transfers and elementary school performance. *Journal of Educational Research, 90,* 3–12.

Allen, M., & Staley, L. (2007). *Helping children cope when a loved one is on military deployment.* Retrieved January 17, 2007, from http://journal.naeyc.org/btj/200701/BTJAllen.asp.

American Association of Retired Persons. (2007). *State fact sheets for grandparents and other relatives raising children.* Retrieved January 20, 2011, from http://www.grandfactsheets.org/state_fact_sheets.cfm.

Armstrong, C. (1997). What to say to bereaved parents. *Principal, 76,* 34–36.

Arnold, R., & Colburn, N. (2006). From a distance: A library program connects inmates and their children through reading. *School Library Journal, 52*(9), 32.

Bagdi, A., & Pfister, I. (2006). Childhood stressors and coping actions: A comparison of children and parents' perspectives. *Child & Youth Care Forum, 35*(1), 21–40.

Barbour, C., Barbour, N. H., & Scully, P. A. (2005). *Families, schools, and communities: Building partnerships for educating children* (3rd ed.). Upper Saddle River, NJ: Pearson.

Bell, D. B., Booth, B., Segal, M. W., Martin, J. A., Ender, J. A., & Rohall, D. E. (2007). *What we know about Army families: 2007 Update.* Washington, DC: Caliber.

Bernstein, N. (2005). *All alone in the world, Children of the incarcerated.* New York, NY: New Press.

Bilchik, S., Seymour, C., & Kreisher, K. (2001). Parents in prison. *Corrections Today, 63*(7), 108–112.

Birenbaum, L. K. (2000). Assessing children's and teenagers' bereavement when a sibling dies from cancer: A secondary analysis. *Child: Care, Health & Development, 26*(5), 381–400.

Blum, L. M. (n.d.). *Building resilient kids.* Web course from Johns Hopkins Bloomberg School of Public Health. Retrieved March 8, 2011, from http://www.jhsph.edu/mci/training_course/.

Blum, R. (2005). *School connectedness: Improving the lives of students.* Baltimore, MD: Johns Hopkins Bloomberg School of Public Health, Retrieved March 8, 2011, from http://www.jhsph.edu/bin/i/e/MCI_Monograph_FINAL.pdf.

Bunting, E. (2000). *The memory string.* New York, NY: Clarion Books.

Bushfield, S. (2004). Fathers in prison: Impact of parenting education. *Journal of Correctional Education, 55*(2), 104–116.

Centers for Disease Control and Prevention. (2009). *Cancer in children.* Retrieved February 3, 2011, from http://www.cdc.gov/Features/dsCancerIn-Children/.

Centers for Disease Control and Prevention. (2011). *2007, United States, Unintentional injuries.* Retrieved February 3, 2011, from http://webappa.cdc.gov/cgi-bin/broker.exe?_service = v8prod&_server = app-v-ehip-wisq.cdc.gov&_port = 5081&_sessionid = DTzmzJe/M52&_program = wisqars.details10.sas&_service = &type = U&prtfmt = STANDARD&age1 = 1&age2 = 14&agegp = 1–14&deaths = 3782&_debug = 0&lcdfmt = custom&ethnicty = 0&ranking = 5&deathtle = Death.

Children's Defense Fund. (2005). *State of American children 2005.* Retrieved August 20, 2008, from http://www.childrensdefense.org/site/PageServer?pagename = research_action_ guides.

Children's Defense Fund. (2007). *Foster care.* Retrieved March 10, 2007, from http://www.childrensdefense.org/site/PageServer?pagename = How_CDF_Works_Child_Welfare_Foster.

Children's Defense Fund. (2009). *Each day in America.* Retrieved February 3, 2011, from http://www.childrensdefense.org/child-research-data-publications/each-day-in-america.html.

Children's Grief Education Association. (2006). *Military families.* Retrieved March 18, 2008, from http://www.childgrief.org/militaryfamilies.htm.

Coulling, N. (2000). Definition of successful education for the "looked after" child: A multi-agency perspective. *Support for Learning, 15*(1), 30–35.

De Vaus, D., & Gray, M. (2003). Family transitions among Australia's children. *Family Matters, 65,* 10–17.

Doran, G., & Hansen, N. D. (2006). Constructions of Mexican American family grief after the death of a child: An exploratory study. *Cultural Diversity and Ethnic Minority Psychology, 12*(2), 199–211.

Doyle, K. W., Wolchik, S. A., Dawson-McClure, S. R., & Sandler, I. N. (2003). Positive events as a stress buffer for children and adolescents in families in transition. *Journal of Clinical Child and Adolescent Psychology, 32*(4), 536–545.

Family & Corrections Network. (2003a). *Conversations: Questions children ask.* Retrieved February 24, 2011, from http://fcnetwork.org/wp/wp-content/uploads/cp1103-conversations-questions.pdf.

Family & Corrections Network. (2003b). *What do children of prisoners and their caregivers need?* Retrieved February 24, 2011, from http://fcnetwork.org/wp/wp-content/uploads/cp1203-whatdochildrenneed.pdf.

Family & Corrections Network. (2009a). *Children and families of the incarcerated fact sheet.* Retrieved February 24, 2011, from http://fcnetwork.org/wp/wp-content/uploads/fact-sheet.pdf.

Family & Corrections Network. (2009b). *The national resource center on children and families of the incarcerated.* Retrieved February 24, 2011, from http://fcnetwork.org.

Farrell, A. F., & Collier, M. A. (2010). School personnel's perceptions of family-school communication: A qualitative study. *Improving School, 13*(1), 4–20.

Friedman, L. B. (2004). *Mallory on the move.* Minneapolis, MN: Carolrhoda Books.

Frieman, B. B. (1997). Two parents: Two homes. *Educational Leadership, 54*(7), 23–25.

Frieman, B. B. (1998). What early childhood educators need to know about divorced fathers. *Early Childhood Education Journal, 25*(4), 239–241.

Goebel, A. J. (2001). Family ties from an 11 year old's viewpoint. *Suite 101.* Retrieved April 16, 2007, from http://www.suite101.com/article.cfm/blended_families/61385.

Haggard, G. (2005). Providing school support for the grieving child. *Delta Kappa Gamma Bulletin, 72*(1), 25–26.

Haine, R. A., Wolchik, S. A., Sandler, I. N., Millsap, R. E., & Ayers, T. S. (2006). Positive parenting as a protective resource for parentally bereaved children. *Death Studies, 30,* 1–28.

Hardy, L. (2006). When kids lose parents in our war in Iraq. *Education Digest, 72*(4), 10–12.

Hartman, C. (2006). Students on the move. *Educational Leadership, 63*(5), 20–24.

Hodak, M. (2003). When parents part. *NEA Today, 21*(4), 36.

Hoffman, H.C., Byrd, A. L., Kightlinger, A. M. (2010, December). Prison programs and services for incarcerated parents and their underage children: Results from a national survey of correctional facilities. *The Prison Journal, 90*(4), 397–416.

Hynson, J. L., Aroni, R., Bauld, C., & Sawyer, S. M. (2006). Research with bereaved parents: A question of how not why. *Palliative Medicine, 20*(8), 805–811.

Johns Hopkins Bloomberg School of Public Health. (2011). *Military child initiative.* Retrieved March 8, 2011, from http://www.jhsph.edu/mci/about/.

Joosse, B. M. (2001). *Ghost wings.* San Francisco, CA: Chronicle Books.

KidsHealth. (2007). Helping your child deal with death. *KidsHealth for Parents: Nemours Foundation.* Retrieved February 7, 2007, from http://kids health.org/parent/positive/talk/death.html.

Kramer, P. A., & Smith, G. G. (1998). Easing the pain of divorce through children's literature. *Early Childhood Education Journal, 26*(2), 89–94.

Krinsky, M.A. (2006, May 30). On foster care: Why foster care reform must happen. *San Francisco Chronicle.* Retrieved March 17, 2011, from http://www.pewtrusts.org/news_room_detail.aspx?id = 18462.

Kübler-Ross, E. (1969). *On death and dying.* New York, NY: Macmillan.

Kübler-Ross, E., & Kesler, D. (2005). *On grief and grieving.* New York, NY: Scribner.

Kurklin, S. (2006). *Families.* New York NY: Hyperion.

Lansky, V. (1998). *It's not your fault, KoKo Bear.* Minnetonka, MN: Books Peddlers.

Mansour, M. (2003). Our mom was in jail. *Scholastic Choices, 19*(3), 6.

Martin, P. Y., & Jackson, S. (2002). Educational success for children in public care: Advice from a group of high achievers. *Child and Family Social Work, 7,* 121–130.

Martinez, C. R., & Forgatch, M. S. (2002). Adjusting to change: Linking family structure transitions with parenting and boys' adjustment. *Journal of Family Psychology, 16*(2), 107–117.

McEntire, N. (2003). *Children and grief* (Report No. EDI-PS-03–06). Champaign, IL: University of Illinois. (Clearinghouse on Elementary and Early Childhood Education; ERIC Document Reproduction Service No. ED 475393)

National Center for Children in Poverty. (2010). *Exploring the Effects of America's Ongoing Wars on the Children of Soldiers.* Retrieved March 8, 2011, from http://www.nccp.org/media/releases/release_114.html.

National Foster Parent Association. (2007a). *FAQ.* Retrieved March 12, 2007, from http://www.nfpainc.org/content/index.asp?page = FAQ&nmenu = 3.

National Foster Parent Association. (2007b). *History of foster care in the United States.* Retrieved March 12, 2007, from http://www.nfpainc.org/content/?page = HISTORYOFFOSTERCARE.

National Network of Partnership Schools. (2006). *Military child initiative.* Retrieved April 16, 2007, from The Center on School, Family, and Community Partnerships at Johns Hopkins University, http://www.csos.jhu.edu/P2000/mci/index.htm.

Newnham, D. (2002). Inside story. *TES: More than a job.* Retrieved March 16, 2007, from http://www.tes.co.uk/section/story/?section = Archive&sub_section = Friday&story_id = 365699&Type = 0.

Noble, L. S. (1997). The face of foster care. *Educational Leadership, 54*(7), 26–28.

Pelton, M. (2004). *When Dad's at sea.* Morton Grove, IL: Albert Whitman.

Pribesh, S., & Downey, D. B. (1999). Why are residential and school moves associated with poor school performance? *Demography, 36*(4), 521–534.

Pryor, J., & Rodgers, B. (2001). *Children in changing families: Life after parental separation.* Oxford, UK: Blackwell.

Quattlebaum, M. (2001). *Grover G. Graham and me.* New York, NY: Delacorte Books for Young Readers.

Roznowski, F. (2010). *Supporting children with family members in prison.* Cambridge, MA: Cambridge Community Partnerships for Children.

San Francisco Children of Incarcerated Parents (2005). A *bill of rights.* Retrieved February 24, 2011, from http://www.sfcipp.org.

Schlozman, S. C. (2003). The pain of losing a parent. *Educational Leadership, 60*(8), 91–92.

Stauffacher, S. (2005). *Harry Sue.* New York, NY: Random House.

Titus, D. (2007). Strategies and resources for enhancing the achievement of mobile students. *NASSP Bulletin, 91*(1), 81–97.

Tragedy Assistance Program for Survivors. (2007). *Tragedy Assistance Program for Survivors.* Retrieved March 18, 2008, from http://www.taps.org.

U.S. Department of Defense. (2008). DoD casualty reports. Retrieved February 3, 2011, from http://www.defense.gov/news/casualty.pdf.

U.S. Department of Health and Human Services. (2010). *The AFCARS Report.* Retrieved March 17, 2011, from http://www.acf.hhs.gov/programs/cb/stats_research/afcars/tar/report17.htm.

U.S. General Accounting Office. (1994). *Elementary school children: Many change schools frequently, harming their education* (No. ED 369 526). Washington, DC: Author.

Weissbourd, R. (2009). The "quiet" troubles of low-income children. *The Education Digest, 74*(5), 4–8.

Willis, C. A. (2002). The grieving process in children: Strategies for understanding, educating, and reconciling children's perceptions of death. *Early Childhood Education Journal, 29*(4), 221–226.

Wood, J. J., Repetti, R. L., & Roesch, S. C. (2004). Divorce and children's adjustment problems at home and school: The role of depressive/withdrawn parenting. *Child Psychiatry & Human Development, 35*(2), 121–142.

Worden, W. J., Davies, B., & McCowen, D. (1999). Comparing parent loss with sibling loss. *Death Studies, 23*(1), 1–15.

CHAPTER 7

Aisenberg, E., & Ell, K. (2005). Contextualizing community violence and its effects: An ecological model of parent-child interdependent coping. *Journal of Interpersonal Violence, 20*(7), 855–871.

American Academy of Pediatrics. (1999). *School issues for children with chronic illness.* Retrieved May 22, 2007, from http://www.aap.org/pubed/ZZZ473VS8FC.htm?%E2%8A%82_cat = 543.

Ashiabi, G. (2005). Household food insecurity and children's school engagement. *Journal of Children and Poverty, 11*(1), 3–17.

Auletta, K. (1982). *The underclass.* Woodstock, NY: Overlook Press.

Beegle, D. M. (2003a). *Communication across the barriers: Building blocks for educating students from generational poverty.* Retrieved May 21, 2007, from http://www.combarriers.com/educating_students.php.

Beegle, D. M. (2003b). Overcoming the silence of generational poverty. *Talking Points, 15*(1), 11–20.

Benard, B. (2004). *Resiliency: What have we learned.* San Francisco, CA: WestEd.

Bohn, A. (2006). A framework for understanding Ruby Payne. *Rethinking Schools Online, 21*(2). Retrieved April 3, 2008, from http://www.rethinking schools.org/archive/21_02/fram212.shtml.

Catholic Charities USA. (2006). *Poverty in America: A threat to the common good.* Washington, DC: Author.

Children's Defense Fund. (2005). *Defining poverty and why it matters for children.* Retrieved March 30, 2008, from http://www.childrensdefense.org/site/DocServer/definingpoverty.pdf?docID = 390.

Daponte, B. O. (2000). Private versus public relief: Use of food pantries versus food stamps among poor households. *Journal of Nutrition Education, 32*(2), 72–83.

DiCosmo, B. (2008, April 3). Officials help flood victims in Marble Hill. *Southeast Missourian,* pp. 1A, 5A.

Drever, A. (1999). *Homeless count methodologies: An annotated bibliography.* Los Angeles: UCLA Weingart Center.

Dryfoos, J., & Maguire, S. (2002). *Inside full-service community schools.* Thousand Oaks, CA: Corwin.

Edwards, C. H. (2000). Moral classroom communities and the development of resiliency. *Contemporary Education, 71*(4), 38–41.

Epstein, J. (2005). Attainable goals? The spirit and letter of the No Child Left Behind Act on parental involvement. *Sociology of Education, 78*(2), 179–182.

Epstein, J., & Dauber, S. (1991). School programs and teacher practices of parent involvement in inner-city elementary and middle schools. *Elementary School Journal, 91*(3), 289–305.

Food Bank for New York City. (2010). USDA reports record food insecurity. Retrieved October 18, 2011, from http://www.foodbanknyc.org/blog/index.cfm/2010/12/10/USDA-Reports-Record-Food-Insecurity-in-2009.

Frey, K. (1998). *Introduction to resiliency.* Retrieved May 21, 2007, from http://www.tucsonresiliency.org/ introduction_to_resiliency.pdf.

Gorski, P. (2005). *Savage unrealities: Uncovering classism in Ruby Payne's framework.* Retrieved May 23, 2007, from http://www.edchange.org/publications/Savage_Unrealities.pdf.

Great-Quotes.com. (n.d.). Marcia Wallace quotes. Retrieved October 18, 2011, from http://www.great-quotes.com/quote/545920.

Greenstein, D. (1998). *Caring for children with special needs: Chronic illnesses.* Raleigh: North Carolina Cooperative Extension Service.

Henderson, N., & Milstein, M. (1996). *Resiliency in schools: Making it happen for students and educators.* Thousand Oaks, CA: Corwin.

Henderson, N., & Milstein, M. (2002). *Resiliency in schools: Making it happen for students and educators* (Updated ed.). Thousand Oaks, CA: Corwin.

Indiana Department of Education. (2007). *Frequently asked questions: McKinney-Vento: Education for homeless children and youths.* Retrieved January 29, 2007, from http://ideanet.doe.state.in.us/alted/mckinney_vento_faq.html.

Johnson, G. M. (1997). Teachers in the inner city: Experience-based ratings of factors that place students at risk. *Preventing School Failure, 42,* 19–26.

Kasindorf, M. (2005, October 12). Nation taking a new look at homelessness, solutions. *USA Today,* p. 1.

KIDS Count Census Data. (2006). *2000 Census data: Income and poverty profile for United States.* Retrieved January 30, 2007, from http://www.aecf.org/cgi-bin/aeccensus.cgi?action = profile results&area = 00N&areaparent = 00N&printer friendly = 0&section = 5.

Lazarus, P. J., Jimerson, S. R., & Brock, S. E. (2002). *Helping children after a natural disaster: Information for parents and teachers.* Bethesda, MD: National Association of School Psychologists.

Molnar, J., Rath, W. R., & Klein, T. P. (1990). Constantly compromised: The impact of homelessness on children. *Journal of Social Issues, 46*(4), 109–124.

National Asthma Education and Prevention Program, National School Boards Association, American School Health Association, American Diabetes Association, American Academy of Pediatrics, Food Allergy and Anaphylaxics Network, & Epilepsy Foundation. (2003). Students with chronic illness: Guidance for families, schools, and students. *Journal of School Health, 73*(4), 131–132.

National Center for Children in Poverty. (2010). Retrieved December 27, 2010, from http://www .nccp.org

National Center on Family Homelessness. (1999). *Homeless children: America's new outcasts.* Newton, MA: Author.

National Center on Family Homelessness. (2010). *What is family homelessness (The problem)?* Retrieved October 18, 2011, from http://www .familyhomelessness.org/facts.php?p = sm.

National Law Center on Poverty and Homelessness. (n.d.). *McKinney-Vento 2001 reauthorization: At a glance.* Retrieved August 20, 2008, from http://64.233.167.104/ search?q = cache:UIudFRDUbKUJ:www.dpi.state .nd.us/title1/homeless/act/glance.pdf + McKinney -Vento + 2001 + reauthorization: + At + a + glance&hl = en&ct = clnk& cd = 2&gl = us.

National Youth Violence Prevention Resource Center. (2003). *What educators can do to prevent youth violence.* Retrieved May 23, 2007, from http:// www.safeyouth.org/scripts/faq/edprevent.asp.

Noddings, N. (1995). A morally defensible mission for schools in the 21st century (adapted from The challenge to care in schools). *Phi Delta Kappan, 76,* 365–368.

Noddlings, N. (2007). Teaching themes of care. *Character, 14*(2), 1–5

Payne, R. (1996). Understanding and working with students and adults from poverty. *Instructional Leader, 9*(2). Retrieved May 23, 2007, from http:// homepages.wmich.edu/ ~ ljohnson/Payne.pdf.

Payne, R. (2003). *A framework for understanding poverty* (3rd Rev. ed.). Highlands, TX: aha! Process.

Payne, R. (2006). *School accreditation and class issues.* Highlands, TX: aha! Process. Retrieved August 20, 2008, from http://www.icsac.org/ enews/enewsfeb06.

Phillips, T. (2009). Teaching is like a box of chocolates: A special story. *Kappa Delta Pi Record, 45*(3), 101–103.

Rosenheck, R., Bassuk, E., & Salomon, A. (n.d.). *Special populations of homeless Americans.* Washington, DC: Department of Health and Human Services. Retrieved January 29, 2007, from http://aspe.hhs.gov/progsys/homeless/ symposium/2-Spclpop.htm.

Ryan, C. A., & Hoover, J. H. (2005). Resiliency: What we have learned [Review]. *Reclaiming Children and Youth, 14*(2), 117–118.

Satcher, D. (2004). Health disparities and the homeless. *Atlanta Foundation Forum.* Atlanta, GA: Community Foundation of Greater Atlanta.

Savelli, L. (2001). *National gang history.* Retrieved June 5, 2007, from http://www.gripe4rkids.org/ his.html.

Scheidlinger, S. (1994). A commentary on adolescent group violence. *Child Psychiatry and Human Development, 25*(1), 3–11.

Schlozman, S. C. (2002). When illness strikes. *Educational Leadership, 60*(1), 82–83.

Scotsman.com. (2004). Dame Sheila McKechnie. Retrieved October 18, 2011, from http://www .scotsman.com/news/obituaries/dame_sheila_ mckechnie_1_500401.

Sheldon, S. B., & Epstein, J. L. (2004). Getting students to school: Using family and community involvement to reduce chronic absenteeism. *School Community Journal, 14*(2), 39–56.

Solorzano, D. G., & Yosso, T. J. (2001). From racial stereotyping and deficit discourse toward a critical race theory in teacher education. *Multicultural Education, 9*(1), 2–8.

Tough, P. (2007, June 10). The class-consciousness raiser. *New York Times Magazine.* Retrieved June 17, 2007, from http://www.nytimes.com/2007/ 06/10/ magazine/10payne-t.html?ex = 13391280 00&en = 374b16587c5596c2&ei = 5090&part ner = rssuserland&emc = rss.

University of Michigan Health System. (2007). *Children with chronic conditions.* Retrieved May 22, 2007, from http://www.med.umich .edu/11ibr/yourchild/chronic.htm#whatis.

U.S. Census Bureau. (2003). *Dynamics of economic well-being: Poverty 1996–1999.* Washington, DC: Author.

U.S. Department of Health and Human Services. (2011). TANF: Total number of families. Retrieved October 18, 2011, from http://www .acf.hhs.gov/programs/ofa/data-reports/case load/2010/2010_family_tan.htm.

U.S. Department of Housing and Urban Development. (2009). The 2009 Annual homeless assessment report to Congress. Retrieved October 18, 2011, from http://www.huduser.org/publications/pdf/5thHomelessAssessmentReport.pdf.

Weller, L., Doren, F. D., Burbach, C., Molgaard, C. A., & Ngong, L. (2004). Chronic disease medication administration rates in the public school system. *Journal of School Health, 74*(5), 161–165.

Wong, J., Peace, J., Wang, A., Feeley, C., & Carlson. (2005). *Safe havens: School, community, and the education of children and youth*

experiencing homelessness. Newton, MA: Education Development Center.

Wong, J., Salomon, A., Elliott, L. T., Tallarita, L., & Reed, S. (2004). The McKinney-Vento Homeless Assistance Act—Education for Homeless Children and Youth Program: Turning good law into effective education. *Georgetown Journal for Poverty Law and Policy, 11*(2), 284–289.

Yeich, S. (1994). *The politics of ending homelessness.* Lanham, MD: University Press of America.

Zagier, A.S. (2011, July 25). Joplin digs out from twister debris. *Southeast Missourian,* pp. 3A.

CHAPTER 8

Alter, C. F. (1985). Decision-making factors in child neglect. *Child Welfare, 64*(2), 99–111.

Alvarez, K., Donohue, B., Kenny, M., Cavanagh, N., & Romero, V. (2004). The process and consequences of reporting child maltreatment: A brief overview for professionals in the mental health field. *Aggression and Violent Behavior, 10,* 311–331.

American Bar Association. (2001). *Know your rights: Domestic violence.* Chicago, IL: Author.

Bancroft, S. (1997). Becoming heroes: Teachers can help abused children. *Educational Leadership, 55,* 69–71.

Berger, E. (2008). *Parents as partners in education: Families and schools working together* (7th ed.). Upper Saddle River, NJ: Pearson.

Besharov, D. J. (1992). A balanced approach to reporting child abuse. *The Child, Youth, and Family Services Quarterly, 15,* 5–7.

Blume, E. (1990). *Secret survivors.* New York, NY: Free Press.

Brown, J., Cohen, P., Johnson, J. G., & Salzinger, S. (1998). A longitudinal analysis of risk factors for child maltreatment: Findings of a 17-year prospective study of officially recorded and self-reported child abuse and neglect. *Child Abuse and Neglect, 22*(11), 1065–1078.

Center for Effective Discipline. (2004). *Proclamation signed by African American leaders.* Retrieved July 25, 2011, from http://www.stophitting.com/index.php?page = afamlead.

Center for Effective Discipline. (2010). *U.S. corporal punishment and paddling statistics by state and race.* Retrieved July 25, 2011, from

http://www.stophitting.com/index.php?page = statesbanning.

Center for Effective Discipline. (n.d.). *School corporal punishment alternatives.* Retrieved July 25, 2011, from http://www.stophitting.com/index.php?page = alternatives.

Chaffin, M., Kelleher, K., & Hollenberg, J. (1996). Onset of physical abuse and neglect: Psychiatric, substance abuse, and social risk factors from prospective community data. *Child Abuse & Neglect, 20*(3), 191–203.

Dalgleish, L. (1988). Application of social judgement theory and signal detection theory. In B. Brehmer & C. R. B. Joyce (Eds.), *Human judgment: The SJT view* (pp. 347–356). Amsterdam: Elsevier-North Holland.

DeBellis, M. D., Broussard, E. R., Herring, D. J., Wexler, S., Moritz, G., & Benitez, J. G. (2001). Psychiatric co-morbidity in caregivers and children involved in maltreatment: A pilot research study with policy implications. *Child Abuse & Neglect, 25,* 923–944.

DePanfilis, D. (2006). *Child neglect: A guide for prevention, assessment, and intervention.* U.S. Department of Health and Human Services, Office on Child Abuse and Neglect. Washington, DC: Government Printing Office.

DHHS (U.S. Department of Health and Human Services, Administration on Children, Youth and Families). 2003. *Child maltreatment 2001.* Washington, DC: U.S. Government Printing Office.

Dube, S. R., Anda, R. F., Felitti, V. J., Croft, J. B., Edwards, V. J., & Giles, W. H. (2001). Growing up with parental alcohol abuse: Exposure to childhood abuse, neglect, and household dysfunction. *Child Abuse & Neglect, 25,* 1627–1640.

Dubowitz, H. (1996). *A longitudinal study of child neglect: Final report.* Washington, DC: U.S. Department of Health and Human Services.

Durant, J. E. (2005). Distinguishing physical punishment from physical abuse: Implications for professionals. *Envision: The Manitoba Journal of Child Welfare, 4*(1), 86–92.

Egeland, B. (1988). *The consequences of physical and emotional neglect on the development of young children.* Child neglect monograph: Proceedings from a symposium. Washington, DC: U.S. Department of Health and Human Services.

Encyclopedia of Children's Health. (2006). *Discipline.* Retrieved April 8, 2008, from http://www.answers.com/topic/discipline.

End Abuse. (2010). *Intimate partner violence and healthy people 2010 fact sheet.* Retrieved October 20, 2011, from http://www.futureswithoutviolence.org/userfiles/file/Children_and_Families/ipv.pdf.

Gaudin, J. (1993). *Child neglect: A guide for intervention* (The User Manual Series). Washington, DC: U.S. Department of Health and Human Services.

Gullatt, D. E., & Stockton, C. E. (2000). Involving educators in the identification and reporting of suspected child abuse. *NASSP Bulletin, 84*(619), 79–89.

Hinson, J., & Fossey, R. (2000). Child abuse: What teachers in the '90's know, think, and do. *Journal of Education for Students Placed at Risk, 5*(3), 251–266.

Kearney, M. (1999). The role of teachers in helping children of domestic violence. *Childhood Education, 75*(5), 290–296.

Kilpatrick, D., & Saunders, B. (1997). *The prevalence and consequences of child victimization.* Washington, DC: Department of Justice, Office of Justice Programs, National Institute of Justice.

Lewis, C. (2000). Emotional abuse: The rearranging of one's mind. *Suite101.com.* Retrieved April 8, 2008, from http://www.suite101.com/article.cfm/teaching_computers/49302.

Lyman, R. (2006, September 30). In many public schools, the paddle is no relic. *New York Times.* Retrieved March 26, 2007, from http://www.nytimes.com/2006/09/30/education/30punish .html?page wanted = 1&ei = 5090&en = 6967bd 5cd7ae3dbc&ex = 1317268800.

Magura, S., & Laudet, A. B. (1996). Parental substance abuse and child maltreatment: Review and implications for intervention. *Children and Youth Services Review, 18*(3), 193–220.

Mass Legal Help. (2011). *Domestic violence and schools.* Retrieved June 11, 2011, from http://www.masslegalhelp.org/domestic-violence/domestic-violence-and-schools.

McClare, G. (1990). The principal's role in child abuse. *Education and Urban Society, 22*(3), 307–313.

McIntrye, T., & Silva, P. (1992). Culturally diverse child rearing practices: Abusive or just different? *Beyond Behavior, 4*(1), 1–6. Missouri Department of Social Services. (2004). *Reporting child abuse and neglect is everyone's responsibility.* Retrieved March 26, 2007, from http://www.dss.mo.gov/cd/rptcan.htm.

Munkel, W. I. (1996). Neglect and abandonment. In J. A. Monteleone (Ed.), *Recognition of child abuse for the mandated reporter* (2nd ed., pp. 105–118). St. Louis, MO: G. W. Medical.

National Association for the Education of Young Children. (2004). *Where we stand on child abuse prevention: NAEYC Position Statement.* Washington, DC: Author.

National Association for the Education of Young Children. (2011). Code of ethical conduct and statement of commitment. Retrieved October 20, 2011, from http://www.naeyc.org/files/naeyc/file/positions/Ethics%20Position%20 Statement2011.pdf.

National Domestic Violence Hotline (2011). *The hotline.* Retrieved June 11, 2011, from http://www.Thehotline.org/.

National Institute of Drug Abuse. (1999). *Drug abuse and addiction research: The sixth triennial report to Congress.* Washington, DC: U.S. Department of Health and Human Services.

Prevent Child Abuse America. (2007). *Recognizing child abuse: What parents should know.* Retrieved February 27, 2007, from http://www.preventchildabuse.org/publications/parents/index.shtml.

Schecter, S. & Edelson, J. (1999). *Effective intervention in domestic violence and child maltreatment cases: Guidelines for policy and practice* (Reno, NV: National Council of Juvenile and Family Court Judges), p. 10. Retrieved June 11, 2011, from Child Welfare Information Gateway http://www.childwelfare.gov/systemwide/laws_policies/statutes/witnessdv.

Sedlack, A. J., & Broadhurst, D. D. (1996). *The third national incidence study of child abuse and neglect (NIS-3)*. Washington, DC: U.S. Department of Health and Human Services.

Smith, S. K. (2006). *Mandatory reporting of child abuse and neglect*. Retrieved February 14, 2007, from http://www.smith-lawfirm.com/mandatory_ reporting.htm.

Smyth, K. (1996). An investigation into teacher's knowledge and awareness of child sexual abuse in single sex national schools in Dublin. *Journal of Child Centered Practice, 3*(1), 23–44.

Spock, B. (n.d.). *Project NoSpank: The web presence of Parents and Teachers Against Violence in Education, Inc.* Retrieved July 18, 2011, from http://www.nospank.net/.

Thomas, L. C. (2003). *Physical abuse or physical discipline: How do clinicians decide?* Doctoral dissertation, Drexel University, Philadelphia.

Tite, R. (1994). Muddling through: The procedural marginalization of child abuse. *Interchange, 25*(1), 87–108.

U.S. Department of Health and Human Services. (1999). *Blending perspectives and building common ground: A report to Congress on substance abuse and child protection.* Washington, DC: Government Printing Office.

U.S. Department of Health and Human Services. (2000). *Child abuse and neglect state statutes elements: Reporting laws, number 1, definitions of child abuse and neglect.* Washington, DC: Author.

U.S. Department of Health and Human Services. (2005). *Child welfare information gateway: Definitions of child abuse and neglect.* Retrieved May 14, 2007, from http://www.childwelfare.gov/systemwide/laws_policies/statutes/define.pdf.

The United States Department of Justice. (May, 2011). *Domestic violence.* Retrieved June 10, 2011, from http://www.ovw.usdoj.gov/domviolence.htm.

Walsh, K., Farrell, A., Bridgstock, R., & Schweitzer, R. (2006). The contested terrain of teachers detecting and reporting child abuse and neglect. *Journal of Early Childhood Research, 4*(1), 65–76.

Warrier, S., Williams-Wilkins, B., Pitt, E., Reece, R. M., McAlister Groves, B., Lieberman, A. F., et al. (2002). "Culturally competent responses" and "Children: Hidden victims." (Excerpts from Day 2 Plenary Sessions). *Violence Against Women, 8*(6), 661–686.

WomensLaw.org. (2008). *Information for the Latino community.* Retrieved October 20, 2011, from http://www.womenslaw.org/laws_state_type.php?id = 14163&state_code = US.

Wurtele, S. K., & Schmitt, A. (1992). Child care workers' knowledge about reporting suspected child sexual abuse. *Child Abuse and Neglect, 16*(3), 385–390.

Zellman, G. (1990). Child abuse reporting and failure to report among mandated reporters: Prevalence, incidence, and reasons. *Journal of Interpersonal Violence, 5*(1), 3–22.

Zellman, G., & Bell, R. M. (1990). *The role of professional background, case characteristics, and protective agency response in mandated child abuse reporting.* Santa Monica, CA: Rand.

CHAPTER 9

Association for Supervision and Curriculum Development. (2007). *A lexicon for learning.* Retrieved May 23, 2007, from http://www.ascd.org/portal/site/ascd/menuitem.5a47c86b3b7b44128716b710e3108a0c.

Barbour, A.C. (2010). *Learning at home PreK–3: Homework activities that engage children and families.* Thousand Oaks, CA: Corwin.

Brent, B. O. (2000). Do classroom volunteers benefit schools? *Principal, 80*(1), 36–43.

Center for School, Family, and Community Partnerships. (2001). *TIPS—Teachers Involve Parents in Schoolwork.* Retrieved May 22, 2007, from the Johns Hopkins University website: http://www.csos.jhu.edu/P2000/tips/index.htm.

Clinton, B. (1994). *State of the Union Address.* Retrieved June 27, 2011, from http://www.presidentialrhetoric.com/historicspeeches/clinton/stateoftheunion.1994.html.

Cooper, H. (2001). Homework for all: In moderation. *Educational Leadership, 58*(7), 34–38.

Cooper, H. (2007). *The battle over homework: Common ground for administrators, teachers, and parents.* Thousand Oaks, CA: Corwin.

Craven, H. S. (2006). Using parent volunteers. *Inspiring Teachers.* Retrieved August 1, 2007, from http://www.inspiringteachers.com/classroom_resources/articles/parent_communication/parent_volunteers.html.

DeCusati, C. L. P., & Johnson, J. E. (2004). Parents as classroom volunteers and kindergarten students' emergent reading skills. *Journal of Educational Research, 97*(5), 235–246.

Delgagdo Gaitan, C. (2004). *Involving Latino families in schools: Raising students' achievement through home-school partnerships.* Thousand Oaks, CA: Corwin.

Epstein, J. L., Sanders, M. G., Simon, B. S., Salinas, K. C., Janshorn, N. R., & Van Voorhis, F. L. (2002). *School, family, and community partnerships: Your handbook for action* (2nd ed.). Thousand Oaks, CA: Corwin.

Family Involvement Partnership for Learning. (1998). *Get involved: How parents and families can help their children do better in school.* Washington, DC: U.S. Department of Education. Retrieved June 18, 2007, from http://www.ed.gov/pubs/PFIE/families.html.

Foster, J. E., & Loven, R. G. (1992). The need and directions for parent involvement in the 90's: Undergraduate perspectives and expectations. *Action in Teacher Education, 14*(3), 13–18.

Gill, B. P., & Schlossman, S. L. (2004). Villain or savior? The American discourse on homework, 1850–2003. *Theory Into Practice, 43*(3). 174–181.

Gonzalez-Dehass, A. R., & Willems, P. (2003). Examining the underutilization of parent involvement in schools. *School Community Journal, 13*(1), 85–97.

Gregg, G. (1996). *A study of parent involvement in Montana public schools: A work in progress* (ERIC Document Reproduction Service No. ED 416 997). Washington, DC: U.S. Department of Education.

Guskey, T. R. (2004). The communications challenge of standards-based reporting. *Phi Delta Kappan, 86*(4), 326–329.

Harry, B., Kalyanpur, M., & Day, M. (1999). *Building cultural reciprocity with families: Case studies in special education.* Baltimore, MD: Brookes.

Henderson, A. T., & Mapp, K. L. (2002). *A new wave of evidence: The impact of school, family, and community connections on student achievement.* Retrieved May 26, 2007, from http://www.sedl.org/connections/resources/evidence.pdf.

Hiatt-Michael, D. B. (2006). Reflections and directions on research related to family-community involvement in schooling. *School Community Journal, 16*(1), 7–30.

Hoover-Dempsey, K. V., & Sandler, H. M. (1997). Why do parents become involved in their children's education? *Review of Educational Research, 67*(1), 3–42.

Inspiring Teachers. (2006). *Tips for using parent volunteers.* Retrieved Aug. 1, 2007, from http://www.inspiringteachers.com/tips/parents/volunteers.html.

Jackson, K., & Remillard, J. T. (2005). Rethinking parent involvement: African American mothers construct their roles in the mathematics education of their children. *School Community Journal, 16*(1), 51–73.

Ladson-Billings, G. (1994). *The dreamkeepers: Successful teachers of African American children.* San Francisco, CA: Jossey-Bass.

Li, G. (2006). What do parents think? Middle-class Chinese immigrant parents' perspectives on literacy learning, homework, and school-home communication. *School Community Journal, 16*(2), 27–46.

Mapp, K. L. (2003). Having their say: Parents describe why and how they are engaged in their children's learning. *School Community Journal, 13*(1), 35–64.

National Network of Partnership Schools. (2006). *TIPS—Math Elementary.* Retrieved June 18, 2011, from http://www.csos.jhu.edu/P2000/tips/tips_download_pdf/Blank/TIPStemplate%20elementary%20math.pdf.

Northwest Regional Educational Laboratory. (2007). The road to success: A rural district in north central Montana finds success by getting parents and community members back in the mix. *Northwest Education, 12*(3), 1–5. Retrieved June 10, 2007, from http://www.nwrel.org/nwedu/12–03.

Ooms, T., & Hara, S. (1991). *The family-school partnership: A critical component of school reform.* Washington, DC: The Family Impact Seminar.

Potter, S., & Davis, B. H. (2003). A first year teacher implements class meetings. *Kappa Delta Pi Record, 39*(2), 88–90.

Richards, R. (2004). *Tool kit for parents: Being an efficient homework helper.* Retrieved May 8, 2007, from http://www.ldonline.org/article/5606.

Shumow, L. (2001). *The task matters: Parental assistance to children doing different homework assignments.* Paper presented at the 2001 annual meeting of the American Educational Research Association, Seattle, WA.

Southeast Missourian. (2010, September 9). *Speak out: Bad grading.* Retrieved June 18, 2011, from http://www.semissourian.com/story/1662897.html.

Thorkildsen, R., & Scott Stein, M. R. (1998). *Is parent involvement related to student achievement? Exploring the evidence.* Phi Delta Kappa International Research Bulletin No. 22. Bloomington, IN: Center for Evaluation, Development, and Research.

Tileston, D. W. (2006*). What every parent should know about schools, standards, and high stakes tests.* Thousand Oaks, CA: Corwin.

Trahan, C. H., & Lawler-Prince, D. (1999). Parent partnerships: Transforming homework into home-school activities. *Early Childhood Education Journal, 27*(1), 65–68.

Truby, D., & Dollarhide, M. (2006). A teacher's guide to sticky situations. *Instructor, 115*(7), 27–29.

Trumbull, E., Rithstein-Fisch, C., & Hernandez, E. (2003). Parent involvement in schooling—According to whose values? *School Community Journal, 13*(2), 45–72.

Turner, J. (2000). Parent involvement: What can we learn from research? *Montessori Life, 12*(2), 37–39.

U.S. Department of Education. (2003). *Homework tips for parents.* Retrieved August 12, 2008, from http://www.ed.gov/parents/academic/involve/homework/index.html.

U.S. Department of Education. (2007). *NCLB (No Child Left Behind): Glossary of terms.* Retrieved June 14, 2011, from http://www.ed.gov/nclb/index/az/glossary.html?src = az.

U.S. Department of Education. (2008). Expectations and reports of homework for public school students in the first, third, and fifth grades. *National Center for Education Statistics Issue Brief,* NCES 2009–033.

Weinstein, C. S., Tomlinson-Clarke, S., & Curran, M. (2004). Toward a conception of culturally responsive classroom management. *Journal of Teacher Education, 55*(1), 25–38.

Williams, E. R. (2007). Unnecessary and unjustified: African American parental perceptions of special education. *Educational Forum, 71*(3), 250–261.

Woolfolk, A. (2001). *Educational psychology* (8th ed.). Boston, MA: Allyn & Bacon.

CHAPTER 10

Alexandria City Public Schools. (2004). *Listening to families and faculty: A report on family involvement in the Alexandria city public schools.* Retrieved March 27, 2007, from http://www.acps.k12.va.us.

Auger, K. W. (2006). Delivering different news to parents: Guidelines for school counselors. *Professional School Counseling, 10,* 134–145.

Bayless School District. (2008). *Bayless school district: Growing and learning together since 1868.* Retrieved May 6, 2008, from http://baylessk12.0rg.

Cazden, C. B., John, V. P., & Hymes, D. (Eds.). (1985). *Functions of language in the classroom.* Prospect Heights, IL: Waveland Press.

Clayton, J. B. (2003). *One classroom, many worlds: Teaching and learning in the cross-cultural classroom.* Portsmouth, NH: Heinemann.

Cohen. D. (1972). *The learning child: Beyond the home to school and community.* Retrieved July 18, 2011, from: http://www.poemhunter.com/quotations/famous.asp?people = Dorothy%20H%20Cohen.

Copeland, A. P. (2007). Welcoming international parents to your classroom. *Kappa Delta Pi Record, 43,* 66–70.

Espinosa, L. M. (2005). Curriculum and assessment considerations for young children from culturally, linguistically, and economically diverse backgrounds. *Psychology in Schools, 42*(8), 837–853.

Evans, J. E., & Hines, P. L. (1997). Lunch with school counselors: Reaching parents through their workplace. *Professional School Counseling, 1,* 45–47.

Gay, G. (2002). Preparing for culturally responsive teaching. *Journal of Teacher Education, 53*(2), 106–116.

Georgiady, N. P., & Romano, L. G. (2002). Positive parent-teacher conferences. *Phi Delta Kappa Fastbacks, 491,* 7–33.

Gonzalez-Mena, J. (2008). *Diversity in early care and education: Honoring differences* (5th ed.). New York, NY: McGraw-Hill.

Gorden, R. L. (1992). *Basic interviewing skills.* Itasca, IL: Peacock.

Henke, L. (2011). Connecting with parents at home. *Educational Leadership, 68*(8), 38–41.

Hirsch, G., & Altman, K. (1986). Training graduate students in parent conference skills. *Applied Research in Mental Retardation, 7,* 371–385.

Howe, F., & Simmons, B. J. (2005). Nurturing the parent teacher alliance. *Phi Delta Kappa Fastbacks. 533,* 7–41.

Huber, L. K. (2003). Knowing children and building relationships with families: A strategy for improving conferences. *Early Childhood Education Journal, 3,* 75–77.

Ingram, P. (2006). Student-led conferences. *Promising Partnership Practices 2006, National Network of Partnership Schools.* Retrieved July 17, 2007, from http://www.csos.jhu.edu/p2000/ppp/2006/pdf/31.pdf.

Ivey, A. E. (1994). *Intentional interviewing and counseling: Facilitating client development in a multicultural society* (3rd ed.). Pacific Grove, CA: Brooks.

Kinney, P. (2005). Letting students take the lead. *Principal Leadership, 6*(2), 33–36.

Kirschenbaum, H. (1999). Night and day: Succeeding with parents at School 43. *Principal, 78*(3), 20–23.

LeBaron, M. (2003, July). *Cross cultural communication.* Retrieved February 25, 2007, from http://www.beyondintractability.org/essay/cross-cultural_ communication.

Minke, K. M., & Anderson, K. J. (2003). Restructuring routine parent-teacher conference: The family-school conference model. *Elementary School Journal, 104,* 49–69.

Moore, K. B. (2002). Policies & practices: Family communications—ideas that really work. *Early Childhood Today.* Retrieved August 14, 2008, from http://www2.scholastic.com.

Poindexter, C. C., Valentine, D., & Conway, P. (1999). *Essential skills for human service.* Belmont, CA: Wadsworth.

Powell, D. (1998). Reweaving parents into the fabric of early childhood programs. *Young Children, 53*(3), 60–67.

PTA issues standards for parent involvement in education. (1997). *Reading Today, 14*(5), 16.

Quintanar, A. P., & Warren, S. R. (2008). Listening to the voices of Latino parent volunteers. *Kappa Delta Pi Record, 44*(3), 119–123.

Quiroz, B., Greenfield, P. M., & Altchech, M. (1999). Bridging cultures with a parent-teacher conference. *Educational Leadership, 56*(7), 68–70.

Ray, J., & Shelton, D. (2004). E-pals: Connecting with families through technology. *Young Children, 59*(3), 30–32.

Ricci, B. J. (2000). How about parent-teacher-student conferences? *Principal, 79*(5), 53–54.

Riggins, C. G. (2003). Families as partners. *Principal, 82*(4), 8.

Simmons, B. J. (2002). Facilitative conferences: Parents and teachers working together. *Clearing House, 76,* 88–93.

Skovholt, T. M., & Rivers, D. A. (2004). *Skills and strategies for the helping professions.* Denver, CO: Love.

Stevens, B. A., & Tollafield, A. (2003). Creating comfortable and productive parent/teacher conferences. *Phi Delta Kappan, 84,* 521–524.

U.S. Department of Education. (2006). *Assessing school-family communication.* Adapted from National Standards for Parent/Family Involvement Programs, National Parent-Teacher Association. Retrieved May 6, 2008, from http://www.ed.gov.

U.S. Department of Education. (2007). *Family Educational Rights and Privacy Act.* Retrieved June 26, 2007, from http://www.ed.gov/policy/gen/ guid/fpco/ferpa/index.html.

Welch, I. D., & Gonzalez, D. M. (1999). *The process of counseling and psychotherapy: Matters of skill.* Pacific Grove, CA: Brooks.

Worthy, J., & Hoffman, J. V. (2001). Home visits, reading engagement, and farewell. *Reading Teacher, 54*(5), 516–518.

Young, M. E. (2005). *Learning the art of helping: Building blocks and techniques.* Upper Saddle River, NJ: Pearson.

CHAPTER 11

Abilities Network. (2010). Abilities Network news. Retrieved April 26, 2011, from http://www.abilitiesnetwork.org/news/.

Al-Hassan, S., & Gardner, R. (2002). Involving immigrant parents of students with disabilities in the educational process. *Teaching Exceptional Children, 34*(5), 52–58.

Autism Education Network. (2011). Welcome to the Autism Education Network. Retrieved October 23, 2011, from http://www.autismeducation.net/.

Batshaw, M. L. (2002). *Children with disabilities.* Baltimore, MD: Brookes.

Blue-Banning, M., Frankland, H. C., & Summers, J. A. (2004). Dimensions of family and professional partnerships: Constructive guidelines for collaboration. *Exceptional Children, 70*(2), 167–184.

Bruder, M. B. (2000). *The individualized family service plan (IFSP).* Retrieved June 15, 2007, from http://www.kidneeds.com/diagnostic_categories/articles/indivfamilyserviceplan.htm.

Byrd, E. S. (2011). Educating and involving parents in the response to intervention process: The school's important role. *Teaching Exceptional Children, 43*(3), 32–39.

The Civil Rights Project. (2002). *Racial inequity in special education.* Retrieved July 15, 2007, from http://www.civilrightsproject.ucla.edu.

Cohen, P. (2006). *Children with disabilities more likely to live with women.* Retrieved July 15, 2007, from http://www.unc.edu/news/archives/ju106/cohen 071106htm.

Concord Special Education Parent Advisory Committee. (2001). *What is an IEP?* Retrieved May 8, 2008, from http://www.concordspedpac.org/WhatIEP.htm.

Davidson, J., & Davidson, B. (with Vanderkam, L.). (2005). *Genius denied: How to stop wasting our brightest young minds.* New York, NY: Simon & Schuster.

Delisle, J. (n.d.). *Texas PBS: Texas gifted/talented education.* Retrieved July 18, 2011, from http://texaspbs.org/gt.php.

Dunn, M.W. (2010). Response to intervention and reading disability: A conceptual model for schools with Reading Recovery. *Learning Disabilities: A Contemporary Journal, 8*(1), 31–50.

Dwight, V. (2001). Aidan's gift. In S. D. Klein & K. Schive (Eds.), *You will dream new dreams: Inspiring personal stories by parents of children with disabilities* (pp. 31–33). New York, NY: Kensington Books.

Ebenstein, B. J. (2001). I wish. . . In S. D. Klein & K. Schive (Eds.), *You will dream new dreams: Inspiring personal stories by parents of children with disabilities* (pp. 156–159). New York, NY: Kensington Books.

Hardman, M. L., Drew, C. J., & Egan, M. W. (2008). *Human exceptionality: School, community, and family* (9th ed.). Boston, MA: Houghton Mifflin.

Hertzog, N., & Bennett, T. (2004). In whose eyes? Parents' perspectives on the learning needs of their gifted children. *Roeper Review, 26*(2), 96–104.

Hoover, J. J., & Love, E. (2011). Supporting school-based response to intervention: A practitioner's model. *Teaching Exceptional Children, 43*(3), 40–48.

Jordan, K. (2005). Discourses of difference and the overrepresentation of black students in special education. *Journal of African American History, 90*(1/2), 128–149.

Kasahara, M., & Turnbull, A. P. (2005). Meaning of family-professional partnerships: Japanese mothers' perspectives. *Exceptional Children, 71*(3), 249–265.

Kaster, K. (2001). Different dreams. In S. D. Klein & K. Schive (Eds.), *You will dream new dreams: Inspiring personal stories by parents of children with disabilities* (pp. 185–186). New York, NY: Kensington Books.

Kim, A., & Yeh, C. (2002). *Stereotypes of Asian American students* (ERIC Document Reproduction Service No. ED462510). New York, NY: ERIC Clearinghouse on Urban Education.

Kübler-Ross, E. (1969). *On death and dying.* New York, NY: Touchstone.

Lamorey, S. (2002). The effects of culture on special education services. *Teaching Exceptional Children, 34*(5), 67–71.

Law and Exceptional Students. (1998). *Education law.* Retrieved July 15, 2007, from http://www.unc.edu/ ~ahowell/exceplaw.html.

Logsdon, P. (2011). Person first language—Focus on the person first is good etiquette. Retrieved May 13, 2011, from http://learningdisabilities.about.com/od/assessmentandtesting/qt/personfirst.htm.

Martin, C. (2002). Serving gifted students through inclusion: A parent's perspective. *Roeper Review, 24*(3), 3–4.

Matuszny, R. M., Banda, D. R., & Coleman, T. J. (2007). A progressive plan for building collaborative relationships with parents from diverse backgrounds. *Teaching Exceptional Children, 39*(4), 24–31.

Milligan, J., & Nichols, J. (2005). Twice-exceptional, twice at risk: Reflections of a mother and son. *Journal of At-Risk Issues, 11*(2), 39–45.

Murray, M. M.; Ackerman-Spain, K.; Williams, E. U. & Ryley, A. T. (2011). Knowledge is power: Empowering the autistic community through parent-professional training. *School Community Journal, (21)*1, 19–36.

Muscott, H. S. (2002). Exceptional partnerships: Listening to the voices of families. *Preventing School Failure, 46*(2), 66–69.

Naseef, R. A. (2001). The rudest awakening. In S. D. Klein & K. Schive (Eds.), *You will dream new dreams: Inspiring personal stories by parents of children with disabilities* (pp. 206–209). New York, NY: Kensington Books.

National Dissemination Center for Children with Disabilities. (2010a). *Response to intervention (RTI).* Retrieved May 18, 2011, from http://nichcy.org/schools-administrators/rti.

National Dissemination Center for Children With Disabilities. (2010b). *Subpart A: General provisions.* Retrieved April 26, 2011, from http://www.nichcy.org/Laws/IDEA/Pages/subpartA-PartBregs.aspx#34:2.1.1.1.1.1.36.24.

National Education Association. (2008). *No Child Left Behind/Elementary and Secondary Education Act: The basics.* Retrieved May 8, 2008, from http://www.nea.org/esea/eseabasics.html.

Nichols, L. A., & Keltner, B. (2005). Indian family adjustment to children with disabilities. *American Indian and Alaska Native Mental Research: Journal of the National Center, 12*(1), 22–48.

North Bay Regional Center. (n.d.). *What is the Individualized Family Service Plan?* Retrieved July 10, 2007, from http://www.nbrc.net/plan.html.

Novita Children's Services. (2007). *Grief and loss.* Retrieved June 15, 2007, from http://www.novita.org.au/Content.aspz?p = 439.

PACER Center. (n.d.). *Understanding the special education process.* Minneapolis, MN: Author.

PACER Center. (2000). *What is the difference between an IFSP and an IEP?* Minneapolis, MN: Author.

Pardini, P. (2002). The history of special education. *Rethinking Schools Online, 5*(3). Retrieved July 15, 2007, from http://www.rethinkingschools.org/archive/ 16_03/Hist163.shtml

Radaszewski-Byrne, M. (2001). Parents as instructional partners in the education of gifted children: A parent's perspective. *Gifted Children Today, 24*(2), 32–42.

Reinisch, S. A. B., & Reinisch, L. (1997). One year at a time: Parents' perspectives on gifted education. *Peabody Journal of Education, 72*(3/4), 237–252.

Salend, S. J. (2006). Explaining your inclusion program to families. *Teaching Exceptional Children, 38*(4), 6–11.

Salomans, L. (2001). Hard choices. In S. D. Klein & K. Schive (Eds.), *You will dream new dreams: Inspiring personal stories by parents of children with disabilities* (pp. 61–64). New York, NY: Kensington Books.

Smutny, J. (2000). *Teaching young gifted children in the regular classroom* (ERIC EC Digest #E595). Retrieved July 7, 2007, from http://www.eric.hoagiesgifted.org/e595.html.

Stephens, K. R. (1999). Parents of the gifted and talented: The forgotten partners. *Gifted Child Today, 22*(5), 38–43.

Strip, C., & Hirsch, G. (2001). Trust and teamwork: The parent-teacher partnership for helping the gifted child. *Gifted Child Today, 24*(2), 26–30, 64.

Tsao, G. (2000). *Growing up Asian American with a disability.* Retrieved June 15, 2007, from http://www.colorado.edu/journals.

Ulrich, M. E., & Bauer, A. M. (2003). Levels of awareness: A closer look at communication between parents and professionals. *Teaching Exceptional Children, 35*(6), 20–24.

U.S. Department of Education. (2002). *Twenty-fourth annual report to Congress on the implementation of the Individuals with Disabilities Education Act.* Retrieved May 9, 2008, from http://www.ed.gov/about/reports/annual/osep/2002/index.html.

U.S. Department of Education. (2004). *Elementary & secondary education: Title IX-general provisions.* Retrieved July 17, 2007, from http://www.ed.gov/policy/elsec/leg/esea02/pg107.html.

U.S. Department of Education. (2006a). *Assessing school-family communication.* Retrieved July 10, 2007, from http://www.ed.gov/admins/lead/safety/training/partnerships/assessing.doc.

U.S. Department of Education. (2006b). *The federal role in education.* Retrieved June 15, 2007, from http://www.ed.gov/about/overview/fed/role.html.

U.S. Department of Education. (2007). *My child's special needs: A guide to the Individualized Education Program.* Retrieved August 14, 2008, from http://www.ed.gov/parents/needs/speced/iepguide/ index.html.

U.S. Department of Education (2011). Response to Intervention framework in primary grade reading. Retrieved May 17, 2011, from http://dww.ed.gov/Response-to-Intervention-Reading/topic/index.cfm?T_ID = 27.

Waldrop, A. (2001). Dreams. In S. D. Klein & K. Schive (Eds.), *You will dream new dreams: Inspiring personal stories by parents of children with disabilities* (pp. 111–113). New York, NY: Kensington Books.

Williams, E. (2007). Unnecessary and unjustified: African American parental perceptions of special education. *Educational Forum, 71*(3), 250–261.

Zeman, L. D.; Swake, J., & Doktor, J. (2011). Strengths classification of social relationships among cybermothers raising children with autism spectrum disorders. *School Community Journal, (21)*1, 37–51.

CHAPTER 12

Administration for Children and Families. (2002). *CCDF FY2000 tables and charts.* Retrieved August 26, 2008, from http://www.acf.hhs.gov/programs/ccb/data/ccdf_data/00acf800/list.htm.

Administration for Children and Families. (2006). *Head Start program performance standards and other regulations.* Retrieved July 14, 2007, from http://eclkc.ohs.acf.hhs.gov/hslc/Program%20Design%20and%20Management/Head%20Start%20Requirements/Head%20Start%20Requirements.

Association for the Education of Young Children—Missouri. (2005). *How to become an advocate.* Retrieved July 13, 2007, from http://www.aeyc-mo.org/public_policy/advocate.asp.

Auerbach, S. (2011). Learning from Latino families. *Educational Leadership, 68*(8), 17–21.

Beck, E. (2007). Why we do it: What keeps you motivated and inspired to help your school, even when the going gets tough? *PTO Today.* Retrieved July 14, 2007, from http://www.ptotoday.com/articles/article.php?article = 0806whydoit.html.

Brookes, S. J., Thornburg, K. R., Summers, J. A., Ispa, J. M., & Lane, V. (2006). Building successful home visitor-mother relationships and reaching program goals in two Early Head Start programs: A qualitative look at contributing factors. *Early Childhood Research Quarterly, 21*(1), 25–45.

Bruder, M. B. (2004). The role of the physician in early intervention for children with developmental disabilities. *Connecticut Medicine, 68,* 507–514.

Children's Defense Fund. (2002). *The state of America's children.* Washington, DC: Author.

Children's Defense Fund. (2004). *The state of America's children.* Washington, DC: Author.

Chrispeels, J. H., & Rivero, E. (2000, April). *Engaging Latino families for students' success: Understanding the process and impact of providing training to parents.* Paper presented at the annual meeting of the Educational Research Association, New Orleans, LA.

Civil, M., Bratton, J., & Quintos, B. (2005). Parents and mathematics education in a Latino community: Redefining parental participation. *Multicultural Education, 13*(2), 60–64.

Cooper, A. (2011). Lunch lessons. *Educational Leadership, 68*(8), 75–78.

Curran, D. (1983). *Traits of a healthy family: Fifteen traits commonly found in healthy families by those who work with them.* Minneapolis, MN: Winston Press.

Damaren, N. (2000). Welcoming, learning school communities. *Kappa Delta Pi Record, 36*(2), 53–55.

David, J. L. (2011). After school programs can pay off. *Educational Leadership, 68*(8), 84–84.

Dempsey, I., & Dunst, C. J. (2004). Help-giving styles as a function of parent empowerment in families with a young child with a disability. *Journal of Intellectual and Developmental Disability, 29*(1), 50–61.

Deojay, T. R., & Novak, D. S. (2001). Power of many. *Journal of Staff Development, 22*(2), 55–57.

DeRose, J. (2005). *A Head Start testimonial.* Retrieved June 30, 2007, from http://www.connectforkids.org/ node/3027.

DeWitt, P. M. & Moccia, J. (2011). *Surviving a school closing.* Educational Leadership, 68(8), 54–57.

Dunst, C. J. (1997). Conceptual and empirical foundations of family-centered practice. In R. Illback, C. Cobb, & H. Joseph Jr. (Eds.), *Integrated services for children and families: Opportunities for psychological practice* (pp. 75–91). Washington, DC: American Psychological Association.

Dunst, C. J. (2000). Revisiting "Rethinking early intervention." *Topics in Early Childhood Special Education, 20,* 95–104.

Dunst, C. J., Boyd, K., Trivette, C. M., & Hamby, D. W. (2002). Family-oriented program models and professional helpgiving practices. *Family Relations, 51,* 221–229.

Dunst, C. J., & Trivette, C. M. (1996). Empowerment, effective helpgiving practices and family-centered care. *Pediatric Nursing, 22,* 334–337, 343.

Dunst, C. J., & Trivette, C. M. (2005). Characteristics and consequences of family-centered helpgiving practices. *CASEmakers, 1*(6), 1–4. Retrieved August 26, 2008, from http://www.fippcase.org/casemakers.php.

Dunst, C. J., Trivette, C. M., & Cutspec, P. (2002). Toward an operational definition of evidence-based practices. *Centerscope, 1*(1), 1–10. Retrieved August 26, 2008, from http://www.researchtopractice.info/productCenterscope.php.

Dunst, C. J., Trivette, C. M., & Hamby, D. W. (1996). Measuring the helpgiving practices of human services program practitioners. *Human Relations, 49,* 815–835.

Dunst, C. J., Trivette, C. M., & Mott, D. W. (1994). Strengths-based family-centered intervention practices. In C. J. Dunst, C. M. Trivette, & A. G. Deal (Eds.), *Supporting and strengthening families: Methods, strategies and practices* (pp. 115–131). Brookline, MA: Brookline Books.

Ferlazzo, L. (2011). Involvement or engagement? *Educational Leadership, 68*(8), 10–14. Cambridge, MA: Brookline Books.

Forum on Child and Family Statistics. (2007). *America's children: Key national indicators of well-being, 2007.* Retrieved August 26, 2008, from http://www.childstats.gov/americaschildren/ec03.asp.

Fromm, S. (2001). *Total estimated cost of child abuse and neglect in the United States.* Chicago, IL: Prevent Child Abuse America.

Ginsberg, M. (2007). Lessons at the kitchen table. *Education Leadership, 64*(6), 56–61.

Gonzalez-Mena, J. (2005). *The young child in the family and community* (4th ed.). Upper Saddle River, NJ: Prentice Hall.

Harvard Family Research Project. (Winter 2006/2007). *Family involvement in elementary school children's education* (No. 2). Family Involvement Makes a Difference, Harvard Graduate School of Education.

Henke, L. (2011). Connecting with parents at home. *Educational Leadership, 68*(8), 38–41.

Howland, A., Anderson, J. A., Smiley, A. D., & Abbott, D. J. (2006). School liaisons bridging the gap between school and home. *School Community Journal, 16*(2), 47–68.

Indiana Department of Education. (2001). *School-parent-community partnerships: Resource book.* Indianapolis: Author. Retrieved August 26, 2008, from http://www.doe.state.in.us/publications/pdf_ other/SFCPnarrative.pdf.

International Reading Association. (2007). *Advocacy manual.* Retrieved July 13, 2007, from http://www.reading.org/downloads/legislative/advocacy_ manua10701.pdf.

Jeynes, W. H. (2011). Parental involvement research: Moving to the next level. *The School Community Journal, 20*(1), 159–187.

Kretzmann, J., & McKnight, J. (1993). *Building community from the inside out.* Evanston, IL: Asset-Based Community Development Institute.

Kugler, E.G. (2011). Is anyone listening to families' dreams? *Educational Leadership, 68* (8), 32–26.

Lewis, K. C. (2004). Instructional aides: Colleagues or cultural brokers? *School Community Journal, 14*(1), 91–111.

McKenna, M., & Willms, J. D. (1998). The challenge facing parent councils in Canada. *Childhood Education, 74*(6), 378–382.

Meyer, J., & Mann, M. B. (2006). Teachers' perceptions of the benefits of home visits for early elementary children. *Early Childhood Education Journal, 34*(1), 93–97.

Miller, M. (2007, July 9). Just one of the guys making a difference. *St. Petersburg Times.* Retrieved July 14, 2007, from http://www.sptimes.com/2007/07/09/Pasco/Just_one_of_the_guys_.shtml

Minnesota School Social Workers Association. (n.d.). *Role of the school social worker brochure.* Retrieved August 7, 2007, from http://www.msswa.org/prof-articles.

National Association for Gifted Children. (2005). *Advocacy and legislation.* Retrieved July 13, 2007, from http://www.nagc.org/index.aspx?id= 970.

National Center for Education Statistics. (2006). *Digest of educational statistics 2005.* Retrieved August 26, 2008, from http://nces.ed.gov/programs/digest/d05.

National Parent Teacher Organization (2011). *PTA in transformation: Meeting the challenge for a new generation.* Retrieved October 30, 2011, from http://www.pta.org/2009_Annual_Report.pdf.

Oakes, J., Rogers, J., & Lipton. M. (2005). *Learning power: Organizing for education and justice.* New York, NY: Teachers College Press.

Pardini, P. (2002). The history of special education. *Rethinking Schools Online, 16*(3). Retrieved July 13, 2007, from http://www.rethinkingschools.org/archive/16_03/Hist163.shtml.

PTO Today. (2007). *Frequently asked questions.* Retrieved July 14, 2007, from http://www.ptotoday.com/ptofaq.html.

Reglin, G. (2002). Project Reading and Writing (R.A.W.): Home visitations and the school involvement of high-risk families. *Education, 123*(1), 153–161.

Sanders, M. (2006). *Building school-community partnerships: Collaboration for student success.* Thousand Oaks, CA: Corwin.

Schumacher, R. (2003). *Family support and parent involvement in Head Start: What do Head Start performance standards require?* Washington, DC: Center for Law and Social Policy.

Senge, P., Cambron-McCabe, N., Lucas, T., Smith, B., Dutton, J., & Kleiner, A., (2000). *Schools that learn: A fifth discipline fieldbook for educators, parents, and everyone who cares about education.* New York, NY: Doubleday.

Strip, C. A., & Hirsch, G. (2000). *Helping gifted children soar.* Scottsdale, AZ: Gifted Psychology Press.

Teasley, M. (2004). School social workers and urban education reform with African American children and youth: Realities, advocacy, and strategies for change. *School Community Journal, 14*(2), 19–38.

Tennessee Early Intervention Services Coordination. (2007). *Partners on a journey of hope.* Retrieved July 14, 2007, from http://www.state.tn.us/education/speced/TEIS/training/module2/1st_4_sections_Module_2.pdf.

U.S. Department of Education. (1997). *Families involvement in children's education: Successful local approaches.* Retrieved July 12, 2007, from http://www.ed.gov/pubs/FamInvolve/Iidex.html.

U.S. Department of Education. (2005). *Digest of education statistics: 2005.* Retrieved September 12, 2007, from http://www.nces.ed.gov/programs/digest/d05/ch_2.asp.

U.S. Department of Health and Human Services. (2007). *Home visiting: Strengthening families by promoting parenting success.* Policy Brief No. 23. Family Strengthening Policy Center. Retrieved August 26, 2008, from http://eclkc.ohs.acf.hhs.gov/hslc/Family%20and%20Community%20Partnerships/Parent%20Involvement/Home%20Visits/HomeVisiting St.htm.

Wagner, M., Spiker, D., & Linn, M. I. (2003). Dimensions of parental engagement in home visiting programs: Exploratory study. *Topics in Early Childhood Special Education, 23*(4), 171–187.

Williams, J. (2011). PTA, PTO . . . What's it all about? *Education.com*. Retrieved from from http://www.education.com/magazine/article/PTA_PTO_Kindergarten_Parents/%3C/IFRAME%3E/.

Worthy, J., & Hoffman, J. V. (2001). Home visits, reading engagement, and farewell. *Reading Teacher, 54*(5), 516–518.

Yellowstone County Head Start. (2001–2002). *Community resource booklet*. Yellowstone, MT: Author.

Zimmerman-Oroco, S. (2011). A circle of caring. *Educational Leadership, 68*(8), 64–68.

CHAPTER 13

Allington, R. L. (2001). *What really matters for struggling readers: Designing research-based programs*. New York, NY: Longman.

Aronson, N. M. (1995). *Building communication partnerships with parents*. Westminster, CA: Teacher Created Materials.

Boost student achievement by enrolling parents in math academies. (2005). *Curriculum Review, 44*(9), 10.

Brent, B. O. (2000). Do classroom volunteers benefit schools? *Principal, 80*(1), 36–43.

Carlson, C. (1991). Getting parents involved in their children's education. *Education Digest, 57*(3), 10–12.

Coates, G., & Stenmark, J. (1997). *Family math for young children*. Berkeley: Lawrence Hall of Science, University of California at Berkeley.

Coates, G., & Thompson, V. (2003). *Family math II*. Berkeley: Lawrence Hall of Science, University of California at Berkeley.

Collins, K. (2006). High five after-school program. *National Network of Partnership Schools*. Retrieved August 1, 2007, from http://www.csos.jhu.edu/p2000/nnps_model/school/sixtypes/type3.asp.

Craven, H. S. (2006). Using parent volunteers. *Inspiring Teachers*. Retrieved August 1, 2007, from http://www.inspiringteachers.com/classroom_resources/articles/parent_communication/parent_volunteers.html.

Darling, S. (2005). Strategies for engaging parents in home support of reading acquisition. *Reading Teacher, 58*(5), 476–479.

Davies, D. (2002). The 10th school revisited: Are school/family/community partnerships on the reform agenda now? *Phi Delta Kappan, 83*(5), 388–392.

Davis, C., & Yang, A. (2005). Investing in parents during the first six weeks of school. *Responsive Classroom Newsletter*. Retrieved August 20, 2008, from http://www.responsiveclassroom.org/newsletter/ 17_3nl_1.html.

DeCusati, C. L. P., & Johnson, J. E. (2004). Parents as classroom volunteers and kindergarten students' emergent reading skills. *Journal of Educational Research, 97*(5), 235–246.

Delgado Gaitan, C. (2004). *Involving Latino families in schools: Raising student achievement through home-school partnerships*. Thousand Oaks, CA: Corwin.

Derman-Sparks, L. (1989). *Anti-bias curriculum: Tools for empowering young children*. Washington, DC: National Association for the Education of Young Children.

Emberley, E. R. (1992). *Ed Emberley's drawing book of faces* (Vol. 1). Boston, MA: Little, Brown.

Feller, T. R., Jr., & Gibbs-Griffith, B. (2007). Teaching content through the arts: Bulldog beat. *Educational Leadership, 64*(8), 48–49.

Ferguson, C. (2005). *Organizing family and community connections with schools: How do school staff build meaningful relationships with all stakeholders?* Strategy brief from National Center for Family and Community Connections with Schools. Retrieved January 4, 2007, from http://www.sedl.org/connections.

Garcia, D. C., & Hasson, D. J. (2004). Implementing family literacy programs for linguistically and culturally diverse populations: Key elements to consider. *School Community Journal, 14*(1), 113–137.

Haynes, J. (2004). Working with bilingual parent volunteers. *EverythingESL.net*. Retrieved August 6, 2007, from http://www.everythingesl.net/inservices/bilingualparents.php.

Hutchins, P. (1986). *The doorbell rang*. New York, NY: Greenwillow.

Kaiser, A. (2000). *Transition to middle school for students and parents*. Promising Partnerships

Practices 2000, National Network of Partnership Schools. Retrieved July 16, 2007, from http://www.csos.jhu.edu/p2000/PPP/2000/pdf/13.pdf.

Kelly, P., Brown, S., Butler, A., Gittens, P., Taylor, C., & Zeller, P. (1998). A place to hang our hats. *Educational Leadership, 56*(1), 62–65.

Kyle, D. W., McIntyre, E., Miller, K., & Moore, G. (2006). *Bridging home & school through family nights: Ready to use plans for grades K–8.* Thousand Oaks, CA: Corwin.

Longwell-Grice, H., & McIntyre, E. (2006). Addressing goals of school and community: Lessons from a family literacy program. *School Community Journal, 16*(2), 115–132.

Lundeen, C. (2005). So, you want to host a family science night? *Science and Children, 42*(8), 30–35.

Markova, D. (2002). How your child is smart: A life-changing approach to learning. York Beach, ME: Conari Press.

McMillan, B. (1992). *Eating fractions.* New York, NY: Scholastic.

National Center for Education Statistics. (1998). Parent involvement in children's education: Efforts by public elementary schools. NCES Publication Number: 98032. Retrieved July 31, 2007, from http://nces.ed.gov/surveys/frss/inc/displaytables_inc.asp.

National Network of Partnership Schools. (2006). *Type 3: Volunteering.* Retrieved August 1, 2007, from http://www.csos.jhu.edu/p2000/nnps_model/school/sixtypes/type3.htm.

Padak, N., & Rasinski, T. (2006). Home-school partnerships in literacy education: From rhetoric to reality. *Reading Teacher, 60*(3), 292–296.

Pallotta, J. (2003). *Apple fractions.* New York, NY: Scholastic.

Promote literacy—and any other skills—through board games. (2004). *Curriculum Review, 43*(6), 9–10.

Quezada, R. L. (2003). Going for the gold! Field reports on effective home-school-community partnership programs. *School Community Journal, 13*(2), 137–155.

Quintanar, A. P., & Warren, S. R. (2008). Listening to the voices of Latino parent volunteers. *Kappa Delta Pi Record, 44*(3), 119–123.

Schussheim, Y. (2004). Large-scale family math nights: A primer for collaboration (A teacher's journal). *Teaching Children Mathematics, 10*(5), 254.

Seefeldt, C. (1998). Family dinner at school involves parents. *Education Digest, 64*(1), 59–62.

Stenmark, K., Thompson, V., & Cossey, R. (1986). *Family math.* Berkeley: Lawrence Hall of Science, University of California at Berkeley.

Thompson, V., & Mayfield-Ingram, K. (1998). *Family math: The middle school years, algebraic reasoning and number sense.* Berkeley: Lawrence Hall of Science, University of California at Berkeley.

Western Upper Peninsula Center for Science, Mathematics and Environmental Education. (2006). *Family science night check list.* Retrieved July 27, 2007, from http://wupcenter.mtu.edu/education/familysciencenight/FSN_CHECKLIST.pdf.

Wheat, J. (2006). *Back to school bash.* Promising Partnership Practices 2006, National Network of Partnership Schools. Retrieved July 19, 2007, from http://www.csos.jhu.edu/p2000/ppp/2006/pdf/50.pdf.

Women's Opportunity and Resource Development, Inc. (n.d.). *Family resource centers.* Retrieved September 7, 2007, from http://www.wordinc.org/FRC/ index.php.

APPENDIX D

California Department of Education. (2006). *Parental involvement flyer.* Sacramento, CA: Author.

National Head Start Association. (2006). *Head Start parental involvement-issue brief.* Alexandria, VA: Author.

No Child Left Behind. (2004). *Parental involvement: Title I, Part A, non-regulatory guidance.* Washington, DC: U.S. Department of Education.

Schumacher, R. (2003). *Family support and parent involvement in Head Start: What do Head Start Program performance standards require?* Washington, DC: Center for Law and Social Policy.

U.S. Department of Education. (2005). *Introduction: Archived information—No Child Left Behind.* Retrieved May 24, 2008, from http://www.ed.gov/nclb/ overview/intro/index.html.

U.S. Department of Health and Human Services, Administration for Children and Families. (2008). *Office of Head Start.* Retrieved May 24, 2008, from http://www.acf.hhs.gov/programs/hsb.

APPENDIX E

Cambridge Public Schools. (2007). *Cambridge Public Schools family involvement procedure for 2007–2008 school year.* Retrieved May 13, 2008, from http://www.cpsd.us/web/Title1/Family_Involvement_ Policy07.pdf.

Davies, D. (2002). The 10th school revisited: Are school/ family/community partnerships on the reform agenda now? *Phi Delta Kappan, 83*(5), 388–392.

Dryfoos, J., & Maguire, S. (2002). *Inside full service community schools.* Thousand Oaks, CA: Corwin.

Epstein, J. L., Sanders, M. G., Simon, B. S., Salinas, K. C., Janshorn, N. R., & Van Voorhis, F. L. (2002). *School, family, and community partnerships: Your handbook for action (2nd ed.).* Thousand Oaks, CA: Corwin.

Missouri Department of Elementary and Secondary Education. (2005). Resolution on parent/family involvement. Retrieved May 13, 2008, from http://www.dese.mo.gov/stateboard/parentinvolvement.pdf.

Patrikakou, E. N., Weissberg, R. P., Redding, S., & Walberg, H. (2005). School-family partnerships: Dimensions and recommendations. In E. N. Patrikakou, R. P. Weissberg, S. Redding, & H. J. Walberg (Eds.), *School-family partnerships for children's success* (pp. 181–188). New York, NY: Teachers College Press.

Seattle Public Schools. (2007). *Family involvement in Seattle Public Schools.* Retrieved May 13, 2008, from http://www.seattleschools.org/area/fam/History.xml.

PHOTO CREDITS

INDEX

Absenteeism, 167
Academic connections, 293
Acceptable Use Policy (AUP), 332 *table*
Accountability, 210 *table*
Acculturation, 114
Achievement, 210 *table*
Active listening, 232
Active parenting, 74–75
Active Parenting of Teens, 75
Active Parenting Today, 75
Adams, Tami, 304
Adequate yearly progress (AYP), 209, 210 *table*
Administrators
    child abuse policy and, 195
    family engagement role, 12, 14, 15 *table*
    family support by, 68
Adolescents
    birthrates of, 17, 18 *table*
    divorced parents, 135
    effective parenting of, 74–75
Adoption and Foster Care Analysis and
    Reporting System (AFCARS), 149
Adoptive families
    challenges of, 102–103
    characterization of, 102
    children's books depicting, 104 *table*
    cross-cultural, 104
    example of, 101
    same-sex, 105 *table*
    working with, 103–104
Adult Education, 74, 298
Adult Education and Family Literacy Act, 74
Advisory councils, 290–301
Advocacy
    activism and, 290
    barriers to, 291–292
    case, 289
    class, 289–291

    definition of, 289
    facts for, 288
    sample letter, 290 *table*
African Americans
    children in poverty, 19, 20 *table*
    corporal punishment and, 197
    disability reactions by, 264
    divorce rate of, 18
    in foster care, 288
    parenting styles of, 66
After-school programs, 338–339
Ainsworth, Mary, 58
Alaska Native, 267
Alignment, 210 *table*
Allington, R. L., 324
Altman, K., 230
Altoona Middle School Partnership
    Committee, 319
Amendment to the Education of the
    Handicapped Act, 259
American Academy of Pediatrics
    (AAP), 173
American Association of Retired Persons
    (AARP), 107
American Bar Association (ABA), 198
American Federation of Teachers, 99
American Indians
    children in poverty, 19, 20 *table*
    disability reactions by, 256
    special education needs of, 267
American School Counselor Association, 99
American School Health Association, 99
The Andy Griffith Show, 79
Asian Americans
    activism by, 290
    disability reactions by, 256
    divorce rate of, 18
    parenting styles, 66

population growth of, 21–22
special education needs of, 267
"Ask the Children" project, 65
Asset-based partnerships
    advocacy in, 288–292
    application of, 284–285 *table*
    benefits of, 282–283
    community resources for, 292–298
    home visits and, 285–288
    parental leadership in, 298–301
Association for Childhood Education
        International (ACEI), 291, 343
At-risk factors, 170
Attachment, 58–59
Authentic contacts, 126 *table*
Authoritarian parenting, 61, 63
Authoritative parenting, 61
Autism, 265
Averill Park Central School District, 300
Avoidant attachment, 58

Babel Fish, 229
Back-to-school events, 316–318
Bandaides and Blackboards for Kids, 167, 174
Barbara Bush Foundation for Family Literacy,
        324, 340
Barbour, A. C., 216
Bauer, A. M., 254
Baumrind, Diana, 60, 62–63
Behavior
    active listening, 232
    classroom, 211–213
    parenting, 60
    styles of, 59
    survey, 212 *table*
Beliefs. *See* Religion
Benchmarks, 210 *table*
Besharov, D. J., 176
Big Love, 80
Bilingual education, 117
Bilingual volunteers, 336
Birthrates, 17, 18 *table*
Bisexuals, 98–99
Blended families
    advantages of, 92–93
    children's books depicting, 94 *table*
    example of, 91
    media portrayal of, 79–80
    portrayal of, 92
    relationships in, 91–92

transitioning to, 135–136
well-functioning, 93
working with, 93–95
Body language, 231–232 *table*
Bond, Julian, 197
Bonding
    caregiver, 59
    concept of, 32–33
    family, 33
    process of, 33–34, 59
    strengths of, 57–58
"Books Without Barriers," 148
"Boot camp" parenting, 148
Boundaries, 31–32
The Brady Bunch, 79–80
Bridging Cultures, 235
Brock, S. W., 169
Bronfengrenner, U., 37–41
Brookes, S. J., 287
Brown v. Board of Education, 258
Bryn Mawr Elementary School, 324
Bulldog Beat class, 320

Cambridge Public Schools, 358
Cambridge Community Partnerships for
        Children, 147
Caretakers, 59
Caring, function of, 172
Carl D. Perkins Vocational and Applied
        Technology Act, 259
Case advocacy, 289
Celebratory back-to-school
        events, 317
Centers for Disease Control, 265
Chess, S., 59
Child abuse
    administrators' role, 197
    advocating against, 191
    cases per year, 176 *figure*
    costs of, 288
    cultural differences and, 190
    discipline *vs.,* 179
    identification of, 175–176
    mandatory reporting of, 185–189
    over reporting of, 189
    prevention agencies, 349–353
    reporting responsibilities, 184–185
    scope of, 177 *table*
    socioeconomic factors, 177
    statistics, 176

substance abuse and, 182–184
types of, 178–183
Child Abuse Prevention and Treatment
Act, 178, 193
Childcare, 54, 59
Child neglect
advocating against, 191
definition of, 181
incidence of, 182–183
prevention agencies, 349–353
risk factors of, 182–184
signs of, 182
substance abuse and, 182–184
Child Protective Services (CPS)
assessments by, 185
caseworker interview, 186 *table*
process overview, 188 *figure*
responsibilities of, 176
state websites, 349–353
substance abuse data, 183
Children. *See also* Infants; Toddlers
behavioral styles of, 59
bonding with, 57–58
chronically ill, 166
death of, 138
divorced parents, 89 *table,* 135
effects of war on, 142 *table*
home alone, 288
with incarcerated parents, 145–148
living in poverty, 19, 20 *table*
maladaptive functioning in, 59
parentification of, 34–35
parenting of, 56–57
parenting views of, 64–66
preschool, 54–55
relatives' death and, 137–140
responsibility for, 51
in single parent households, 87–88
temperament of, 59
Children's Defense Fund, 127, 291
Children, Youth and Families Consortium, 307
Chronic illness
absenteeism from, 167
children affected by, 166
common types of, 166 *table*
definition of, 165
teacher's approach to, 166–168
Chronosystem, 38 *table, 39–40*
Civil Rights Act of 1964, 258
Class advocacy, 289–291

Class meetings, 211
Classrooms
behavior in, 211–213
community collaboration with, 292–296
cultural audits in, 125–126 *table*
diversity in, 22–23
new students in, 132–133
parents' perspective, 29
volunteers in, 213–215
Clinton, Bill, 164, 211
Closed questions, 233 *table*
C. M. E. Middle School, 320
Cohen, Dorothy H., 225
Coleman, James, 43–44
Collaboration
barriers to, 207–208
on behavioral challenges, 211–213
classroom/community, 292–296
community, 46 *figure,* 47
conferences and, 233
on cultural events, 320–321
scenario of, 205–206
Comer School Development Program, 50
Comer, James, 48–49, 62
Communication. *See also* Conferences
assessment of, 248 *table*
barriers to, 243–246
community networks, 293
cultural issues, 241–243
documentation of, 238, 239 *table*
exceptional needs, 262–265
facultative, 321
with hostile families, 246
linguistically issues, 241–243
mass media, 228
nonverbal, 231–232 *table*
parent-teacher conferences, 227–228
partnership involvement, 46 *figure,* 47
print, 226–229
reciprocal, 230–232
RTI, 273
skills building, 225–226
skills checklist, 247 *table*
on standards-based curriculum, 208–211
technology, 239–241
Community
collaboration with, 46 *figure,* 47
conferences, 238
cultural diversity of, 126 *table*
curriculum development and, 208–209, 211

engagement barriers of, 9–10, 13 *table*
event liaisons, 315
family definitions of, 28
neighborhoods in, 292
resources of, 296–298
schools role in, 70
support in, 292
violence in, 164–165
volunteers from, 213–215
Community partnerships
    child abuse prevention and, 190, 192 *table*
    classroom collaboration with, 292–296
    communication via, 228
    curriculum-based projects for, 294–295
    family support by, 69
    potential, 293–294 *table*
    successful, 70
Community Resource Booklet, 296
Complementary learning, 285
Conferences
    alternatives to, 233–238
    community, 238
    considerations for, 231–232 *table*
    example of, 227–228
    group, 235–236
    home visits, 237–238
    misconceptions of, 244
    overview of, 230
    planning for, 233
    special-needs related, 253
    student involvement in, 234–235
    suggestions for, 234 *table*
    telephone, 236–237
    three-way, 235
    workplace, 238
Confidentiality, 195, 339
Connection Collection, 50
Contexts, model of, 37
Corporal punishment, 196–197
The Cosby Show, 80
Coulling, N., 151
Council for Exceptional Children, 279
The Courtship of Eddie's Father, 79
Cultural audits, 125–126 *table*
Cultural deficit model, 158
Cultural diversity
    adoptive families, 104
    child abuse and, 190
    conferences and, 241–243
    events-based on, 312–313

exceptional need students, 267
family engagement and, 11–12, 22–24
family structures, 82
family-centeredness and, 33
knowledge funds of, 44–45
parenting and, 64
responding to, 123–126
school activities bridging, 69
within cultures, 112
Cultural events
    benefits of, 312
    checklist for, 315–316 *table*
    family math as, 325–326
    planning for, 320–321
    scenario, 320, 325–326
Culturally response teaching (CRT), 23–24
Culture. *See also* Language; Religion
    child abuse and, 177
    definition, 112
    dominate perspective of, 116
    factors of, 113
    key concepts of, 113–114
    paraphrases and, 232 *table*
    poverty, 158
Curious George, 324
Curriculum
    community projects for, 294–295
    religious studies in, 120
    standards-based, 208–211
    tourist, 320
"Customer friendly" teachers, 285

Darling, S., 322
Death
    child, 138
    children's books about, 153 *table*
    coping with, 139
    grandparent, 138–139
    parent, 137–140
    remarriage following, 18–19
    sibling, 138
    war related, 144
Decision making, 46 *figure,* 47
Delarm, Martha, 186 *table*
Delgado Gaitan, C., 66, 221, 337
Delisle, Jim, 251
Department of Education, 196, 258, 275
Department of Health and Human Services, 182
Department of Justice, 191
Derman-Sparks, L., 320

Differentiated parenting, 66, 115
Differentiating instruction, 210 *table*
Digital e-mail devices, 241
Disability categories, 252–253 *table*
Disaggregated data, 210 *table*
Discipline
    abuse *vs.,* 179
    corporal, 196–197
    effective, 197
    shaming, 66
Disengagement, 33
Displays, 125–126 *table*
Diversity, 22–23
Divorce
    children affected by, 136–137
    children's books on, 89 *table,* 152 *table*
    classroom impact, example of, 131
    engagement practices for, 90–91
    rates of, 18, 134
    remarriage after, 91
Domestic violence. *See also* Child abuse
    ABA commission on, 198
    affects of, 191, 193–194
    definitions of, 193
    immigrants and, 194–195
    statistics on, 193
Drama projects, 295
Drawing Book of Faces (Emberley), 323
Dual-language programs, 117
Dunst, Carl, 41–43, 45
Dysfunctional, 37

Early Childhood STEP, 74
Early Intervention Act, 259
Eaton, Sherry, 168
Ebenstein, B. S., 254
Ecological systems theory
    development of, 37
    levels of, 38–40
    resources of, 40
Economic status. *See* Socioeconomic status
Edelman, Marion Wright, 197
Ed Emberlye's Drawing Book of Faces, 323
Education. *See also* Special education
    adult, 74, 298
    homeless, 162
    opportunities for, 297 *table*
    parental level of, 64
    parental, models of, 71–75
    poverty and, 157–158

Education for All Handicapped
    Children's Act, 258
Education of the Handicapped Act
    Amendments, 258
Education World, 341
Educators. *See* Administrators; Teachers
Edwards, P. A., 115
Elementary and Secondary Education Act,
    3, 258, 355,
E-mails, 241
Emily Dickinson Elementary School Family
    Resource Center, 323
Emotional abuse, 180–181
Emotionally disturbed, 267, 271
Empowerment model
    simplified version of, 42 *figure*
    social capital, 43–44
    understanding, 42–43
Enabling and Empowering Families, 41
English immersion, 117
English language learners (ESL), 11. *See also*
    Non-English speakers
    backgrounds of, 110 *table*
    home environment, example of,
        111–112
    instructional programs for, 117
    percentage of, 117
    by state, 111 *table*
Enmeshed families, 32–33
Epstein, Joyce L., 45, 47–48, 358–359
Espinosa, Linda, 109, 243
Ethics
    family engagement, 24
    mandatory reporting, 189
    NAEYC, 189, 345–357
Ethnicity. *See also* Cultural diversity; *specific
        groups*
    diversity of, 21–22
    knowledge funds of, 44–45
    world view-based on, 32
Even Start, 74
Events. *See also* Cultural events
    back-to-school, 316–318
    community liaisons for, 315
    examples of, 313 *table*
    exit questionnaire for, 314
    interactive, 311
    literacy, 321–324
    math nights, 325–326
    preparation for, 314–315

programs for, 318 *table*
school-based, 310–311
science nights, 327–330
technology nights, 330–331, 332 *table*
transition, 318–320
Exceptional needs students. *See also* Gifted and
   talented students; Special education
   autism, 265
   categories of, 252
   considerations for, 251–252
   cultural considerations for, 256–257, 267
   family communication and, 262–265
   family's reaction to, 254–256
   homework for, 222
   parent-teacher conferences and, 253
   referrals for, 266
   RTI and, 272–273
   screening for, 266–268
   in single-parent households, 90
Exosystem, 39
Exploratorium, 329–330
Extended families, 84–85, 105 *table*

Facilitative communication, 321
Families. *See also* Households; Single-parent
   families
   adoptive, 101–104
   advocacy by, 70
   birthrates of, 17, 18 *table*
   blended, 91–95
   bonding in, 32–34
   books depicting diversity in, 106 *table*
   boundaries of, 31
   census data on, 15
   child-rearing responsibilities of, 51
   cultural diversity in, 115–119
   definitions of, 14
   disengagement by, 33
   diversity in, 109
   ecological systems theory, 37–40
   economic status of, 19, 20 *table*
   enmeshed, 32–33
   ethnic diversity of, 21
   extended, 84–85, 105 *table*
   foster, 105–106
   grandparents role in, 19
   hierarchical structures of, 34–35
   hostile, 246
   "ideal," self-evaluation, 23 table
   interventionists, 116

kinship care, 95–98, 105 *table*
life cycles of, 130–131
linguistic diversity in, 117–118
media portrayal of, 79–80
morphogenesis of, 35
newly immigrated, 118–119
nontraditional configurations of, 16
nuclear, 81–84, 105 *table*
positive relationships with, 68
as program resource, 68, 70
racial diversity of, 21
religious diversity in, 120–123
same-sex, 98–101, 105 *table*
school-based initiatives for, 70
single-parent, 79, 85–91
traditional configurations of, 15–16
trends in, 14
worldview of, 31–32
Families in Action, 75
Family and Community website, 25
Family and Work Institute, 107
Family-centered partnerships
   advocacy in, 288–292
   application of, 284–285 *table*
   basis of, 282
   community resources for, 292–298
   home visits and, 285–288
   parental leadership in, 298–301
Family Center on Technology and Disability, 279
Family Communications, 249
Family Education Network, 76
Family empowerment model, 41–42
Family engagement
   administrators role in, 12, 14
   attitude survey, 7 *table*
   benefits of, 8–9
   coordinator for, 302 *table*
   culturally responsive, 22–24, 123–126
   curriculum development and, 208–209
   definition of, 6
   ecological systems model for, 37–40
   empowerment model for, 41–42
   ethical, 24
   funds of knowledge model for, 44–45
   high-poverty schools, 10–11
   mission statement sample, 357–360
   partnership framework for, 45–48
   plan for, example, 5–6
   priority of, 10–11
   program mandates, 355–356

school development program model for,
    48–49
standards for, 343
systems conceptual framework for, 30–37
teachers commitment to, 27–28
websites for, 344
Family engagement barriers
community-based, 10–11, 13 *table*
conventional, 116
culturally-based, 11–12
district based, 10–11
educators, 9–10, 207–208
family-based, 10, 13 *table*
group-based, 10
individual-based, 10
linguistic-based, 11–12
programmatic, 13 *table*
school-based, 10–11, 13 *table*
Family information center (FIC), 332
Family interview questionnaire, 57 *table*
Family Involvement Network, 107
Family Math Program, 325–326
Family Night Out, 319–320
Family outreach specialists (FOS),
    305–306
Family resource centers (FRCs)
definition of, 332
function of, 334–335
volunteers at, 335
Family-school partnerships, 1
child abuse prevention and, 190–191
development of, 45
forming, 6–7
guidance for, 48
involvement types, 46 *figure,* 47
network for, website, 50
preparation for, 4–6
website for, 25
Family science night
benefits of, 330
goals of, 328
ideas for, 329–330
planning checklist for, 328–329 *table*
scenario of, 327
Family support
characterization of, 72
definition of, 67
premises of, 67 *table,* 68
program activities for, 72
in school, principles of, 68–72

Family Violence Prevention Fund (FVPF), 198
Fathers, 16
Federal Educational Rights and Privacy Act,
    231*table*
Fetal alcohol syndrome, 183–184
Foreign language projects, 295
Foster care
African Americans in, 288
challenges of, 150–151
children's books about, 152 *table*
emotional problems and, 150
families, 105–106
family tree example, 148–149
issues, 149–150
outcomes for, 149, 150 *table*
potential of, 150
working with, 151
Foxworthy, Jeff, 65
A Framework for Understanding Poverty
    (Payne), 158
Free and appropriate public education (FAPE), 260
Friday folders, 228
Funds of knowledge model, 44–45

Gangs, 164
Gays, 98–99
Generational poverty, 157–158
Gifted and talented students
definition of, 275
encounters with, example, 277–278
IDEA categorization of, 273, 275
identification of, 275–276
insights to, 276–277
placement of, 276
Gilbert, N., 83
"Girl Scouts Beyond Bars," 148
Goals
improvement, 283–284
science night, 328
system, 36
Good News Notebook, 229
GrandCare Support Locator, 107
Grandparents. *See also* Kinship care families
caregivers, 19
contributions of, 97–99
death of, 138–139
financial constraints of, 96–97
parental role of, 81
parenting styles of, 95–96
Spanish-speaking, 69

Grief, 254–255
Group conferences, 235–236
Guskey, T. R., 209

Habits. *See* Rituals; Traditions
Habitudes, 115–116
Handicapped Children's Protection Act, 259
Harvard Family Research Project, 50, 285
Head Start, 55, 356
Head Start Information and Publication
    Center, 249
Health class projects, 295
Healthfinder, 174
Health resources, 297 *table*
Henderson, N., 172
Henderson, A., 10
Henke, L., 285
Hiatt-Michael, D. B., 292
Hierarchical structures, 34–35
High Five After-School Program, 338
Highland Park Elementary School, 300
Highly effective teachers, 210 *table*
Highly qualified teachers, 261
High-poverty schools, 10–11
High-stakes testing, 209, 210 *table*
Hirsch, G., 230
Hispanic Americans
    activism by, 290
    children in poverty, 19, 20 *table*
    disability reactions by, 256, 264
    divorce rate of, 18
    knowledge funds of, 44–45
    parenting styles, 66
    population growth of, 21–22
Home and School Institute, 76
Home Instruction for Parents of Preschool
    Youngsters (HIPPY), 75
Homeless liaison, 162
Homelessness
    educating, 162
    effects of, 160–162
    face of, 161
    moving by, 162
    teachers and, 163
Home School Association (HSA), 299
Home-school coordinators, 301–303
Home visits
    benefits of, 287–288
    concept of, 237
    considerations for, 237

reasons for, 285, 286 *table*
    training sessions for, 238
Homework, 204
    age-based benefits of, 216
    assignment flexibility, 219
    common parents comments on, 222–223
    definition of, 215
    parents concerns, 219–220
    signature form, 220 *figure*
    special needs students and, 222
    traditional assignments, 216
Honor, Respect, and Responsibility (HR2) Grant
    Project, 209
Hospice website, 154
Hostile families, 246
Households. *See also* Families
    adults living in, 14
    gay-lesbian, 98
    size of, 17 *table*
    two-parent, 15–16
Hunger, 160

IDEA. *See* Individuals With Disabilities Education
    Act (IDEA)
IEP. *See* Individualized education
    programs (IEP)
IFPS. *See* Individual family service plan (IFPS)
Immigrants
    children in poverty, 19, 20 *table*
    diversity of, 118
    domestic violence and, 194–195
    home visits to, 287
    working with, 118–119
Improvement goals, 283–284
Incarcerated parents
    children's books about, 152 *table*
    children's reaction to, 145–148
    percentage of, 145
    visits to, 146
Individual family service plan (IFPS)
    IEP *vs.*, 269, 270 *table*
    meeting preparation, 271
    preparation for, 272
Individualized education programs (IEP)
    development of, 266
    IFPS *vs.*, 269, 270 *table*
    parents involvement in, 268–269
    placement for, 266–267
    plan authors, 269
    purpose of, 260

students' adjustment of, 271–272
team make-up, 268
Individualized family service plan (IFSP), 260
Individuals With Disabilities Education
	Act (IDEA)
	categories developed by, 252
	components of, 260
	original provisions of, 259
	part C, provisions of, 269
	reauthorization of, 252
Infants
	drug-affected, 183–184
	parental attachment to, 58
	parenting of, 53–54
Information
	24-hour line for, 226
	center for, 334
	difficult, 245, 246 table
	on websites, 240
Insecure attachment, 58
Instructional aides, 305
Intellectual disability, 255
Interactive events, 311
Interactive home learning activities
	characteristics of, 216
	scenario of, 216
	successful, keys to, 219–220
Interstate New Teacher Assessment and Support
	Consortium (NTASC), 343
Interventions
	families, 116
	programs for, 171
	response to, 210 table
Intimate partner violence, 193
Irreplaceable value, 256–257
Ispa, I. M., 287

Janshorn, N. R., 359
Jehovah's Witness, 34
Jimerson, S. R., 169
Julia, 79

Keeping Children and Families Act, 178
Kennedy, J. W., 80
Kicking Woman, Luanne, 304
Kidshealth, 167, 174
Kinship care families
	challenges of, 96
	children's books depicting, 97
	origins of, 95

quotable minute paper, 105 table
	working with, 96–98
Kit Kat Club, 142
Kübler-Ross, Elisabeth, 139, 254

Ladson-Billings, G., 67, 115, 211
Lally, J. R., 59
Lamorey, S., 256
Lane, V., 287
Language arts projects, 294
Languages. See also English language
	learners (ESL)
	acquisition of, 55
	bilingual, 117, 336
	diversity in, 117–118
	expressive, 242
	family engagement limits of, 11–12
	Spanish, 69
	spoken in schools, 110 table
Laosa, L. M., 66–67
Lasting restrictive environment
	(LRE), 260
Lawrence Hall of Science, 325
Lazarus, P. J., 169
Leaders. See Parent leaders
Learning
	complementary, 285
	disabled, 267
	preschool years, 55
LearnNC, 341
Leave It to Beaver, 79
Legal terms, 28
Lesbians, 98–99
Letter writing campaigns, 290–291
Lewis, A., 10
Lewis, K. C., 305
Lieberman, A. F., 113
Life cycles, 35, 130–131
Limits. See Boundaries
Listening, 232
Literacy
	acquisition strategies for, 323 table
	development of, 322
	events for, 321–324
	organizations supporting, 324
Literacy Involves Families Together (LIFT)
	Act, 74
Livingston, Jonathan, 168
Luther Burbank High School, 290
The L Word, 80

Macrosystem, 39
Maladaptive functioning, 59
Mama Loves Me From Away, 147
Mandatory reporting
    complexity of, 189
    consequences of, 189
    educators role following, 195
    ethical responsibility of, 189
    facts on, 187–189
    laws, 185
    process of, 185
Mann, M. B., 285
Married . . . With Children, 80
Mastery, 210 *table*
Math and Parent Partnership in the Southwest
        (MAPPS), 301
Math projects, 294
Maude, 79
McAlister Groves, B., 113
McKinney-Vento Homeless Education Act, 162
Media
    communication via, 228
    letters to, 291
    portrayal of families on, 79–80
    print, 226, 228–229
Mental health, 297 *table*
Mental retardation, 255
Mesosystem, 39
Meyer, J., 285
Microsystems, 38–39
Military Child Initiative, 154
Military families
    deployments and, 143–144
    issues facing, 144–145
    reassignments of, 140–142
    teachers and, 145
    websites for, 143
Milstein, M., 172
Minnesota School Social Workers
        Association, 304
Missouri Department of Social Services, 189
Missouri Parent/Family Involvement Policy,
        358–360
Models
    contexts, 37
    cultural deficit, 158
    ecological systems, 37–40
    funds of knowledge, 44–45
    partnership framework, 45–48
    school development program, 48–49
    systems conceptual framework, 30–37

Modern Family, 80
Moll, Luis, 44–45
Morphogenesis, 35
Mothers
    infant attachment to, 58
    postpartum depression in, 53
    single head of household, 16
    stay-at-home, 83
    support system for, 71
    unmarried, 17
Moving residences
    children's books about, 152 *table*
    by homeless families, 162
    normal, 132–133
Mt. Jumbo Elementary School, 334
Multigenerational families. *See* Extended
        families
Multnomah County Library, 148
Murphy Brown, 80
Music projects, 295

NAEYC. *See* National Association for the
        Education of Young Children (NAEYC)
National Association for Gifted Children, 279
National Association for the Education of Young
        Children (NAEYC)
    advocacy efforts by, 289
    advocacy tips from, 291
    creation of, 343
    ethical guidelines of, 24, 189 *table,* 345–357
    ideals of, 345–346
    principles of, 346–347
National Board Certified Teachers (NBCT), 343
National Board of Professional Teaching
        Standards (NBPTS), 343
National Center for Children in Poverty, 15
National Center for Educational Statistics, 338
National Child Abuse and Neglect Data System
        (NCANDS), 182
National Child Traumatic Stress Network, 198
National Coalition for the Homeless (NCH), 174
National Council on Child Abuse and Family
        Violence (NCCAFV), 199
National Even Start Association, 306
National Foster Parent Association, 154
National Incidence Study-3 (NIS-3), 182
National Institute of Early Education
        Research, 55
National Mental Health Association
        (NMHA), 174
National Network of Partnership Schools, 50

National Parent Teacher Association (PTA), 299

National Resource Center on Children and Families of the Incarcerated at Family & Corrections Network, 154

National School Lunch Program, 160

Native language programs, 117

Natural disasters, 168–170

Neglect. *See* Child neglect

Neighborhoods, 292

Newsletters, 226, 227 *table*

A New Wave of Evidence: The Impact of School, Family, and Communications on Student Achievement (Henderson, Mapp), 8

No Child Left Behind Act, 3
    Even Start and, 74
    family engagement mandate of, 356
    IDEA linkage to, 260–261
    terms used in, 210 *table*

Noddings, Nel, 171

Nondiscriminatory, multidisciplinary assessment, 260

Non-English speakers, 69
    community resources for, 296, 298 *table*
    conferences with, 241–243
    exceptional need students of, 267
    family engagement limits of, 11–12
    homework issues and, 221–222
    volunteer translators for, 336

Nonnormative transitions
    characteristics of, 133–134
    death-related, 137–140
    foster care, 148–151
    marriage-related, 134–137
    military-related, 140–145
    prison-related, 145–148

Nontraditional families, 16

Normalization, 255

North Idaho Correctional Institution, 148

Notes to parents, 226

Nuclear families
    disadvantages of, 82–83
    example of, 81–82
    ideal of, 82
    quotable minute paper, 105 *table*
    working with, 83–84

Obama, Barack, 3

On Death and Dying (Kübler-Ross), 254

One Day at a Time, 79

Online events, 311

Ooms, Theodora, 203

Opening Doors: Lesbian and Gay Parents and Schools, 99–100

Open questions, 233 *table*

Optimal positive development, 59

Oregon Education Service District (EDS), 70

Ostrich phase, 255

Pacific Islanders, 267

Paraphrasing, 232 *table*

Paraprofessionals, 305–306

Parental Information and Resource Center, 307

Parental Involvement website, 224

Parental safeguards and involvement, 260

Parent Communication Councils (PCC), 290

Parent education
    models of, 73–75
    resources for, 71–72

Parent Effectiveness Training (P.E.T), 74

Parentification, 34–35

Parent Information and Resource Centers Grantees (PIRCS), 341

Parenting
    active, 74–75
    "boot camp," 148
    children's view of, 64–66
    community support for, 297 *table*
    cultural aspects of, 64, 190
    definition of, 57
    differentiated, 66, 115
    effective, training for, 74
    partnership involvement, 46 *figure,* 47
    situational aspects of, 63–64

Parenting styles
    characterization of, 60
    classification of, 61–62
    effects of, 62–63
    grandparents, 95–96
    research, criticisms of, 63–64
    teachers' acceptance of, 66–67

Parent Institute, 107

Parent leaders
    advisory councils, 290–301
    development of, 298–299
    in organizations, 299–300

Parent Teacher Home Visit Project, 127, 306

Parent Teacher Organizations (PTOs), 290, 341

Parents. *See also* Fathers; Mothers
    attachment and, 58–59
    bonding and, 57–58
    death of, 137–140

disinterest of, 116
educational levels of, 64
first meeting with, 52
golden years of, 57
homework concerns of, 219–220, 222–223
incarcerated, 145–148
involvement of, 6
negative school experiences of, 10, 244–245
notes to, 226
stages of, 53–57
Parents Action for Children, 76
Parents as Teachers (PAT) program, 73–74
Parents Toolkit, 224
Participatory support, 283
Payne, R., 158
Peer harassment, 98–99
Permissive/indulgent parenting, 61, 63
Permissive/neglectful parenting, 61–63
Pervasive Development Disorder-Not Otherwise
    Specified (PDD-NOS), 272
Perverse triangle, 35
Phillips, T., 113, 155
Physical abuse, 178–179
Physical education projects, 295
Popkin, M., 75
Positive Connections, 94–95
Postpartum depression, 53
Poussaint, Alvin, 62, 197
Poverty
    compassion for, 158
    culture of, 158
    definition of, 19
    educational levels and, 157–158
    homelessness, 160–163
    hunger and, 160
    impact of, 19
    misconceptions about, 159
    school supplies and, 157
    students of, working with, 159–160
    wage earns in, 156–157
Powell, D., 71
Power structures, 35
Preschoolers, 54–55, 75
Prevent Child Abuse America,
    180–183, 288
Primary language programs, 117
Principals. See Administrators
Print communication
    approaches to, 226, 228
    creation of, 229
    successful strategies for, 229

Protective factors, 170–173
Psychological abuse, 180–181
PTA. See National Parent Teacher
    Association (PTA)
PTO Today, 341
Public school choice, 210 table
Public School Night Out, 319–320

Quayle, Dan, 80
Questionnaires
    events, 314 table
    family interview, 57 table
    student behavior, 212 table
    using, 56
Questions, 233 table
Quintanar, A. P., 337
Quotable minute paper, 105 table

Race. See also specific groups
    diversity of, 21–22
    worldview-based on, 32
Reading is Fundamental (RIF), 324, 341
Reading projects, 294
Reciprocal communication, 230–232
Recreational resources, 297 table
Recruitment, 336–338
Reece, R. M., 113
Reflection, 232 table
Rehabilitation Act of 1973, 258
Reid, Cicely, 205–206
Relational support, 283
Relationships
    blended families, 91–92
    mutually respectful, 4–5
    nurturing, 4
    positive, 68
Religion
    constitutional protection, 120
    dilemma scenarios, 122–123
    holidays, 120–121 table
    practices of, 120
Remarriage. See also Blended families
    children's books about, 152 table
    effects of, 134–137
    rates of, 18–19
Report cards, 210 table
Resilience
    environmental factors, 171–172
    fostering, 172–173, 172 table
    research on, 171
Resistant attachment, 58

Resources
    center for, 332–335
    community, 292–298
    families as, 68
    home school, 301–303
    mental health, 297 *table*
    paraprofessionals, 305–306
    physical/medical needs, 297 *table*
    social workers, 303–305
    teachers as, 285
Respect, 4–5
Respeto, 66
Response to intervention (RTI)
    approach of, 272–273
    definition of, 210 *table*
    diagram of, 274 *figure*
    explaining, tips for, 273
Richards, R., 222
Ringgold Elementary School, 142
Rites of passage, 133
Rituals
    family bonding and, 33–34
Roles
    administrators, 12, 14, 15 *table*
    social system, 36
    volunteers,' 214–215
Rosa's Law, 255
Roseanne, 80
RTI. *See* Response to intervention (RTI)

Salinas, R, 359
Same-sex families
    challenges of, 98–99
    characterization of, 98
    children's books depicting, 101 *table*
    media portrayal of, 80
    quotable minute paper, 105 *table*
    teachers' fears of, 99–100
    teachers' working with, 100–101
Sanders, M. G., 359
Sanders, Mavis., 293
Saylors, Chuck, 299
Scholastic Parents, 249
School Breakfast Program, 160
School Days Top Ten Classroom Websites, 240
School district report cards, 210 *table*
School effectiveness team (SET), 357
Schools. *See also* Classrooms
    atmosphere, 231
    corporal punishment in, 196–197
    development program, 48–49

    domestic violence and, 193–194
    engagement barriers of, 9–11, 13 *table*
    engagement benefits for, 9
    high-poverty, 10–11
    negative experiences in, 10
    social workers for, 303–305
    sponsored programs, 72
Science Family Fun Night, 341
Science projects, 295
Seattle Public Schools, 357–358
Secure attachment, 58–59
Self-actualization, 255
Separation, 135–137, 152 *table*
Sexual abuse, 180
Shaming discipline, 66
Shoemake, Joyce, 299
Siblings, 138
Silent child, 111–112
Simon, B. S., 359
Single-parent families, 16
    child rearing issues, 87–88
    children's books depicting, 89 *table*
    example of, 85
    geographical distribution of, 86 *figure*
    history of, 85–86
    media portrayal of, 79
    quotable minute paper, 105 *table*
    special needs members of, 90
    trends leading to, 86–87
    working with, 88, 90
Skiba, Justin, 145
Smartphones, 241
Social capital model, 43–44
Social studies projects, 295
Social workers, 303–305
Socioeconomic status. *See also* Poverty
    child abuse and, 177
    grandparents, 96–97
    home visits and, 233–234
    loss of, 134
    parenting and, 64
    remarriage and, 92
Southwest Elementary School, 323–324
Spanish, 69
Special designation, 255
Special education. *See also* Individualized
        education programs (IEP)
    eligibility for, 266
    legislation relating to, 258–259
    practices and standards for, 267
    teachers' role in, 257

Spooner Elementary School, 338
St. Bernard-Elmwood Place School, 311
Stand for Children, 307
Standardized tests, 210 *table*
Standards for Culturally Responsive Schools,
      123–124
Standards-based curriculum
   development of, 208–209
      explanation guidelines, 209, 211
      key terms in, 210 *table*
Stay-at-home mothers, 83
Stein, Scott, 204
Stein, Thorkildsen, 204
Stepfamilies. *See* Blended families
STEP/Teen, 74
Steve Spangler Science, 330
Stevens, B. A., 230
Stress
   homelessness and, 160
   in nuclear families, 83
   transition-related, 134
Student Behavioral Survey, 212 *table*
Students. *See also* Exceptional needs students
   conference involvement by, 234–235
   engagement barriers of, 9–10
   engagement benefits for, 8
   foster care, 148–151
   languages spoken by, 117
   special needs, 99, 117, 222
   success, events for, 310–311
Substance abuse, 182–184
Successful Local Approaches website, 25
Sugarland Elementary School, 299
The Suite Life of Zac and Cody, 80
Summers, J. A., 287
Supplemental services, 210 *table*
Surveys. *See* Questionnaires
Systematic Training for Effective Parenting
      (STEP), 74
Systems theory
   bonding/buffering in, 32–34
   boundaries of, 31–32
   dynamically changing in, 35
   family as, 30
   goals of, 36
   hierarchy of, 34–35
   roles of, 36
   self-government in, 34
   self-regulation of, 36–37
   sum of parts, 31
   well-functioning, 31

TANF. *See* Temporary Assistance for Needy
      Families (TANF)
Teachers
   adoptive families and, 103–104
   attitudes of, 244
   beliefs of, 244
   blended families and, 93–95
   body language of, 232 *table*
   certification of, 343
   child abuse reporting by, 184–185, 187–189
   children bonding to, 59
   chronically ill students and, 166–168
   corporal punishment by, 197
   cultural attitudes toward, 11
   customer friendly, 285
   domestic violence and, 193–194
   expectations of, 172
   extended families and, 85
   family engagement view of, 9–10
   family support by, 68
   fears of, 99
   foster care students and, 151
   habitudes of, 115–116
   highly qualified, 261
   homeless students and, 163
   kinship care families and, 96–98
   linguistically diversity and, 117–118
   military families and, 145
   natural disasters and, 169–170
   notes from, 226
   nuclear families and, 83–84
   poor students and, 159–160
   religious families and, 123
   same-sex families and, 99–101
   single-parent families and, 88, 90
   special education role of, 257
Teachers Involve Parents in Schoolwork (TIPS)
      program, 220, 224
Teaching
   culturally response, 23–24
   parenting styles and, 66–67
   standards for, 343
   toddler classroom, 54–55
Teaching Diverse Learners (TDL), 127
Technology
   class projects for, 295
   communication via., 239–241
   nights, 330–331, 332 *table*
Technology-Related Assistance for Individuals
      Act, 259
Telephone conferences, 236–237

Temperament, 58–59
Temporary Assistance for Needy Families
    (TANF), 39
Testing
    achievement, 260–261
    exceptionality, 266–268
    high-stakes, 209, 210 *table*
    intervention after, 272–273
    mandatory, 304
    special services, 253
    standardized, 210 *table,* 359
Theodore Roosevelt Elementary School, 236
Third National Child Abuse Incidence study, 180
Thomas, A., 59
Three-way conferences, 235
Thornburg, K. R., 287
Through the Looking Glass, 279
Tileston, D., 208
Timing, 133
Title I, 355
Title IX, 258
Toddlers, 54–55
Tollafield, A., 230
Tourist curriculum, 320
Traditions, 33–34
Tragedy Assistance Program for Survivors
    (TAPS), 144
Transition events, 318–320
Transitions. *See also* Nonnormative transitions
    moving, 131–133, 152 *table*
    normal, 130–131
Turner, J., 214

Ulrich, M. E., 254
Underclass, 158
University of California, Berkeley, 325
Unmarried mothers, 17, 18 *table*
Urban Institute, 128
U.S. Census Bureau
    family definition of, 28
    family demographics of, 14–15
    linguistic diversity data, 117
    stay at home mothers data, 83

Van Voorhis, F. L., 359
Verbal ignorance, 103
The Very Hungry Caterpillar, 324
Violence
    community, 164–165
    domestic, 191, 193–195
    gang, 164

Visiting Day, 147
Volunteers
    benefits, 213–214
    bilingual, 336
    confidentiality and, 339
    definition of, 213
    partnership involvement, 46
        figure, 47
    policies for, 338–339
    recruitment of, 336–338
    retaining, 339–340
    roles for, 214–215
    tasks for, 335–336
    training of, 338–339
von Bertainffy, L., 30

Wallace, Marcia, 165
Warren, S. R., 337
Warrier, S., 113
Wars, 144
Websites
    communication via, 239–241
    CPS, 349–353
    family and community, 25
    family engagement, 344
    family-school partnerships, 25, 50
    hospice, 154
    information on, 240
    military families, 143
    parental Involvement, 224
Welfare. *See* Temporary Assistance for Needy
    Families (TANF)
Welfare Reform Law of 1996, 39
"What my kids taught me," 65
The Whole Child, 250
Williams, E. R., 213, 267
Williams-Wikers, B., 113
Women's Opportunity and Resource
    Development, Inc., 304, 332
Woolfolk, A., 206
Working poor, 156–157
Workplace conferences, 238
Worldviews, 31–32
Worry doll, 142
Worrying unit, 142
Wrightslaw, 279

Yankviak, Chris, 334
Yellowstone County Head Start, 296

Zero to Three, 76

ABOUT THE AUTHORS

Kathy B. Grant, EdD, is Associate Professor of Curriculum and Instruction at SUNY Plattsburgh's School of Education. She has taught undergraduate courses in family involvement, as well as graduate courses in educational psychology and child development. She also worked as a home-school coordinator through Title 1 in the Missoula School District in Missoula, Montana. During her six years in this position, she oversaw the development of family resource centers at the elementary and middle school levels, worked with family outreach specialists and social workers, established parent libraries, and conducted home visits. As home-school coordinator, she helped develop an Even Start program serving children and parents. Having taught second, fifth, sixth, seventh, and eighth grades, as well as high school, she has worked collaboratively with families for more than 30 years.

She conducted statewide research on teacher preparation in family involvement through coursework initiatives and generated a model that schools of education can use to effectively prepare candidates. *An Emerging Model for Preservice Teacher Education in Family Involvement* has been presented at several national and state conferences. Through a Goals 2000 grant, she coauthored the Teacher and Parents (TAP) website and consulted for Montana Parent Information Resource Centers (MPIRC) on preservice teacher strategies to increase family involvement through the University of Montana School of Education.

Julie A. Ray, PhD, is Professor of Education at Southeast Missouri State University in Cape Girardeau, where she has taught early childhood education undergraduate and graduate courses, including Family-School Collaboration, since 2002. She also currently serves as the Interim Chair of the Elementary, Early Childhood, and Special Education Department at Southeast Missouri State. She has been in the field of education for more than 31 years as a teacher educator, as well as an early childhood teacher, school librarian, and teacher of the gifted. She continues to work with classroom teachers in improving their family engagement practices in their classroom and school districts.

She has been actively involved in the National Association for the Education of Young Children (NAEYC) for several years and currently serves as a program reviewer for early childhood programs seeking NAEYC Recognition from NCATE. She has done numerous presentations at state, regional, and national conferences on topics such as supportive family engagement practices, working with diverse families and families in crisis, organizing successful family events, effective teaching strategies in higher education, and using case study methodology.

ABOUT THE CONTRIBUTORS

Josephine C. Agnew-Tally, EdD, is department head of Childhood Education and Family Studies at Missouri State University in Springfield, Missouri. Her research areas include teacher education, the socialization of elementary school teachers, teacher research, Scholarship of Teaching and Learning (SoTL), early childhood equity, early intervention, and family support. She has served on several state and national executive boards in the field of education. She has published and presented nationally as well as internationally in the field of teacher education, early childhood, and early childhood special education.

Keith Anderson, PhD, is a staff psychologist and adjunct faculty member at Rensselaer Polytechnic Institute. He frequently teaches classes in abnormal psychology, human sexuality, community psychology, and group counseling. He is the chair of the Mental Health Best Practices Task Force of the American College Health Association, and, as such, is a frequent consultant to the media. His research has focused on human-computer interaction, group counseling, and academic achievement and has been published in the *Journal of American College Health* and the *Journal of College Student Psychotherapy.*

Sheila Brookes, PhD, is an assistant professor in the Child and Family Studies Department and the executive director of the Center for Child Development at the University of Southern Mississippi. She teaches child development courses in the undergraduate Child Development emphasis area and in the Master's in Child and Family Studies program, in addition to supervising student teachers in their Student Teaching Practicum. Her research interests include early care and education program quality and child maltreatment prevention. Dr. Brookes coauthored several chapters of *Keepin' On: The Everyday Struggles of Young Families in Poverty,* which was the culmination of a longitudinal, qualitative study of mothers in the Early Head Start Program. Formerly, Dr. Brookes was a senior policy research analyst at the Center for Family Policy and Research at the University of Missouri–Columbia, where she worked on numerous research projects, including the national Early Head Start study; a nine-state welfare reform project, The Impacts of Welfare Reform on Young Children and Their Families, which culminated in a briefing on Capitol Hill; and the Preschool Curriculum Evaluation Research funded by the U.S. Department of Education. Prior to her work at the university level, she had extensive experience working with teachers, parents, and children in early childhood programs.

George Cliette, EdD, is an associate professor and director of the North Carolina Central University (NCCU) Parent Training study (Boston University). His specialty area is community psychology with an emphasis on community mental health and action research. He joined the NCCU faculty in 1993, and is the recipient of the NCCU Teaching Excellence Award. He has maintained a focused and productive research agenda in areas such as African American mental health, parent training, rites of passage programs, and the psychohistory of oppression. In addition, he is a health service provider approved by the National Register of Professional Psychologists and a licensed psychologist.

Jewell Cooper, PhD, is an associate professor at the University of North Carolina at Greensboro in the Department of Curriculum and Instruction. Her research interests include equity education, specifically community-based learning in teacher education, culturally relevant pedagogy, and high school reform. She has conducted professional development activities in K–12 public and private schools for over a decade. She has published research in journals such as *Journal of Teacher Education, High School Journal, Evaluation Review,* and *Science Teacher.*

Sherry Eaton, PhD, after teaching kindergarten for one year, decided to pursue a doctorate in school psychology, which she received in 1988. She served as director of the North Carolina Central University Testing Center from its inception in 1987 until 1997. She has taught many of the courses in the undergraduate curriculum as well as measurement and assessment courses. She has independently developed and taught a cultural diversity course in the graduate program. She is a professionally licensed psychologist with her research focusing on academic achievement for culturally diverse youth and parental socialization.

Suzanne George, PhD, is a faculty member in the Early Childhood and Family Development Department at Missouri State University in Springfield. She has been a special education classroom teacher and college faculty member in special education and early childhood education for more than 30 years. Her ambitious research agenda has resulted in numerous publications and frequent presentations to professional organizations.

Joyce Goddard, MEd, literacy/reading specialist, has years of experience partnering with families of diverse cultures in many states. Through workshops, she assisted teachers in developing parent involvement projects and teamed with colleges to provide opportunities for teacher candidates to participate in family nights. As a literacy coach, she was involved in developing a cultural audit classroom checklist. She has done presentations at state and national conferences that promoted understanding of families of diverse cultures. Currently, she is a reading recovery teacher in a rural school in North Carolina.

Luis Hernández, T/TAS (Training & Technical Assistance Services) early childhood education specialist, holds an MA in bilingual/multicultural education from the University of San Francisco. He is a regular speaker at national, state, and local conferences, and his special interests include early literacy, second-language learning, collaboration and partnerships, changing demographics and diversity, adult learning, and ECE management topics. He is active in a number of national organizations that support children and family interests, serving on the board of the Parent Services Project in California, the advisory board of the McCormick Tribune Center for Early Childhood Leadership, and the United Way's Center for Excellence in Early Education.

Jonathan Livingston, PhD, is an assistant professor of psychology and codirector of the Institute for the Study of Children, Youth, and Families. His current research focuses on social and psychological factors associated with positive mental health outcomes for African Americans. He is currently serving as Director of Outreach for the Export Grant, a project of the Julius Chambers Biomedical Bio-Technical Research Institute, evaluating the effectiveness of their efforts to reduce health disparities and educate the African American community about alcohol, substance abuse, and cardiovascular risk factors. He has authored and coauthored peer-reviewed journal articles, book chapters, and newspaper articles on race, psychology, mental health, health disparities, and education, as well as presented his research at many national and international conferences.

Catherine Matthews, PhD, is a professor of science education at the University of North Carolina in Greensboro in the Department of Curriculum and Instruction, with a focus on K–12 science education and environmental education. She has worked extensively in the Professional Development Schools in Guilford County for the past 14 years. She has published in journals such as the *Journal of Research in Science Teaching, Science Teacher, Science and Children, Science Scope, Science Activities,* and *American Biology Teacher.*

Pamela Moses-Snipes, PhD, is an assistant professor of mathematics education and the secondary mathematics education coordinator of the Mathematics Department at Winston-Salem State University in North Carolina. Her professional accomplishments include presenting at numerous state and national conferences, organizing undergraduate research, conducting mathematics professional development workshops for public school teachers, organizing family math nights, and receiving funding from grants to coordinate a Mathematics Leadership Academy. Her research interests are ethnomathematics, the mathematics education of African American students, literature in the mathematics classroom, and technology.

Donald Mott, MA, is chief clinical officer at Catawba Valley Behavioral Healthcare in Hickory, North Carolina. He also operates a private practice in psychology in the western North Carolina area and has worked with children, adults, and families for more than 30 years. He has spent many years in the fields of early childhood development, family support, developmental disabilities, and community mental health. He has authored numerous publications, including journal articles, book chapters, and one book. He has an MA in educational psychology from the University of Nebraska–Lincoln.

Helen Nissani, MA, is a faculty member at Edmonds Community College, Lynnwood, Washington. She currently is department chair of the Family Life Education Department, offering an online, certificate program in family support studies to professionals nationwide. In the recent past, she was an education researcher for ICFI Consulting and Senior Education Advisor to Family Support America. She has extensive experience in integrating public education and human services, education research, teacher training, and migrant/bilingual education.

Carole Robinson, EdD, is a distance education specialist at Pasadena City College, California. She is an active researcher and author. Her recent work is a California State University team effort—*Assessing Online Facilitation (AOF) Instrument.* The AOF is used to objectively evaluate online course facilitation for strengths and areas for improvement and to guide facilitator peer evaluation of their performance in an online classroom. She also collaborated with Kathy Grant to develop the TAP website through the Montana Parent Information Resource Center and an Education 2000 grant.

Dorothy Singleton, PhD, is director of the Institute for the Study of Minority Issues and Codirector of the Institute for the Study of Children, Youth, and Families at North Carolina Central University, Durham. She is also chair of the Department of Curriculum and Instruction and Professional Studies in the H. M. Michaux, Jr., School of Education. She has published several reviews in the *Mental Measurement Yearbook;* a book forthcoming on *The Aftermath of Hurricane Katrina: Educating Traumatized Children PreK Through College.* She has published several articles in refereed journals on minority children. She is coeditor of the *Journal of Minority Issues and Economic Development.* She is cochair of the annual North Carolina Central University African American Male Conference in Education. She has also written several funded grants on research in education, African American males in education, and literacy.

Vincent Snipes, PhD, is an associate professor of mathematics at Winston-Salem State University. His professional accomplishments include organizing family math nights, producing several research publications, presenting at numerous national and state conferences, and conducting mathematics professional development workshops for public school teachers. His research interests include the mathematics education of African American students, policy and equity issues, ethnomathematics, and technology.

Jeannine Studer, EdD, is a professor of Counselor Education/Program Coordinator at the University of Tennessee, Knoxville. She has published more than 30 articles in various adjudicated journals and presented at numerous state and national conferences. She has authored *School Counselor: An Advocate for Students* and *A Guide for Supervising the School Counselor Trainee.*

Kathy R. Thornburg, PhD, is Emerita Professor and Director of the Center for Family Policy and Research at the University of Missouri–Columbia. She also leads the Division of Early Learning at the Missouri Department of Elementary and Secondary Education. She has been a tireless advocate for high-quality early-childhood education at the state and national levels, and an Association for the Education of Young Children-Missouri scholarship fund for leadership development was named in her honor. As President of the National Association for the Education of Young Children from 2000 to 2002, she testified before the U.S. Senate about compensation for the child-care workforce. She has more than 36 years of experience teaching, directing early childhood programs, and conducting research.

Manuel Vargas, PhD, is an associate professor and associate dean in the School of Education and Human Performance at Winston-Salem State University. His research and writing interests revolve around issues of educational equity, cultural and linguistic diversity, and bilingual education. His professional experiences include K–12 teaching and administration, teacher education curriculum development, and strong advocacy for educational excellence of underserved populations.

John Wong, PhD, specializes in education and training for severely disadvantaged communities and populations. His recent publications include a 12-step manual for adults who are homeless to recover from addiction and alcoholism, a case study of an innovative life skills and job-readiness training program for adults suffering from codisorders of mental illness and substance abuse, and an article and a guidebook on the education of children and youth in homeless situations. He received his PhD from the Massachusetts Institute of Technology.

Lynn Zubov, PhD, is currently an associate professor at Winston-Salem State University where she teaches both graduate and undergraduate courses in special education. As a practitioner, she has had a wide variety of practical experiences. She has worked with children with behavioral disorders, learning disabilities, mental and physical disabilities, children at risk of school failure, and children without handicapping conditions. She received her PhD from Vanderbilt University.